Na Masu'u kia 'i Kwara'ae

Tualaka 'i Solomon Islands fa'inia
logo na rū bulao kī saena fanoa kia

Our Forest of Kwara'ae

Our life in Solomon Islands and
the things growing in our home

Michael Kwa'ioloa and Ben Burt

Published for the Trustees of The British Museum by
THE BRITISH MUSEUM PRESS

© 2001 The Trustees of the The British Museum

First published in 2001 by The British Museum Press
A division of the The British Museum Company Ltd
46 Bloomsbury Street, London WC1B 3QQ

ISBN 0 7141 2556 3

Designed and typeset by Ben Burt
Cover by John Hawkins Book Design
Printed and bound by Henry Ling Ltd, Dorchester, England

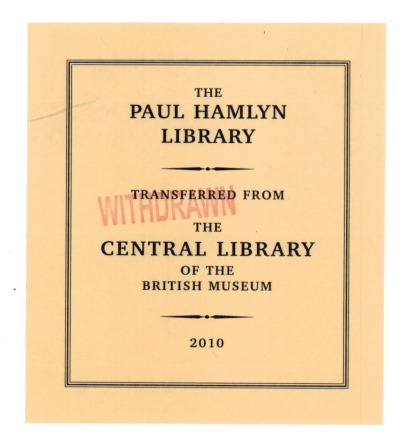

Acknowledgements

We wish to thank many people for helping us to research and write this book, including:

Senior members of the research team:
Frank Ete Tuaisalo, Adriel Rofate'e Toemanu, Rocky Tisa Sugumanu, Nelson Konabako, Mark Merlin

Research associates:
Michael Ngidu'i, Ben Idufa'asia, Stephen Binalu, Leslie Matthew Gereniu, John Langi, Gibson Misitana, Japhlet I'ana, Michael Ngidu'i, Ramo Benjamin.

Chiefs meeting at Mu'usunga Cultural Centre:
Fangamae, Moses Mae'alea, Sylvanus Maniramo, Muaua, Gulungwane, Peter Fini'a, Jack Kena, Abraham Maeongoa, Silas Labukwasi, Michael Butu, John Ko'ore'a.

Chiefs meeting at Gwa'iliki:
Arnon Ngwadili, George Bola, Codrington, Ben Gwaufungu, Alfred Kaki, Kosomo, Kosote'e, Malcolm Maefilia, Niukwao, Ramosui, Gabriel Timi, Ashley Tome

Research associates in Britain:
Ethel Maeābu Bush, Helen Maen'īa, Rose Gwao.

Colleagues who generously contributed academic advice (including some we did not take):
David Akin, Graham Baines, Chris Henderson, Paul Sillitoe, Arthur Whistler

Susan Wickison, whose drawings from *A Guide to the Useful Plants of Solomon Islands* illustrate Part 2 of the book.

We are also grateful to the institutions and individuals who contributed essential practical support for the project:

The research was approved by the Kwara'ae chiefs, the local and Provincial authorities of Malaita and the government of Solomon Islands.

Research expenses were provided by:
The Nuffield Foundation
The British Academy
The Forest Management Foundation
Avenir des Peuples des Forêts Tropicales, with the support of Christin Kocher-Smid

Lawrence Foana'ota and his staff at the Solomon Islands National Museum facilitated Michael Kwa'ioloa in his research in Honiara.

The British Museum supported Ben Burt in writing and producing the book in London.

Our wives Bizel Fanenalua and Annette Ward provided kind hospitality on our visits to each other's home countries.

Carolyn Jones was very supportive as editor of the book for The British Museum Press, Molly Davis gave secretarial help, Sue Vaccary assisted with typing, and Pauline Khng with copy editing.

The Grove public house, Balham, (known to some as The Grave and to others as the Balham Reading Rooms) provided a quiet congenial setting, with refreshment, for much of the translation work.

Mr Nick Hurley, New Zealand High Commissioner to Solomon Islands, has kindly provided for copies of the book to be distributed free to people in Kwara'ae and Solomon Islands, with funding from New Zealand's Official Development Assistance programme.

Notice to readers in Solomon Islands:
We receive no royalties from the sale of this book. The sale price is to cover the cost of publication.

Michael Kwa'ioloa
Secretary, Kwara'ae House of Chiefs

Ben Burt
Education curator, Ethnography Department, The British Museum

Rū saena 'abafola ne'e kī

Contents

Ma'e Fata'a Etaeta   Foreword

Michael Kwa'ioloa, Secretary to the Kwara'ae House of Chiefs

Na keresilana 'abafola ne'e fuana to'a 'i Kwara'ae, fuana talata'i ngwae ta'ena ma talata'i ngwae lō ma'i 'i kira ke lia sai ana malitana masu'u kira kī. Sulia ki daoto'ona ngwae fi'i doe 'oro kira 'iri sai na'a ana satana rū kira kī saena masu'u, ne'e ka kwatea kira ke malatikoa masu'u kira kī, ma kira ke tufu dale'a o'ofilana kula kī. Kaimili fikuta'i ngwae rao 'i Kwara'ae fa'inia gwaunga'i kī, kaili ogā ki alua saena 'abafola 'i ne'e ki to'oma'i olioli ana fa'asia ta talata'i ngwae 'uana ta talata'i ngwae. Fuana logo ngwae kwaifa'amanata kī ke fa'ananau 'ania kaela ngela kī saena primary, secondary, colleges ma institute kī. 'Unari mala tua'a nini 'i Kwara'ae kira ka fi'i manata doe ana malitana masu'u kira kī, ma kira ka sai ana kira ke ogani ani ma kira ke saunga'i fanoa 'i saeni ma ke tua ni fuli 'i saeni, ita nama ma'i na'o ka dao ana kaida'i ta'ena.

Masu'u ke la'u fuana tuafilana ke le'a. Nia kwatea ano ke gwarigwari'a fuana fanga ke 'inoi, ma kafo ke āfe fuana kwa'ufilana. Nia fuana logo 'ai fuana 'anilana fa'irū kī, fa'inia logo tatabu kwasi kī ma sibolo kwasi kī. Masu'u fuana logo rū fuana saunga'i luma'a kī di'ia 'ai ma kwalo ma ra'i rau kī. Masu'u ke teo logo fuana 'ai fuana fa'amauri'a kī fuana guralana mata'inga kī. Fuana logo tua nunufi-'anga ka tasa ana fulitua'a kī ma ma'e fanoa kī.

Masu'u fuana tuala'i ngwae bore nia ke teo logo fuana no'o lofolofo kī ke nu'i ana 'ai kī, ma no'o akaka'u ma sakwalo kī ke kale saena leko 'ai kī. Logo fuana fi'i fari, tatale'ole'o kī ke teo fuana no'o akaka'u kī ke tuafi'i ma ke kale 'i saeni, fa'inia logo fi'i bula kī ke bulao ana 'ai kī. 'Unu kī bore ogā logo ke tua ana masu'u bono 'i ke 'ania rauna 'ai saena dukwasi. Masu'u logo fuana rū angoango kī, ma siko, ma rū to'o ana fa'i 'a'erū kī.

'I nini'ari ki lisia ne'e masu'u kia kira malitako. Na fikuta'i ngwae rao ne'e kī fa'inia gwaunga'i kī, kira daoto'ona 'atolana ne'e masu'u karangi fuirū'anga ki ke fa'asuia na'a di'ia o'ofilana ma tufu dalelana fuana fa'i niu, fokai buluka, kaukau, ma roto kī logo ka tasa ana o'ofilana. Fa'inia logo ne'e ngwae kī ke tufua 'ai kī saena kwata'ato fasi 'i ke kwa'i ka ngwali'igi ka kirida'i. 'Olelana rebana 'ai ne'e le'a fuana saunga'i luma'a ma kabani doe kī, kira ke foli 'ani'i 'i 'a'e asi noema 'i fanoa 'a'ana. Rū ne'e fa'alia na'a 'ai ne'e loging kambani kī kira tufu dalea fuana foli 'afu'afu'anga ani boborū kī 'uana 'i 'a'e asi.

This book is written for the people of Kwara'ae, for the present generation and future generations to understand the nature of their forests. Because we come upon many young people who do not know the names of things in the forest, which leads them to destroy their forests and to chop them down destructively in gardening. Our group of Kwara'ae workers and chiefs want to put it into a book so we can come back and read it from generation to generation. Also for teachers to train small children in primary and secondary education, colleges and institutes. So that the inhabitants of Kwara'ae think seriously about the nature of their forests and know how to conserve them and build their homes in them and establish their living in them, beginning long before until the present day.

Forest is for living to be good. It makes the land moist for crops to be large and waters to flow for drinking. It is also for trees with fruit for eating, also for wild greens and wild animal-protein. Forest is also for things for building houses such as wood and vine and leaf. Forest is also there for trees for saving life, for curing illnesses. It is also for staying in the shade, especially at rest-sites and homes.

Forest is for man's living, but it is also there for birds to nest in the trees, and cuscus and bats to give birth in hollows in trees. Also for clusters of *fari*-orchids and *takale'ole'ò*-fern to be there for cuscus to live in and give birth in, and also for clusters of *bula*-vine to grow on the trees. Even lizards like to live in dense forest to eat the leaves in the wilderness. Forest is also for creeping things and hoppers and things which have tubers.

At present we see our forest being destroyed. This group of workers and chiefs have come to the conclusion that the forest has almost been finished off by our developments such as gardening and destructive cutting for coconuts, cattle fields and roads, but especially for gardening. It is also people chopping down trees on steep places so that they fall with a tremor and crash. Cutting planks of wood is good for building houses and large buildings and they sell them overseas or in town. What destroys the trees are logging companies which cut destructively for the sale of entire logs overseas.

Rū ne'e kia'a to'a Kwara'ae, ki lisia ma ki ka rao fa'inia ara'ikwao kī fuana fa'ita'ilana rū kī saena masu'u 'ania fata'a Kwara'ae fa'inia logo fata'a English. 'I ne'e ta ngwae bore 'ana ke sai ana to'oma'ilana ma ka tasa logo fuana ngwa'i ngela kī.

Kerekere'anga ne'e, kula etaeta ne'e idumilana malitana masu'u fa'inia fuirū'anga ma saunga'irū-'anga 'ania rū saena masu'u, di'ia o'ola, fanga fasia ma fanga kwasi kī, ma saunga'ilana rū di'ia luma ma rū fuana tualana ngwae kī saena fanoa 'i Kwara'ae ma'i 'i na'o, kaida'i ki tua talaka. Na ruana kula ana kerekere'anga ne'e sulia rū bulao saena masu'u di'ia satana 'ai, lisilana nonina, rauna, takana, sūla ma fuana, ma kula ni'i ke bulao ani kī, ma tae ne'e bolo fa'inia ki sasi'i 'ani'i, fuana ngela kī ke to'oma'i sulia saena sukulu 'i kira ke sai logo ani fuana rao'a 'ani'i ana fa'i asoa ke dao ma'i kī.

This is what we the Kwara'ae people see, and we work with the whitemen to explain the things in the forest in Kwara'ae language and in English language. So that anyone can read it, and especially the children.

Of this writing, the first part details the nature of the forest and developing and building with things in the forest, such as gardens, planted foods and wild foods, and building things such as houses and things for people's living in Kwara'ae formerly, when we lived by ourselves. The second part of the writing is about the things which grow in the forest, such as the names of trees, the appearance of their trunk, their leaf, their flower, sap and fruit, and the places they grow in, and what they can be used for, for children to read in school and to understand about working with them in days to come.

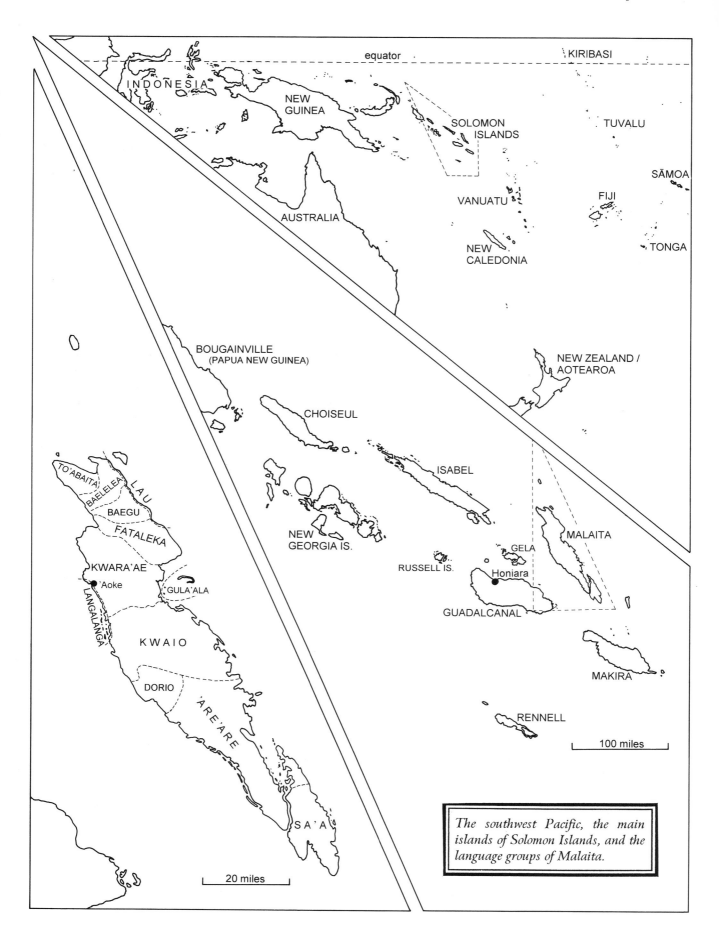

equator

KIRIBASI

INDONESIA

NEW
GUINEA

SOLOMON
ISLANDS

TUVALU

SĀMOA

VANUATU

FIJI

AUSTRALIA

TONGA

NEW
CALEDONIA

BOUGAINVILLE
(PAPUA NEW GUINEA)

NEW ZEALAND /
AOTEAROA

CHOISEUL

ISABEL

TO'ABAITA

LAU

BAELELEA

BAEGU

FATALEKA

MALAITA

KWARA'AE

NEW
GEORGIA IS.

GELA

'Aoke

RUSSELL IS.

Honiara

LANGALANGA

GULA'ALA

KWAIO

GUADALCANAL

DORIO

'ARE'ARE

MAKIRA

RENNELL

100 miles

SA'A

20 miles

*The southwest Pacific, the main
islands of Solomon Islands, and the
language groups of Malaita.*

Introduction

Ben Burt, The British Museum

This book describes a little of what the Kwara'ae people of Malaita in Solomon Islands know about the forest resources which have formed the basis of their livelihood for centuries past, and should ensure it for the future. As authors, Michael Kwa'ioloa and I bring the very different experiences of a Kwara'ae community activist and an English anthropologist to the task of documenting this knowledge in a way which retains a Kwara'ae cultural perspective but is intelligible and useful to members of both our cultures. We have been supported in this project by a local research team and numerous associates, as well as by the Kwara'ae chiefs who have approved our work as a contribution to the cultural development of their people. This Introduction explains how we set about writing the book and considers some of the issues raised by our presentation of Kwara'ae ecological knowledge and material culture.

Books about plants are something of a speciality for the English, whose understanding of our own environment, often termed 'natural history' has long been shaped and authorised by writings based on scientific disciplines such as botany, which are well integrated into our popular culture. Most books about tropical forests, and about local knowledge of them, are written from a similar Western scientific perspective. But the culture of science is very different from that of most tropical forest peoples, whose knowledge of such matters is seldom reduced to writing in terms which reflect their own culture rather than a foreign author's view of it. This is hardly surprising for a people like the Kwara'ae, who have gradually adopted writing only during the last three or four generations, and have used it mainly as a means to assimilating Western culture. The present book is intended as a contribution to a Kwara'ae language literature, to serve the development of their own culture while sharing it with others.

Kwara'ae culture as 'local knowledge'

The Kwara'ae are the largest of about eighty ethnic groups in Solomon Islands, numbering more than 20,000 people. Their name applies at once to the people, their language and their territory, which forms a band across the island of Malaita, like most of the dozen or so language groups of the island. In language and culture the Kwara'ae closely resemble other peoples to the north and are rather less similar to their neighbours to the south. Like most Malaitans, they are an inland or 'bush' people who live mainly by gardening, agroforestry and foraging on forested lands which belong to an indefinite number of local clan communities.

It is not the purpose of this book to review Kwara'ae culture in general, or its transformation during more than a century of growing involvement in the world beyond Solomon Islands. More may be learned from our other publications (Burt 1994a, 1994b, Kwa'ioloa & Burt 1997). Nor will we examine how an expanding population and economy is putting pressure on Kwara'ae land and forests, leading to the problems mentioned in Kwa'ioloa's Foreword. These are experiences which the Kwara'ae share with other Pacific Islanders, just as they share a far longer history of creative adaptation to their island environments and forests. Such ancient adaptations and recent problems, and the dynamic relationship between them, are now increasingly researched in fields such as anthropology, botany, zoology, geography and agriculture in various fruitful combinations, with an emerging common focus on 'local knowledge'. It is with such local knowledge that this book is concerned.

The notion of 'local' applies to both the knowers and the known, with a particular emphasis on the ecological relationships between people and places. As Sillitoe reviews this approach (1998), it owes much to the rise of development studies, which has encouraged academic research to involve local people in addressing practical concerns. This can be seen as part of a historic shift from 'top down' attitudes to development, which assume the superiority of Western economic and ecological knowledge, to 'bottom up' approaches which encourage people to build upon their local knowledge and experience, rather than replace it. Western-educated professionals are likewise encouraged to respect local cultures as alternative ways of understanding and dealing with ecological questions, rather than merely as objects of academic study or impediments to development. The implications of this approach, and the rationale for our book, are aptly summarised in the title *Traditional Ecological Knowledge: Wisdom for Sustainable Development* (Williams & Baines 1993), a book which emphasises the importance of foreign researchers working in partnership with local people to learn from them, rather than merely about them.

The kind of ecological knowledge we have tried to learn from our Kwara'ae colleagues derives from a far-flung and ancient tradition, described as follows by Clarke and Thaman in a wide-ranging survey of *Agroforestry in the Pacific Islands* (1993):

Pacific Islanders have selected for incorporation in their agroforestry systems a wide range of tree and tree-like species that meet their particular environmental and cultural needs. The use of these species is the cumulative result of a selection process that has occurred over thousands of years, beginning in the ancestral homelands of today's Pacific Islanders in South-East Asia and the archipelagic areas of Indonesia, the Philippines, and Papua New Guinea, whence valuable cultigens and accumulated knowledge of wild species were transferred to the smaller Pacific oceanic islands.

After they arrived, early settlers domesticated previously unknown indigenous species or else incorporated them as wild species into agro-forestry systems prior to European contact . . . Similarly, post-European contact introductions, including food plants, timber trees, and ornamentals, have been tested, selected, and incorporated into today's systems to such an extent that the undiscerning visitor or agricultural "expert", and many of the current generation of islanders, believe the introduced trees to be traditional or even indigenous. (1993:194-5)

Clarke and Thaman refer to a total 419 of what the Kwara'ae would call kinds of trees, planted and wild, identified as 'useful components of local agroforestry systems' in the Pacific Islands, of which about 272 or 65% have pre-colonial origins in the region (1993:96). Not all of these are represented in our Kwara'ae sample of about 360 trees and plants. Our book is not intended to be comprehensive, and it concentrates on those regarded as from 'formerly' (*ma'i na'o*, implying pre-colonial) and omits many of the 'foreign' (*faka* or 'ship') introductions of recent generations. There is little doubt that further research would yield a total for Kwara'ae to match Clarke and Thaman's count for the Pacific Islands as a whole, nor is there any reason to suppose that the Kwara'ae are exceptional in this respect.

The Kwara'ae have also made important contributions to research on Pacific Islands agro-forestry. A study by Manner of Kwara'ae gardening (1993) is among the dozen case studies of Pacific Islands agroforestry presented by Clarke and Thaman, while studies of plant succession and soil properties on Kwara'ae garden sites have been published by Nakano and Miyauchi (1992, 1996).

Kwara'ae experts have also made a major contribution to the most comprehensive study of Solomon Islands ethnobotany, Henderson and Hancock's *Guide to the Useful Plants of Solomon Islands* (1988).

Our book provides data for comparison with such research but makes no claim to comparable scientific status. Instead we have tried to present Kwara'ae culture in its own terms, as far as this can be done in writing. This results from a conviction that, even in translation, their own descriptions of environment and culture will convey insights which would be lost in an academic study of the subject. Hence the text is based not on my direct observations as a foreign researcher, but on notes written or dictated by Kwa'ioloa and other members and associates of the local research team, who describe what 'we', the Kwara'ae, know of and do with the resources of 'our' forest. This 'we' is the first person plural inclusive *ki*, meaning 'you and me' (Pijin *iumi*), rather than the 'we' (*kami*, Pijin *mifala*) which excludes the hearer or reader. These notes helped to clarify the cultural categories which guided me in editing the Kwara'ae text and in making the English translation, and my own research experience of their culture enabled me to ask useful questions of my Kwara'ae colleagues.

Since my understanding of botany goes only a little further than English folk knowledge, we were particularly fortunate in being able to draw on the botanical identifications of Solomon Islands plants published in Henderson and Hancock's *Useful Plants* (1988), which uses Kwara'ae as the standard local vernacular, and on the botanical drawings by Susan Wickison which illustrate it. But this information serves to situate our Kwara'ae data for those more familiar with botany, rather than to inform the contents of the book as a whole.

Although we have not attempted to present Kwara'ae culture in the terms of either natural or social science, in writing a book we have inevitably been influenced by Western perspectives. Part 2 of the book is a catalogue of what the Kwara'ae describe as the 'growing things' (*rū bulao kī*) of their forests, the only general expression which covers the English category of 'plants'. This is presented on the lines of a botanical dictionary, but focusing on the characteristics and uses which give these things their significance in Kwara'ae life. Since this information only makes sense within a broader understanding of this way of life, Part 1 of the book describes areas of technical knowledge, in a way which reflects an anthropological interest in material culture. We have tried to write all this in terms familiar to the Kwara'ae themselves, to make their contributions accessible both to their own communities and to foreigners. But doing so in a medium so different from the social and practical contexts in which this knowledge was devised, used and shared among the Kwara'ae themselves presents certain problems.

The kinds of questions raised in reducing Kwara'ae knowledge of their forest resources to writing, presenting it in their own language and interpreting it in English, can best be dealt with by reviewing the contents of the book.

Part 1: Our Living in the Forest

Kwara'ae understanding of their land and environment is founded on the practical considerations of making a living. This does not make them uninterested in other kinds of environmental knowledge, but their expertise focuses on providing food and shelter, manufactures and medicines, ensuring spiritual support and avoiding hazards. As an 'inland people' (*to'a ni tolo*) they understand best the forests of the Malaita inland and make little use of the sea and offshore islands and reefs. These are the territory of 'sea people' (*to'a ni asi*) of other language groups, who depend on fishing.

As farmers living and working in temporary clearings in the forest, the Kwara'ae distinguish between things which are 'planted' (*fasia*) and 'wild' (*kwasi*), but their living depends on both. The relationship between the two may appear to resemble the European distinction between culture and nature which some anthropological studies make so much of, but for the Kwara'ae this is a very fluid relationship, and it tends to be cyclical. 'Gardens' (*o'olā*) and 'homes' (*fanoa* or 'habitation', often translated as 'village') are laboriously cleared from 'forest' (*masu'u*) but, under a lifestyle of shifting cultivation and shifting homes, the boundaries between inhabited spaces and forest are also constantly shifting. New garden plots are cleared as old ones become depleted after about a year, and when houses decay after five years or so they are often rebuilt in new clearings. The forest soon covers abandoned sites, restoring soil fertility and supplies of raw materials in a cycle of human activity and forest growth which may climax in 'wilderness' (*dukwasi*, implying 'covered with the wild'). Kwara'ae wilderness is more or less equivalent to primary forest, but is neither as dreadfully deserted nor as naturally pristine as these European concepts tend to imply. Wilderness is regularly traversed and foraged in, as part of home (*fanoa*) in the sense of 'country' belonging to local people.

Kinds of forest (*malinga'ilana masu'ū kī*), the habitat of the Kwara'ae people and the growing things and creatures they depend on, introduces Part 1 of the book. Until the colonial period Kwara'ae territory was almost completely forested, with only some small inland areas showing signs of ancient deforestation. The Kwara'ae distinguish several main geographical zones, in which distance from the coast generally coincides with increasing altitude. 'On the sea' (*fafona asi*) includes dry coastal land as well as tidal 'stilt-roots' (*kabara*), brackish 'saltmarsh' (*asirufarufa*) and (freshwater) 'swamp' (*kunukunu'a*). The stilt-roots are named for the roots of the *Rhizophora* mangrove (*ko'a ngwane*), but also called 'scraping swamp' (*kunu ko'a*) for the *Bruguiera* mangrove (*ko'a kini*) whose fruits are scraped for pudding, as well as 'mangrove' (*maguru*), from the English. From on the sea, we go up to intermediate 'lowlands' (*to'ona'oa*) and thence to the highest areas of 'inland' (*tolo*, more usually translated as 'bush'). 'Inland' is actually a relative term, in Kwara'ae as in English, but in the mountainous island of Malaita it also implies increased altitude. In relation to on the sea and lowland, it refers particularly to the higher 'central inland' (*tofungana tolo* or 'middle bush'), including the distinctive 'misty inland' (*tolo goro*) of the highest mountains, which rise to over 700 metres. Inland can also mean 'local', as distinct from foreign or modern things, which come from 'overseas' (*'a'e asi*).

Differences between these areas tend to be identified in terms of suitability for gardening and homes, but lists of growing things regarded as characteristic of different zones show variations between the extremes of on the sea and inland which reflect the exaggerated climatic effects of altitude characteristic of tropical islands. The Kwara'ae geographical categories resemble botanical accounts of vegetation formations, distinguished in Hancock and Henderson's *Flora of the Solomon Islands* as saline and freshwater swamps, lowland rainforest and montane forest (1988:2-6). Other features of the landscape identified as habitats for particular growing things include 'hills' (*ua*), valleys (*ote*), rocky areas (*kwaru*), 'gullies' (*dodo*) and 'waters'. 'Water' (*kafo*) covers all fresh water, from rivers and streams to a few drops, as distinct from 'sea' (*asi* or 'saltwater'), which also means 'salt' and 'sweet'.

Gardening (*o'onga'a*) is described in the second chapter as a basic use of the forest, and the main source of food. Garden crops are the primary meaning of 'food' (*fanga*), just as 'gardening' can also be translated as 'work'. Garden knowledge includes the suitability of local garden sites as well as of different kinds of soil, and the various methods of clearing and burning forest growth in preparation for planting. Formerly, the main garden crops were taro and yam, supplemented by leaf 'vegetables' (*tatabu*, equivalent to Pijin *kabis*, from English 'cabbage'), and bananas. But since Malaitans began to travel overseas during the colonial period they have taken every opportunity to introduce foreign crops and diversify their food supply. Taro, the most esteemed food, has suffered much from blight in recent generations, despite the use of protective plants, an important feature of gardening technology. Sweet potato, introduced in the late 19th century and easier to grow, has become the main crop since the mid 20th century, with cassava also important on poorer soils. New varieties of bananas and vegetables (not just leaf-vegetables but also things like green beans), sugar cane and an ever increasing range of fruit are also grown among and around the staple crops.

When gardens are exhausted they soon revert to forest, beginning with the emergence of the 'points' (*raku*) of new growth. This we translate as 'shoots', to convey the Kwara'ae concept in a way that 'secondary forest' cannot. Shoots are usually cleared for new gardens before they develop into wilderness, after perhaps five, ten or fifteen years, periods which are shortening with increasing demands on the land in recent generations. Our general description of this process according to Kwara'ae perceptions may be compared with Nakano's quantitative study of plant succession on Kwara'ae garden fallows (1992).

Pig-keeping (*sare gwata'a* or 'pig-feeding') also depends on garden foods, which are used to tame and fatten them while they forage for other foods in the forest. Pigs have great symbolic as well as economic importance in Kwara'ae culture for feasting and sacrifice, but pig-keeping practices are dealt with only briefly here. These include important uses of forest materials for fencing gardens and homes to keep pigs out, or pens or paddocks to keep them in (the colonially introduced alternative).

Chickens, introduced in the early colonial period, are the only other domestic food animal, fed on scraps but given little other attention. Cattle have been kept by some families since the 1960s but as a source of cash rather than as a regular contribution to the diet. Neither of these feature in our book, with its emphasis on former times.

Foods in the forest (*fanga saena masu'u ki*), that is crop or vegetable foods, complement garden foods. Here the Kwara'ae distinction of wild from planted becomes rather ambiguous, for the same reason that the Western distinction between 'natural' and 'artificial' environments is confounded by studies of human ecology. Things planted in gardens and homes can grow wild, as abandoned sites become overgrown with forest, and wild things can be planted in, or 'transferred' (*salinga'i*, implying to take and claim) to forest, gardens or homes. In many cases there are planted and wild varieties of the same thing, including wild varieties of planted fruit trees and of root crops, taro and especially yam, which are both gathered in the forest and transferred to gardens. Presumably some planted varieties also

revert to the wild. (David Akin discerns a long-term cycling between planted and wild varieties of yam and taro in neighbouring Kwaio; pers. com.).

Of course there are other things which do not survive long on overgrown sites, such as bananas and sweet potatoes. But planted things which will grow in forest, particularly larger fruit trees and palms, continue to be claimed by those who planted or tend them, becoming long-term signs of human habitation and claims to the land. The same applies to wild non-food plants which are transferred or tended, such as sago-palm (for leaf), bamboo (for containers and building), and certain trees, particularly when planted as site or boundary markers. In such cases the significant distinction between 'planted' and 'wild' is mainly that people claim (*firia*) the right to decide on the use of the things which they have either planted or found and tended. None of the forest of Kwara'ae is completely 'wild' in the sense of untouched by human activity and unaffected by human claims, any more than it is a strictly 'natural' environment in the popular Western sense.

Our book lists the trees and other things growing in the forest, including those planted in homes and gardens, which 'bear' (*fungu'ania* or 'fill with') edible 'fruit' (*fuana, fa'irū*). Most of these are regarded as being from former times, but there are also many which are foreign and recently introduced. The most important for the food supply are seasonal 'nuts' (*ngali*), strictly speaking a type of canarium almond but also covering several others with individual names. Coconuts, which grow well only on the sea and in the lowland, have increased in importance since they became a cash crop early in the 20th century. Other forest foods include mangrove fruit, yams and many kinds of wild vegetables, including ferns, treeferns, trees, vines, taros and fungi. Formerly some of these foods were particularly important in times of famine when gardens failed. They tend to be regarded as inferior to garden products, which represent the values of hard work and domestic stability, although this does not reflect on their nutritional value. Again, for the Kwaio, whose limited involvement in the cash economy resembles the Kwara'ae situation several generations ago, these wild foods form a significant, if unacknowledged, proportion of the diet, even for industrious gardeners (Akin pers. comm.)

Wild protein (*sibolo kwasi*, as distinct from vegetable 'food'), is another important resource of the forest. The importance of this subject lies in the limited amount of animal protein in the Kwara'ae diet, making protein-hunger (*sibolo'a*) a common experience in former times. Pigs are eaten mainly on special occasions, formerly especially by men as sacrificial meals for ancestral ghosts, and chickens are now eaten hardly more often. Until the 1910s, men also sometimes ate people killed in restitution and feuding. Sea fish has to be traded from the sea people by those able to attend regular coastal markets, once or twice a week in recent times. These foods have been supplemented in recent generations by relatively expensive supplies of tinned fish and meat, with effects which are evident in the greater stature of many younger people. But formerly people gathered many wild creatures which are equally nutritious but less valued and now rather neglected. The list amounts more or less to a catalogue of Malaitan fauna of a size worth eating, apart from a few creatures regarded as unclean or tabu for religious reasons.

Creatures can be classed as 'living things' (*rū mauri kī*), as plants are 'growing things. Those the Kwara'ae eat include *no'o*, both 'flying' and 'clinging' ones or birds and cuscus (several kinds of *Phalanger orientalis*, related to possum); a large rat (*ngwari*); bats (*sakwalo*); lizards (*īunu*); frogs and toads (*gwere*); grubs, including caterpillars and wood-borers (*ngwa-ngwarū*); 'hoppers' (*siko*) such as locusts; 'creeping and flying things' (*rū angoango ma rū lofo kī*) which covers other insects; and land snails (*kuru*). As inland people with little access to the sea and reefs, the Kwara'ae obtain protein also from (fresh) waters, coastal inlets and mangrove swamps. They distinguish winkles (water snails / *karango*); clams (*tutu*); crabs (*u'a*); fish (*ī'a*, one of which, *moro*, covers a variety of zoological species); eels (*dolo*); and prawns or crayfish (*denge*). Most of these creatures were probably eaten mainly as occasional snacks, but in some cases they were also gathered in quantity for substantial meals or feasts, with measures taken to conserve habitats and stocks.

It has not been easy to identify many of these living things, especially the insects, in English or zoological terms, and there are few publications on Solomon Islands fauna to assist (McCoy's *Reptiles of the Solomon Islands*, 1980, is one). The Solomon Islands postage stamps which illustrate this book are some of the clearest images of these creatures available, but they should not be taken as precise guides to appearance or to scientific identity. This applies especially to the attractive set of reptiles and amphibians (McCoy pers. com.). Although the Kwara'ae research team had no difficulty in putting names to the stamp illustrations, they may not have been considering all the characteristics which distinguish each of these living things.

Preparing food (*rao fanga'a*) requires supplies of disposable forest materials. Fuel (*so'i*) for cooking comes from a wide range of trees, which 'burn' (*du'a*) in various ways, such as 'flaming' (*kwasukwasu*), 'dying' (*maemaela*) or 'till day' (*dangi*) by smouldering overnight. Burning also describes the way trees are killed and left to dry in preparation for felling for fuel, as well as the cooking of food. Ways of burning food range from roasting on an open fire, 'flasking' (*dodoa*), which means stuffing into a tube of bamboo to be laid on the fire, and boiling in a saucepan (*kukia*, from 'cook'). 'Oven-cooking' (*gwa'abia*) with heated stones is suitable for larger quantities of food and includes 'baking' (*kō*), the term applied especially to cooking pigs. The most elaborate preparations are several kinds of pudding (*sau'a* or 'pounded' foods), made particularly for feasts.

Most of these processes require leaf from a range of suitable plants to lay out or 'spread the way' (*safa talana*) for food, or to wrap or seal it for cooking. Until recently the essential supply of water for drinking and cooking depended on bamboo for bottles and ducting to water spouts (*mā na kafo*, the water's 'face' or 'eye'). Since piped water was widely introduced in the 1980s, it has saved women much labour in carrying water home from selected clean springs. Other drinks are also mentioned, including water from growing things, and honey.

House-building (*saunga'ilana luma*) depends on particular forest materials, which the book deals with in some detail. Formerly, under the ancestral religion, ordinary dwelling houses (*luma*), men's 'sanctum' houses (*fera*) and women's seclusion houses (*bisi*) were segregated to protect the tabu qualities of men and ancestral ghosts from the defiling reproductive qualities of women. But all were usually simple four-square buildings with pitched roof, earth floor and hearth, much like the separate 'cooking house' or 'kitchen' (*luma ni du'urū'a*, *kisina*) which most households still retain. It is this basic house which we focus on in an account of building materials and techniques.

'Building houses' (*saunga'i luma'a*) implies using small trees or saplings as poles for the house frame, as distinct from setting the 'posts' (*diro*, *funu*) which are sunk into the ground and require more specialised kinds of durable wood. Best quality trees for both purposes are in increasingly short supply as shoots replaces wilderness in the most populous areas, although chainsaws and saw-milling now allow building timber to be cut from larger trees which were unusable in the past. The house frame is tied with strips of rattan or 'winds-far' (*kalitau*) or certain types of vine (*kwalo*) and thatched with panels of 'sago' (*sao*) stitched from sago palm leaves. It may also be walled with sago leaf, or with bamboo, entire or flattened into boards, or occasionally with decorative plaiting for special buildings such as sanctums and churches.

For several generations now Kwara'ae Christians have also been experimenting with colonial architectural forms. In particular, the more modern or 'important' house has a raised floor to assist ventilation and cleaning (forbidden by ancestral ghosts to avoid women going above things they might defile, particularly sacrificial pigs), as well as internal rooms, verandas and occasionally even a second storey. It usually has no hearth and often stands apart from the kitchen, being used for sleeping and living quarters but not for cooking. This means that the frame requires more durable trees, which are now distinguished from those suitable only for cooking-houses where the smoke inhibits worm and rot. However, a raised floor does also reduce the need for the most durable trees required for posts, which need only be long enough to support the floor joists on which the house frame stands.

Most of these architectural innovations have developed from older building techniques, including the raised flooring which derives from and is named for the 'platform' benching (*tatafe*) of palm or bamboo slats which serves as seats, shelves and beds in the basic house. Only the increasing minority of houses with timber frames, iron roofs and board walls are a real departure from local architecture, but these are beyond the scope of this book.

Making things (*saunga'ilana rū kī*), apart from houses, covers manufactures from forest materials such as wood, bamboo, fibre and leaf. Durable hardwood from a small range of preferred trees is used for 'carving things' (*kalakalalana rūkī*), from axe-handles, paddles and clubs to slit-gongs, bowls and canoes. Palmwood is used for bow staves and arrow foreshafts, including a palm named for this function (*basibasi*, from *basi*, bow). Bamboo is used for durable storage containers for precious objects such as personal ornaments and for the lime eaten with betel.

Binding and twining (*fi'iri'anga ma dadalo'anga*) is a more complex subject covering a wide range of techniques and materials. Most techniques can only be distinguished in translation by a very approximate use of English terms. The basic material is usually 'vine' (*kwalo*), a word which implies cordage as well as vines as growing things (hence the Pijin translation of vine as *rop*, from English 'rope'). Some vines are used entire but lengths of certain vines, as well as various kinds of tree-bark, can also be made into flat 'vine-strip' (*'aba kwalo*, which includes, for instance *'aba sula*, a strip of *sula* tree bark). These in turn may be split into fine 'shreds' (*sisilirū*) for sewing or threading beads, or twined by rubbing on the thigh into two-ply 'twine' (*dadalo*), or plaited into 'braid' (*gwa'i nili*) of three or more elements.

Vines or vine-strips are used to tie (*itoa*) house frames and to lash (*fo'ota*) or bind (*fi'iria*) bundles, as well as for making durable cordage for many purposes such as fishing line and nets, bow strings, for threading shell-money beads and other purposes.

'Plaiting' (*faosia*), including what may be distinguished as 'weaving' (*folia*), employs bark vine-strip for shoulder-bags, coconut leaf for plaited baskets and other utensils, and vine for coiled baskets. We have used English words to distinguish the various named kinds of bags, baskets and other plaited utensils, although these are often very imperfect translations.

'Wrapping' (*'afurū'a*) includes the multi-purpose mat, bag and cover known in Solomons English as an 'umbrella', made of and named for the 'mat' or pandanus leaf (*fa'u*). Other purposes are served by 'cloth' (*la'ua*), a coarse barkcloth, and by sheets of untreated bark. 'Staining' (*atongilana rū kī*) includes the use of red 'dye' (*dilo* or Indian mulberry, *Morinda*) for fibre, and black stains for wood. Red-stained coconut cuticle and yellow orchid-stem were used for 'patterned things for decoration' (*rū gwaroa fuana laungilana kī*), mainly costume ornaments, which were the finest products of Malaitan fibre arts. 'Patterned' (*gwaroa*) is a general term to cover embroidery, plaiting and weaving, as well as engraving. 'Growing things for personal decoration' (*rū bulao kī fuana laungi ngwae'a*) lists decorative and scented plants.

Many of the things described in this chapter are no longer made. Personal decorations are regarded as 'heathen' by fundamentalist Christians and as unfashionable by most others, and many fibres have been substituted by plastics such as nylon fishing-line or string. The illustrations of patterned fibrework; combs, ear-reeds and armbands, are mostly from neighbouring Kwaio, where these crafts are still alive, but they are recognised by the Kwara'ae as hardly different from those they once made themselves.

Things used for ghosts and curing (*rūfuana rao akalo'anga ma gura'anga kī*) include a wide range of growing things which are used to affect people's lives and well-being in more or less mysterious and esoteric ways. Plants are so characteristic of these processes that *'ai* (tree) also serves as a general term for magic and magical substances, even when they are not derived from trees or other growing things. But so also does *akalo* (ghost), which more precisely refers to spiritual beings, especially dead ancestors. In this context neither 'tree' nor 'ghost' should be taken too literally, and either could also be translated as 'magic' or 'medicine'.

The Kwara'ae do recognise a distinction between the inherent properties of magical or medicinal substances and the spiritual agency of ghosts, or God, who are often invoked in their use. But this can be rather ambiguous and does not necessarily coincide with the distinction between tree and ghost. Nor does it necessarily reflect the Western distinction between the therapeutic properties of some of the substances used and their symbolic and possibly psychosomatic values. Furthermore, 'things used for ghosts and curing' can also be rather ambivalent, some being used to harm as well as help, to kill as well as cure, whether through various kinds of manipulative magic such as love magic, or through deadly 'sorcery' (*kelema*). In the absence of English translations to convey the Kwara'ae concepts effectively, 'tree' and 'ghost' should be read with this range of meanings in mind. The ambiguities in translation seem appropriate to the esoteric mystery which surrounds medicine and magic in Kwara'ae culture.

In this section we list some growing things which have quite well-known protective or ritual properties, often associated with the ancestral religion, as well as certain wild creatures generally known to have religious or magical associations. But the publication of more esoteric magical and medicinal knowledge poses important problems. In writing this book we have had to recognise the risk of such knowledge being misused by some and disapproved of by others, as well as concerns over unauthorised exploitation for economic gain both locally and by outside commercial interests. As we explain, only general information is included, with details reserved for a separate reference document to be made accessible only at the discretion of the Kwara'ae chiefs.

Caring for our forest (*tagi'a sulia masu'u kia*) concludes Part 1 of the book with some general observations on resource management. Considering the range of uses which the Kwara'ae make of the forest, we may suppose that efforts to ensure their own well-being would have had a major long-term impact on the forest ecosystem which they have inhabited, according to their own histories, for up to 30 generations (perhaps 600 - 900 years?). It would be difficult even for detailed botanical surveys to demonstrate what effect this might have had on the composition of the forest, in the absence of uninhabited forest for comparison. But our book does indicate some of the ways that useful things have been planted and conserved to make the forest more habitable and economically productive. From this we may deduce that even forest which the Kwara'ae would regard as 'wilderness' and Westerners as a 'natural' environment must have been given a cultural form by many hundreds of years of clearance and regeneration, gardening, agroforestry and foraging, enhancing the proportion of useful trees. Shifting cultivation would also have maintained a higher proportion of the forest as 'shoots', with trees particularly adapted to secondary forest, than would occur in uninhabited forest. Until the colonial period these processes seem to have reached a balance which avoided much forest degradation, with only a few small areas reduced to

the infertile grassland which is becoming ever more common in tropical forest regions today, including parts of Solomon Islands.

This is not to say that Kwara'ae culture was intrinsically conservationist, or that even those most true to its ancient values are immune from the pressures and temptations which are now leading some Melanesians to participate in the degradation of their lands and forests. For all the faith that some Western conservationists have in the wisdom of indigenous rainforest peoples, they can become, as Filer suggests for Papua New Guinea, '. . . willing partners in a process which makes perfect economic sense to people who believe that they have tried and failed in all other efforts to achieve a reasonable increase in living standards' (1996:295). But as long as it was conservation of forest resources which made 'perfect economic sense' to the Kwara'ae, they showed themselves able to achieve this by maintaining a stable and productive ecosystem.

Part 2: Things which grow in the Kwara'ae area
The introduction to the forest resources and material culture of Kwara'ae in Part 1 of the book is supported by a catalogue of more than 360 named growing things in Part 2. This may represent only about half of those recognised by the Kwara'ae, albeit mainly the well-known and important ones. As an inland forest people, we might expect the Kwara'ae to have an extensive and detailed knowledge of such things. This is confirmed by botanical research in Solomon Islands as a whole, which uses Kwara'ae as the standard local vernacular for plant names. Henderson and Hancock's *Guide to the Useful Plants of Solomon Islands* (1988) lists over 800 Kwara'ae names which correspond to one or more of 3,210 botanical species which have been identified and named, from an estimated total of 4,500 species (Hancock & Henderson 1988:9). No doubt studies of most other Solomon Islands language groups could produce equally impressive inventories.

But the invaluable catalogue of Kwara'ae names in *Useful Plants* does not reveal much about Kwara'ae cultural categories or taxonomy, as its approach is basically Western and botanical. The botanists also misinterpret significant features of the language which the Kwara'ae use to describe growing things (as can be seen by comparing what follows with Henderson & Hancock 1988:13 and Whitmore 1966:120). In this book we have tried to provide a Kwara'ae rather than a botanical perspective by basing our dictionary on descriptions by the Kwara'ae research team of how each growing thing looks and grows, where it grows, and what it is used for. These descriptions provided insights into Kwara'ae categories which have enabled us to standardise the descriptions of common characteristics of growing things in terms which should make sense to Kwara'ae readers.

However, this has not completely solved the problem of how to classify these things in a way which is also appropriate for a purpose for which the Kwara'ae categories were never devised; listing and grouping growing things in a book. This exercise raises a number of interesting questions which should be taken into account in reading Part 2 of the book.

Kwara'ae botanical classification

How people describe and classify plants depends on their interest in them. The Kwara'ae are particularly concerned with the functions, whether uses or problems, material or symbolic, which they have attributed to growing things under a lifestyle based on forest-farming and foraging. The emphasis on (cultural) function is shared by English and other folk classifications, but it stands in contrast to Linnean botanical classifications based on perceived (natural) form (including genetic parameters) which serve scientific purposes such as cataloguing and tracing evolutionary relationships. Of course functions are closely related to perceptions of form and the two cannot be categorically distinguished in the Kwara'ae classification of growing things. But neither do function and form always correlate from one growing thing to another. It is also important to recognise that people may acknowledge similarities between things without necessarily assigning them to named categories, as the scientific culture of the West considers it important to do. In devising a classificatory scheme for an ethnobotanical catalogue such as this, it is also useful to identify 'covert' categories, as Sillitoe calls them (1995:204-5). These may be referred to in terms of a common characteristic or similarity to a named example when required, for instance, to deal with questions from an anthropologist.

All in all, Kwara'ae categories are less mutually exclusive and suitable for a catalogue than botanical categories are designed to be. But although the Kwara'ae classify plants mainly for pragmatic and utilitarian purposes, we have been able to adapt their existing categories or devise new ones for the equally pragmatic purpose of providing descriptions for this book. As with Sillitoe's ethnobotanical work in Papua New Guinea, this 'expands the indigenous scheme in a way that local people can understand and appreciate' (1995:209). Even if our classification is not wholly derived from Kwara'ae culture, it should make sense in Kwara'ae terms. A look at some Kwara'ae descriptions of growing things will help to explain the rationale for this approach.

First it is worth noting that the Kwara'ae word 'thing' *(rū)* allows all kinds of words to be converted quite conveniently into nouns (which accounts for what, in English terms, is the overuse of the word 'thing' in this book). 'Growing things' *(rū bulao kī)* is the simplest and perhaps the only way to describe all those things which grow as English 'plants' do. Most named growing things can also be termed 'tree' *('ai)*, although not always according to the strict meaning of the word. But there are few convenient general descriptions available for many of the things which are not trees in the strict sense, and many of these refer to functional categories which are not mutually exclusive.

'Tree' also has the functional meaning of 'wood', as a basic building and working material, and in form a tree has a hard *(ngasi* or 'strong') trunk and branches (making Kwara'ae trees rather like English ones). But in practice many of the things referred to as trees do not share all these characteristics. As Kwara'ae colleagues explain, strictly speaking, palms, soft-cored trees like pawpaw, small trees like cordyline shrubs and things like gingers and ferns are *not* trees, although they may be referred to as such. Then again, hard-stemmed shrubs like cordylines are more like trees than are leafy-stemmed plants like gingers. This is rather like a native English-speaker saying we don't normally refer to trees as plants, although we recognise that this is what they are.

The Kwara'ae language also uses various words as classifiers; particles which precede a word to indicate membership of a class (as distinct from qualifiers such as adjectives which follow it) and these can make important distinctions of meaning. Something which generally distinguishes the form of a tree is that it can be classed as a discrete 'item' by preceding it with the classifier *fa'i*, which also applies, among other things, to a fruit, a stick or a grove of a particular tree. Hence *fa'i 'ai* is a tree or a stick of wood, while *fa'i ngali* is a nut *(Canarium)* tree, a nut fruit, a nut grove, or a nut season (meaning a year). By contrast, many other growing things usually form a 'clump' or cluster of stems as items growing from a common base, which is indicated by the classifier *fi'i*. Hence *fi'i ka'o* is a bamboo clump, as distinct from *fa'i ka'o*, a bamboo stem. Of course, there are also trees which grow as clumps, but most do not, which makes the term 'clump' (clump-thing, *fi'irū*) a large and convenient descriptive category distinct from trees. A third important category is 'vine' *(kwalo)*, also used as a classifier, as in *kwalo a'ata*, a derris vine (although the vines of edible tubers are distinguished as *kwala)*. *Kwalo* also reflects the function of tying, as mentioned above. Of course vines can also grow in clumps, and the stem of a vine is also *fa'i*.

Although 'trees', 'clumps' and 'vines' cover the forms of the majority of growing things, these are not exclusive categories, nor are they always a useful basis for smaller categories. In distinguishing among the large number of trees, they can conveniently be divided into those which 'get really big' (*ke doe mala*), which 'don't get very big' (*kesi doe liu go ȯ*), and those which are 'just small' (*ti'iti'i go ȯ*), the last including things which strictly speaking are not trees in Kwara'ae or in English terms. But other categories are less easy to name. Although palms are not really trees and do not grow as clumps or vines, there is no Kwara'ae expression which conveniently describes their distinctive characteristics. Palms are normally referred to by their individual names, although their similarities are readily acknowledged, if necessary by using the English word. As a covert category, the search for an appropriate general description produces, for instance, 'things we tear into flats' (*rū ki gasi'i rebani*) for slatting and battens, a function which they share with other quite different things.

It is equally difficult to define other groups of similar things below the most general level of clumps or vines. Bamboos and certain other clumps can be grouped as 'clumps having sections' (*fi'irū kasirū'a kī*), reflecting the fact that they can be cut into convenient internode lengths, but some palms and vines could also be described thus. Gingers, heliconia and bananas can be grouped as having a 'leaf-tube sheathing the stem' (*boeboena ne 'e ofi fafia nonina*), but there is no simple descriptive term for this. Then there are things which are 'tubered' (*afurū'a*), particularly taros and yams, but also gingers, each of which could be assigned to other categories too. Small plants in general may be described as 'weeds' (*laua*), which means that they can (and often should) be 'pulled up' when they grow in places like gardens, but these also include seedlings or saplings (*ti ȧtlana*, smallness) of trees.

Although such descriptions help to clarify how the Kwara'ae perceive and classify growing things, the clearest categories below the level of trees, clumps and vines are small groups based on resemblances between particular named things. In some cases one thing is regarded as the 'proper' or 'right / correct' (*to'o* or *saga*) or 'important' (*'inoto'a*) example of a group of similar things, generally because it is the most useful or culturally significant. Fruit-bearing trees in particular give their names to 'false' or pseudo (*mala*) varieties which, although similar in appearance, do not bear edible fruit, a distinction also often made between a fruiting 'female' tree and a similar but non-fruiting 'male' one. Hence 'nut proper' (*ngali saga*) is 'female', as distinct from 'false nut' (*malangali*), which is also 'male nut' (*ngali*

ngwane). The male-female distinction may also have other implications, as with taro, of which male varieties are superior eating while female ones are more robust. In other cases utility may be less significant than how common or familiar things are. Hence 'true treefern' (*kwa'e saga*) is distinguished from 'dark treefern' (*kwa'e bulu*) and *gwaea*-treefern, all of which have similar uses.

Broader categories are formed when one thing can be said to represent or 'stand for' (*ū fuana*) other similar things. Degrees of similarity can range from 'like it' (*di'ia*) to 'a kind of it' (*malitana*) or 'equivalent to it' (*bolo fa'inia*). This solves the problem of naming the covert category of palms, allowing *niniu* (*Gulubia*) to be translated as 'palm' and to stand for things such as bow (*basibasi*) as a kind of *niniu*, and set-solid (*bōfau*) as equivalent to bow (all *Arecaceae*), as well as for cycad (*baibai*). Alpinia (ginger)(*'age*), bamboo (*ka'o / Nastus*), fern (*takuma / Diplazium*) and mat (*fa'u / Pandanus*) also serve to represent groups of similar things. As we might expect, more kinds are likely to be identified for more useful or important things. We include about 20 kinds of yam and things like it, some of which also have several kinds, but this is probably just a sample of all those known. (Akin estimates over 50 varieties of yam in neighbouring Kwaio; pers. com.). Of course some acknowledged similarities may be less significant than implicit differences. 'Apple vine' (*kwalo 'afi'o*) is named for its fruit's similarity to (Malay) apple tree (*'afi'o*), although it is a vine, and 'derris tree' (*'aiuka*) for similarity to the derris vine (*kwalo uka*), although it is a tree.

How appropriate it is to group things by these kinds of resemblance for the novel exercise of writing a book is bound to be a matter of debate. If a bundle of several kinds of edible ferns is called *takuma* when it includes this particularly important fern, this would seem to make 'like *takuma*' a useful general expression. But it might also be argued that strictly speaking ferns should be called by their individual names, or perhaps likened instead to another important fern, 'head' (*gwau / Cyclosorus*), which itself has several kinds. If pressed to find a common term for all, people are as likely to call them 'vegetables', a category which does not distinguish the common features of ferns at all, since it includes also the leaves of certain trees, clumps, vines and taros. Then there are things which are so distinctive and common that likening them to other things would normally serve no useful purpose. It would not make much sense to call coconut (*niu*), 'like palm' (*niniu / Gulubia*) when it is so ubiquitous and important, although the similarity in their names does suggest some cultural association between them.

Cataloguing 'growing things'

To organise the description of about 360 different named growing things in this book in a way which makes sense in Kwara'ae terms, we have identified them within the three major categories of 'trees', 'clumps' and 'vines' and then grouped them quite loosely into smaller categories as follows: big trees; trees which don't get very big; trees which are just small; weeds; things like palm; clumps with a leaf-tube sheathing the stems (like gingers and banana); clumps with (internode) sections (like bamboo); clumps like fern; other clumps; vines; tubered things (like taro and yam). Within these categories things are grouped together according to similarities recognised in the Kwara'ae descriptions. For trees, this means that not very big trees sometimes fall among big trees when they are similar to them. However, the distinction between tree, clump and vine is judged more significant than the comparisons drawn between them. So, for instance, apple vine (*kwalo 'afio*) comes under vines, not trees. In the apparent absence of similarities in Kwara'ae terms, growing things are grouped by botanical families, on the presumption that this is more likely to reflect Kwara'ae perceptions than would alternatives such as random or alphabetical order.

These categories should be recognised as more a literary contrivance than a reflection of common Kwara'ae usage. The Kwara'ae are more likely to refer to things in terms of the functions listed in Part 1, such as 'wood' (*'ai*), 'fuel' (*so'i*), 'fruit for eating' (*fa'irū fuana 'anilana*), 'vegetable' (*tatabu*); 'protector' (*oto'a*); 'thing for decorating the village' (*ru fuana laungilana fanoa*) and so on. Some functional associations are so strong that names are synonymous with the purposes they serve, so that 'mat' (*fa'u*) refers not only to the common mat/bag/umbrella, but also to the pandanus it is made from; 'derris' (*uka*) means 'to dope fish', *saia* means 'to caulk' with putty from the *saia* fruit, and *somota* means 'to abrade' with *somota* leaf, or even with sandpaper.

The reason we have not listed things according to such functional categories is because they are seldom mutually exclusive. Hence most of the things for 'building houses' are also for 'fuel', but there are also things used only for one or the other, while some are also for edible fruit, or vegetables, like other things which provide neither building nor fuel. Vegetables may be more salient and useful category in everyday life than a general name for ferns, but it is less useful for the essentially Western exercise of cataloguing growing things as elements of the Kwara'ae environment. Our catalogue inevitably misrepresents Kwara'ae culture insofar as it is the nature of documentation to distort culture as lived, the more

so for a society without a strong literary tradition. Culture is indeed 'reduced' to, or by, writing.

Within the catalogue these descriptive categories provide a starting point for identifying the appearance of each named growing thing and how it grows, based on the kind of distinctions drawn in Kwara'ae speech. These are rather vague by comparison with the detailed criteria devised by botanic science, but important in showing how the Kwara'ae perceive the appearance and structure of growing things. Descriptions usually begin with the appearance of its 'body' (*nonina*), which includes the trunk or main stem (*'ingatana*) of trees and clumps and the branches (*rarana*) of trees, the sections (*kasina*) of bamboos and the vines (*kwalona*) of vines. (The suffix -*na* to such words is the inalienable possessive pronoun 'his' or 'its'.) Leaves (*rauna, ra'irū*) are described as more or less long or short, wide or narrow, rounded or divided, and green or some other colour. Less is usually indicated by reduplication; hence *reba*, 'wide' and *rebareba*, 'wideish', *marako*, 'green' and *maramarako'a*, 'greenish'. The colour of the flower (*takana*) and the size or shape of the fruit (*fa'irū, fa'ina*) are usually mentioned, as is the climbing or creeping habit of vines and the appearance of an edible tuber (*afuna*) or 'bottom' (*oni onina*, from *oni*, which also means shit or arse). Less usual distinguishing features include the sap or juice (*suluna*), the smell (*mokofana*), irritant properties and peculiar forms of growth.

Where something grows may be distinguished in terms of on the sea, in the lowland or inland, as well as in more specialised places such as in scraping-swamp (mangroves), along waters or among rocks. In some cases it is the distinction between wilderness, shoots and 'about the home' (*nonina fanoa*) which is more important, or whether it is wild, planted or 'transferred' (*salinga'i*). Many thing just grow 'in all places' or 'everywhere' (*kula kī ta'ifau* or *kula kī sui*).

We conclude each entry with what 'we' do with the thing, or what it is 'for' (*fuana*), implying its 'work' (*raolana*) or use. This repeats, usually in abbreviated form, much of the information given in Part 1, which gives more technical details of uses which are common to a number of different things.

Questions of translation

Translating all this information for the English side of the book has presented several problems. As the purpose of the book is to convey a Kwara'ae perspective to readers in both languages, the English text attempts to give some sense of Kwara'ae conceptual categories by translating more literally than a conventional use of English might allow. Where conventional English seems inadequate we have used English words in unfamiliar constructions or with specialised meanings, rather than obscure significant Kwara'ae categories or treat Kwara'ae words as untranslatable. The only exceptions are certain proper names, which appear in Kwara'ae in italics. Fortunately English is a flexible language which can still be comprehended even when it borrows unfamiliar grammar or syntax and invents new compound words.

The term 'growing thing' for what in English is usually called a 'plant', with all that word's ambiguous range of meanings, is an obvious example of the rather clumsy English this kind of translation entails. But many English common names seem inappropriate because they draw precise distinctions where Kwara'ae uses only general expressions. Hence the kernel of a nut in English is in Kwara'ae simply the 'inner thing' (*sa'erū*) of a 'fruit' (*fa'irū / fuana*) and, as discussed above, 'tree' in Kwara'ae (*ai*) may mean tree, shrub, pole, stick or wood in English. Similarly, Kwara'ae terms for the parts of growing things also sometimes have no precise English or botanical equivalent. *Boeboe* is the base of a leaf or palm frond where it broadens to encase the parent stem, and although leaf-tube is an inadequate translation, it is at least more comprehensible to an English reader than the Kwara'ae term. Where such translations seem to require clarification, this is given in brackets. Hence when the Kwara'ae use something to 'conduct with' (*sabangi 'ania*), the implication is explained as 'conduct (yam vines)' or 'duct (water)'. Of course some literal translations would stretch the English language too far for little purpose. Although trees 'fill' (*fungu*) with fruit in Kwara'ae, this does not tell us much more than that they 'bear' fruit. 'Flats' (*reba / rebarū*), which covers slats, battens, wooden steps and other flat pieces of trees, is translated as 'planks' in repeated references to cutting trees for timber. Although the Kwara'ae 'burn' food, the 'burning house' (*luma ni du 'urū'a*) where they do so can less ambiguously be termed a 'cooking house.'

There are special problems in translating the Kwara'ae names for growing things, most of which do not have even generic names in common English. Many of these names are descriptive and as such convey important information on Kwara'ae cultural perceptions which are absent from the English names (if there are any) and from the botanical names (which most do have). To avoid ambiguity, references to particular growing things in the English text include, where available, three kinds of names: an English name, the Kwara'ae name and the botanical genus. It is the English name, or rather the name to be read as part of the English text (without brackets) which requires most explanation, since it may be (in order of preference) a direct translation of the Kwara'ae name; an English common name; the

botanical genus name; or the Kwara'ae name itself. The other names follow in brackets, unless they already appear as the English-text name. Where the Kwara'ae and English-text names are emphasised in capitals in facing columns, the Kwara'ae name is omitted from the English text, and where a name is repeated in the same paragraph, only the English-text name appears.

In devising this system, the priority has been to translate literally into English those Kwara'ae names which describe the cultural significance of a thing, and this has resulted in strange alternatives to some common English names. Many Kwara'ae names clearly describe commonly held perceptions, and are preferred to English common names for this reason. Hence 'winds-far' (*kalitau*) refers to the way rattan (*Calamus*) winds among the trees, and 'scraping' (*ko'a*) to the preparation of mangrove (*Bruguiera*) fruits by scraping them to make 'scraping' pudding, just as 'bindweed' or 'blackberry' reflect significant characteristics in English culture. But not all translations are so simple.

One problem is to assess what is the primary referent of the name. When Kwara'ae first used sandpaper they called it *samota* after the leaf used for smoothing carved wood, which we translate as 'abrasive' (*Ficus*). But in translating *saia* (*Parinari*) as 'putty' or *dilo* (*Morinda*) as 'dye', we have to recognise that such properties may not be referred to by these words, even metaphorically, when they derive from other things. The Kwara'ae language allows nouns to be used as verbs much as English does, so the fact that people 'derris' (*uka*) a pool to kill fish may no more justify the translation 'fish-poison' for the *uka* vine (*Derris*) than 'whip' translates the English name for the tree used to 'birch' criminals. In other cases names may be homonyms rather than evidence of cultural associations. 'Butterfly-tree' (*'aibebe*) is so called because it attracts butterflies and scatter-tree (*'aitakalo*) because it sheds and scatters its leaves. But *dolo* vine (*Caesalpina*) seems to have no more association with the eel (*dolo*), or *alo*-tree (*'aialo / Gomphandra*) with taro (*alo*), than the English ash tree does with the ash of a fire, at least so far as speakers of each language are aware. Then again, the association may be obscure or archaic, although still significant, like the many English plant names ending in 'wort' which represent medicinal knowledge now lost to most native English-speakers.

No doubt exhaustive research would find further translatable names, but where we have been unable to translate Kwara'ae names literally, English names are used as available and appropriate. Preference is given to common names, which are usually generic for tropical plants. Sometimes there is a fortunate coincidence between English generic names and

Kwara'ae specific names which can be used generically, such as 'nut' for *ngali* (*Canarium*) or 'bamboo' for *ka'o* (*Nastus*). However, many English common names are also descriptive in ways which make for inappropriate translations. 'Stinking passion-flower' has several connotations for English speakers (including perhaps varying understandings of 'passion') which would make it a quite inappropriate translation for *kwalo kakali* (*Passiflora*), even if that name were otherwise untranslatable.

A balance has to be struck between the benefit of assisting comprehension and the risk of mis-representing Kwara'ae concepts. Hence 'sago' in English is almost as devoid of secondary meanings as *sao* (apart from an archaic association with milk pudding), while the familiar 'coconut', although more descriptive than *niu*, hardly distorts the Kwara'ae concept. But 'heliconia-ginger' (*fiu rako* / *Curcuma*) is preferred to 'turmeric' because it reflects an explicit Kwara'ae description, in this case the similarity between two different growing things. Likewise, instead of stinking passion-flower we have 'hornstedtia vine (*kwalo kakali* / *Passiflora*)'. This conveys both the Kwara'ae perception of its resemblance to hornstedtia (ginger)(*kakali*) and the botanical distinction between them, rather than the cultural associations and natural characteristics conveyed by the English name.

In the absence of appropriate English names, botanical names may provide useful translations. For English speakers these will be more familiar than the Kwara'ae names but almost as devoid of cultural associations. Where used, they are treated as English names (without italics or proper-name capitals) but for the sake of brevity only the genus is used as an English-text name or a botanical referent in the English text. If only part of the Kwara'ae name is translatable, particularly with prefixes like *'ai* (tree) or *kwalo* (vine) then it may appear, for instance, as 'sarufi-tree (*'aisarufi*)' (hyphenated to show a compound word) or 'green glochidion (*'o'a marako*)'. Sometimes it seems useful to clarify Kwara'ae or botanical names by suffixing (bracketed) English generic names, as with 'mixture(bamboo)(*dodola* / *Bambusa*)' and 'caryota(palm)(*dai'i*).' Only where several untranslatable Kwara'ae names are of the same genus, where one Kwara'ae name is equivalent to botanical names from several genera, or where no botanical equivalent has been identified, do we fall back on using Kwara'ae names, distinguished by italics. (The names of living creatures, mainly included in Chapter 5 as 'wild protein', are treated in the same way, except that their scientific names are mostly unavailable or uncertain.)

However, there are a few growing things which occur so frequently in the text and have such familiar and unambiguous translations that their English names can stand without Kwara'ae or botanical references throughout most of the book. These are:

nut = *ngali* / *Canarium indicum* /canarium almond
palm = *niniu* / *Gulubia*
sago = *sao* / *Metroxylon* / sago palm / ivory nut
coconut = *niu* / *Cocos nucifera*
banana = *ba'u* / *Musa*
bamboo = *ka'o* / *Nastus* (as well as *'au*, the generic term for bamboo as a material)
sugar = *ufu* / *Saccarum* / sugar-cane
winds-far = *kalitau* / *Calamus* / rattan / lawyer cane
fern = *takuma* / *Diplazium*
treefern = *kwa'e* / *Cyathea*
taro = *alo* / *Colocasia esculenta*/ cocoyam
yam = *kai* / *Dioscorea alata* / greater yam
potato = *kumara* / *Ipomoea batatas* / sweet potato

But when all's said and done, the Kwara'ae names for growing things are the basic referents for the book and the key to the botanical identifications given in Part 2. If there is any doubt about the status of names used in the book, all names, Kwara'ae, English and botanical, are listed together at the end of each catalogue entry in Part 2 and again in the Index. We hope that this system of translation will be simpler to comprehend in reading than it has been to explain. If English-speaking readers will tolerate the rather unusual use of the language which it entails, they may come a little closer to understanding how the Kwara'ae express themselves in describing their environment and culture.

Finally, it may be useful to add a note on the Kwara'ae language itself, as used in the book. Most of the research team and associates are from East Kwara'ae, so their words may reflect the slight differences in speech between the east and west sides of the island. For clarity we have written Kwara'ae words in the long form which underlies the quicker but less precise usage of everyday conversation, in which end-vowels are usually clipped or switched to shorten the words. We have used a system of spelling recommended by Simons (1977) which involves, among other things, long vowels being shown as ā, ē, ī, ō, ū, rather than as double vowels, which result from reduplicated or compound words. For simplicity, 'f' is always used instead of 'h', although the two are usually interchangeable in Kwara'ae speech.

What is the book for?
Much of this book is about what growing things are 'for' (*fuana*), but it is also worth considering in more detail what the book itself is for. The cultural knowledge it contains is the kind that both Kwara'ae and Westerners tend to regard as 'tradition' (Kwara'ae *falafala*, Pijin *kastom*), a concept often

identified with idealised notions of the past in contrast with the rapidly changing circumstances of the present day. But although the Kwara'ae share this tendency their attitude to tradition is more sophisticated. This is not the place to explore questions about how people reconstruct their traditional culture, essentialise it, idealise it and play politics with it (although it may be worth noting that the Kwara'ae also identify the 'traditional' with the 'local', as we do in this book). But one reaction to change is to seek for continuity by incorporating interpretations of the receding past into plans for an otherwise uncertain future. This is the approach to tradition which gives our book its purpose, and we can conclude by considering what it may hope to achieve.

The changes which have come over Kwara'ae society since the beginning of the colonial period have been unprecedented in their long history. From the 1870s, when Europeans began taking Malaitans to work on overseas plantations, Kwara'ae horizons widened beyond the neighbouring islands and they rapidly adopted previously unimagined new goods and technologies. Their capacity to clear forest for gardens and building was considerably increased by steel cutting tools (from a detailed study in the Papua New Guinea Highlands, Sillitoe (1979) estimates an increase in efficiency of about 50% for steel over stone). At the same time, new forms of wealth could now be exchanged for their labour and local products. Then in the first half of the 20th century they experienced the loss of political autonomy under the British colonial administration, the transformative power of Christianity and the destructive power of mechanised warfare in the Second World War.

From the 1960s, foreign investment in primary production for export enabled the Kwara'ae to improve their material standard of living by longer term clearance of larger areas of forest for coconut and cacao plantations, market gardening, cattle farming and logging. With improved public health leading to rapid population growth, gardening for subsistence as well as for marketing has also put greater pressure on their forest, especially in areas accessible to the coast and to the new roads which have penetrated some inland areas since the 1970s. In some places this is leading to progressive degradation of the forest, reducing areas of wilderness and even of mature shoots. Ever shorter cultivation cycles produce areas of scrub with only small patches of mature trees around sites which are protected as tabu by association with the traditional religion.

Although so much of their working lives are devoted to clearing forest land to create their homes, gardens and cash-earning projects, the Kwara'ae do agree with ecologists on the importance of forest in maintaining a viable ecosystem. In Kwara'ae terms this means maintaining the conditions for human life. In recent generations they have seen the most extreme consequences of deforestation in the hills around Honiara, the capital of Solomon Islands on the neighbouring island of Guadalcanal, where many Malaitans have migrated to gain the benefits of the capitalist economy and urban life. It is they who are largely responsible for extending the barren grasslands and shrunken streams inland of the town by careless over cultivation of land not their own, to support themselves and supplement their cash incomes.

Perhaps the Kwara'ae are prepared to accept such environmental degradation as long as their livelihood does not depend entirely on the land and they still have the option of retreat to their own land at home. But on Malaita too a rapidly growing population and opportunities to earn cash from their land is degrading or replacing forest over increasing areas, especially in West Kwara'ae. Like people everywhere, many seem to have difficulty in looking far beyond their short-term needs. While the availability of imported goods reduces the need to conserve local resources, it also creates incentives to despoil them for the sake of the cash to buy these goods, and local people may not appreciate the risks outsiders perceive in eroding their forest resource base. In fact the ecological questions raised by inappropriate development tend to be overshadowed by its political repercussions. Competition for land and economic resources has recently provoked armed conflict between the peoples of Malaita and Guadalcanal and threatened the future of the whole country.

It is to address such development issues in various parts of the world that local knowledge is now increasingly being researched and published for the benefit of the communities it derives from. This is intended both to inform the theory and practice of foreign development professionals, and to enhance the culture of local people by preserving and transmitting their knowledge through the medium of writing. Of course this approach to local knowledge is not without problems of its own. In a review of 'returning results' of ethnobotanical research, Martin and Hoare (1997) warn of the risks of undermining the local control of knowledge which depends partly on restricted access to it, of failing to communicate effectively in communities unaccustomed to written resources, and of distorting oral traditions in the process of reducing them to writing. In many cases a local botanical tradition might benefit more by promoting its transmission, with associated technical skills, through the social relationships in which it can be put to use within the community. In Kwara'ae this might entail work such as auditing and planning the use of forest resources at the level of local land-holding clans under the guidance of chiefs' organisations, supported by training workshops and school programmes. But, as Martin and Hoare point out, there is also a demand for published documentation in such communities, in reaction to the way Western education undermines the appreciation and transmission of local knowledge. This is one opportunity for overseas researchers to collaborate with local people.

In the Pacific there are already some publications on traditional ecological knowledge for local readers which have the rationale that, while the value of local knowledge is increasingly challenged, its application diminished and its transfer to younger generations threatened, a corresponding development of literacy provides new opportunities for preserving and communicating this knowledge within the societies concerned as well as beyond. Such work varies between what we may call academic or etic and local or emic approaches to the documentation of traditional ecological knowledge.

On the one hand there is a programme led by one of our associates, Mark Merlin, to publish textbooks for the islands of Micronesia to educate school students in the botany and environments of their own islands through the English-language curriculum (Merlin et al. 1992,1993,1994). On the other, there is Edvard Hviding's *Dictionary of Environment and Resources in Marovo Lagoon*, presenting Solomon Islands local ecological knowledge in local language according to local categories, '. . . written primarily to be used by the Marovo people in village schools and in community-level environmental education' (1995:8). The one provides systematic environmental descriptions from a scientific perspective, the other provides local perspectives in a dictionary format which avoids the problems of describing broader cultural structures.

Our book attempts to combine aspects of both approaches by presenting a systematic description from a local perspective. It is written in response to the Kwara'ae concern to document knowledge which is being lost to many members of their rapidly changing society. We have had to decide what kind of knowledge is useful to include and how far to make it explicit when it is self-evident to Kwara'ae readers, even though it may be quite obscure to others. We have tried to strike a balance which reflects the fact that an increasing number of Kwara'ae young people are no longer brought up to learn much of what their parents and grandparents know about life in the forests of their homeland. Kwara'ae associates of our project assert that even

quite mundane information on the everyday uses of common trees for basic raw materials, which every child still learns in the more conservative rural communities, is worth documenting for the sake of educated and especially urban youngsters who do not gain this information in their upbringing. The question is whether they have the opportunity or motivation to learn it from books either.

The documentation and publication of their culture has an important symbolic value for the Kwara'ae. They have come to appreciate the value of literacy through the sacrosanct tabu texts of the Bible and the codified social norms of biblical and colonial law, experiencing written culture as a powerful tool for social transformation. In their efforts to take control of this process from the authority of government and missions, they have been codifying their genealogical history and law as tradition or *kastom* since the 1940s or earlier. This has contributed to the success of political movements in regaining some of the cultural and political autonomy lost in colonisation. But, with this experience, are the Kwara'ae now in danger of over-estimating the power of documentation for cultural conservation? Will anyone but academics, foreign and local, be interested in reading about the uses of the hundreds of plants listed in our book, whether through the Kwara'ae or English language text? Are ordinary peasant farmers, the custodians and dependants of the forest, likely to benefit from such a book, or only outsiders who may use it to serve their own interests, whether academic or commercial?

Kwara'ae and other Malaitan political movements have a good record of mobilising their communities in the cause of cultural and political autonomy, formerly focused on anti-colonial resistance and self-government, now particularly on asserting inherited land rights and local law. Perhaps these movements will also take up the issues of retaining traditional ecological knowledge and managing forest resources. The potential at least is implied in the name of the 1990s organisation which supported research for this book, the *Kwara'ae Traditional Culture and Environmental Conservation Foundation*. The activists and community leaders or 'chiefs' involved in this organisation have welcomed enthusiastically our earlier work documenting Kwara'ae land tenure in a bilingual booklet (Burt & Kwa'ioloa 1992). Will the ordinary people who support them be willing or able to draw upon this much larger work on their traditional material culture?

And what can we expect from the educated minority? The future of the Kwara'ae and their forests will also depend upon the policies and efforts of the educated elite of Islanders who can influence the economic and environmental future of Solomon Islands at a state level, within an increasingly global economic system. The more such people become estranged from the culture of the rural majority and influenced instead by their Western education, the more they may be prepared to draw upon written sources of information on their own culture. The English text of our Kwara'ae book could provide material for school teachers and curriculum writers, or for the organisers of conservation and development projects and policies. As Clarke and Thaman explain the purpose of their book *Agroforestry in the Pacific Islands*, 'If indigenous agroforestry is to be encouraged, the character and value of the many existing agroforestry systems needs to be more deeply appreciated' (1993:203).

Apart from these possibilities, the symbolic value of documentation may itself have some practical impact. Perhaps it will help local people to appreciate and assert the value of a body of knowledge too easily depreciated as old-fashioned and irrelevant by those who are immersed in or dazzled by the culture of modernity. The Kwara'ae community leaders who have given their consent and co-operation for our project claim it as a product of their own culture. If they or their descendants do decide to review the use of their forests, to plan their economic development so as to maintain a viable forest ecosystem, to build upon their traditional ecological knowledge rather than discard it, the fact that some of this knowledge has been published may help them to value it as well to use it, in the future as in the past.

References

Burt, B. 1994a *Tradition and Christianity: The Colonial Transformation of a Solomon Islands Society*. Harwood Academic Publishers, New York.

Burt, B. 1994b Land In Kwara'ae and Development in Solomon Islands. *Oceania* Vol.64 pp.317-35

Burt, B. & M. Kwa'ioloa 1992 *Falafala ana Ano 'i Kwara'ae / The Tradition of Land in Kwara'ae*. Institute of Pacific Studies and Honiara Centre, University of the South Pacific

Clarke, W.C. & R.R. Thaman 1993 *Agroforestry in the Pacific Islands: Systems for Sustainability*. United Nations University Press.

Filer, C. 1996 The Social Context of Renewable Resource Depletion in Papua New Guinea. Ch.20 in R. Howitt, J. Connell & P. Hirsch (eds.) *Resources, Nations and Indigenous Peoples: Case Studies from Australasia, Melanesia and Southeast Asia*. Oxford University Press.

Hancock, I.R & C.P. Henderson 1988 *Flora of the Solomon Islands*. Dodo Creek Research Station, Research Department, Ministry of Agriculture and Lands, Honiara.

Henderson, C.P. & I.R. Hancock, 1988 *A Guide to the Useful Plants of Solomon Islands*. Research Department, Ministry of Agriculture and Lands, Honiara.

Hviding, E. 1995 *Of Reef and Rainforest: A Dictionary of Environment and Resources in Marovo Lagoon*. Centre for Development Studies, University of Bergen in co-operation with Western Province Division of Culture, Gizo, Solomon Islands.

Kwa'ioloa, M. & B. Burt 1997 *Living Tradition: A Changing Life in Solomon Islands*. British Museum Press, London, and University of Hawaii Press, Honolulu. (autobiography of Kwa'ioloa)

Manner, H. I. 1993 Buma Village, West Kwara'ae, the Solomon Islands. Ch.3 in W.C. Clarke & R.R. Thaman, *Agroforestry in the Pacific Islands: Systems for Sustainability*. United Nations University Press

Martin, G.J. & A.L. Hoare 1997 Returning Results: Community and Environmental Education. In *People and Plants Handbook* issue 3. WWF, UNESCO, RBG Kew.

McCoy, M. 1980 Reptiles of the Solomon Islands. *Wau Ecology Institute Handbook* No.7

Merlin, M., D. Jano, W. Raynor, T. Keen, J. Juvik & B. Sebastian 1992 *Plants of Pohnpei*. East-West Center, Honolulu.

Merlin, M., A. Capelle, T. Keene, J. Juvik & J. Maragos 1994 *Plants and Environments of the Marshall Islands*. East-West Center, Honolulu.

Merlin, M., R. Taulung & J. Juvik 1993 *Plants and Environments of Kosrae*. East-West Center, Honolulu.

Nakano, K. 1992 On the Vegetational Change in Fallows at a Hamlet in a Northwestern Region of Malaita, Solomon Islands. *South Pacific Study* Vol.12:113-27

Nakano, K. & N. Miyauchi, 1996 Changes in Physical and Chemical Properties of Surface Soil in a Swidden and Subsequent Fallow in a Northwestern Region of Malaita Island, Solomon Islands. *South Pacific Study* Vol.17:1-20

Sillitoe, P. 1979 Stone Versus Steel. *Mankind* Vol.12:151-61.

Sillitoe, P. 1995 An Ethnobotanical Account of the Plant Resources of the Wola Region, Southern Highlands Province, Papua New Guinea. *Journal of Ethnobiology* Vol.15:201-35.

Sillitoe, P. 1998 What, Know Natives? Local Knowledge in Development. *Social Anthropology* Vol.6:203-220

Simons, G. 1977 *A Kwara'ae Spelling List*. Working Paper for the Language Variation and Limits to Communication Project, No.6, Summer Institute of Linguistics.

Whitmore, T.C. 1966 *Guide to the Forests of the British Solomon Islands*. Oxford University Press, London.

Williams, N.M. & G. Baines 1993 *Traditional Ecological Knowledge: Wisdom for Sustainable Development*. Centre for Resource and Environmental Studies, Australian National University.

Na kula etaeta ana 'abafola ne'e nini'a

Tualaka ma fuirū'anga
saena masu'u kia

The first part of this book is

Our life and developments
in our forest

1
Malitana masu'u kī

Masu'u rū fuana tuafilana ma fulirū'anga 'i saena di'ia o'onga'a ma 'oi fanoa'anga 'i saena, fa'īnia logo ngalilana rū bulao kwasi kī ma rū mauri fuana 'anilani ma saunga'inga 'ani'i. Masu'u ke bulao ke susuto'o bore 'ana, 'ai doe kī ne'e bulao to'oto'o ma 'ai ti'iti'i ma fi'irū kī ma ti rū bore 'ani ne'e bulao 'i safitani. Bore ma saena bubunga kia masu'u nia to'o ana ti malita'i afu masu'u. Di'ia ki leka fa'asia fafona asi ma maguru, ki ra'e saena to'ona'oa ma ki ra'e la'u 'uana tofungana tolo, ki lisia ne'e masu'u ke rokisi. 'Unari, ana ti kula 'i nai'ari ka mamata logo fa'asia logo ti kula. Ti 'ai ne'e bolo fa'inia kula kī sui, ti 'ai ne'e bolo fa'inia go'o ti kula. Fulirū'anga ma ngalirū'anga, na masu'u mamata to'oto'o, ti kula ka bolo fa'inia ti rū ma ti kula ka bolo lala fuana ti rū.

'I na'o bore ma'i aka, di'ia ki tuafia masu'u nia ke rokisia logo 'ania ta malita'i masu'u. Ki tabua o'olā kī, ki tabua fanoa kī, ki tufua 'ai kī fuana saunga'irū'anga, ki fasia logo 'ai kī saena masu'u. 'Unari na masu'u ana gwa'i dukwasi nia mamata fa'asia masu'u ana fuli o'olā ma fuli fanoa, na 'ai ne'e ke bulao ana fuli raku ni'i mamata logo.

Fafona asi
Masu'u 'i fafona asi to'o go'o ana bara 'ai doe kī di'ia alita kī, fa'i fū kī, 'ai doe ne'e teo ana kula kunu'a kī di'ia dafo, 'ai saena kabara kī di'ia ko'a kī. Bore ma rū ne'e 'oro ana fafona asi ne'e fi'i fa'u kī, fi'i tara kī, mamafu'ai kī, madakware'a kī, 'ai ana raku faolu kī. Saena bubunga to'a asi lisilana masu'u di'ia logo 'i fafona asi. Masu'u 'i fafona asi, lisilana nia satola ka le'a liu, kaida'i ki ungalia ma ki fisia, sungilana nia te'e sasala. Bore ma 'i na'o ma'i noa'a kia kesi tuafia kula nai'ari sulia ti kula ni'i kunukunu'a ka simi'a, ma sulia mae kī ke fuli logo 'i safitani to'a asi fa'inia kulu'a to'a tolo.

Kabara
Na kula kunukunu'a ne'e teo 'i fafona asi ma sulia su'u kī, ne'e asi ke fungu logo fafia kaida'i nia ke lua, kula nai'ari ko'a kī ke bulao saena, ki saea 'ania kula kabara'a sulia 'ai kabara'a 'oro ni'i ana. Ki saea logo 'ania kunu ko'a sulia ko'a ngwane ma ko'a kini, 'ai ne'e kī 'oro ka tasa saena kabara. 'I nini'ari ki saea logo 'ania maguru.

1
Kinds of forest

Forest is for living in and for developments such as gardening and home-building in, and also for taking wild growing things and living things to eat and work with. Although the forest grows and covers everything, the big trees grow individually and small trees and clumps and other things grow among them. But in our island the forest is of several kinds. If we go from on the sea and the mangroves and climb into the lowlands, and we climb further into the central inland, we see that the forest changes. So in some of those places it is different from others. Some trees are suitable for all places, some trees are suitable for some places only. For developing and taking things the forest differs, some places are suitable for some things and some places are suitable for others.

Even formerly, if we lived in the forest it changed the nature of the forest. We clear gardens, we clear homes, we chop down trees for building, we also plant trees in the forest. So then, the forest of the wilderness is different from forest on garden sites and home sites and the trees that grow on shoots sites are also different.

On the sea
The forest on the sea has only a few big trees like almond (*alita* / *Terminalia*), barringtonia (*fū*), big trees in swampy places like terminalia (*dafo*) and trees in the stilt-roots like scrapings (*ko'a* / mangroves). But things which are plentiful on the sea are mat clumps (*fa'u* / *Pandanus*), *tara* clumps (*Pandanus*), *mamafu'ai* (*Onagraceae*), croton (*madakware'a*) and trees of the new shoots. On the islands of the sea people the forest looks like on the sea. The forest on the sea looks fine and very nice and when we clear it and cut it up it is quite light to scorch off (for gardening). But formerly we didn't live in this area because some places are swampy with mosquitoes, and because feuds would develop between sea people and inland people.

Stilt-roots
The swampy places which are on the sea and along inlets, which the sea fills during high tide, the places scrapings (*ko'a* / mangroves) grow in, we call the stilt-root area because stilt-rooted trees are plentiful there. We also call it scraping swamp because male scraping and female scraping trees (*ko'a ngwane* and *ko'a kini* / *Rhizophora* and *Bruguiera*) are especially plentiful in the stilt-roots. At present we also call it mangroves.

Kabara fuana go'o dē'a ma ngalilana fa'īrū kī fuana ko'alani ma fi'i tutu kī, fa'inia logo tufulana 'ai fuana saunga'i luma'a ma tufulana bobo fita'u ma safao kī.

Stilt-roots is just for fishing and taking fruits for scraping (as pudding) and clams, and also for chopping trees for house building and chopping logs for *fita'u* (mangrove-worms) and *safao* (grubs).

Ti malita'irū ne'e ke bulao 'i fafona asi ana kula 'eke'eke ne'e satani 'uri:
Some kinds of things which grow on the sea in dry places are named:

fa'i alita	almond tree (*Terminalia*)	fa'i ba'ula	banyan tree (*Ficus*)
fa'i dalo	portia tree (*Calophyllum*)	fa'i uaua	light-weight tree (*Cordia*)
fa'i dafo	terminalia tree	fa'i 'airamo	*ramo*-tree
fa'i u'ula	ipil tree (*Intsia*)	fa'i sao	sago palm (*Metroxylon*)
fa'i 'aisisiu	*sisiu*-tree (*Excoecaria*)	mamafu'ai	*mamafu'ai* (*Onagraceae*)
fa'i mamufua	securinega tree	fa'i madakware'a	croton tree
fa'i salu	casuarina tree	fi'i afaafamanu	*afaafamanu* clump (*Flagellariaceae*)
fa'i fū	barringtonia tree	fi'i rako	heliconia clump
fa'i rārā	*rārā* tree (*Erythrina*)	fi'i fa'u	mat clump (*Pandanus*)
fa'i totongwala	*totongwala* tree (*Cerbera*)	fi'i tara	*tara* clump (*Pandanus*)
fa'i 'aibebe	butterfly-tree (*Messerschmidia /Scaevolay*)	fi'i fa'u da'i	*da'i* mat clump (*Pandanus*)
fa'i 'aimarako	green-tree (*Mastixia / Pongamia*)	kwalo a'ata	*a'ata* vine (*Derris*)
fa'i 'aibulu	dark-tree (*Diospyros*)	kwalo maemae	dies vine (*Medusanthera*)
fa'i 'ai'afae	bitter-tree	kwalo dolo	caesalpinia vine
fa'i aikame	monitor-tree (*Putranjiva / Ziayphus*)	kwalo kauburu	*kauburu* vine (*Calamus*)
fa'i 'ai'ofa	pepper-tree (*Pittosporum*)	kwalo fuara	*fuara* vine
fa'i 'aiba'asi	*ba'asi*-tree	kwalo afaafola	*afaafola* vine (*Ipomoea*)
fa'i 'aida'afi	sunshine-tree (*Desmodium*)	kwalo daudau	hold-on vine
fa'i fata	vitex tree		

Ti malita'irū ne'e ke bulao saena kabara ne'e satani 'uri:
Some kinds of things which grow in stilt-roots are named:

fa'i ko'a ngwane	male scraping tree (*Rhizophora*)	fa'i 'ailali	kidney-tree (*Inocarpus*)
fa'i ko'a kini	female scraping tree (*Bruguiera*)	fa'i totongwala	*totongwala* tree (*Cerbera*)
fa'i bubula	*bubula* tree (*Sonneratia*)	fa'i 'aikuku	*kuku*-tree (*Myristica*)
fa'i oneone	sandy tree (*Heritiera*)	fi'i tasisi	*tasisi* clump (*Cyperaceae*)
fa'i lalato	genitals tree (*Xylocarpus*)	fa'i dingale asi	sea *dingale* tree (*Lumnitzera*)
fa'i futu	*futu* tree (*Barringtonia*)		

Asirufarufa

Asirufarufa, kunukunu'a nini'a doe ka teo fafona asi kī, tala ana kula kabara'a. Kaida'i asi nia lua fafia kabara, di'ia na asi ka mai kula kabara'a ka langalanga logo, bore ma asirufarufa nia kasi mai ma kasi lua logo, kafona fafari asila'a. 'Ai ne'e ki saea 'ania rufa nia 'oro liu saena asirufarufa, fa'inia logo 'ai kī di'ia 'aininiu ma ngwano.

Saltmarsh

Saltmarsh, this is a big swamp lying on the sea, by stilt-roots places. When the sea rises it is over the stilt-roots, if the sea ebbs the stilt-roots is dry, but saltmarsh doesn't have ebb or high tide, its water is slightly salty. The tree we call marsh (*rufa / Eugenia*) is plentiful in saltmarsh, as well as trees like palm-tree (*'aininiu / Horsfieldia*) and eleocharis-grass (*ngwano*).

Kunukunua

Ti kula ne'e 'i sulia kafo kī ne'e asi kesi fungu bore fafi'i kī ni'i kunukunu'a logo, bore ma kaida'i ana da'afi na ano ke 'eke'eke, ka 'unari kula nai'ari mamata logo ana kula kabara'a.

Swamp

Some places along waters, although the sea doesn't fill them up, are also swampy, but during droughts the ground dries, and so these areas are different from stilt-roots.

Ti malita'irū ne'e ke bulao saena kunukunua ne'e satani 'uri:
Some kinds of things which grow in swamp are named:

fa'i lamilami	archidendron tree (*lamilami*)	fa'i susura	*susura* tree (*Rhizophoraceae*)
fa'i dafo	terminalia tree	fa'i mamalade	alanguim tree
fa'i kaumanu	*kaumanu* tree (*Calophyllum*)	fi'i luluka	*luluka* clump (*Dennstaedtiaceae*)
fa'i gwarogwaro	calophyllum tree	fi'i fa'u da'i	*da'i* mat clump (*Pandanus*)
fi'i tasisi	*tasisi* clump (*Guettarda / Cyperaceae*)		

To'ona'oa

Saena to'ona'oa lala ne'e gwa'i dukwasi ki ke teo ana, ma 'ai doe kī 'oro ani, di'ia akwa, ba'ula, fata, liki, ma masu'u bono ne'e suma ke fanga ana. Bore ma kula ne'e ki lisia 'ai doe 'oro ana ka gwa'i dukwasi'a ne'e sulia kafo doe kī ma gwa'i kafo kī, saena ote kī, ma fa'i ua kī, ma dododoa kī. Saena lelete ua kī go'o ne'e di'ia ki tuafia ma ano ka 'eke'eke ma noa'a ta 'ai doe kesi bulao ani, ma di'ia 'ai kī bulao bore ma kesi 'oro go'o. Saena to'ona'oa masu'u nia sasala logo, kaida'i ki fisia ma ke sinafia, sungilana nia te'e kwasukwasula.

Lowland

In lowland there is wilderness and big trees are plentiful, such as *akwa*, *ba'ula* (*Calophyllum*), vitex (*fata*), *liki* (*Pterocarpus*), and dense forest in which grubs eat. But the places where we see plentiful big trees and wilderness are along big waters and headwaters, levels, hills and valleys. On the ridges of hills where we live and the ground is dry, no big trees will grow and even if trees grow they are not plentiful. In lowland the forest is also light and when we cut it up and sun (dry) it, it scorches off with a bit of a flame.

Ti malita'irū ne'e ke bulao ka 'oro saena to'ona'oa, satani 'uri:
Some kinds of things which grow plentifully in the lowland are named:

fa'i ba'ula	*ba'ula* tree (*Calophyllum*)	fa'i sala	smooth tree (*Ficus*)
fa'i liki	pterocarpus tree	fa'i borabora	purple tree (*Leea*)
fa'i gwarogwaro	calophyllum tree	fa'i 'ako'ako	stinger tree (*Dendrocnide*)
fa'i ako	shout tree (*Pometia*)	fa'i 'amau	*'amau* tree (*Ficus*)
fa'i fata	vitex tree	fa'i 'aitea	tea-tree (*Ficus*)
fa'i mala'o	*mala'o* tree (*Trichospermum*)	fa'i niniu	palm (*Gulubia*)
fa'i tangafino	macaranga tree	fi'i kwakwako	kava clump (*Piper*)
fa'i sikimā	squirt-eye tree (*Homalanthus*)	fi'i alangia	*alangia* clump (*Ficus*)
fa'i rebareba	wideish tree (*Macaranga*)	fi'i faefae	kleinhovia clump
fa'i su'amango	breath-wipe tree (*Macaranga*)	fi'i katakata	*katakata* clump (*Nephrolpis*)
fa'i ba'aba'a	*ba'aba'a* tree (*Euodia*)	fi'i lai	imperata(grass) clump
fa'i kete	rattle tree (Planchonella)	fi'i ka'o	bamboo clump (*Nastus*)
fa'i bala	euodia tree	fi'i keketo	schizostachyum(bamboo) clump
fa'i akwa	*akwa* tree	fi'i rade	reed clump (*Poaceae*)
fa'i mamu	*mamu* tree (*Euodia*)	fi'i rako	heliconia clump
fa'i keto	*keto* tree (*Macaranga*)	fi'i 'age	alpinia(ginger) clump
fa'i 'o'a	glochidion tree (*Antidesma*)	fi'i folota	guillainia(ginger) clump
fa'i dadame	*dadame* tree (*Commersonia*)	fi'i kakali	hornstedtia(ginger) clump
fa'i milo	*milo* tree (*Elaeocarpus*)	fa'i kalitau	winds-far (rattan / *Calamus*)
fa'i 'ama	*'ama* tree (*Terminalia*)	kwalo sata	lygodium vine

Tofungana tolo

Saena tofungana tolo, masu'u kesi doe liu go'o sulia 'ai ne'e ke bulao ana kī ne'e fi'i goea kī, kwa'e kī, baliu, sakosia, fa'ibeabea, sigoria. 'Ai doe ki baru'a go'o di'ia ba'ula ma dingale. Masu'u saena tofungana tolo nia ke kulu ke isila, sungilana nia te'e ato. Saena tolo goro nia gwari liu ana dangi bore 'ana ma saena logo rodo, 'ai lokiri bolo logo fa'inia tofungana tolo bore ma noa'a ni'i kesi keta liu go'o ma ni'i lumulumu'a lala.

Central inland

In the central inland the forest doesn't get very big because the trees that grow there are *gwaea* (treefern) clumps (*Cyathea*), treefern, timonius (*sakosia*), *fa'ibeabea* (*Schizomeria*) and *sigoria* (*Araliaceae*). There are a few big trees like *ba'ula* (*Calophyllum*) and *dingale* (*Podocarpus*). The forest in the central inland is heavy and wet and quite hard to scorch off. In the misty inland it is very damp, whether by day or night and even trees suited to the central inland don't get very tall but are mossy.

Tofungana tolo, ti malita'irū ne'e ke bulao ka 'oro ana satani 'uri:

In the central inland, some kinds of things which grow plentifully are named:

fa'i baliu	*baliu* tree (*Ascarina*)	fi'i fitafita	*fitafita*(fern) clump (*Blechnum*)
fa'i sigoria	*sigoria* tree (*Plerandra / Schefflera*)	fi'i gwau bulu	dark head(fern) clump (*Cyclosorus*)
fa'i dingale	*dingale* tree (*Podocarpus*)	fi'i 'unu'unu	dennstaedtia(fern) clump
fa'i simidi	*simidi* tree	fi'i fo'oka	worship-clump (*Euodia*)
fa'i madakware'a	croton tree	fi'i dili	cordyline clump
fa'i mudu	*mudu* tree (*Dillenia*)	fi'i kwa'e	treefern clump (*Cythera*)
fa'i beabea	*beabea* tree (*Schizomeria*)	fi'i kurako	*kurako* (treefern) clump (*Cythera*)
fa'i 'aialo	gomphandra-tree	fi'i gwaea	*gwaea*(treefern) clump (*Cythera*)
fa'i 'aibū	*bū*-tree (*Myrtaceae*)	fi'i rīdo	hydnophytum (antplant) clump
fa'i akama	finschia tree	fi'i dionga	*dionga* clump (*Loranthaceae/Dendromyza*)
fa'i sakosia	timonius tree	fi'i fari	liparis (orchid) clump
fa'i akwasi	with-ease tree (*Rhus*)	fi'i ri'i	*ri'i* clump (*Euodia*)
fa'i sarufi	*sarufi* tree (*Lauraceae*)	fi'i falefalefau	*fafalefau*(yam) clump (*Dioscorea*)
fa'i sula	*sula* tree (*Trichospermum*)	fi'i kwalekwale	*kwalekwale* clump (*Flagellaria*)
fa'i 'ama rodo	night *ama* tree (*Terminalia*)	fi'i kwasakwasa	*kwasakwasa* clump (*Flagellaria*)
fa'i mamu	*mamu* tree (*Euodia*)	fi'i dangidangi	*dangidangi*(fern) clump
fa'i niniu	palm (*Gulubia*)	'ama'ama	selaginella(fern)
fi'i baliu	*baliu*-clump (*Ascarina*)	fi'i mafusu	*mafusu*(ginger) clump (*Alpinia*)
fi'i ka'o	bamboo clump (*Nastus*)	kwalo farakau	raspberry vine (*Rubus*)
fi'i gwa'igwa'i	*gwa'igwa'i* clump (*Angiopteris?*)	kwalo ufuufu	*ufuufu* vine (*Urticaceae*)
fi'i mumudala	*mumudala* clump	kwala ufi'abe	*ufi'abe*(yam) vine (*Dioscorea*)
fi'i kakara	*kakara* clump (*Alpinia*)	kwalo 'abe	anondendron vine
fi'i fulu	*fulu* clump	kwalo kaulata	*kaulata* vine (*Uncaria*)
fi'i folota	guillainia(ginger) clump	fa'i kalitau	winds-far (rattan / *Calamus*)
fi'i mamani	*mamani* clump (*Urticaceae*)		

2
O'onga'a

Masu'u ne'e kwatea ano ka ngwangwako'a ka bolo fa'inia o'ofilana, rū nai'ari ana tualaka 'i na'o, ki tua go'o ani o'olā. O'onga'a, rū ki sai le'a mala ana sulia ki ti'iti'i ma'i, na kula ne'e ki leleka ana fa'inia ma'a ma te'a kī ana asoa kī ta'ifau, ne'e o'ola na'a. 'I na'o ma'i, o'olā ne'e 'inoto'a aka, alo fa'inia kai ma fana, fa'inia logo rū kī di'ia tatabu ma ba'u. 'I nini'ari bore ki o'olia logo fanga ne'e dao ma'i 'a'e asi, rū kī di'ia kumara ma kaibia.

Kula ne'e bolo fa'inia o'olā
O'ofilana o'olā, ki efoa mala kula ne'e bolo fa'inia fanga. Kula nai'ari kī, kia'a sai go'o ani sulia ki ti'iti'i ma'i, ki leka na'a saena o'olā, ki malinga'inia na'a kula ne'e ki fasia alo ka le'a ana, kula ne'e le'a logo fuana falisi. Kula ba ko'o kia kī kira daoto'oni 'i na'o ma'i. Kaida'i ki leka sulia ta'itala, ma'a fa'inia te'a kī kira ke fa'ata'inia logo afu ano ne'e na ano sa rū, 'ai fasia ne'e 'ai sa rū, kula ne'e ki fasia fanga 'uri 'i saena 'i na'o, kula ne'e nia totolia fanga 'uri, kula ne'e noa'a nia kesi bolo fa'inia rū 'uri. Kia'a ngela kī, ana sa'ulafi ma'a kia kī kira ke fa'amanata kia 'uri, ano 'oe nia 'uri, fa'i biru kī ni'i 'uri, kula ābu 'oe kī ni'i 'uri, rū 'uri kī. Kini 'afe, kaida'i nia tua tau fa'inia ara'i nia, funga ma luma'a nia kī kira ke fa'ata'inia ano kira kī 'i ne'e nia ke o'ofia o'olā nia 'i nai'ari. Ngwae faolu ne'e tua ma'i fa'asia ta kula, ka fi'i dao kia ke fa'ata'inia logo rū nai'ari kī fuana, 'iri ne'e nia ke sai logo ana ano faolo nai'ari.

Ka 'unari ki sai ana malita'i ano ne'e bolo fa'inia fasilana fanga to'oto'o kī ni'i 'uri, kula ne'e bolo fa'inia malita'i fanga 'uri ne'e 'uri.

Malita'i ano kī
Ki sai bore ana kula, ki lia sai logo ana ano ne'e bolo fa'inia fanga noema ka noa'a go'o. 'I na'o ma'i ngwae nia ke ngalia afu ano saena limana ke mokoto'ona fuana ke sai le'a ana, di'ia nia mokole'a ka bolo fa'inia fasilana alo, di'ia nia mokoboso'a ka noa'a go'o.

2
Gardening

Forest makes the land fertile and suitable for gardening, which was our way of life formerly, when we just lived on gardens. Gardening is what we know best because since we were small the place we went with our fathers and mothers every day was the garden. Formerly the garden-crop most important to us was taro, with yam and pana(yam) and also things like vegetables and bananas. But at present we also garden foods which arrived from overseas, things like (sweet) potato and *bia*-yam (cassava).

Places suitable for gardens
To make a garden we must choose a place which is suitable for the food-crop. These are places we know of because since we were small we have gone into gardens and distinguished places where the taro we planted was good, and places which were good for yams. Those were places our grandparents discovered formerly. When we went along the path our fathers and mothers also showed us that this piece of land was so-and-so's land, this planted tree was so-and-so's tree, this area we planted such-and-such a crop in formerly, this area is fitted for such-and-such food, this area is not suitable for such-and-such a thing. As children, in the evenings our fathers and mothers would teach us so; your land is so, the boundaries are so, your tabu places are so, things like that. When a married woman comes from afar to live with her husband, her in-laws show her their lands so she can make her gardens there. With a newcomer who comes to live from elsewhere, on arrival we also show these things to him so that he'll know about the new land.

So that's how we know the kinds of land suitable for planting each food are like so, and the places suitable for such kinds of food are like so.

Kinds of ground
Although we know the places, we also know how to see if ground is suitable for food or not. Formerly a man would take a piece of ground in his hand and smell it to be sure of it, and if it smelled good it was suitable for taro planting, if it smelled rotten it was not.

Ki lia sai go'o ana ne'e malita'i ano kī to'oto'o ni'i 'uri:

ANO SAGA ne'e nia 'i tolo, nia to'o go'o ana rerede ti'iti'i, nia bolo fa'inia alo ma falisi logo.

ANO BULU ne'e gwā nia bolo ka tasa fuana fanga kī ta'ifau, fuana o'ofilana ma fasilana 'ai fufungu kī.

ANO KAOLE'A ne'e meo nia le'a logo fuana fasilana fanga kī, nia bolo logo fa'inia ti malita'i alo di'ia mamala sa'oga. Fuana logo saunga'ilana fanoa 'i saena ma fuana gwata kī kira ke kiu 'uana lalirū ma ngwalidai, ke 'ania logo ano fuana kira ke kubu.

ANO BŪ ne'e ngwara'u ma noa'a nia 'iri moge, nia bolo fa'inia falisi ma alo ma ti rū bore 'ana, di'ia kumara ma ba'u.

ANO NGWANGWAKO'A, nia bolo fa'inia alo fa'inia ta rū go'o 'ana di'ia ki fasia 'i saena.

ANO ONEONE'A ne'e 'i fafona asi, nia teo logo 'i ninimana kafo kī, ne'e ngwara'u ma kesi meme, nia bolo fa'inia alo ma falisi logo.

ANO FULAKO'A, di'ia ki fula 'ania limaka nia ke 'asi ma ke ngwafulafula go'o, nia di'ia logo memena ko'a kaida'i ne'e ki saungia 'ania fa'i saua. O'ofilana le'a liu sulia fanga le'a liu ana.

ANO DAFUDAFU, lisilana saena afu ano nia mole'a ma ka moge, nia one'a ka ngwara'u, ka moko burero. Nia bolo go'o fa'inia ti fanga di'ia kumara.

ANO KA'AKA'A 'ILA'A , lisilana gwā ma ti kula ana afu ano kī ta'i sakosako'a ma ka kwalakwala-kwao'a, ma ka ngwara'u liu mala. O'ofilana le'a logo fuana ti fanga, nia bolo fa'inia ba'u ma ufu fa'inia alo kunu, nia bolo logo fa'inia fasilana tatabu kī, bore noa'a kesi bolo fa'inia alo saga ma falisi.

ANO RATA ne'e dola fa'inia ano gwā, nia bolo fa'inia falisi ma sangai ma kumara, bore ma alo ne'e noa'a.

ANO NAKINAKI ne'e bolo fa'inia fasilana fanga kī ta'ifau.

ANO KWARU'A ne'e rakurakua noema rerede'a, noa'a kesi bolo fa'inia alo sulia nia kata 'eke'ekea. Ano kwaru'a bore, di'ia ano 'oro safitana gwa'i kwaru kī, nia ke bolo go'o fa'inia ti malita'i alo ngwane di'ia 'anigao, kōnare, beronunufi. Bore ma ano kwaru'a noa'a kesi bolo fa'inia falisi sulia gwa'i fau kī ni'i fonea 'oni'onina kesi doe. Ano kwaru'a ne'e 'eke'eke nia bolo go'o fa'inia kumara.

GWA'I KWARU kī ana kula di'ia gwauna ua, noa'a kisi o'ofia sulia noa'a ta ano to'o ana, 'i na'o ma'i ki labu kalia go'o fuana fa'i labu saena.

We recognise that the different kinds of ground are:

NORMAL GROUND which is in the inland and just has fine gravel is suitable for taro and yam too.

DARK GROUND is black and specially suitable for all foods, for gardening and planting (fruit) bearing trees.

CLAY GROUND is red and also good for planting food and suitable for some kinds of taro such as yellow-itch (*mamala sa'oga*). It is also for building houses on and for pigs to grub for roots and earthworms, and also to eat the soil so they'll be stout.

CLOTTED GROUND which is soft and not soggy is suitable for yam and taro and anything else, like potato and banana.

SOFT-MOIST GROUND is suitable for taro and for anything else if we plant it on it.

SANDY GROUND which is on the sea and also besides waters, which is soft and not soggy, is suitable for taro and also yam.

SCRAPING-POWDERY GROUND, if we powder it in our hands it falls as powder, like scraping (mangrove) paste when we pound it with a pounder. It is very good to garden as food does very well on it.

DUSTY GROUND, the inside of a piece of ground looks granular and soggy, it is sandy and soft, and it smells off. It is only suitable for foods like potato.

FLECKED-MASH GROUND looks black with some parts of the ground a bit yellowish and striped white, and it is very soft. It gardens well for some foods, it is suitable for banana and sugar (cane) and swamp taro, but it is not suitable for normal taro or yam.

CHALKY GROUND which is mixed with black ground is suitable for yam and alocasia (*sangai*) and potato, but not taro.

FLINTY GROUND is suitable for planting all foods.

ROCKY GROUND which has sharps or is gravelly is not suitable for taro because it can be dry. But even rocky ground, if there is plenty of ground between the rocks, is suitable for some kinds of male taro such as eat-Gao ('*anigao*), *kōnare* and *beronunūfi*. But rocky ground is not suitable for yam because the stones block the tubers from becoming big. Rocky ground which is dry is only suitable for potato.

ROCKS on places such as the heads of hills, we don't garden because there is no ground, formerly we staked it around for a palisade.

O'onga'a

O'ofilana kula faolo, ki lia le'a basi ana masu'u, si di'ia 'ai kī doe na'a, rū bulao ana raku faolo kī ke fi'i mae na'a, masu'u nia kwaena'anga, ka 'unari, kula nai'ari fi'i bolo fa'inia o'olā. Ki lisia logo ti rū ne'e fa'ata'inia malitana ano. Ka 'unari na kula ne'e 'ama'ama'a nia 'oro ana ne'e le'a fuana kilulana alo, si ne'e nia ka fa'ata'inia kula nai'ari gwarigwari'a.

Tabulana o'olā, ki tufua basi 'ai kī, ki fi'i fisi'i, ki sikilia kwalo kī ma fi'irū kī, ki ungalia laua kī. 'I na'o ma'i, kaida'i noa'a ta akisi ma naifi, ki tufua go'o 'ania naki, ki diua go'o fa'i kwalo kī 'ania 'abala'i 'ai. Ki ogā tufulana 'ai kī ta'ifau, kwatea o'ola ke madako le'a, 'i kesi nunufia rū fasi'i kī ma kesi bulao le'a. Te'e 'ai fasia noima kasirū fasia ta ngwae matamata go'o ne'e ke ogani ana ke alā, ki ala 'ania ke ū 'ani. 'Ai fuana so'i bore ki ogani logo ani, ki sungia ki ala 'ania ke teo fuana kwa'ilana 'i buri. Ki tufua rū kī ka sui, ki fi'i ungalia tafurū du'a kī, ki erea mafula, ki tadilia 'ifi' ai sasala kī, ti kaida'i ki sada 'ania tanga 'ai, kwatea gwa'i mafula ke aka'u, mala ki fi'i to'osia tafu kī fafia.

O'onga'a to'o ana malita'irū to'oto'o kī. Ta o'onga'a ne'e bolo fa'inia dukwasi ma masu'u bono, ne'e tafu kī kulu, ki eta sirua basi masu'u mala ki tufua 'ai kī, ka sui ki fi'i ungalia go'o ki sada fuana gwa'i mafula ki to'osia fafia. Ta malita'i o'onga'a ne'e bolo fa'inia masu'u sasala, ki ungalia laua kī ka sui ki fisia kula ka sinafia mala ki fi'i sungia. Ta malita'i o'onga'a ne'e ki ungalia masu'u ka sui, ki fisia ka teo sulia bara asoa 'i ke sinafia mala, ki fi'i alu ana, go'o ki ukua tafu du'a ore'e kī 'i 'aena gwari 'ai kī 'i ki do'ofi'i. Ta malita'i o'onga'a ne'e ki unga go'o talana gwa'i talafa, go'o ki sada gwa'i mafula ki ere le'a go'o ana 'ania 'ifi 'ai du'a le'a kī go'o ki ungalia masu'u ma'ā ki to'osia fafia gwa'i mafula.

Kaida'i mafu ke du'afia ka tali mala ana gwa'i fu'afu'a, ki fi'i alata'inia 'ania 'ai ni talatala. Alata'ilana fuana ke 'akofia ano 'i ke saungia rū angoango kī 'i kesi 'ania rū fasi'i kī, fuana logo ne'e ke 'akofia lalina 'ai kesi bulao, fa'inia logo 'i ke lia le'a. Di'ia ti rū bulao 'oro kī ne'e fura 'ali'ali ma rū ne'e kesi du'a talangwara'u kī, ki fiku'i sulia biru ma 'i 'aena gwari 'ai doe kī, 'i ne'e kaida'i ni'i fura ka sui, ano ke ngwangwako'a na'a, kwatea fanga saena fa'i bō ke bulao le'a. Rū bulao ne'e bolo fa'inia ka di'ia fi'i folota, fi'i 'age, fi'i gwa'igwa'i, ufuufu, sasao, fa'inia logo isifura kī.

Gardening

To garden a new place, we first have a good look at the forest and if the trees are big, the growing things of the shoots are dying off and the forest is mature, so then that place will be suitable for a garden. We also look at anything which shows the nature of the ground. Thus a place where selaginella(fern) (*'ama'ama*) is plentiful is good for planting taro, as it shows the place is damp.

To clear a garden, we first chop down the trees and cut them up, we cut off the vines and clumps and clear the weeds. Formerly when there were no axes and bush-knives, we just chopped with flint and smashed vines with a plank of wood. We like to cut down all the trees to make the garden good and light, so as not to shade the planted things, or they won't grow well. Only planted trees or planted canes belonging to other people do we conserve and let stand. Trees for fuel we also conserve, we scorch them and let them remain for felling later. We chop down everything and then we clear off the dry rubbish, we kindle a fire and trim off the logs of light wood, sometimes we stack it on a forked stick to make the fire catch, and then throw on the rubbish.

Gardening has different kinds. In gardening which is suitable for wilderness and dense forest, where the rubbish is heavy, we first slash the forest and then chop down the trees, then we clear it off and stack it for a fire and throw it on. In a kind of gardening which is suitable for light forest, we clear the weeds and then we cut up the area to be well sunned and then we scorch it off. In a kind of gardening where we clear off all the forest, we cut it up to lie for several days to be well sunned, we then set fire to it, then we heap up the remaining dry rubbish at the foot of the tree stumps to burn them. In a kind of gardening where we just clear the way for an ash-patch, we stack a fire and kindle it well with well-dried logs of wood, then we clear off the unburned forest and throw it on the fire.

When the fire has burned and all that's left is ash, we then spread it with a raking-stick. The spreading is to heat the ground to kill creeping things so they won't eat what is planted, and also to heat the roots of trees so they won't grow, and also to look good. If there are plenty of growing things which rot quickly and won't burn easily, we gather them along the boundaries and at the stumps of big trees so that when they have rotted the ground is soft and moist, to make food in the plot grow well. Suitable growing things are like guillainia(ginger) clumps (*folota*), alpinia(ginger) clumps (*'age*), *gwa'igwa'i* (*Angiopteris*) clumps, *ufuufu* (*Cyrtandra / Urticaceae*), *sasao* (*musa*), and also rotten logs.

1   *A view over lowland forest from Na'oasi in 'Aita'e, looking towards the east coast of Kwara'ae and the offshore islands of Kwai and Ngongosila. On the hill to the right a home can just be seen among coconut palms. (1983)*

2   *A path through the scraping swamp (mangroves) near Faumamanu. The people are returning from market and the last man is carrying mat (pandanus) leaves. (1979)*

3   *Lowland forest, viewed from a taro garden at the same place as (1) but looking inland, with other garden clearings in the distance. (1983)*

4   *Trees of wilderness in the lowland, in Latea. (1983)*

5   *Forest of the central inland, looking west towards Siale, the ancient headquarters of Kwara'ae. (1984)*

6   *Adriel Rofate'e clearing a garden in lowland forest in Latea, and burning the rubbish around a tree stump. (1983)*

7   *Riomea and his wife planting a new plot to extend a taro garden, near Lama. (1979)*

8   *Adriel Rofate'e training the vines in his yam-plot.(1984)*

9   *A mature old-fashioned garden in 'Ere'ere, belonging to the tabu-speaker (priest) Timi Ko'oliu. It includes taro and yam, with bananas, sugarcane and leaf-vegetables, fenced with bamboo against pigs. (1984)*

10 *Some living things of the forest as portrayed in Solomon Islands postage stamps, with Kwara'ae identifications.*
(see Chapter 5)

fau

kongeo

ku'i

no'o akaaka'u

sura'au

surao fauboso

dangisato

'unu

kame

kwasa

adaadafunu

gwereano

gwerekafo

'ik'iki

'ufu'ufu

u'a tōtō

u'a kakarafau

alimango

latokaeso

loi kakala'a

gwaubonobono

fa'i ngwalada

fa'i tafo

Ki sungia o'ola ka sui, ki fi'i bōngia 'ania fa'i bō kī 'ania fa'i 'ai saga kī. Bōngilana o'olā nia fuana fasilana ma'e o'ola to'oto'o 'i kaida'i ta'i fa'i bō nia ka lango fuana 'anilana, ka sui ta fa'i bō nia ke fi'i lango la'u 'i burina. Logo ma fuana di'ia ta fa'i bō ne'e bolo fa'inia mani tolo di'ia tafuli'ae, ta ma ngwae kī ke foli'i logo. Logo fuana o'olā ke lia le'a, kwatea kaida'i ngwae kī ke liu saena ta'itala, kira ke lia sai ana ngwae ne'e sai le'a ana o'onga'a nini'a. Ki saunga'inia logo babala kī 'i māna o'ola fuana tua nunufi'a ma ki tua langalanga fa'asia uta. Babala nai'ari, ki barabara ka sui 'ania fa'i 'ai kī, ki fi'i to'osia fafona 'ania ra'i rū di'ia uli 'age kī, uli folota kī, uli kikiru kwasi kī, ra'i rako kī.

Fasilana o'olā

Ki tabua o'olā ka sui, ki fi'i fasia fanga 'i saena. O'onga'a 'i na'o, fanga 'inoto'a ko'o kia kī ne'e alo fa'inia logo kai, ki saea 'ania falisi. 'I ta'ena o'onga'a nia rokisi fa'asia kaida'i 'i na'o, sulia ki fasia fanga faolu kī ne'e dao ma'i fa'asia 'a'e asi. Kumara ne'e fanga 'inoto'a 'i nini'ari, rū ko'o kia kī kira salinga'inia bore ma'i, fa'inia logo ti fanga faka. Kaida'i ki fasia o'olā, ki fasia logo na fanga matamata kī 'i safitana alo ma saena falisi kī. Rū di'ia ba'u kī ma fi'i ufu kī ma ti tatabu ne'e di'ia fi'i ba'era ma fi'i 'ofenga, ki fasia rū nai'ari kī sulia biru kī ma 'i 'aena logo gwari 'ai kī ma gwa'i fau kī. Ki fasi'i logo 'i safitana kumara ma kaibia kī.

Ta o'onga'a ki o'o matamata logo talana fanga to'oto'o kī ana kula ne'e bolo fa'inia, di'ia koli, ba'u, bini, baenafa, kiukaba, 'ufu, losi, kakama, melene. Di'ia fa'i ba'u, ki fasia ke matamata, nia kata nunufia alo kī. Alo bore ki kilu mamata logo ana ta'i malita'irū'anga, ka tasa ana alo fuana logo sarelana 'ania gwata kī. Kaida'i o'olā nia ke bulao, laua ta'a kī ke ra'e safitana fanga, ka 'unari ki failia basi, leleka o'olā ka lango, ki fi'i 'ilia fuana 'anilana.

Fanga fasia saena o'olā kī ni'i 'uri:
ALO ne'e fanga 'inoto'a ko'obora kia kī, ki to'o ana alo 'oro kī, satani to'oto'o, ti ai ki saea 'ania alo ngwane kī, ti ai alo kini kī. Alo ngwane nia doe ka ra'e ka ūlua ka liufia mala alo kini kī. 'Anilana alo ngwane nia le'a ma ka moko le'a liu ka tasa ana alo kini kī, ti alo ngwane ni'i alo sata mala. Ta rū bore, gwa'i mata'inga ne'e ki saea 'ania 'eo nia kata fa'alia alo ngwane, nia ke dula. Alo kini, noa'a ni'i kasi alo sata'anga bore 'ana maurilana nia ngasingasi'a, noa'a 'iri talangwara'u fuana 'eo ke saungia ana kaida'i gwa'i mata'inga ne'e 'eo ka liu.

After we have scorched the garden we set it out in plots with straight poles. Setting out the garden is for planting each garden separately so when one plot ripens for eating, then another plot will ripen after it. Also so that if a plot is worth a local (shell) money such as a ten-string, then people can buy it. Also so that the garden will look good, so that when people pass by on the path they'll recognise that it's a person who knows well how to garden. We also build shelters in front of the garden for staying in the shade and staying dry from rain. For these shelters we make a frame with poles and then roof it with leaves such as alpinia(ginger)('age) fronds, guillainia(ginger) (folota) fronds, wild betel (Areca) fronds and heliconia (rako) leaves.

Planting a garden

We clear the garden and then plant food-crops in it. In gardening formerly, the most important food of our ancestors was taro and also yam, called yam-plot (falisi). Today gardening has changed from former times, because we plant new foods which arrived from overseas. Potato is the important food at present, something our ancestors transferred here, as well as other foreign foods. When we plant a garden, we also plant other foods among taro and in yam-plots. Things such as bananas and clumps of sugar and vegetables such as clumps of cabbage (ba'era / Hibiscus) and pseuderanthemum (ofenga), we plant these things along the boundaries and also at the foot of tree stumps and rocks. We also plant them among potato and bia-yam (cassava).

Some gardens we also make separately for individual foods in places which suit them, such as maize, banana, bean, pineapple, cucumber, sugar, pitpit (losi / Saccharum), cyrtosperma (kakama) and melon. If it's a plot of bananas, we plant it separately lest it shade the taro. Even taro we bury (plant) separately in one variety, especially taro for feeding pigs. When the garden grows, weeds come up among the food, so then we weed it, and eventually the garden wilts and we dig it up to eat.

The foods planted in gardens are these:
TARO (Colocasia) is the most important food of our forebears and we have many taros with different names, some we call male taro and some female taro. Male taro is big and upstanding, much more so than female taros. Male taro is good eating and smells very good, better than female taro, and some male taros are really prime taro. However, the disease we call poison may spoil male taro with stem-rot. Female taro is not prime taro but its life is stronger, it is not easy for poison to kill it when there is an epidemic of poison.

O'ofilana alo nama ana kula ne'e bolo fa'inia, kula gwarigwari'a kī go'o, ano te'e moge go'o, ano gwā bore 'ana, ano kaole'a, ano nakinaki'a, ano saga, ma kula ano to'onga. Saena kula 'eke'eke noa'a nia kesi ūlua le'a ana, noa'a kisi kilua la'u ana ano ne'e kwaru'a ma ka rerede'a ma ka gwara ofoofo. Fasilana alo, ki kilua a'una 'ania suba'e. Alo ngwane, ki kilua nama saena gwa'italafa kī, di'ia langa 'ani kula nia kata simora'a. Alo kini ki kilua bore ma saena langa ani kula. Saena o'olā alo ki fasia logo 'asaka kī 'i 'aena gwari ai kī ma saena gwa'i talafa kī ma gwauna fa'i alo kī, rū nai'ari fuana ulikwa'ima nari.

FALISI ne'e 'inoto'a logo 'i na'o, nia to'o ana malita'irū 'oro kī, di'ia kai ma fàna ma 'arakai, ti ai ke kwasila'a logo, ki salinga'ini'i ma'i 'i masu'u. O'ofilana, na o'olā faolu ana kai ma fana ma arakai go'o, ki saea 'ania fa'i falisi, ma di'ia ki fasi fuli ana ta ma ki saea 'ania fa'i kukuli. Ti kaida'i ki fasi'i logo safitana alo.

Kula ne'e bolo fa'inia falisi, ano bū'a ne'e noa'a kesi moge, kula ngwangwakwa'a kī, ma ti kula 'i fafona asi ne'e ano oneone'a ma afu ano fulako'a kī. Noa'a kai kesi bulao saena kunukunua. O'ofilana falisi, kaida'i 'oni'onirū ni'i karangia bulao ana August noema September, ki o'o na'a talani fuana fasilana. Fasilana, ki afita ano ka le'a mala, ki fi'i ru'unga'inia 'uli kai kī saena afita fuiri, nia ke bulao na'a ma'i. Teoteo sulia ūlu madamo ka sui, ki fi'i tufu sabangi na'a fuana sabangilana falisi. Sabangi ki lia nama 'uana fa'i 'ai ne'e ngasi kī, di'ia 'ai ne'e bolo fa'inia saunga'i luma'a: fa'i mamalade, fa'i 'aisirufarufa, fa'i gwarogwaro, fa'i kaumanu, fa'i ba'ula, fa'i mamufua, fa'i fata. Ki sabangi logo 'ania fa'i keketo ma lalana ka'o kī. Ki 'ili talana basi ta kwato go'o ki fi'i katanga'inia fa'i sabangi kī ni'i egola'inia sulia fa'i kwato fuana kwalana kai ke ra'e kalia.

Leleka ana kaida'i ana April leleka ana June, karangi falisi nia ke lango na'a, nia ka sa'o ru'uru'u na'a, ki saunga'inia babala 'i falisi fuana alulana falisi saena ke teo langalanga fa'asia uta. 'I na'o falisi nia ke lango ana July, 'i nini'ari nia ke lango na'a ana August ma September. Nia lango mala, ki fi'i 'ilia kai kī, ti ai ki ngalia fuana 'anilana, ti ai ki alua ke ma'asia sulia rō madamo kī noema ūlu madamo kī fuana la'u fasilana.

Taro gardening must be in a suitable place, in damp places, quite soggy ground, whether black ground, clay ground, flinty ground, normal ground or a place with proper ground. In a dry place it won't stand up well, nor can we bury (plant) it in ground which is rocky and gravelly or on landslides. To plant taro we bury the stock with a dibble. Male taro we have to plant on ash-patches, lest on the dry (unfertilised) area it grow unhealthily. But we bury female taro on the dry area. In the taro garden we also plant coleus (*'asaka* / *Blumea*) at the foot of tree stumps, in ash patches and at the head of the taro plot, as a protector-plant.

YAM was also important formerly and has many kinds such as yam (*kai* / greater yam / *Dioscorea alata*), pana(yam) (*fana* / lesser yam / *D. esculenta*) and *arakai*(yam) (*D. pentaphylla*), and others growing wild which we transfer from the forest. In gardening, a new garden of yam, pana(yam) and *'arakai*(yam) is called a yam-plot (*falisi*) and if we plant it on an existing site then we call it *kukuli*. Sometimes we plant them among taro.

A place suitable for yam is clotted ground which is not soggy, soft and moist places and some places on the sea where the ground is sandy with bits of scraping-powdery ground. Yam won't grow in swamp. To garden yam, when the tubers are about to grow in August or September we garden the space for planting. To plant, we mound the ground well before we insert the yam skin into the mound when it is already growing. It lies for three months and then we cut conductors (props) to conduct the yams. For conductors we have to look for trees which are strong, like trees suitable for house-building: *mamalade* (*Alangium*), *sirufarufa*-tree (*Myrtaceae*), *gwarogwaro*, *kaumanu*, *ba'ula* (all *Calophyllum*), securinega (*mamufua*), and vitex (*fata*). We also prop with schizostachyum(bamboo) (*keketo*). We first dig in the main pole and then thrust in the conductors to lean on the main pole for the yam vines to climb around.

Eventually, during the time from April to June when the yam has almost wilted and has yellowed throughout, we build a yam shelter to put the yams to stay dry from the rain. Formerly yam would wilt in July, at present it wilts in August and September. Once it wilts we dig up the yams, some we take for eating, some we put to wait for two or three months for planting again.

KUMARA, rū faka nini'a, nia to'o ana bara malita'irū, nia 'inoto'a nini'ari sulia talata'i kaida'i saena fa'i ngali kī rokisi ne'e ka kwatea ano bore ka 'iri bolo logo fa'inia alo ma kai ma fana. Kaida'i ki lafua alo ka sui, ki fasia logo kumara 'i fuila raku.

KAIBIA, rū faka logo nini'a, nia to'o ana bara malita'irū, nia 'inoto'a logo sulia nia bolo fa'inia kula kī sui, kula fanga kesi bulao le'a bore ana, ki fasia go'o 'aka kasina kaibia ana.
FILA, alo doe mala nini'a.
KAKAMA, ki saea logo 'ania ALO KUNU, alo faka nini'a, ki fasia seana kula fungu.
KONGKONG ALO, ta sata KALAFERA, alo faka nini'a.
BA'U, nia to'o ana malita'irū 'oro kī, ti ai rū 'inoto'a 'i na'o, ti ai rū 'i 'a'e asi kī lala.
'OFENGA ne'e tatabu 'i na'o, nia to'o ana malita'irū kī.
BEROBERO ne'e tatabu 'i na'o.
    Ki to'o logo ana tatabu ma fa'irū 'oro ne'e rū faka, ti ai satani 'uri:
BA'ERA, nia to'o ana malita'irū 'oro kī.
TANAFA, ta sata WATAKABIS
SILATA
BINI, nia to'o ana malita'irū 'oro kī.
UFU
LOSI
BAENAFA
KIUKABA
KOLI

Fa'amaurilana o'olā
Saena o'olā ki fasia logo rū kī fuana ulikwa'ima, rū ne'e ke fa'amauria o'olā, 'i ke tagi sulia ke bulao le'a, ke fonea mata'inga nia kata takisia fanga kī, ngwae nia kata ngali ma'i ma'e akalo fuana fa'alilana o'olā. Rū fuana ulikwa'ima kī ne'e rū di'ia fi'i 'asaka ma fi'i gwagwasu ma fa'i bala. Rū mokole'a nai'ari kī, mokofani ne'e fonea mata'inga. Ni'i fuana logo laungilana o'ola 'i ke kwanga. Ulikwaimā, ki fasia ana kula di'ia gwa'i talafa ma 'aena gwari 'ai ma gwauna fa'i bō kī. Si ne'e 'asaka nia teo safitana alo kī ma ka tagi sulida fa'asia alo kata mae ana 'eo noima ka simora'a, ka kwatea o'olā kī ka 'inoi lala. Nia teo logo safitana falisi 'i ne'e nia ke fonea mata'inga ne'e ke takisia falisi fuiri. 'I na'o ma'i, kaida'i ki fasia ulikwaimā ki fasia ana 'ofodangi, ki fo'osia basi akalo fuana nia ke mamanā, kwatea nia ke ngasingasi'a. 'Unari, kula ulikwaimā nai'ari ke teo ana, noa'a ta kini kesi liu ana, nia kata fa'asuā. Nia ke teo nama leleka o'olā ka lango ma ka mau'a.

(Sweet) POTATO is foreign, it has several kinds and is important at present because at certain times of the year changes make the ground unsuitable for taro and yam and pana(yam). When we have lifted the taro then we plant potato in the shoots site.
BIA-YAM (cassava) is foreign, it has several kinds and is also important because it is suitable for all places and even in places where food won't grow we can plant a length of *bia*-yam cane.
ALOCASIA is a really big taro.
CYRTOSPERMA, also called SWAMP TARO, this is a foreign taro, we plant it in flooded places.
KONGKONG TARO, also called *KALAFERA*, this is a foreign taro.
BANANA has many kinds, some of them were important formerly and some are from overseas.
PSEUDERANTHEMUM is a vegetable from before, it has different kinds.
BEROBERO (*Araliaceae*) is a vegetable from before.
    We also have many vegetables and fruits which are foreign, some are named:
CABBAGE (*Hibiscus*) has many different kinds.
TANAFA, also called WATERCRESS
SHALLOT
BEAN has many different kinds
SUGAR (*Saccharum*)
PITPIT (*Saccharum*)
PINEAPPLE
CUCUMBER
MAIZE

Making the garden live
In the garden we also plant things as protector-plants, things to give the garden life, to ensure it grows well and block the sicknesses that might attack the food, and the person who might bring magic to damage the garden. Protector-plants are things like coleus clumps (*'asaka* / *Lamiaceae*), hediotis clumps (*gwagwasu*) and euodia trees (*bala*). These are good-smelling things and it is their smell which blocks the sickness. They are also to decorate the garden to be pretty. We plant protector-plants in places like ash patches and the foot of tree stumps and at the head of the plots. So the coleus is among the taro and protects it against dying from poison or stunting, making the garden fruitful. It is also among the yams to block the sickness which attacks yams. Formerly, when we planted a protector-plant we planted it in the morning and first prayed to the ghosts to be true, to make it powerful. So then, the place a protector-plant was, no woman could pass by lest she defile it. It has to stay until the garden wilts (yam) or matures (taro).

Ti rū la'u ki sasia fuana guralana o'olā 'i ke le'a. Taba'a, ki koria butarū, ki lalia ma ki taka 'ania saena kula langa, ki ngīa fa'asia saena falisi, ki kilua 'ania alo, ka sui fanga kī ke ūlua go'o. Ki fi'i koria mumudala, ki ba'ata ki fi'i taka 'ania saena o'olā 'i ke su'usia 'eo 'i kesi takisia alo.

Bulaolana masu'u burina o'olā

Kaida'i o'olā ki 'ania ka sui na'a, ti fanga ke teo 'ua di'ia kai ma ba'u ma fi'i ufu, bore ma laua ta'a kī ke ore ke fi'i bulao, ki ngalia nama 'aka fanga kī saena raku. Ngwae sai ana ke tabu 'afi'i ma ka 'ani'i logo bore ma di'ia masu'u buru na'a fafi'i ta ngwae bore 'ana ke ngalia fuana 'anilana.

Laua ne'e ke eta bulao ne'e rū di'ia mamafu'ai, garagara, maraburabu, kwakwalu bebe, kuikuita, ma karasi. Leleka raku faolu ka bulao la'u, na 'ai kī ma fi'irū kī ma kwalo kī ke bulao na'a fuana ni'i ke buru fafia fuli o'olā.

'Ai ne'e ke bulao saena raku faolu ne'e rū di'ia fa'i karefo, fa'i sikima, fa'i sungasunga, fa'i mala'o, fa'i su'amango, fa'i kakafae, fa'i akwasi, fa'i fae, fa'i fifikulu, fa'i tangafeno, fa'i mangomango, fi'i agalu.

Fi'irū ne'e ke bulao saena raku faolu ne'e rū di'ia fi'i 'age, fi'i folota, fi'i kakali, fi'i rako, fi'i kwakwako, fi'i kokoi. Fi'i ka'o saena masu'u, lalina ke garagara ma'i 'i fafona ano nia fi'i bulao saena fuli raku.

Fa'i kwalo ne'e ke bulao saena raku faolu ne'e rū di'ia kwalo 'abui, kwalo farakau, kwalo oli, kwalo lolosi, kwalo kakali, kwalo sa'a.

Raku faolu nai'ari nia ke bulao sulia rō fa'i ngali noema ūlu fa'i ngali noema fai fa'i ngali kī, leleka 'ai kī ke doe la'u, nia ke fi'i masu'ula la'u. Go'o nia ke bulao sulia lima fa'i ngali kī, sali ka leka ana karangia akwala ma lima fa'i ngali kī, leleka 'ai ana raku faolu nai'ari kī ke mae ka sui na'a, 'ai ana dukwasi ka tata'e ka doe na'a, masu'u kwaena, nia ka bolo la'u fa'inia o'ofilana.

We also do other things to benefit a garden. With gigantic (*taba'a* tree / *Alstonia*), we scrape a parcel (of bark), make an invocation and scatter it in the dry area, we break bits off in a yam garden and we bury it with taro, then the food-crop will be upstanding. We then scrape *mumudala* (bark), package it and then scatter it in the garden to resist poison so it won't attack the taro.

Forest growth after the garden

When the garden has all been eaten, some food is still there such as yams and bananas and sugar clumps, but the remaining weeds then grow and we have to take the food from in the shoots. The person can clear around it and eat it, but if the forest thickens over it anyone may take it to eat.

The weeds which grow first are things like *mamafu'ai* (Onagraceae), *garagara* (fern) (*Nephrolepis*), *maraburabu* (*Crassocephalum*), clingers (*kwakwalubebe*/ Asteraceae), swarm (*ku'iku'ita*) and grass. Eventually new shoots grow too, the trees, clumps and vines grow to cover over the garden site.

Trees which grow in the new shoots are things like flare (*karefo* / *Shleinitzia*), squirt-eye (*sikimā* / *Homalanthus*), pipturus (*sungasunga*), *mala'o* (*Trichospermum*), breath-wipe (*su'amango* / *Macaranga*), *kakafae* (*Clerodendrum*), with-ease (*akwasi* / *Rhus*), mimosa (*fae*), *fifikulu* (*Trema*), macaranga (*tangafeno*), breathing (*mangomango* / *Ficus*) and *agalu* clump (*Ficus*).

Clumps which grow in the new shoots are things like alpinia (ginger) (*'age*), guillainia (ginger) (*folota*), hornstedtia (ginger) (*kakali*), heliconia (*rako*), kava (*kwakwako* / *Piper*), *kokoi* clump. Bamboo clump in the forest, its roots come spreading under ground and it then grows in the shoot-site.

Vines which grow in new shoots are things like convolvulus vine (*'abui* / *Ipomoea*), raspberry vine (*farakau* / *Rubus*), return vine (*oli* / *Ipomoea*), mikania vine (*lolosi*), hornstedtia vine (*kwalo kakali* / *Passiflora*) and *sa'a* vine (*Papilionatae*).

The new shoots will grow for two or three or four years until eventually the trees grow bigger and it then becomes forested. Then it will grow for five years, perhaps it will go on for nearly fifteen years, and eventually those trees of the new shoots will have all died off and the trees of the wilderness will have become big, the forest is mature, and it is again suitable for gardening.

3
Sare gwata ʼa

Gwata, rū ʼinotoʼa ana tuaʼa ʼi Kwaraʼae, ta neʼe ki tagi leʼa mala sulia gwata ana falafala kia. Kaidaʼi uikiti, gwata neʼe rū ki kōngia mala ana akalo fuana mauriʼa. Diʼia ta ngwae ke mataʼi, ki daua nama ta gwata ki leka kōngia ana akalo, ʼiri ke kwate ngwae fuiri ke mauri. Gwata rū logo fuana folilana ma folosilana ʼania mani tolo ma mani faka.

Gwata, ki laga ana sarelana. ʼI naʼo maʼi, gwata tiʼitiʼi ki tagi leʼa sulia ka diʼia logo ngela, ki alua ana kula ʼakoʼako saena luma, ʼunari ki meme ʼana, ki ʼalataka ʼana, ki fulā logo ʼana. Diʼia nia ʼaba-ʼabaʼa naʼa ta ma ki tufu tiʼitiʼi naʼa ana fanga nia kī. Diʼia nia doe naʼa ta ma ki ʼui naʼa ʼania fanga kī fuana, ki tufu afu sao kī fuana, goʼo nia ka leka kiu naʼa saena makelaʼa. Diʼia fanga nia ʼato ana kaidaʼi ana fioloʼa, ki tufua logo kwaʼe fuana sarelana. Ti ngwae ke sare gwata logo ʼania ʼai, ti ai ki siufia ʼania gwata ma ti ai ki dola memena ʼania fanga gwata ʼi ke doe ʼaliʼali. Ti kaidaʼi ki ke sare gwata ʼania rū saena asi kī.

Ki sarea bore gwata kī niʼi ke talafanga goʼo ʼana saena logo masuʼu. Diʼia kira kiu kira ke lulu ʼuana fangalada, rū diʼia ngwalidai kī, gogoromalau, ngwaingwai ʼi folota, rako, ʼage, kaʼo, kaʼo asi, lalirū diʼia lalina kaʼo, kikiru, faʼinia ti lali ʼai neʼe totolia nia ke ʼania, lali keketo, folota, rako, kakali, ʼage, daiʼi, niu, niniu, bofau, diʼa, basibasi, filu, tali, fiʼi leo, nia ʼania logo ʼisifura. Fanga neʼe gwata kwasi doe ana naʼiriʼa.

Sarelana gwata fuana ke doe ma ka kubu mala, ʼi ke kwatea gwata ke raʼo ma ka tua toʼo nia kata leka kwau ka ʼania faʼalia oʼolā ti ngwae kī. ʼI naʼo maʼi ki sarea gwata naʼa ʼania alo goʼo ʼana bore ma niniʼari ki sarea ʼania kaibia ma kumara. Ki saungaʼinia logo luma gwata ʼi nonina fanoa fuana teoʼa ma na fangaʼa saena.

Faʼi ngongō ki falasia ʼi neʼe ke kubu ma ka doe ʼaliʼali, logo ma fuana noaʼa nia kesi moko taʼa. Diʼia ngwae toʼo goʼo ana gwata kini kī, ta ma nia ke ngalia maʼi faʼi ngongo ta ngwae ʼi ke raʼefia, goʼo nia ke kwatea logo ngwanengwanelasu.

3
Keeping pigs

Pigs are very important in Kwaraʼae life, hence we care for pigs very well in our culture. In pagan times pigs were what we had to bake to the ghosts to have life. If a person was sick we had to take hold of a pig and go and bake it for a ghost so that he'd make that person live. Pigs were also for selling and purchasing for local shell-money and foreign money.

With pigs, we work hard to feed them. Formerly, we cared for a piglet like a child, we put it in a warm place in the house, so then we chewed up its food, we bit off pieces, and we crumbled it up. If it was half-grown then we chopped its food up small. If it was big then we threw food to it, we chopped pieces of sago (pith) for it, and it went grubbing in the pen. If food was hard to get in times of hunger, we also chopped treefern to feed it. Some people feed pigs with tree (medicine) too, some trees we bathe the pigs with (infusions) and some trees we mix a paste (of bark, leaf etc.) with the pigs' food to make them grow big quickly. Sometimes we feed pigs with things from the sea.

Although we feed pigs they also feed them-selves in the forest. If they grub they search for food, things like worms, beetle-grubs, sprouts of guillainia(ginger)(*folota*), heliconia (*rako*), alpinia (ginger)(*ʼage*), bamboo, sea bamboo (*kaʼo asi*); roots like bamboo and betel(palm)(*kikiru / Areca*), and tree roots suitable to eat; roots of schizostachyum (bamboo)(*keketo*), guillainia(ginger), heliconia, hornstedtia(ginger)(*kakali*), alpinia (ginger), rhopaloblaste(palm)(*daiʼi*), coconut, palm, set-solid (palm) (*bōfau / Ptychosperma*), bow(palm) (*basibasi / Arecaceae*), bright(palm)(*filu / Livistona*), split bright (palm)(*filu tali / Licuala*), barren (*leo / Dioscorea*), and they also eat rotten logs. That's the food wild pigs grow big on.

Feeding pigs is so they'll be big and stout, to make the pig be tame and stay put, lest it go off and despoil other people's gardens. Formerly we fed pigs with just taro but at present we feed them with *bia*-yam (cassava) and potato. We also build a pig house in the home area for it to sleep and eat in.

A boar we castrate so it will get stout and big quickly, and also so it won't smell bad. If a person only has female pigs, then he will bring someone else's boar to mount it, and then he will give a piglet for the insemination.

Sakalilana gwata

'I na'o o'olā, ki sakali 'usia gwata kata 'ania fanga kī. Kaida'i uikiti ki sakalia logo fanoa 'i ne'e gwata kesi ru'u ma'i kata kiufia fanoa ma luma kī, ka tasa ana luma bisi kī, nia kata sua, rū ki kōngia ana akalo. Ki labua logo bā gwata ma ki sakalia logo luma gwata.

Saunga'i bā'anga, ki labua 'ania 'ai ngasi kī, 'ai di'ia mamufua ma fata ma ngara, fa'inia logo fa'i 'au kī. 'Ai kī, ki tufua ki tadili'i go'o ki katani labulaburū kī. Ti 'ai, di'ia ki tufua ma ki labua 'ania ma'e bā, nia ke bulao fuana fonelana gwata kī. Bore 'ana ki lia nama 'i safitana 'ai ne'e mae kī, ki talafuli'i 'ania ti 'ai faolu. 'Ai ne'e ke bulao kī 'uri: fa'ola, 'alabusi, fata, 'ako'ako, iloi, tatali, 'o'a. Itolana bā ne'e bolo nama fa'inia kwalo ne'e kesi fura 'ali'ali ana kula ne'e to'ea ma ka sinafia, ki itoa 'ania kwalo rara, kwalo sata, fa'i kwalekwale, ti kaida'i fa'i leo. 'Aba kalitau bore noa'a kesi teo tau, ta ne'e ki kwa'ia 'ania fa'i kalitau la'ula'u kī, ti kaida'i ki sisi'i 'ania rō rebarū'anga.

Ta malita'i bā, ki sufungia logo fofo 'au kī, ki labua to'o rō ma'e sakali 'i ki ludangia fa'i 'au kī 'i safitana rō ma'e bā kī ma ki fi'i itobakasia fa'i 'ai fafia fa'i 'au kī.

Ta malita'i bā, ki saea 'ania satana sakali ko'oko'o, ki saunga'inia ana kula ne'e noa'a ta fi'i ka'o ana. Ki alua bobo 'ai ta'i doe ka teo 'i ano, ki fi'i labunga'inia fa'i 'ai kī ke ū kwairokisi fafia, ki taidīa mala, ki fi'i ludangia ti fa'i 'ai saena ma'e sakali fuiri ki itoa 'ania fa'i kwalo, mala ka fi'i ngasi ma ka teo tau fuana gwata ke tua 'i saena.

Ta malita'i bā, ki saunga'inia logo 'ania 'ai ne'e ngasi liu kī, di'ia mamufua, fata, u'ula, liki, kwa'u, 'o'a. Ki tufua ki kwa'igasia 'ania akisi ma ki tadilia, ka sui ki 'ilia kakaloa talani ki labunga'ini'i ki taidīa mala, noa'a kisi itoa na'a bā ne'e 'ania ta fa'i kwalo.

Ta malita'i bā, ki 'ilia go'o kakaloa 'usia gwata. Ti malita'i bā, ki 'ili ofotā kula 'ato 'i gwata kesi ra'e ana.

Ti malita'i bā, ki 'uia sulufaua 'usia gwata. Sulufaua, ki saunga'inia 'ania ano ma gwa'i kwa'e kī fa'inia gwa'i fau kī. Ki 'ilia kakaloa, ki ludangia gwa'i fau kī ka ra'e ma'i fafona ano, ki alua ano fafia fau fuiri, sui ki kwalea ma'i gwa'ina kwa'e. Ki ludangia fafia ano fuiri, sui ki 'uia la'u ta kula 'i fau

Fencing pigs

Formerly we fenced gardens against pigs lest they eat the food. In pagan times we also fenced homes so that pigs wouldn't enter, lest they grub up the homes and houses, especially the seclusion houses, and be defiled, as things we bake to ghosts. We also stake a pig barrier to fence the pig house.

To build a barrier we stake with strong trees, like securinega (*mamufua*), vitex (*fata*) and prickly (*ngara / Fagraea*) as well as bamboos. We chop and trim the trees and stick them in as fence stakes. Some trees, if we chop them down and stake a barrier with them, they'll grow to block the pigs. But when we can see between the dead trees we have to replace them with new trees. Trees which will grow are: mallow (*fa'ola / Hibiscus*), *'alabusi* (*Euphorbiaceae*), vitex, stinger (*'ako'ako /Dendrocnide*), *iloi* (*Urticaceae*), hibiscus (*tatali*), glochidion (*'o'a*). Tying the barrier requires vines which won't rot quickly in a place which is soaked and sunned and we tie with heliconia vine (*kwalo rārā/Stenochlaena*), lygodium vine (*sata*), *kwalekwale* vine (*Flagellaria*) and sometimes with barren vine (*leo / Dioscorea*). But winds-far strip won't last long so we use the winds-far entire and sometimes split it into two flats.

One kind of barrier, we cut a bundle of bamboos and stake the fence posts in pairs to stack the bamboos in between the two barrier posts and we then tie and clamp trees against the bamboos.

One kind of barrier which we call an owl fence, we build in place where there are no clumps of bamboo. We lay quite big logs of wood on the ground and then stake trees to stand crosswise over them, very close together, we then stack trees inside those fence posts and tie them with vine, and then it is strong and long-lasting for pigs to live in.

One kind of barrier we also build with trees which are very strong such as securinega (*mamufua*), vitex (*fata*), ipil (*'u'ula / Intsia*), pterocarpus (*liki*), drink (*kwa'u / Premna*), glochidion (*'o'a*). We chop and split them with an axe and trim them and then we dig a trench for them and stake them in very close together, we don't tie the barrier with vine.

One kind of barrier, we just dig a ditch to stop the pigs. For one kind of barrier we dig away at a steep place so the pigs can't climb it.

Some kinds of barrier, we build stone walling to stop the pigs. We build stone walling with earth and treefern (*kwa'e / Cyathea*) trunks with stones. We dig a trench and heap up stones in it to rise above ground level, we put earth on the stones and then we carry up a treefern trunk. We stack it on 'i fafona, mala ka fi'i bolo fa'inia ne'e gwata ke tua 'i saena ma noa'a nia kesi lofo noima ke ru'u 'i mā.

Ta sakali'a la'u ne'e ki saea 'ania satana fa'i labu, sulia ki labu 'usia na fanoa fa'asia ta malimae kata saungia ngwae kī, 'i ra'efilana ke 'ato. Ki saunga'inia 'ania na gwa'i kwa'e kī noema sasa 'i kwa'e, ki 'ilia kakaloa talani. Ki saunga'inia fa'i labu logo 'ania sulufaua.

top of the earth, then we throw another layer of earth on top and then it is suitable for pigs to live in and they can't jump over or get through.

One other fence we call a palisade (*fa'i labu*) because we stake (*labu*) the home against enemies who might kill people, so that it is hard to climb up. We build it with treefern trunks or close-set treeferns and dig them into a trench. We also make palisades of stone walling.

Fanga saena masu'u kī

Saena masu'u rū 'oro kī ne'e bulao fuana 'anilana; rū to'o ana fa'irū kī, tatabu kī, kai kī, gero kī. Ti ai ni'i bulao kwasila'a, ti ai ki fasi'i lala, ti ai ki tagi logo suli'i.

'Ai fungu fuana 'anilana fa'irū kī

'Ai fungu fuana 'anilana, ki to'o ana ai 'oro kī, ti ai ne'e bulao kwasila'a, ti ai ne'e ki fasi'i. 'Ai fasia fuiri kī, ana kula di'ia nonina fanoa, sulia ta'itala kī, māna kafo kī, fuli tua'a kī. Ti kaida'i ki fasia logo saena o'olā kī. Ki fasia fa'irū noima ki salinga'inia bubirū, ki efoa go'o 'ai ne'e fuana doe noima 'uilana lasirū talangwara'u noima 'anilana mamasia ma ka asila liu. 'Ai fasi'i kī bore ti ai ke bulao kwasi logo.

'Ai fuana 'anilana fa'irū kī, satani 'uri:
NGALI, ti aï fasi'i, ti ai ni'i kwasi logo, ta malita'i ai ne'e kwasi lala. Ngali ne'e fanga 'inoto'a fuaka, ki 'uia lasirū, ki okea sa'erū kī nioma ki saungia 'ania kata.
FALA, rū fasia go'o, nia bolo logo fa'inia ngali faka. Ki 'ania sa'erū, 'anilana le'a liu logo di'ia sa'e ngali kī.
ADO'A, rū fasia logo. Fa'irū di'ia logo ngali, ki okea sa'erū kī, ki sau kata logo 'ania, di'ia ngali.

ALITA, ti ai fasi'i, ti ai ni'i kwasi logo. Fa'irū di'ia logo ngali, ki okea sa'erū go'o, noa'a kisi do'ofia, noa'a kisi sau kata 'ania.
'AFI'O, ti ai ki fasi'i, ti ai ni'i kwasi logo. Ki okea fuana, 'anilana le'a liu.
'AFI'O BŪ ne'e rū kwasi lala, 'anilana 'eo'eo ana 'afi'o saga.
'ASAI, ti ai ki fasi'i, ti ai ni'i kwasi logo. Ki okea fuana, 'anilana asila liu.
'AIO, ti ai fasi'i, ti ai ni'i kwasi logo. Ki okea fa'irū, anilana asila liu ma ka 'eo'eo

AKAMA, rū kwasi go'o. Ki 'ania fuana, ki usu'ia afuna sulia ma'e 'ai fuana du'afilana, 'anilana rakufa di'ia ngali ma ka 'ero'ero.
BALE'O, ta sata RAU'AI, ti ai ki fasi'i ma ti ai ka kwasi logo, ta malita'i ai kwasi lala. Ki du'atelea fa'irū kī ma ki resia ka faolo mala ki fi'i 'ani'i, 'anilana le'a liu.
RAKONA, rū kwasi go'o. Ki 'ania fa'irū, 'anilana ka asila liu.
KO'A KINI, rū kwasi go'o. Fa'irū kī ki ko'ā ki du'afia fuana 'anilana.

Foods in the forest

In the forest there are many things which grow to be eaten; things which have fruits, vegetables, yams and fungi. Some of them grow wild, some we plant, and some we care for.

Trees bearing fruit for eating

Of (fruit) bearing trees for eating we have many, some of which grow wild, some of which we plant. The planted trees are in places like home areas, along paths, at water-spouts and rest-sites. Sometimes we also plant them in gardens. We plant fruits or transfer seedlings, we just choose trees which have big fruit or easy-to-crack shells or are tasty to eat or very sweet. Although trees are planted, some of them also grow wild.

Trees for eating the fruit are named:
NUT (*Canarium indicum*), some are planted, some are wild and some kinds are just wild. Nut is an important food for us, we crack the shell and eat the inside raw or we make it into nut-pudding.
CUTNUT (*Barringtonia*) is a planted tree, it is equivalent to a foreign nut. We eat its inside, it is very good to eat like the inside of nut.
JOINED (*Canarium*) is also planted. Its fruit is like nut, we eat the inside raw and we also make nut-pudding with it, like nut.
ALMOND (*Terminalia*), some are planted, some are wild. The fruit is like nut, we just eat the inside raw, we don't burn it or make nut-pudding with it.
APPLE (*Eugenia*), some we plant, some are wild. We eat the fruit raw, it is very good to eat.
SOUR APPLE is wild, it is more acid to eat than apple proper.
MANGO (*Mangifera*), some we plant, some are wild. We eat the fruit raw, it is very sweet to eat.
ACID (*Spondias*), some are planted, some are wild. We eat the fruit raw, it is very sweet to eat but acid.
FINSCHIA is just wild. We eat the fruit, we thread pieces of it on a stick to burn, it is appetizing to eat like nut, and oily.
BREADFRUIT (*Artocarpus*), also called *RAU'AI*, some are planted, some are also wild and some kinds are only wild. We roast the fruit and scrape it clean, then eat it, it is very good to eat.
PARATOCARPUS is just wild. We eat the fruit, it is very sweet to eat.
FEMALE SCRAPING (*Bruguiera* mangrove) is just wild. We scrape and burn the fruit to eat (as pudding).

DAE, ti ai fasi'i, ti ai ni'i kwasi logo. Ki 'ania fa'irū, 'anilana le'a ka asila ma ka 'ero'ero, ki dodoa, ki du'atelea logo, 'i ne'e ke ngwara'u.
TO'OMA, rū kwasi go'o. 'Anilana fa'irū nia asila liu, fa'irū ngasi ki do'ofia, fa'irū make ki 'ania logo.

'EBO, ta malitarū ne'e fasia, ta malita'irū ne'e kwasi go'o. Ki 'ania fa'irū ma'ā ma ki do'ofia logo.
'IBO, tai kwao, tai ka meo, ni'i rū kwasi kī ta'ifau. Ki 'ania fa'irū.
KATAFO, rū fasia go'o. Ki 'ania fa'irū, 'anilana asila ka le'a liu.
NIU, rū fasia go'o. Ki koria sa'erū fuana lofalana ma sau gwasu 'ania.
KIKIRU, ta malita'irū ne'e fasia, ta malita'irū ne'e kwasi go'o. Ki damia fa'irū kī.
FARAKAU, ru kwasi go'o. 'Anilana fa'irū asila liu.

KAKALI, rū kwasi go'o. Ki okea magarū, 'anilana mamasia liu ka asila.
KWALO KAKALI, rū kwasi go'o. Ki 'ania fa'irū kī, 'anilani asila liu, noa'a kisi do'ofia.

KWALO 'AFI'O, rū kwasi go'o. Fa'irū di'ia logo 'afi'o, ki 'ania logo.
　　Ki to'o logo ana ti malita'irū fuana tagi'a sulia 'ai fungu kī. Di'ia 'ai nia ke rara'aufisi'a, ti kaida'i ki ke ragia ta'eta'ena kalikalia 'aena ana bara kula kī, 'i ke kwatea suluna ke āfe, ka sui nia ka fi'i fungu 'ania fa'irū kī. Ka sui mala ta'eta'ena ke fi'i lalisusu la'u. Di'ia 'ai fungu ma ka noa'a nia kesi bulao le'a noema ka keta liu fuana loilana fuana, ta ma ti kaida'i ki likisia rarana. Ka sui mala nia ka fi'i birabira la'u 'ania fa'i 'ai sasabe'a ma ka te'e dokodoko kī, 'i ne'e loilana fuana ke talangwara'u la'u. Loilana fuana 'ai di'ia fofo ngali kī, ki loia 'ania kauala. Ki kania bilinga ta reba 'au ridi ana māna fa'i 'au keta 'i ke alua kauala mala ki fi'i kaua 'ania fofo ngali kī.

Kai kwasi kī
Ti kai fuana 'anilana ni'i bulao kwasi logo saena masu'u. Ti ai go'o ne'e ki fasi'i logo saena falisi. Kai kwasi saena masu'u satani 'uri:
'ARAKAI, ki fasia logo.
SAULU, ki salinga'inia logo fuana fasilana saena falisi.
GWA'UFI nia to'o ana ti malita'i gwa'ufi fa'inia logo ti malita'irū kī di'ia malafau, falefalefau.
Ti ai kwasi go'o, ti ai ki fasi'i logo.
AFĀ, rū kwasi go'o.
UFI'ABE, rū kwasi go'o.
KAMO, rū kwasi go'o.
DA'U, ta malita'irū kwasi, ta malita'rū ki fasia.
GWAUGWAUMELA, rū kwasi go'o.

GNETUM, some are planted, some are wild. We eat the fruit, it is good to eat, sweet and oily, we flask-cook and also roast it so it is soft.
TO'OMA. (*Terminalia*) is just wild. The fruit is very sweet to eat, we burn the hard fruits and eat the ripe fruits too.
'EBO, one kind is planted, one kind is just wild. We eat the raw fruit and we also burn it.
CORYNOCARPUS, one is white, one is red and they are both wild. We eat the fruit.
PAWPAW is just planted. We eat the fruit, it is sweet and very good to eat.
COCONUT is just planted. We grate the inside for cream and pound coconut-pudding with it.
BETEL (*Areca*), one kind is planted, one kind is just wild. We chew the fruit.
RASPBERRY (*Rubus*) is just wild. The fruit is very sweet to eat.
HORNSTEDTIA (ginger) is just wild. We eat the seed raw, it is very tasty to eat and sweet.
HORNSTEDTIA-VINE (*Passiflora*) is just wild. We eat the fruits, they are very sweet to eat, we don't burn them.
APPLE-VINE (*Medinilla*) is just wild. The fruit is like apple (*'afi'o* / *Eugenia*), we eat it too.
　　We also have ways of caring for (fruit) bearing trees. If a tree is barren sometimes we strip the skin around its foot in several places to make the sap flow, and then it will bear fruit. Afterwards the skin will grow together again. If a tree bears but won't grow well or it is too tall to pick the fruit, then sometimes we lop off the branches. Then afterwards it will sprout again as straight trees which are a bit shorter, so picking the fruit is easy again. To pick the fruits of a tree, like bunches of nuts, we pick with a hook. We lash a tip of *ridi* bamboo flat (*'au ridi* / *Decospermum*) to the end of a long bamboo to make a hook and then hook the bunches of nuts with it.

Wild yams
Some yams for eating also grow wild in the forest. Some of them we also plant in the yam-plot. Wild yams in the forest are named:
'ARAKAI (*Dioscorea pentaphylla*), we also plant it.
HIGH, we also transfer it for planting in the yam-plot.
GWA'UFI (*D. aff. alata*) includes many kinds of *gwa'ufi* as well as some other kinds like *malafau* and *falefalefau*. Some are just wild, some we also plant.
AFĀ (*D. aff. esculenta*) is just wild.
UFI'ABE is just wild.
KAMO (*D. alata*) is just wild.
DA'U (*D. bulbifera*), one kind is wild, one we plant.
BROWN-HEAD is just wild.

Tatabu kwasi kī

Ti rū ne'e bulao kwasila'a saena masu'u, ki 'ania rauni noima gwa'irū di'ia tatabu, satani 'uri:

'AMAU, 'ai ne'e, nia to'o ana malita'irū to'oto'o kī, ki 'ania ngwasana.
MALIFU, 'ai ne'e, ki 'ania gwangona.
DAE, 'ai ne'e, ki 'ania gwangona.
NGO'ONGO'O, 'ai ne'e, ki 'ania gwangona.

'OFENGA, 'ai fasia nini'a bore ma nia ke bulao kwasi logo, nia to'o ana ti malita'irū, ki 'ania rauna.

RONGORONGOLUA, 'ai ne'e, ki 'ania gwa'irū kī.
TEKO, alo kwasi ne'e, ki 'ania rauna.
fi'i KOKO'OE, ki 'ania gwa'irū kī.
fi'i DIUDIUDARA, ki 'ania gwa'irū kī.
     Fi'i takuma nia to'o ana ti malita'irū to'oto'o kī, satani 'uri:
fi'i TAKUMA to'o, ki 'ania rauna.
fi'i 'UNU'UNU, ki 'ania gwa'ina.
MĀBILI, ki 'ania gwa'irū kī .
fi'i 'ORO KWADI, ki 'ania gwa'irū kī.

fi'i SISIRABA'U, ki 'ania gwa'irū fi'i ra'e kī.
fi'i SITOI, ki 'ania gwa'irū kī
fi'i GWAU saga, ki 'ania gwa'irū fi'i ra'e kī.

fi'i GWAU BALA, ki 'ania rauna.
fi'i FITAFITA, ki 'ania gwa'irū kī
KWA'E, nia to'o ana ti malita'irū to'oto'o, ki 'ania gwangoni di'ia logo takuma kī.
RĀRĀ TOLO, kwalo ne'e ki 'ania gwa'irū kī.

INA ne'e kwalo, ki 'ania gwangona kī.

Gero kī

Gero 'oro kī ni'i bulao saena masu'u fuana 'anilana. Ti gero ni'i ala ana nonina 'ai mae fura kī, ti kaida'i ki tufua 'ai kī fuana gero ke ala ana. Ti gero ne'e bulao go'o ana ano. Gero fuana 'anilana satani 'uri:

GERO NGINGI'O nia ke bulao go'o ana isifura ta 'ai go'o 'ana.
GERO TABA'A nia ke bulao go'o ana isifura ta 'ai go'o 'ana.
GERO 'OI'OI nia ke bulao ana bobo sakosia ma malanunu.
GERO SATA fa'inia logo GERO SATA 'A'EAFA ni'i ke bulao ana bobo sakosia ma malanunu.

Wild vegetables

Some things growing wild in the forest, of which we eat the leaf or the crown as vegetables, are named:
'AMAU (*Ficus*) is a tree, it has different kinds, we eat its shoot
MALIFU (*Ficus*) is a tree, we eat its leaf-shoot
GNETUM is a tree, we eat the leaf-shoot
NGO'ONGO'O (*Ficus*) is a tree, we eat its leaf-shoot.
PSEUDERANTHEMUM, this is a planted tree but it also grows wild, it has many kinds, we eat its leaf.
RONGORONGOLUA (*Acanthaceae*) is a tree, we eat the crowns.
TEKO is a wild taro, we eat its leaf.
WEDELIA clump, we eat the crowns.
SMASH-BROW clump, we eat the crowns.
     Fern clump has many separate kinds, which are named:
FERN clump proper (*Diplazium*), we eat its leaf.
DENNSTAEDTIA clump, we eat its crown.
DIRTY-EYE, we eat the crowns.
'ORO KWADI clump (*Cyclosorus*), we eat the crowns.
SISIRABA'U clump, we eat the emerging crowns.
SITOI clump (*Blechnum*), we eat the crowns
HEAD clump proper (*Cyclosorus*), we eat the emerging crowns.
PALE HEAD clump (*Cyclosorus*), we eat its leaf.
FITAFITA clump (*Blechnum*), we eat the crowns.
TREEFERN (*Cythera*) has many separate kinds, we eat their leaf-shoots like ferns.
LOCAL *RĀRĀ* (*Stenochlaena*) is a vine, we eat the crowns.
OPERCULINA is a vine, we eat the leaf-shoots.

Fungi

Many fungi grow in the forest for eating. Some fungi sprout from the trunks of rotten dead trees and sometimes we chop down trees for fungi to sprout from. Some fungi just grow on the ground. Fungi for eating are named:
NGINGI'O FUNGUS just grows on a rotten log of any tree at all.
GIGANTIC FUNGUS just grows on a rotten log of any tree at all..
'OI 'OI FUNGUS grows on timonius (*sakosia*) and nonauclea (*malanunu*) logs.
SATA FUNGUS and *SATA 'A'EAFA* FUNGUS grow on timonius and nonauclea logs.

GERO 'ULAU nia ke bulao ana bobo sakosia.
GERO SAO nia ke bulao ana bobo sao.
GERO BUBŪ nia bulao ana ano saena tolo.

GERO FAUKALA nia bulao ana ano.
GERO TAFU nia bulao saena tafu.
GERO BANIA nia ka la'umi di'ia 'aba'abana bebe kī, nia ke bulao saena ano.

'*ULAU* FUNGUS grows on timonius logs.
SAGO FUNGUS grows on sago logs.
BUBŪ FUNGUS grows on the ground in the inland.
FAUKALA FUNGUS grows on the ground.
RUBBISH FUNGUS grows on rubbish.
BANIA FUNGUS is bendy like butterfly wings, it grows on the ground.

5
Sibolo kwasi kī

'I na'o ma'i sibolo nia te'e 'ato, ki kōgwata mala fuana akalo ma fanga'a doe, ki usia go'o ī'a kī ana to'a asi. Ka 'unari sibolo kwasi ne'e rū 'inoto'a aka, rū kī di'ia no'o lofolofo, no'o akaka'u, sakwalo, unu, gwere, ngwangwa, siko, ī'a, fi'i tutu, fa'i karango.

No'o lofolofo kī

No'o lofolofo, ti no'o doe ki 'ania, ti no'o ne'e lisilana kwanga ki sare'e, ti no'o to'o ana rao'a to'oto'o kī. Ti malita'i no'o fuana 'anilana, satada 'uri:

fa'i BOLA nia di'ia logo fa'i kurukuru bore ma nia tua saena tolo.

KURUKURU nia di'ia logo fa'i bola bore ma nia tua 'i fafona asi.

FAU nia di'ia logo fa'i bola bore ma nia ti'iti'i ana.

BINA, afaafa'a ana rakana kī fa'ata'inia fa'i ngali nia tua suli'i. 'Anilana nia saela ka le'a liu.

GEO nia doe, nia di'ia karai. Ki 'ania logo fakalena.

KONGEO, nonina midimidi'a melamela'a. Nia tua saena lalano.

fa'i KU'I, lisilana di'ia logo geo ma karai, nonina gwā, aena keta, gwauna meo. Nia tua saena kunukunu'a fa'inia logo raku faolu.

KAURA, nonina melamela'a, 'aena keta liu. Nia 'ania rū ana kafo kī, di'ia denge kī, gora 'i ī'a ti'iti'i kī.

fa'i KAKA to'o ne'e kwao. Ti ngwae ke 'ania, ti ngwae kesi 'ania sulia 'anilana ngwangwā'a. Ki sarea logo.

fa'i KAKA BORA ne'e marako, kwakawana ka fau, kalikalia luana ka meo kwalakwala, kalikalia māna ka meo logo. Ki 'ania, ki sarea logo.

fa'i DANGISATO, ta sata KAKA BORA MEO, ai ngwane nia meo ta'ifau, ai kini ka marako ta'ifau.

fa'i SURA'AU, 'aba'abana fa'inia ku'iku'ina marako, nonina ka meo, tofungana gwauna ka gwā, nia to'o ana lua 'i sao, ma na alingana ka gwā.

fa'i SURAO, luana sakosako'a. Nia 'iri doe liu go'o ma nia kwanga liu. Ki sarea go'o, nia ke fata logo.

fa'i SURAO FAUBOSO, nia doe ka liufia sura'ao, nonina bolo go'o.

fa'i SURAKĒ nia di'ia logo surao bore ma nia maramarako'a lala ma ka ti'iti'i go'o, kwakwana ka melamela, fa'inia logo 'aena. Tualana nama ana gwauna niu kī. Ki sarea logo.

5
Wild proteins

Formerly protein was quite hard to get, we baked pigs for ghosts and big feasts and just bartered some fish from the sea people. Thus wild protein was important to us, things like flying birds, cuscus, bats, lizards, frogs, grubs, hoppers, fish, clams, snails.

Flying birds

Of flying birds, some big birds we eat, some birds which look pretty we feed (as pets), and some birds have particular uses. Some kinds of birds for eating are named:

PIGEON is like dove but it lives in the inland.

DOVE is like pigeon but it lives on the sea.

FAU (fruit dove) is like pigeon but it is smaller.

HORNBILL, the lines on its beak show the years it has lived. To eat, it is greasy and very good.

MEGAPODE is big, it is like a chicken. We also eat its eggs.

QUAIL, its body is speckled brown. It lives in the forest.

RAIL also looks like megapode and chicken, its body is black, its legs are long, its head is red. It lives in swamp and also in the new shoots.

HERON, its body is brownish and its legs are very long. It eats things in the waters, like prawns and small fish.

True COCKATOO (*Cacatua*) is white. Some people eat it, some people don't because it is worm ridden to eat. We also feed it.

BORA COCKATOO is green, its mouth is solid, around its neck it is light red, around its eye is red too. We eat it and we also feed it.

SUNNY-DAY, another name RED BORA COCKATOO (eclectus parrot), the male one is all red, the female one is all green.

SURA 'AU (yellow-bibbed lori), its wings and tail are green, its body is red, the top of its head is black, it has a yellow throat and its ear is black.

SURAO, its neck is yellow. It is not very big but it is very pretty. We feed it, and it also talks.

HOGSTONE *SURAO* (duchess lorikeet), it is bigger than *surao*, its body is similar.

SURAKE (Meek's lorikeet) is like *surao* but it is greenish and only small, its beak is brownish as well as its legs. It has to live at the head of coconut palms. We feed it too.

fa'i KILA nonina marako, gwauna sakosako'a, kwakwana fa'inia 'aena meomeo'a, kwakwana fau di'ia kaka.

fa'i SUBA, nia ti'iti'i liu ma nonina ka te'e kwanga.

fa'i SUBA SANE nia ti'iti'i go'o, nia di'ia logo suba. bore ma nia gwā lala.

fa'i FAO nia kesi doe liu go'o bore ma nia rafurafu'a di'ia bola.

fa'i LA'E, nia kasi doe liu go'o, lakelakena keta, nia ka eloeloa ku'iku'ina.

fa'i SINGILO nia gwā ta'ifau, kalikalia māna ka meo.

fa'i BIBISU māna ka meo, nonina ka gwā ma ka nunura. Tualana 'i gwauna 'ai doe nama, ka tasa ana ako, nia saunga'inia nu'i doe ma kira ke nu'i nama ana ta'i 'ai.

fa'i KWADU, lisilana karangia ka di'ia logo bibisu bore ma doelana liufia mala bibisu.

fa'i 'ABA RAUNGALI nia 'iri 'oro liu, kaida'i ana fa'i ngali nia ke 'idufa'i angi.

AFA nia doe ana no'o kī ta'ifau. Ki 'ania bore ma ti fū'ingwae kesi 'ania sulia kira ke kō 'ania.

fa'i ALAFAU nia kesi doe liu go'o, nia ke bilia karai kī ma fangalana ana ti no'o lofolofo.

fa'i FIU, nia doe, nonina gwā, 'aena ka ka te'e keta.

No'o akaaka'u

No'o akaaka'u nia aka'u ana 'ai kī, nia tua saena leko ma saena 'ai o'ala kī, fa'inia logo saena fi'i fari ma fi'i tatale'ole'o kī, nia ke 'ania rauna 'ai kī di'ia sikima ma salu. Ki ra'efia fuana 'anilana, ki gwa'abīa, ki dodoa, ki du'atelea, ma ki kukia logo. 'Anilana eroero ka le'a ka mamasia.

Nia to'o ana lima malita'rū kī, satani 'uri:

GUI, nonina gwā ta'ifau.

NO'O KWAO, nonina gwā ta'ifau.

fa'i REKO, ai ngwane ne'e.

fa'i SUSU, ai kini ne'e.

fa'i DANGE, nia tua saena lekona 'ai, nonina te'e melamela'a liu mala, olofana ka balabala'a.

Ngwari

Ngwari nia di'ia logo 'asofe bore ma nia doe liu mala. Nia ke 'ania rū di'ia fa'i ngali ma fa'i 'ado'a kī. Ki 'ania logo ngwari.

KILA (palm lorikeet) has a green body and its head is yellow, its mouth and its legs are red, its mouth is solid like the cockatoo (*kaka*).

SUBA is very small and its body is quite pretty.

SUBA SANE is only small and like *suba*, but it is black.

FAO is not very big and it is powdery-white like pigeon.

LA'E (willy wagtail) is not very big, it has a long tail and waves its tail.

SINGILO is black all over and surrounding its eye is red.

BIBISU has a red eye, its body is black and shiny. It lives at the head of big trees, especially shout (*ako / Pometia*), it makes a big nest and they will all nest in one tree.

KWADU looks almost like *bibisu*, but its size is greater than *bibisu*.

NUT-LEAF-WING is not very common, during the nut season it cries continually.

EAGLE is biggest of all birds. We eat it, but some clans won't eat it because they bake (pigs) to it.

ALAFAU-HAWK is not very big, it steals chickens and the food of other flying birds.

FIU-HAWK is big, its body is black and its legs are quite long.

Clinging bird (cuscus / *Phalanger oreintalis*)

Clinging bird clings to trees, it lives in cavities and in hollow trees as well as in clumps of liparis(orchid)(*fari*) and *tataleoleo*(orchid) and eats the leaves of trees like squirt-eye (*sikimā / Homalanthus*) and casuarina (*salu*). We climb after it for eating, we oven-cook it, we flask-cook it, we roast it, and we also boil it. To eat it is oily, good and delicious.

It has five kinds, their names are:

GUI, its body is all black.

WHITE CUSCUS, its body is all white.

REKO is a male one.

BREAST is a female one

DANGE lives in cavities in trees, its body is very brownish and underneath it is paleish.

Ngwari

Ngwari is like rat but it is really big. It eats things like nuts and joined (nuts)(*'ado'a / Canarium*). We also eat *ngwari*.

Sakwalo kī

Sakwalo kī ki 'ania fuana 'ai kī, di'ia bale'o, 'afi'o, kaipok, fa'u, ba'u, katafo, 'agiru kwasi, salu. Sakwalo kī ke durufia leko 'ai kī ma faoda kī. Ki 'ania sakwalo kī, 'anilana ka le'a ka di'ia no'o akaaka'u. 'I na'o ki saunga'i 'ania sulina rū di'ia ma'e nanga ma fuana tailana fa'u kī, ki efoa logo lifana fuana laungilana nonina ngwae. Kaida'i ngwae ke daoto'ona leko sakwalo, nia ke kwa'ia sakwalo ka sui, nia ke alua ke la'u sulia ta'i fa'i ngali noema rō fa'i ngali kī fuana sakwalo ke durufia la'u.

Ti malita'i sakwalo satani 'uri:
GWAUGWAUTALI nia doe ana sakwalo kī ta'ifau.
OFI'AFU ruana malita'i sakwalo doe.
RAKAGIFIGIFI ūla sakwalo ne'e te'e doe, rakana gifigifi'a.

SAKWALO LIKO nia ke lofa ana sa'ulafi kī.
'ABAKUTUKUTU nia ka ti'iti'i go'o.
'ABISINGWANEFALA nia ti'iti'i go'o, kira teo fiku usuusu'a ana ta'i kula 'i ilina ra'i rū kī di'ia kwalo salu, 'a'afae, rako, sasao.

'Unu kī

'Unu kī ki 'ania logo ai doe kī, te'e 'unu ti'iti'i kī noa'a kisi 'ani'i go'o. Ti malita'i 'unu satani 'uri:
'UNU to'o nia doe, gwauna ba'u, kwakwana ka fau. Nia ke tua ana 'ai kī, sulia nia ke 'ania rauna kwalo salu ma 'ai 'oro kī.
GWALI'UNU nia doe, lisilana di'ia logo 'unu bore ma nia ti'iti'i lala. Nia tua ana 'ai kī.
KAME, ti sata AMARI, KOKOMA'Ā, nia doe liu mala, ketalana bolo fa'inia ta'i tafanga ma nia ka maramarako'a. Nia ke tua saena faoda kī ma kula fau'a ma saena 'ai o'ala kī, saena masu'u. Nia 'inoto'a ka tasa fuana 'anilana, te'e saena ti fū'ingwae saena tolo nia ābu sulia kira ke kō ana. Ta sata ne'e kokōma'ā, sulia di'ia nia doe ka tasa, ki kōngi'i ma nia ke ma'ā logo. Kame nia di'ia logo kwasa, kaida'i ni'i ke kalea fakale'erū kī, ta'i fakalena ka alua kwasa, ta'i ke alua kame.
KWASA nia doe liu, nia ka keta nonina ka ngarangara'a ma ka aliali'a, lifana ka raku liu mala. Nia ke tua logo saena asi ma kafo ma kunu ma logo ana kula 'eke'eke. Kaida'i nia ke kalea fakala'irū nia kī, nia ke saunga'inia nui nia 'ania rauna tasisi ma rauna masu'u fafona kukunua kī. Nia ke kalea fakela'irū 'oro kī, ti fakela'iai ke abota 'ania bibi kwasa kī, ta fakela'iai ka abota 'ania bibi 'unu kī. Ki 'ania logo, fasina di'ia gwata ma buluka ma ī'a. Te'e saena ti fū'ingwae 'i fafona asi nia ābu sulia kira ke kō ana. Na kwasa rū ke saungwae.

Bats

Bats eat the fruit of trees like breadfruit (*bale'o / Artocarpus*), apple (*'afi'o / Eugenia*), kapok, mat (*fa'u / Pandanus*), banana, pawpaw (*katafo*), wild betel (*'agiru kwasi / Areca*) and casuarina (*salu*). Bats congregate in tree cavities and caves. We eat bats, they are good to eat, like cuscus. Formerly we made their bones into things like fish-hooks and (needles) for sewing mats (*fa'u / Pandanus*) and we also extracted their teeth for decorating the body. When a man comes upon a bat cavity, he kills all the bats and then leaves it for a year or two for the bats to congregate again.

Some kinds of bats are named:
GWAUGWAUTALI is the biggest of all the bats
OFI'AFU is the second kind of big bat
WIDE-NOSTRILS (tube-nosed bat / *Nyctimene*) is the third bat which is quite big, its nose has wide nostrils.
CAVITY-BAT flies in the evenings.
WRAPPED-WING is only small.
'ABISINGWANEFALA is only small, they gather to lie in a row in one place at the back of leaves such as *salu* vine (*Araceae*), bitter (betel)(*'a'afae / Areca*), heliconia (*rako*) and sasao (*musa*).

Lizards

Of lizards we eat the big ones, only small lizards we don't eat. Some kinds of lizards are named:
LIZARD proper (skink / *Corucia*) is big, its head is swollen, its mouth is solid. It lives in trees because it eats *salu* vine leaves (*Araceaea*) and many trees.
GWALI-LIZARD (*Lamprolepis*) is big, it looks like lizard but is smaller. It lives in trees.
MONITOR (*Varanus*), also called *AMARI* and RAW-BAKE, is really big, up to a fathom in length, and it is green. It lives in caves and rocky places and in hollow trees, in the forest. It is especially important for eating, only in some clans in the inland it is tabu because they worship it. The name raw-bake is because if it is especially big, we bake it but it is still raw. Monitor is like crocodile and when they lay eggs one of its eggs will produce a crocodile and another will produce a monitor.
CROCODILE is very big, it is long and its body is rough and wrinkled, its teeth are very pointed. It lives both in the sea and the waters and swamp and also in dry areas. When it lays its eggs it builds a nest of *tasisi* (*Cyperaceae*) leaves and forest leaves on the swamp. It lays many eggs, some eggs hatch into baby crocodiles, some eggs hatch into baby lizards. We eat it, its flesh is like pig, cow and fish. Only in some clans on the sea it is tabu because they worship it. Crocodile is a thing which kills.

KOANA, nia doe, nia teo saena 'ai o'ala kī. 'Anilana le'a.
gwa'i ADAADAFUNU, ki saea 'uri 'ania sulia nia teo nene ka di'ia na'a rū ne'e mae. Di'ia ki ma'u 'ania nonina ke sikifia nonimu, lisilana nonimu ka di'ia nonina adaadafunu logo. Ti ngwae go'o ne'e ke 'ania, ti ngwae noa'a go'o. Noa'a kesi 'oro go'o.

gwa'i ADATOLI lisilana di'ia logo gwa'i adaadafunu ma nia ke fa'ita'inia nama toli gwauna, nia tua ana 'ai.
GWALIKELA nia doe ka maramarako'a, nia ke tua ana tego 'ai ma 'ai kī ta'ifau.
NGONGORA nia tua saena kilu ma saena gwa'i kwa'e, saena likona 'ai mae ma 'ai o'ala kī, ki ru'ufia 'ania kui kī fuana 'anilani.
NGWADADALA nonina nunura.

'Anilana 'unu kī, ki unuunulia ana mafula ki fi'i karasia ta'eta'ena ka sui ki falasia ogana fa'asia, ki dodoa fa'inia tatabu di'ia ba'era ma ofenga saena fa'i ka'o kī, 'anilana ka le'a liu. Ti kaida'i ki gwa'abia logo fa'inia tatabu di'ia gwangona kwa'e bulu 'i ne'e ke moko le'a fuana 'anilana di'ia logo ba'era. 'I nini'ari ki kukia na'a saena fa'i sosobini kī, ki saunga'inia 'ania sufusufu ma ki lofa na'a fa'i niu fuana 'i ne'e kwa'ufilana suluna ke rakufa le'a.

Gwere kī
Gwere kī ki 'ania logo ai doe kī, te'e gwere ti'iti'i noa'a kisi 'ani'i go'o, fa'inia logo gwere faka. Gwere kī fuana anilani'i, satani 'uri:
GWERE, nia ke tua go'o ana kula kī ta'ifau saena go'o ano.
GWEREBOROSAKO nia kesi doe liu go'o, borosirana sakosakoa.
GWEREANO nia ti'iti'i go'o, nia ke tua ana ano.

GWEREKAFO nia doe liu mala, ro mā nia kī doe liu mala, angilana doe liu, lofolana tau. Ti ai ki saea 'ania FI'IFAFALUMU sulia ilina ka di'ia na'a fi'i lumulumu kī. Nia ke tua 'i fafona kafo kī olofana ra'i rau kī, saena faoda kī, ma kula ngwangwakwa'a kī. 'Anilana le'a liu.
'IKI'IKI nia ti'iti'i, 'aena keta ma nonina ka didila. Nia ke tua saena namo kī ma ninimana kunu kī. Kaida'i nia ka saele'a ke angi ka 'uri:
'iki'iki'iki'iki'iki, bore di'a ta ngwae ka liu, no'a nia kesi 'angi go'o. We eat it too.
DE'ODE'O, ta sata TUATUAFIKWALO, karangi nia ke di'ia 'iki'iki bore ma nia tua ana fa'i kwalo kī.

IGUANA is big, it lives in hollow trees. It is good to eat.
EXPIRED-WATCHER (*Gonocephalusi / Cyrtodactylus*), we call it this because it lies quietly like a dead thing. If we are afraid of its body it leaps on your body and your body will look like the body of the expired-watcher. Some people eat it, some don't. It is not very plentiful.
DOWNWARDS-WATCHER looks like expired-watcher but it always holds its head downwards, and it lives in trees.
GWALIKELA is big and green, it lives in shrivelled leaves and in all trees.
NGONGORA (*Eugongilus*) lives in caves and in treefern crowns, in dead tree cavities and hollow trees, and we go for it with dogs, to eat it.
NGWADADALA (*Sphenomorphus*) has a shiny body.

To eat lizard, we scorch it on the fire and then scrape off the skin and then cut out its guts, we flask it with vegetables like cabbage (*ba'era / Hibiscus*) and pseuderanthemum (*ofenga*) in a bamboo, it is very good to eat. Sometimes we also oven-cook it with vegetables like dark treefern leaf-shoots (*kwa'e bulu / Cyathea*) to smell good to eat like cabbage. Nowadays we boil it in a saucepan, we make it into stew and we cream coconut so that the juice will be appetising to drink.

Frogs
Of frogs we eat the big ones, only the little frogs we don't eat, and the foreign frog (cane toad). Frogs for eating are named:
FROG, it lives in every place, just on the ground.

YELLOW-BELLIED-FROG is not very big, its lower belly is yellow.
GROUND-FROG (horned frog / *Ceratrobatrachus*) is only small, it lives on the ground.
WATER-FROG (Guppy's frog / *Rana*) is very big indeed, its two eyes are very big indeed, its cry is very loud and it jumps a long way. Some we call MOSS-BEARER because its back is like a clump of moss. It lives on waters under leaves, in caves and soft moist places. It is very good to eat.
'IKI'IKI (marsh frog / *Platymantis*) is small, its legs are long and its body is slippery. It lives in pools and beside swamps. When it is happy it cries 'iki'iki'iki'iki'iki, but if anyone passes by it won't cry. We eat it too.
DE'ODE'O, also called VINE-DWELLER is rather like *'iki'iki* (marsh frog) but it lives on vines.

'OTOFAO, nia doe ka melamela'a, tualana ana fi'i rako kī ma fi'i lā kī ma ke ra'efia 'ai kī. 'Anilana le'a.

'ARA nia di'ia logo 'otofao bore ma nia ti'iti'i ma 'aena ka keta. Nia bolo logo fa'inia 'iki'iki bore ma nonina ne'e mamata ma angilana ka mamata logo fa'asia 'iki'iki.

'UFU'UFU nia doe mala, nonina ka melamela'a. Nia tua saena masu'u ma safitana tematema rau kī. Di'ia ana rodo ma ke tua saena ta'i tala. 'Unari ki unu logo 'uani ki dau'i fuana 'anilani, 'anilana le'a liu.

OGEOGE, noa'a kesi doe liu go'o, nia ke tua ana ano ma ana bobo 'ai kī.

'U'URU nia ti'iti'i go'o, nia ke tua logo saena masu'u saena ano. Ki 'ania logo ma 'anilana le'a.

MAMASAFI, malata'i gwere to'oto'o kī nini'a, ni'i ti'iti'i go'o, lisilada ka mamata, angilada mamata to'oto'o. Ti ngwae ke 'ania bore ma ti ngwae noa'a go'o.

Ngwangarū kī

'I na'o ti ngwangarū di'ia numa ma ganafu ma safao, ki 'ania di'ia sibolo. Ngwangarū fuana 'anilana, satani 'uri:

NUMA kī ke bura ana 'ai kī di'ia akwasi, mamu, akama, kwanasia, 'aisiko, fo'a, sakosia, ni'i 'ania rauni. Ta malita'i numa mamata ne'e ke 'ania rauna akama, nonina kwanga liu. Numa nai'ari kī, 'anilana le'a liu ta'ifau.

Numa kī to'o ana kaida'i ana July ma August. 'Ai ne'e numa ke fanga ana, ki tabu 'afia, leleka kaida'i numa kī 'oro ka doe ki orosia rarana 'ai ne'e numa bura ana, ki 'oia. Kaida'i ki 'oia ki daria 'i ne'e sūla 'ai 'afae ke afe mala, ki felerotoa ngwangwarū 'i ogana ke busu. Ki dodoa numa saena fa'i ka'o, ki fi'i do'ofia fuana 'anilana. 'I na'o numa ne'e sibolo 'inoto'a, ki folia logo, akwala bi'i numa ka bolo fa'inia la'usu'u.

LAULAUGWAU nia tua ana rauna sungasunga. Nia di'ia logo numa bore ma nia ti'iti'i ma ka di'ia go'o ngwangwa alo kī bore ma nia kerekere'a lala.

GANAFU nia fanga saena fa'i sao ma fa'i di'a. Kaida'i fa'i 'ai ka 'asia noema ki tufua, ki folofolo ana kwatea kudi ke alua fakela kī ana, nia ke teo 'i ano leleka nia ka ganafu'a logo, ki fi'i tufua 'uana ganafu fuana 'anilana. Ki dodoa, ki du'atelea, ki buta ki gwa'abia ma ki sufusufua saena fa'i sosobini. Ki 'ania logo kudi.

'OTOFAO is big and brownish, it lives in heliconia (*rako*) and cominsia (*lā*) clumps and climbs trees. It is good to eat.

'ARA is like *'otofao* but it is small and its legs are long. It is also similar to *'iki'iki* (marsh frog) but its body is different and its cry is different from *'iki'iki*.

BURPER (giant toad / *Bufo*) is really big and its body is brownish. It lives in the forest among leaf litter. At night it sits on the path. So then we use a light to catch it for eating, it is very good to eat.

OGEOGE is not very big, it lives on the ground and on logs of trees.

'U'URU is only small, it also lives in the forest, on the ground. We also eat it, it is good to eat.

MAMASAFI, these are separate kinds of frogs, they are only small, they look different and each has a different cry. Some people eat them but some don't.

Grubs

Formerly grubs like caterpillars and *ganufu* and *safao* we ate as protein. Grubs for eating are named:

CATERPILLARS swarm on trees like with-ease (*akwasi* / *Rhus*), odour (*mamu* / *Euodia*), finschia (*akama*), *kwanasia* (*Alphitonia*), hopper-tree (*'aisiko* / *Elaecarpus*), *fo'a* (*Timonius*), timonius (*sakosia*), they eat the leaves. A different kind of caterpillar which eats the leaves of finschia has a very pretty body. These caterpillars are all very good to eat.

Caterpillars have a time in July and August. The trees which caterpillars eat we clear around and eventually when the caterpillars are plentiful and big we bend down the tree branches which the caterpillars swarm on and pick them. When we pick them we cleanse them so that the bitter tree juice flows out, we wring a grub so its stomach bursts. We flask caterpillars in a bamboo and then burn them to eat. Formerly caterpillars were an important protein and we bought them, ten tubes of caterpillars were worth an elbow-length (shell-money).

HEAD-SHAKER lives on pipturus (*sungasunga*) leaves. It is like a caterpillar but smaller and like a taro grub but it has markings.

GANAFU eats the inside of sago(palm) and caryota (palm)(*di'a*). When the tree falls or we chop it down, we score across it to make the weevil (*kudi*) lay eggs on it, it lies on the ground until it is *ganafu*-ridden and we then chop out the *ganafu* to eat. We flask them, we roast them, we parcel them and oven-cook them or we stew them in a saucepan. We also eat the weevil.

SAFAO nia fanga saena 'ai kī di'ia fa'i bale'o, fa'i 'amau, fa'i mala'o, ruana fa'i la'ela'e. Ki do'ofia 'aena fa'i 'ai ki alua ke ū fuana safao kī ke fanga 'i saena. Leleka kaida'i nia ka safao'a, ki fi'i angia ma ki tufua 'uana safao fuana 'anilana. Ki du'afia saena mafula, noima ki dodongia.

NGWARIMADEKO, na ngwangarū doe ne'e sau ana fa'i kwalo 'ai ma kwalo roto, nia ke fanga saena kwalona, ka bubuta. Ki tufua fuana 'anilana, 'anilana le'a liu. Di'ia nia ke matai'a nia ke manua ka alua bebe fufumalao, ne'e ma'e kedokedo'a ka sakasako'a ka kwao ka gwāgwā.

FITA'U, ngwangarū ne'e keta liu mala ka kwao ma saena ngwangwarū fungu 'ania kafo, to'o ana gwauna nia to'o ana 'oni'onirū gwā kī, ma rū mela kī. Nia fanga saena bobo ko'a 'asi ka teo saena mo'amo'a ka tau mala ana. Ki folosia boborū, ki kakasia ka ti'iti'i ka sui mala ki tara ngwangarū kī fa'asia rebena 'ai. Sui ki dana ka sui ki ta'ufia ma ki dodoa, noima ki kukia ma ti kaida'i ki kōngia 'ania meme ko'a fuana 'anilana.

Siko kī

Ti malita'i siko 'oro ni'i tua saena masu'u. Ti siko ni'i ke tua saena tegotego rau kī. Di'ia 'aba'abarū nia beta ka mae ma ka 'asia ka orea ana kala 'ai ti'iti'i kī, na siko kī ke teo saena tego 'i rau ni'i ke tua logo saena gwango 'i rū ma saena fa'i ka'o tufu'i kī. Na 'ai ne'e siko kī ke tua ana ne'e 'age, kakali, kakara, rako, afaafamanu, lā, folota, kwa'e, ma ana ta ra'irū ne'e mae. Ti siko ni'i tua lala saena ano ma ana kula mamata kī. Siko kī, ki 'ania ta'ifau, te'e siko ti'iti'i simiga, ti ngwae saso go'o ke 'ania.

Siko fuana 'anilani, satani 'uri:
gwa'i DU'U, siko 'inoto'a nini'a, nia doe ka melamela'a, nia sai ana lofo saga, noa'a kasi sakasaka la'u. Kaida'i nia abota ka ti'iti'i 'ua, borona dadara, ki saea 'ania fa'i lake lala. Nia ke tua saena tego. 'Anilana nia le'a ka tasa ana siko kī ta'ifau.
KIKISITA, ai ngwane nini'a, ka sakosako'a, nia ke angi ka 'uri; sīsīsīsī. Nia ke tua saena tego.
SUSULITA nia di'ia logo kikisita bore ma nia ti'iti'i ana. Nia ke tua ana fi'i fa'u kī. Ti ngwae ke 'ania, ti ngwae noa'a go'o.

SAFAO eats the insides of trees like caryota(palm) (*di'a*), breadfruit (*bale'o / Artocarpus*), cabbage ('*amau / Ficus*), *mala'o* (*Trichospermum*) and the second celtis (*la'ela'e / Leucosyke*). We burn the foot of the tree and leave it standing for the *safao* to eat inside. Eventually when it is *safao*-ridden we fell it and chop out the *safao* to eat. We burn them on the fire or flask them.

NGWARIMADEKO is a big grub which develops on tree-vine (*kwalo 'ai / 6 genera*) and entada vine (*kwalo roto*), it eats the inside of the vine and swells it. We chop it out to eat, it is very good to eat. If it matures it transforms and begets a *fufumalao* butterfly which is colourful, yellow, white and black.

FITA'U (mangrove worm), this grub is very long, it is white and the inside of the grub is full of water, at the head it has a black bottom-part and brown things. It eats the insides of scraping (*ko'a / Rhizophora / Bruguiera*) logs which have lain in the mud a long time. We cut the logs crosswise and split them small, then we drag out the grubs from the planks of wood. Then we squeeze them out and then we wash them and flask them, or we boil them and sometimes we bake them in scraping paste (mangrove pudding), to eat.

Hoppers

Many kinds of hoppers live in the forest. Some hoppers live in shrivelled leaves. If strips (leaves) wither and die, drop and remain on little small trees, hoppers will live in the shrivelled leaf, and they also live in leaf-shoots and in chopped-off bamboos. The trees which hoppers live in are alpinia(ginger)('*age*), hornstedtia(ginger)(*kakali*), heliconia (*rako*), *afaafamanu* (*Flagellariaceae*), cominsia (*lā*), guillainia (ginger)(*folota*), treefern, and other dead leaves. Some hoppers live on the ground instead, and in other places. Hoppers, we eat them all, only tiny little hoppers, just people who'll try anything eat them.

The names of hoppers for eating are:
LOCUST, this is the most important hopper, it is big and brownish and it can fly properly, it doesn't leap. When it is hatched and still small its bottom is naked (without wings) and we call it a *lake*. It lives in shrivelled leaves. To eat it is the best of all hoppers.

KIKISITA is a male one, it is yellow, it cries sīsīsīsī. It lives in shrivelled leaves.

SUSULITA is like *kikisita* but it is smaller. It lives in mat clumps (*fa'u / Pandanus*). Some people eat it, some don't.

KUIKUITA, nonina te'e rebareba'a, nia ke kalafu 'ania limana di'ia ki kusua 'ania ma'erū. Nia ke tua saena tego.

FONOFONOTA nia kesi doe liu go'o, nonina te'e kwaokwao'anga. Nia ke tua saena tego.

DIDILINGWĀ, nonina gwā ka nura, ki saea logo 'ania NGWAE KWA'I'O noima NGWAE FUANA FUANGA'A, sulia lifana doe ka raku, nia 'ala'ala liu, ngela kī ma'u 'ania. Nia ke tua saena tego.

GWA'IBAITA, nia doe ma ka gwagwā'a. Nia ke tua saena tego.

BOBOROGAFU nia te'e ti'iti'i, nonina marako, gwauna te'e raku, 'aba'abana te'e raku logo. Nia ke tua saena tego.

fa'i DORI nia doe ka marako, 'aba'abana doe liu, nia to'o ana du'u gwau. Nia tua ana rauna 'aidori ma ta 'ai bore 'ana.

gwa'i DADA, nia doe ka gwagwā'a, ilina 'aba'abana maramarako'a, sirana kwao sakosako'a. Nia ke lofo tau liu, di'ia ki daua ki rongoa nia ke angi 'uri; ngēngēngē. Nia tua saena ano ka tasa ana karasi.

'USU nia doe ka mela. Tualana saena faoda kī saena kafo ma saena ma'e rū kī ninimana kafo.

'ARANGOGE nia ta'i sakosako'a, ka di'ia logo 'usu bore ma nia ta'i ti'iti'i ana. Nia ke tua saena tego.

KIKIDORA nia 'iri doe liu go'o, ka gwā. Nia ke angi 'uri ītītītīt. Nia ke tua saena ano ana ma'erū kī.

SIKITAU nia gwā, 'aba'abana ka dokodoko go'o, bore nia ke lofo go'o 'ania 'aena, nia ka siki tau liu ma ka lofo 'ali'ali. 'Aena to'o ana 'ala'alarū kī, di'ia nia to'o aka, nia ke 'abula. Nia ke tua saena tego.

SIKOSI, nia kesi doe liu go'o, 'aba'abana keta. Nia ke tua saena leko.

SIKOSAKWARI, ta sata SIKO 'AMAU, nia marako, olofana 'aba'abana meo. Tualana nama ana sakwari.

FUAFUARAU nia doe mala, 'aba'abana ka talata'irū'a 'i fafona, nia ka marako. Nia tua saena dukwasi bono sulia siko ne'e kesi 'oro ma lisilana 'iri talangwara'u.

RA'O, nia kesi doe liu go'o, nonina te'e kwao. Nia ke tua saena tego.

Ele siko'anga, ana kula ne'e nia 'oro ani ti kaida'i ki 'oiduruna siko, fada 'ania ki 'oia rauna fi'irū kī kwatea ke tigo'a fuana siko kī ke duru 'i saena, ma ki sikilia lala ka'o kī fuana siko ke ra'e ke duru 'i saena kasina. 'Unari ki ke ngali'i ne'e ni'i tatakola'a ka bolo fa'inia fanga'a. Ki dodoa fuana do'ofilana noema ki usu'ia 'ania ma'e 'ai fuana do'ofilana noema ki kukia ma sufusufua.

MANTIS, its body is quite wide, it punches with its hands if we prod it with a stick. It lives in shrivelled leaves.

FONOFONOTA is not very big and its body is a bit whitish. It lives in shrivelled leaves.

BLACK-*DIDILI*, its body is black and shiny and we also call it STRIKE-YOU MAN or FIGHTER MAN because its teeth are big and pointed, it bites a lot and children fear it. It lives in shrivelled leaves.

GREAT-CROWN is big and dark. It lives in shrivelled leaves.

BOBORAGAFU is quite small, its body is green, its head is quite pointed and its wings are quite pointed too. It lives in shrivelled leaves.

DORI is big and green, its wings are very big and it has a head covering. It lives on the leaves of *dori*-tree (*'aidori* / *Antidesma*) and other trees.

CRICKET is big and blackish, the back of its wings is greenish, its belly is yellowish white. It can jump very far and if we hold it we hear it cry ngēngēngē. It lives on the ground, especially in grass.

'USU is big and brown. It lives in caves in waters and in sticks beside waters.

'ARANGOGE is all yellow, it is like *'usu* but it is smaller. It lives in shrivelled leaves.

KIKIDORA is not very big, it is black. It cries ītītītīt. It lives on the ground and in sticks.

LEAPS-FAR is black, its wings are just short, but it leaps with its legs, it leaps very far and jumps quickly. Its legs have spikes and if it catches us we bleed. It lives in shrivelled leaves.

SIKOSI is not very big, its wings are long. It lives in cavities.

SAKWARI-HOPPER, also named *'AMAU*-HOPPER is green, underneath its wings is red. It lives on *sakwari* (*'amau* / *Ficus*).

LEAF-BURDEN is really big, its wings overlap each other and it is green. It lives in dense wilderness because it is not plentiful and it is not easy to see.

RA'O is not very big, its body is a bit white. It lives in shrivelled leaves.

To hunt hoppers, in places where they are plentiful, sometimes we 'break for congregations of hoppers' meaning we break the leaves of clumps to make them shrivel for hoppers to congregate inside, and we cut off lengths of bamboo for hoppers to climb and congregate inside the internodes. So then we can take them when they are abundant enough for a feast. We flask them for burning or we thread them on a stick to burn or we boil and stew them.

Rū lofo ma rū anogango kī

Ti rū lofo ma rū anogango fuana 'anilana ni'i tua saena masu'u ka di'ia logo siko kī, satani 'uri:
KUAKUAFILU ki saea logo 'ania RARA 'AI, nia ti'iti'i go'o ka keta liu ma 'aena ka keta liu. Nia ke tua saena tego ma ka kaua 'ania limana ana rarana 'ai.
'AI'AITA nia di'ia logo kuakuafilu bore ma nia doe mala, aena keta, nia borabora'a.
TATARAKUNU, ta sata GWAUGWAUBA'U, nia mela, nonina keta ma ka tatara liu, gwauna ba'u ma tufungana ka dokodoko. Nia ke tua sulia kafo kī ana rara 'ai ma ana ta kula bore 'ana.
TATARASIBOLO, karangia nia di'ia logo tatarakunu bore ma nia ti'iti'i go'o ma nonina kesi doe. Di'ia nia ke ru'u ma'i saena luma, ki saea karangia ti sibolo kī ke dao ma'i fa'inia.
SĪSĪ, nonina gwā, ka te'e ngwangwasina.
KUDI, lisilana nia di'ia logo sīsī bore ma nia ti'iti'i ana. Na kudi nini'a ke alua ganafu kī fuana 'anilana.
'ORO'ORO, nia di'ia logo sīsī, nia tua saena ano, fangalana nama ana alo noima 'isifura. Ki fa'asata 'uri ana sulia nia ke sotea alo ke 'oro'oro'a ka leka saena alo kī.

Kuru kī

Na malita'i kuru fuana 'anilana kī ne'e teo saena masu'u satani 'uri:
KURU to'o nia ti'iti'i ka angofia fi'irū kī di'ia rako, folota ma sulia 'ai kī.

KURU BALA nia kesi doe liu go'o, nia ango ana rauna 'ai.
KURU BULU nia doe ka tasa, ka tuafia ma ka angofia ano.
KURU FO'OKA nia kesi doe liu go'o, nia ka marako. Nia ke angofia fo'oka ma ti 'ai bore 'ana.

KURU INAMAE nia keta, ka tuafia tolo. Ki fa'asata sulia nia ke tua inamae'a saena tolo, noa'a nia kesi tua ata go'o 'ana.
NGWALA nia ti'iti'i'i go'o ma ta'eta'ena ka nemanema'a.

    'Anilana kuru, di'ia ki oga liua na'a 'anilana, ki alata'inia mafula onaonala'a ki fi'i alua fa'i kuru kī 'i saena, go'o ki 'ania. Bore ma dodolana na'a ne'e le'a ka tasa.

Fa'i karango kī

Fa'i karango fuana 'anilani kī ne'e teo saena kafo ana gwa'ifau ma ana rama 'ai, satani 'uri:
fa'i KARANGO to'o, noa'a kesi doe liu go'o, mamā'irū kwao.
fa'i KARANGO BULU, mamā'irū meo ma fa'irū ka gwā.

Flying and creeping things

Some flying things and creeping things for eating live in the forest, like hoppers, their names are:
KUAKUAFILU, also called TREE-BRANCH (stick-insect), is just small and is very long and its legs are very long. It lives in shrivelled leaves and hooks with its hands on tree branches.
STICK is like *kuakuafilu* but it is much bigger, its legs are long and it is dark red.
SWAMP-TRAILER, also named SWOLLEN-HEAD (dragonfly), is brown, its body is long and trailing, its head is swollen, its middle is short. It lives along waters on tree branches and anywhere.
PROTEIN-TRAILER is almost like swamp-trailer but it is just small and its body is not big. If it comes into the house, we say that some protein-food will soon arrive.
BEETLE, its body is black and a bit shiny.
WEEVIL looks like beetle (*sīsī*) but it is smaller. It is the weevil which begets *ganafu* (grubs) for eating.

SO-MANY (taro beetle) is like beetle (*sīsī*), it lives in the ground and eats taro or rotten wood. We name it thus because it bores into taro and so many of them go inside the taros.

Snails

The kinds of snails for eating which live in the forest are named:
SNAIL proper is small and crawls on clump-plants like heliconia (*rako*) and guillainia (ginger) (*folota*) and on trees.
PALE SNAIL is not very big, it crawls on tree leaves.
DARK SNAIL is especially big, it lives and crawls on the ground
WORSHIP SNAIL is not very big, it is green. It crawls on worship (*fo'oka / Euodia*) trees and any other trees.
SOLITARY SNAIL is long, it lives inland. We name it because it lives solitarily in the inland, it won't live just anywhere.
NGWALA is only small and its skin (shell) is thin.

    To eat snails, if we very much want to eat them we spread the embers of a fire and put the snails in it, then we eat them. But flask-cooking is especially good.

Winkles (water-snails)

Winkles for eating which live in the waters on stones and sticks of wood, are named:
WINKLE proper is not very big, its face (cover) is white.
DARK WINKLE, its face is red and its fruit (shell / body) is black.

fa'i KOKOROBA'ULA nia doe liu mala.
fa'i SISIKAFO noa'a kesi doe liu go'o, mamā'irū kwao.
fa'i MARE, fuana kesi doe liu go'o bore ma nia ngarangara'a.
ta'e FAURA'O nia molimoli'a, nia teo ana gwa'i fau, ngalilana fa'asia nia ato.
fa'i MENGO nia ti'iti'i ka keta. Nia teo olofana gwa'i fau kī saena kafo kī.

Fa'i karango fuana 'anilani kī ne'e teo saena su'u ma kunu ko'a ma asi, satani 'uri:
fa'i 'AURAGU nia doe ka keta, ta'eta'erū gwā. Nia tua saena kunu ko'a.
fa'i SUKU nia doe ka gwā. Nia teo saena su'u.
fa'i TOTOBA nia tua ana lalina ko'a.
fa'i GWALIU nia doe. Nia ka tua saena kunu ko'a.

Fa'i karango kī, ki dodoa ma ki kukia go'o ki diua 'oni'onirū kī, ki lotofia, ki 'agalia logo sa'erū kī, ki 'ani'i.

Fi'i tutu kī

Fi'i tutu fuana 'anilani kī ne'e teo saena su'u ma kunu ko'a, satani 'uri:
fi'i TUTU BULU nia teo saena kafo 'i aena 'uana su'u.
fi'i KE'E, nia teo saena kunu ko'a ma 'aena kafo kī. Ta'eta'erū, to'a asi kira saunga'inia 'ania maga mani kī fuana tafuli'ae, kira fi'i 'akofi'i kwatea ni'i ke meomeo'a.
fi'i GWARIGWARI nia teo saena kunu ko'a, ki saea logo 'ania fi'i URIURI sulia ki uria 'uana saena mo'amo'a. Ta'eta'erū, to'a asi kira saunga'i-nia 'ania maga mani kwao kī fuana tafuli'ae.
fi'i BA'UBA'U nia doe ka kwao, nia teo saena kunu ko'a.
fi'i 'ADOMA ka molimoli'a ka kwaokwao'anga, nia teo saena su'u ma kabara. Ki fa'asata 'uri ana sulia rō balibali kī 'ado. Ki garua ki gwa'ia 'ania memena ko'a fuana 'anilana.
RATATAI nia tua saena asi ana mai. Fa'irū kī ta'ta'ena ratai ana nonini. Ki 'ania logo.
SASALI, fa'irū kī kesi doe liu go'o, māna fa'irū bota ma ka kwao. Nia tua saena asi ma saena mai. 'Anilana le'a liu.

Ti fi'i tutu di'ia tutu bulu, gwarigwari, ba'uba'u, adoma, ki uria 'uana saena mo'amo'a ana kunu ko'a. Saunga'ilana fuana 'anilana, ki garua basi noima ki kukia fi'irū kī, 'i ke akafoa, ki fi'i dodoa noima ki lulungā sa'erū kī fuana 'anilana.

U'a kī

U'a fuana 'anilana kī, satani 'uri:
U'A KINI nia kesi doe liu go'o bore ma nia farifono mala. Nia ke 'ili 'i fafona asi saena one. Kaida'i ana fa'i u'a, ti ai saeni farakau'a, 'anilani ka rakufa ka 'ero'ero mala, nia le'a dangalu. Kaida'i fa'i u'a ke

KOKOROBA'ULA is really big.
SISIKAFO is not very big, its face is white.

MARE, its fruit is not very big but it is prickly.

LIMPET is round, it lives on stones and is hard to take off.
MENGO is small and long. It lives under stones in the waters.
Winkles for eating which live in inlets, scraping swamp (mangroves) and sea are named:
'AURAGU is big and long, its shell is black. It lives in scraping swamps
SUKU is big and black. It lives in inlets
TOTOBA lives on scraping (*Rhysphoraceae*) roots.
GWALIU is big. It lives in scraping swamps.

Winkles, we flask-cook them and we boil them and then we hammer the bottoms (shells) and suck them up or turn out the insides and eat them.

Clams

Clams for eating which live in the inlets and scraping swamps are named:
DARK CLAM lives in waters at the mouths of inlets.
MUSSEL lives in scraping swamps and the mouth of rivers. The sea people make the shell into money beads for ten-string (shell-money), and they heat them to make them reddish.
COCKLE lives in scraping swamp, we also call it TREADING because we tread for it in the mud. Its shell the sea people make into white money beads for ten-string (shell-money).
SWOLLEN is big and white, it lives in scraping swamp.
JOINED is rounded and whitish, it lives in inlets and stilt-roots. We name it thus because its two sides are joined together. We cut it open and mix it with scraping paste (mangrove pudding) for eating.
STICKY lives in the sea on the reef. The shells of other things stick to its body. We eat it too.
SASALI is not very big, its face is bulging and white. It lives in the sea and on the reef. It is very good to eat.

Some clams like dark clam, cockle, swollen and joined we tread for in the mud of the scraping swamp. To prepare them for eating, we first de-hinge them or boil the shells to open them up, we then flask-cook or parcel-cook the insides to eat.

Crabs

Crabs for eating are named:
FEMALE CRAB is not very big but it is really full of meat. It digs in on the sea in the sand. During the crab season some are raspberry-coloured inside, appetising and really oily to eat, it is extremely

sui na'a, buri 'ana nia ke lami'a na'a sulia ofiofirū
ana guruna, ki oia ki efoa go'o lamina fuana
'anilana, ki to'osia itanga'irū. 'Anilana ka saela
liu mala.
U'A NGWANE nia doe liu, 'u'una ka doe liu. Nia
ke 'ili saena kula kunukunu'a ma fafona one.
'Anilana nia kesi saela liu go'o.
U'A TŌTŌ nia kesi doe liu go'o bore ma nia
kwanga liu, nia ma'e tōtō'anga tōtō kwao ma tōtō
meo kī. Nia tua saena asi. 'Anilana rakufa ka asila.

GIFU, 'anilana nia di'ia logo u'a tōtō.
U'A KAKARAFAU nia kesi doe liu go'o, lisilana
nonina ka ngasi ka di'ia logo gwa'i fau. Tualana 'i
ninimana kafo ma safitana gwa'i fau kī, sulia dodo
kī, saena bore tolo logo ana kula isila kī.
OGALA nia doe ana u'a kī ta'ifau bore ma 'anilana
kesi le'a liu go'o sulia nia gufugufu. Nia ke tua 'i
ninimana kunu, ke 'ili fafona kunu.
U'A BULU nia kesi doe liu go'o, nia bulu mala. Nia
ke 'ili 'i fafona asi, ke lae ana December January.
ALIMANGO nia doe liu ana u'a kī ta'ifau, nia
tuafia su'u kī ma kunu ko'a kī. 'Anilana le'a ka tasa.

LATOKAESO, ta sata LATOKASUSU, 'itangana
ka doe, nia to'o ana rū ne'e di'ia fa'i lato kī, nia
la'umia ma'i 'i olofana 'ingata'irū. Nia ke ra'efia niu
kī, ka tua 'i gwauni fuana 'anilana fa'irū kī, nia ke
'alasote'e go'o. 'Anilana le'a ka tasa.

RA'ERA'E, nia ke tua 'aena fa'i ko'a kī ma tasisi kī.

Ī'a kī
Kia'a to'a tolo ki sai go'o ana ī'a saena kafo fa'inia
logo ī'a saena su'u ma kunu ko'a. Ī'a saena asi to'a
asi logo ne'e kira sai le'a ani. Malita'i ī'a saena kafo
ne'e ki 'ani'i, satani 'uri:
MORO, ī'a ne'e kī, ti ai ti'iti'i go'o, ti ai ke doe
di'ia limana ngwae, ti ai gwā, ti ai mela, ti ai
kedokedo'a. Ni'i tua saena kafo kunukunu'a. Moro
kī ke alua fakelana fuana kafo ke āfea 'uana saena
asi, kaida'i fakelana abota, bibirū kī fi'i 'arango ma'i
saena kafo, ki fa'asata 'ania mamamu. Mamamu
ti'iti'i ka miga kī dēa saena su'u 'ania taunamu, ki
butā 'ania ra'irū, ki gwa'abia noema ki dodoa,
kaida'i nia du'a lisilana ka di'ia lulunga 'i losi.

BUKURU, moro ne'e, nia gwā.
MORO 'ADI'ADI nia doe mala ka ma'e toto'anga.
DADALI nia kesi doe go'o, nia dau ana fau 'ania
kwakwana.
MAMĀ lisilana ka sina, kaidai ki siu saena kafo,
nia ke te'e kumulia 'aeka.
Ī'A SINA, ta sata Ī'A MARAKO, nia ke doe, lisilana
ka sina.

good. When the crab season is finished, afterwards
it has an egg-pouch along the case on its belly, we
break it and uncover the egg-pouch to eat and we
throw away the main part. It is very fatty to eat.
 MALE CRAB is very big and its claws are very big.
It digs in swampy places and on the sand. It is not
very fatty to eat.
SPOTTED CRAB (red-spotted crab) is not very big
but it is very pretty, it is spotted with white spots
and red spots. It lives in the sea. It is appetising
and sweet to eat.
GIFU is like spotted crab to eat.
STONE-*KAKARA* CRAB is not very big, its body
looks hard like a stone. It lives beside waters and
among stones, along gullies, even in the inland in
wet places.
OGALA is bigger than all other crabs but it is not
very good to eat because it is meatless. It lives
beside swamps and digs in the swamp.
DARK CRAB is not very big and is really dark. It
digs on the sea and runs in December to January.
RED-EYED CRAB is bigger than all other crabs, it
lives in inlets and scraping swamps. It is especially
good to eat.
KAESO-GENITALS, another name *KASUSU*-
GENITALS (coconut crab), its body is big and it
has things like (male) genitals, it folds them up
under its body. It climbs coconuts and lives at the
heads to eat the fruit, it bites holes in them. It is
especially good to eat.
RA'ERA'E lives at the foot of scraping trees
(*Rhysophoraceae*) and *tasisi* (*Cyperacea*e).

Fishes
We inland people just know about the fish in the
waters, as well as the fish in the inlets and scraping
swamps. The kinds of fish in the waters, which we
eat, are named:
MORO, of these fish some are just small, some are
as big as a man's arm, some are black, some are
brown, some are colourful. They live in swampy
waters. *Moro* lay their eggs for the waters to wash
them to the sea and when the eggs hatch the babies
come swimming into the waters and we call them
mamamu. Tiny little *mamamu* we catch in inlets
with a fine net, we parcel them in leaf and oven-
cook or flask-cook them and when burned they
look like a parcel of pitpit (*losi* / *Saccharum*).
BUKURU is a *moro*, it is black.
MORO 'ADI'ADI is really big and spotted.
LOACH is not very big, it holds onto stones with
its mouth.
MAMĀ looks shiny, when we bathe in the water it
nibbles our legs.
SHINY FISH, also called GREEN FISH is big and
looks shiny

Dolo kī

Dolo nia ke tua saena kafo ma saena logo su'u. Na dolorū ke futa ke doe, ka leleka ka fualanga'a, ki fa'asatā sulia doelana, ki 'ania ta'ifau. Na sata nai'ari 'uri:

KUSUKUSUFILADE nia ti'iti'i go'o, ka ru'u saena lade ka no'ana kisi lisia.

FODALIMA, di'ia ki daua nia ke fodalia limaka.

KWARAKWARA nia ke doe liu mala, ketalana ka tasa ta'i tafanga, nia tua saena su'u kī.

NANGANANGASIKAFO nia doe liu mala. Di'ia ki daua saena rodo nia ke nangasia kafo aka 'ania ribiribina go'o ka tafi.

DONGA TA'I NGWAE, doelana di'ia ki dau 'afua nonina nia bolo fa'inia ta'i lima ngwae.

DONGA RŌ NGWAE, di'ia ki dau 'afua nonina nia bolo fa'inia rō lima ngwae kī.

Fa'i Ū nia doe logo, ke ū 'ania ribiribina saena mo'amo'a, nia ka tua saena su'u kī.

'ABALOGELOGE, karangi nia ka di'ia logo dolo, lisilana ka di'ia 'aba kwalo, nia ti'iti'i go'o ka rebareba'a ka sakosako'a, ti ai ni'i gwā lala. Ti ngwae go'o ne'e ke 'ania.

Denge kī

Denge nia tua saena kafo 'i olofana gwa'i fau kī ma saena rama 'ai kī ma bobo 'ai kī.

DENGE to'o, di'ia nia doe liu na'a ki saea logo 'ania KA'UKA'URARA.

'U'UBA'U, ta denge nini'a, nia ti'iti'i ana denge kī bore ma 'u'una ba'u lala.

Dērū'a

Dēlana ī'a ma dolo, ki dēa 'ania ma'e nanga ma furai, ki fanasia ma ki ukā logo.

Dēlana 'ania a'au, ki itoa ta bali gwa'i nili ana ta bali fa'i 'au, go'o ki alua ma'e nanga ana ta bali, go'o ki 'a'ao ī'a 'ania. 'I na'o, ma'e nanga ki saunga'inia 'ania sulina sakwalo. Ki 'olea boeboena fi'i afaafamanu noima boeboena fi'i afole ke di'ia ī'a sokesoke kī fuana alulana ana ma'e fina'u fuana dē'a saena asi, ki saea 'ania arakao. Ti kaida'i ki tua rodo fuana dēlana ī'a ma dolo 'ania ma'e nanga. Ti kaida'i ki ngalia fuana fū ne'e langalanga ki bulasia logo dadalo fuana dē'a sulia nia ke fa'ofa'o, ki itoa ma'e nanga ana dadalo. Na ngwae dē ke danga 'ania fa'i fū kī saena asi kalikalia iolo nia ka daudau 'ana ka lia go'o 'uana ne'e di'ia ī'a to'o ana ka 'idua nia ka 'ali'ali ka lafua logo ī'a ka danga logo 'ania s aena asi.

'I na'o furairū kia fuana dē'a saena kafo, ki saunga'inia 'ania dadalorū di'ia kwalo 'abe, ki itoa ana rō ifi 'ai ana rō bali kī fuana ki lalafia saena kafo. 'I ta'ena ki dēa 'ania ma'e fu'a, ki saea logo

Eels

Eels live in waters and also in inlets. As eels are born and become big and eventually become enormous, we name them according to their size, and we eat them all. These names are:

GRAVEL-POKER is only small, it disappears into the gravel and we can't see it.

RESIST-HAND, if we catch it, it resists our hands.

KWARAKWARA is very big indeed, its length is over a fathom, it lives in inlets.

DASH-WATER is very big indeed. If we catch it in the night it dashes water at us with its tail-fin and escapes.

ONE-MAN-ROUND, its size when we grasp its body fits a man's one hand.

TWO-MAN-ROUND, if we grasp its body it fits a man's two hands.

STANDER is also big, it stands on its tail-fin in the mud, it lives in inlets.

LOGELOGE -STRIP is almost the same as eel, it looks like a vine-strip, it is small and wide and yellow, but some are black. Only some people eat it.

Prawns

Prawns live in waters under stones and among sticks of wood and logs.

PRAWN proper, if it is very big we also call it *KA'UKA'URARA*.

SWOLLEN-CLAW, this is a prawn which is smaller than other prawns but its claws are swollen.

Fishing

In fishing for fish and eels we fish with hook and net, we shoot and we also dope them.

In fishing by angling we tie the end of a fish-hook on the end of a bamboo and we angle for fish with it. Formerly we made the fish-hook from bat's bone. We cut off the leaf-tube of *afaafamanu* clump (*Crinum*) or curved clump (*afole / Pandanus*) to be like imitation fishes for putting on the hook for fishing in the sea, we call it a lure. Sometimes we spend the night fishing for fish and eels with a fish-hook. Sometimes we take a barringtonia (*fū*) fruit which is dry and wind fishing twine around it, because it floats, and tie a fish-hook to the twine. The fisher-man drops the barringtonia fruits into the sea around the canoe and he holds on and watches for fish to get it and move it and he quickly pulls up the fish and drops it (the fruit) into the sea again.

Formerly our nets for fishing in waters were made of twine like anondendron vine (*'abe*) and we tied two sticks, one to each side, to pull it through the water. Today we fish with a fish-trap (*ma'e* 'ania atola, fa'i tatari, ne'e ki saunga'inia 'ania kalitau noema lali salu.

Di'ia ki ogā namo ke gwa'u fuana daulana ī'a ma denge ma dolo, ki nalufia 'ania ra'ī ra'u noima ra'i felofelo. Di'ia tata ka 'ato fuana nalufilana namo, ta ma ki sabangia 'ania 'uli'uli 'ai di'ia fai, mala'o, sula, noima 'aba ka'o ma boeboena sasao, fuana lililana kafo 'i ke gwa'u.

Daulana dolo ma denge, ki sama'ia logo. Dolo, ki daua 'ania ra'i 'amau 'i ke 'ala fuana lafulana 'i langi, ti kaida'i ki rorā logo ī'a 'ania ma'e nanga noima fa'i kwalo. Ti kaida'i ki fanasia ī'a ma dolo 'ania basi, ka tasa saena kunu ko'a. Rū doe kī, ti kaida'i ki kwa'ifolosia noima ki kwa'imaelia 'ania naifi doe.

Daulana ī'a 'oro kī, ti kaida'i ki afua agi kafo, rū nai'ari ka bolo fa'inia fanga'a. 'I na'o ma'i ki ke fonea ki lu'ia agi kafo fuana ke ī'anga'a 'i ki ke sasia 'ania fanga'a, ne'e ki saea 'ania siufa, leleka ki afua. Rū fuana afulana, ki diu'i ka meme, ti kaida'i ki to'ongi'i saena ngwa'i kī, ki fi'i danga 'ania uka saena kafo fuana ī'a, ī'a ma dolo ma denge ni'i ke mae ta'ifau.

Rū kī ne'e ki afu 'ani'i ni'i 'uri:
Kwalo UKA, ki siki dokodoko ana kwalo ne'e bolo fa'inia rō malafunu kī, go'o kī diu le'a mala ani'i leleka ni'i ka meme kī losia 'i gwauna kafo, go'o sūla ka saungia ī'a kī ma dolo kī ma ti rū la'u. Ta rū ne'e tasa ana ne'e kaida'i kī ngalia, ki diua noima ki losia ma ki kwalanga'inia kasirū saena ngwa'i kī, noa'a kisi mimi fa'inia sulia na uka kata dalakwai ma kesi saungia go'o ta ī'a. m
Kwalo A'ATA, ki diua kwalona ki afua logo 'ania 'ego'egora kī 'uana ī'a, ka di'ia logo uka.
Kwalo KOKOLOME, ki 'inia rauna ki diua ki fi'i danga 'ania saena kafo fuana afulana ī'a.
FŪ, ki diua fa'irū kī ka meme ki to'ongi'i saena ngwa'i kī, ki fi'i afua'ania ī'a saena kafo.

Ti rū mauri ne'e noa'a kisi 'ania kī
'ASOFE noa'a kisi 'ania si ne'e kira ke leka ana kula ta'a kī di'ia kabara.
fa'i LOI kī, noa'a kisi 'ani'i sulia 'i na'o ma'i ti fū'ingwae kira fo'osi ana.
'UNU kī, ti malita'i ai ne'e noa'a kisi 'ani'i, satani 'uri: fa'i KWARIKWARI, nia ti'iti'i go'o, tualana sulia ta'itala kī, lisilana talangwara'u liu.
KAUFURU nonina ngwasinasina, nia ke ra'e, gwa'i Ā'A nia ti'iti'i go'o, tualana nama ana luma,
GWALI-MANGOMANGO nia ti'iti'i, ka tatalaasia.

fu'a), called *atola* and *tatari*, which we make from winds-far (*kalitau* / *Calamus*) or *salu* root (*Araceaea*).

If we want a pool to empty for catching fish and prawns and eels, we bale it out with a leaf or *felofelo* (*Calamus*) leaf. If there is a waterfall and it is hard to bale out the pond, then we duct it with the bark of a tree like mimosa (*fai*), *mala'o* or *sula* (both *Trichospermum*) or flattened bamboo or *sasao* (*musa*) leaf-tube, to divert the water so it empties.

To catch eels and prawns we also feel for them. Eels we catch with an *'amau* (*Ficus*) leaf so it will bite and be pulled up, and sometimes we also lure the fish with a fish-hook or a vine. Sometimes we shoot fish and eels with a bow, especially in the scraping swamp. For big ones we sometimes hack it or beat it to death with a bush-knife.

To catch many fish, sometimes we dope a stretch of water, and this is suitable for a feast. Formerly we'd shut off and prohibit a stretch of water to become full of fish to make a feast called a *siufa*, and eventually dope it. The thing for doping we hammer to a paste and sometimes we pack it in bags and then drop the dope into the water for the fish, and the fish, eels and prawns will all die.
The things we dope with are:
DERRIS vine, we cut the vine into short lengths of two spans, then we hammer it well until it is a paste and wring it out at the head of the water, then the juice kills the fish and the eels and other things. Something special is that when we take it and hammer it or wring it out and collect the internodes in bags, we don't pee by it, lest the derris be ineffective and won't kill any fish.
A'ATA vine (*Derris*), we hammer its vine too, to dope tidal pools for fish, as with derris (*uka*).
GEOPHILA vine, we pick the leaf and hammer it and then drop it into the water to dope fish.
BARRINGTONIA, we hammer the fruits to a paste, pack it in bags and dope fish with it in the waters.

Some living things we don't eat
RATS we don't eat because they go in bad places like the latrine.
SNAKES we don't eat because formerly some clans prayed to them.
LIZARDS, some kinds we don't eat are named: *KAUFURU* (similar to *Eugongylus rufenscens*) has a shiny body, it climbs. *KWARIKWARI* (*Emoia*, *Sphenomorphus* etc.) is only small, it lives along the paths and is very easy to see. GECKO is just small and it lives in the house. *GWALIMANGOMANGO* is small and multi-coloured.

6
Rao fanga 'anga

Ki to'o ana ti malita'irū 'oro fuana rao fanga'a ma du'afilana fanga. Ti rū ne'e 'inoto'a fuana rao fanga'a ana tualaka ne'e so'i, rau kī, fa'i ka'o.

So'i
Du'afilana fanga, ki efoa mala 'ai ne'e bolo fa'inia so'i, ki erea basi mafula fuana du'urū'a. 'Ai ne'e ki efoa fuana so'i saena o'ola noema saena masu'u, ki sungia noema ki ragia, leleka kaida'i nia du'a ki fi'i kwa'ia fuana so'i. 'Ai ne'e totolia so'i ni'i ke du'a kwasukwasu mala ma noa'a kesi du'a maemaela.

Ti 'ai ni'i totolia so'i sulia ni'i ke du'a 'ali'ali, ni'i bolo fa'inia du'urū'a ma gwa'abi'a. 'Ai nai'ari kī ne'e fa'i ako, fa'i karefo, fa'i mala'o, sikimā, fenofeno.

Ti 'ai ni'i totolia so'i sulia ni'i ke du'a dangi. Di'ia ki ogni ana bobora'i'ai kī kata du'a ka sui ta ma ki kiki fa'amaea 'i kesi du'a 'ali'ali. 'Ai ne'e du'adangi ka tasa ne'e fa'i aialo, ki saea logo 'ania satana sofonga'i mafula. Ti 'ai du'a dangi'a la'u ne'e fa'i fasa, fa'i sakosia, fa'i 'aitea, fa'i daufau, fa'i kwalo'ai. 'Ai du'a dangi ne'e bolo fuana du'urū'a saena onala'a, ki du'afia 'ania rū di'ia ī'a doe ma dolo kī.

Ti 'ai ni'i ke du'a maemaela kaida'i ki du'urū ani ne'e tangafenofeno. Ti 'ai ne'e du'a maemaela ne'e fa'i bale'o, sungasunga, sikima, gwa'ugwa'u, lofa.

Ere mafula'a, 'i na'o ki ba'o go'o 'ania rō fa'i 'ai kī. Te'e fa'i 'ai go'o ne'e ki tadilia logo 'ania ma'erū ma ki ba'o logo 'ania ana fa'i 'ai ne'e ki alua ' i ano, leleka mafula ka du'a nama. 'Ai ne'e bolo nama fa'inia ba'onga'a, 'ai di'ia faefae, kwa'u, isu. Ba'onga'a 'uana mafula ne'e rao'a doe logo, ta ne'e ki ngalia nama mafula 'uana o'ola ma kula kī sui. 'Ai ne'e totolia ne'e 'aialo, sulia nia sao ma ka du'a sofonga'i ka du'adangi. Ki ogani ana ifirū kī 'i moko sasu noima sulia 'odoa kī, ki leka go'o 'i o'olā ki tufua ta kula ana fuana mafula 'i ne'e noa'a nia kesi talangwara'u fuana ke mae sulia ta'itala. Di'ia ki fītala ne'e nia kata do'ofia ka sui, ki buta 'ania ra'irū di'ia 'age ma folota 'usia kula mafula du'a ka dao ana 'i nia ke du'a safa'i.

6
Preparing food

We have many ways to prepare and burn (cook) food. Things which are important for preparing food in our way of life are fuel, leaves and bamboo.

Fuel
To burn food we must select trees which are suitable for fuel and first kindle the fire for burning. The tree we select for fuel in the garden or in the forest we scorch or ring-bark, and eventually when it is burned we fell it for fuel. Trees which are fit for fuel must burn flaming and not burn dying.

Some trees are fit for fuel because they burn quickly, they are suitable for burning (food) and oven-cooking. These trees are shout (*ako / Pometia*), flare (*karefo /Shleinitzia*), *mala'o* (*Trichospermum*), squirt-eye (*sikimā / Homalanthus*), *fenofeno* (*Macaranga*).

Some trees are fit for fuel because they burn till day. If we want to conserve the firewood lest it burn out, we sprinkle water to make it die down so it won't burn quickly. The tree which burns till day the best is gomphandra-tree (*aialo*), which we also name fire-hider. Other burns till day trees are vitex (*fata*), timonius (*sakosia*), tea-tree (*aitea /Ficus*), *daufau* (*Neoscortechninia*), *kaulata* (*Uncaria*). A burns till day tree is suitable for burning things in embers, we burn things like big fish and eels with it.

Some trees burn dying when we burn with them with sticks protruding (from the fire). Some trees which burn dying are breadfruit (*bale'o / Artocarpus*), pipturus (*sungasunga*), squirt-eye (*sikimā / Homalanthus*), sterculia (*gwa'ugwa'u*), *lofa* (*Sterculia*).

To raise a fire, formerly we just rubbed with two trees (sticks). One tree we trim into a thin piece and we rub it on the tree which we put on the ground and eventually fire will burn. Trees suitable for rubbing are trees like kleinhovia (*faefae*), drink (*kwa'u / Premna*) and callicarpa (*isu*). Rubbing for fire is a big job and so we must take fire to the garden and everywhere. The tree which is fitted is gomphandra-tree (*aialo*), because it is soft and burns-hidden and burns till day. We store logs in the smoke or along the wall and when we go to the garden we chop off a piece for fire so it won't easily die out along the path. If we suspect it may burn out, we wrap leaf like alpinia(ginger) (*age*) or guillainia(ginger)(*folota*) against the place the fire has reached so it will burn slowly.

Du'afilana fanga'a

Du'afilana fanga to'o ana ti malita'i rū to'oto'i kī
di'ia du'atele'a, dodo'a, gwa'abī'a, kuki'a ma sau'a.
DU'ATELE'ANGA nia talangwara'u go'o, nia bolo
fa'inia du'afilana 'oni'onirū di'ia alo kī, kai kī, fa'i
butete, 'a'e kaibia. Ki alua fanga ma'a saena
mafula, ki ri'ita'inia 'ania korefe, ki fi'i resia 'ania
tutu, ki balafia ka du'a ki resikasika mala ana, ki fi'i
'ania. Du'atelelana ti sibolo di'ia no'o akaaka'u,
karai, 'unu, gwere, ī'a, dolo, denge, ki kedea mafula
ke du'afia ka onaonala'a mala, ki fi'i du'atelea 'i
saena. Du'atelelana sibolo ti'iti'i kī di'ia siko,
numa, karango, ma sa'e ngali logo, ta ma ki usu'ia
'ania ma'e sasalo fuana du'afilana, ki unala'inia
mafula, ki fi'i balafia, leleka ni'i ke du'a ki fi'i ani'i.
Ti kaida'i ki sarufu'a fanga, ki 'ili fafia fanga ma'a
saena fu'a, ki kedea mafu fafona, nia du'a ki fi'i
'ania logo.

DODO'A nia bolo fa'inia ti fanga ne'e ke du'a
'ali'ali, ki dodongia saena fa'i ka'o fanga di'ia alo,
kai, kumara ma tatabu, ki dodongia logo sibolo
kwasi di'ia numa ma siko, fa'inia logo afu gwata
noema 'uli gwata ne'e ki gwa'abia ka sui ma'i 'i
ro'oki. 'Oi ka'o'anga, ki filia lala ka'o ne'e kasina
keta, ki tufua ki dumulia gwauna, ka sui ki usua
nonina 'ania ra'i rau 'i kesi momote mala, ki fi'i
'oia kasirū kī 'i ke kwakwa ana ta bali, ta bali
gwagirū ka fonea. Ki dodongia fanga ka sui, ki
gu'utā bi'irū 'ania ra'i rau, ki fi'i do'ofia saena
mafula, ki ri'ita'inia leleka na moko ka kwatea
fanga ka du'a mala, ki fi'i folea bi'irū fuana
'anilana.
GWA'ABĪ'ANGA nia le'a fuana fanga ke moko le'a
ma 'anilana ka fulakwa'a ma ka le'a liu, logo ma
fuana fanga kī ke tatakola'a ke bolo fa'inia sarelana
tua'a doe kī, ma kaida'i ana fanga'a kī. Sulia
lulunga 'i tatabu ma fanga gwata kī bore ke liu
ta'ifau saena gwa'abī, na gwata 'oro kī bore ki
gwa'abī'i ta'ifau saena, lakeno ma 'ara 'i kaibia
ka 'unari.

   Gwa'abī'anga, ki goea gwa'i umu saena kafo
doe kī. Gwa'i fau ne'e ki efo'i, ni'i ngasi mala, noa'a
kesi busu, noa'a kesi mangisi saena mafula, ta ma
gwa'i fau boso ne'e totolia. Di'ia ni'i noa'a bore, fau
bala nia le'a logo, bore ma nia kata mangisi ma ka
busu ka siki ka to'e kia. Mafula, ki sada basi ki
erea, ki fi'i alua faifolo ana ti 'ifi so'i mala ki fi'i
ludangia gwa'i umu kī 'i fafona. Nia ke do'ofia ka
ofo, ki alata'inia mala ki fi'i safilia 'ania ra'i rau kī.
Ka sui ki fi'i alua fanga kī 'i saena, la'u ki fi'i alua
ra'i rau kī fafia mala, ki fi'i alua la'u gwa'i umu kī
fafia fanga kī. Ka sui mala ki alua la'u ra'i rū kī
fafia, mala ki fi'i bibi fafia. Leleka ka du'a mala, ki
fi'i īlia gwa'abi, mala ki ta'ea 'ita fanga fuana
'anilana.

Burning (cooking) food

To burn food there are different ways like roasting,
flasking, oven-cooking, boiling and pounding.
ROASTING is an easy way, it is suitable for
burning tubers like taros, yams, potatoes and *bia*-
yam (cassava). We put the raw food in the fire and
turn it with tongs, we then scrape it with a
clamshell and heat it on stone to burn and scrape it
really clean, and then eat it. To roast protein like
cuscus, chicken, lizard, frogs, fish, eel and prawn,
we kindle a fire and burn it to embers and then
roast in it. To roast small protein like hoppers,
grubs, winkles, and also nut insides (kernels), we
thread them on a broom-spine to roast, we stoke
up the fire, we heat them on stone and eventually
when they are burned we eat them. Sometimes we
hearth-cook food, we dig the raw food into the
hearth and kindle a fire above it and when it is
burned we eat it.
FLASKING is suitable for foods which burn
quickly, we flask in bamboo foods like taro, yam,
potato and vegetables. We also flask wild protein
like grubs and hoppers, as well as pieces of pig or
belly-pork which we have already oven-cooked the
previous day. To cut the bamboo we select bamboo
lengths with long internodes, we chop and trim off
the top and then we rub the body with a leaf so it
won't be too scratchy, and then break the section
open at one end, the other end the node closes off.
We flask the food and then we plug the tube with
leaf and then burn it on the fire, we turn it over
until the smell (vapour) makes the food burn and
then split open the tube to eat.
OVEN-COOKING is good for food to smell nice
and appetizing and very good, and also for an
abundance of food for feeding big families, and at
times of feasts. Because parcels of vegetables and
pig's food can all go into the oven, even lots of pigs
can be oven-cooked in it, and cream-pudding and
bia-yam (cassava) grating likewise.

   To oven-cook we gather cooking-stones in the
big waters. The stones we select are really hard,
they won't burst and won't shatter in the fire, so
hog-stones (basalt) are fitted. However if there are
none, pale stones (limestone) are alright, but they
may shatter and burst, fly out and wound us. The
fire, we first stack and kindle it, then we put on
fuel logs crosswise and then we heap the cooking-
stones on top. It burns and collapses, we rake it
well and then spread it over with leaves. After that
we put the food on it, we then put more cooking-
stones on top of the food. After all that we put
more leaves onto it, then we secure it in place.
Eventually when it is well burned we unwrap the
oven and bring out the food to eat.

LOFA fuana du'afilana ti malita'i fanga kī. Saunga'ilana lofa, ki koria fa'i niu saena dako, ki kikia 'ania kafo, ki fi'i losia meme niu nia teo saena dako noima ta'e disi ma fa'i sosobini. 'I na'o ki kori niu 'ania tutu ma ta'e gwarigwari, 'i nini'ari ki koria 'ania sauka'e, ki saea logo 'ania kari, faro. Sufusufu, kaida'i ki lofa mala, ki kikia 'ania fa'i asi noima solo, ki fi'i do'ofia fa'inia tatabu noima ī'a noima ta rū bore 'ana ne'e ki saunga'inia 'ania sufusufu. Lofa fuana sau'a, ki lofa ka sui ki kisita'inia saena fa'i ka'o mala ki fi'i do'ofia ka bū, ki fi'i 'ototafa ana ka āfe ma'i fuana lakeno.

MĀ 'I GWATA, ki rari ti'iti'i ana, ki kukia fa'inia solo noima fiki asi 'i noa'a kesi moko, nia ka kutukutufia ka du'a le'a mala, ki fi'i kisita'inia sūla saena fa'i 'au noima ta'e soso 'i ke bū mala, ki fi'i saunga'i fanga 'ania. Ti kaida'i ki ke alua sulia bara asoa'anga, nia ke teo ka le'a ua. Saunga'ilana fanga 'ania mā 'i gwata, ki kaea ta kula 'i ki ngwoia 'ania gwa'i tatabu kī, ki fi'i dodo'i fuana ki du'afia, ki dola logo 'ania gwa'i tatabu kī kaida'i ki buta lulunga 'i ki kōngia fania. 'Anilana tatabu fa'inia mā 'i gwata nia 'ero'ero ma ka mamasia liu, ki 'adomia fa'inia alo ma kumara ma kaibia.

Sau'a

Ti kaida'i ana fanga'a ki saunga'inia logo sau'a, ne'e to'o ana malita'irū to'oto'o kī. Lakeno fa'inia logo gwasu, ki saungia alo fa'inia niu, kata ma tadili mamata logo, ki saungia lala alo fa'inia ngali. Ti sau'a ki saungia lala rū di'ia ba'u noema ki ko'ā fa'i ko'a kī noema ki arā lala kaibia.

Saunga'ilana sau'a, ki saungia ka'aka'a saena dako 'ania fa'i sau'a. Di'ia noa'a ta dako, ki saungia lala saena 'uli 'ai. 'Ai ne'e bolo fuana fa'i sau'a nia ke 'eke'eke ma ke ngasi ma ke maomao'a. Sulia di'ia 'oko sau 'ania 'ai ngwara'u na ngisingisin̄a ke ru'ufia ka'aka'a ka ta'a fuana 'anilana. Ka di'ia 'oko sau 'ania 'ai fungufungula na sūla ke leka saena ka'aka'a 'unari nia ka moko ta'a ma ka fa'alia siraka ka kwatea ki moa ma ki siri. Na fa'i 'ai maomao'a kesi fa'alia limaka kaida'i ki saungia ka'aka'a. 'Ai ne'e bolo fa'inia fa'i sau'a ne'e 'aitea ne'e le'a ka tasa, fa'adi'ila ma ko'a ngwane bore le'a logo. Na lofa ngwaingwai'a ne'e fuana ngwailana fa'i sau'a 'i kesi 'eke'eke fuana sau'a 'ania.

'I na'o ma'i lakeno ma kata, rū ne'e kī bolo fa'inia fanga'a doe kī di'ia siufa. Ki 'agania sau'a saena ra'i rau rarangia, ki fi'i daua ka ketaketa'a mala ki fi'i ngīa ka sui fuana daro'ilana fuana 'anilana. Ki daro'ia ana ngwae kī fa'inia ī'a, denge, gwata, karai, no'o akaka'u ma sakwalo.

CREAM is for burning certain kinds of food. To make cream we scrape a coconut into a bowl and sprinkle it with water, we then squeeze out the coconut paste into a bowl, dish or saucepan. Formerly we scraped coconut with a clamshell or cockle shell, at present we scrape it with a scraper (*sauka 'e*), also called a *kari* or *faro*. For stew, when we've made the cream we sprinkle it with seawater or salt and then burn it with vegetables or fish or whatever we are making the stew with. For cream for pudding we make the cream and then pour it all into a bamboo and burn it till it thickens, and we poke it to flow out for cream-pudding.

PIG FAT, we slice it small and boil it with salt or a bit of seawater so it won't smell, and when boiled and really well burned we then tip out the juice into a bamboo or dish to thicken and then prepare food with it. Sometimes we leave it for several days and it still stays good. To prepare food with pig fat we scoop out a bit to smear on vegetables and flask them for burning, we also mix it with vegetables when we package a parcel for baking. To eat, vegetables with pig fat is oily and very tasty, we serve it with taro, potato and *bia*-yam (cassava).

Pudding (pounding)

Sometimes at feasts we also make pudding, which has separate kinds. For cream-pudding and coconut-pudding we pound taro with coconut, but for nut-pudding and cured-pudding we pound taro with nut. For other puddings we pound things like banana or scrape scraping (*ko 'a* / mangrove) fruit or grate *bia*-yam (cassava).

To make pudding we pound the mash in a bowl with a pounder. If there is no bowl we pound it in tree bark instead. Trees suitable for pounders are dry, strong and smooth. Because if you pound with a soft tree, fragments will enter the mash and it will be bad to eat. If you pound with a full (wet) tree the sap will go into the mash, so then it will smell bad and upset our bellies, make us vomit and give us diarrhoea. A smooth wood won't damage our hands when we pound the mash. Of trees suitable for pounders, tea-tree (*'aitea* / Ficus) is especially good but *fa'adi'ila* (Ficus) and male scraping (*ko 'a ngwane* / Rhizophora) are also good. The oily cream oils the pounder so it won't be dry to pound with.

Formerly cream-pudding and nut-pudding were things suitable for big feasts like *siufa* (feasts). We turn the pudding out onto warmed leaf and then hold (hand-mould) it to lengthen it and afterwards break it up to portion out for eating. We portion it out for people with fish, prawn, pig, chicken, cuscus or bat.

Di'ia ki saungia sau'a doe fuana ki koko fāfia 'ania ngwaefuta kia kī ana fanga'a, ka 'unari ki saunga'inia tafe fuana ngalilana. Ki tufua rō 'itanga'irū kī di'ia fa'i niniu kī, ki kwa'i folo 'ania 'ifi 'ai dokodoko kī, ki fi'i rebasia fa'i ka'o 'i fafona ka sui ma ki saunga'inia sau'a doe 'i fafona, ki fi'i buta fāfia 'ania ra'irū kī. Ka sui mala ki ngalia kwau fuana koko'a fāfia ngwaefuta kī ana fanga'a.

Saunga'ilana sau'a to'oto'o kī ni'i 'uri: LAKENO, ki gwa'abia alo ka du'a, ki lofā niu. Lofa, ki 'ongia saena fa'i ka'o, ki do'ofia ka du'a, ki alua ke gwari mala, ki fi'i labutafa ana boroni 'i lofa kafokafola ke āfe ka tali mala ana lofa bū ne'e bolo fa'inia saunga'ilana lakeno. Kaida'i alo ka du'a mala, ki fi'i saungia ka sui, ki fi'i alu kwairoki ana 'aba kwalo kī 'i ki ito fafia, mala ki fi'i safatalana ka molimolia 'ania ra'i lā kī, ka sui ki fi'i safa la'u 'ania ra'i sasao rarangi'i kī. Go'o ki kaea ka'aka'a 'alo, ki alua 'i saena safa fuiri, ki fi'i ebesia 'ania ra'i rau ne'e ki afua logo 'ania ta'eta'e niu. Ka sui mala ki fi'i kwa'ia lofa 'i saena, mala ki fi'i ebesia la'u ti afu ka'aka'a 'i ki alua fafia ke bonobono mala ki fi'i 'afu fafia ki fi'iri fafia, mala ki fi'i gwa'abia. Ta malita'i lakeno ki dodoa lala.

GWASU, ki koria niu, ki ridoa memena saena dako ka sui ki kikia 'ania kafo ma kala fiki asi ka bolo logo fa'inia ne'e ke ngwalotoloto ma ka lofa'a le'a ma ke mamasia. Ka sui ki dodoa ririro fuiri saena fa'i ka'o go'o ki du'afia. Ki susulia alo, ki fi'i du'afia, ka sui ki fi'i saungia saena dako. Ka sui ki safatalana, ki ngwinua ka'aka'a 'ania lofa ma meme niu, ki fi'i alua saena safa, ki bebesia 'ania ta'eta'e niu ne'e ki buta 'ania ra'irū nai'ari. Ki fi'i angania bi'i niu saena ka'aka'a ebesi'a, ki fi'i la'umia rō bali kī fafia niu mala, ki fi'i ngia fuana 'anilana.

GWASU BIBISU, ki do'ofia alo, ki fi'i saungia, ki koria niu ki alua memena saena titiu, ki fi'i du'afia saena mafula, ka sui ki kaea ma'i ka'aka'a 'ania tutu, ki fi'i bunia fa'inia meme niu saena titiu, ki 'ania logo saena titiu.

GWASU TAUMANGA, saungilana nia di'ia gwasu bibisu bore ma ki rokisia meme niu 'ania lofa bū lala, noa'a kisi ebesia la'u fa'inia.

KATA MANUMANU'I, ki 'uia fa'i ngali kī, ki manumanua, ka sui ki dodoa. Ki dadafia bị'i ngali ka sui ki karia go'o ki 'agania ki 'otosusulia mala saena dako, ki fi'i saungia ka mangisi le'a mala.

If we make a big pudding to present to our kinsmen at a feast, then we make a board to take it on. We chop down two trunks like palms, we lay short sticks across, we then flatten bamboo over it and after that we make the big pudding on it and then package it in leaves. After all that we take it away to present to our kinsmen at the feast.

The making of different puddings is like this: CREAM-PUDDING, we oven-cook the taro and we cream the coconut. The cream we pour into a bamboo, we burn it till burned, we put it to cool and then poke to the bottom so the watery cream flows out and leaves the thick cream which is suitable for making cream-pudding. When the taro is burned too, we pound it and then we first put vine-strips crosswise to tie it up and after that we spread a round area for it with cominsia leaf (*lā*) and then we spread again with warmed *sasao* leaf (*musa*). Then we scoop the taro mash and put it on the spread, and we then knead it with leaf wrapped round a coconut husk. After that we put the cream in and we knead in some more pieces of mash, put over it to close it well in, and then wrap it up and tie it up, and then we oven-cook it. Another kind of cream pudding we flask instead.
COCONUT-PUDDING, we scrape coconut, we crush the mash in a bowl, then we sprinkle it with water and a little sprinkling of seawater, enough to be juicy, good and creamy and tasty. Then we flask the crushings in bamboo and burn it. We pare taro, we burn it and then we pound it in a bowl. Then we spread (leaves) for it and hand-roll the mash with cream and coconut paste, then put it on the spread and flatten it with a coconut husk wrapped in the leaf. We knock out the tube of coconut into the kneaded mash, we fold the two sides right over the coconut and we break it up to eat.
BIBISU-PUDDING, we burn taro and then pound it, we scrape coconut and put it in a (coconut-shell) cup and then burn it on the fire, then we scoop out the mash with a clamshell and we roll it into a ball with the coconut paste in the cup and eat it from the cup.
TAUMANGA-PUDDING is made like *bibisu*-pudding but we replace the coconut paste with thick cream and we don't knead it.
BLANCHED NUT-PUDDING, we hammer nuts, we blanch them, then we flask them. We warm the tube of nuts and then we turn it out and poke it all out into a bowl and then pound it so it is really well broken up.

Ki fi'i du'atelea alo, noa'a kisi kōngia, ki fi'i resikasika ana ki ida'i ki danga ani'i saena dako fa'inia ngali saungia fuiri, ki sau le'a ana ka to'o, ki fi'i 'igi'iginia dako 'i ka'aka'a ke alifa'i. Ka sui mala ki 'agania saena ra'i rau rarangia fuana 'anilana, noema ki ke dodoa ki do'ofia la'u, 'i ne'e ke teo tau fuana 'anilana sulia ta bara asoa kī. Kata nia nunura liu, di'ia nia to'o le'a sūla nia ke afe mala. Kata ki sasia logo 'ania rarada 'au ki saungia alo ma ngali saena fa'i ka'o.

KATA 'I TADILI, ki fa'asasufia fa'i ngali saena bara 'i tadili, nia ke teo sulia ta rō madamo noema ta ulu madamo, ka me'e mala, ki fi'i 'uia. Noa'a kisi manumanua si ne'e sa'erū kī me'e na'a bore ma ki dodongia go'o fa'inia reforefona, go'o ki alua bi'irū kī saena bara ka sasufia la'u. Go'o ki 'agania saena dako, ki ridoa, alua kala kafo ti'iti'i saena, ki ridoa la'u, ka leleka ka le'a mala, ka sui ki alua ka teo. Ki do'ofia bi'i alo ma ki sau mamata lala ana ka'aka'a alo saena ta dako, ka sui ki fi'i 'iroa rirido 'i saena go'o ki akoa 'ania ka'aka'a fuiri 'ania tutu noima ki maia ki fa'ita'inia 'ania fa'i sau'a. Ka sui mala ki saungia ka leleka ka le'a mala, ki fi'i alua saena ra'i rau rarangia fuana 'anilana.

GWASU 'I BA'U, ki du'atelea ba'u baba kī ka du'a, ki songea ka sui, ki fi'i saungia saena dako. Ki fi'i ebesia ka'aka'ana fa'inia niu di'ia logo ka'aka'a alo.

LAKENO 'I BA'U, saungilana di'ia logo lakeno 'i alo bore ma ba'u ne'e talafuila alo.

'ARA 'I KAIBIA nia di'ia logo lakeno alo te'e ki eta 'arā kaibia mala. Ki songe'e afuna kaibia kī, ka sui ki 'arā ana 'uli kaba ka sui ki losia memerū, kī kisita'inia sūla ne'e kwao ma ka 'afae, nia kata kwaifungu. Ka sui ki bō talana 'ania ifi so'i kī, ki fi'i safa talana 'ania ra'irū rarangi'i kī, mala ki fi'i takalonga'inia meme kaibia 'ara'i kī saena safa, ki fi'i kwa'ia lofa do'ofia 'i saena ne'e ki ebasia, ki fi'i takalonga'inia la'u ti meme kaibia fāfia mala ki fi'i butā go'o ki fi'iri fāfia, ki fi'i kōngia.

GWASU 'I KAIBIA nia bolo logo fa'inia gwasu alo bore ma nini'ari kaibia ne'e talafuila alo.

KO'A, ki gwaea fa'i rū kī, ki garasia basi ta'eta'ena 'ania 'u 'i tutu, ki fi'i ko'ā sa'erū saena dako noima fa'i tini, ta'e soso, ne'e fungu 'ania kafo. Ki ko'ā saena kafo, ka sui ki losia memena ko'a sulia nia ta'i 'afae'anga, ki likita'inia kafo fa'asia. Ka sui ki alua memena saena dako, ki fi'i saungia 'ania fa'i sau'a, ka sui ki dolā 'ania sa'e tutu kī. Ka sui ki rarangia ra'i fa'u kī, ki safa talana 'ania, ki alua ra'i rū di'ia ra'i lā ma ra'i ba'u talana ko'a fuiri. Ki fi'i alua na'a memerū fuiri kī saena safa fuiri.

We then roast taro, we don't bake it, and then scrape it clean and soften it and drop it into the bowl with the pounded nuts, we pound it properly and then shake the bowl so the mash turns over. After that we turn it out onto warmed leaf to eat, or we flask it and burn it again, so it will be long-lasting for eating over several days. Nut-pudding is very oily and if done properly the juice flows out. We also make nut-pudding by bamboo-ramming, we pound the taro and nuts in a bamboo.

CURED-PUDDING, we smoke the nuts on a curing rack, to lie for two or three months, and when they are well parched we hammer them (to shell them). We don't blanche them as the insides are parched but we flask them with the scale (endocarp) on, then we put the tube on the rack and smoke it again. Then we turn them out into a bowl and crush them, put a little bit of water in, crush them more and eventually when it is well done, then we put it by to stand. We burn tubes of taro and we pound the taro mash separately in a bowl, then we ease the crushings into it and stir it into the mash with a clamshell or mix it and turn it over with a pounder. After that we pound it until it is well done, then put it on warmed leaf to eat.

BANANA COCONUT-PUDDING, we roast *baba* bananas until burned, we peel them and then pound them in a bowl. We then knead the mash with coconut as with taro mash.

BANANA CREAM-PUDDING is made like taro cream pudding but banana replaces the taro.

BIA-YAM (cassava) GRATING is like taro cream-pudding only we begin by grating *bia*-yam. We peel *bia*-yam tubers and then grate them on a (perforated) sheet of iron and then wring out the paste and pour off the juice which is white and bitter, lest it be full of it. Then we set out a space with sticks of fuel-wood, we then spread a space for it with warmed leaves and after that we scatter the grated *bia*-yam mash on the spread and then add burned cream to it and knead it and then scatter more *bia*-yam mash over it, then parcel it and tie it up and then bake it.

BIA-YAM PUDDING is like coconut-pudding, but nowadays *bia*-yam replaces the taro.

SCRAPING (*Bruguiera* mangrove), we collect the fruits, we first scrape off the skin with a clamshell and we scrape (*ko'a*) the inside into a bowl or tin or dish full of water. We scrape it all into the water and then wring out the scraping mash because it is quite bitter, and pour the water away. Then we put the mash in a bowl and pound it with a pounder, then mix it with clam meat. Then we warm mat leaves (*fa'u* / *Pandanus*) and spread them out and put leaves like cominsia leaf (*lā*) and banana leaf in place for the scraping.

Sui go'o, ki kwa'ia ma'i lofa 'i niu 'ania ta titiu, ki alua saena ko'a fuiri, go'o ki 'afua na'a buta ko'a, ka sui ki gwa'abia fuana 'anilana.

Rau furana rao fanga'anga

Rao fanga'a, ti ra'i rau ne'e 'inoto'a fuana ki buta fanga 'ani'i ma gwa'abi'a ma gu'utalana bi'i fanga ma safa'atalana fanga kī. Ra'i rū ne'e ki efoa ne'e totolia, nia ke doe ke reba ke keta, nia lia le'a ma ke kwatea fanga kaida'i nia du'a ke moko le'a, noa'a nia kesi 'afae logo nia kata fa'alia na fanga kī. Kaida'i ki butarū 'ania ra'i rau, ki rarangia basi 'i ne'e ke mabe fuana la'umilana, di'ia noa'a kisi rarangia nia ke gā. Ra'i rū ne'e bolo fa'inia saunga'i fanga'a, satani 'uri:
Ra'i LĀ, ki 'afu 'ania fanga kī ka tasa ana sau'a, nia bolo fa'inia sulia nia lia le'a la'u ma kaida'i fanga ka du'a 'anilana ka moko le'a. Ki gwa'abi logo 'ania rauna bore ma nia te'e le'a go'o sulia ti ra'irū ti'iti'i go'o. Rū gwa'abi le'a ka tasa fuana tolo gwari, kula noa'a rau kesi 'oro ana.

Ra'i RAKO, ta sata RĀRĀ, nia totolia gwa'abi'a ma safa'atalana fanga sulia rauna reba ma ka keta mala, ka dada ma ka moko le'a logo, noa'a kesi 'afae. Ki rao fanga 'ania ka tasa ana tolo gwari, kula ne'e rau kesi 'oro ana.
Ra'i BA'U fa'inia ra'i SASAO ni'i le'a logo sulia ni'i doe mala ka reba bore ma mokolani te'e 'afae. Ra'irū ne'e kī, ki sisia logo sisilirū kī, sulia sisilina doe nia kesi mabe fuana la'umilana.

Ra'i FOLOTA, ki rarangia fuana butālana fanga di'ia kata ma ta rū bore 'ana, fuana logo gwa'abi'a, ki gu'uta logo 'ania bi'i fanga. Nia moko le'a ka noa'a kesi 'afae.
Ra'i 'AGE, ki buta 'ania ti fanga di'ia sa'e ngali kī, ki gwa'abi logo 'ania bore ma ra'irū ni'i ti'iti'i go'o, noa'a 'iri le'a kesi bolo fa'inia ti ra'irū doe kī.

Rauna KAKAMA, ki gwa'abi 'ania, ki safa logo 'ania talana fanga kī, ki afua logo 'ania buta ko'a kī.

Rauna FA'U, ki butā 'ania ko'a fuana 'anilana, ki buta logo 'ania 'ara Ki rarangia basi ra'i fa'u 'i ne'e nia ke mabe, ki fi'i safalia la'u 'ania ra'i rū di'ia ra'i lā ma ra'i ba'u, ka sui ki buta 'ania. Ki karusua logo 'ania maga ī'a kī fuana gwa'abilani, ka tasa ana imola.

Rauna DEDELA, ki gwa'abi 'ania ma ki butarū logo 'ania.

We then put the mash on the spread. And then we get coconut cream in a cup and put it in the scraping and wrap the scraping parcel, then we oven-cook it for eating.

Leaf for food preparation

For preparing food, leaves are important for wrapping food in and oven-cooking and plugging (bamboo) tubes and spreading the way for food. The leaf we select as fitting is big and wide and long, it looks good and makes the food smell good when burned, and it is not bitter either lest it spoil the food. When we wrap things in leaf we warm it so it will be flexible to fold, if we don't warm it it will tear. Leaves which are suitable for food-making are named:
COMINSIA leaf, we wrap food in it, especially pudding, it suitable because it both looks good and when the food is burned it smells good to eat. We also oven-cook with the leaf but it is only quite good because some leaves are small. For oven-cooking it is especially good in the damp inland, a place where leaf is not plentiful.
HELICONIA is fitted for oven-cooking and spreading for food because the leaf is wide and really long, it is smooth and it smells good too and is not bitter. We prepare food with it especially in the damp inland, a place where leaf is not plentiful.
BANANA leaf and *SASAO* leaf (both *musa*) are also good because they are really big and wide but their smell is a little bitter. With these leaves we strip out the (midrib) strip, because the strip is big and not flexible to fold.
GUILLAINIA (ginger) leaf we warm for parcelling food like nut-pudding and anything else, also for oven-cooking, and we also plug tubes of food with it. It smells good and not bitter.
ALPINIA (ginger), we also wrap food like nut insides (kernels) with it, we also oven-cook with it but the leaves are just small and it is not as good and suitable as big leaves.
KAKAMA (swamp taro / *Cyrtosperma*) leaf, we oven-cook with it, we also spread the way for food with it and wrap parcels of scraping (mangrove pudding) with it.
MAT (*Pandanus*) leaf, we parcel scraping (mangrove pudding) with it for eating and we also parcel grated *bia*-yam (cassava pudding) with it. We warm the leaf first so it will be flexible and then also spread out leaves like cominsia leaf (*lā*) and banana leaf, and then we parcel it up. We also package tiny fish in it to oven-cook them, especially *imola*.
DEDELA leaf (*Ficus*), we oven-cook with it and also parcel with it.

Rauna TANGAFINO ki gwa'abi 'ania.
Rauna kwalo SALU, ki gwa'abi 'ania ma ki 'afua
logo 'ania buta ko'a ti'iti'i kī.

Rauna kwalo BABĀ, di'ia rau le'a nia ato ki gwa'abi
logo 'ania.
Rauna DILI, ki dodoa 'ania ngongora kī 'i 'anilana
ke moko le'a liu.
Rauna REBAREBA, ki gwa'abi 'ania.
Rauna 'AKO'AKO, ki gwa'abi 'ania. Ki rarangia
rauna basi kwatea noa'a nia kesi 'akofikia na'a.
NIU, ki 'afu ī'a 'ania rauna fuana gwa'abilana.

Kafo

Kafo, ngalilana ma'i luma fuana kwa'ufilana ma
kukilana fanga, ki ufi fungu ana gwagi ka'o. Ki
tufua lala ka'o, ki sikilia ta'i kasirū 'i ne'e nia ke
fonea 'ania na rō gwaugwau kī, ka sui ki fi'i sotea ta
gwaugwau. 'I na'o gwa'i sosote ne'e ki sotea 'ania,
na gwa'i fau raku ki saena kafo. Ka sui ki ūfia 'ania
kafo, ki 'uru'urua fuana ke tabua fulafulana fa'inia
rū kwao ana gwaugwau ne'e kwate ka'o kwa'ufilana
ka mingaminga. Ki tabua ka sui, ki 'uru'uru'a, 'uru
ana ne'e ki ūfi ūru logo ana ka'o. Ka sui ki ūfi fungu
ana ka'o, mala ki fi'i sigorā na'a. Sigorilana, ki talia
ra'irū di'ia ra'i 'age noema ra'i folota, ka sui ki
sigorā, ki silifa'inia sigora saena gwagi ka'o, ka sui
ki gu'utā la'u 'ania ra'irū sigora'a 'i fafo mala, kini
kī fi'i foea 'uana 'i luma.

Di'ia ki ogā ufilana kafo 'oro ki tufua 'aurua
noima ladelade. Ki tufua lala ka'o 'ania rō
kasirū'anga noima kasi ka'o 'oro kī, ki ladea sufulia
'ania fo 'i 'au saena kasi ka'o kī 'ania ma'e 'ai keta,
ki fi'i tabua mala ki fi'i ufi fungu ana, ki sigorā ki
gu'utā logo. Ngwae kī nini'a rao'a kira tufu
ladelade'a.

Ti kaida'i ki sabangia ma'i kafo fuana siu'a ma
kwa'unga'a. Ki tufua basi fa'i ka'o noima fa'i
dodola, bore ma fa'irū ona kī nama 'i kesi fura
'ali'ali. Go'o ki gasia 'ania rō rebarū kī, ki tufusisilia
gwagirū kī ne'e kafo ke afe ka daofa'iliu sulia saena
kasirū kī, mala ki ngalia ki labunga'inia 'ala'a 'i
māna ma'e busu. Ki fi'i tufua rō gwa'i tanga ngasi
kī, ki kata'ini'i ana kula kafo ke to'o ana, ki alu
faifolo ana ta fa'i 'ai ana rō gwa'i tanga kī. Mala ki
fi'i alua 'aba sasaba 'i fafona, mala kafo fi'i afe 'i
sulia. Ka sui ki 'ilia afu ano ki bulia 'adoa safitana
'aba sasaba fa'inia māna busu fuana kafo kesi loto.

Di'ia ki sabangia go'o kafo fuana kaida'i
dokodoko, 'īra ki boea go'o ofiofina sasao, go'o ki
sabangia logo 'ania kafo fuana kwaunga ma siu'a.

MACARANGA leaf, we oven-cook with it.
SALU-vine leaf (*Araceae*), we oven-cook with it and
also wrap small parcels of scraping (mangrove
pudding) with it.
BABĀ-vine leaf (*Euodia*), if good leaf is hard to get
we also oven-cook with it.
CORDYLINE leaf, we steam *ngongora*(lizards) in it
so they will smell very good to eat.
WIDEISH leaf (*Macaranga*), we oven-cook with it.
STINGER leaf (*Dendrocnide*), we oven-cook with it.
We warm the leaf first so it won't sting us.
COCONUT, we wrap fish in it for oven-cooking.

Water

Water, to bring it to the house for drinking and
boiling food we fill up internodes of bamboo. We
chop down a length of bamboo, we cut off a
section so it is shut off by two nodes, then we bore
one node. Formerly the borer we bored with was a
pointed stone from the water. Then we fill it with
water, we shake it up to clear out the dust and
white stuff from the node which would make
drinking from the bamboo foul. We clear it out, we
shake it up, three times we fill and shake the
bamboo. Then we fill up the bamboo, before we
roll a spout. To roll a spout we split a leaf like
alpinia(ginger)(*'age*) or guillainia(ginger)(*folota*),
then we roll it up, we insert the roll into the
bamboo node, then we plug it with leaf at the top
and then women carry it to the house.

If we want to fill up with a lot of water we
chop a double-bamboo or a knocked-through-
length. We chop a length of bamboo of two
sections or many sections of bamboo, we jab and
pierce through the nodes in the bamboo with a
long stick, we then clear it out well and fill it up,
we roll a spout and plug it. It is men's work to
make knocked-through-lengths.

Sometimes we duct water to bathe and drink.
First we chop bamboo or mixture (bamboo)(*dodola /
Bambusa*), but it must be tough ones so it won't rot
quickly. Then we tear them into two strips and
chop along the nodes so the water can flow past
along the sections, after that we take it and stake
it up in front of a spring. We then chop two strong
forks and stake them at the place the water gets
to and put a tree across the two forks. Then we
put the duct on it, then the water will flow along
it. After that we dig earth and stamp it down to
join the duct to the spring so the water won't
seep away.

If we are ducting water for a short time, then
we make a tube of *sasao* stem-sheath (*Musa*) and
duct water with it for drinking and bathing.

Rū fuana kwa'ufilani kī

Kafo ne'e rū talinga'i ne'e ki kwa'ufia, bore ma ki kwa'ufia logo ti rū mamata.

NIU, ki kwa'ufia fa'irū kī.

KA'O, ki kwa'ufia 'ausura kaida'i kafo fungu saena kasirū, ki tufua 'uana ana gwagirū fuana kwa'ufilana.

Kwalo KAULATA, ki tufua fa'irū fuana kafo ke āfe ma'i fa'asia fuana kwa'ufilana.

NGINGIDUA, ki tufu 'uana saena liko 'ai noima saena 'ifi 'ai fuana kwa'ufilana latalatarū.

UFU, ki tufua kasirū ki tadilia fuana totofia noima ki losia fuana kwa'ufilana.

Ti FA'IRŪ FAKA di'ia lamana, oronisi, baenafa, ki losi'i fuana kwa'ufilani.

Things to drink

Water is the main thing we drink, but we also drink some other things.

COCONUT, we drink the fruits.

BAMBOO, we drink the bamboo-liquid when water fills the sections, we chop it out at the node to drink.

KAULATA (*Uncaria*) vine, we chop a piece for water to flow from to drink.

HONEY-BEE, we chop it out of tree cavities or logs to drink the honey.

SUGAR(cane), we chop a section and trim it for sucking or squeeze it for drinking.

Some FOREIGN FRUITS like lemon, orange and pineapple we squeeze for drinking.

7
Saunga'ilana luma kī

Na taki fuana tuafilana fanoa kī

Tuafilana fanoa, 'i na'o ma'i ki fa'amanata 'ania taki fuana tualaka 'i ke o'olo ma rū kī ke saga, 'i ne'e kia'a ke tua le'a saena fanoa ne'e. Ka 'unari ki saunga'inia malita'i luma to'oto'o kī, kwatea akalo ma ngwae ma kini kira ke tua to'oto'o ana kula mamata kira kī. Ki fasia logo 'ai fuana laungi'a kī saena fanoa ma fuana logo 'oto'a kī, fa'inia logo ti 'ai fufungu ma ti 'ai fuana saunga'irū'anga. Ki sakalia logo fanoa fa'asia gwata kesi kiufia.

Luma kī, feraābu ne'e 'inoto'a, kula nini'a fuana akalo ke teo ana fuana fo'osilana, ki saunga'inia 'i burina fanoa, ki sakalia mala kula ne'e ābu fuana ngwae ma kini kira kesi liu ata ana, kira kata fa'asuā. Fulisango, kula ne'e fuana ngwa'enga kaida'i ana maoma, nia karangia logo ferāabu.

Saena fanoa ki saunga'inia fera ana kula 'i langi. Fera ne'e kula ngwangwane kī fuana tua'a ma teo'a, nia ābu logo fuana kini kī kesi ru'u 'i saena. Di'ia fataābu, nia ke tua go'o ti'ana ana fera nia, nia ābu liu fuana kini kī ke liu 'uana. Di'ia ngwae 'inoto'a ti kaida'i nia ke saunga'inia fera gwaroa fuana fa'ata'ilana satana. Fera 'i na'o kī, ki alua nama sinama 'olofolo 'i burina fera fuana tafi'a kaida'i mae ke dao.

Ne'e ki koso toli fa'asia fera 'uana luma ne'e kini ma ngela kī tua ana, ma kira ka do'ofia fanga ana, fuana sarelana to'a kī ma gwata kī. Saena logo luma nai'ari ne'e ki ke alua buta mani saena usausa. Ti ka'idai ki saunga'inia logo luma fuana gwata kī ke tua 'i saena.

Kaida'i kini ke saka 'i fu'a rafi nia ke koso 'i īlina sakali, ke tua 'i luma bisi sulia kaida'i nia ke taka. Kula nai'ari sua fuana ngwae kī ke liu ana. Ta luma ne'e bisi kale nia teo ta'u liu fa'asia fanoa saena masu'u, karangia kabara kini. 'Afe kī go'o ne'e kira saunga'inia bisi kale fuana kale'a. Nia sua dangalu ngwae kī kesi liu 'uana. Na afu masu'u mala ne'e fonea bisi kale, nia kata fa'aolā to'a ta'ifau, ma akalo ka geosida kira ka mae.

Na kula fuana kabara ngwane ma ai kini kī teo to'oto'o logo ka teo te'e tau fa'asia fanoa saena masu'u, ma na koto mimi kī bore teo to'oto'o logo.

7
Building houses

The rules for living at home

To live at home, formerly we taught rules for our living to be straight and things to be correct, so we would live well in the home. And so we built separate kinds of houses, to make ghosts and men and women live separately in their different places. We also planted trees for decoration in the home and as charms, as well as fruit-bearing trees and trees for making things. We also fenced the home against pigs grubbing it up.

Of the houses, the tabu-sanctum (shrine) was most important, it was the place for the ghosts to stay for praying, we built it behind the home and fenced the area which was tabu so that men and women wouldn't pass by at random, lest they defile it. The dance-site, the place for dancing during festivals, was also near the tabu-sanctum.

In the home we built a sanctum in a high place. The sanctum was the males' place for living and sleeping and it was tabu for women to enter. If there was a tabu-speaker (priest) he'd live by himself in his sanctum and it was very tabu for women to go to. If there was an important man, sometimes he'd build a patterned sanctum to show off his name. With sanctums formerly, we had to put a doorway directly behind the house for escape when a feud-band came.

So we go downwards from the sanctum to the (dwelling) house, where the women and children lived and burned their food, to feed the people and the pigs. In this house we also put parcels of shell-money on a storage-rack. Sometimes we also built a house for pigs to live in.

When a woman went out from the hearth she went down at the back of the fence to live in a seclusion house while she menstruated. This place was defiling for men to go by. The house of birth seclusion was far away from the home, in the forest, near the women's latrine. It was the wives who built the birth seclusion-house for a birth. It was extremely defiling for men go to. A piece of forest had to shut off the birth seclusion-house lest it pollute all the people and the ghosts overthrow them and they die.

The place for the men's latrine and the women's one were also separate and quite far from the home in the forest, and peeing places were also separate.

Saunga'ilana luma'a

'I na'o ma'i luma kī, ki du'arū 'i saeni ta'ifau, ka 'unari saunga'ilana luma nai'ari kī mamata fa'asia luma nini'ari kī sulia ki saunga'ini'i go'o 'i ano. Luma 'i ta'ena kī, fa'asia bara talata'ingwae fa'asia na'a ko'o ma ma'a kia kī, nini'a ki lisia luma ara'ikwao kī ma ki saunga'i sulia luma 'i 'a'e asi ma fanoa doe kī. Ka 'unari, luma kia 'i nini'ari, ki saunga'inia luma tatafe'a ne'e to'o logo ana ma'e luma kī, ma'e luma 'i mā, ma'e sinama kī, rū 'unari kī. Ki rokisia logo rū fuana saunga'i'anga, ka di'ia tiba ne'e talafuila na'a fa'i 'ai, reba 'ai ne'e talafuila na'a reba niniu, nila ne'e talafuila na'a 'aba kalitau, kaba ne'e talafuila na'a ra'i sao.

'I na'o ko'o ki kesi saunga'inia safisi sulia gwata kī kata ru'u 'i olofana rū kini kī ke tua 'i fafona, kwatea ni'i ke sua. Na luma ne'e ko'o ki saunga'ini'i 'i na'o ma to'a 'i buri ke saunga'inia ua, ni'i lia di'ia luma ni du'urū'a kia kī 'i nini'ari bore ma luma 'i ano kī ne'e, noa'a la'u safisi kī.

Saunga'ilana luma, ki efoa mala rū ne'e bolo fa'inia kī, kwatea luma ke ngasi ke teo ta'u ma ke lia le'a, na rū le'a nai'ari kī ne'e 'ai ma kwalo ma 'au ma ra'i rau ma ta rū bore 'ana. Ti luma ni'i teo gwari go'o 'ani noa'a kisi eforū fuana, luma di'ia gwaurau kī noema babala saena o'ola kī, fuana tua nunufi'anga ma tua'a go'o fa'asia uta, babala logo fuana tua'a saena lalano kaida'i ana fa'i ngali ma fuana 'ui ngali'a kī. Gwaurau nai'ari kī, noa'a kisi fili 'ai go'o fuani'i, 'atona go'o 'ana 'ai di'ia fa'i sa'osa'o, fa'i faefae, fa'i sungasunga, fa'i lofa, fa'i gwa'ugwa'u, fa'i nunuba, fa'i melo, 'ai niniu.

House-building

Formerly we burned (food) inside all houses, so we built houses differently from houses at present because we just built them on the ground. Today's houses are from a few generations ago, from our grandfathers and fathers, because we saw white-men's houses and built according to houses from overseas and big countries. And so for our houses today we build platformed houses which also have rooms, verandas, doors and things like that. We also change the things we build with, like timbers replacing tree-poles, wooden planks replacing palm flats, nails replacing winds-far strip, sheet-iron replacing sago leaf.

Formerly our ancestors wouldn't build a raised floor lest pigs enter under things women had been above, making them defiled. The houses which our ancestors built formerly, and old-fashioned people still build, look like our cooking houses at present, and they are houses on the ground, not with floors.

To build a house we must select suitable things to make the house strong, long-lasting and look good, and these good things are tree, bamboo, vine, leaf and whatever. Houses which are just damp we don't select things for, houses like leaf-shelters and shelters in gardens, for staying in the shade and out of the rain, and also shelters for staying in the forest during the nut season and for hammering nuts. For these leaf-shelters we don't choose the trees, the rafters are just trees like yellow (*sa'osa'o / Cananga*), kleinhovia (*faefae*), pipturus (*sungasunga*), sterculia (*gwa'ugwa'u*), lofa (*Sterculia*), squirt-eye (*sikimā / Homalanthus*), beetle-turner (*bulasīsī / Ulmaceae*) and palm-tree (*'aininiu / Myrsinaceae*).

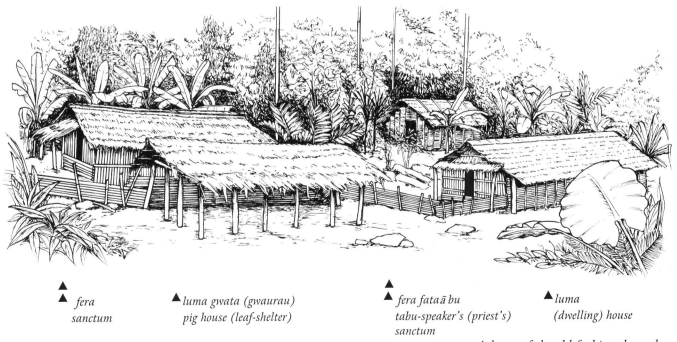

▲ *fera*
  sanctum

▲ *luma gwata (gwaurau)*
  pig house (leaf-shelter)

▲ *fera fataā bu*
  tabu-speaker's (priest's)
  sanctum

▲ *luma*
  (dwelling) house

Ma'e fanoa to'a 'i buri.   *A home of the old-fashioned people*

Rau fuana to'osilana babala kī, noa'a kisi usa bore ra'irū kī ma ki tolea go'o ulirū ma ra'irū 'i fafona barabara 'ai, ra'irū di'ia uli kikiru kwasi kī, uli bofau kī, rauna sao kī, ra'i rako kī, uli 'age kī ma uli folota kī.

Barabaralana luma

Saunga'ilana luma, ki tabua basi kula, ki 'otomia rebalana ma ketalana luma 'ania tafanga 'ai ne'e ki tafangā 'ania limaka. Di'ia ki ogā ketalana ne'e ta fita tafanga, rebalana ta fita tafanga, ki alu laelae ana ta fita kasi 'au funi'a 'i ne'e ke bolo fa'inia ta fita tafanga ne'e ki ogā. Di'ia luma ti'iti'i ne'e sali ke bolo fa'inia fai tafanga ana ketalana, ulu tafanga ana rebalana, di'ia luma doe ne'e sali ke bolo fa'inia fiu tafanga ana ketalana ma fai tafanga ana rebalana.

Ki efoa basi 'ai kī fuana diro'a kī. Na 'ai ne'e bolo fa'inia diro nia ke ngasi mala, kaida'i ki 'ili fa'inia nia ke teo tau, noa'a nia kesi fura 'ali'ali noima ke 'akofolo. 'Ai ne'e le'a ka tasa fuana diro fuana luma kī ne'e fa'i tō, fa'i 'u'ula, fa'i malanunu fau, fa'i mamufua. Ti 'ai ne'e totolia logo diro ne'e fa'i fata, fa'i kwa'o, fa'i 'u'ufi, fa'i kwa'e, fa'i dingale, fa'i 'aidori, fa'i fa'ulu, fa'i baliu, fa'i ngara, fa'i 'o'a meo ma fa'i 'o'a marako. 'Ai fuana diro'anga ni'i 'oro saena to'ona'oa bore ma saena tofungana tolo ni'i kesi 'oro liu go'o, ki tufua ma'i diro fa'asia to'ona'oa. Ti 'ai fuana diro ne'e bulao saena tolo ne'e fa'i kwa'e, fa'i ngara, fa'i baliu, fa'i o'a meo ma fa'i o'a marako.

Tufulana diro, ki tafangā 'ania limaka ka bolo fa'inia ta fita tafanga, ki aea ta'eta'ena, ki ngalia ma'i. Gwauna diro kī, ki tufua ka tanga'a fuana alulana fa'i gwaofa fa'inia fa'i 'idi'idi kī ani, ki saea 'ania nia di'ia alingana kui fa'inia gwauna. Ka sui ki 'ilitalana diro gwaofa ki fa'inia diro 'idi'idi kī, ki fi'i fa'asagā fuana saunga'i luma'a.

Fa'i 'ai fuana saunga'i luma'a, ne'e fada 'ania tufulana fa'i gwaofa fa'inia fa'i 'idi'idi kī, fa'i falo kī, fa'i 'ato kī. Fa'i 'ai fuana luma ne'e bolo nama fa'inia, 'ai saga le'a kī ma ka keta sasabe'a ma ka ona ka ngasi logo, noa'a suma kesi 'ania, noa'a gwagwao kesi sotea. Ti 'ai ne'e le'a ka tasa fuana saunga'inga ne'e fa'i kasibulu, fa'i mamalade, fa'i gwarogwaro, fa'i ba'ula, fa'i 'aika'o, fa'i kaumanu. 'Ai nai'ari kī ta'ifau ne'e bolo fa'inia saunga'i luma'a bore ma noa'a kesi bolo fa'inia funu. Ta'i fa'i gwaofa ne'e 'ai ne'e bolo nama fa'inia na 'ai ngasi kī ne'e bolo fa'inia diro. Fa'i 'ato kī, ma fa'i 'au ne'e le'a liu logo fuana 'ato'a. 'Ai fuana saunga'i luma'a kī ni'i 'oro ana kula kī sui, ma 'ai ne'e 'oro

The leaf for roofing shelters, we don't stitch the leaves but just thatch fronds and leaves on the tree-frame, leaves like wild betel fronds (*kikiru kwasi / Areca*), set-solid (palm) fronds (*bōfau / Arecaeae*), sago leaf, heliconia leaf (*rako*), alpinia(ginger) fronds (*'age*) and guillainia(ginger) fronds (*folota*).

Framing the house

To build a house we first clear the area, we fathom (measure) the width and length of the house with a fathom-stick which we fathom with our (outstretched) hands. If we want a length of so many fathoms and a width of so many fathoms, we lay it out with however many lengths of bamboo to meet the number of fathoms we want. If it's a small house it might be four fathoms in length and three fathoms in width, if it's a big house it might be seven fathoms in length and four fathoms in width.

We first select trees for posts. A tree suitable for posts is really strong and when we dig it in it is long-lasting, it won't rot quickly or break off. Trees which are especially good for posts for houses are streblus (*tō*), ipil (*'u'ula / Intsia*), *malanunu fau* (*Neonauclea*), securinega (*mamufua*). Some trees which are also fit for posts are vitex (*fata*), drink (*kwa'u / Premna*), *'u'ufi* (*Moraceae*), treefern (*kwa'e / Cythera*), dingale (*Podocarpus*), *dori*-tree (*'aidori / Antidesma*), *fa'ola* (*Hibiscus*), baliu (*Ascarina*), prickly (*ngara / Fagraea*), red and green glochidion (*'o'a*). Trees for posts are plentiful in the lowland but in the central inland they are not very plentiful and we chop posts from the lowland. Trees for posts which grow in the inland are treefern, prickly, *baliu*, red and green glochidion.

To chop posts, we fathom with our hands to so many fathoms, we peel the skin and bring them back. The heads of the posts we chop into a fork to lay the ridge-beam and the eave-beams on; we say it's like a dog's ears and head. Then we dig in the ridge-beam post and the eave-beam posts and straighten them up to build the house.

Trees for house building means for chopping the ridge-beam and eave-beams, bearers and rafters. Trees suitable for the house must be good straight trees, long and even and also tough and strong, which worms won't eat and wasps won't bore. Some trees which are especially good for building are dark-section (*kasibulu / Melochia*), alangium (*mamalade*), calophyllum (*gwarogwaro*), *ba'ula*, *kaumanu* (all *Calophyllum*) and bamboo-tree (*'aika'o / Xylopia*). All these trees are suitable for building houses but not suitable for posts. Only the ridge-beam should be of the strong trees which are suitable for posts. For rafters, bamboos are also very good. Trees for house-building are plentiful saena tolo ne'e fa'i ba'ula, fa'i kaumanu, fa'i gwarogwaro.

Ti 'ai ne'e kesi le'a liu fuana saunga'i luma'a sulia noa'a nia kesi ngasi go'o, nia ka ngwara'u go'o, nia 'iri teo tau sulia suma ke 'ania ma gwagwao ke sotea, noima uta ka fa'aisila ma ke fura aliali go'o, ni'i kesi bolo fa'inia luma tua ni fuli kī. Ti 'ai ana raku faolu kī ne'e 'unari. Bore ma ti ai ana 'ai nai'ari kī ni'i bolo lala fa'inia luma sasufi'i kī ka di'ia luma ni du'urū'a kī, si ne'e mafula ke sasufia ke 'eke'eke 'i ne'e ke ngasi la'u. 'Ai nai'ari kī ni'i di'ia fa'ola, sula, mala'o, faefae, bala, rebareba, karefo, su'amango, keto, fenofeno, sa'osa'o. Ti 'ai, di'ia ki saunga'inia bore 'ania babala 'i luma fuana du'arū'anga, sasu ka sasufia bore 'ana, nia suma'ala nama. 'Ai kī di'ia ngali ni'i 'unari.

Saunga'ilana luma, ki alua basi fa'i gwaofa ma fa'i 'idi'idi kī, ki ito fafia diro kī, ka sui ki alua logo fa'i falo kī, ki itoa ke teo fafona fa'i 'idi'idi kī, ka sui ki alua fa'i ato kī, ki itoa ta'i bali ana fa'i gwaofa. Sui mala ki fi'i alua la'u fa'i fafo 'i falo, ki saea logo 'ania fa'i falo daudau, ke teo fafia fa'i falo kī ka donga sulia fa'i 'idi'idi kī. Fa'i falo daudau kī ki daudau ana 'i ne'e ki lia talana kula ne'e ke bolo fa'inia fafona falo ma olofana fa'i ato kī. Fa'i falo daudau nia fuana susu'ilana fa'i 'ato kī, ki itoa fafia fa'i falo, ki itoa la'u fa'i ato kī fafia fa'i falo daudau fuiri. Di'ia ki oga to'osilana luma ke lia le'a ma ka madako ma'i saena luma, ta ma ki tufu dokodoko ana ti fa'i ato, ki alua 'i fafona fa'i 'idi'idi kī ma ki ru'unga'inia 'i olofana fa'i fafo 'i falo, ki itotaia gwauna fa'i ato dokodoko nai'ari kī 'i 'aena fa'i ato kī ta'ifau. Ki atoa luma ka sui mala, ki fi'i itoa la'u fa'i 'ai kī ni'i ke teo faifolo olofana fa'i ato kī, ki saea 'ania fa'i laelae 'asofe.

everywhere and the trees which are plentiful in the inland are *ba'ula*, *kaumanu* and calophyllum.

Some trees are not very good for building houses because they are not strong, just soft, they are not long-lasting because worms eat them and wasps bore them or rain wets them and they rot quickly, they are not suitable for dwelling houses. Some trees of the new shoots are like this. But some of these trees are suitable for smoky houses like cooking houses, as the fire smokes them dry so they get stronger. These are trees like mallow (*fa'ola / Hibiscus*), *sula*, *mala'o* (both *Trichospermum*), kleinhovia (*faefae*), euodia (*bala*), wideish (*rebareba*), flare (*karefo / Shleinitzia*), breath-wipe (*su'amango*), *keto* (all *Macaranga*), macaranga (*tangafeno*), yellow (*sa'osa'o / Cananga*). Some trees, even if we build house shelters for cooking and smoke smokes them, they get worm-eaten. Trees like nut are like this.

To build a house we first lay the ridge-beam and eave-beams and tie them onto the posts, then we also lay the bearers and tie them to lie on top of the eave-beams, then we lay the rafters and tie one end to the ridge-beam. After that we also lay the over-bearers which we also call the hold-bearers, to lie on the bearers following along the eave-beams. The hold-bearers we hold onto to see that they fit in place over the bearers and beneath the rafters. The hold-bearer is to secure the rafters; we tie it onto the bearer and tie the rafters onto the hold-bearer. If we want the house roofing to look good and let light into the house, we chop some rafters short and lay them on top of the eave-beams and insert them underneath the over-bearers and tie up the heads of these short rafters to the foot of all the rafters. After we have raftered the house, then we also tie trees to lie across underneath the rafters, we call them rat-runs.

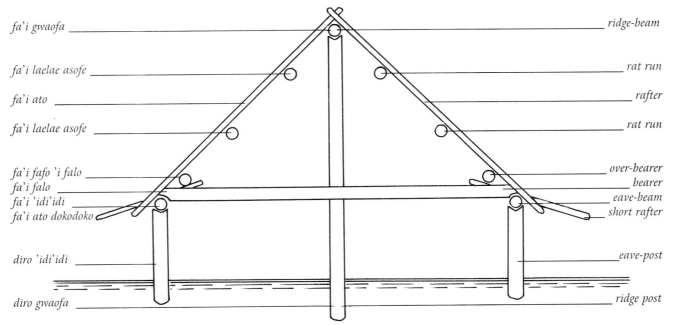

Fonelana kifikifi, ki 'oi sulia rebalana kula funi'a ana kifikifi ke teo ana, ki saunga'inia 'ania ana ūlu fa'i 'ai kī ne'e ki itoa ana fa'i 'ai raurau'a 'oro kī, ka sui ki lafua ki susu'ia 'i gwauna luma.

Itolana luma

Itolana luma, ki itoa 'ania malita'i kwalo to'oto'o kī, ni'i 'uri:

'Aba KALITAU ne'e 'inoto'a fuana itolana luma sulia nia keta ka ngasi le'a ka mabe le'a logo, obi'a 'ania ka lia le'a liu. Ki usa logo sao 'ania. Ki sisia ma ki toea saena 'abarū ka dada mala, ki fi'i ito 'ania. Bore ma ki firi go'o 'ania ana kula langalanga kī, di'ia ki itoa 'ania ti rū ana kula isila nia ke fura 'ali'ali logo. Kalitau ne'e nia fi'i doe, ki saea 'ania fi'i felofelo, noa'a nia kesi bolo 'ua fa'inia ito luma'a sulia noa'a nia kesi ngasi le'a go'o ma noa'a kesi mabe go'o, si ne'e di'ia ki sisia noema ki aea nia mafusifusi'anga. Bore ma di'ia kalitau noa'a kesi tatakolo'a ana ti kula, ta ma ki ito logo 'ania ti kwalo mamata.

Kwalo RĀRĀ TOLO, ki itoa 'ania luma ma sao fuana to'osilana luma, ki rao 'ania di'ia logo kalitau, di'ia nia 'oro ka liufia kalitau 'i nonina fanoa ta ma ki rokisia 'ania kalitau. Ki itoa 'ania fa'i kwalo la'ula'u, noa'a kisi sisia la'u di'ia kalitau. Ti kaida'i ki rarangia go'o 'i ne'e ke mabe fuana ito'a, nia kata ma'oi. Ngasilana rarā tolo nia bolo logo fa'inia kalita'u, bore ma ki ito 'ania ana kula langalanga kī go'o si ne'e nia ke fura ana kula isila kī.

Fi'i KWASAKWASA, fa'ina ki aea 'ania 'abarū fuana itolana luma, fuana logo usalana sao, di'ia logo kalitau.

Fi'i KWALEKWALE nia di'ia logo kwasakwasa bore ma kwasakwasa ne'e fa'irū doe ana. Ki aea logo 'ania 'abarū kī fuana itolana luma, ma fuana logo usulana sao.

Kwalo SATA nia ngasi ka bolo fa'inia kalitau bore ma nia dokodoko go'o, noa'a kesi bolo fa'inia ta'i tafanga. Fa'i sata, ki ito 'ania fa'i kwalo la'ula'u kī, di'ia ki sisia nia ke fura 'ali'ali. Ki susu'ia 'ania kokoba ana luma, 'i ne'e uta ke to'ea ke isila bore 'ana, noa'a kesi fura 'ali'ali. Bore ma ta'i malitana sata ne'e ki saea 'ania sata 'u 'i afa ne'e noa'a kesi bolo fa'inia susu'ilana luma sulia di'ia ki ito 'ania fa'i kwalo la'ula'u īra, nia ke ma'oi.

Kwalo SALU ki firi 'ania ngwakona, nia le'a ka tasa sulia 'aba ngwako kī ngasi liu, ki itoa 'ania sao kī fuana to'osilana luma.

To close the gable we gauge the width of the area where the gable will be and build it of three trees which we tie to many slender trees and then we lift it up and secure it at the top of the house.

Tying the house

To tie the house we tie with different kinds of vines, which are:

WINDS-FAR strip (rattan / *Calamus*) is important for tying houses because it is long, good and strong and good and flexible too, and lashings of it look very good. We also stitch sago (leaf) with it. We split it and pare the inside of the strip really smooth and then tie with it. But we only tie with it in dry places and if we tie something with it in a wet place it will rot quickly. Winds-far which is still young, which we call *felofelo*, is not yet suitable for tying a house because it is not good and strong and not flexible, so if we split it or peel it, it snaps. But if winds-far is not abundant in an area, we tie with other vines.

INLAND *RĀRĀ* vine (*Stenochlaena*), we tie the house and sago (leaf) for thatching the house with it, we work it like winds-far and if it is more plentiful than winds-far in the home area, then we change to it from winds-far. We tie with the entire vine, we don't split it like winds-far. Sometimes we warm it to be flexible for tying, lest it snap. The strength of inland *rārā* is equal to winds-far, but we only tie with it in dry places as it rots in wet places.

KWASAKWASA (*Flagellaria*), we peel it into strips for tying the house, and also for stitching sago (leaf), like winds-far.

KWALEKWALE (*Flagellaria*) is like *kwasakwasa*, but *kwasakwasa* has a bigger stem. We also peel strips from it for tying the house and also for stitching sago (leaf).

LYGODIUM vine is equivalent in strength to winds-far but it is only short, not equal to a fathom. With lygodium we tie with the entire vine and if we split it, it rots quickly. We secure the roof-crest with it, as even when the rain soaks it, it won't rot quickly. But the kind of lygodium which we call eagle's claw lygodium (*sata 'u 'i afa*) is not suitable for securing the house because if we tie with the entire vine it will snap.

SALU-vine (*Araceae*), we bind with the tendril, it is especially good because the tendril-strips are very strong and we tie the sago (leaf) to roof the house with it.

To'osilana luma

Ki saunga'inia barabara luma ka sui, ki fi'i to'osia 'ania sao. Ana ko'o kia kī bore ma'i 'i na'o, kira ke usa go'o rauna felofelo noima rauna mafusu tolo, ki tolea 'ania luma kī, ka leleka sao ka dao, kira salinga'inia ma'i 'i Kwara'ae.

Usalana sao, ki ngalia basi ta reba 'au, ki 'oi sulia ketalana luma nia bolo fa'inia ta fita 'oi'oi 'i sao, mala ki fi'i sikilia reba rū kī 'i sulia fuana usa sao'anga, ka di'ia ta'i tafanga fuana ta'i sao. Usalana sao, ki usa ana reba raforafo kī di'ia 'aba 'au ta'i reba ti'iti'i kī, 'aba kikiru kwasi, 'aba dai'i, 'ali'ali 'alabusi. Ta'ena ki usā lala ana rū di'i fa'i rade kī noema reba dodola kī, rū fukiri noa'a kesi le'a liu. Usalana, ki ngalia ra'i sao, ki aea sisilina, ki la'umia ta'i ra'irū fafia raforafo, ki usā 'ania 'aba kalitau. Di'ia ki ogā sao ke ngasi le'a ki la'umia rō ra'i sao kī ki saea 'ania usa rō 'aba. Di'ia kalitau nia 'ato, ki usa logo 'ania 'aba kwalekwale. Ta'ena ki usa lala 'ania ma'e midi sao, ta sata kutakuta, bore 'ana noa'a kesi ngasi liu go'o, kesi bolo fa'inia usā rō 'aba'a.

To'osilana luma, ki itoa sao fukiri ana 'ato kī 'ania 'aba kalitau, ki kalia 'ania 'ato kī ka tala'ae ana 'aena 'ato, leleka ka dao karangia fa'i gwaofa. Gwauna luma, ki la'umia ra'i sao fuana ra'itai ne'e ki alua 'i fafona.

Di'ia luma ni fuli, ki alua la'u na kokoba ke teo di'ia ra'itai, kwatea sao ke teo tau ma ke lia le'a logo. Kokoba, ki eta barabara talana 'ania ma'e 'ai kī ke di'ia sakali ko'oko'o, ka sui ki fa'aūa la'u sao usa'i kī sulia ki fi'iri'ini, ka sui ki fi'i fa'aūa la'u ti reba raforafo. Ka sui ki fa'aūa la'u ta talata'i sao usa, mala ki fi'i susu'ia fa'inia reba raforafo noima lala keketo kī 'i fafona. Ki fi'iri'ia 'ania fa'i sata kī 'i ne'e kesi fura 'ali'ali ne'e uta ke to'ea. Mala ki fi'i la'umia na'a ra'i sao kī, ki alua kwairokisi ani ne'e ki saea 'ania bula ī'a, mala ki fi'i fi'iribakasi'i fafia kokoba fuiri. Ka sui mala ki fi'i lafua ki to'osia fafia gwaofana luma.

Di'ia gwaurau fuana tua'a fa'asia sina ma uta go'o 'ana, nia ke teo 'ofa'ofa go'o 'ana. Di'ia luma mala, ki fi'i odoa na'a.

'Odolana luma

'Odolana luma, ki to'o ana ti malita'i 'odo'a, di'ia susu'ilana fa'i 'au kī noema sao 'o'o kī go'o, ti kaida'i ki 'odo 'ania 'aba au noema sisinga noema ti rū la'u ne'e ke ngasi la'u noema ke lia kwanga. 'Odolana, ki susu'ia basi fa'i 'ai ki saea 'ania daudau 'oto'oto kī, ki itoa ke teo faifolo ana diro 'idi'idi kī fuana susubakasilana 'odo ana.

Roofing the house

When we finish building the frame of the house we roof it with sago (leaf). But our ancestors formerly just stitched *felofelo* (*Calamus*) leaf or inland *mafusu* (*kakara* / *Alpinia*) leaf and thatched houses with it, until sago came and was transferred to Kwara'ae.

To stitch sago we take a bamboo flat and gauge the length of the house as suiting how many panels of sago, then we cut flats accordingly for stitching the sago at maybe one fathom for one sago (panel). To stitch sago we stitch on battens like quite wide small bamboo strips, wild betel strips (*kikiru kwasi* / *Areca*), strips of rhopaloblaste(palm)(*dai'i*), *'alabusi* shoots (*Euphorbiaceae*). Today we stitch on things like reeds (*rade* / *Poaceae*) or mixture(bamboo) flats (*dodola* / *Bambusa*) instead, which are not so good. To stitch, we take a sago leaf, peel off the (spine) strip, fold a leaf over the batten and stitch it with winds-far strip. If we want the sago to be good and strong we fold two sago leaves (at once) and call it a stitched double layer, If winds-far is hard to get we also stitch with *kwalekwale* strip (*Flagellaria*). Today we stitch with sago leaf-spine instead, called *kutakuta*, but it is not very strong and not suitable for stitching a double layer.

To roof the house we tie the sago to the rafters with winds-far strip, we wind it around the rafters starting at the foot of the rafter, going on almost to the ridge-beam. At the head of the house we fold sago leaf for the ridge which we put on the top.

If it is an established house we also put a crest to lie as a ridge, making the sago (leaf) long-lasting and also to look good. For the crest, we first frame it with tree-sticks like an owl fence (chevrons) then we stand stitched sago (panels) along it and bind them, then we also stand up some battens. Then we stand another row of stitched sago and we then secure it with battens or schizostachyum(bamboo) poles (*keketo*). We bind it with lygodium(vine)(*sata*) so it won't rot quickly as the rain soaks it. Then we fold sago leaves and put them crosswise on it, which we call fishes, and then we bind and clamp them onto the crest. After that we raise it and roof it onto the ridge of the house.

If it is just a leaf-shelter for sitting away from the sun and rain, it will just stay open-sided. If it is really a house, we then wall it.

Walling the house

To wall the house we have kinds of walling like securing bamboos, or sago (leaf) alone, and sometimes we wall with bamboo strips or stripy or other things which are stronger or look pretty. To wall we first secure trees which we call wall-holders and tie them to lie across the eave-posts for clamping the walling to.

Ti malita'i 'odo'a ni'i 'uri:
'ODOA 'I SAO, ki eta fi'iria basi na rebarū 'i 'aena 'odoa fa'inia fa'i 'oto'oto kī fuana ta'elana 'aena sao 'i ke teo saga kaida'i ki bakasia. Rō sao etaeta kī 'aena 'odoa ki bulasia ke teo ka lia 'ala'a.
Ka sui ki fi'i susu'ia sao kī ne'e ki fa'ita'inia toli, ki itoa ana daudau 'oto'oto kī ma ki bakasia na'a 'ania reba raforafo ma 'aba kalitau. Di'ia ki ogā luma ke lia le'a, ta ma ki eta alua sao 'i fafona fa'i 'ai 'i ano fuana ki sikilia mudimudina ra'i sao kī ke bolo, mala ki fi'i odo'a 'ania.

'ODOA 'I 'AU, di'ia ki ogā ki fa'aūa fa'ina 'au, ki susubakasi'i ana daudau 'oto'oto kī. Di'ia ki ogā fa'ina 'au ke teo ka ra'e ma ka teo faifolo ana diro 'idi'idi kī, ki fa'aūa basi fa'i 'oto'oto kī 'i safitana diro 'idi'idi kī, ke bolo go'o fa'inia ta'i gwau'aba-'anga, ka sui mala ki fi'i susubakasia fuana 'au ana. 'ABA 'AU fuana saunga'ilana 'odoa, ki saea 'ania 'au kara, ta sata 'au karako. Fa'i 'au ne'e bolo fa'inia botakwalekwalelana fuana 'au kara, nia ke doe ma kasina ka keta nama. Ka'o saga ne'e le'a ka tasa fuana 'au kara bore ma dodola noa'a kesi bolo fa'inia sulia kasina dokodoko, gwagina ka doe, na rebana ka baba'ula ma suma ke 'ania. Ti 'au ni'i ti'iti'i liu kesi bolo fa'inia botakwalekwalelana, di'ia ka'o asi, 'au fīrū fa'inia logo keketo. Saunga'ilana 'au kara, ki tufua basi fa'i 'au doe kī, go'o ki fa'asinafi'i noema ki alua ke du'a mala, ki fi'i botakwalekwalea. Ki alua fa'i 'au fafona ta afu 'ai te'e doe, ki diungisia 'ania 'abala 'i 'ai, ka sui ki tagā 'i ke reba, ki fi'i tabua, ka sui nia bolo fa'inia saunga'ilana rū di'ia 'odo'a ma tatafe.

Some kinds of walling are:
SAGO WALLING, we begin by binding flats at the foot of the wall onto the uprights to set up the foot of the sago so it will lie straight when we clamp it on. The first two sagos (panels) at the foot of the wall we reverse to lie (leaf-ends) facing upwards. Then we fix the sagos which we turn downwards and tie them to the wall-holders and clamp them with battens and winds-far strip. If we want the house to look good, we first lay the sago on a tree on the ground to cut the tips of the sago leaves even, and then we wall with it.
BAMBOO WALLING, if we want to stand the bamboos up we clamp them against the wall-holders. If we want the bamboos to go up crosswise to the eave-posts, we first stand uprights between the eave-posts at a distance of one arm-length, and only then do we clamp the bamboo poles to it.
BAMBOO STRIP for making walling is called scored bamboo ('scored' with splits). Bamboo suitable for smashing flat for scored bamboo must be big with long internodes. Bamboo proper is especially good for scored bamboo but mixture (*dodola* / *Bambusa*) is not suitable because its inter-nodes are too short, the nodes are big, the flats are thick and worms eat it. Some very small bamboos are not suitable for smashing flat, like sea bamboo (*ka'o asi*), tangled bamboo (*'au fīrū* / *Poaceae*) and schizostachyum(*keketo*). To make scored bamboo we first chop down big bamboos, we sun them or put them to dry out, then we smash them flat. We put the bamboo on a quite large piece of tree and hammer it with a tree plank, then we open it out flat, we clean it up and then it is suitable for building things like walls and platforms.

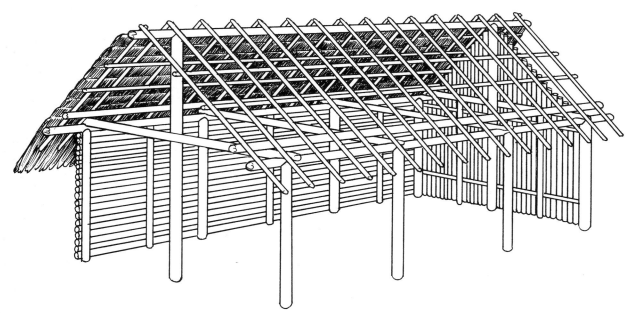

▲ *Barabara luma fa'inia logo sao ma 'odo'a 'i 'au*   ▲ *House frame with sago (leaf roof) and bamboo walling*

'Odolana luma 'ania 'au kara ki to'o ana ti malita'i odo'a.

'AU KARA, ki fa'aūa ta afu'ai, go'o ki ladoa fa'inia ta afu'ai.

'AU KAKARO, ki alua 'ala'a ti reba 'au, 'unari ki alu fa'ifolo ana ti reba 'au, ki faosi'i.

SISINGA, di'ia ki ogā 'au kakaro ke lia le'a, ki alua logo 'aba kwasakwasa ne'e gwā kī, ke teo'i ninimana 'au kara ana ro bali afu'ai ū 'ala'a kī, ki saea 'ania sisinga. Noima ki ngalia lala 'au kara ne'e bala, ki faosia fa'inia 'au kara ne'e du'a ana mafula noema 'aba kwasakwasa. 'Abarū fuana sisinga ni'i te'e reba ma kwa'ilana ka 'ali'ali ma kesi 'ato liu go'o.

KENIAILA, karangia ka di'ia logo sisinga bore ma 'aba kwaskwasi kī kesi 'oro go'o ana nonina.

SISIMA ne'e 'odo'a 'ania kwanga ka tasa. Ki saea 'uri 'ania sulia ki silia 'abarū 'i ki kwa'i 'ania, ma ki fada logo 'ania di'ia ki lia fuana ka ta'i tau ki sisilia māka nama fuana lisilana ke madako. Sisima, ki kwa'ia logo 'ania 'au kara ne'e bala le'a ma ka sisili'a go'o, ki faosia fa'inia 'abarū ne'e gwā, rū nai'ari 'aba kwasakwasa ne'e totolia, ma di'ia ka noa'a, ki rikisia 'ania ana 'abana kwalo ongi. Bore ma 'abarū fuana faosilana 'ania te'e ti'iti'i go'o ma kwa'ilana ka 'ato liu, ka tasa ana sisinga. Bara ngwae kī go'o ne'e sai nama 'ada ana, bore ma ki foli doe logo ada.

To wall a house with scored bamboo we have several kinds of walling.

SCORED BAMBOO, we stand a piece up and then adjoin it to another piece.

FRAME BAMBOO, we place some pieces upright so as to put other pieces crosswise and plait them.

STRIPY, if we want frame bamboo to look good we also put *kwasakwasa* (*Flagellaria*) strips, which are black, to lie alongside the scored bamboo at both sides of the upright pieces, and we call it stripy. Or otherwise we take scored bamboo which is pale and plait it with scored bamboo which is burned by fire, or *kwasakwasa* strip. Strips for stripy are quite wide and it is quick and not very difficult to do.

KENIAILA is almost like stripy but the *kwasakwasa* strips are less plentiful on the body.

NARROW, walling with this is especially pretty. We call it this because we shred the strips to do it with, and we also mean if we look at it from quite far away we have to narrow our eyes (squint) to see it clearly. Narrow we also make with scored bamboo which is nice and pale and only narrow, and plait it with strips which are black, something which *kwasakwasa* (*Flagellaria*) strip is fitted for, but if there isn't any we change it for strips of *ongi* vine. But the strips for plaiting with are quite small and it is very hard to do, more so than stripy. There are only a few men who know how to do it, but we pay them a lot.

▲ *Ma'e 'odo'a ana sisinga ne'e 'i saena fera*
Walling section of stripy inside a sanctum

▲ *Ma'e 'odo'a ana sisima ne'e 'i saena fera ni fo'o*
Walling section of narrow inside a church

ITOGEREA, lisilana ka kwanga logo, ki saunga'inia 'ania 'au kara fa'inia 'aba kwasakwasa kī, ki ru'unga'inia 'aba kwasakwasa kī 'i olofana lima 'aba ka'o'anga ka sui mala nia fi'i saka. Lisilana ma'ei'a kī kesi madako liu ana ma'e'ia ana sisma ma kwa'ilana nia te'e ngwara'u ana kwa'ilana sisima. Ki saea 'ania itogerea sulia kira eta kwa'ia sulia fu'ufu'una ito 'i fanoa 'i Gerea, tofungana tolo 'i Kwara'ae.

Sisinga fa'inia sisima noima itogerea ni'i bolo fa'inia kwa'ia ana fera ni fuli, ka tasa fuana fera gwaroa ne'e 'inoto'a. Sisima noima itogerea , ki kwa'ia 'i māna kifikifi, go'o ki kwa'ia 'au kakaro 'i saena 'i safitana tala 'i diro, ki bakasia 'ania reba dai'i noima reba niniu ne'e ki tadikalakalā ma ki rafu'i 'ania fau kwao. Na fa'i falo ne'e daro'ia sisima fa'inia 'au kakaro, ki tadikalakalā logo.

Bōngilana 'odoa 'i 'au ma 'au kara bore, ki 'uia logo talana 'aena 'odoa 'ania kala sulufaua, noema ki bongia 'aena 'ania ti 'ifi 'ai go'o 'ani. Bore ma 'ifi kwa'e nama fa'inia logo 'ifi gwaea ne'e bolo fa'inia bō'a talana 'odoa sulia ni'i ke teo tau, noa'a kesi fura 'ali'ali.

Ki fone 'usia luma 'ania babalita noima kilafa kī. Babalita ki saunga'inia 'ania sao usa'i kī. Kilafa ki saunga'inia 'ania kobakoba 'ai di'ia fa'i fata, ruana fa'i lamilami, ma fa'i ketekete, noima ki tadilia kobakoba 'i taba'a.

Saena luma

Saena tofungana luma ki saunga'inia bara fafona fu'a fuana alulana so'i fafona ma gonilana fa'u kī ana usausa 'i olofana bara, 'i ne'e ke sasufia ma ka ngasi. Ki alua logo fa'u isila fuana fa'asasufi-lana 'i ke langalanga. Ki gonia logo bi'i ngali ki, dako kī fa'inia buta mani kī 'i safitana 'ifi so'i kī 'i saena.

Saunga'ilana bara, ki 'ili talana fai gwa'i tanga 'ai kī noema ono tanga 'ai kī, ki fi'i alua tatafe'e 'ai 'i gwauna. 'Ai ne'e bolo fa'inia tanga fuana bara, ni'i ngasi mala ka di'ia 'ai ona fuana diro bore ma ni'i ti'iti'i go'o, 'ai kī di'ia fa'i 'alabusi, fa'i 'o'a, fa'i 'aika'o, fa'i mamalade, fa'i madakware'a. Noima ki itoa bara ke dau tatara ana fa'i falo kī 'ania fa'i kalitau, 'i noa'a kesi ofo sulia ki ludangia so'i fafona.

Saena luma ki saunga'inia tatafe ni tua noema gwaru'a. Tatafe'anga, 'i na'o ki saunga'inia go'o ti tatafe bore ma ki alua go'o rebarū fuana gwaru'a ma teo'a fafona saena ano.

ZIGZAG also looks pretty, we make with scored bamboo and *kwasakwasa* (*Flagellaria*) strip, we insert the *kwasakwasa* strip under five strips of bamboo and then it emerges. The design does not look so clear as the design of narrow and it is a bit easier to make than making narrow. We call it zigzag (*itogerea*) because they first made it to follow the chest (markings) of an *ito*-bird at the home at Gerea in the central inland of Kwara'ae.

Stripy and narrow or zigzag are suitable to do on established sanctums, especially for an important patterned sanctum. The narrow or zigzag we do on the front of the gable, then we do frame bamboo in between the posts and clamp it with flats of rhopaloblaste (palm)(*dai'i*) or palm which we trim and carve and paint with white stone. The bearer dividing the narrow from the frame bamboo we also trim and carve.

To fix a wall, whether of bamboo or scored bamboo, we also position the foot of the wall with a small stone wall, or we fix the foot with tree logs. But treefern and *gwaea* (treefern) (both *Cyathea*) are most suitable for fixing the position of a wall because they are long lasting and don't rot quickly.

We close up the house with a leaf door or board door. A leaf door we make from stitched sago. A board door we make from the buttress of a tree like vitex (*fata*), the second archidendron (*lamilami*), campnosperma (*ketekete*), or we trim down a gigantic buttress (*taba'a* / *Alstonia*).

Inside the house

In the centre of the house we make a rack over the fire for putting fuel on and keeping mats (*fa'u* / *Pandanus*) on a shelf underneath the rack, so they will be smoked and strong. We also keep tubes of nuts, bowls, and parcels of shell-money among the fuelwood on it.

To build the rack, we dig in four or six forked trees and lay a platform of trees at the top. The trees suitable for forks for a rack are really strong, like the tough trees for posts, but only small; trees like *'alabusi* (*Euphorbiaceae*), glochidion (*'o'a*), bamboo-tree (*'aika'o* /*Xylopia*), alangium (*mamalade*), croton (*madakware'a*). Or we tie the rack to hang from the rafters on winds-far, so it won't collapse when we stack fuel on it.

Inside the house we build platforms for resting or seating. For platforms, formerly we made some platforms but we just laid flats for sitting and lying on, on the ground.

▲

*Māna fera gwaroa ni fo'oa ne'e
'odoa 'ania sisima fa'inia logo
sisinga.*
Front of a patterned prayer
sanctum (church) walled with
narrow and stripy.

▶

*Māna fera gwaroa ni fo'oa ne'e
'odoa 'ania itogerea fa'inia logo
sisinga.*
Front of a patterned prayer
sanctum (church) walled with
zigzag and stripy.

Tatafe fukiri, ki ragia go'o bae kī ana fa'i 'ai doe ka di'ia fa'i mala'o, noema ti kaida'i ki tufua logo ofiofirū di'ia ofiofina rara sao kī ka di'ia logo bae, noema ki saunga'inia logo 'ania fifiko di'ia fifiko 'i niniu, noima 'abarū lala di'ia 'aba niniu.

Saunga'ilana 'abarū di'ia 'aba niniu, ki tafanga fa'i niniu 'ania ta fita tafanga ne'e ki ogā, ki tufua ta mafora'irū. Go'o ki botekwalekwalea 'ania kwa'ikwa'i, ka sui ki gasia sulia ta'i bali noema ki kwa'igasia 'ania rō balirū kī. Ka sui ki fi'i rebasia noema ki gasia 'ania rebarū ti'iti'i ne'e ki fili'i kī. Go'o ki fi'i tufua ki 'isiria sa'esa'erū fuiri ma kula bulibuli 'i nonina, 'i nia ke ta'i dada. Ka sui ki bulasia rebarū ngasi fuiri ma ki ito basi fafia fuana ngalilana 'uana 'i luma. Ki fi'i rebata'inia fuana saunga'ilana tatafe, ki alua 'i ne'e saena rebarū ka lia toli, ilina ka lia ala'a. Ma sali ki saunga'inia 'ania 'odoa.

Tatafe ta'ena, ki alua ka teo fafona barabara 'ai. Ki tufua basi ma'i tanga 'ai kī noema ki tufua fa'i 'ai tanga'a kī, ki 'ilitalani saena luma sulia 'odoa, ka sui ki alua ramarama 'i gwauni'i, ki fi'i alua fafona tatafe, na rū ne'e di'ia rebarū noema lalarū noema bae.

'Ai ne'e bolo fa'inia tatafe'anga ne'e reba niniu ma reba dai'i, ni'i ka le'a ka tasa. 'Ai kī ne'e le'a logo ne'e reba kikiru, reba bofau, reba sao, fa'i keketo, fa'i rade. 'Au kara ne'e bolo logo fa'inia tatafe'anga, ka di'ia bore reba ka'o ma reba dodola.

Luma tatafe'a

Luma tatafe'a ne'e ki saunga'inia fuana teo'a 'i saena ma tuafilana ana ābula'a ta'ena, saunga'ilani nia 'uri. Ki 'ili talana basi diro dokodoko go'o kī, ka sui ki fi'i alua falo kī, sui ki alua faifolo na ramarama 'i fafona fa'i falo. Ka sui mala ki fi'i fa'aūa 'oto'oto kī, ki foto'ia fa'i 'idi'idi ma ki faloa 'ania fa'i falo, ki alua la'u fa'i gwaofa, sui mala ki fi'i atoa. Sui ki to'osia na'a sao fafia mala ki fi'i alua tatafe fafona ramarama fuana tatafe ka fi'i sui. Ka sui ki fi'i 'odoa 'ania 'odo 'i sao.

Laungilana fanoa

Ki fasia logo 'ai kī fuana laungilana nonina fanoa, 'ai ne'e di'ia asaka, fi'i fiu, fi'i fo'oka, dili, 'ala'ala, fi'i ri'i, gisobala, mamala 'alako, bulao rauna, berobero, danisato, tatali. 'I na'o ma'i ti rū di'ia berobero ki fasia 'i māna fera 'i ke daro'ia fa'asia luma ma fera fataābu.

For these platforms we just stripped bark-boards from big trees like *mala'o* (*Trichospermum*) and sometimes we also chopped leaf-stems like sago branch leaf-stem as bark-boards and we also made it from the frond-stems like palm frond-stem or strips like palm strip.

To make strips of things like palm we measure a palm to as many fathoms as we want and chop off a length. Then we smash it flat with an axe and then we tear it down one side or tear it into two halves. Then we flatten it out or tear it into small flats as we choose. We then chop away the inside bit and the dirty part of the body (stem) so it is quite smooth. Then we roll up the hard flats and just tie it up to take to the house. We then flatten it out to make platforms and lay it so the inside of the flat faces downwards and the back (outer part) faces up. Or we may make walling from it.

The platforms of today we lay on a frame of trees. We first chop trees into forks, or chop forked trees, and dig them in inside the house along the wall, then we lay joists on their heads and then lay a platform on top; things like flats or cane-poles or bark-board.

Trees suitable for platforms are flats of palm and rhopaloblaste(palm)(*dai'i*), which are especially good. Also good are flats of betel(palm)(*kikiru / Areca*), *bōfau* (palm)(*Arecaceae*), sago, schizstachyum (bamboo)(*keketo*) and reeds (*rade / Poaceae*). Scored-bamboo is also suitable for platforms, like flats of bamboo and mixture (bamboo)(*dodola / Bambusa*).

Platformed (floored) houses

Platformed houses which we build for sleeping in and for living in the fashion of today are made like this. We first dig in short posts and then lay bearers, then we lay joists crosswise on top of the bearers. After that we stand the uprights, we bang the eave-beams on, put on the bearers, and we also lay the ridge-beam, and after that we put on the rafters. Then we roof with sago (leaf) and we then lay the platform (floor) on the joists to finish it off. Then we wall it with sago (leaf) walling.

Decorating the home

We also plant trees to decorate the home area, trees like coleus clumps (*asaka / Lamiaceae*), ginger (*fiu / Zingiber*), worship (*fo'oka / Euodia*), cordyline (*dili*), instant (*'ala'ala / Codiaeum*), ri'i (*Euodia*), gisobala (*Ocimum*), mamala 'alako (*Verbenaceae*), leaf-grower (*bulao rauna*), berobero (*Araliaceae*), sunny-day (*danisato*) and hibiscus (*tatali*). Formerly some things like *berobero* we planted in front of the sanctum to divide it from the (dwelling) house and the tabu-speaker's (priest's) sanctum.

▲ *Luma tatafe'a, fa'inia logo luma ni du'urū'a.*　　　　　▲ *Platformed house, with cooking house.*

▲ *Saena luma ni du'urū'a. 'Afe ne'e 'ui ngali'a.*　　　　　▲ *Inside a cooking house. The woman is hammering nuts.*

Kalakalalana rū kī

'I na'o ma'i ki saunga'i 'ania 'ai ti rū 'oro ne'e ki kalakala'i ne'e 'inoto'a fuana tualaka, di'ia rū ana luma kī, rū fuana rao'a kī, ra'unga kī.

Kalakalalana rū kī, tufulana 'ania kwa'ikwa'i, rū 'i ta'ena go'o, 'i na'o ki tufua go'o 'ania tufutufu ne'e ki saea 'ania nguru. Nguru, ki uia naki, ki itoa ana ka'ika'irū ne'e ki saunga'inia ana matafa tanga'a, ki obia 'ania 'aba kalitau. Ki tufu 'ai logo 'ania nguru, go'o ki koria 'ania gwa'i nakinaki noima ta'eta'e tutu 'i ne'e ke dada, ki somota logo 'ania ra'i rau 'ala di'ia ra'i samota noima ra'i raranga. Ki 'inia rauna samota ki alua ka bala fuana samotālana rū kī.

'Ai ne'e bolo fa'inia rū kala'i kī, nia ngasi mala, nia ke teo tau mala, noa'a nia kesi fura 'ali'ali, noa'a nia kesi foga logo. 'Ai ne'e bolo fa'inia, fa'i 'ai kī ne'e bolo logo fa'inia diro fuana luma. Ta'i 'ai ne'e liufia 'ai kī ne'e fa'i fata, nia ngasi ka le'a liu, nia le'a logo sulia nia ke bulao ka te'e 'oro ana kula kī ta'ifau. Fa'i tō ne'e le'a ka tasa fuana saunga'i-lana rū kī di'ia ra'unga ma kakata, sulia nia ngasi liu ma noa'a nia kesi foga, bore ma fa'i 'ai nai'ari kī baru'a go'o. Ti 'ai ne'e le'a logo ne'e dingale, maoa, kwa'u.

Ti rū ne'e ki kalakala'i 'ania 'ai ne'e 'uri: dako, 'o'a, ngingi kata, fote, fa'i kuba, subi, 'alafolo, ka'ika'ina kwa'ikwa'i, taba, kakata fa'inia ngingilo.

Ti rū ne'e ki kalakala'i, saunga'ilani ni'i 'uri: BASI, ki saunga'inia 'ai'ai 'i basi 'ania rū di'ia fa'i basibasi, fa'i bofau, fa'i filu. Ki gasia fa'irū, ki tadilia saena reba rū ka sui ki tadilia rō gwa'i rū kī ka ti'ti'i, tufungana ka doe, go'o ki itoa gwa'i nili ana ta gwa'igwa'i ai go'o ki dosia ki itoa ana ta gwa'igwa'i ai fuana inalana basi.

Ma'e SIMA, 'ingatana ne'e fa'i rade, ki bilingā ma'e rū to'o 'i māna ne'e ki tadilia ana fa'i basibasi noima fa'i bōfau, fa'i filu. Ma'e sima kī fuana fana ī'a'anga saena su'u ma kula kabara'a kī kaida'i asi ke nononga ma'i, ni'i logo fuana fanasilana sakwalo kī.
SUA, ki tadilia logo ana rū di'ia fa'i bōfau.

Carving things

Formerly we made from trees many carved things which were important for our living, like household things, things for work, and weapons.

For carving, chopping with an axe is just a present-day thing and formerly we chopped with a chopper called an adze. For an adze we hammered a flint, we tied it to a handle which we made from a forked branch and ringed it with winds-far strip. We chopped tree (wood) with an adze then scraped it with a flint or a clam shell to be smooth and abraded it with biting leaf like abrasive leaf (*samota*) or *raranga* leaf (both *Ficus*). We pick abrasive leaf and leave it to fade for abrading things.

A tree suitable for carving is really strong, it is long-lasting, it won't rot quickly, nor will it crack. The trees which are suitable are trees which are also suitable for posts for the house. One tree which surpasses other trees is vitex (*fata*), it is good and strong and also good because it grows quite plentifully everywhere. *Tō (Streblus)* is especially good for making things like weapons and (betel) mortars, because it is very strong and it won't crack, but the tree is scarce. Trees which are also good are *dingale (Podocarpus)*, *maoa (Meliaceae)* and drink (*kwa'u / Premna*).

Some of the things we carve from trees are: bowls, gongs, nut-pudding slicers, paddles, walking sticks, angle-clubs, deflector-clubs, axe handles, (dance) batons, pestle and mortars (for betel).

Some of the things we carve are made like this: BOWS, we make the bow stave from things like bow (palm)(*basibasi*), set-solid (palm)(*bōfau*) and bright(palm)(*filu*)(all *Arecaceae*). We tear the stem and trim the inside of the flat and then trim the two tips small, the middle big, and tie a braided cord to one tip, bend it and tie it to the other tip to string the bow.
ARROWS, the main shaft is a reed (*rade / Poaceae*) and we tie to the end a striking part which we trim from bow(palm)(*basibasi*), set-solid(palm)(*bōfau*) or bright(palm)(*filu*) (all *Arecaceae*). Arrows are for shooting fish in the inlets and stilt-root places when the sea tide is in, and also for shooting bats.
SPEARS we also trim from things like set-solid (palm)(*bōfau / Arecaceae*).

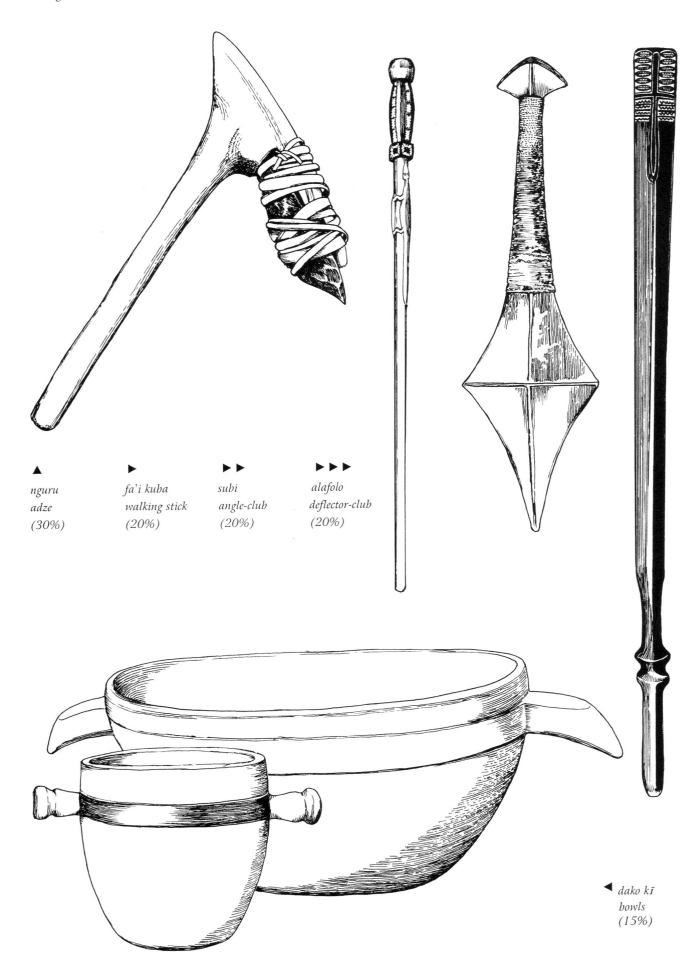

▲
nguru
adze
(30%)

►
fa'i kuba
walking stick
(20%)

►►
subi
angle-club
(20%)

►►►
alafolo
deflector-club
(20%)

◄ *dako kī*
bowls
(15%)

▲ *iolo ne'e saunga'i 'ania reba 'ai kī*   ▲ *canoe built of planks*

IOLO, 'i na'o ma'i ki saunga'ini'i 'ania reba 'ai 'oro kī, ki firi'ia 'ania 'aba kalitau noima kwalo sata, ka sui ki mokea safitana reba 'ai 'ania meme saia fuana fonelana kafo. Ti 'ai ne'e le'a ka tasa fuana reba 'ai fuana iolo ne'e arakoko, 'aisiko, maladala.

Iolo ne'e ki tufua 'ania ta'i bobo 'ai doe ne'e rū 'i nini'ari go'o. 'Ai ne'e bolo fa'inia iolo nai'ari, fa'i 'ai doe mala ne'e nia ngasi le'a ma ka mabe, kwatea noa'a nia kesi foga, nia ke teo tau logo sulia ta fita fa'i ngali bore 'ana saena asi ma kafo. Ngwae ne'e sai le'a ana saunga'ilana ne'e ke saunga'ilana iolo, ka tasa na'a ana ngwae asi kī.

MOKELANA rū foga kī, ki mokea 'ania saia. Ki koria fa'ina saia noima ki saungia saena titiu ke meme fuana ki mokea 'ania kula foga ana rū kī di'ia dako foga ma iolo ne'e te'e foga, fuana fonelana kafo kesi afe 'i saena. Kaida'i 'i na'o ki mokea logo 'ania kula foga safitana reba 'ai ana iolo kī. Ti kaida'i ki mokea logo kula foga ana iolo kī 'ania buli ana ngali.

KASI KA'O, ki goni'i saeni rū kī di'ia rū fuana noni laungi'a kī ma fena ma rū ābu kī, ki fonotā logo 'ania ana ma'e ka'o. Di'i fa'i fena, ti kaida'i ki rokoa logo fuana laungilana 'i ke lia kwanga.

CANOES, formerly we built them of many tree planks and tied them with winds-far-strip or lygodium vine (*sata*), then we caulked between the tree planks with putty mash (*saia / Parinari*) to stop the water. Some trees which are especially good for tree planks for canoes are *arakoko* (Gmelina), elaecarpus-tree(*'aisiko*), *maladala* (Gmelina).

The canoes which we chop from one big tree log (dugouts) are just a thing of the present. Trees suitable for these canoes are really big, good and strong and flexible so that they won't crack, and also long-lasting for however many years they are in the sea or water. Men who know all about building build canoes, especially the sea people. For CAULKING cracked things, we caulk with putty (*saia / Parinari*). We scrape the putty fruit or pound it in a cup into a paste for caulking things such as cracked bowls or canoes which are a bit cracked, to stop water flowing in. In former times we also caulked the cracks between the tree planks of canoes with it. Sometimes we also caulk cracks in canoes with nut resin (*ngali / Canarium*).

BAMBOO SECTIONS we keep things in, like things for body decoration and lime (for betel) and tabu things, and we also close them with a piece of bamboo. If for lime, sometimes we also engrave them for decoration to look pretty.

▲ *kasi ka'o fuana gonilana fa'i rade kī (60%)*   ▲ *bamboo section for keeping (ear) reeds (60%)*

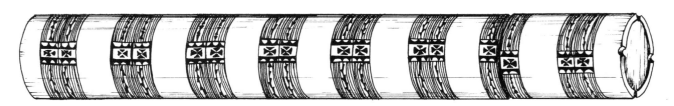

▲ *fa'i fena (100%)*   ▲ *lime (container) (100%)*

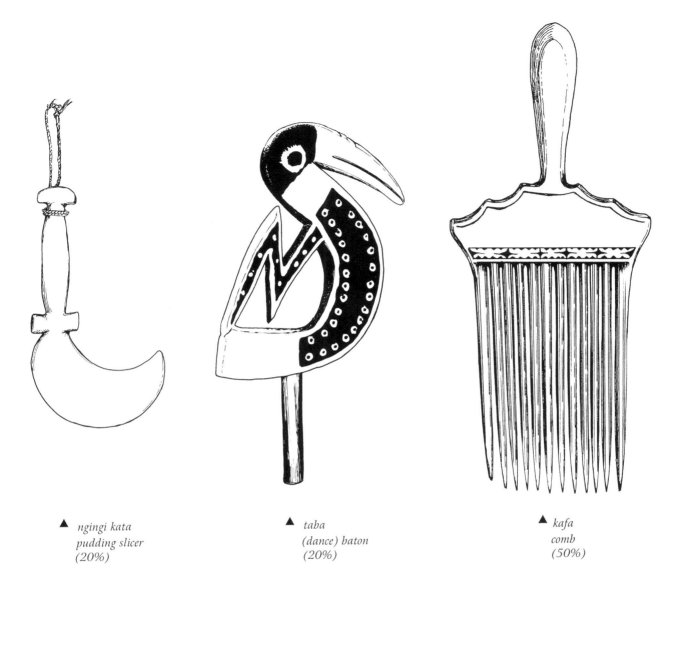

▲ *ngingi kata*
  pudding slicer
  (20%)

▲ *taba*
  (dance) baton
  (20%)

▲ *kafa*
  comb
  (50%)

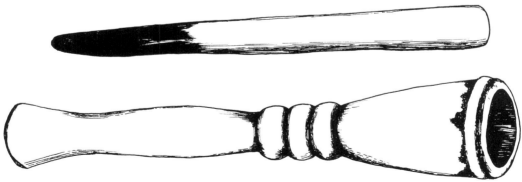

▲ *ma'e kakata fa'inia ngingilo (50%)*

▲ *pestle and mortar (for betel) (50%)*

Fi'iri'anga ma dadalo'anga

Rū ki fi'iri 'ani'i kī ne'e fa'i kwalo, 'aba kwalo, dadalo, gwa'i nili, sisilirū, kwalo dae'e.

FA'I KWALO fuana fi'iri'a kī, malita'irū ni'i to'oto'o kwailiu. Ki fi'iri 'ania fa'i kwalo ana foforū kī, ki itoa logo 'ania luma ma rū di'ia tala'au, ki fo'ota logo 'ania 'ai doe kī fuana ra'efilani. Ki fo'ota 'ania foforū di'ia fofo sao, ka'o, so'i, a'u, sabangi, rau fuana gwa'abi, rade. Rū nai'ari kī, ki fo'ota'i 'ania fa'i kwalo lau'ula'u, ki kali ro rū ana foforū, go'o ki nikia 'i ke nekeneke le'a, mala ki fi'i fi'iria 'ania 'aba kwalo fuana ngalilana.

'ABA KWALO ne'e ki aea fa'asia ti fa'i kwalo noima ta'eta'ena ti 'ai, nia bolo fuana 'aba kwalo fuana fua'a, kabileta fuana ra'enga'a, fi'irilana lakeno, 'ara, buta ko'a. 'Abakwalo, ki aea ana 'ai kī 'ania naki to'o le'a kī.

SISILIRŪ, ki silia ana 'aba kwalo 'ania gwa'i naki to'o fuana taialana rū ka tasa fuana fa'u, ki usu'ia logo 'ania maga mani kī.
DADALO, ki dalofia 'ania 'aba kwalo, nia bolo fuana rū kī di'ia firai, dadalo basi, usu mani'a, ti rū fuana laungi'anga kī. Saunga'ilana dadalo, ki eta sisia sisilirū fa'asia 'a'e kwalo ma ki aea 'abarū kī. Di'ia ki ogā 'aba kwalo ke mabe fuana dalofilana, ta ma ki usuusunga'inia ana fa'i 'ai, noima ki daubakasia ta bali go'o ki tarusua safitana saka'i. Ti 'aba kwalo ki koria lala 'ania ta'e tutu 'i ke mabe. Di'ia ki ogā dadalo ke mabe le'a, ti kaidai'i ki dodoa logo, ki ongia kafo fafia ki fi'i du'afia, noima ki kukia saena sosobini. Nia mabe, mala ki fi'i dalofia 'ania dadalo.

GWA'I NILI, nia bolo fa'inia rao'a di'ia tagilana gwata ma fi'irilana iolo. Nililana gwa'i nili, ki silia ulu 'aba kwalo'anga noima fairū noima limarū'anga, mala ki fi'i nili'i.
KWALO DAE'E, 'i na'o ma'i ki rao logo 'ania 'abarū dae'e ka kwanga kī fuana faosirū'a ma folilana rū kī. Rū ne'e lia le'a ka tasa ne'e gwaroa sakosako'a ma ka meo.

Malita'irū fuana fi'irilana rū kī

KALITAU, ki aea 'abarū fuana itolana luma bore ma ki fi'irirū logo 'ania. Ki faosia 'ania obi fuana obilana limaka ma 'aeka, ti kaida'i ki 'atongia 'abarū 'ania dilo.
OBI, ta kalitau doe nini'a, ki sikilia ki sisia ta'eta'ena fuana saunga'ilana rū di'ia obi kī fuana laungilana limana ngwae ma 'aena ngwae kī. Kaida'i ki tua uikiti, nia logo fuana obi'a fuana kini sari'i kī, obi nai'ari ki atongia 'ania dilo.

Bindings and twine

The things we bind with are vine, vine strip, twine, plaited cord, shreds and coloured vine.
VINES for binding are of all different kinds. We bind with vine to bundle things, we also tie houses and things like bamboo-rows (panpipes) and we also lash big trees with it to climb them. We lash bundles of things with it like sago (leaf), bamboo, fuelwood, cane, yam-conductors, leaf for ovens and reed (*rade / Poaceae*). These things we lash with the entire vine, we wind it twice round the bundle and tighten it to compress it well and then we bind it with vine strip for carrying.
VINE STRIP which we peel from a vine or the skin of some trees is suitable for vine strip for carrying burdens, foot-straps for climbing and for tying up cream-pudding, grating (cassava pudding) and scraping (mangrove pudding) parcels. Vine strip, we peel it from the trees with a good sharp flint.
SHREDS, we shred vine strip with a sharp flint for sewing things, especially for mats (*Pandanus / fa'u*) and we also thread shell-money beads on it.
TWINE we twine from vine strip, it is suitable for things like nets, bow strings, threading shell-money and things for decoration. To make twine we first split shreds from a length of vine and peel off strips. If we want the vine strip to be flexible for twining we pull it to and fro on a tree or clamp the end between a pair of tongs and pull it through. Some vine strips we scrape with a clam shell to make them flexible. If we want the twine to be really flexible, sometimes we also flask it (in bamboo), pour water on it and burn it, or we boil it in a saucepan. When it is flexible, then we twine it into twine (by rubbing on the thigh).
BRAIDED CORD is suitable for work like caring for pigs and tying up canoes. To braid a cord we split three vine strips or four or five and then braid them.
COLOURED VINE, formerly we worked with pretty coloured strips for plaiting and weaving things. What looks especially good is yellow and red patterning.

Kinds of things for binding

WINDS-FAR, we peel off strips for tying houses but we also bind things with it. We plait bands from it to band our arms and legs and sometimes we stain it with dye (*dilo / Morinda*).
BAND (*Calamus*), this is a big winds-far, we cut it off and split off the skin for making things like bands to decorate a person's arms and legs. When we were pagans it was also for (waist) bands for maidens, bands which we stained with dye (*dilo / Morinda*).

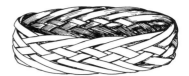

▲ *obi kī (50%)*

▲ *(arm) bands (50%)*

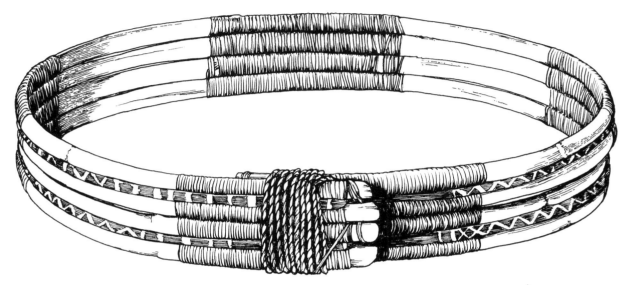

▲ *fo'osae (50%)* ▲ *(man's) girdle (50%)*

Ki saunga'inia logo fo'osae kī 'ania fai 'abarū kī, ki itoa 'ania 'aba kwalo di'ia ongaonga noima luluka, ti kaida'i ki obia logo 'ania rō 'aba kalitau meo kī.

Kwalo A'ATA, kwalana le'a ka tasa fuana firi'a noima ito'a sulia nia ngasi liu. Ki ito rū 'ania ma ki fo'ota rū 'ania, di'ia kaida'i ana kwa'isao'anga, ki fo'ota 'ania fofo sao kī. Ki saunga'i nia logo 'ania kabileta kī fuana ra'efilana 'ai. Ki fi'iri 'ania fa'i kwalo la'ula'u kī bore ma di'ia fa'irū doe ki sisia nama ki fi'i ito 'ania.
Kwalo ABU, kaida'i nia ma'ā nia le'a ka tasa fuana fo'otalana 'ania rū di'ia fofo sao kī ma ta rū bore 'ana.
Kwalo SALU, ngwakona ki sisia ki fi'iria 'ania rū kī di'ia to'osilana sao, nia ngasi ka le'a liu. Ki fi'iri logo 'ania ka'ika'ina kaida'i nia ngwaka, ti kaida'i ki dalofia logo. Nia le'a ka tasa fuana usu'ilana 'ania rū di'ia maga mani ma fa'i sila kī, sulia sisilina ti'iti'i ka ngasi liu.

Kwalo GWARI, ki fi'iri 'ania rū di'ia foforū kī, bore ma noa'a kisi itoa luma 'ania sulia nia ke fura 'ali'ali.

We also make (men's) girdles from four strips, we tie it with vine strip like *ongaonga* or *luluka* (*Dennstaedtiaceae*) and sometimes we also band it with two strips of red winds-far.
A'ATA-DERRIS vine, its vine is especially good for binding and tying because it is very strong. We tie and lash things with it, as when sago (leaf) felling we lash bundles of sago (leaf) with it. We also make foot-straps with it for climbing trees. We tie with the whole vine but if it is a big stem we have to split it to tie with.
BLOOD vine (*Merremia*), when fresh it is especially good for lashing things like bundles of sago (leaf) and other things.
SALU vine (*Eprimemnum*), we split the tendrils and bind things like sago roofing with it, it is very good and strong. We also bind with the stem when it is soft and sometimes we also twine it. It is very good for threading things like shell-money beads and coix seeds (*sila*) because the small shreds are very strong.
GWARI vine (*Tetrastigma*), we bind things like bundles with it, but we don't tie houses with it because it rots quickly.

Kwalo FAUDUMU, ki fi'iri rū 'ania, di'ia fofo sao kī, fofo 'ai kī, ma ta rū go'o 'ana ne'e fuana fi'irilana. Fa'i kwalo doe ki gasia fuana fi'iri'anga 'ania rō 'abarū doe kī .

Kwalo 'ARI'ARI, ki firi 'ania fa'irū kī. Ki sisia 'ari'ari di'ia kalitau bore ma na rō afurū'anga go'o ne'e bolo fa'inia ki firi 'ania. Bore ma kisi aea saena 'aba rū ma kisi firi 'ania ta'eta'e rū. Ki rao 'ania fuana fo'otalana fofo sao kī ma fofo 'ai kī ma fofo ka'o kī ma ti rū la'u. Kaida'i ki firi 'ania fa'i 'ari'ari, ki alialita'inia ro agiagirū'anga kalia go'o ki lala ngiringiri ana ki fi'i fi'iri ka'uka'u du'unga ana, ta firi'a 'i 'aena, ta firi'a 'i gwauna, ti kaida'i ta firi'a 'i tofongana.

Kwalo SA'A nia le'a ka ngasi fuana fi'iri'anga 'ania. rū kī di'ia fofo 'i sao kī, fa'inia logo to'osi'anga ngali kī fuana ra'efilana.

Kwalo 'ADI'O, ki firi 'ania kwalona, nia le'a ka tasa fuana fo'otalana rū di'ia fofo sao, fofo 'au, fofo so'i. Nia le'a sulia nia 'alata'a noa'a kesi didilia, nia kesi langalanga bore ki fi'iri go'o 'aka 'ania. Di'ia ki ogā ki itoa 'ania rū le'a kī, ki aea mala fa'i adi'o le'a kī, ka sui ki aea ta'eta'ena, ki saunga'i rū 'ania sa'esa'erū. Fa'i 'adi'o le'a fukiri, ki susu'ia 'ania fa'i 'au fuana saunga'ilana tala'au fuana ūfilani, ki susu'ia 'ania fa'i 'ai kī fuana kafa, ki bulasia 'ania 'aba kalitau fuana fo'osae kī, kī obia logo 'ania kauala fuana loi ngali'a.

Kwalo 'ABE nia le'a ka tasa fuana itolana rū kī. Ki sikilia kasirū kī, ki aea ta'eta'ena fuana rebarū sisili'a kī, ki fi'i dodoa saena fa'i ka'o, ki 'ongia kafo saena fuana du'afilana, noima ki kukia saena sosobini. Ki du'afia ka sui, ka teoteo ka gwari mala sulia rō fa'i bongi kī noima ulu fa'i bongi kī, ka sui ki lafua fa'asia kafo, ki koria 'ania tutu 'i ne'e rebarū ke faolu ma ka mabe 'i ki silia to'oto'o 'abana, ka sui ki itoa rebarū kī, ki fa'asinafi'i leleka ni'i ka langa. Ka sui ki fi'i dalofia 'ania dadalo, na dalofilana ne'e ngasi ka tasa liu mala, ka le'a ka tasa fuana usu mani'a ma inalana 'ania basi kī ma gaulana 'ania ta rū bore 'ana. 'Abarū ka bolo logo fuana gwarosangisangi, ki atongia 'ania dilo noima bunabuna, ki fi'i faosia 'ania gwarosangisangi fuana laungilana limaka. Ti kaida'i ki kwa'i dadalo 'ania kwalona la'ula'u, ki garasia go'o ta'eta'ena fa'asia, ki fi'i dalofia.

Kwalo SUSURU, kaida'i uikiti ki saunga'i 'ania gwa'i susuru fuana 'afe kī ke abisia. Noa'a kisi sisia, noa'a kisi garasia, ki saunga'i 'ania fa'i kwalo la'ula'u. Ki ngalia ti fa'i susuru, ki usa 'ania ti maga mani kwao fuana laungi'anga ma ki faosia kalikalia ti fa'i susuru.

CLEMATIS vine we bind things with, like bundles of sago (leaf) and trees and anything for binding. For tying with a big vine, we tear it into two big strips.

FREYCINETIA vine, we bind things with it. We split freycinetia like winds-far but only into two parts suitable for binding with. But we don't peel off the inside of the strips and don't tie with the skin. We use it for lashing bundles of sago (leaf) and bamboos and other things. When we bind with freycinetia we wind two lengths around and tug it tight and then hold the binding with a knot, one binding at the foot, one at the head and sometimes one in the middle.

SA'A vine (*Papilionatae*) is good and strong for tying things with, like sago (leaf) bundles and also for throwing onto nut trees for climbing.

'ADI'O vine (*Vitaceae*), we tie with its vine, it is especially good for lashing things like bundles of sago (leaf), bamboo and fuelwood. It is good because it grips and isn't slippery, and even when it isn't dry we bind with it. If we want to tie something good with it we peel good *'adi'o* and then peel off the skin and make things with the inside part. This good *'adi'o* we secure bamboos with to make bamboo-rows (panpipes) for blowing, we secure sticks for combs, we wind it round winds-far strips for girdles and band it on hooks for nut picking.

ANONDENDRON vine is especially good for tying things. We cut off sections and peel off the skin to get narrow flats, we then flask it in a bamboo and pour in water to burn it, or we boil it in a saucepan. When we have burned it, it lies there cold for two or three days and then we lift it from the water and scrape it with a clam (shell) so the flats will be clean and flexible to shred into separate strips, then we tie up the flats and sun them until they are dry. After that we twine it into twine, a twine which is very strong indeed, especially good for threading shell-money and stringing bows and binding up anything else. The strips are also suitable for ring-patterns (armbands), we stain it with dye (*dilo / Morinda*) or *bunabuna* (*Cyclosorus*) and then plait it into ring-patterns to decorate our arms. Sometimes we make twine with the whole vine, we just scrape the skin off and then twine it.

SUSURU vine, in pagan times we made into a *susuru*-belt for women to wear. We don't split it, we don't scrape it, we work with the entire vine. We take a piece of *susuru* and thread white shell-money beads on it for decoration and plait (twine) *susuru* vine around it.

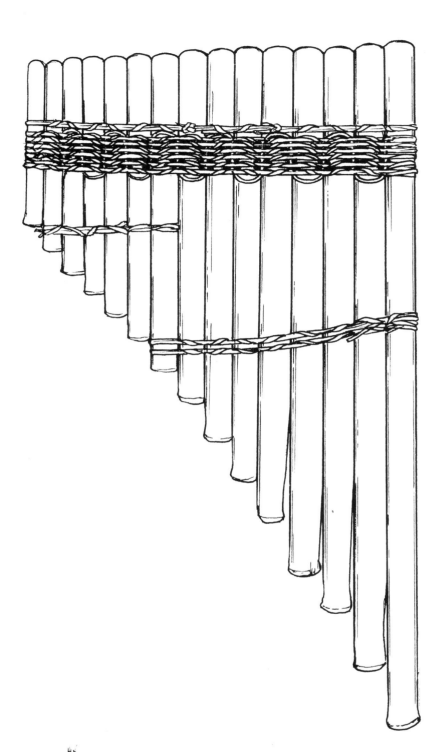

▲ *kafa*
comb
(50%)

◀ *tala'au*
bamboo-row (panpipes)
(50%)

▼ *gwa'i susuru*
susuru *belt*
(50%)

FA'OLA, 'ai nini'a nia kesi doe liu go'o, ki tufua fa'i 'ai fi'i doe noima 'a'erū, ki aea 'abakwalo ana ta'eta'ena. 'Abakwalo nia bolo fa'inia fi'irilana foforū kī. Saunga'inga 'ania 'abakwalo, ki furia ki fi'i aea ta'eta'erū ngasi ma ki to'osia, ki alua 'abakwalo ngwara'u ka teo langalanga.
Noima ki do'ofia kasirū kī, ki fi'i alu'i saena kafo, ka teoteo ta'eta'erū ngasi ke a'efo mala, ki fi'i aea 'abakwalo, ki fa'alangā. 'Abakwalo ki kwa'ia 'ania dadalo fuana furai ma dadalona basi, ki foli ngwa'i logo 'ania.
FA'OLA ASI, 'ai nini'a kesi doe liu go'o, ki aea 'abarū, ki do'ofia, ki fi'i dalofia fuana gwa'i nili.

SULA fa'inia MALA'O, rō 'ai ne'e kī ki aea 'aba kwalo fa'asia fa'i 'ai ti'iti'i kī fuana saunga'ilana rū 'oro kī. Sula ne'e nia le'a ka tasa ana mala'o sulia ta'eta'ena malao di'ia nia ke isila 'ua nia ke didila lala, bore ma kaida'i nia ka 'eke'eke ni'i bolo logo. 'Abakwalo kī fuana kini kī ke fua 'ani'i, ki aea 'abana, ki fa'alangā go'o ki sosotea ki fi'i fa'asasufia go'o ki fua na'a 'ania. Nia le'a logo fuana foli ngwa'inga ma nililana ma dalofilana, ki kata do'ofia 'abana 'i ne'e ke mabe ke ngwafeafea. Ki aea ta'eta'ena, ki efoa kula 'i saena, ki sosotea ki dodoa saena fa'i ka'o, ki kiki sulia 'ania kafo, ki do'ofia saena mafula. Ka gwari go'o ki fi'i 'agania ki karasia giragirana, ki fi'i fa'alangā, go'o ki silia na'a 'ania ma'e naki fuana saunga'i rū 'anga 'ania. Sisilirū ki dalofia 'ania dadalo, ki nilia 'ania gwa'i nili kī, ki faosia 'ania ngwa'i kī di'ia guiaguia ma gwanagwana ma ngwa'i fa'a. Dadalo nai'ari ki saunga'inia 'ania rū di'ia furai fuana dē ī'a 'anga saena asi. Ki silia logo sisilirū ti'iti'i kī, ki tai fa'u logo 'ania, ki usu'ia logo 'ania maga la'usu'u kī.
NIÚ, taketakena fuana kwa'ilana rū fuana laungilana ma gwarolana rū kī. Ki aea taketakena ana gwango niu, ki kanusua ka sui ki aea la'u, ki dodoa, ki do'ofia ka sui, ki 'ongia kafo saena, ka sui ki alua ka teo 'ana. Teoteo ka bila mala, ka sui ki kanusua fa'asia na kafo, ki fi'i atongia taketake 'ania dilo 'i ne'e ke meo. Ka sui mala ki talia, ki gwarorū 'ania fa'inia logo kwalo 'adi fuana saunga'ilana rū gwaroa kī di'ia kafa gwaroa ma fa'i rade. Kaida'i uikiti, ki saunga'inia logo 'ania 'aba obi fuana laungilana kini sari'i kī.

Fi'i 'ADI ne'e nonina sakosako'a, ki efoa kwalona fuana gwarolana 'ania rū kī 'i ke kwanga, rū di'ia kafa gwaroa ma fa'i rade ma fo'osae, fuana laungi'anga. Ki fa'asinafia kwalo 'adi 'i ke langa, ki toea ta'eta'ena, ka sui ki fi'i gwaro 'ania, ki faosia fa'inia taketake niu ne'e ki atongia ke meomeo-'anga, lisilani kwanga liu.

MALLOW (*Hibiscus*), this is a tree which is not very big, we chop down the young tree or a length of it and peel a vine-strip from the skin. The vine-strip is suitable for tying bundles. To make vine-strip we saw it and then peel off the hard skin and throw it away and we put the soft vine-strip to dry out. Or we burn the sections and then leave them in water to lie until the hard skin comes away and then peel off the vine-strip and dry it. We make the vine-strip into twine for nets and bow-strings and also weave bags with it.
SEA MALLOW (*Thespesia*), this is a tree which doesn't get very big, we peel off strips and burn them, then twine them for braided cord.
SULA and *MALA'O* (both *Trichospermum*), with both these trees we peel vine-strips from the small trees for making many things. *Sula* is better than *mala'o* because when the skin of *mala'o* is still wet it is slippery, but when it is dry they are the same. For vine-strips for women to carry burdens we peel off the strip, we dry it and coil it up, then smoke it and then carry with it. It is also good for weaving bags and plaiting cords and twining and we may burn the strips so they will be flexible and soft. We peel off the skin, we remove the inside part, we coil it up and flask it in a bamboo, we sprinkle in some water and burn it on the fire. When it is cool we tip it out and scrape off the sticky sap and then dry it, then we shred it with a piece of flint for making things. The shreds we make into twine, we braid into braided cord, we weave into bags like sacks and satchels and hanging bags. The twine we make into things like nets for fishing in the sea. We also shred it small and sew mats (*fa'u / Pandanus*) with it and we also thread shell-money beads on it.
COCONUT, the cuticle is for doing things for decorating and patterning. We peel off the cuticle of a coconut leaf-shoot, we remove it and peel it again, we flask it and burn it and then we pour water into it, then we leave it lying there. It lies until it stinks, then we remove the water from it and then stain the cuticle with mulberry (*dilo / Morinda*) to go red. Afterwards we split it and pattern things with it and with orchid vine (*'adi*), to make patterned things like combs and ear-reeds. In pagan times we also made (waist) band strips for decorating maidens.
ORCHID clump, which has a yellow stem, we choose its vine for patterning pretty things, like patterned combs, ear-reeds and girdles, for (personal) decoration. We sun the orchid vine so it is dry, we pare off the skin and then we pattern with it, we plait it with coconut cuticle which we stain red, and it looks very pretty.

LULUKA, ki aea 'abarū ne'e gwā. Ki ngalia luluka, ki dodoa, ki do'ofia ka sui, ki ongia kafo saena, ka sui ki alua ka teo 'ana. Teoteo ka bila mala, ka sui ki kanusua fa'asia na kafo. Ki itoa 'ania ma'e kafa kī, ki faosia logo 'ania 'aba obi kī fuana saunga'ilana fo'osae kī.

Kwalo ONGAONGA, ki saunga'irū 'ania 'abana ne'e gwā. Ki sisia 'abana ka sui ma ki alasia, ka sui ki la'umia fuana dodoa, ki kiki sulia 'ania kafo, ki fi'i du'afia. Ka sui ki alua nia ke teo sulia akwala bongi kī, ki fi'i saunga'i 'ania rū kī. Ki faosia 'ania sangesange ne'e ki gwaro 'ania 'adi ma taketake niu, ki faosia logo 'ania 'aba obi fuana saunga'ilana fo'osae.

BUNABUNA, 'ai ti'iti' nini'a, ki saunga'i dadalo gwā 'ania itangana ka'ika'ina. Ki dodoa saena fa'i ka'o, ki kiki suli'a 'ania kafo, ki alua ka teo sulia bara bongi kī, 'iri ke ngwaka. Ka sui ki lafua ma ki karasia fuana ki efoa ta'ta'ena, ki fi'i fa'alangā. Ka sui mala ki fi'i dalofia kala dadalo kī 'ania. Dadalona bunabuna nia ti'iti' liu ka ngasi liu. Ki faosia logo 'ania sangesange ne'e ki gwaro 'ania 'adi ma taketake niu, ki faosia logo 'ania fo'osae. Ki obia 'ania usuusu, ki fi'i saia 'ania meme saia fa'inia fulafulana gwa'i leleo.

GLEICHENIA, we peel off strips which are black. We take the gleichenia and flask it, we burn it and then pour water inside, then we leave it to lie. It lies until it stinks and then we tip away the water. We tie the sticks of combs with it, and we also plait strips of band (*obi / Calamus*) with it to make (men's) girdles.

ONGAONGA vine, we make things with its strips, which are black. We split off strips and then we shave them, we then fold them for flasking, we sprinkle it with water and then burn it. Then we put it to lie for ten days and then make things with it. We weave (arm) rings with it which we pattern with *'adi*-orchid and coconut cuticle and we also plait it with strips of band (*obi / Calamus*) to make (men's) girdles.

BUNABUNA (*Cyclosorus*), this is a small tree, we make a black twine from its main stem. We flask it in a bamboo and sprinkle it with water, we put it to lie for several days, so it rots. Then we lift it out and scrape it to remove the skin and then dry it. After that we twine a fine twine with it. *Bunabuna* twine is very small and very strong. We also make armbands from it which we pattern with orchid (*'adi*) and coconut cuticle, and we also plait (men's) girdles with it. We band nose-pins with it and then putty it with putty (*saia / Parinari*) paste and powdered charcoal.

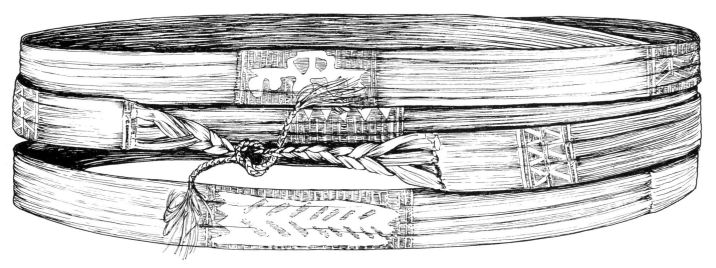

▲ *'aba obi fuana kini sari ĭ (100%)*   ▲ *(waist) band strip for a maiden (100%)*

Faosirū'anga

KUKUDU 'I NIU fuana gonilana fanga ma rū kī saena luma, ki faosia 'ania ūli niu. Ki sisia basi ūli niu 'ania ro rū kī, ki ngalia ta kula, ki sisia la'u 'ania ulu afurū kī, ki fi'i ngalia la'u ro kula 'i ilina kī fuana faosilana kukudu. Nia le'a ka tasa fuana ki fa'asinafia basi ūli niu sisia 'i ke kwao le'a ma nia kesi luku kaida'i ki faosia ka sui, nia kata bara kwakwa. Ro kula sisili'i kī ki alua kwairokisi, ki fi'i tobia fuana fi'iri'adolana, mala ki fi'i faosia kwairokisi sisilirū kī toli, ka dao mala 'i fauna, ki fi'i safalia, ki ta'ea ti sisilirū ki ru'unga'ini'i kwailiu mala ki fi'i sikilia sisilirū ore'e kī, kukudu ka fi'i sui. Faosilana kukudu, ki to'o ana rō malita'i faosi'anga kī, tai ne'e ki saea 'ania ta'e rō 'aba, tai ne'e ki saea 'ania ta'e ta'i 'aba.

'ITA, ki sisia ta kula ana ūli niu 'ania rō afurū kī, go'o ki alu bolo ana, ki fi'i faosia rō bali kī to'oto'o 'uana 'i fauna, go'o ki fi'i foli'adoa fuana safa'atalana fauna. Go'o ki nili'adoa rō bali kī, ka sui ki fi'i itoa gwa'i nili ana rō bali kī fuana fa'alana.

KAKARO, saunga'ilana nia di'ia logo 'ita bore ma ki folia 'ania ūli niu ne'e ra'irū kī la'ula'u, ki foli'adoa rō afu ūli niu kī ana ta'i bali, ta rō ai ana ta bali. Nia fuana go'o ngalilana fanga kī, ai doe bolo fa'inia fanga 'oro, ai ti'iti'i bolo go'o fa'inia fanga barū'a kī. Ki ngalirū ani, ka sui ki to'osia logo.

LAFA fuana alu fanga 'i saena, ki saea logo 'ania LABENGO, ki sisia ūli niu 'ania rō balibalirū kī, ka sui ki safali kwairokisi 'ani'i, mala ki fi'i faosia ra'irū ana ta bali kī 'uana ta bali, logo ki faosia logo 'unari ta bali. Mala ki fi'i nilia gwauna ra'irū kī ta'ifau mala ki fi'i ru'unga'ini'i sulia rō bali kī.

TIRUTIRU, ta sata BEBETE, ki sikilia gwauna ūli niu ka sui ki sisia logo 'ania rō balibalirū kī, go'o ki alu kwairokisi 'ania go'o ki foli'i toli. Ka reba ma ka keta ka bolo go'o, ki fi'i sikimusia ra'i niu kī fa'asia mala ki fi'i tirutiru 'ania.

KUKUDU NGASI, saunga'ilana mamata fa'asia kukudu niu, na malita'i kukudu ne'e to'a 'i Western Solomon ne'e kira fadā fuaka. Ki saunga'inia 'ania fa'i kwalo sata noima 'aba kalitau, nia ngasi liu ka le'a 'inoto'a fuana alurū'anga ma ngalirū'anga. Saunga'ilana, ki sosotea fa'i kwalo, ki susu'adoa fa'inia fa'i ai eta'erea 'ania 'aba sata ne'e kalikalia ro fa'i kwalo kī, ki tala'ae ki safalia fauna kukudu mala ki fi'i susuia ka ra'e kalikalia 'uana māna.

Plaiting

COCONUT BASKETS for storing food and things in the house, we plait from coconut frond. We first split the coconut frond into two, we take one part and split it again into three pieces and we then take the two outer parts for plaiting the baskets. It is best to sun the split coconut frond first so it will be good and white and won't shrink after we have plaited it, lest it (the basket) have a few holes. The two shredded parts we lay across one another and then bend them in a circle to tie them together, then we plait the shreds across one another downwards until we reach the base, then lay it out and we raise some strips and insert them past one another and then cut off the remaining shreds, and the basket is finished. For basket weaving we have two kinds of weaving, one which we call raising two strips (twill), one we call raising one strip (plain).

POUCHES, we split a piece of coconut frond into two parts and we treat them the same, we plait the two halves separately towards the base and we then weave them together to lay out the base. Then we braid the two sides together and after that we tie a braided cord to the two sides for hanging.

FRAMES are made like pouches but we weave them from coconut frond with the leaves entire, we weave together two pieces of coconut frond for one side and two for the other side. They are just for carrying food, big ones suitable for a lot of food, small ones suitable for a little food. We carry things with them and then throw them away.

TRAYS for putting food on, we split a coconut frond into two sides and then we lay them across one another, then we plait the leaves of one side towards the other side and also plait the other side the same. We then braid the tops of all the leaves and then insert them along the two sides.

FANS, also called FLAPS, we cut off the top of a coconut frond and then we also split it into two sides, and we put them across one another and weave them downwards. When the width and the length are equal we cut the coconut leaves away and then we fan with it.

STRONG BASKETS are made differently from a coconut basket, it is a kind of basket the people of Western Solomons explained to us. We make it with lygodium vine (*sata*) or winds-far strip, it is very strong and important for putting things in and carrying things. To make it we coil a vine and secure it to the previous coil with a lygodium strip which winds around the two vines, we start by laying out the base of the basket and we then secure it, winding around towards the face (rim).

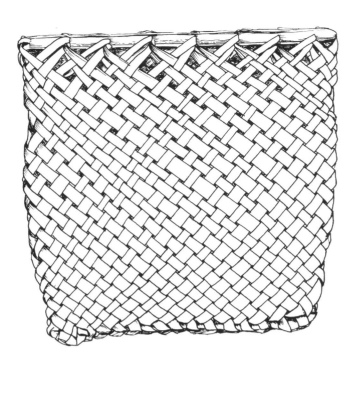

▲ *'ita*
pouch
(30%)

▲
▲ *kukudu 'i niu ana ta'e ta'i 'aba*
coconut basket of one raised strip
(30%)

▲ *kukudu 'i niu ana ta'e ta'i 'aba*
coconut basket of one raised strip
(30%)

◄ *kukudu ngasi*
strong basket
(30%)

NGWA'I fuana ngalilana ma foelana rū kī, ki faosi'i ania 'aba kwalo, di'ia gwanagwana ma guiaguia, ngwa'i doe fuana foelana rū fualanga'a kī, ngwa'i fa'a fuana rū kia kī, ngwa'i firu'a fuana ke lia le'a. Na 'aba kwalo fuana ngwa'i ne'e bolo logo fuana fi'irilana rū, ka tasa ana sula ma malao. 'Aba kwasikwasi nia le'a ka tasa fuana ngwa'i firua sulia nia kwao ka lia le'a. 'Aba fa'ola ne'e ki faosi ngwa'i logo 'ania, ki du'afia basi 'a'e kwalo saena mafula noima ki aea 'aba kwalo ki fi'i dodoa noima ki kukia 'i ke ngwara'u ma ke mabe fuana faosilana 'ania rū kī. Faosilana ngwa'i, ki ngalia rō 'aba kwalo reba kī, ki sili'i ka ti'iti'i ka 'oro mala, ki fi'i folia ki safalia fauna ngwa'i, ka sui mala ki fi'i faosia 'ingata'irū ka dao mala 'i māna, ki fi'i nili kalikalia ka sui ki dalofia na'a dadalona ngwa'i 'ania sisirū ore kī, ki fi'i 'itoa fuana fa'alana.

Fa'i SAKUSAKU fuana sakusakulana ma gelosilana 'ania 'aena, ki saunga'inia 'ania ra'i niu. Ki tafia rō ra'i niu kī ka sui ki silia sisilina fa'asia, ka sui ki ru'unga'inia fūna ta ra'i niu fafia ta ra'i 'ai, mala ki fi'i folia ka molimolia di'ia fa'i bolo, go'o ki sikilimusia gwauna ra'irū tamatama kī.

'Afurū'anga

FA'U ne'e rū 'inoto'a ne'e kini kī ke saunga'inia ma ke goni'i. Fa'u ne'e rū fuana dukulana fanga kī ma ti rū bore 'ana 'i saena, ki fua logo 'ania. Kaida'i uta ke to'o ki sū 'ania fa'u fa'asia uta kesi to'e kia, ki 'isita'inia logo fuana teo 'i saena ma māliu'anga. Ki sū logo 'ania fāfia ngela ti'iti'i kī fonea 'ania sina ma uta. Kaida'i kini ke 'afe ki safa logo 'ania talana 'ania kini faolu ke tala'u 'i saena 'uana 'i luma. Kaida'i ngwae ka mae, ki karia logo fuana 'afulana 'ania ngwae mae.

Saunga'ilana fa'u, ki 'olea 'abana, ki silia logo sisilina rauna, ki rarangia ana mafula, ki samota ra'irū kī 'ania rauna raranga kwate 'aba fa'u kī ke kwao, ki fi'i fa'asinafi'i ka kwao, ki fi'i koria 'ania tutu 'i ne'e ke mabe. Ki sosotea ka sui ki firi'ia 'abakwalo kī 'ania 'ere'ere fa'u. Ki fi'i ngalia 'aba kwalo di'ia ta'eta'ena sula ne'e ki silia ke bolo fa'inia ma'e kwakwa ana suli sakwalo, ki fi'i taia 'adoa 'ania 'abana. Ki la'umia ki tai gwauna la'u ta la'unga'a la'u ki fi'i tai faufauna Ka sui mala nia ka fi'i bolo fa'inia dukuru 'ania ma sū'a 'ania.

BAGS for carrying and loading things we plait from vine-strip, like satchels and sacks, big bags for loading great burdens, hanging bags for our belongings, and fringed bags to look good. Vine-strips for bags are the same as for tying things, especially *sula* and *malao* (both *Trichospermum*). *Kwasikwasi* strip (*Abroma*) is especially good for fringed bags because it is white and looks good. Mallow strip (*fa'ola / Hibiscus*) we also plait bags from, we first burn the vine-strip on the fire or peel the vine-strip and flask-cook it or boil it so it will be soft and flexible for plaiting. To plait a bag we take two wide vine-strips and shred them many and small, we then weave them and lay out the bottom of the bag, and after that we plait the main part up to the face (rim), we then braid around it and then we twine the bag strings from the remaining strips and tie them for hanging.
BALLS for playing ball and rolling with the foot we make from coconut leaf. We pull off two coconut leaves and then we shred strips from it, then we insert the base of a coconut leaf over another leaf and we then weave it round like a ball, and cut off the tops of the protruding leaves.

Wrapping

MATS (*Pandanus / fa'u*) are an important thing which women make and store. A mat is for bundling up food and anything else inside and we carry burdens with it. When rain falls we cover with a mat from being soaked by the rain, and we lay it as a bed for lying and sleeping on. We also cover small children to shut out the sun and rain. When a woman marries we also spread them on the path for the new woman to traverse to the house. When a person dies we split it open to wrap the dead person in.

To make a mat we cut off the strip (leaf) and split out the spine of the leaf, we warm it on the fire, we abrade the leaves with warmed-up leaf (*raranga / Ficus*) to make the strips of mat white and then sun it white and then scrape it with a clam(shell) so it will be flexible. We coil it up and then we tie vine-strips round the mat coils. We then take a vine-strip like *sula* skin (*Trichospermum*) which we shred to fit the hole in a bat's bone and sew the strips together with it. We fold it and sew the top and another fold we sew as the bottom. After that it is suitable for bundling things and covering with.

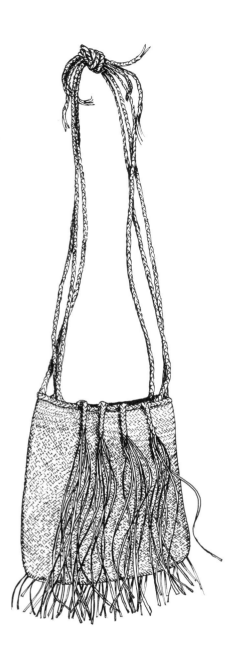

▲

gwanagwana
satchel
(30%)

▶

guiaguia
sack
(30%)

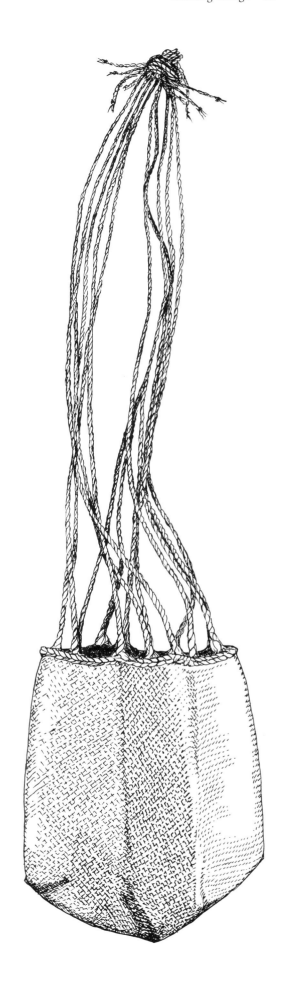

'ULI'ULI 'AI, ki rao logo 'ania. Ki 'afua 'ania ngwae mae, 'ulina fa'i fai ne'e le'a ka tasa. 'I na'o ma'i, kwaiatolana ngwae mae, ki 'afua 'ania 'uli 'ai, ki alua ka ngwaka 'i fafona tatafe ne'e ki saunga'inia fuana kwa'iato'a. Ki ragia logo 'uli 'ai fuana saungilana kata, ki la'umia ki fi'i tai'adoa ro bali kī fuana sau kata saena, saena fa'i ngali.

'Aba LA'UA fuana to'ilana ngela bibiu'a kī ma buta-lana mani kī. Kaida'i 'i na'o 'afe kī ke alua la'ua kī fuana sofonga'ilana na'ofada. La'ua, ki saunga'inia 'ania 'uli'ulina 'ai kī di'ia sala ma bubulia, la'ua ana bubulia nia ke ngasi ana la'ua ana fa'i sala. Ki 'uia fa'i 'ai fi'i doe kī, ki tufua kasirū sasabe'a go'o ki koria 'uli'uli ngasi ma ka bulibuli, ki fi'i diua 'ania fi'i gwarigwari noima gwa'i fau, leleka ta'eta'ena ka mabe mala, ki fi'i furia la'ua ma ki fa'asinafia 'i ke langa. Di'ia ki ogā nia ke ngwafeafea ka bolo fa'inia toro'a 'ania, ki kurua saena kafo noima saena asi, nia teo sulia lima asoa kī, ki fi'i sau'ua ki ngilosia, ka sui ki fa'asinafia 'i ke langa.

Rū gwaroa fuana laungi'anga kī
'I na'o ma'i ki saunga'inia rū kī ne'e ki gwaro'i 'ania kwalo dae'e 'i ke kwanga fuana laungilana nonika.

FA'I RADE fuana sa'ingilana ana alingaka, ki gwaroa 'ania 'adi fa'inia taketake niu meo, ti kaida'i ki kwa'ia logo 'ania luluka ne'e gwā. Ki saea logo 'ania fa'i 'au gwaroa ma ki saunga'inia logo 'ania fa'i 'au ti'iti'i.

KAFA GWAROA, ki tadilia ma'erū kī 'ania 'itangana kwa'e ne'e taliore'a ka ona. Ma'erū gwā fukiri ne'e ki dau saorani'i mala ki fi'i itoa 'ania 'aba luluka mala ki fi'i gwaroa 'ania 'adi fa'inia taketake niu meo.
GWAROSANGISANGI fuana obilana ana limaka, ki faosia 'ania 'aba ongaonga ne'e gwā, ka sui ki gwaroa 'ania 'adi fa'inia taketake niu meo.

FO'OSAE, di'ia ki oga nia ke lia kwanga liu, ta ma ki fi'i gwaroa ti kula ana 'ania 'adi fa'inia taketake niu meo.

TREE-BARK we also work with. We wrap a dead person in it, and mimosa (*fai*) bark is especially good. Formerly to deposit a dead person we wrapped him in tree bark and left him to rot on a platform which we built for depositing. We also strip off tree bark for making nut-pudding, we fold it over and sew the two ends together to pound the nut pudding inside, in the nut grove.
CLOTH is for cradling babies and wrapping shell-money. Formerly wives put cloth to conceal their fronts. We make cloth from the bark of trees like smooth (*sala*) and *bubulia*, (both *Ficus*) and cloth from *bubulia* is stronger than cloth from smooth. We hammer half-grown trees, we chop a straight section and scrape off the hard and dirty (outer) bark and hammer it with a cockle shell or a stone until the bark is really flexible and then cut off the cloth and sun it to dry out. If we want it to be soft, suitable for dressing in, we sink it in water or in the sea, it lies there for five days and we then rub and wring it and then we sun it to dry out.

Patterned things for decoration
Formerly we made things which we patterned with coloured vine to be pretty for decorating our bodies.
REEDS (*rade / Poaceae*) for inserting in our ear (lobe) we pattern with orchid (*'adi*) and red coconut cuticle, sometimes we also make them with *luluka* (*Dennstaedtiaceae*), which is black. We also call them patterned bamboos and we also make them with small bamboo.
PATTERNED COMBS, we trim sticks of treefern trunk which has a tough heartwood. These black sticks we hold in place and then we tie them well with gleichenia (*luluka*) strip and then we pattern it with orchid (*'adi*) and red coconut cuticle.
RING-PATTERNS for banding our arms, we plait from *ongaonga* strip which is black, then we pattern (embroider) it with orchid (*'adi*) and red coconut cuticle.
GIRDLES (for men), if we want it to look very pretty, then we pattern some parts of it with *'adi*-orchid and red coconut cuticle.

▶ *gwarosangisangi kī*
(100%)

◀ *ring-patterns*
(100%)

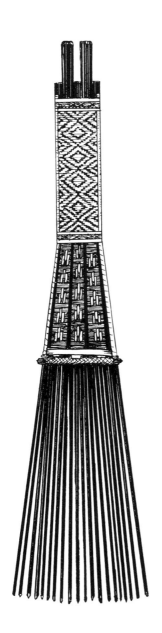

▲ *fa ì rade kī*
 (ear) reeds
 (100%)

▲ *kafa gwaroa kī*
 patterned combs
 (100%)

Atongilana rū kī

DILO, ki atongirū 'ania lalina ma ta'eta'ena 'i ke meo. Ki atongia rū kī di'ia takataka niu ma 'aba obi fuana saunga'ilana rū fuana laungi'a kī ma rū gwaro'i kī. Ki 'ilia lalina ma ki koria 'uli'ulina lalirū, ki dodoa memena fa'inia 'abarū kī, ki kisita'inia kafo saena, ki do'ofia, leleka 'abarū kī ke meo.

BUNABUNA, ki atongia rū kī 'ania rauna 'i ke meo, ka di'ia logo dilo. Ki saungia rauna saena dako fa'inia kafo ti'iti'i, go'o ki dodoa saena fa'i ka'o, ki du'afia, ka sui ki kanusua saena dako, ki fi'i alua rū ne'e kī, ki atongia 'i saena fuana atongilana. Ki atongia 'ania rū di'ia ta'eta'e 'ai ma kwalo 'abe, rū fuana saunga'inia 'ania dadalo ma sangisangi kī.

SASAO, ki atongirū 'ania sūla 'i ke gwā. Ki atongia rū di'ia dako kī ma la'ua fuana sofonga'ilana na'ofana kini kaida'i 'i na'o, ma fa'i singisingi kī, rū fuana laungi'anga ana maoma kī. Ti ngwae bili ke atongia māna, kwatea ngwae kī noa'a kesi lia sai ada.

SAIA, ki atongia logo 'ania memena ne'e ki dola fa'inia nanao 'i ke gwā, ki saia 'ania rū di'ia nonina dako kī, kwate ke gwā.

ATONGILANA RŪ KALAKALA'I KĪ di'ia subi ma alafolo ma fa'i kuba, ki kilua saena kunu ko'a sulia ti fa'i madamo, kwate ke gwā.

Rū bulao kī fuana laungilana ngwae

Ki to'o ana rū bulao 'oro kī ne'e rauni noima takani ni'i bolo fuana laungilana nonika ma ngwa'i ni fa'a. Na rū moko le'a ma ka lia le'a fuana laungi'a kī ni'i 'uri:

MUDU, ki 'oia uila fuana laungilana 'ania ngwa'i kī ka tasa fuana ngwae 'alako kī, sulia di'ia rauna ngwati'ula nia ke moko le'a ma ka lia le'a.

BALA, ūluna ki laungia 'ania ngwa'i kī.

BALIU, na uila nia bolo fuana laungilana ngwa'i kī, 'i ke lia 'olo'olo ma ka mokomoko.

FO'OKA, ki laungi ngwa'i 'ania ūlirū.

SAEBALA, ki laungi ngwa'i 'ania ūlirū.

KAKARA, ki silia gwangona fuana laungi'anga.

GWAGWASU, ki laungia 'ania nonika ma ngwa'i fa'ani kī fuana ke moko le'a, fuana logo bulasilana manatana ngela kini 'i nia ke manata fifī to'ona ngwae.

RI'I, ki laungia 'ania ngwa'i fa'ani kī, ti kaida'i ki 'oia ulirū 'i ki fa'abala'i fuana laungi'anga.

Staining things

DYE (*Morinda*), we stain things with the root and the bark to go red. We stain things like coconut cuticle and band strip (*obi / Calamus*) for making things for decoration and patterned things. We dig up the root and scrape the bark of the root, we flask the paste with the strips and pour water inside, and burn it until the strips go red.

BUNABUNA (*Cyclosorus*), we stain things with the leaf to go red, like dye (*dilo / Morinda*). We pound the leaf in a bowl with a little water and we flask it in a bamboo, we burn it and then we tip it out into a bowl and then put the things we are staining inside to stain. We stain things with it like tree bark and anondendron vine (*'abe*), things for making twine with and armbands.

SASAO (*Musa*), we stain things with the sap to be black. We stain things like bowls and (bark) cloth for concealing women's fronts in former times, and armbands for decoration at festivals. Thieves stain their faces with it so that people won't recognise them.

PUTTY (*Parinari*), we also stain with the paste, which we mix with charcoal to be black, and putty things like the body of bowls with it to make them black.

TO STAIN CARVED THINGS like angle-clubs and deflector-clubs and walking sticks, we bury them in a scraping (mangrove) swamp for a month to make them black.

Growing things for personal decoration

We have many growing things with leaves or flowers suitable for decorating our bodies and hanging bags. Things which smell good and look good for decoration are:

MUDU (*Dillenia*), we pick fronds for decorating bags, especially for young men, because when the leaves are dried they smell good and look good.

EUODIA (*bala*), we decorate bags with the fronds.

BALIU (*Ascarina*), the fronds are suitable for decorating bags, to look right and smell.

WORSHIP (*Euodia*), we decorate bags with the fronds.

SAEBALA (*Aglaia*), we decorate bags with the fronds.

KAKARA (*Alpinia*), we shred the leaf-shoot for decoration.

HEDYOTIS, we decorate our bodies and hanging bags with it to smell good and also to turn the mind of a girl so she will think intensely of a man.

RI'I (*Euodia*), we decorate hanging bags with it and sometimes we pick fronds to fade for decoration.

BULA, kaida'i takana ke 'asi ki usu'ia sulia 'aba kwalo ka sui ki fa'ā 'i luaka.

SA'OSA'O, ki laungi 'ania ūlina.
GISOBALA, ki laungia 'ania ngwa'i kī 'i ke moko le'a.
　　Na rū no kesi moko bore ma ni'i logo fuana laungi'anga 'i ke lia le'a, satani 'uri:
'ALA'ALA, ki 'inia ūluna fuana laungilana nonika kaida'i ana ngwa'enga kī. Kaida'i 'i na'o ngwae kī ke fonea 'ania na'ofada kaida'i ana laungi noni'anga.
'AMA'AMA, 'i na'o ma'i ki 'oia ūlina fuana laungi'anga 'i ke lia le'a, ki daura'ini'i sulia ngwa'i. Ki alua logo saena gwauna ngwae, fada 'ania ngwae nai'ari nia saungia ngwae.
TATARAKWASI, gwangona nia le'a ka tasa fuana laungilana ngwa'i kī. Ki sikilia ra'irū kī, ki fa'asinafi'i, ki sili'i mala, ki fi'i laungia 'ania ngwa'i kī.
DANGISATO, ti kaida'i ki ngalia ūlirū kī fuana laungilana ngwa'i ngwangwane kī.
DILI MARAKO fa'inia DILI MEO, ki laungi logo 'ania nonika ma ngwa'i kia kī.
TATALI, takana ki silifa'inia saena gwauka ma ki sa'ingia ana alingaka fuana laungi'anga 'ania.

FILU TALI, ki talia rauna ki fa'asinafia ke kwao 'i ki laungia 'ania ngwa'ī kī.
AFAAFAFOLA, ki laungi 'ania takana, nia le'a fuana laungilana 'ania ngwa'i.
BEROBERO, ki laungi 'ania ngwa'i kia kī.

BULA (*Fagraea*), when the flowers fall we thread them on vine-strip and then hang it round our necks.
YELLOW (*Cananga*), we decorate with the fronds.
GISOBALA (*Ocimum*), we decorate bags with it to smell good.
　　Things which don't smell but which are also decorative because they look good are named:
INSTANT (*Croton / Codiaeum*), we pick fronds for decorating the body during dances. In former times men shut off their fronts with it when they decorated their bodies.
SELAGINELLA (fern), formerly we picked fronds for decoration to look good and hang them from the bag. We also put them on a man's head, meaning that the man had killed someone.
TATARAKWASI (*Pleocnemia*), the leaf-shoot is especially good for decorating bags. We cut off the leaves and sun them, we shred them and then decorate bags with them.
SUNNY-DAY, sometimes we take the fronds for decorating men's bags.
GREEN CORDYLINE and RED CORDYLINE, we also decorate our bodies and our bags with.
HIBISCUS, we insert the flowers in our heads (hair) and stick them behind our ears for decoration.
SPLIT BRIGHT (palm)(*Licuala*), we split the leaf and sun it white to decorate bags with.
AFAAFAFOLA, we decorate with the flower, it is good for decorating bags
BEROBERO (*Araliaceae*), we decorate our bags with it.

Rū fuana raolana akalo ma gura'a kī

Things for ghost work and curing

'I na'o ma'i ti rū bulao fuana fa'amaurilana ngwae kī noima fa'alilana ngwae kī, ki kwaiguragura 'ania noima akalo ke manu ani fuana ki rao 'ani'i.

Formerly some growing things were for saving people's lives or damaging people, we cured with them or ghosts empowered them for us to work with.

Rū fuana raolana akalo kī

Ti 'ai, 'i na'o ma'i ki fasi'i nonina fanoa fuana 'oto'a 'ania ma'e akalo, rū ne'e fonea akalo kwasi ma kelema ma malimae kī. 'Oto'a nai'ari kī, ki fasi'i nonina fanoa, nonina logo fera ma feraābu, fa'inia logo sulia ta'itala kī, ma kula di'ia 'i māna sakasaka'a ana fanoa ma māna kafo, ana fulitua'a kī. Ki 'oto 'ania rū kwanga noema ka moko le'a, ki laungia logo 'ania ngwa'i kī, 'i nini'ari ki fasi'i go'o fuana laungilana fanoa ma fera ni fo'o. Bore ma ta'ifilia go'o fataāabu ne'e sai ana ma'e fata'a fuana fasilana ana 'oto'a. Ki 'oto logo 'ania gwa'i fau boso.

Things for ghost work

Some trees, formerly we planted them in the home area to charm by ghost-magic; things which block wild ghosts and sorcery and enemies. These charms we plant in the home area, and also about the sanctum and tabu-sanctum, as well as along paths and places like in front of the entrance to the home (clearing) and at water-spouts and rest-sites. We charm with things which are pretty or smell good, we also decorate bags with them and at present we also plant them to decorate the home and prayer-sanctum (church). But it was only the tabu-speaker (priest) who knew the words for planting the charm with. We also charm with hog stones (basalt pebbles).

Ti 'ai ne'e 'inoto'a fuana ki rao ani fuana akalo, satani ma raolani 'uri:

'ALA'ALA, ki 'oto 'ania, nia logo fuana laungilana nonina fanoa.

DILI, kaida'i 'i na'o, fataāabu ke 'ilala 'ania ra'irū, ki saea 'ania sango ni 'ilala'a. Nia ke rarangia ra'irū 'ania mafula, ka itoa ka'uka'udu'ua ka lalafia ka fafato'o 'uana tae ne'e kwatea mata'inga fuana ngwae. Di'ia ra'irū mū kaida'i fataāabu saea rū ne'e kwatea mata'inga ta ma gwata kī kōngia na'a ana akalo fuana gura'a. Di'ia ra'i dili ngasi ta ma rū kī le'a go'o 'ani sulia mata'inga saga go'o ne'e takisia ngwae. Ki 'oto logo 'ania dili, nia fuana logo laungilana nonina fanoa.

ASAKA, ki 'oto 'ania, nia fuana logo laungilana nonina fanoa.

GWAGWASU, ki 'oto 'ania, nia fuana logo laungilana nonina fanoa. Gwagwasu bulu, 'i na'o ma'i ki du'afia rauna kwate sasuna ke fa'amāliua malimae kia kī, fuana saungilada. Ngwae sai ani ke lalia 'ania ma'e fata'a ne'e ki saea 'ania fa'abulu.

FO'OKA, ki 'oto 'ania, nia fuana logo laungilana nonina fanoa.

DINGALE, ki 'oto 'ania

KWA'U, ki 'oto 'ania

Some trees which are important for working with ghosts, their names and uses are:

INSTANT (*Croton / Codiaeum*), we charm with it and it is also for decorating the home area.

CORDYLINE, in former times a tabu-speaker would divine with the leaf, we call it sango-divination. He'd warm the leaf on the fire and tie a hook and tug on it and concentrate on what was causing sickness for a person. If the leaf broke when the tabu-speaker said what caused the sickness, then pigs would be baked to the ghost for a cure. If the cordyline leaf was strong (didn't break) then things were good because a straight-forward sickness had attacked the person. We also charm with cordyline and it is also for decorating the home area.

COLEUS (*Lamiaceae*), we charm with it and it is also for decorating the home area.

HEDYOTIS, we charm with it and it is also for decorating the home area. Dark hedyotis, formerly we burned the leaf to make the smoke send our enemies to sleep, for killing them. A man who knew how would invoke it with words, which we call dark-making.

WORSHIP (*Euodia*) we charm with it and it is also for decorating the home area.

DINGALE (*Podocarpus*), we charm with it.

DRINK (*Premna*), we charm with it.

RI'I, ki 'ilua 'ania manatana ngela kini kī 'ania 'i ne'e kira ke ogā ngwae.

BALA, rū fuana kelema ne'e, ki fa'alia ngwae 'ania, ki kwaiguragura logo 'ania 'usia kelema.

FIU, rū fuana fonelana akalo ne'e, na ngwae tua fuana akalo ke lalia afurū kī 'ania ma'e fata'a ka damia ka busura'inia 'usia akalo kwasi ma rū ke takisi kia kī.

SASATO'O, ki fasia nonina fa'i labu ana fera , nia ke teo fuana fafato'o'anga ana malimae kī. Di'ia ki lisia ne'e rauna ni'i kuku, ta ma karangia ta mae ke fuli na'a, noima mae ke alasika na'a.

Rū fuana fo'osi'anga kī
FA'I LOI KĪ, 'i na'o ma'i ti fū'ingwae kira fo'osi ana. Fa'i loi kī satada 'uri:

fa'i NGUNGURU, nia ke doe liu mala, noa'a kesi 'ala'ala.

fa'i LOI KAKALA'A, nia bolo go'o fa'inia fa'i ngunguru, bore ma nonina to'o ana ma'e tōtō kī.

MALO, ba'eko ne'e, kerekere'a ti kula kwao ti kula ka gwā, nia ke tua saena asi.

MALO 'I TOLO, lisilana nia di'ia logo malo bore ma nia tua saena tolo. Nia ke 'alangwae, ngwae ke mae 'ali'ali ana.

GWAUBONOBONO, nia ti'iti'i ka keta mala, ka lia nunura, ti ai ka meo, ti ai ka gwā. Nia to'o ana kwakwa ana rō bali kī ta'ifau. Ba'eko saena ano nini'a, di'ia nia ka 'alekia, ki 'ania nama 'oni gwata ki fi'i mauri.

NGWALADA nia keta liu, lekalana ka 'ali'ali liu, noa'a kesi 'ala ngwae.

fa'i OLO nia ke tua 'i gwauna 'ai kī, noa'a kesi 'ala'ala bore ma kaida'i ngwae ke ra'efia 'ai ka ma'u go'o 'ani nia ka olo.

fa'i TAFO, nia keta liu, noa'a kesi 'ala ngwae.

NO'O LOFOLOFO KĪ
AFA nia doe ana no'o kī ta'ifau, nia ka lofo ka ra'e ana no'o lofolofo kī ta'ifau, nia ngasingasia ana no'o kī ta'ifau. Ti fū'ingwae kira ke kō 'ania, ta ma nia ābu noa'a kira kesia 'ania.

fa'i KUSI nia angi ka 'uri, kusi kusi fuana ke fa'abasua ngwae 'ania rū fuli kī.

fa'i KOROKORO nia gwā ta'ifau, nia kesi doe liu go'o, nia angi ka 'uri, korokoro. Ngwae kī ke fo'osia fuana kelema'anga.

MANU TOLO, no'o ne'e inamaemū mala rongoa angilana ma ka lisia nonina, kwatea nia ke ngwangwane'a.

RI'I (*Euodia*), we bespell girls' minds with it so they will want a man.

EUODIA (*bala*), this is for sorcery, we damage a person with it and we also use it as a cure for sorcery.

GINGER (*Zingiber*), is something for stopping ghosts, a man who deals with ghosts will invoke the tubers with words, chew it and spray it out against wild ghosts and things which attack us.

DEFENDER (*Trichadenia*), we plant it about the yard of the sanctum, it is there for the prediction of enemies. If we see its leaves wilt, then a feud is close to happening, or a band will raid us.

Things for prayer
SNAKES, formerly some clans prayed to them. Snakes are named:

BOA (*Candoia*) is very big, it doesn't bite.

MARKED SNAKE is the same as the boa but its body has markings.

MALO (sea snake / *Loveridgerlaps*) is a menace with white and black parts, it lives in the sea.

INLAND *MALO* looks like *malo* but it lives inland. If it bites a person, the person will quickly die from it.

SHUT-HEAD (burrowing snake / *Ramphotyphlops*) is small and very long, it looks shiny, some are red and some are black. It has a mouth at both ends. This is a menace of the land, if it bites us we have to eat pig shit and then we live.

NGWALADA (whip snake / *Dendrelapis*) is very long and it goes very quickly, it doesn't bite people.

TUMBLER (*Boiga*) lives at the heads of trees, it doesn't bite but when a man climbs a tree he is frightened by it and tumbles.

TAFO (Guppy's snake / *Salomonelaps par*) is very long, it doesn't bite people.

FLYING BIRDS
EAGLE is bigger than all other birds, it flies higher than all other birds, it is stronger than all other birds. Some clans bake (pigs) by it, so it's tabu for them to eat it.

I-CAN'T (greybird) cries kusi kusi (I-can't I-can't) to warn a person of things happening.

KOROKORO is black all over, it is not very big and it cries korokoro. People pray to it for sorcery.

INLAND *MANU*, this bird, when a kinless man hears its cry and sees its body, it makes him blessed.

Rū fuana guralana mata'inga kī

Guralana mata'inga, ki to'o nama ana malitana
rao'a 'ania 'ai kī. Ki gura 'ania rauna ti 'ai ma 'ulina
ti 'ai noima ti kula ani.

Guralana 'ania 'ai, ti ai ki karasia ta'eta'ena, ti
ai ki 'inia rauna noima gwangogwangorū noima
takarū, ti ai ki ngalia fa'irū kī, ti ai ki tufua 'uana
sula, ti ai ki fata fuana 'ania ma'e fata'a. Raolana
'ai fuana gura'a, ti rū ki 'ani'i, ti rū ki dola fa'inia ti
'ai ki fi'i 'ani'i, ti rū ki dami'i fa'inia agiru, ti rū ki
losia fuana kwa'ufilana, ti kaida'i ki eta du'afia
mala fuana 'anilana noima kwa'ufilana. Ti rū ki
losia ki dola 'ania kafo fuana siufilana 'ania nonika,
ti rū ki dami ki busura'inia 'i nonika, ti rū ki ofia
'onia nonika ki fi'i fi'iri fafia, ti rū ki alu'i go'o 'i
nonika di'ia saena ngwa'i fa'a, ti rū ki mumu fafi'i
kaida'i ki ala'a fa'inia ngwae kelema fuana fa'adala-
kwailana ngasingasi'anga. 'I na'o kaida'i ki gurā
mata'inga kī, ki fo'osia akalo fuana nia ke fa'angasi-
ngasia 'ai 'i ke mamana. Nini'ari ki fo'osia lala
satana na'a sa God.

Fuana falafala to'a Kwara'ae fadalana 'ai fuana
gura'a nia 'ato ka ago, ma ngwae kī ta'ifau 'iri sai
ana 'ai fuana gura'a kī. Ka 'ato fuana ta ngwae ke
fada 'ai fuana gura'a fuana ta ngwae noima kira ke
keresia 'ania 'abafola. Ta rū ana ne'e di'ia ngwae
'oro sai ana rū fuana gura'a nia kesi ngasingasi ma
kesi fa'amauria ngwae. Ma ti ngwae kira gura ani
ma ki foli doe logo ada. Logo ma ti ngwae ili'i kesi
rao sulia sali kira ngali rora 'ania ma kira ka kwate
fuana ngwae mata'i ma nia ka fi'i ta'a liu ma ngwae
kata mae ma ngwae nia kata gania toto'a.

Saile'a ana ne'e kabani doe kī 'i fanoa doe kī,
kira ngalia 'ai nini ki gura 'ani'i kī, kira ka
saunga'inia fuana selene doe liu. Ta nini'a rū fuana
guragura'a 'i Kwara'ae ki keresi'i ki alu'i mamata
ani 'i kisi fa'ata'inia kwailiu. Sasi 'ubani ti kabani
kata ngali'i fuana saunga'ilani fuana selene.

'Unari, saena ruana kula ana 'abafola ne'e, di'ia
kaili keresia rū fuana guralana kī, mili kere 'afu'afu
go'o ana rū tae ne'e bolo fa'inia ki gurā 'ania
mata'inga. Ta 'abafola mamata ne'e kaili ke kere
madako ana rū tae ma ki ngali fa'uta ana ma ki
saunga'i fa'uta ana ma ki kwate fa'uta ana fuana
guralana 'ania ngwae mata'i. Na 'abafola nai'ari kisi
fa'ata'i kwailiu ana sulia ki fadangisia ma ki
talikwakena na'a malitana rū fuana kwaigurai'anga
kī 'i Kwara'ae.

Things for curing sickness

To cure sickness we have ways of using trees. We
cure with the leaves of some trees and the bark of
other trees or other parts of them.

To cure with trees, with some we scrape the
bark, some we pick the leaf or leaf-shoot or flower,
some we take the fruit, some we chop for the sap,
some we speak words to. To use a tree for curing,
some things we eat, some things we mix with other
trees and then eat them, some things we chew with
betel, some things we squeeze to drink and
sometimes we first have to burn them to eat or
drink. Some things we squeeze and mix with water
for bathing the body, some things we chew and
spray on the body, some things we wrap round the
body and then tie them on, some things we just
put on the body, like in a hanging bag, some things
we put in the mouth while talking with a sorcerer
to make the power ineffective. Formerly when we
cured sicknesses we prayed to a ghost to make the
tree powerful and true. At present we pray instead
to the name of God.

In the tradition of the Kwara'ae people,
explaining trees for curing is difficult and secret
and not everyone knows about trees for curing. It is
hard for someone to explain trees for curing to
someone else or to write it in a book. For one
thing, if too many people know about a tree for
curing it won't be powerful and won't save people's
lives. Some people cure with them and we pay
them a lot for it. Also people shouldn't try to use it
because they might take it the wrong way and give
it to a sick person who then gets very ill and the
person may die and someone may ask for
compensation.

To be sure, big companies from big countries
can take the trees we cure with and use them to get
very big money. This is why the things for curing in
Kwara'ae we are putting separately so as not to
reveal them indiscriminately. This is in case
companies take them to use them for money.

Thus in this book we are writing only part of
what we need to cure sickness with. In a separate
book we will write clearly what things are and how
we take them and work them and give them to cure
a sick person. That book will not be shown
indiscriminately because we detail and go to the
heart of the kinds of things used for curing in
Kwara'ae.

11 *George Bako shooting fish. (1983)*

12 *Stephen Binalu rubbing to raise a fire. (1979)*

13 *The family of Adriel Rofate'e making an oven by heaping hot stones around the food. (1983)*

14 *Le'akini flask-cooking vegetables in bamboos. She is dressed in the old-fashioned maiden's waist-band. (1979)*

15 *William Kware pounding coconut-pudding. (1983)*

16 *A feast set out on a spread of banana leaves, celebrating the completion of a piped water-supply to Nafinua. (1984)*

17 *Samuel Alasa'a stitching sago-leaf thatch. (1979)*

18 *Nelson Salole roofing a house. He is tying sago panels to the short rafters, which in this case rest on top of the over-bearer. The rafters can be seen lying on the over-bearer, which lies on the bearer, which lies on the eave-beam. (1983)*

19 *Stephen Binalu plaiting a coconut basket. (1979)*

20 *Adriel Rofate'e beginning to plait a bag by laying out the bottom with two strips of sula bark shreds. (1979)*

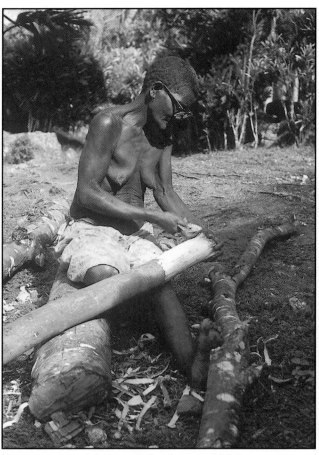

22 *Making barkcloth, at Taba'akwaru. (1984)*

23 *Maefatafata sewing a mat (pandanus). (1987)*

24 *Some of the* Forest of Kwara'ae *research team: Rocky Tisa Sugumanu, Michael Kwa'ioloa, Ben Burt, Adriel Rofate'e Toemanu, Frank Ete Tuaisalo. (1991)*

Tagi ʾa sulia masu ʾu kia

Caring for our forest

Saena masu'u bore, rū 'oro ne'e ki fasi'i ma ki salinga'ini'i 'i ke bulao fuana 'anilana noima raolana. Ko'o kia ki kira ke sasi 'uri fa'asia ta talata'ingae 'uana ta talata'ingwae leleka ka dao 'i ta'ena, kwatea masu'u ka te'e rokisi ke bolo fuana tualaka ka te'e ngwara'u ka le'a, sulia rū ne'e ki ogā ni'i bulao ka 'oro saena masu'u. Ti rū ne'e ki fasi'i ma ki salinga'ini'i saena masu'u, ni'i 'uri:

KA'O ma ti 'au logo, ki salinga'ini'i ma'i 'i fanoa fuana ki rao 'ani'i.

NGALI ma ti 'ai fufungu logo, ki fasi'i 'i ke 'oro fuana 'anilani fa'irū kī.

'AMAU, ki ogani ana kaida'i ki tabua o'olā fuana 'anilana rauna.

MAMUFUA ma ti 'ai ne'e ona le'a, ki ogani logo ana fuana rao 'ania.

DINGALE ma ti 'ai logo, ki fasi'i fuana fa'ata'ilana toto ana rū 'inoto'a kī.

LOFA ma ti 'ai logo, ki fasia sulia fa'i ngali kī ma fa'i sao kī fuana ra'enga'a sulia 'i ne'e ki loia fa'i ngali kī ma ki tufua rara sao ki.

DANGISATO ma ti 'ai logo, ki fasia 'i nonina fanoa 'i ke lia kwanga ma fuana logo tuafia nunufi'anga, leleka nia ke bulao saena masu'u.

LĀ, ki fasia saena kula ngwangwakwa'a fuana rao fanga'a 'ania rauna.

Na masu'u fa'inia rū kī ta'ifau ne'e bulao kwasi ana kula kī ta'ifau, ne'e rū ngwae fu ano rū kira. Ma di'ia ta ngwae ke fasia ta rū, ta ma rū ngwae nai'ari na'a. Ngwae nai'ari kī kira to'o ana ngasingasi'a fuana kira ke fata nama sulia rū bulao saena masu'u kī, kira ke tagi nama sulia masu'u kira. Fuana rū kī ta'ifau ngwae kī 'iri madafia malatikolana rū 'inoto'a ne'e bulao saena masu'u, sulia ni'i ke teo ani fuana rao'a 'ani'i. Fuana ke fonea falafala nai'ari ngela fi'i doe kī ke no fa'inia ra'efilana 'ai fuana likisilana ma tufu 'o'o'anga ani 'i ke kwa'i kirida'i go'o fuana masa'a. Ma 'uifogalana gerogero ka'o kī ma tufulana fa'i 'ai kī fuana labulani. Si ke tufu'i ka bala kisi su fafia gwarirū, na akalo kwasi ke tua ani ma ke daua ngwae kī ne'e ke liu ta ne'e ki su nama fafia gwari 'ai tufu'i kī 'i kesi 'unari. Rū bulao saena masu'u kī, ni'i 'inoto'a fuana rao'a 'ani'i, ni'i kwasila'a noima ki fasi'i bore, ki tagi nama suli'i ma ki 'ogani nama ani.

Ti 'ai kwasi bore ki fasi'i logo fuana 'anilana fa'irū kī noema fuana saunga'irū'anga 'ani'i. 'Ai fufungu saena masu'u kī, ki tabu 'afi'i 'i ne'e ni'i ke

Even in the forest there are many things which we plant or transfer to grow for eating or work. Our ancestors did this from generation to generation until today, making the forest change a bit to enable our living to be a bit easier and better, because the things we want grow plentifully in the forest. Some of the things we plant and transfer in the forest are:

BAMBOO (*Nastus*) and other bamboos we transfer to the home for us to work with.

NUT (*Canarium*) and other bearing trees we plant to be plentiful to eat the fruit.

'AMAU (*Ficus*) we conserve when we clear gardens to eat the leaf.

SECURINEGA (*mamufua*) and other trees which are good and tough we also conserve to work with.

DINGALE (*Podocarpus*) and other trees we plant as markers showing important things.

LOFA (*Sterculia*) and other trees we plant alongside nut trees and sago trees for climbing them so we can pick nuts and chop sago branches.

SUNNY-DAY and other trees, we plant in the home area to look pretty and also for sitting in the shade, and eventually they grow in the forest.

COMINSIA we plant in moist places to prepare food with the leaf.

The forest with all things which grow wild everywhere are the things of the person whose land it is. But if a person plants something, then it's a thing of that person. The people who have power to speak about things growing in the forest must care for their forest. So that of all these things, people will beware of destroying the important things growing in the forest, because they are there to work with. So as to stop the custom of young boys climbing trees to lop them and chop them down pointlessly to fall with a crash for play. And cracking bamboo shoots and chopping down trees for spears. If they chop them down and they fade and we don't cover up the stumps, a wild ghost can sit on them and grab people who pass by, so we must cover up chopped tree stumps so they won't do that. The growing things in the forest are important for working with, whether they are wild or planted, and we must care for them and conserve them.

We also plant wild trees to eat the fruit or to make things with. Bearing trees in the forest we clear around so they'll grow well. We also clear bulao le'a. Ki tabu logo 'afia 'ai ne'e numa ke ani'i fuana ki 'ani'i. 'I ta'ena ki tabu logo 'afia 'ai fuana saunga'irū'a kī sulia ni'i barū'a na'a, 'i na'o ni'i 'oro liu, noa'a kisi tabu go'o 'afi'i. Kaida'i ki o'ofia bore o'olā, 'ai 'inoto'a kesi bolo fa'inia tufulani ki ogani logo ani, ka tasa ana 'ai fuana gura'a kī ma 'ai fuana saunga'inga kī. Ka 'unari, fa'i mamufua ki ogani ani fuana diro, ki birā 'ali'ali rū kī 'i ke doe 'ali'ali.

Ti 'ai ne'e ko'o ki fasi'i fuana fa'i bōlana 'ano kī kisi tufu'i sulia ni'i fa'asaga tualaka ke saga. Na 'ai ū sulia tala ki ogani ani fuana ke nunufi ma ngwae kī ke saunga'inia nama fuli tua'a kī ka tasa ana tala doe 'uana kula ni usi'a. Nia le'a ki 'uia sulufaua fuana mango'a ma ki fasia 'ai kī ani. Ma ti fuli tua'a 'i na'o ma'i ka dao 'i ta'ena ne'e ti fa'i bō logo ana afu ano kī.

Māna kafo kī sikasika ma ka satola ta ma nia fa'ata'inia ne'e ki dau sulia taki kia ne'e kula ni siu ma kwa'unga'a ke satola ma ka sikasika nama, kula ngwae 'oro ke liu ana. Na 'ai bore sulia kafo kī fuila kisi tufu'i sulia ni'i nunufia kafo ka gwarigwari'a, fuana logo ne'e ni'i ke teo 'i ke daua ano kesi ofo ma uta ka toea ano kata fa'afungua kafo ka gwa'u 'ali'ali ne'e gwari 'ai kī ke fura na'a. Ka tasa ana kafo ni kwa'u kī, noa'a kisi tufudalea māni, ki 'auābua kini kī kesi ra'e 'i gwauna ma'e kafo ma kisi mimisia māna ma kisi siu 'ania sufu ka kwate ka mokosi'i sufu'a 'i māna, ma kwa'ufilana ka mingaminga.

Ki ogani logo ana ti rū ne'e 'inoto'a ana tualaka ana bali ana akalo. Ka 'unari, ki 'ogani ana 'ai ne'e ki 'oto 'ani'i kī ma ki alua 'oto'a 'i 'aeni fuana fonelana rū di'ia akalo kwasi ma kelema. Ki 'ogani logo ana fi'irū kī ma gwa'i fau kī ne'e ki alu'i fuana su'usilana fanoa fa'asia gwa'i mae'a kesi saungi kia. Afu masu'u safitana fera'ābu, ki ogani logo ani sulia rikwa'anga, sasuna mafula ma busulana fi'i ka'o noima maladalafalana feraābu kwatea akalo ke saeta'a ma ke ketolanga'inia tua'a.

Bolo fa'inia ki fa'amanata 'ania na taki 'inoto'a nai'ari 'i ke fa'ama'ua ngwae malangaingai kī 'i rū ne'e ki 'ogani ani kī ke teo 'ani fuana ki rao 'ani'i, ka tasa ana kaida'i ana fanga'a doe di'ia siufa ma maoma kī. Ka 'unari, ki ogani ana kula kī 'i bolo la'u fa'inia o'onga'a talana malita'i fanga ne'e bolo fa'ini'i kī. Ki ogani logo ana fangala fuana no'o akaka'u ma rū kī di'ia 'unu ni'i ke gwa'ita'alu'a ma ngwae ki kesi saungi'i. Ki ogani logo 'ai kī ni'i ke teo logo fuana numa ke fanga ani ma liko kī fuana sakwalo ma futo ke tua ana ma 'ai kī fuana no'o lofolofo kī ke nu'i ani. Ki 'ogani logo ana agi kafo

around trees which grubs eat for us to eat them. Today we also clear around trees for making things because they are scarce, formerly they were very plentiful and we didn't clear around them. Even when we make gardens, important trees should not be chopped down and we conserve them, especially trees for curing and trees for building. Thus securinega (*mamufua*) we conserve for posts and pollard it to sprout and get big quickly.

Trees which our ancestors planted to set land boundaries we don't chop down because they keep our living correct. Trees standing along a path we conserve for shade and for people to build rest-sites, especially along a big path to a market place. It is good to throw down stone platforms for resting and plant trees at them. And some rest-sites, from the past to today, are also boundaries of pieces of land.

When water spouts are clean and pretty it shows we are upholding our law that the bathing and drinking place be pretty and clean, as a place many people pass by. Even trees along the water we should not chop down because they shade and cool the water and also for them to stay and hold the ground so it won't collapse, and when rain strikes the ground it won't make the water fill up and empty quickly where the tree stumps rot. Especially with drinking waters, we don't chop and damage beside them and we make it tabu for women to climb to the head of a water or pee beside it and we don't bathe in it with soap to make it smell soapy at the watering place and foul to drink.

We also conserve important things for our living to do with ghosts. Thus, we conserve trees which we charm with or put charms at the foot of to block things like wild ghosts or sorcery. We also conserve the clumps and stones which we put to protect homes from sickness striking us. The piece of forest separating the tabu-sanctum we also conserve because raised voices, smoke from fire and bursting bamboo clumps or disrespect for the tabu-sanctum makes ghosts angry and troubles our lives.

It is appropriate for us to teach this important law to frighten vandals so the things we conserve will remain for us to work with, especially at times of big feasts like pudding-feasts and festivals. So it is that we conserve places which are suitable for gardens for the kinds of foods which suit them. We also conserve foraging areas for cuscus and things like lizards to become abundant without people killing them. We also conserve trees to remain for caterpillars to eat and cavities for bats and cuscus to live in and trees for birds to nest in. We also conserve a stretches of water so that fish will ke la'u 'i ne'e ī'a ke 'oro ka rerefo 'i saena. Rū nai'ari kī, 'i na'o ma'i ni'i 'inoto'a ana tua'a. Ki lu'ini sulia bara fa'i ngali'anga, ki 'ogani ani ka tasa fuana siufa.

Di'ia ki ogā ki ogani ana ta 'ai di'ia 'ai fufungu, 'ai ni numa, 'ai ne'e ngwangwa ni'i fanga ana, ta ma ki ke gwa'i bu fuani 'ania uli 'ai ne'e ki kanga'inia ki 'oia fafia. Di'ia ki ogā ki ogani ana afu masu'u noima agi kafo, ta ma ki eta fa'arongo logo 'ania fuana ngwae kī ta'ifau ke sai ana mala, ki fi'i gwa'i bū usia 'ania 'uli 'ai, ki itoa ana gwauna ba'e 'ai.

become plentiful in it. These things were important for our living formerly. We prohibit them for several years and conserve them specially for feasts.

If we want to conserve a tree like a (fruit) bearing tree, a caterpillar tree or a tree which grubs eat, then we put a block on it with a tree frond which we thrust in and break over. If we want to conserve a piece of forest or a stretch of water, we first announce it so that everyone knows about it and then we block it with a tree frond, we tie it to the top of a post.

▲ *sa'osa'o*   ▲ *ako*   ▲ *fa'ola*   ▲ *alita*
yellow   *shout*   *mallow*   *almond*
(*Cananga*)   (*Pometia*)   (*Hibiscus*)   (*Terminalia*)

Na ruana kula ana 'abafola ne'e nini'a

Na rū ne'e bulao saena aba 'i kula 'i Kwara'ae kī

Satana rū bulao kī ma lisilani ma kula ne'e ni'i ke bulao ani kī, fa'inia logo rū to'oto'o ne'e ki saunga'ini 'ani'i kī fuana tualaka.

The second part of the book is

The things which grow in the Kwara'ae area

The names of growing things, their looks and the places they grow, with the various things we make with them for our living.

'Ai doe kī *(fai'inia logo ti 'ai ne'e bolo logo fa'ini'i)*

NGALI, 'ai ne'e ke doe liu mala, nonina kwaokwao'anga, rauna nia ketaketa'a ka marako, takana kwao ka ti'iti'i go'o. Nia ka taka mala, fa'irū kī ka fi'i sau ana takana. Nia ke fungu ana kaida'i nia ke fi'i doe, ki saea 'ania atokale, ma doe to'olana ma ngwarolana logo. Nia ke fungu go'o ana unita'irū kī, ti kaida'i nia ke fungu ta'irū go'o saena fa'i ngali nama ana kaida'i nia ke fungu. Kaida'i nia ke make nia ke fa'ata'inia ana ta'eta'ena fa'irū ne'e nia ke gwā. Na ta'eta'erū ne'e ofia lasirū, na lasirū ka ofia reforefona, na reforefona ne'e ka ofia sa'erū. Kaida'i ki 'uia fa'irū, nia foga 'ania ulu lasirū kī 'afia sa'erū. Ti ngali sa'erū kī molimoli'a, ti ngali sa'erū kī te'e keta bore ma ni'i kesi keta liu go'o, na ngali 'au sa'erū keta liu mala.

○ Nia ke bulao go'o ana kula kī ta'ifau, fa'asia fafona asi 'uana tolo, ana logo kula kaole'a ma ano bulu, te'e saena kunu kī ma saena tolo goro ne'e noa'a nia kesi bulao ana. Ki salinga'inia fuana fasilana ma nia ke tala bulao logo, nia ke bulao ka 'oro liu funia ki saea 'ania fa'i ngali.

• Ngali ne'e fanga 'inoto'a fuaka. Ki ke ra'efia ma ki loia fa'ina 'ania kauala, ki goea ki ukua saena gwaurau 'i ngali, ki fi'i 'uia lasirū, ki efoa ta'eta'erū. Faulā fuana 'uilana fa'i ngali ki saunga'inia mala 'ania nakinaki, ma'e fau ani 'ui ngali'a ki efoa mala gwa'i fau boso noima gwa'i nakinaki. Di'ia ki 'uia fa'i ngali ka sui na'a, ki fi'i manumanua ka sui ki fi'i dodoa sa'erū kī saena fa'i ka'o, ki labu le'a ana ki satea ke fungu ma ka nekeneke, ki fi'i gu'utā. Bi'i ngali kī ki fi'i do'ofi'i fuana saungilana 'ania kata manumanua. Saukata'a, ki saungia fa'inia alo saena dako.

• Di'ia ki oga ki alua bi'i ngali ke tau lala ta ma ki alu 'i go'o 'i mokosasu saena bara noima usausa fuana ta kaida'i go'o 'ana ne'e ki oga saungilana kata 'ania, 'i noa'a nia kesi moko. Di'ia ki oga fuana tadili ta ma ki goea fa'i ngali ki to'ongi'i lala saena ngwa'i noima ki kisita'inia saena bara 'i tadili, ki fa'asasufia nia ke teo sulia ta bara madamo noima fa'i ngali, ka me'e mala ki fi'i 'uia, ka sui ki 'efoa sa'erū kī ki dodo'i logo, ki fi'i saungia 'ania kata 'i tadili.

• Sūla ngali alua logo buli fuana du'a madako'a saena luma. Ki tufua sūla ke afe ka bū go'o, ki 'oto susulia ki dodoa saena fa'i ka'o du'a, ki alu ana 'ania mafula, nia ke du'a madako saena luma ana kaida'i rodo'a, ma ki kede mafula logo 'ania.

Big trees *(with some other trees similar to them)*

NUT, this tree gets very big indeed, its body is whiteish, its leaf is longish and green, its flower is white and just small. It flowers and fruits then develop from the flower. It bears while almost grown, we call it begetting, and fully grown and in old age. It bears a single crop, sometimes it bears just once a year (nut-season) at the time it bears. When it is ripe it shows by the skin of the fruit, which becomes black. The skin covers a shell which covers a scale (endocarp), and this scale covers the inside (kernel). When we hammer the fruit it cracks into three shells surrounding the inside. With some nuts the inside is round, with some nuts the inside is quite long but not very long, with bamboo-nut the inside is very long indeed.

○ It just grows everywhere, from on the sea to the inland, on both clay ground and dark ground, only in swamps and in the misty inland it won't grow. We transfer it for planting and it also grows by itself, and where it grows very plentifully we call a nut (grove).

• Nut is a very important food for us. We climb and pluck the fruit with a hook, pick them up and gather them in a nut shelter, then hammer the shell and remove the skin. The stone to hammer the nuts we make from flint, for the stone to hammer the nuts on we select a hog-stone (basalt) or lump of flint. When we have finished hammering the nuts we blanche them (remove the scale) and then flask the insides in bamboo, we tap it down well and press it till full and compressed and we plug it. The tubes of nuts we cook for pounding into blanched nut-pudding. For nut-pudding we pound it with taro in a bowl.

• If we want to leave the flasks of nuts for longer we just put them in the smoke on a rack or shelf for whenever we want to make nut-pudding, so they won't smell. If we want cured-pudding we pick up the nuts and keep them in a bag or tip them onto a curing rack and smoke them there for several months or a year, and when well parched we hammer them, then we take out the insides and flask-cook them and pound them into cured nut-pudding.

• Nut sap leaves a resin to burn brightly in the house. We chop it for the sap to flow and thicken, we poke it off and flask it in a dry bamboo and set fire to it, it burns brightly in the house at night, and we also kindle the fire with it.

- Buli fuana logo mokelana kula foga ana iolo kī.
- Na lasina ngali nia du'a dangi, ki du'a logo 'ania 'i olofana bara 'i tadili kī.
- Noa'a kasi bolo fa'inia saunga'ilana luma sulia nia ke suma'ala'a, luma sasufi'a bore 'ana noa'a kasi bolo fa'inia.
- Na 'ingata'irū du'a ki kwa'ia logo fuana so'i, nia le'a sulia nia ke du'a kwasukwasu bore ma noa'a nia kesi du'a dangi.

MALANGALI, ki saea logo 'ania NGALI NGWANE, BULUNGALI, 'ai ne'e lisilana ka di'ia logo ngali, mokofana ka di'ia ngali. Bore ma rauna ne'e matamata, rauna keta liu ma ka reba, ma nia kesi fungu le'a, fa'irū kī ka ti'iti'i go'o. Kaida'i fa'irū kī ke make, lisilani ka borabora'a, ta ne'e ki saea 'ania bulungali.
- Nia ke bulao fa'asia fafona asi 'uana 'i tolo.
- Fa'irū, noa'a kesi 'ania.
- Noa'a kesi saunga'i luma 'ania sulia nia ke suma'ala, ka di'ia logo ngali saga.
- Ki kwa'ia fuana so'i.
- 'I nini'ari ki tufua fuana rebarū kī bore ma ki rafua nama 'ania feda ara'ikwao.

- Resin is also for caulking cracks in canoes.
- Nut shells burn till day, we also burn them under the curing rack.
- It is not suitable for building houses because it gets worm-eaten, even for smoky houses it is not suitable.
- The dry trunk we also fell for fuel, it is good because it burns flaming but it won't burn till day.

NGALI = NUT / ngali-nut / galip nut / pili nut / canarium almond / java almond / *Canarium indicum* L. (*Burseraceae*)

FALSE-NUT, also called MALE NUT and DARK-NUT, this tree looks like nut and smells like nut. But the leaf is different, the leaf is very long and wide and it doesn't bear well, the fruits are only small. When the fruits are ripe they look purple, that's why we call it dark-nut.

- It grows from on the sea to the inland.
- We don't eat the fruit.
- We don't build houses with it because it gets worm-eaten, like nut proper.
- We fell it for fuel.
- At present we chop it down for planks but we have to paint it with whiteman's paint.

MALANGALI / NGALI NGWANE / BULUNGALI = FALSE-NUT / MALE NUT / DARK-NUT / *Canarium asperum* Benth. / *C. hirsutum* Willd. / *C. liguliferum* Leenh. / *C. vitiense* A. Gray / *Haplolobus sp.* (*Burseraceae*)

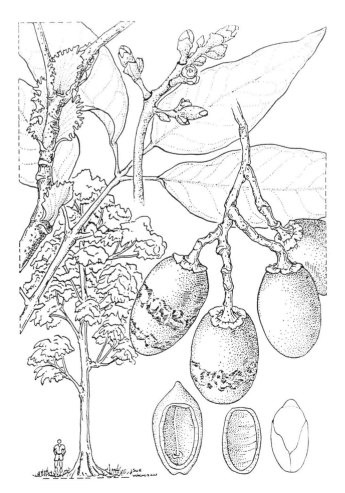

◄ ngali / nut

FALA, ta sata 'AIKENU, 'ai ne'e ka ta'i keta mala, nonina gwagā'a, rauna ta'i reba ka ketaketa'a ka nura. Ki saea logo 'ania MAMALANGALI FAKA si ne'e nia bolo logo fa'inia ngali faka.
○ 'Ai fasia ne'e, ki fasia go'o 'i fafona asi, nia ke bulao go'o ana ano ngwangwakwa'a ma ana kula kunukunu'a kī.
• Ki 'ania sa'erū, 'anilana le'a liu logo di'ia sa'e ngali kī.
• Ki saunga'i 'ania luma ni du'urū.
• Ki kwa'ia fuana so'i.
• Ki gura logo 'ania ti mata'inga.

'ADO'A, ki saea logo 'ania 'ADO'A KINI, 'AIKWASI, 'ai ne'e lisilana karangi ka di'ia ngali bore ma rauna te'e molimoli'a ka te'e dokodoko ma kesi reba liu go'o. Fuana 'ado'a ne'e karangi ka di'ia fuana ngali, bore ma nia te'e lia matamata sulia nia dokodoko ka te'e 'ere lala. Kaida'i ki 'uia fa'irū nia foga 'ania rō lasirū kī 'afia sa'erū, ta ne'e ki saea 'ania 'ado'a.
○ 'Ai fasia ne'e, ki fasia logo di'ia ngali ana kula kī ta'ifau. Nia ke bulao ka 'oro ana ti kula, ti kula nia ke bulao fiku sulia ua 'i 'aikwasi.

• Ki 'ania fa'irū kī, nia di'ia logo ngali bore ma lasina 'ado'a ka ngasi ana ngali saga, sa'erū kī, na 'anilana noa'a kesi gwari di'ia fuana ngali bore ma nia 'ero'ero ma ka mamasia mala. Ki sau kata 'ania sa'erū kī, ki dodo'i logo fuana fa'asasufilani 'i mokosasu saena usausa, di'ia ngali.
• Na 'ado'a fa'inia ngali, rao'a 'ani'i bolo go'o, noa'a kesi matamata go'o. Noa'a kasi bolo fa'inia saunga'ilana luma sulia nia suma'ala logo, ki labua 'ania biru kī, ki kwa'ia fuana so'i bore ma nia kesi du'a dangi go'o.

MALA'ADO'A, 'ai ne'e ke doe mala, lisilana karangi ka di'ia logo na 'ado'a kini. Nia ke fungu 'ania fa'irū kī di'ia nia ke make nia ke gwā. Kaida'i nia taka nia kesi alua go'o ti fa'irū.
○ 'Ai kwasi lala nini'a, nia ke bulao saena to'ona'oa ma fafo 'i asi kī.
• Fuana mala 'adoa noa'a ki kesi 'ania go'o, sulia ni'i 'iri to'o ana sa'erū di'ia 'ado'a kini.
• Fa'i 'ai ki rao 'ani'i nia bolo logo fa'inia 'ado'a kini.

CUTNUT, this tree is quite tall, its body is blackish, its leaf is quite wide and longish and shiny. We also call it FOREIGN PSEUDO-NUT as it is equivalent to a foreign nut.
○ This is a planted tree, we plant it on the sea, it just grows on moist ground and in swampy places.
• We eat its fruit, it is very good to eat like the inside (kernel) of nut.
• We build cooking houses with it.
• We fell it for fuel.
• We also cure some sickness with it.
FALA / 'AIKENU= CUTNUT / *Barringtonia aff. edulis* Seem. / *B. edulis* Seem. / *B. neidenzuana* (Schum.) Kunth / *B. novae-hyberniae* Ltb. / *B. oblongifolia* Kunth / *B. procera* (Miers) Kunth. / *B. sp.* (DCRS 492)

JOINED, also called FEMALE JOINED and WILD-TREE, this tree looks almost like nut but the leaf is a bit rounded and a bit shortish and not very wide. Joined fruit is almost like nut but it looks a bit different because it is shortish and a bit curved. When we hammer the fruit it cracks into two shells surrounding the inside (kernel), that's why we call it joined.
○ This is a planted tree, we plant it like nut, everywhere. It grows plentifully in some places and in some places it grows crowded along wild-tree hills.
• We eat the fruit, it is like nut but the shell of joined-nut is stronger than nut proper and the inside is not cool like nut fruit but it is oily and really tasty. We make nut-pudding with the insides, we also flask them for smoking to smell smoky on a shelf, like nut.

• Joined and nut are equal to work with, not at all different. It is not suitable for building houses because it gets worm-eaten, we stake out boundaries with it, we fell it for fuel but it doesn't burn till day.
'ADO'A / 'ADO'A KINI / 'AIKWASI = JOINED / FEMALE JOINED / WILD-TREE / *Canarium salomonense* Burtt. ssp. (*Burseraceae*)

FALSE-JOINED, this tree gets really big, it looks almost like female joined (*ado'a kini / Canarium*). It bears fruits and if ripe they are black. While flowering it will not bear fruit.
○ This one is a wild tree, it grows in the lowlands and on the sea.
• The fruits of false-joined we don't eat because they don't have an inside like female joined.
• We use the trees as equivalent to female joined.
MALA'ADO'A = FALSE-JOINED / *Canarium harveyi* Seem. / *Haplolobus canarioides* Leenh. / *H. floribundus* (Schum.) Lamk. (*Burseraceae*)

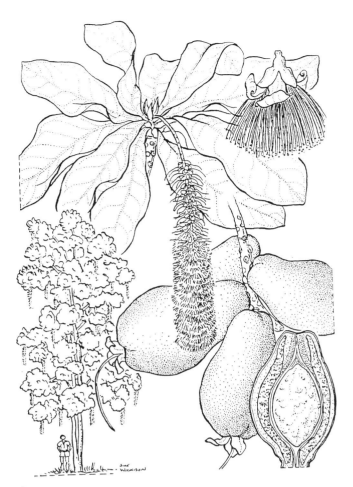

▲ *fala / cutnut*

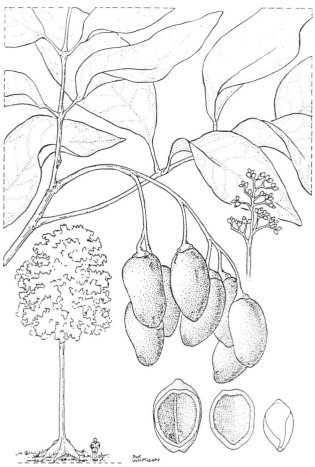

▲ *'ado'a / joined*

mala 'ado'a / false-joined ▶

ALITA, 'ai ne'e nonina meomeo'anga, rauna reba ka keta, takana kwao. Nia ke fungu, fa'irū ka di'ia ngali bore ma nia rebareba'a lala ma sa'erū ka molimoli'a. Nia to'o ana rō malita'irū kī.
ALITA saga, 'ai ne'e ke doe liu mala.
○   'Ai kwasi nini'a, nia ke bulao go'o 'i fafona asi.
ALITA FASIA nia kesi doe liu go'o, fa'irū ta'i doe ka liufia fuana ai kwasi.
○   Ki fasia fa'irū bulao kī 'i nonina fanoa kī fafona asi, ana ano oneone'a ma ano fenamae'a, ma ki fasia logo saena tolo.
•   Rō alita kī ta'ifau ki ni'i bolo go'o fa'inia ki sasia 'ania rū kī.
•   Fa'irū kī, ki 'uia di'ia ngali fuana 'anilana sa'erū kī. Ki okea go'o, noa'a kisi do'ofia, noa'a kisi saungia fuana kata di'ia ngali.

•   Saunga'i luma'a 'ania, noa'a kesi le'a liu go'o sulia ti'iti'ilana 'iri ngasi, nia ke suma'ala, nia bolo go'o fa'inia luma ni du'urū kī.
•   Bore ma doelana nia bolo fuana 'olelana 'ania rebarū kī.
•   Ki kwa'ia logo fuana so'i bore ma nia ke du'a maemaela go'o, nia kesi du'a kwasukwasu.
•   Ki gurā 'ania ti mata'inga.

ALMOND, the body of this tree is reddish, its leaf is wide and long and its flower is white. It bears, the fruit is like nut but it is wideish and the inside is rounded. It has two kinds.
True ALMOND, this tree is really big.
○   This one is a wild tree, it just grows on the sea.
PLANTED ALMOND is not very big and its fruit is a bit bigger than the fruit of the wild one.
○   We plant the growing fruits in home areas on the sea, on sandy ground and dead-coral ground, and we also plant it inland.
•   Both the almonds are equal for us to do things with.
•   The fruits we hammer like nut to eat the insides. We just eat them raw, we don't burn them and we don't pound them for nut-pudding like nut.
•   For house-building it is not very good because when small it is not strong, it becomes worm-eaten and is only suitable for cooking houses.
•   But when big it is suitable for cutting into planks.
•   We also fell it for fuel but it only burns dying, it doesn't burn flaming.
•   We cure some sickness with it.

ALITA = ALMOND / sea almond / indian almond / *Terminalia catappa* L. / *T. copelandii* Elmer / *T. samoensis* Rech.
ALITA FASIA = PLANTED ALMOND / *Terminalia kaernbachii* Warb. (*Combretaceae*)

▼ *alita / almond*

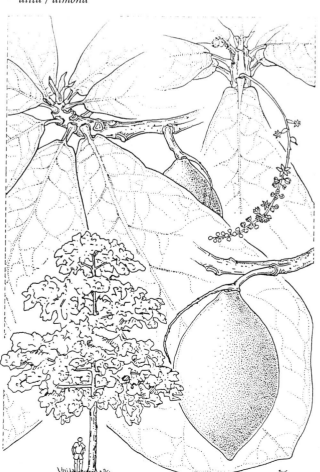

▼ *alita fasia / planted almond*

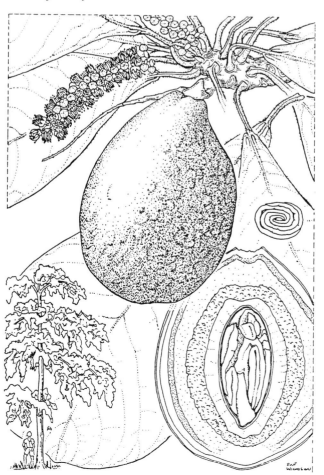

DAFO, 'ai ne'e kaida'i nia doe nia ke liufia 'ai kī ta'ifau. Ta'eta'ena te'e melamela'anga, ka baba'ula ka ngasi liu, reforefona ta'eta'ena ke a'efo talangwara'u. Rauna ketaketa ka sisili'a go'o.
- ○ Nia ke bulao go'o saena kula kunukunu'a kī ma saena ote kī.
- • Ki saunga'i luma 'ania fa'i 'ai raurau'a kī, ni'i sasabe'e ma ka gwalagwala'a.
- • Ki saunga'i iolo logo 'ania 'ai doe kī.

KAKO, ki saea logo 'ania SUA'ISALO, 'ai ne'e ke doe liu mala, 'ingata'irū gwalogwalo'a ke doe, rarana kesi doe liu go'o, nia ne'e ki saea 'ania sua'isalo. Nonina te'e lololia na ta'eta'ena ka te'e nemanema'a go'o, rauna sisimia ka mela, sūla te'e sakosakoa ma kesi fungufungula di'ia taba'a. Nia ke bulao ana fuana.
- ○ Nia ke bulao saena dukwasi, ana to'ona'oa ma tolo.
- • Ki saunga'i luma 'ania.
- • Nia totolia so'i sulia nia ke du'a 'ali'ali.
- • Ki kwaiguragura 'ania.

NULI, 'ai ne'e ke doe mala ma ka te'e keta mala, ki saea 'ania bobi nuli, nia ka di'ia logo dafo. Nonina mela ka dada goligolia, rauna di'ia mamufua.

- ○ Nia ke bulao nama sulia kafo doe kī, ka tasa ana kula oneone'a kī.
- • Ti'iti'ilana ki saunga'i luma 'ania .
- • Na 'ai doe ka bolo logo fuana 'olelana 'ania reba 'ai kī.
- • Ki kwa'ia logo fuana so'i.

'AMA, 'ai ne'e ke doe ka keta liu mala, akwasi kera'a bolo bore ma nia doe ana akwasi ma rauna mamata logo fa'asia. Nonina melamela'a ka goligoli'a, rarana babala'a, rauna ka ti'iti'i go'o. Nia ke bulao ana fa'irū kī. Nia ka to'oa fa'i ngali sulia nia ke aragwata ke ala faolu logo, di'i ki lisia rauna 'ama nia tegotego'a na'a 'i ano, fada 'ania ne'e fa'i ngali make na'a ma ka 'asia logo ne'e ke fotobulitai ki 'uia fa'i ngali.
　'Ama nia to'o ana rō malita'irū kī.
'AMA saga, ki saea logo 'ania 'AMA KAREFO, rauna ta'i raurau'a ka fisifisila go'o, lisilana ka te'e balabala'a. Ai kini nini'a, kaida'i nia taka na no'o kī ke saele'a, kira ke fiku ta'ifau fuana 'anilana fa'irū kī.

TERMINALIA, this tree when big exceeds all other trees. Its skin is brownish, thick and very strong, the scales of the skin fall off easily. The leaf is longish and narrow.
- ○ It only grows in swampy places and in the levels.
- • We build houses with the slender trees, they are straight and erect.
- • We also build canoes from the big trees.
DAFO = TERMINALIA /swamp oak / brown terminalia / *Terminalia brassii* Exell (*Combretaceae*)

KAKO, also called SPEARS-THE-SKY, this tree gets very big indeed, its main stem is erect and big and its branches are not very big, which is why we call it spears-the-sky. Its body is veined and its skin is quite thin, its leaves are narrow and brown, the sap is quite yellow and not wet, like gigantic (*taba'a / Astonia*). It grows from its fruit.
- ○ It grows in wilderness, in the lowland and inland.
- • We build houses with it.
- • It is fit for fuel because it burns quickly.
- • We cure with it.
KAKO / SUA'ISALO = *KAKO* / SPEARS-THE-SKY / *Terminalia calamansanai* (Bl.) Rolfe (*Combretaceae*)

ALBIZIA, this tree gets really big and quite tall, we call it albizia log, it is like terminalia (*dafo*). Its body is brown, smooth and wrinkled, its leaf is like securinega (*mamufua*).
- ○ It has to grow along big waters, especially in sandy places.
- • When small we build houses with it.
- • The big tree is also suitable for cutting into wooden planks.
- • We also fell it for fuel
NULI = ALBIZIA / *Albizia salomonensis* C.T.White (*Fabaceae*)

'AMA, this tree gets big and very tall indeed, with-ease (*akwasi / Rhus*) and it are similar but it is bigger than with-ease and the leaf is also different. The body is reddish and wrinkled, the branches are sheltering, the leaf is only small. It grows from its fruit. It marks the year because it sheds its leaves and sprouts anew, if we see *'ama* leaves shrivelled on the ground it means nuts are ripe and falling too, so there will be hard work hammering nuts.
　'Ama has two kinds.
True *'AMA*, also called SOFTWOOD *'AMA*, the leaf is slender and only narrow and it looks paleish. This is the female one, when it flowers the birds are happy and they all gather to eat the fruit.

'AMA FAU, ki saea logo 'ania 'AMA RODO, lisilana bolo logo fa'inia 'ama saga bore ma rauna go'o ne'e doe ka molimoli'a ma ka lia rorodo'a mala. Ai ngwane nini'a, bore ma nia ke fungu logo 'ania fa'irū ne'e gwagina di'i logo gwagi to'oma kī. Kaida'i ki tufua nia ngasi ka liufia 'ama karefo.

○ Nia ke bulao fa'asia fafona asi 'uana 'i tolo, nia 'oro saena to'ona'oa. Ki lia mala sulia 'i gwauna ua kī, nia keta ana 'ai kī, ka di'ia baola kī.

• Ti'iti'ilana ki saunga'i luma 'ania.
• Ti'iti'ilana ki aea logo ta'eta'ena ki rigoa fuana nalufilana kafo fuana kwa'ufia ma logo fuana sabangi kafo'a ma'i 'i luma.
• Ki ragi bae ana fuana susu'ilana babala 'i ngali kī ma luma kī.
• Na 'ai doe ki saunga'i iolo 'ania, nia ka bolo logo fuana 'olelana 'ania reba 'ai kī.
• Ki kwa'ia fuana so'i.
• Ki guragura logo 'ania.

SOLID *'AMA*, also called NIGHT *'AMA*, looks similar to true *'ama* but the leaf is rounded and it looks dark. This is the male one but it also bears fruit which has a pit like a *to'oma* (*Terminalia*) pit. When we chop it, it is hard, more so than softwood *'ama*.

○ It grows from on the sea to the inland and is plentiful in the lowland. We can see it along the hilltops, it is taller than other trees, like banyans (*baola / Ficus*).
• The small tree we build houses with.
• The small tree we also peel the skin from to make a cone to bail water for drinking and also for ducting water to the house.
• We strip bark-board from it for fixing down in nut shelters and houses.
• The big tree we make canoes from and it is also suitable for cutting into wooden planks.
• We fell it for fuel.
• We also cure with it.

'AMA = *'AMA* / swamp oak / *Terminalia microcarpa* Decne. / *T. aff. rubiginosa* Schum. / *T. complanta*. K Schum.
'AMA FAU / 'AMA RODO = SOLID *'AMA* / NIGHT *'AMA* / *Terminalia* Diels. / *T. rerei* Coode / *T. whitmorei* Coode (*Combretaceae*)

AKWASI, 'ai ne'e noa'a kesi doe liu go'o, nonina kwaokwao'anga, nia ke fungu, no'o akaaka'u kī ke 'ania fuana ma ngwasana. Ki saea 'ania akwasi sulia ne'e di'ia nia teo ma ka 'eke'eke na'a, karilana nia talangwara'u go'o ma nia ke foga saga go'o 'i sulia.

○ Nia ke bulao saena raku faolu, ana fafo 'i asi ma saena to'ona'oa, ka tasa saena tolo.
• Numa ke fanga, ta ma ki 'oia ma ki ra'e ki tikitikingia 'i ne'e ngwangarū kī ke 'asi'i 'i ki ngalia fuana 'anilana.
• Ngwasana fuana okolana lifana ngwae ke ngasi ma ka gwā bisibisi 'ala. Ki didia saena gwa'i oko, ki doalia 'ania bi'i ngwasa akwasi, ki fi'i alua ngwaia 'ania lifaka.
• 'Uli'uila ki do'ofia ki sungia 'ania ifu 'i fufula māna gwata kī 'i ne'e kira ke ra'o.

WITH-EASE, this tree doesn't get very big, its body is whiteish, it bears and cuscus eat the fruit and shoots. We call it with-ease because if it lies and has dried out, it will split easily and it will crack straight along.

○ It grows in the new shoots, on the sea and in the lowland, and especially in the inland.
• Caterpillars eat it so we pick them and we climb and shake it so the grubs fall and we can take them to eat.
• The shoot is for staining a person's teeth to become strong and shiny black. We powder a stain-stone and mix it with a tube of with-ease shoots and then put the mixture on our teeth.
• The bark we burn and singe the eyebrow hairs of pigs with it so they'll be tame.

AKWASI = WITH-EASE /island sumak / *Rhus taitensis* Guill. (*Anacardiaceae*)

'AFI'O, 'ai ne'e to'o ana malita'irū kī.

'AFI'O saga, ki saea logo 'ania KABIRAI, SA'AU, 'ai ne'e ti ai ke doe liu, nonina ka melamela'a, rauna ka te'e reba ka dokodoko go'o, takana meo. Nia ke fungu, fa'irū ka marako ma ka kwao, di'ia nia ke kwasā nia ke meo lala. Ti ai ne'e fungu 'ania fa'irū ketaketa'a kī, ki saea 'ania 'AFI'O NGWA-FILA, ti ai ne'e fa'irū kī ka molimoli'a ki saea 'ania 'AFI'O KO'OKO'O.

APPLE, this tree has several kinds.

APPLE proper, also called BUNCH and *SA'AU*, this tree sometimes gets very big, its body is brownish, its leaf is quite wide and shortish, its flower is red. It bears and the fruit is green and white but if it is ripe it is red. Some which fill with longish fruits we call CENTIPEDE APPLE, some with fruits which are rounded we call OWL APPLE.

▲ *akwasi / with-ease*

▲ *'afi'o / apple*

'Afi'o nia ke fungu nama ana kaida'i ana fa'i 'afi'o, ta'i fa'i fungu'a go'o ana fa'i ngali, ti kaida'i rō fa'i fungu'a. Sakwalo kī ke 'ania takana fa'inia logo fuana ana rodo, no'o lofolofo ke 'ania ana dangi. Nia ke bulao logo ana gwagirū.

○ 'Ai fasia nini'a, nia ke bulao ana kula kī sui te'e ana kunukunua go'o ne'e noa'a. Ki ngalia gwagirū ki fasia mala 'i nonina fanoa kī ma o'olā kī ma saena logo lalano.
• Kaida'i fuana ka make 'anilana le'a liu, ngela kī ma ngwae kī ogā liu.
• Noa'a kesi le'a fuana saunga'i'anga sulia nia ke fura 'ali'ali.
• Ki kwa'ia fuana so'i, nia ke du'a kwasukwasula.
• Ki gurā 'ania ti mata'inga.

'AFI'O BŪ nia di'ia logo 'afi'o saga bore ma 'afi'o ne'e kwasi lala.

○ Nia ke bulao go'o saena lalano.
• Ki 'ania fuana bore ma nia eoeo ana 'afi'o saga.

Apple always bears during the apple season, one bearing a year, sometimes two bearings. Bats eat the flower and also the fruit at night, birds eat them by day. It grows from the core.

○ This one is a planted tree, it grows in all places, only in swamps it will not. We take the core and plant it in the home area and gardens and also in the forest.
• When the fruit is ripe it is very good to eat, children and other people like it very much.
• It is not good for building because it rots quickly.
• We fell it for fuel, it burns flaming.
• We cure some sicknesses with it.

'AFI'O / KABIRA'I / SA'AU = APPLE / BUNCH / SA'A'U / Malay apple / mountain apple / *Eugenia malaccensis* L. (*Myrtaceae*)

SOUR APPLE is like normal apple, but this apple is wild.

○ It just grows in the forest.
• We eat the fruit but it is more acid than apple proper.

'AFI'O BŪ = SOUR APPLE

MALA'AFI'O, 'ai ne'e to'o mala ana ūlu malita'i 'ai kī, ūlu 'ai kī ta'ifau ni'i di'ia nama 'afi'o bore ma lisilani te'e matamata ma noa'a kisi 'ania fa'irū kī. Ta ai ne'e MALA'AFI'O saga, ta ai ne'e MALA-'AFI'O BALA, nonina te'e kwaokwao'a, ta ai ne'e MALA'AFI'O BORA, nonina meomeo'a ma rauna ka te'e meo logo.

○ Nia ke bulao ana kula kī ta'ifau, fa'asia fafona asi ka dao 'i tolo.
• Saunga'inga ma du'alana nia bolo logo fa'inia ti malita'i 'afi'o.
• Di'ia nia doe liu ka bolo logo fuana 'olelana 'ania reba 'ai kī.

RUFA ne'e 'ai doe liu mala, nonina ka te'e meo kwalakwala'a ma ka 'efo'efoa ma ka maomaoa. Nia to'o ana rararū 'oro kī, rauna molimoli'a ka ti'iti'i go'o. Nia ke fungu 'ania fa'irū molimolia ma kesi doe liu go'o ma ka marakoa, di'ia ne'e nike make ke meo ka 'asia ka teo na'a 'i ano ka fi'i gwā na'a. Di'ia nia fungu ma ka make ta ma tala uta doe ke to'o na'a 'i ke āfelanga'inia fuana 'uana saena asi 'i leleko ke fanga ana, ki saea 'ania āfetafa.

○ Nia ke bulao ana ano to'o ma sulia kafo kī, ka 'oro ana ti kula reba ote 'i 'aena kafo doe ne'e ki saea 'ania asirufurufa. Di'ia nia ke bulao saena to'ona'oa ma tolo logo, fada 'ania ngwae ka salinga'inia fa'asia kafo.
• 'Ai nunufi ne'e, ki salinga'inia fuana fasilana ana fulitua'a kī ma māna kafo kī ma nonina fanoa kī ma fulisango kī. Ki fasia logo ana biru ana ano kī, ka di'ia logo dingale, sulia lisilana le'a ka mamata fa'asia 'ai ana tolo kī.
• Ki gurā 'ania ti mata'inga.

'ASIRUFARUFA, 'ai ne'e lisilana ka di'ia logo rufa 'inoto'a bore ma nia ti'iti'i go'o.
○ Nia ke bulao saena asirufarufa, ta ne'e ki fa'asata 'uri ana.
• Ki saunga'i luma 'ania.
• Ki sabangi logo 'ania.

FALSE-APPLE, this tree really has three kinds, all three trees are very like apple but they look a bit different and we don't eat the fruits. One is FALSE-APPLE proper, one is PALE FALSE-APPLE, its body is a bit whiteish, and one is PURPLE FALSE-APPLE, its body is reddish and its leaf is also quite red.

○ It grows in all places, from on the sea to the inland.
• For building and burning it is the same as other kinds of apple.
• If it is big it is also suitable for cutting up into wooden planks.

MALA'AFI'O = FALSE-APPLE / *Eugenia* sp. / *Syzygium aqueum* (Burm.f.) Alston / *S. aff. synaptoneuron* Merr. & Perry (*Myrtaceae*)

MARSH is a really big tree, its body is brownish-red and scaly and smooth. It has many branches and its leaf is just small, its fruit is rounded and not very big. It bears fruit which are rounded and not very big and green, if they ripen they are red and fall and lie on the ground and are then black. If it bears and ripens, a heavy rain falls to wash the fruit towards the sea so *leleko*(fish) can eat it, and we call it a wash-out.

○ It grows on proper ground and along waters and is plentiful in some wide levels at the foot (mouth) of big waters, which we call saltmarsh. If it grows in the lowland or inland it means that someone has transferred it from the water.
• This is a shade tree, we transfer it for planting at rest-sites and water spouts and in home areas and dance-grounds. We also plant it on land boundaries, because it looks good and different from the trees of the inland.
• We cure some illnesses with it.

RUFA = MARSH / *Eugenia lauterbachii* (18730) / *E. tierneyana* Muell. / *Mearnsia salomonensis* C.T. White / *Syzygium leerneyanum* Muell. (*Myrtaceae*)

SALTMARSH, this tree looks like the important marsh (*rufa* / *Myrtaceae*) but it is just small.
○ It grows in saltmarsh, that's what we name it after.
• We build houses with it.
• We conduct (yam-vines) with it.

'ASIRUFARUFA = SALTMARSH / *Eugenia effusum* A. Gray / *Syzygium decipiens* (Koord. & Val.) Amsh. (*Myrtaceaea*)

MALARUFA, 'ai ne'e noa'a kesi doe liu go'o, nonina ta'i meomeo'a, lisilana rauna ma fa'irū kī te'e mamata logo fa'asia rufa. Nia ka fungu ka 'asi ma ka bulao ana fuana.

○   Nia ke bulao ana kunukunu'a, ka tasa saena ote lafa. •Ki labua 'ania sakali sulia nia ke birabira.
•   Ti'iti'ilana ki saunga'i luma 'ania.
•   Nia ke mae, ki kwa'ia fuana so'i.
•   Na 'ai doe ka bolo logo fuana 'olelana 'ania reba 'ai kī.

'AINIGAO, 'ai ne'e te'e doe mala, nonina ka sasabe'a ka le'a mala, na rauna sisili'a ma takana ka kwao ka ti'iti'i.

○   'Ai ne'e 'ai fasia fuana fa'akwangalana nonina fanoa kī. Ki salinga'inia logo fa'asia ti fanoa 'uana ti ma'e fanoa, saena tolo ma logo 'i fafona asi. Ti gwaunga'i ngwae kira fata 'uri 'ai ne'e ki salinga'i-nia fa'asia 'i Gao, kaida'i 'i na'o, ti ai 'iri ala fāfia.
•   Ki saunga'i rū 'ania di'ia ma'e kakata kī fa'inia logo ngingilo ma fa'i kuba kī.
•   Ki saunga'i luma 'ania.

FALSE-MARSH, this tree doesn't get very big, its body is a bit reddish, its leaf and fruit look a bit different from marsh (*rufa / Myrtaceae*). It bears (fruit) and they fall and it grows from its fruit.

○   It grows in swamp, especially in the levels.
•   We stake fences with it because it sprouts.
•   When small we build houses with it.
•   When dead we fell if for fuel.
•   The big tree is also suitable for cutting into wooden planks.

MALARUFA = FALSE-MARSH / *Metrosideros parviflora* C.T.White / *Eugenia buettneriana* Schum. / *E. effusa* A. Gray / *E. onesima* (Merr. & Perry) Whitmore / *E. tierneyana* Muell. (*Myrtaceae*)

TREE-OF-GAO, this tree gets really quite big, its body is good and straight, its leaf is narrow and its flower is white and small.

○   This tree is a tree planted to beautify the home area. We also transfer if from one home to another, in the inland and also on the sea. Some headmen (elders) say that we transferred this tree from Gao (Isabel) in former times, some disagree.
•   We make things with it like (betel) pestles and mortars and walking sticks.
•   We build houses with it.

'AINIGAO = TREE OF GAO / *Xanthestemon* sp. (*Myrtaceae*)

'ainigao / tree of Gao ▶

'AIBŪ, 'ai ne'e te'e doe, nonina ka gwā ma rauna marako ka te'e rebareba'a go'o, takana ka kwao ma fuana ka molimoli'a.
○ Nia ke bulao saena tolo ma saena to'ona'oa, bulaolana kesi 'oro liu go'o.
• Ki saunga'i luma 'ania.
• 'Ifirū sasala kī ki du'a logo 'ania, nia du'a maemaela go'o.

'AISARUFI, 'ai ne'e ke doe mala, nonina bulu, ngwasana meo.
○ Nia ke bulao ana kula kī ta'ifau, fa'asia fafona asi ka dao 'i tolo.
• Ti'iti'ilana ki saunga'i luma 'ania .
• Ki kwa'ia logo fuana so'i.
• Na 'ai doe ka bolo logo fuana 'olelana 'ania reba 'ai kī.

'O'A, 'ai ne'e ke te'e doe go'o, ta'eta'ena ka ta'i momote. Nia to'o ana rō malita'i 'o'a kī. 'O'A BULU ki saea logo 'ania 'O'A MEO, ngwasana meo, saena 'ai ka meo logo. 'O'A BALA, ki saea logo 'ania 'O'A MARAKO, ngwasana bala, saena 'ai ka bala logo.

○ Nia ke bulao ana masu'u sasala kī ma raku buru, ka 'oro saena to'ona'oa.
• Ki tufua diro kī ana fuana saunga'i luma'a.
• Ki sakali 'ania sulia kaida'i ki katanga'inia fa'i 'ai kī nia ke bulao logo.

'AISALINGA, 'ai ne'e ke doe mala, nonina te'e gwāgwa'anga ma nia ka ngasi. Rauna to'o ana alinga'irū kī 'aena rauna, ta ne'e ki fa'asata 'uri ana. Nia ke taka ka fungu logo, fa'irū molimoli'a nia kesi doe liu go'o.
○ Nia ke bulao saena tolo ma saena kaole ma fafona logo kafo kī.
• Ki saunga'i luma 'ania.
• Ki kwa'ia fuana so'i.

BŪ-TREE, this tree gets quite big, its body is black and its leaf is green and a bit wideish, its flower is white and its fruit is round.
○ It grows in the inland and in the lowland, it doesn't grow very plentifully.
• We build houses with it.
• We cook with the light logs, it just burns dying.
'AIBŪ = BŪ-TREE / *Diospyros ebenum Koen* (Ebenaceae) / *Eugenia buettneriana* Schum. / *E. onesima* (Merr. & Perry) Whitmore / *Syzgium aqueum* (Burm. f.) Alston (*Myrtaceae*)

SARUFI-TREE, this tree gets really big, its body is dark, its leaf-shoot is red.
○ It grows in all places, from on the sea to the inland.
• When small we build houses with it.
• We also fell it for fuel.
• The big tree is also suitable for cutting into wooden planks.
'AISARUFI = SARUFI-TREE / *Eugenia effusa* A.Gray (*Myrtaceaea*)

GLOCHIDION, this tree is quite big and its skin is a bit scratchy. There are two kinds of glochidion. DARK GLOCHIDION, also called RED GLOCHIDION, its shoot is red and the inside of the tree is also red. PALE GLOCHIDION, also called GREEN GLOCHIDION, its shoot is pale and the inside of the tree is also pale.
○ It grows in light forest and thick shoots, it is plentiful in the lowland.
• We chop posts of it for house-building.
• We fence with it because when we stake with the tree it will grow.
'O'A = GLOCHIDION / *Glochidion angulatum* C.B. Rob. / *G. arborescens* Bl. / *G. perakense* Hook. f. / *G. philippicum* (Cav.) C. B. Rob. / *G. aff. ramiflorum* J. R. & G. Forst. / *Antidesma polyanthum* Schum. & Ltb. (*Euphorbiaceae*)

TRANS-EAR-TREE, this tree gets really big, its body is darkish and it is strong. Its leaf has ears at the base of the leaf, that's why we name it thus. It flowers and bears, its fruit is rounded and not very big.
○ It grows in the inland and on clay and also on the waters.
• We build houses with it.
• We fell it for fuel.
'AISALINGA = TRANS-EAR-TREE / *Aporosa papuana* Pax & Hoffm. (*Euphorbiaceae*)

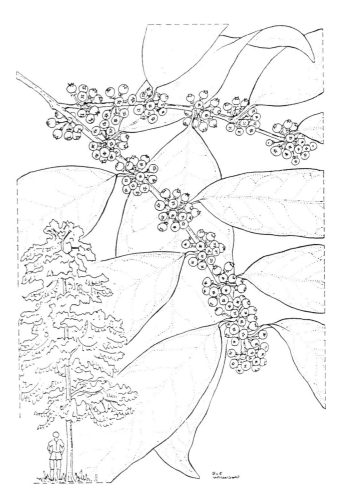

mamufua / securinega ▶

MAMUFUA, 'ai te'e doe ne'e, fa'i 'ai kī sasabe'a mala, ta'eta'ena te'e nemanema'a go'o, nia ka reforefo'a, rauna ketaketa'a ka sisili'a. Doelana ka 'ali'ali liu ma tufulana ka te'e ngwatobitobi'a.

○   Nia ka bulao go'o 'ana ana kula kī sui, bore ma tofungana tolo ne'e noa'a ana. Noa'a kesi 'oro liu, 'i nini'ari nia baru'a go'o.

•   Na 'ai ne'e le'a ka tasa ana 'ai kī sui sulia nia ngasi liu bore ma noa'a kisi saunga'inia 'ania rū kala'i kī sulia nia ke foga.

•   Ki saunga'i funu 'ania fuana saunga'i luma'a.

•   Ki tadilia logo 'ifirū kī fuana labulana 'ania bā noima foka gwata kī.

•   Ki sabangi logo 'ania fa'i 'ai ti'iti'i kī.

•   Na 'ai doe ki bongia logo 'ania kabara tolo kī.

•   Ki kwa'ia logo fuana so'i, nia kesi du'a dangi go'o.

SECURINEGA, this is quite a big tree, the tree is really straight, its skin is quite thin and it is scaly, its leaf is longish and narrow. It becomes big very quickly and it is quite soft to chop down.

○   It just grows in all places, but not in the central inland. It is not very plentiful and at present it is scarce.

•   This tree is the best of all trees because it is very strong, but we don't make carved things with it because it will crack.

•   We make posts with it for house-building.

•   We also trim the logs for staking pig barriers or pens.

•   We also conduct (yam-vines) with the small trees.

•   The big tree we also use as a foundation for local latrines.

•   We also fell it for fuel, it doesn't burn till day.

MAMUFUA = SECURINEGA / *Securinega flexuosa Muella. Arg. / Securinega samoana Croizat (Euphorbiaceae)*

'AISUBU, 'ai ne'e ke doe liu, nonina te'e kwao melamela'a, sūla tongatonga'a ka kwao. Nia ke fungu 'ania fa'irū kī ma fuana molimoli'a ka ti'iti'i go'o, nia ke bulao ana fuana.
○　Nia ke bulao saena to'ona'oa.
•　Ki saunga'i 'ania bore ma luma sasufi'i go'o.
•　Na 'ai doe ka bolo logo fuana 'olelana 'ania reba 'ai kī.
•　Ki gurā 'ania ti mata'inga.

FATA, ki saea logo 'ania FASA, 'ai ne'e ke doe liu mala, nonina kwao, nia kobakoba'a, rauna moli-moli'a ka marako, takana kwaokwao'anga, nia ke bulao ana fa'irū kī. Kaida'i fa'i fata nia mae ki saea 'ania fa'i akeake, boborū kī kesi fura, nia ngasi liu.
○　Nia ke bulao ana kula kī ta'ifau, fa'asia fafona asi ka dao 'i tolo ma saena logo kunukunua.
•　'Ai doe nia ngasi liu, ka le'a ka liufia 'ai kī fuana saunga'ilana rū kala'i di'ia dako, 'o'a, ngingi kata, fote, ma rū ne'e ki ogā ke teo tau kī.

•　'Ai ti'iti'i noa'a kesi bolo fa'inia saunga'ilana 'ania rū kala'i sulia nia girogiro liu, bore ma ki saunga'i luma 'ania.
•　Nia le'a logo fuana diro'a.
•　Nia totolia saunga'i iolo'anga logo sulia nia kesi fura 'ali'ali.
•　Kobakobana ki saunga'i kilafa 'ania.
•　Ki sabangi logo 'ania, ki labua 'ania sakali.

•　Ki kwa'ia logo fuana so'i, nia ke du'adangi ka onaona'a.
•　'Ai doe ki olea 'ania reba 'ai kī.

'AIULUULU, 'ai ne'e doe liu mala, nia di'ia logo fata bore ma rarana ma rauna ka uluulu'a lala. Takana kwao, nia ke bulao ana takana.
○　Nia ke bulao saena tolo.
•　Na 'ai ti'iti'i kī ki saunga'i luma 'ania.
•　Ki kwa'ia logo fuana so'i.

ARAKOKO, 'ai ne'e ke doe liu mala, nonina kwao, saena bore kwao logo, rauna reba ka marako, burina ra'irū kī kwao. Nia ke bulao ana fingirū.

○　Nia ke bulao 'i fafona asi fa'inia saena to'ona'oa.
•　Ti'iti'ilana ki saunga'i luma 'ania.
•　Na 'ai doe ki filia mala fuana saunga'i iolo-'anga sulia nia sasala go'o, ka mabe, noa'a nia kesi foga.

PIMELEODENDRON-TREE, this tree gets very big, its body is a bit white-brownish, its sap is sticky and white. It bears fruit and the fruit is rounded and small, it grows from its fruit.
○　It grows in the lowlands.
•　We build with it, but just smoky houses.
•　The big tree is suitable for cutting into wooden planks.
•　We cure some illnesses with it.
'AISUBU = PIMELEODENDRON-TREE / *Pimeleodendron amboinicum* Hassk. (*Euphorbiaceae*)

VITEX, this tree gets very big indeed, its body is white, it is buttressed, its leaf is rounded and green, its flower is whiteish and it grows from its fruits. When the vitex tree dies we call it an *akeake*, the logs won't rot and it is very strong.
○　It grows in all places, from on the sea to the inland and also in swamp.
•　The big tree is very strong and better than other trees for making carved things like bowls, gongs, pudding-slicers, paddles and things we want to be long-lasting.
•　The small tree is not suitable for making carved things from because it is too tender, but we build houses with it.
•　It is also good for posts.
•　It is ideal for canoe-building too because it won't rot quickly.
•　The buttresses we make boards from.
•　We conduct (yam-vines) with it and stake fences with it.
•　We also fell it for fuel, it burns till day with embers.
•　The big tree we cut into wooden planks.
FATA / FASA = VITEX / *Vitex cofassus* Reinw. ex Bl. (*Verbenaceae*)

BUSHY-TREE, this tree gets very big indeed, it is like vitex (*fata*) but its branches and leaves are bushy. Its flower is white, it grows from its flower.
○　It grows in the inland.
•　The small tree we build houses with.
•　We also fell it for fuel.
'AIULUULU =BUSHY-TREE / *Vitex cofassus* Reinw. ex Bl. (*Verbenaceae*)

GMELINA, this tree gets really very big, its body is white and even its inside is white, its leaf is wide and green and the back of the leaf is white. It grows from bunches (of fruit).
○　It grows on the sea as well as in the lowland.

•　When small we build houses with it.
•　The big tree we choose for canoe-building because it is light and flexible and won't crack.

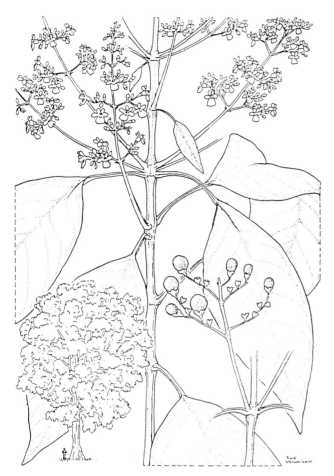

▲ *fata / vitex*

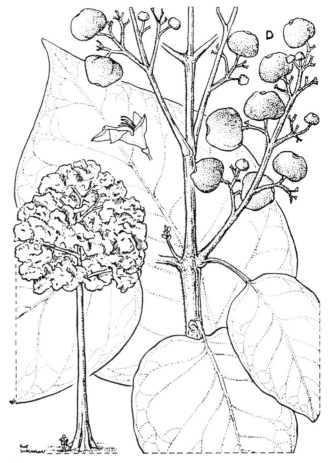

▲ *arakoko / gmelina*

- Ki kwa'ia fuana so'i.
- Na 'ai doe ka bolo logo fuana 'olelana 'ania reba 'ai kī.

A'ASA ne'e 'ai doe, lisilana karangi ka di'ia arakoko bore ma rauna a'asa nia kwaokwao'anga lala. Taka-na ka kwao, nia fungu 'ania fa'irū molimoli'a kī.
- Nia ke bulao fa'asia fafona asi 'uana 'i tolo, ana kula gwa'i kwaru'a kī ma ana kula kunukunu'a. Nia ke bulao ka tasa ana ti kula bore ma nia kesi 'oro liu go'o.
- Ti'iti'ilana ki saunga'i luma 'ania, noa'a kesi le'a dangalu sulia nia ke te'e suma'ala.
- Na 'ai doe ki saunga'i 'ania iolo sulia nonina ka sagasaga'a ka doe.
- Nia ka bolo logo fuana 'olelana 'ania reba 'ai kī.

- Ki kwa'ia logo fuana so'i, du'urū'a 'ania a'asa ne'e le'a liu sulia nia du'a sarafa'i ma ka onaona la'a bore ma nia kesi du'a dangi go'o.

- We fell it for fuel.
- The big tree is also suitable for cutting into wooden planks.

ARAKOKO = GMELINA / white beech / *Gmelina moluccana* (Bl.) Baker (*Verbenaceae*)

ENDOSPERMUM is a big tree, it looks almost like gmelina (*arakoko*) but endospermum leaf is whiteish. Its flower is white and it bears rounded fruit.
- It grows from on the sea to the inland, in rocky places and swampy places. It grows especially in some places but it is not very plentiful.

- When small we build houses with it, it is not particularly good because it gets worm-eaten.
- The big tree we make into canoes because it is straightish and big.
- It is also suitable for cutting into wooden planks.
- We also fell it for fuel, burning with *'a'asa* is very good because it burns slowly and with embers, but it doesn't burn till day.

A'ASA =ENDOSPERMUM cheesewood / milkwood / *Endospermum medullosum L.S.Sm.* (*Euphorbiaceae*)

FELOFELO, 'ai ne'e ke doe liu mala, nonina melamela'anga, rauna te'e ketaketa'a. Nia ke fungu ka bulao ana fuana.
○   Nia ke bulao ana kula kaole'a ki ne'e saena logo tolo kī noima 'i fafona asi kī bore 'ani.
•   Ki saunga'i 'ania rū di'ia ka'ika'ina akisi ma fa'i kuba ma alafolo kī.
•   Ti'iti'ilana ki saunga'i luma logo 'ania.
•   Ki du'a logo 'ania.

MALADALA ne'e 'ai doe mala, nonina kwao-kwao'anga, rauna ka sisili'a ka keta, fuana ti'iti'i.

○   Nia ke bulao 'i tolo ana ano to'o ma gwa'i kwaru logo bore ma saena kunukunu'a ne'e noa'a. Nia kesi 'oro liu go'o.
•   Ti'iti'ilana ki saunga'i luma 'ania.
•   Ki kwa'ia fuana so'i.
•   Na 'ai doe ka bolo logo fuana 'olelana 'ania reba 'ai kī.
•   Nia 'inoto'a fuana guragura'ana, di'ia nia doe ki gurā 'ania du'adu'a atokilu kī ma kū logo. Di'ia ki tufua o'olā nia ābu fuana tufulana, ta ne'e ki saea 'ania maladala.

'AIKAME, 'ai ne'e ke doe liu mala ma ka gwalo-gwalo'a, rauna keta mala. Ta'eta'ena nia ona ka ngarangara'a ka di'ia nonina kame kī. Kaida'i kame ke tafi fa'asia kui ke ra'e sulia, nia 'afita'i liu fuana kui ke ra'e sulia ma ka saungia. Ta ne'e ki fa'asata 'uri ana.
○   'Ai ana dukwasi nini'a, nia ke bulao ana to'ona'oa ma fafona asi.
•   Noa'a kisi saunga'i luma 'ania sulia nia ke suma'ala ma ka fura 'ali'ali.
•   Tufulana ngasi ka te'e ngwasikisikila.
•   Nia le'a fuana so'i, nia du'a kwasukwasu bore ma nia kesi du'a dangi.

KWANASIA, 'ai ne'e ke doe mala, Nonina ka kwao rafurafu'anga nia kusi'a, rauna marako, ilina ra'i rau kī raforafoa.
○   Nia ke bulao ana fa'i ua kī saena fafona asi ma to'ona'oa ma saena logo tolo.
•   Na numa kī ke 'ania rauna ma ki 'oia ki 'ania.
•   Ti'iti'ilana ki saunga'i luma 'ania.
•   Ki kwa'ia logo fuana so'i.

TEYSMANNIODENDRON, this tree gets very big indeed, its body is brownish, its leaf is a bit longish. It bears and grows from its fruit.
○   It grows in clay places, whether they are on the sea or in the inland.
•   We make things with it like axe handles and walking sticks and deflector-clubs.
•   When small we also build houses with it.
•   We also burn with it (as fuel).
FELOFELO =TEYSMANNIODENDRON / *Teijsmanniodendron ahernianum (*Merr.) Bakh. (*Verbenaceae*)

DISREGARD is a really big tree, its body is whiteish, its leaf is narrow and long, its fruit is small.
○   It grows in the inland, whether in proper ground or rocks, but not in swamp. It is not very plentiful.
•   When small we build houses with it.
•   We fell it for fuel.
•   The big tree is also suitable for cutting into wooden planks.
•   It is important for curing, if it is big we cure ulcerous sores with it and also leprosy. If we chop a garden it is tabu to chop it down, that's why we call it disregarded.
MALADALA = DISREGARD / *Gmelina lepidota* Scheff. (*Verbenaceae*)

MONITOR-TREE, this tree gets very big indeed and is erect and branchless, its leaf is really long. Its skin is tough and prickly like the body of a monitor (lizard). When a monitor flees from a dog, it climbs it and it is very difficult for the dog to climb it and kill it. That's why we name it thus.
○   This is a tree of the wilderness, it grows in the lowland and on the sea.
•   We don't build houses with it because it becomes worm-eaten and rots quickly.
•   It is hard to chop and the chips fly a bit.
•   It is good for fuel, it burns flaming but it won't burn till day.
'AIKAME = MONITOR-TREE / *Putranjiva roxburghii* Wall. (*Euphorbiaceae*) / *Ziayphus angustifolius* Harms (*Rhamnaceae*)

ALPHITONIA, this tree gets really big, its body is white with a greyish bloom, its leaf is green and the back of the leaf has a bloom.
○   It grows on hills on the sea and lowland and also in the inland.
•   Grubs eat the leaves and we pick and eat them.
•   When young we build houses with it.
•   We also fell it for fuel.
KWANASIA = ALPHITONIA / *Alphitonia incana* (Roxb.) T.&B. ex Kurz / *A. philippinensis* Braid. (*Rhamnaceae*)

'AIKUSI, 'ai ne'e ke doe liu mala, nonina rafurafu'a. Rauna ka sisili'a, saena ra'irū ka marako. Īla ra'irū ka rafurafu'a ka di'ia nonina fa'i no'o ne'e ki saea 'ania kusi, ta ne'e ki fa'asata 'uri ana. Fa'irū kī ti'iti'i ka bababa'a, magarū ti'iti'i miga kī ni'i marako.

- Nia ke bulao 'i fafona asi ma ana to'ona'oa ma saena logo tolo.
- Ti'iti'ilana ki saunga'i luma 'ania .
- Nia ka le'a fuana so'i ki du'a 'ania.

SARUFI, ta sata NGWANGWAOGALE'A, ne'e 'ai doe mala, nonina reforefo'a ka melamela'a, rauna molimoli'a ka marako.

- Nia ke bulao go'o saena tofungana tolo.
- Na rauna le'a fuana rarafono'anga 'usia 'ai ni fali'a 'i ke fa'agwaria ma ka olita'inia ka saungia ngwae fu saungwae 'ania. Nia ne'e asoa sui ki alua 'i nonika.
- 'I na'o ma'i ngwae kī ke alua rō ra'irū noima ūlu ra'irū'anga fonea na'ofada ma latoda ana kaida'i ana maoma kī, kira ke 'abisia uli 'ai kī ana fo'osae 'i ke fa'agwaria manatana ngwae ne'e ogata'a fuaka kī 'i kira ke ogale'a fuaka. Nia ne'e 'ai ne'e ki saea 'ania ngwangwaogale'a.
- Kaida'i fataābu ke koria gwata ka unuunulia nia ke do'ofia 'ania uli sarufi kī 'i ke kwatea aroaro'anga ma fo'osi nia ka ngwangwane'a.

- Na 'afe 'i na'o kī kira sofonga'inia na'ofada 'ania 'aba la'ua, kaida'i kira siu kira ke 'abisia lala uli sarufi kī.
- Ki saunga'i logo 'ania.
- Ki kwa'ia logo fuana so'i.

'AIKA'O, 'ai ne'e ke doe, itanga'irū ka sasabe'a ka sagasaga ka gwalogwalo'a mala, ta ne'e ki fa'asata sulia ka'o. Rauna ka ketaketa'a, fa'irū kī ka moli-moli'a ma ka marako, nia ke bulao ana fa'irū kī.

- 'Ai ana raku faolu ne'e, nia ke bulao nama 'i fafona asi ma saena to'ona'oa, noa'a nia kesi 'oro liu go'o.
- Ti'iti'ilana ki saunga'i luma 'ania sulia nia sasabe'a bore ma noa'a nia kesi le'a liu go'o sulia di'ia nia isila nia ke fura 'ali'ali.
- Ki kwa'ia fuana so'i.

I-CAN'T-TREE, this tree gets very big indeed, its body has a bloom, its leaf is narrow and the front of the leaf is green. The back of the leaf has a bloom like the body of the bird we call I-can't (*kusi* / greybird), that's why we name it thus. The fruit is small and flat, the seeds are tiny and green.

- It grows on the sea and lowland and also in the inland.
- When small we build houses with it.
- It is good for fuel to burn with.

'AIKUSI = I-CAN'T-TREE / *Cryptocarya alleniana* C.T.White / *C. mackinnoniana* Muell. / *C. medicinalis* C.T.White (*Lauraceae*)

LITSEA, also named GOODWILL-EASER, is a really big tree, its body has a bloom and is brownish, its leaf is rounded and green.

- It only grows in the central inland.
- The leaf is good for putting a block against damaging tree-magic to cool it and return it to kill the person who would kill with it. So every day we'd put it on our bodies.
- Formerly men would put two or three leaves to shut off their fronts and genitals during festivals, they wore fronds of the tree in their girdles to cool the thoughts of men who ill-wished them so they'd wish them well. That's why this tree is called goodwill-easer.
- When a tabu-speaker (priest) scraped a pig and singed (the bristles) he would burn it with litsea fronds to bring peace and make his prayers easy.
- Wives formerly hid their fronts with cloth, but when they bathed they wore litsea fronds instead.
- We also build with it.
- We also fell it for fuel.

SARUFI / NGWANGWAOGALE'A = LITSEA / GOODWILL-EASER / *Litsea alba* Kost. / *L. chysoneura* Kost. / *L. domarensis* Schmidt. / *L. griseo-sericea* Kost. / *L. ramiflorus* Kost. / *L. subcordata* Kost. / *L. subsessilis* Kost. / *L. whiteana* C.K. Allen / *Cryptocarya medicinalis* C.T. White (*Lauraceae*)

BAMBOO-TREE , this tree gets big, the trunk is smooth and straight and erect, that's why we name it after bamboo. Its leaf is longish, the fruit is rounded and green and it grows from the fruit.

- This is a tree of the new shoots, it grows on the sea and in the inland, it is not very plentiful.

- When small we build houses with it because it is straight but it is not very good because if it is wet it rots quickly.
- We fell it for fuel.

'AIKA'O = BAMBOO TREE / *Xylopia papuana* Diels (*Annonaceae*)

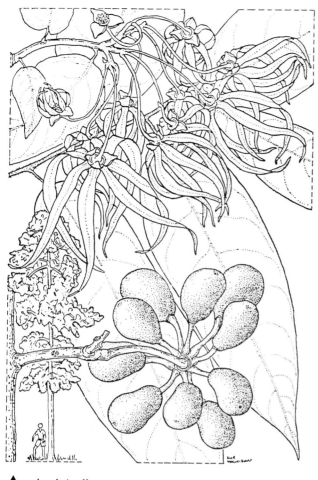

▲ *sa'osa'o / yellow*

▲ *'ailali / kidney tree*

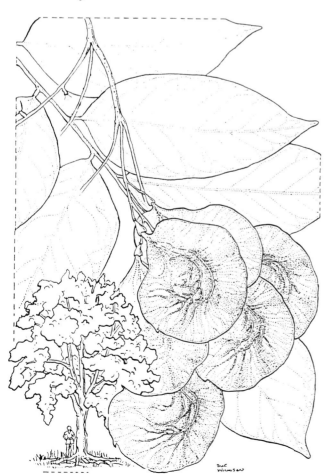

◄ *liki / pterocarpus*

SA'OSA'O, 'ai ne'e ke te'e doe mala, nonina gwagwā'a, rarana ka ti'iti'i, rauna ka ketaketa'a. Ki saea 'ania sa'osa'o sulia takana sakosako'a, ma ka moko le'a liu. Fuana ka marako ka molimoli'a.
- ○ Nia ke bulao fa'asia fafona asi 'uana 'i tolo.
- • Ki saunga'i luma 'ania, bore ma nia bolo go'o fa'inia luma sasufi'i ma babala kī.
- • Noa'a kisi 'idufa'i du'a 'ania bore ma di'ia kula 'ai 'ato ana ki du'a logo 'ania sulia nia le'a logo fuana so'i.
- • Ūluna ki laungia 'ania nonika sulia nia mokole'a.
- • Ki guragura logo 'ania.

'AILALI, 'ai ne'e ke doe mala, nonina gwagwā'a, rauna keta ka reba ka marako, ka maomao'a ma ka nura. Nia ke fungu, fa'irū kī molimoli'a ka rereba'a di'ia fa'i lalina karai, ka marako, kaida'i nia maua nia ta'i sakosako'a.
- ○ Nia ke bulao saena kunu ko'a ma fafona kafo kī.
- • Ki 'ania fuana. Ki do'ofia saena mafula, ki fi'i 'uia lasirū di'ia ngali. 'Anilana di'ia ngali.
- • Ki kwa'ia fuana so'i.
- • Ki guragura 'ania kwatea ngwae ke ngasingasi'a.

LIKI, 'ai ne'e ke doe liu mala, nonina kwaokwao'a, rauna te'e dokodoko, gwauna ra'irū ta'i raku. Nia ke fungu 'ania fa'irū ti'iti'i go'o, nia bulao ana rarana fa'inia fuana.
- ○ Nia ke bulao ka 'oro liu ana kula kī ta'ifau, fa'asia fafona asi 'uana 'i tolo, ka tasa 'i ninimana su'u kī.
- • Ti'iti'ilana ki saunga'i luma 'ania, nia ngasi liu ka di'ia gwarogwaro.
- • Ki saunga'i iolo 'ania boborū doe.
- • Ki tadilia fuana labulana 'ania sakali sulia nia ke birabira ma ka ngasi.
- • Ki kwa'ia logo fuana so'i.
- • Na 'ai doe ka bolo logo fuana 'olelana 'ania reba 'ai kī.

YELLOW, this tree gets really quite big, its body is blackish, its branches are small, its leaf is longish. We call it yellow because its flower is yellow, and it smells very good. Its fruit is green and rounded.
- ○ It grows from on the sea to the inland.
- • We build houses with it, but it is just suitable for smoky houses and shelters.
- • We don't usually burn with it but in a place where trees are hard to get we burn with it because it is quite good for fuel.
- • Its fronds we decorate our bodies with because it smells good.
- • We also cure with it.

SA'OSA'O = YELLOW / ylang-ylang / perfume tree / *Cananga odorata* (Lamk.) Hook.f. & Thoms. (*Annonaceae*)

KIDNEY-TREE, this tree gets really big, its body is blackish, its leaf is long and wide and green, smooth and shiny. It bears and the fruit is rounded and wide like a chicken's kidney and green, and when mature it is a bit yellow.
- ○ It grows in scraping swamps and on waters.

- • We eat the fruit. We burn it in the fire and hammer the shell, like nut. To eat it is like nut.
- • We fell it for fuel.
- • We cure with it to make a person strong.

'AILALI = KIDNEY-TREE / polynesian chestnut / tahitian chestnut / *Inocarpus fagiferus* (Park.) Fosb. (*Fabaceae*)

PTEROCARPUS, this tree gets very big indeed, its body is whiteish, its leaf is quite shortish, the top of the leaf is a bit pointed. It bears small fruit and it grows from its branch as well as its fruit.
- ○ It grows very plentifully in all places, from on the sea to the inland, especially beside inlets.

- • When small we build houses with it, it is very strong like calophyllum (*gwarogwaro*).
- • We build canoes with the big logs.
- • We trim it for staking fences because it sprouts and is strong.
- • We fell it for fuel.
- • The big tree is also suitable for cutting into wooden planks.

LIKI = PTEROCARPUS / new guinea rosewood / bluewater / sang dragon / padaouk / *Pterocarpus indicus* Willd. (*Fabaceae*)

'AININIU, 'ai ne'e ke doe liu mala ma ka keta mala, nonina ka fulafula'a ka te'e gwāgwā'a, takana ka 'afu'afu'a go'o ka alua na'a fa'irū kī, go'o ofiofirū ka 'asi go'o fa'irū ni'i make. Kaida'i fa'irū nia make, lisilana sakosako'a di'ia logo fingi niniu kī, ta ne'e ki fa'asata sulia niniu.
- ○ Nia ke bulao saena kunukunua ma ana ano 'eke'eke logo, ana to'ona'oa ma saena tolo.
- • Ki saunga'i luma 'ania.
- • Ki kwa'ia logo fuana so'i.
- • Na 'ai doe ka bolo logo fuana 'olelana 'ania reba 'ai kī.

KAKALA'A, 'ai ne'e doe mala, nia keta ka saga, nonina bulu, rauna ketaketa'a ka sisili'a go'o, ka mela ma burina ra'irū kī ka kwaokwao'anga, fuana molimoli'a ka marako. Nia ka fungu 'ania fa'irū kī, nia ke bulao ana fuana. 'Ai ne'e noa'a kesi ngasi go'o nia ngwara'u go'o.
- ○ Nia ke bulao ana dukwasi.
- • Ki saunga'i luma 'ania.
- • Ki kwa'ia fuana so'i.

'ASAI ne'e 'ai doe mala, rauna marako, fuana ka ta'i rebareba'a ka marako, kaida'i ni'i make ka sakosako'anga. Nia ke bulao ana gwagirū. Nia to'o ana rō malita'irū kī. 'ASAI TOLO, rū kwasi nini'a, 'ASAI FAKA, rū fasia lala.
- ○ 'Asai tolo, nia ke bulao saena to'ona'oa. 'Asai faka, ki fasia 'i nonina fanoa ana ta kula bore 'ana, ma di'ia fa'i no'o kī laua fa'irū kī saena masu'u, ma ni'i ke bulao ka kwasi na'a.
- • Kaida'i fuana ke ngeso 'anilana asila liu.
- • Ki saunga'i 'ania 'o'a kī.
- • Noa'a kisi saunga'i luma 'ania si ne'e nia ngwara'u.
- • Ki kwa'ia fuana so'i.
- • Na 'ai doe ka bolo logo fuana 'olelana 'ania rebarū kī.

MALA'ASAI, 'ai ne'e lisilana di'ia nama 'asai bore ma kala fa'irū kī fuana ta'i raurau'a go'o ka 'iri di'ia la'u 'asai, noa'a kisi 'ania si ne'e nia'a mamala 'asai lala.
- ○ Nia ke bulao saena to'ona'oa.
- • Ki saunga'i luma 'ania.
- • Na 'ai doe ka bolo logo fuana 'olelana 'ania reba 'ai kī.

PALM-TREE, this tree gets very big and tall indeed, its body is dusty and quite blackish, its flower is covered and it sets fruit, then the sheath falls and the fruit is ripe. When the fruit is ripe it looks yellow like a palm bunch, that's why we call it after palm (*niniu / Gulubia*).
- ○ It grows in swamp and on dry ground too, in the lowland and in the inland.
- • We build houses with it.
- • We also fell it for fuel.
- • The big tree is also suitable for cutting into wooden planks.

'AININIU = PALM-TREE / *Horsfieldia irya* (Gaertn.) Warb. / *H. novo-guineensis* Warb. / *H. palauensis* Kaneh / *H. whitmoreii* Sinclair / *Myristica paleuensis* Kaneh. (*Myristicaceae*)

NUTMEG, this tree is really big, it is tall and straight, its body is dark, its leaf is longish and narrow, it is brown and behind the leaf is whiteish, its fruit is rounded and green. It bears fruit and it grows from its fruit. This tree is not strong, it is just soft.
- ○ It grows in wilderness.
- • We build houses with it.
- • We fell it for fuel.

KAKALA'A = NUTMEG / *Myristica fatua* var. papuana Houtt. / *M. hollrungii* Warb. / *M. insipida* R.Br. / *M. kajewski* A.C.Sm. / *M. petiolata* A.C. Smith / *M. schlenitzii* Engl. (*Myristicaceae*)

MANGO is a really big tree, its leaf is green, its fruit wideish and green and when ripe they are yellow. It grows from the core. It has two kinds. LOCAL (inland) MANGO is wild but FOREIGN MANGO is planted.
- ○ Local mango grows in the lowland. Foreign mango we plant about the home and in any place at all, and if the birds snatch the fruit off into the forest it will grow wild.
- • When the fruit is ripe it is very sweet to eat.
- • We make gongs from it.
- • We don't build houses with it as it is soft.

- • We fell it for fuel.
- • The big tree is suitable for cutting into planks.

'ASAI = MANGO / *Mangifera indica* L. / *M. minor* Bl. (*Anacardiaceae*)

FALSE-MANGO, this tree looks just like mango (*'asai*) but with little fruits, the fruits are a bit slender, unlike mango, and we don't eat them as it is a false mango.
- ○ It grows in the lowland.
- • We build houses with it.
- • The big tree is also suitable for cutting into wooden planks.

MALA'ASAI = FALSE MANGO / *Mangifera mucronulata* Bl. (*Anacardiaceae*)

'aio / acid ▶

'AIO, 'ai ne'e doe liu mala, nonina melamela'anga, rauna ka fisifisi'a ka marako. Nia ke fungu, fa'irū kī molimoli'a ka doe, kaida'i ni'i ke make fa'irū kī ke sakosako'a.
○ Nia ke bulao saena to'ona'oa. Ti ai ki fasi'i, ti ai ni'i bulao kwasi lala.
• Ki 'ania fa'irū, 'anilana asila liu ma ka eoeo, ta ne'e ki fa'asata 'uri ana. 'Afe ina kī kira ogā liua 'anilana.
• Noa'a kisi saunga'i luma 'ania ma kisi kwa'ia fuana so'i, sulia 'aio rū fuana 'anilana, la'u ma fa'i 'ai ti'iti'i kī ni'i ngwara'u liu kesi bolo fa'inia saunga'i luma'a.
• Bore ma na 'aio doe kwasi ka bolo fa'inia 'olelana 'ania reba 'ai kī.

ACID, this tree is very big indeed, its body is brownish, its leaf is thin and green. It bears and the fruit are rounded and green, and when they are ripe the fruit are yellow.
○ It grows in the lowland. Some we plant and some grow wild.
• We eat the fruit, it is very sweet to eat and acid, that's why we name it thus. Pregnant women very much like to eat it.
• We don't build houses with it and we don't fell it for fuel, because acid is for eating, and also the small trees are very soft and not suitable for building houses.
• But the big wild acid is suitable for cutting into wooden planks.

'AIO = ACID / hog plum / polynesian plum / wild apple / otaheiti apple / golden apple / *Spondias cyatherea* Sonn. / *S.* Sol. ex Park. (*Anacardiaceae*)

KWAILASI, 'ai ne'e ke doe, nonina kwaokwao'a, rauna ka doe ka reba mala ma ka keta, takana kwao, nia ke to'o ana magarū ti'iti'i kī ma ka gwā logo. Di'ia ki tufua kwaikwaina ka āfe ka gwā bore ma nia ke lofo'ia noni ngwae ka du'a di'ia logo ne'e mafula milia ngwae ka du'a.

POTENT-WATER, this tree gets big, its body is whiteish, its leaf is big and really wide and long, its flower is white and it has seeds which are small and black too. If we chop it, liquid (sap) flows black and if it flies onto a person's body it burns like fire scorching the person and burning.

○ Nia ke bulao fa'asia fafona asi 'uana 'i tolo, noa'a nia kesi 'oro liu go'o.
• Di'ia nia ke mae mala safao kī ke fanga 'i nonina bore noa'a kisi tufu 'uana fuana 'anilana sulia sūla ne'e ta'a.
• Nia ta'a fuana saunga'inga ma du'urū'a.

○ It grows from on the sea to the inland, it is not very plentiful.
• If has died *safao*(grubs) eat the body but we don't chop them out to eat because the sap is bad.
• It is bad for building and burning.
KWAILASI = POTENT-WATER / *Semecarpus brachystachys* Merr.& Perry / *S. forstenii* Bl. (*Anacardiaceae*)

'AIRADE, 'ai ne'e ke doe mala, nonina ka mela-mela'a, rauna ketaketa'a ka marako. Nia ke taka ka fingifingi'a sulia nonina ka leka sulia rarana ma 'itangana. Takana ka kwao, mokofana ta'i moko fifī. Di'ia ki tufua ta'ta'ena nia ke moko ta'a ka di'ia logo mokofana ngwae ne'e kesi siu ma'udi, ta ne'e ki saea 'ania 'airade. Kaida'i ngwae mokofana ta'a liu, ki saea 'ania nia moko di'ia 'airade kī.
○ Nia ke bulao 'i fafona asi ma saena tolo ana ta kula bore 'ana.
• Ki tufua diro kī ana fuana saunga'i luma'a sulia nia ngasi.
• Ki kwa'ia logo fuana so'i.
• Na 'ai doe ka bolo logo fuana 'olelana 'ania reba 'ai kī.

STINK-TREE, this tree gets really big, its body is brownish, its leaf is longish and green. It flowers in bunches along its body from its branches to its trunk. Its flower is white, its scent smells quite intense. If we chop its bark it smells bad, like the smell of a man who is unwilling to bathe, that's why we call it stink-tree. When a man smells very bad, we say he smells like stink-tree.
○ It grows on the sea and in the inland in any place at all.
• We chop posts from it for house-building because it is strong.
• We also fell it for fuel.
• The big tree is also suitable for cutting into wooden planks.
'AIRADE = STINK-TREE / *Aphanamixis polystachya* (Wall.) Park. / *Dysoxylum cauliflorum* Hiern. / *D. caulostachyum* Miq. / *D. gaudichaudianum* (Juss.) Miq. / *D. mollisimum* Bl. ssp. molle (Miq.) Mabb./ *D. parasticum* (Osbck) Kost. / *D.* aff. *randianum* Merr.& Perry / *D. variabile* Harms. (*Meliaceae*)

LALATO, ki saea logo 'ania LATOA, 'ai ne'e ke doe liu mala, nonina fa'i rufa'a, ka meomeo'a. Nia ke fungu ana gwangona ulirū, fuana ka moli-moli'a ka daukulukulu ka doe ana 'ai kī ta'ifau, ki saea 'ania nia di'ia logo farufaruna ngwae. Nia bulao ana fuana.
○ Nia ke bulao sulia su'u kī ma fafona asi ma saena kunu ko'a kī.
• Ti'iti'ilana ki saunga'i luma 'ania.
• Ki kwa'ia logo fuana so'i.

GENITALS, this tree gets very big indeed, its body is like a marsh tree (*rufa* / *Eugenia*), reddish. It bears on its branches frond-shoots, its fruit is rounded and hangs heavily and is bigger than all trees, we say it is like a man's testicles. It grows from its fruit.
○ It grows along inlets and on the sea and in the scraping swamps.
• When small we build houses with it.
• We also fell it for fuel.
LALATO / LATOA = GENITALS / *Xylocarpus granatum* Koen. / *X. moluccensis* (Lamk.) Boehm. (*Meliaceae*)

'AISIKISIKI, 'ai ne'e doe liu mala, nonina meo-meo'a, rauna te'e reba ma kesi keta liu go'o. Nia ke fungu 'ania fa'irū kī , nia ke bulao go'o ana fuana.
○ Nia ke bulao saena to'ona'oa ma tolo logo.
• Ki saunga'i luma 'ania.
• Ki kwa'ia logo fuana so'i, nia ke du'a sikisiki, ta ne'e ki fa'asata 'uri ana.
• Na 'ai doe ka bolo logo fuana 'olelana 'ania rebarū.

SPARKING-TREE, this tree gets very big indeed, its body is brownish, its leaf is quite wide and not very long. It bears fruits and it grows from its fruit.
○ It grows in the lowland and also in the inland.
• We build houses with it.
• We also fell it for fuel, it burns sparking, that's why we name it thus.
• The big tree is suitable for cutting into planks.
'AISIKISIKI = SPARKING-TREE / *Maranthes corymbosa* Bl. (*Chrysobalanaceae*)

'AISIKO, 'ai ne'e ke doe liu mala, nonina te'e kwaokwao'anga, takana kwao ka ti'iti'i.

○ Nia ke bulao fa'asia fafona asi 'uana 'i tolo.
• Na numa ke 'ania rauna ma ki 'oia fuana 'anilana.
• Ti'iti'ilana ki saunga'i luma 'ania .
• Di'ia nia du'a ki kwa'i fuana so'i.
• Na 'ai doe ka bolo logo fuana 'olelana 'ania reba 'ai kī.

MILO, ki saea logo 'ania MELO, 'ai ne'e ke doe liu mala, rauna marako ka te'e ketaketa'a ka raku, di'ia rauna beta na'a ta ma nia meo na'a, takana ti'iti'i ka kwao, fuana ka marako ka ti'iti'i ma ka magarū'a logo.
○ Nia bulao ka 'oro 'i fafona asi, saena to'ona'oa ma saena tolo.
• Ti'iti'ilana ki saunga'i luma 'ania bore ma luma sasufi'i kī go'o ma babala kī ne'e bolo fa'inia, nia 'iri le'a liu go'o sulia na suma ma gwagwao ke 'ania.
• Ki kwa'ia logo fuana so'i bore ma nia du'a maemaela go'o.
• Na 'ai doe ka bolo logo fuana 'olelana 'ania reba 'ai kī.

TABA'A, ki saea logo 'ania SUALA, 'AITONGA, 'ai ne'e ka keta ka tasa ana 'ai kī, nia ne'e ki saea 'ania rū ne'e doe ka tasa kī, rū taba'a ne'e. Nia ka ra'e ka saga, ta ne'e ki saea logo 'ania suala. Nonina kwaokwao'anga, sūla kwao ka tongatonga'a, ta ne'e ki saea logo 'ania 'aitonga. Takana ka kwao ma nia ka fungu, fuana molimoli'a ka marako. Di'ia ki tufua nia ke birabira.
○ Nia ke bulao ana kula kī sui.
• Fa'i 'ai ti'iti'i kī ne'e kisi saunga'i 'ani'i sulia noa'a nia kesi ngasi bore ma fa'i 'ai te'e doe kī ki saunga'i 'ani'i.
• Fa'i 'ai gwa'i tanga'a kī ki tufu'i ki ragia ta'eta'ena fuana daura'ilana tila lamb kaida'i ngū kī ke ngū saena rodo.
• Ki tadilia kobakobana lalirū kī fuana baba 'i kilafa fuana fono'a 'usi luma.
• Ki du'a logo 'ania.
• Ki 'olea 'itanga'irū fuana rebarū kī.
• Ki gurgura 'ania ana ti mata'inga to'oto'o 'oro kī, ma di'ia ba'eko tolo ke 'alea ngwae.
• Kaida'i ana tua'a 'i buri, ki koria logo ta'eta'ena, ki lalia butarū kī fuana siufilana 'afe kale 'i nia ke ra'e 'i luma.

ELAECARPUS-TREE, this tree gets very big indeed, its body is a bit whiteish, its flower is white and small.
○ It grows from on the sea to the inland.
• Caterpillars eat the leaves and we pick them to eat.
• When small we build houses with it.
• If it is dry we fell it for fuel.
• The big tree is also suitable for cutting into wooden planks.
'AISIKO = ELAECARPUS / *Elaeocarpus multisectus* Schltr. / *E. salomonensis* Kunth (*Elaeocarpaceae*)

MILO, also called *MELO*, this tree gets very big indeed, its leaf is green and quite wideish and pointed, if the leaf withers it is red, its flower is small and white and its fruit is green and small and has seeds.
○ It grows plentifully on the sea, in the lowland and in the inland.
• When small we build houses with it but only smoky houses and shelters are suitable, it is not very good because worms and wasps eat it.
• We also fell it for fuel but it just burns dying.
• The big tree is also suitable for cutting into wooden planks.
MILO = *Elaeocarpus sphaericus* (Gaertn.) Schum. (*Elaeocarpaceae*)

GIGANTIC, also called LANCE-LIKE and GUM-TREE, this tree is taller than other trees, that's why we call especially big things gigantic. It climbs up straight, that's why we call it lance-like. Its body is whiteish, its sap is white and gummy, that's why we call it gum-tree. Its flower is white and it bears, its fruit is rounded and green. If we chop it down it sprouts.
○ It grows in all places.
• The small trees we don't build houses with because they are not strong but the bigger trees we build with.
• The forked trees we chop and remove the skin for hanging a tilley-lamp on when singers sing in the night.
• We trim the buttress-roots for board doors for closing the house.
• We also burn with it (as fuel).
• We cut the trunk for planks.
• We cure many different sicknesses with it, and if an inland menace (snake) bites a person.
• During the former way of life we also scraped the skin and made an invocation over the package (of scrapings) to bathe a woman who had given birth so she could go up to the house (from seclusion).

- Kaida'i fa'i alo ke 'eo, ki taka logo 'ania buta taba'a saena o'olā 'i ke mauri le'a.

'AITONGATONGA, 'ai ne'e ke doe mala, nonina ta'i gwā melamela'a, rauna sisilia ka marako, sūluna kwao ka tongatonga'a. Nia ke fungu, fa'irū kī molimoli'a ka marako.
- Nia ke bulao go'o saena to'ona'oa ma saena logo tolo.
- Ti'iti'ilana ki saunga'i luma 'ania.
- Ki sakali foka gwata logo 'ania.
- Ki du'a logo ani fuana so'i di'i ni'i du'a.

'AIKIKIRU, 'ai doe ne'e nonina ka borabora'a. Nia ke fungu, fa'irū molimoli'a ka di'ia logo kikiru, ta ne'e ki fa'asta 'uri ana.
- Nia ke bulao saena to'ona'oa.
- Ki saunga'i luma 'ania.
- Nia le'a fuana so'i ki du'a 'ania.

AKAMA ne'e 'ai doe mala, nonina ka gwagwā'a, nia ke fungu 'ania fa'irū kī ma fuana molimoli'a, nia ke bulao ana talina.
- Nia ke bulao fa'asia fafona asi 'uana 'i tolo, nia 'oro saena tolo.
- Ki 'ania fuana, ki tufua, ki usu'ia afuna sulia ma'e 'ai fuana du'afilana. Na 'anilana rakufa di'ia ngali ma ka 'irio'iro.
- Na numa kī ke 'ania rauna ma ki 'oia fuana 'anilana.
- Ti'iti'ilana ki saunga'i luma 'ania.
- Ki kwa'ia logo fuana so'i.
- Na 'ai doe ka bolo logo fuana 'olelana 'ania reba 'ai kī.

AKO, ki saea logo 'ania DANGWA, 'ai ne'e ke doe liu ka keta liu mala, nonina melamela'anga, nia ke fungu 'ania fa'irū molimoli'a kī, nia ke bulao ana fa'ina. Kaida'i nia 'oro ana ta'i kula, ki saea 'ania busubusu 'ako, di'ia iru nia foto ana, rauni'i rongolana ka di'ia lingalinga 'ako'a kī, ta ne'e ki fa'asata 'uri ana.
- Nia ke bulao ana kula kī ta'ifau, fa'asia fafona asi ka dao 'i tolo, nia 'oro saena to'ona'oa.

- When a taro-plot is poisoned we also scatter a package of gigantic (scrapings) in the garden so it will live.
TABA'A / SUALA / 'AITONGA = GIGANTIC / LANCE-LIKE / GUM-TREE / *Alstonia scholaris* (L.) R.Br. (*Apocynaceae*)

GUMMY-TREE, this tree gets really big, its body is black-brown, its leaf is narrow and green, its sap is white and gummy. It bears, its fruit is rounded and green
- It just grows in the lowland and also in the inland.
- When small we build houses with it.
- We also fence pig pens with it.
- We also burn it for fuel if it is dry.
'AITONGATONGA = GUMMY-TREE / *Cerbera floribunda* Schum. (*Apocynaceae*)

BETEL-TREE, this tree gets big and its body is purplish. It bears and its fruit is rounded like betel (*kikiru / Areca*), that's why we name it thus.
- It grows in the inland.
- We build houses with it.
- It is good for fuel to burn with.
'AIKIKIRU = BETEL-TREE / *Ochrosia elliptica Labill.* / *O. glomerata* (Bl.) Muell. / *O. manghas L.* / *O. oppositifolia* (Lamk.) Schum. / *O. parviflora* (Forst.) Hemsl. / *O. sciadophylla* Mgf. (*Apocynaceae*)

FINSCHIA is a really big tree, its body is blackish, it bears fruit and the fruit is rounded, it grows from its pit.
- It grows from on the sea to the inland, it is plentiful in the inland.
- We eat the fruit, we chop it up and thread the pieces on a stick to burn. It is appetising to eat, like nut, and oily.
- Caterpillars eat the leaves and we pick them to eat.
- When small we build houses with it.
- We also fell it for fuel.
- The big tree is also suitable for cutting into wooden planks.
AKAMA = FINSCHIA / *Finschia chloroxantha* Diels. / *Finschia waterhousiana* Burtt (*Proteaceae*)

SHOUT, also called *DANGWA*, this tree gets very big and very tall indeed, its body is brownish, it bears rounded fruits and it grows from its fruit. When it is plentiful in one place, we call it a shout thicket, if the wind hits it the sound of the leaves is like shouting voices, that's why we name it thus.

- It grows in all places, from on the sea to the inland, it is plentiful in the inland.

- Ki saunga'i rū 'ania, di'ia adele akisi.
- Ki kwa'ia fuana so'i, nia du'a kwasukwasu.
- Na 'ai doe ka bolo logo fuana 'olelana 'ania rebarū.
- Ki gurā 'ania ti mata'inga.

'AISAFUSAFU, 'ai ne'e ke doe mala, nonina te'e kwaokwao'anga, rauna ka dokodoko.
- Nia ke bulao ana kula kī ta'ifau, fa'asia fafona asi ka dao 'i tolo.
- Ki saunga'i luma 'ania, bore ma 'ai ne'e ngwara'u go'o.
- Ki kwa'ia 'ai du'a fuana so'i.

- We make things with it like axe hafts.
- We burn it for fuel, it burns flaming.
- The big tree is also suitable for cutting into planks.
- We cure some sicknesses with it.

AKO / DANGWA = SHOUT / oceanic lychee / island lychee / pacific maple / *Pometia pinnata* Forst.f. (*Sapindaceae*)

SAFUSAFU-TREE, this tree gets really big, its body is whiteish, its leaf is shortish.
- It grows in all places, from on the sea to the inland.
- We build houses with it, but the tree is just soft.
- We fell the dry trees for fuel.

'AISAFUSAFU = *SAFUSAFU*-TREE / *Harpullia arborea* (Bl.) Radlk. (*Sapindaceae*) / *Euodia elleryana* Muell. (*Rutaceae*)

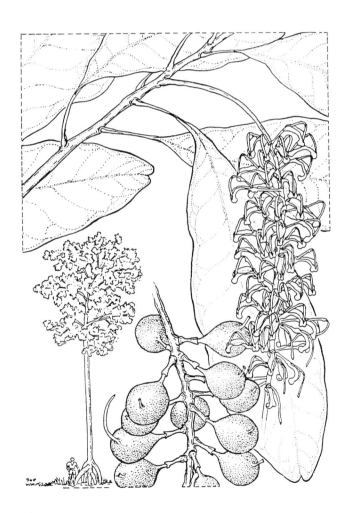

▲ *akama / finschia*

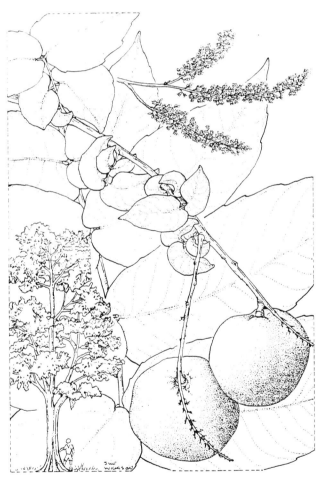

▲ *ako / shout*

BALE'O nia to'o ana ulu malita'irū kī.

BALE'O saga, ki saea logo 'ania RAU'AI, 'ai ne'e ke doe mala, rauna reba ka marako, kaida'i ki tufua, suluna kwao. Nia ke fungu 'ania fa'irū kī, fuana molimoli'a ka doe, ka to'o ana farū 'oro kī. Fuana marako, kaida'i nia kesi make saena kwao, kaida'i nia ke make, nonina ka sisirafu'a, saena ka sakosako'a. Nia ke bulao ana faruna.
- ○ 'Ai fasia nini'a, nia ke bulao saena to'ona'oa. Ki fasia faruna ma ti ai ke bulao logo saena masu'u si ne'e sakwalo ke lofota'ini'i kwau faruna ke danga 'ania go'o ka bulao.
- • Ki 'ania fa'irū kī, 'anilana le'a liu. Ki du'atelea fa'irū kī ma ki resia ka faolo mala ki fi'i 'ania.

BALE'O KWASI, lisilana bolo logo fa'inia ai fasia bore ma fa'irū kī mamata lala, ni'i ti'iti'i ma ti ai 'anilani ka isiisi'a lala ma di'ia ki du'afia nia ka ngoe lala ma ka ngasi, 'anilani noa'a kesi le'a liu di'ia ai fasia.
BALE'O FAKA, 'ai ne'e kira salinga'inia ma'i 'i 'a'e asi, karangi ka di'ia bale'o saga bore ma nia ke fungu go'o 'i ano, fa'irū kī ka molimoli'a ka doe liu mala ana bale'o saga ma ke fungu go'o 'i ano.
- ○ 'Ai fasia nini'a, ki fasia saena fanoa ma o'olā ma ta kula bore 'ana. Fasilana bale'o faka ka matamata ana bale'o saga sulia ki fasia lala lalina fa'inia logo faruna.
- • Fa'irū kī, 'anilana di'ia logo bale'o saga bore ma 'anilana ngwagafu mala.
- • Bale'o kī ta'ifau, raolana fa'i 'ai ni'i bolo logo.
- • Kaida'i 'ai ke mae safao kī ke fanga ana nonina, ki tufua fuana 'anilana.
- • Ki kwa'ia logo fuana so'i bore ma noa'a nia kesi le'a sulia nia du'amaemaela.
- • Ki ngalia sūla ma rauna ma memena fuana guralana 'ania ti mata'inga.

BAOLA, 'ai ne'e nia ke ra'e ma ka kalia sulia 'ai kī, ma 'itangana ka di'ia logo 'ai kī. Nia ke fungu ma fuana sakosako'a, nia ke bulao ana fa'irū kī. No'o kī kike 'ania fa'irū kī, di'ia kira fi'i 'onita'inia magana 'i 'aena 'ai, baola fi'i bulao ka kalia 'ai nai'ari, leleka 'ai ke mae go'o, baola ka ū na'a ti'ana.

- ○ Nia ke bulao fa'asia fafona asi 'uana 'i tolo, ka tasa na'a ana tolo goro, bore ma nia kesi 'oro liu.
- • Ki fasia 'i nonina fuli feraābu kī ma fuli tua'a kī sulia 'ai ne'e doe liu ma ka satola fuana tua nunufi'anga.

BREADFRUIT has three kinds.

BREADFRUIT proper, also called RAU'AI, this tree gets really big, its leaf is wide and green, when we chop it its sap is white. It bears fruit, the fruit is rounded and big and has many small pips. The fruit is green and when it is unripe the inside is white, when it is ripe its body has a bloom and the inside is yellow. It grows from its fruit.
- ○ This one is a planted tree, it grows in the lowland. We plant the pips and some also grow in the forest as bats fly away with the pips and let them drop and they grow.
- • We eat the fruit, it is very good to eat. We roast the fruit and scrape it really clean and then eat it.

WILD BREADFRUIT looks the same as the planted one but the fruit is different, it is small and fibrous to eat and if we burn it, it is underdone and hard, it is not as good to eat as the planted one.

FOREIGN BREADFRUIT, this tree they transferred here from overseas, it is quite like breadfruit proper but it just fruits at the ground.

- ○ This one is a planted tree, we plant it in homes and gardens and anywhere. Planting foreign breadfruit is different from breadfruit proper because we plant its root as well as its pip.
- • The fruit is like breadfruit proper to eat but it is really tasty to eat.
- • For all breadfruits, using the tree is the same.
- • When the tree dies *safao*(grubs) eat the body and we chop them out to eat.
- • We also fell it for fuel but it is not good because it burns and dies out.
- • We take the sap and leaves and mash them up for curing some sicknesses.

BALE'O = BREADFRUIT / *Artocarpus communis* Forst. / *A. altilis* (Park.) Fosb. (*Moraceae*)

BANYAN, this tree climbs and winds around trees and its main stem is like trees. It bears and its fruit is yellow, it grows from its fruit. Birds eat the fruit and if they shit the seeds at the foot of a tree a banyan will then grow around the tree and eventually the tree will die and the banyan will stand on its own.
- ○ It grows from on the sea to the inland, especially in the misty inland, but is not very plentiful.
- • We plant it in the area of tabu houses and rest-sites because the tree is very big and fine-looking for sitting in the shade.

Baola to'o ana malita'irū to'oto'o kī:
BAOLA GARAGARA, itangana garagara.

- Ki lalafia lalirū kī, ki itoa ana 'ai matamata ne'e ū logo tala ana baola doe fuiri, nia ne'e ki saea logo 'ania BAOLA LĀLĀ sulia rū masa go'o 'ada.
- Na lalirū saga ma ka keta kī ki tufui'i fuana fa'i gwaofa ma fa'i 'idi'idi sulia nia keta ma ka saga le'a fuana saunga'inga.

BAOLA FAU, nonina ka gwāgwā'a ma nia doe ana 'ai kī ta'ifau, lalina sūsū go'o, ta ne'e ki saea 'ania baola fau.

- Nia ke kalia fau lifu kī ma ka bulao ani.

BAOLA SUSUSU, ta sata SIRIFENA, noa'a kesi doe liu go'o di'ia baola garagara ma baola fau kī, lalina ka tatara kwailiu go'o ana rarana.

- Nia ke bulao go'o ana kwaru kī.

Banyan has separate kinds:
SPREAD BANYAN, its main stem spreads.

- We tug the roots and tie them to another tree which stands by the big banyan, which is why we also call it TUG BANYAN, because it's a plaything.
- The straight long roots we chop for ridge-beams and eve-beams because they are long and good and straight for building.

SOLID BANYAN, its body is blackish and it is bigger than all other trees, its roots cover over, that's why we call it solid banyan.

- It winds round huge stones and grows on them.

SUSUSU BANYAN, also called SIRIFENA, is not very big like spreading banyans and solid banyans, its roots just hang about from the branches.

- It just grows on rocky areas.

BAOLA = BANYAN / strangler fig / Ficus microcarpa L.f ssp. naumannii Engl. / F. prasinicarpa Elmer. / F. glandulifera Summerh.
BAOLA GARAGARA / BAOLA LĀLĀ = SPREAD BANYAN / TUG BANYAN / Ficus benjamina L. var nuda (Miq.) Braith. / F. subcordata Bl.
BAOLA FAU = SOLID BANYAN / Ficus drupacea Thunb. ssp. glabrata Corner / F. obliqua Forst. f. / F. xylosycia spp. cylindricarpa Diels / F. crassiramea Miq. ssp. patellifera Warb.
BAOLA SUSUSU / SIRIFENA = SUSUSU BANYAN / Ficus tinctoria Forst. f.
(Moraceae)

BUBULIA ne'e 'ai doe liu ka keta logo, nonina gwagwā'anga, rauna molimoli'a ka te'e reba, nia ka taka ka fungu ka bulao ana fuana.

- Nia ke bulao 'i fafona asi ma saena to'ona'oa ma saena logo tolo.
- 'Uli'ulina ki saunga'inia 'ania 'aba la'ua, nia ngasi ka liufia la'ua ana fa'i sala.
- Ti'iti'ilana ki saunga'i luma 'ania.
- Kaida'i nia doe ki kwa'i logo fuana so'i.
- Ki gura logo 'ania mata'inga kī.

BUBULIA is a very big tree and also tall, its body is blackish, its leaf is rounded and quite wide, it flowers and bears and grows from its fruit.

- It grows on the sea and in the lowland and also in the inland.
- Its bark we make cloth from, it is stronger than cloth from smooth tree (sala / Ficus).
- When small we build houses with it.
- When it is big we also fell it for fuel.
- We also cure sicknesses with it.

BUBULIA = BUBULIA / Ficus austrina Corner / F. hombroniana Corner / F. pachystemon Warb. / F. smithii Horne (Moraceae)

LASI, 'ai ne'e ke doe liu mala ka keta logo, 'uli'ulina ka ngwātobitobi, di'ia nia du'a nia ke sao. Nia ke fungu 'ania fa'īrū ti'iti'i kī.

- Nia ke bulao ana kula gwa'i kwaru'a kī.
- Ki saunga'i luma 'ania, nia le'a sulia nia ngasi.

- Nia le'a liu fuana so'i sulia nia du'a kwasukwasu ma ka du'adangi.

LASI, this tree gets very big indeed and tall too, its bark is easy to break and if it is dried it is soft. It bears small fruits.

- It grows in rocky places.
- We build houses with it, it is good because it is strong.
- It is good for fuel because it burns flaming and burns till day.

LASI = LASI / Ficus hombroniana Corner / F. polyantha Warb. (Moraceae)

MALIFU, 'ai ne'e ke doe, nonina ka maramarako'a, rauna ka marako ka molimoli'a, di'ia nia fi'i ala rakuna sakosako'a. Di'ia ki tufua nia ke tongatonga-'anga ka ta'i kwao, di'ia nia tongalia māka ke rodo.
○   Nia ke bulao sulia kafo kī ana kula fau boso-'anga kī ma ka fau la'anga.
•   Tatabu kwasi ne'e, ki 'ania rakuna.
•   Ki kwa'ia fuana so'i.

MALIGONA ne'e 'ai doe mala, nia di'ia fa'i totofua, nonina gwagwā'a, rauna marako ka ti'iti'i go'o ka ta'i molimoli'a ma ka ketaketa'a, takana lisilana kwaokwao'a.

MARAGONA ne'e 'ai doe mala, nia di'ia fa'i totofua, nonina gwagwā'a, rauna marako ka ti'iti'i go'o ka ta'i molimoli'a ma ka ketaketa'a, takana lisilana kwaokwao'a.
○   Nia ke bulao ana raku faolu, ana kula kī sui.
•   Sūlana ki tabua 'ania laungi kī di'ia sa'ela'o kī sulia nia ke kanusua bulibuli kī.
•   Ki kwaiguragura logo 'ania.

RAKONA ne'e 'ai doe mala, nonina sakosako'a, rauna rebareba'a ka molimoli'a. Nia ke fungu 'ania fa'irū doe liu kī ka fi'ifi'ila, kaida'i nia kwasā ka 'asi 'i ano nia moko le'a liu, di'ia nia teo ka ago saena lalano, ki eta saia go'o ne'e nia ke mokofi kia.
○   Nia ke bulao fafona asi. Ki fasia logo sulia ta'i tala kī ma māna kafo kī ma nonina fanoa kī.
•   Ki fasia logo sulia ngali kī, 'i ne'e ki ra'e sulia ki fi'i aka'u ka talangwara'u ana ngali.
•   Ki 'ania fa'irū, 'anilana ka asila liu.

TŌ, 'ai ne'e ke doe liu mala, nia to'o ana rō malita'irū kī.
ETANA TŌ, nonina bulu nunura, rauna ka molimoli'a ka te'e rebareba'a go'o. Nia ka fungu logo, fa'irū kī molimoli'a ka ti'iti'ii go'o.
○   Nia ke bulao go'o saena kula tolo'a kī, nia te'e 'ato fuana lisilana dalafa.
RUANA TŌ, nonina ka kwaokwao'a, rauna ka sisili'a ka ketaketa'a, nia ke fungu, saena fa'irū kī meomeo'a noima ka sakosako'a.
○   Nia ke bulao saena tolo ma saena to'ona'oa ma kula kunukunu'a kī bore, nia baru'a logo.
•   'Ai ngasi liu nini'a, ka liufia ti 'ai, noa'a kesi foga, ta ne'e nia ka totolia saunga'ilana 'ania rū kala'i kī di'ia alafolo, subi, kakata, fa'i kuba, adele fuana akisi.
•   Nia le'a ka tasa fuana diro.
•   Ki kwa'ia logo fuana so'i.

MALIFU, this tree gets big, its body is greenish, its leaf is green and rounded, if sprouting its shoot is yellow. If we chop it, its sap is gummy and quite white and if it gums up our eyes they'll go blind.
○   It grows along waters in places with hog-stones (basalt) and light (coloured) stones.
•   This is a wild vegetable, we eat its shoots.
•   We fell it for fuel.
MALIFU = *MALIFU* / *Ficus cristobalensis* Corner / *F. edelfeltii* ssp. *bougainvillei* King / *F. novae-georgiae* Corner / *F. novo-guineensis* Corner (*Moraceae*)

MARAGONA is a really big tree, it is like *totofua* tree, its body is blackish, its leaf is green and just small and a bit rounded and longish and its flower looks whiteish.
○   It grows in the new shoots, in all places.
•   Its sap we use to clean ornaments like shell-disks because it removes dirt.
•   We also cure with it.
MARAGONA = *MARAGONA* / *Ficus smithii* Horne (*Moraceae*) / *Melastoma affine* D.Don / *M. malabathricum* L. / *M. polyanthum* Bl. (*Melastomataceae*)

PARATOCARPUS is a really big tree, its body is yellow, its leaf is rounded and wideish. It bears very big knobbly fruit and when it is ripe it falls to the ground and smells very good and if it lies hidden in the forest the first we know of it is its smell.
○   It grows on the sea. We also plant it along paths, at water spouts and in home areas.
•   We also plant it alongside nuts so we can climb it, cling to it and easily get to the nuts.
•   We eat the fruit, it is very sweet to eat.
RAKONA / RAKWANA = PARATOCARPUS / *Parartocarpus venenosa* (Zoll. et Mor.) Becc. (*Moraceae*)

STREBLUS, this tree gets very big indeed, it has two kinds.
The FIRST STREBLUS, its body is dark and shiny, its leaf is rounded and a bit wideish. It also bears and the fruits are rounded and just small.
○   It just grows in inland places and is quite hard to see at random.
The SECOND STREBLUS, its body is whiteish, its leaf is narrow and longish, it bears and the inside of the fruit is reddish and yellow.
○   It grows in the inland and in the lowland and even in swampy places, and it is scarce.
•   This is a very strong tree, more than other trees, it won't crack, so it is ideal for making into carved things like deflector-clubs, angle-clubs, (betel) mortars, walking sticks and hafts for axes.
•   It is especially good for posts.
•   We also fell it for fuel.
TŌ = STREBLUS / *Streblus glaber* (Merr.) Corner (*Moraceae*)

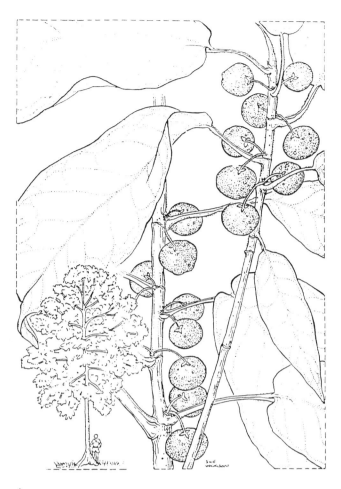

▲   *malifu* / malifu

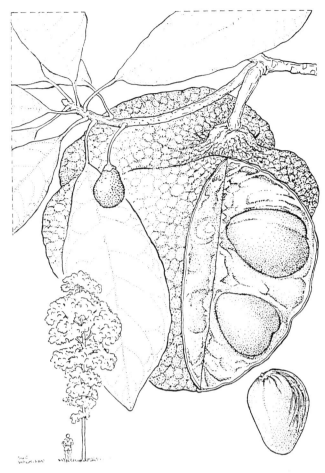

▲   *rakona* / paratocarpus

'U'UFI,'ai ne'e ti 'ai doe liu, nonina mela, saena
sakosako'a, sūla ka kwao, rauna ka ketaketa'a.

○   Nia ke bulao go'o 'i fafo 'i asi ma saena
    to'ona'oa, ti kaida'i saena logo tolo kī.
•   Kaida'i nia ke doe kula gwā fu 'i saena nia ngasi
    liu, ka di'ia mamufua, u'ula ma fata. Ta ma ki
    saunga'i diro 'ania fuana luma.

•   Ki o'o 'afi'i fuana fasi gwa'ufi'anga, fuana ni'i
    ke kali sulia.

ANTIARIS, this is a very big tree, its body is
brown, the inside is yellow, its sap is white, its leaf
is longish.
○   It just grows on the sea and in the lowland,
    sometimes also in the inland.
•   When it is big the black part inside it is very
    strong, like securinega (*mamufua*), ipil (*u'ula /
    Instia*) and vitex (*fata*). So we make posts from
    it for houses.
•   We garden around it to plant *gwa'ufi* (yam)
    (*Dioscoresa*), for them to wind round it.
'U'UFI =ANTIARIS / *Antiaris toxicaria* (Pers.) Lesch. / *Artocarpus
vriesianus* Miq. var. *refractus* (*Moraceae*)

KAUMANU, 'ai doe ne'e, nonina melamela'anga, rauna ketaketa'a ka sisilia go'o. Nia bulao ana takana.
- Nia ke bulao ana kula kī ta'ifau.
- 'Ai ti'iti'i kī ki saunga'i luma 'ania sulia nia saga le'a fuana saunga'inga.
- Ki sabangi logo 'ania.
- Nia le'a logo fuana so'i.

'AURIDI, 'ai ne'e kesi doe liu go'o, lisilana karangia ka di'ia logo kaumanu, nonina melamela'a, rauna ti'iti'i go'o, karangia ka di'ia logo rauna kaumanu.
- Nia ke bulao saena dukwasi, ana to'ona'oa ma 'i tolo logo.
- Nia le'a ka tasa fuana saunga'inga, sulia nia ona ka mabe le'a.
- Di'ia nia mae ka du'a ki kwa'ia fuana so'i.

BA'ULA, 'ai ne'e keta liu, 'uli'ulina ngasi ka borabora'a, rauna ka baba'ula ka ketaketa'a. Nia ka fungu 'ania fa'irū kī molimoli'a ka doe ka to'o ana ta'eta'erū ne'e ofi fāfia talirū kī, nia to'o go'o 'ana te'e sa'erū.
- Nia ke bulao ana kula kī ta'ifau, saena kunu fa'inia logo ano to'o, nia 'oro saena to'ona'oa. Kaida'i fa'irū kī ke make, sakwalo ki ke 'ani'i logo. Nini'a ba'ula ke bulao ana ta kula bore 'ana, sulia sakwalo kī kira ka 'onita'inia fa'irū kī.
- Ti'iti'ilana ki saunga'inia luma 'ania, ka tasa sulia ka sagasaga ka ngasi logo.
- Ki sabangi logo 'ania.
- Na 'ai doe ki saunga'i iolo 'ania.
- Nia ka bolo logo fuana 'olelana 'ania reba 'ai kī.

- Ki kwa'ia logo fuana so'i, nia ke sao ke du'a dangi ma ka du'a kwasukwasu logo.
- Fuana ngela kī ke masa 'ania di'ia fa'i bolo kī, ki saunga'i logo 'ania rebarū fuana kwa'i bolo'anga.

GWAROGWARO, 'ai ne'e ke doe liu mala, nonina sakosako'a, fuana di'ia logo ba'ula bore ma rauna ti'iti'i liu.
- Nia ke bulao ana kula fungufungula kī, nia 'oro saena to'ona'oa.
- Ki saunga'i luma logo 'ania di'ia ba'ula, nia le'a ka tasa sulia nia sagasaga ma ka ngasi logo.

- Ki sabangi logo 'ania.

KAUMANU, this is a big tree, its body is brownish, its leaf is longish and narrow. It grows from its flower.
- It grows in all places.
- The small trees we build houses with because it is good and straight for building.
- We also conduct (yam vines) with it.
- It is also good for fuel.
KAUMANU = *KAUMANU* / *Calophyllum cerasiferum* Vesque. (*Clusiaceae*)

'AURIDI, this tree does not get very big, it looks almost like *kaumanu* (*Calophyllum*), its body is brownish, its leaf is just small and looks almost like *kaumanu* leaf.
- It grows in the wilderness, in the lowland and in the inland.
- It is especially good for building, because it is tough and good and flexible.
- If it is dead and dried we fell it for fuel.
'AURIDI = *'AURIDI* / *Decaspermum fruticosum* J.R. & G. Forst. / *D. salomonense* Scott / *Metrosideros eugenioides* (Schltr.) Steere / *Metrosideros salomonense* C.T. White (*Myrtaceae*)

BA'ULA, this tree gets very tall, its bark is strong and purplish, its leaf is thick and longish. It bears fruits which are rounded and big and have a skin which sheaths the pits and it has only a small inside (kernel).
- It grows in all places, in swamp and also in proper ground, and it is plentiful in the lowland. When the fruits are ripe bats eat them, and that's why *ba'ula* grows in any place, because the bats shit out the seeds.

- When small we build houses with it, especially because it is straight and also strong.
- We also conduct (yam vines) with it.
- The big tree we make canoes from.
- It is also suitable for cutting into wooden planks.
- We also fell it for fuel, it is soft and burns till day and also burns flaming.
- The fruit children play with as balls and we also make a flat (bat) from it for striking the ball.
BA'ULA = *BA'ULA* / *Calophyllum kajewskii* A.C.Sm. (*Clusiaceae*)

CALOPHYLLUM, this tree gets very big indeed, its body is yellow, its fruit is like *ba'ula* (*Calophyllum*) but the leaf is very small.
- It grows in wet places and is plentiful in the lowland.
- We also build houses with it, like *ba'ula*, it is especially good because it is straightish and strong too.
- We also conduct (yam vines) with it.

- Fa'i 'ai ti'iti'i kī ki saunga'inia 'ania fa'i kuba.
- 'Ai doe ki saunga'i iolo 'ania.
- Ki kwa'ia logo fuana so'i.
- Nia bolo logo fuana 'olelana 'ania reba 'ai kī.

FA'IBEABEA, 'ai ne'e doe mala, rauna rebareba'a, burina ra'irū kwao. Nia ke fungu 'ania fa'irū kī, fuana gwā borabora'a. Nia ke bulao ana magana. Bina kī ke 'ania fuana.
- Nia ke bulao saena to'ona'oa saena letena ua kī, nia 'oro logo saena tolo.
- Ki saunga'i luma 'ania.
- Ki kwa'ia fuana so'i.

BOTALIGWAU, ki saea logo 'ania TATAREBA, nia 'ai doe, nonina gwagwā'a, rauna keta.
- Nia ke bulao fa'asia fafona asi 'uana 'i tolo.
- Ti'iti'ilana ki saunga'i luma 'ania.
- Ki kwa'ia logo fuana so'i.

LATOREKO, 'ai ne'e kesi doe liu go'o, nonina ka mela ka 'efo'efo'a, rauna reba ka dokodoko, fuana ka molimoli'a ni'i saulaelae sulia nonina, nia bulao ana fa'irū kī.
- Nia ke bulao saena to'ona'oa ma saena logo tolo.
- Ki tufua diro kī ana fuana saunga'i luma'a.
- Ti'iti'ilana ki saunga'i luma 'ania.
- Ki kwa'ia logo fuana so'i.
- Nia le'a logo fuana guragura'a.

NONO'O, 'ai ne'e ke doe liu mala, nonina kwaokwao'a, rauna te'e dokodoko ka molimoli'a, nia ke fungu. Rauna, no'o akaka'u ke 'ania, ta ne'e ki fa'asata 'uri ana.
- Nia ke bulao go'o ana kula kī sui bore ma fafo'i asi fa'inia kunukunua ne'e noa'a go'o.
- Ti'iti'ilana ki saunga'i luma 'ania.
- Ki saunga'i 'ania rū kī di'ia ka'ika'ina akisi ma sele kī ma fa'i kuba kī logo.
- Ki kwa'ia logo fuana so'i.
- Ki gura logo 'ania ti mata'inga.

- The small trees we make into walking sticks.
- The big trees we make canoes with.
- We also fell it for fuel.
- It is also suitable for cutting into wooden planks.

GWAROGWARO = CALOPHYLLUM / *Calophyllum neo-ebudicum* Guill. / *C. pseudovitiense* Turrill / *C. Solomonensis* A. C.Sm. / *C. vitiense* Turrill (*Clusiaceae*)

SCHIZOMERIA, this tree gets really big, its leaf is wideish and the back of the leaf is white. It bears fruit and the fruit is purplish-black. It grows from its seed. Hornbills eat the fruit.
- It grows in the lowland on the ridges of hills and it is plentiful in the inland.
- We build houses with it.
- We fell it for fuel.

FA'IBEABEA =SCHIZOMERIA / *Schizomeria brassii* Mattf. / *S. ilicina* (Rdl.) Schltr. / *S. serrata* Hochr. (*Cunoniacaea*)

BOTALIGWAU, also called *TATAREBA*, is a big tree, its body is blackish and its leaf is long.
- It grows from on the sea to the inland.
- When small we build houses with it.
- We also fell it for fuel.

BOTALIGWAU / TATAREBA = *BOTALIGWAU* / *Timonius pulposus* C.T.White / *T. solomonensis* Merr. & Perry (*Rubiaceae*)

LATOREKO, this tree doesn't get very big, its body is brown and scaly, its leaf is wide and shortish, its fruit is rounded and grows all along its body, and it grows from its fruit.
- It grows in the lowland and also in the inland.

- We chop posts from it for house-building.
- When small we build houses with it.
- We also fell it for fuel.
- It is also good for curing.

LATOREKO = *LATOREKO*/ *Timonius pulposus* C.T. White / *T. solomonensis* Merr. & Perry (*Rubiaceae*)

CUSCUS, this tree gets very big indeed, its body is whiteish, its leaf is quite shortish and rounded, and it bears (fruit). The leaf, the cuscus eats it, that's why we name it thus.
- It grows in all places but not on the sea and in swamp.
- When small we build houses with it.
- We make things with it like handles for axes and knives and also walking sticks.
- We also fell it for fuel.
- We also cure some sicknesses with it.

NONO'O = CUSCUS / *Canthium cymigerum* (Val.) Burtt / *C. korrense* (Val.) Kaneh (*Rubiaceae*)

BULASĪSĪ, ki saea logo 'ania MELO noima MILO,'ai ne'e ke doe mala, nonina melamela'a, rauna ka marako, kaida'i rauna karangia mae nia ke meo. Takana kwao, fuana ka gwā ka afae. Sīsī kī ke fiku ana ma ka 'ania nonina. Kaida'i sīsī ke lofo ka liu, di'ia nia mokofia 'ai ne'e, nia ke abula ma'i 'uana, ta ne'e ki saea 'ania bulasīsī.

- o Nia ke bulao go'o saena to'ona'oa ma saena logo tolo, nia 'oro liu.
- • Ti'iti'ilana ki saunga'i luma 'ania.
- • Ki sabangia falisi logo 'ania.

FIFIKULU, 'ai ne'e doe liu mala, nonina gwagwā'a, rauna ka keta ka te'e reba go'o. Nia ke fungu, ke bulao ana fa'irū.
- o Nia ke bulao saena raku faolu, fa'asia fafona asi 'uana 'i tolo.
- • Ti'iti'ilana ki saunga'i luma 'ania.
- • Ki kwa'ia fuana so'i.
- • Ki gura logo 'ania mata'inga kī.

DALO, 'ai ne'e ke doe liu mala, nonina gwagwā'a, ta'eta'ena ka baba'ula, rauna ka molimoli'a ka te'e reba la'u ka nunura mala. Nia ke fungu 'ania fa'irū kī ne'e marako ka molimoli'a ka talirū'a, nia ke bulao ana talirū.
- o Nia ke bulao go'o 'i fafona asi, ka 'oga musia sulia one. Ti kaida'i sakwalo kī ke ngalia fuana saena masu'u nia ke 'asia ka bulao. Ti kaida'i ki fasia logo fuana tua nunufi'anga ma fuana saunga'irū'anga.
- • Ti'iti'ilana ki saunga'i luma 'ania.
- • Na ai doe ki saunga'i iolo 'ania.
- • Ki kwa'ia logo fuana so'i.
- • Na ngela ti'iti'i kī ke goea talirū fuana masa 'ania, kira ke sakusaku 'ania.
- • Na 'ai doe ka bolo logo fuana 'olelana 'ania reba 'ai kī.
- • Ki gurā 'ania ti mata'inga.

MOKOFANIASI, 'ai ne'e ke te'e doe, nonina kwaokwao'a, lisilana ka di'ia dalo bore ma nia te'e mamata, noa'a kesi moko di'ia fa'i dalo. Noa'a 'iri moko la'u di'ia asi bore ma satana na'a, noa'a kisi fada 'ania fadalana satana.

- o Nia ke bulao ana to'ona'oa.

BEETLE-TURNER, also called *MELO* or *MILO*, this tree gets really big, its body is brownish, its leaf is green and when the leaf is almost dead it goes red. Its flower is white and its fruit is black and sour. Beetles (*sīsī*)gather on it and eat its body. When a beetle flies past, if it smells this tree it turns towards it, that's which we call it beetle-turner.
- o It only grows in the lowland and in the inland, it is very plentiful.
- • When small we build houses with it.
- • We also conduct yam-gardens with it.

BULASĪSĪ / MELO = BEETLE-TURNER / poison peach / *Parasponia andersonii* (Planch.) Planch. / *Trema aspera* Bl. / *T. orientalis* (L.) Bl. (*Ulmaceae*)

TREMA, this tree gets very big indeed, its body is blackish, its leaf is long and quite wide. It bears and grows from its fruit.
- o It grows in the new shoots, from on the sea to the inland.
- • When small we build houses with it.
- • We fell it for fuel.
- • We also cure sicknesses with it.

FIFIKULU = TREMA / poison peach / *Trema cannabia* Lour / *T. orientalis* (L.) Bl. (*Ulmaceae*)

PORTIA, this tree gets very big indeed, its body is blackish, its skin is thick and its leaf is rounded and quite wide too and really shiny. It bears fruit which are green and rounded and have a pit, and it grows from its pit.
- o It only grows on the sea, it shades all along the sand. Sometimes bats take the fruit into the forest to fall and grow. Sometimes we also plant it for sitting in the shade and for building things.
- • When small we build houses with it.
- • The big tree we make canoes with.
- • We also fell it for fuel.
- • Small children pick up the pits for playing with, they play catch with it.
- • The big tree is also suitable for cutting into wooden planks.
- • We cure some sicknesses with it.

DALO = PORTIA / portia tree / alexandrian laurel / beach mahogany / *Calophyllum inophyllum* L. (*Clusiaceae*)

SMELL-OF-THE-SEA, this tree gets quite big, its body is whiteish, looks like portia (*dalo* / *Calophyllum*) but is a bit different and doesn't smell like a portia. It doesn't smell like the sea either but that's its name, we don't know the meaning of its name.
- o It grows in the lowland.

- Ki saunga'i luma 'ania.
- Ki kwa'ia logo fuana so'i.

- We build houses with it.
- We also fell it for fuel.

MOKOFANI ASI = SMELL-OF-THE-SEA / *Avicennia alba* Bl. / *A. eucaptifolia* Zipp. ex Miq. / *A. marina* (Forst.) Vierh. (*Avicenniaceae*)

FAI ne'e 'ai doe mala, nonina kwaokwao'anga, kaida'i ki ragia saena ta'eta'ena ke melamela'a. Nia ke fungu 'ania fa'irū keta ma ka reba.

○ Nia bulao saena raku faolo kī, saena fuli fanoa kī, saena lefoka'o kī, ana kula sasala kī ne'e noa'a ti dukwasi doe ani kī.

- Rarana ka satola ne'e na bola ma bina kī ke mamalo ana rarana ma ke 'onita'inia fa'i ngali ma fa'i uku kī fuana 'anilana, ki saea 'ania 'oni'onita.

- 'Ai ta'i doe ki tufua ki ragia ta'eta'ena fuana saunga'i rū 'anga. Ki safalia 'ania gwaurau 'i ngali kī, ki susu'ia fa'inia ano 'ania ma'e 'au kī fuana 'uilana ngali saena.

- Ta'eta'ena ki tolea logo 'ania kafo fa'asia namo 'i ki nalufia denge ma ī'a kī.

- Ta'eta'ena le'a ka tasa fuana gwaru'a 'i luma, fuana logo 'afulana 'ania ngwae mae kī.

- Ti'iti'ilana ki saunga'i luma logo 'ania.

- Ki kwa'ia logo fuana so'i.

SIRIS is a really big tree, its body is whiteish and when we strip it (the bark) the inside of the skin is brownish. It bears long and wide fruit.

○ It grows in the new shoots, at home-sites, in bamboo thickets, in light places where there is no big (full-grown) wilderness.

- Its branches look fine so pigeons and hornbills rest on the branches and shit out nuts and *uku* (*Gnetum*) seeds for us to eat, we call it a shitting.

- The quite big tree we chop and strip the skin for making things with. We spread it (as flooring) for nut leaf-shelters and fix it to the ground with bamboo sticks, for hammering the nuts on.

- The skin we also channel water with from ponds, so we can bale out prawns and fish.

- The skin is especially good for seating in the house, and also for wrapping dead persons.

- When small we also build houses it.

- We also fell it for fuel.

FAI = SIRIS / siris tree / woman's tongue / *Albizia falcataria* (L.) Fosb. / *Serianthes minahassae* ssp. *fosbergii* Kanis. (*Mimosaceae*)

dalo / portia ▶

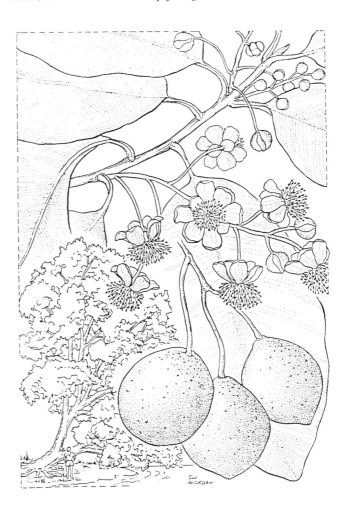

LAMILAMI, 'ai ne'e ke doe mala, nia to'o ana rō malilta'irū kī.
ETANA LAMILAMI, nonina mela, rauna ka reba. Nia taka ka sakosako'a ka moko fifī.

○   Nia ke bulao 'i ninimāna kafo doe kī ma saena to'ona'oa.
•   Na 'ai doe ki saunga'i iolo 'ania.
•   Ti'iti'ilana ki saunga'i 'ania luma ni du'urū'a kī.
•   Ki kwa'ia logo fuana so'i, nia kesi du'a dangi go'o.
•   Na 'ai doe ka bolo logo fuana 'olelana 'ania reba 'ai kī.
RUANA LAMILAMI nia kobara'a ka doe mala, nonina kwaokwao'a.
○   Nia ke bulao saena kunukunua ana maguru.
•   Fa'i 'ai ti'iti'i nia le'a fuana saunga'ilana luma.
•   Kobakobarū 'i fa'i 'ai doe liu mala ne'e ki saunga'inia 'ania baba 'i 'ai noima kilafa kī.
•   Ki kwa'ia logo fuana so'i.
•   Na 'ai doe ka bolo logo fuana 'olelana 'ania reba 'ai kī.

DAUFAU, ki saea logo 'ania 'AIASILA, 'ai ne'e doe mala, nonina melamela'a, ta'eta'ena di'i ki tufua nia ka ta'i sikisikila ma ka mafusifusi, rauna mara-marako'a ka keta ma kesi reba liu go'o, takana kwao, fa'irū marako.
○   Nia ke bulao saena dukwasi ana to'ona'oa ma fafona asi ma kunukunua, saena tofongana tolo ne'e noa'a ana.
•   Ti'iti'ilana ki saunga'i luma 'ania, bore ma noa'a kasi le'a sulia nia ke suma'ala.
•   Ki kwa'ia fuana so'i, nia le'a liu sulia nia ke du'adangi.
•   Doelana ki 'olea 'ania rebarū kī.

DINGALE, 'ai ne'e doe mala, nonina melamela'a, rauna sisili'a ka ketaketa'a. Nia to'o ana rō malita'irū kī.
DINGALE ASI, rauna ta'i rereba'a ka ta'i baba'ula ti'iti'i.
○   Nia ke bulao saena kabara.
DINGALE TOLO, rauna ti'iti'i go'o.
○   Nia ke bulao ka 'oro saena tolo.
•   'Ai ne'e ki fasia ana fuli tua'a kī ma māna kafo kī ma fuli fera kī. Ki fasia sulia biru kī 'i ne'e ke fa'ata'inia fa'i bōlana afu ano. Fa'i dingale asi, di'ia nia bulao saena tolo ki lia sai nama ana rū ne'e ngwae fasia, ka fada 'ania ta rū ana rū 'inoto'a kī.
•   Ki tufu diro 'ania fuana saunga'i luma'a.

ARCHIDENDRON, this tree gets really big and it has two kinds.
The FIRST ARCHIDENDRON, its body is brown and its leaf is wide. It has yellow flowers with an acute smell.
○   It grows beside big waters and in the lowland.

•   The big tree we make canoes from.
•   When small we build cooking houses with it.
•   We also fell it for fuel, it won't burn till day.

•   The big tree is also suitable for cutting into wooden planks.
The SECOND ARCHIDENDRON is buttressed and really big, its body is whiteish.
○   It grows in swamps in the mangroves.
•   The small tree is good for building houses.
•   The buttress of the very big tree we make into doors or boards.
•   We also fell it for fuel.
•   The big tree is also suitable for cutting into wooden planks.
LAMILAMI = ARCHIDENDRON / *Archidendron oblongum* (Hemsl.) de Wit (*Mimosiaceae*)

DAUFAU, also called *ASILA*-TREE, this tree gets really big, its body is brownish, its skin if we chop it chips fly and it snaps, its leaf is greenish and long and not very wide, its flower is white, the fruit is green.
○   It grows in wilderness in lowland and on the sea and in swamp, not in the central inland.

•   When small we build houses with it, but it is not good because it gets worm-eaten.
•   We fell it for fuel, it is good because it burns till day.
•   When big we cut it into planks.
DAUFAU / 'AIASILA = DAUFAU / *Neoscortechninia forbesii* (Hook.f.) C.T. White (*Euphorbiaceae*)

DINGALE, this tree gets really big, its body is brownish, its leaf is narrow and longish. It has two kinds.
SEA *DINGALE*, its leaf is quite wideish and quite thick and small.
○   It grows in the stilt-roots.
INLAND *DINGALE*, its leaves are just small.
○   It grows plentifully in the inland.
•   This tree we plant at rest-sites, water spouts and sanctum sites. We plant it along boundaries to show the layout of a piece of land. If sea *dingale* grows in the inland we see it as something a person planted, meaning it has to do with something important.
•   We chop posts from it for house-building.

- Ti'iti'ilana ki saunga'i luma 'ania.
- Ki saunga'inia 'ania subi ma fote ma rū di'ia salu gwaro'i kī.
- Ki kwa'ia logo fuana so'i.
- Na 'ai doe ka bolo logo fuana 'olelana 'ania reba 'ai kī.

- When small we build houses with it.
- We make angle-clubs and paddles and things like patterned lances from it.
- We also fell it for fuel.
- The big tree is also suitable for cutting into wooden planks.

DINGALE ASI = SEA *DINGALE* / red terentum / *Lumnitzera littorea* (Jack.) Voigt (*Combretaceae*)
DINGALE TOLO = INLAND *DINGALE* / *Podocarpus insularis del.* / *P. neriifolius* D.Don / *P. pilgeri* Foxw. / *P. salomoniensis* Wassch. (*Podocarpaceae*)

FAEFAE, 'ai ne'e ka te'e doedoe'anga, ka fi'irū'a sulia 'ingatana fi'ifi'ila 'i ano ma ke birabira ana 'ai 'oro kī. Rauna ka ta'i molimoli'a ka marako, takana sakosako'a.
- Nia ke bulao fa'asia fafona asi 'uana 'i tolo, nia 'oro saena to'ona'oa.
- Ti'iti'ilana ki saunga'i luma 'ania, bore ma luma sasufi'a go'o, sulia suma ke 'ania.
- 'Ai ne'e le'a fuana so'i sulia kakasilana ka ngwara'u u ma nia du'a kwasukwasu.
- Ki ba'o logo ana, nia di'ia logo isu.

KLEINHOVIA, this tree gets quite big, it forms clumps because its main stem clusters at the ground and it sprouts with many trees. Its leaf is a bit wideish and green and its flower is yellow.
- It grows from on the sea to the inland, it is plentiful in the lowland.
- When small we make houses with it, but only smoky houses because worms eat it.
- This tree is good for fuel because it is easy to split and it burns flaming.
- We also rub (for fire) with it, it is like callicarpa (*isu*).

FAEFAE = KLEINHOVIA / puzzle tree / guest tree / *Kleinhovia hospita* L. (*Sterculiaceae*)

faefae / kleinhovia ▶

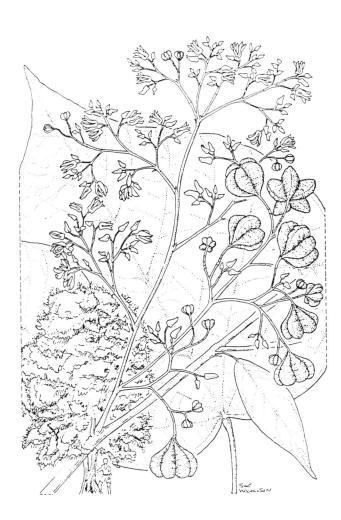

ONEONE, 'ai doe ne'e, nonina gwagwā'a, rauna reba ka keta.

- ○ Nia ke bulao fafona asi ma saena kabara ma kunukunu'a. Nia bulao ka tasa ana kula oneone'a, ta ne'e ki fa'asata 'uri ana.
- • Ki saunga'i luma 'ania
- • Ki kwa'ia fuana so'i
- • Ki gura logo 'ania.

SULA, 'ai ne'e ke doe mala, nonina ka kwaokwao'a ma rauna ka sisili'a. Lisilana karangi ka di'ia logo mala'o.

- ○ Nia ke bulao saena raku faolo kī, ka 'oro liu saena tolo.
- • Ta'eta'ena nia totolia saunga'irū'anga, ki aea 'aba kwalo fa'asia fa'i 'ai ti'iti'i kī.
- • 'Abarū ki aea 'ania 'aba kwalo ni fua'a, ki sisia 'ania sisirū fuana faosilana ngwa'i kī. Sisirū ti'iti'i fuana ki tai fa'unga 'ania, ki usu maga mani logo 'ania, ki dalofia logo 'ania dadalo. Na 'abana sula nia'a le'a ka tasa fuana saunga'ilana rū nai'ari kī ka tasa ana ti 'ai di'ia mala'o.
- • Ki saunga'i luma 'ania bore ma luma ni du'urū'a go'o, sulia di'ia nia sasufia ka 'eke'eke nia ke ngasi liu ma noa'a kesi suma'ala.
- • Na safao ke fanga logo ana di'ia nia du'a, ki tufua fuana 'anilana.
- • Ki kwa'ia logo fuana so'i, sulia nia le'a liu fuana du'arū'a 'ania.

MALA'O, 'ai ne'e noa'a kesi doe liu go'o, nonina nia meo gwagwā'a, ta'eta'ena ka ta'i ngasi mala ka 'abakwalo'a mala, fa'i a'oa'ona no'iri ngasi go'o ka sasala. Rauna keta ka te'e reba, takana kwao, nia ke fungu 'ania fa'irū molimoli'a ka alua maga rū 'oro ti'iti'i kī ana.

- ○ Nia ke bulao ana kula kī ta'ifau, fa'asia fafona asi ka dao 'i tolo, nia 'oro saena to'ona'oa. Nia bulao saena raku buru, ka bulao logo fuila 'ai ifu kī ana logo kaole.
- • Ki aea fa'i 'ai ti'iti'i kī fuana saunga'irū'anga di'ia dalalo ma ngwa'i, nia di'ia fa'i sula. Bore ma 'abakwalo ana sula nia le'a ka tasa ana, sulia ta'eta'ena mala'o di'ia nia isila nia ke didila lala.
- • Ki ragia bae fuana teo 'i saena ana fa'i 'ai doe kī, ma ki fono logo 'ania, ma ki saunga'inia logo 'ania talo kī fuana ofo'a 'i na'o ma'i.

SANDY is a big tree, its body is blackish, its leaf is wide and long.

- ○ It grows on the sea and in the stilt-roots and swamp. It grows especially in sandy places, that's why we name it thus.
- • We build houses with it.
- • We fell it for fuel.
- • We also cure with it.

ONEONE = SANDY / *Heritiera novo-guineensis* Kost. / / *H. salomonensis* C. T. White. / *H. littoralis* Ait. (*Sterculiaceae*) / *Parinari solomonensis* Kost. (*Crysolbalanaceae*)

SULA, this tree gets really big, its body is whiteish and its leaf is narrow. It looks almost like *mala'o* (*Trichospermum*).

- ○ It grows in the new shoots, it is plentiful in the inland.
- • Its skin is fitted for making things, we peel vine-strips from the small trees.
- • The strips we peel into vine-strips for burdens and we split them into narrow shreds for plaiting bags. The small shreds are for sewing mats (*fa'u* / *Pandanus*) and we also thread shell-money beads on it, and also twine it into twine. *Sula* strip is especially good for making these things and better than trees like *mala'o*.
- • We build houses with it but only cooking houses, because if it is smoked dry it is strong and will not become worm-eaten.
- • *Safao* (grubs) also eat it if it is dried out and we chop it to eat them.
- • We also fell it for fuel because it is very good for burning with.

SULA = SULA / *Trichospermum arachnoideum* Kost. / *T. incaniopsis* Kost. / *T. incanum* Merr. & Perry / *T. kajewskii* Merr. & Perry / *T. rhamnifolius* Kost. / *Triumfetta nigricans* F.M. Bail. (*Tiliaceae*)

MALA'O, this tree doesn't get very big, its body is blackish-red, its skin is quite strong and forms vine-strips but the bare pole is not strong and is light. Its leaf is long and quite wide, its flower is white, it bears rounded fruit which have many small seeds.

- ○ It grows in all places, from on the sea to the inland, it is plentiful in the lowland. It grows in the new shoots, and also grows on uprooted tree sites on clay.
- • We peel the small trees for making things (from the bark) like twine and bags, like the *sula* tree (*Trichospermum*). But *sula* vine-strip is better because when *mala'o* skin is still wet it is slippery.
- • We strip bark-board for lying on from the big trees, and we also shut with it (as doors etc.), and we also made shields from it for fighting, formerly.

- Ki saunga'i 'ania bore ma ana luma sasufi'i kī go'o.
- Ki kwa'ia fuana so'i, nia ke du'a kwasukwasu.
- Kaida'i nia mae ka du'a, safao kī ke fanga 'i saena, ki tufua fuana 'anilana.
- Ki guragura logo 'ania.

FOTEFOTE, 'ai ne'e doe mala, nonina ta'i kwaokwao'anga, rauna ta'i di'ia logo na malao fa'inia sula. Nia ke bulao ana takana.
- Nia ke bulao go'o ana raku buru, ana kula kī ta'ifau, fa'asia fafona asi ka dao 'i tolo.
- Ki kwa'ia logo fuana so'i.
- Nia le'a logo fuana guragura'a.

FŪ, 'ai ne'e ke doe liu mala, nia kesi ngasi liu go'o. Rauna reba ka keta, nia ke fungu go'o 'i fūna ra'irū kī, fuana te'e doe mala ka molimoli'a, ka to'o ana fai ninima 'i rū kī. Nia ke bulao ana fuana.

- Nia ke bulao ka 'oro 'i fafona asi. Ki fasia logo saena fanoa ma kula kī sui, nia'a fuana tua nunufi'anga 'i fafona asi.
- Fa'irū kī fuana afulana 'ania ī'a. Ki diua fa'irū kī ka meme ki to'ongi'i saena ngwa'i kī, ki fi'i uka 'ania ī'a saena kafo.
- Kaida'i fuana ke langalanga ki bulasia logo dadalo fuana dē'a kī ana sulia nia ke fa'ofa'o, ki itoa ma'e nanga ana dadalo fuana dēlana ī'a.

KETE, 'ai ne'e ke doe liu mala, rauna ketaketa'a, fa'irū marako, talirū ketaketa'a nia 'i saena .
- Nia ke bulao ana kula kī ta'ifau, nia 'oro saena to'ona'oa.
- Talirū kī fuana ketekete 'ania, ta ne'e ki fa'asata 'uri ana. Ki kakasia talirū, ki 'otomia sa'erū kī ki fi'i sotea ki usu'ia 'ania 'aba kwalo ki fi'i itoa fa'irū 'oro kī ana abala 'i 'ai, ki fi'i ketekete ani kaida'i ki ngwa'elia 'au 'i sango ma ki kwa'ia kana.
- Ti'iti'ilana ki saunga'i luma 'ania.
- Ki kwa'ia logo fuana so'i.
- Na 'ai doe ka bolo logo fuana 'olelana 'ania reba 'ai kī.

- We build with it, but only smoky houses.

- We fell it for fuel, it burns flaming.
- When it's dead and dry, *safao* (grubs) eat its inside and we chop it to eat them.
- We also cure with it.

MALA'O = *MALA'O*/ *Trichospermum fauroensis* Kost. / *T. psilocladum* Merr. & Perry / *T. peekelii* Burret (*Tiliaceae*)

COLONA, this tree gets really big, its body is quite whiteish, its leaf is a bit like *mala'o* and *sula* (*Trichospermum*). It grows from its flower.
- It just grows in dense shoots, in all places from on the sea to the inland.
- We fell it for fuel.
- It is also good for curing.

FOTEFOTE = COLONA / *Colona scabra* (Sm.) Burret / *C. velutina* Merr. & Perry (*Tiliaceae*)

BARRINGTONIA, this tree gets very big indeed, it is not very strong. Its leaf is wide and long and it bears at the base of the leaves, its fruit is quite big and rounded and has four sides. It grows from its fruit.
- It grows plentifully on the sea. We also plant it in homes and all places, for staying in the shade on the sea.
- The fruits are for doping fish with. We hammer the fruit into a paste and put it in bags and then dope fish with it in the water.
- When the fruit is dry we also roll twine for fishing on it because it floats, and we tie a hook to the twine for catching fish.

FŪ = BARRINGTONIA / fish-poison tree / *Barringtonia asiatica* (L.) Kurz (*Barringtoniaceae*)

RATTLE, this tree gets very big indeed, its leaf is longish, its fruit is green and a longish pit is inside.
- It grows in all places and is plentiful in the lowlands.
- The pits are for rattling with, that's why we name it thus. We split the pits and poke out the insides and then bore them and thread them on vine-strip and tie many of them to a length of wood, and then we rattle them while we dance panpipe dances and perform chants.
- When small we build houses with it.
- We also fell it for fuel.
- The big tree is also suitable for cutting into wooden planks.

KETE = RATTLE / *Planchonella thyrsoidea* C.T. White (*Sapotaceae*)

KETEKETE, 'ai ne'e keta ka doe liu ana ti 'ai, nia kobakoba'a 'i 'aena, nonina mela, rauna ketaketa'a gwauna ra'irū ka raku.

- ○ Nia ke bulao ana kunukunua ma māna kafo doe kī.
- • Ti'iti'ilana ki saunga'i luma 'ania .
- • Na 'ai doe ki saunga'i iolo 'ania.
- • Ki tufua kobakobana fuana saunga'ilana baba 'i kilafa kī ana, kaidai 'i na'o.
- • Ki kwa'ia logo fuana so'i.
- • Na 'ai doe ne'e bolo logo fuana 'olelana 'ania reba 'ai kī.

KO'A (ki fa'asatā logo 'ania KWA'A) nia to'o ana ti malita'irū.

KO'A KINI ne'e ko'a 'inoto'a, 'ai ne'e ke doe liu mala, nonina ka gwā, rauna keta ka sisilia. Lalina ne'e mamata fa'asia lalina ko'a ngwane, ni'i sau saga go'o 'aena itanga'irū. Nia ke fungu 'ania fa'irū keta liu, kaida'i nia kesi afisu 'ua nia to'o ana ofiofirū, kaida'i nia doe ka make na'a nia meosakosako'anga, ka asia 'i ano. Nia ke bulao ana fa'irū kī.
- ○ Nia bulao saena kabara ma 'i ninimana asi ma sulia logo su'u kī.
- • Fa'irū kī ki goea ki garasia ta'eta'ena ka sui, ki fi'i ko'ā ki du'afia fuana 'anilana. Ta ne'e ki saea 'ania ko'a.
- • Ti'iti'ilana ki saunga'i luma 'ania, nia le'a sulia nia ngasi ka tasa.
- • Ki tufua boborū fuana ta'itala liu saena maguru, nia le'a ka tasa sulia nia ke teo tau.
- • Ki tufua fuana fa'i sau'a.
- • Ki kwa'ia logo fuana so'i.
- • Ki guragura logo 'ania.

KO'A NGWANE, ki saea logo 'ania KWA'I-KWA'IALI, KABARA'A 'ai ne'e ke doe liu mala, lalina kabakaba liu, ta ne'e ki fa'asatā 'uri ana. Rauna ka keta, noa'a nia kesi fungu.
- ○ Nia ke bulao saena maguru ma 'i ninimana asi ma sulia logo su'u kī.
- • Rao'a 'ania fuana saunga'ilana luma noima fa'i sau'a nia bolo logo fa'inia ko'a kini.
- • Ki tufua logo fuana ta'itala saena maguru.
- • Ki kwa'ia logo fuana so'i.

CAMPNOSPERMA, this tree gets tall and much bigger than other trees, it is buttressed at the foot, its body is brown, its leaf is longish and the top of the leaf is pointed.
- ○. It grows in swamp and at the mouth of big waters.
- • When small we build houses with it.
- • The big tree we make canoes from.
- • We cut the buttresses for making door-boards, in former times.
- • We also fell it for fuel.
- • The big tree is also suitable for cutting into wooden planks.

KETEKETE = CAMPNOSPERMA / solomon islands maple / *Campnosperma brevipetiolata* Volkens (*Anacardiaceae*)

SCRAPING has several kinds.
KO'A / KWA'A = SCRAPING / mangrove

FEMALE SCRAPING is the important scraping, this tree gets very big indeed, its body is black, its leaf is long and narrow. Its root is different from the root of male scraping, it emerges straight from the foot of the main stem. It bears very long fruit, when it has not yet dropped it has a sheath and when it is big and ripe it is yellowish-red and falls to the ground. It grows from its fruit.
- ○ It grows in the stilt-roots and beside the sea and also along inlets.
- • The fruits we gather up and scratch off the skin, then we scrape it and burn it to eat. That's why we call it scraping.
- • When small we build houses from it, it is good because it is especially hard.
- • We chop logs for paths through the mangroves, it is especially good because it is long-lasting.
- • We chop it for (food) pounders.
- • We also fell it for fuel.
- • We also cure with it.

KO'A KINI = FEMALE SCRAPING / brown mangrove / oriental mangrove / *Bruguiera gymnorrhiza* (L.) Lamk. (*Rhizophoraceae*)

MALE SCRAPING, also called LONG-*KWA'I-KWA'I*, STILT-ROOT, this tree gets very big indeed, its roots are very stilt-like, that's why we name it thus. Its leaf is long and it doesn't bear.
- ○ It grows in the mangroves and beside the sea and also along inlets.
- • Its uses for building houses or making pounders are the same as female scraping.
- • We also chop it for paths in the mangroves.
- • We also fell it for fuel.

KO'A NGWANE / KWA'IKWA'IALI / KABARA'A = MALE SCRAPING / LONG-*KWA'IKWA'I* / STILT-ROOT / red mangrove / *Rhizophora apiculata* Bl. / *R. stylosa* Griff. (*Rhizophoraceae*)

KO'A DILA, ta sata MALAKO'A, 'ai ne'e kesi doe liu go'o, lisilana te'e gwagwā'anga karangi ke di'ia logo ko'a 'inoto'a bore ma rauna te'e molimoli'a lala, lalina kesi garagara. Nia ke fungu 'ania fa'irū ketaketa'a, nia ke bulao ana fa'ina.

- Nia ke bulao saena maguru ma 'i ninimana asi.
- Ki saunga'i luma 'ania kasi 'ai saga kī.
- Ki saunga'i fote 'ania

KO'A FANEFANE, 'ai ne'e kesi doe liu go'o, nonina borabora'a, rauna nunura ka ta'i baba'ula ana rauna ko'a saga. Takana ka sisimia ka kwao nia ke bulao ana fuana.

- Nia ke bulao ana kula kī ta'ifau, saena dukwasi kī, te'e saena kula kunukunu'a nia noa'a, nia ne'e saea 'ania ko'a fanefane.
- Ki saunga'i luma 'ania.
- Ki sabangi 'ania.
- Ki kwa'ia logo fuana so'i.

DILA SCRAPING, also called FALSE-SCRAPING, this tree doesn't get very big, it looks quite blackish almost like the important scraping (*Bruguiera*) but its leaf is a bit rounder and its roots don't spread. It bears longish fruit and it grows from its fruit.

- It grows in the mangroves and beside the sea.
- We build houses with straight lengths of tree.
- We make paddles from it.

KO'A DILA / MALAKO'A = DILA SCRAPING / FALSE SCRAPING / pemphis / *Pemphis acidula* J. R. & G. Forst. (*Lythraceae*)

RISING SCRAPING, this tree doesn't get very big, its body is purplish, its leaf is shiny and a bit thicker than the leaf of scraping proper. Its flower is narrow and white and it grows from its fruit.

- It grows in all places, in wilderness, only not in swamp, which is why we call it rising scraping.

- When small we build houses with it.
- We conduct (yam vines) with it.
- We also fell it for fuel.

KO'A FANEFANE = RISING SCRAPING / *Garcinia hollrungii* Ltb. / *G. aff. platyphlla* A.C.Sm. / *G. aff. pseudoguttifera* Seem. / *G. sessilis* (Forst.) Seem. / *Pentaphalangium solomonense* A.C. Sm. / *G. celebica* L. (*Clusiaceae*)

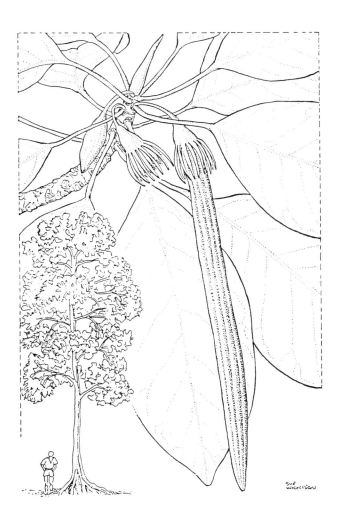

ko'a kini / female mangrove ▶

MABURA, 'ai ne'e noa'a nia kesi doe go'o, nonina 'efo'efo'a, rauna ka ketaketa'a ka marako, ka di'ia rauna ko'a, bore ma nia ta'i raurau'a go'o.
- ○ Nia ke bulao sulia su'u kī ma saena kunukunua kī, ka tasa ana kula ne'e ko'a ke bulao ana.
- • Ki saunga'i luma 'ania.
- • Ki kwa'ia fuana so'i di'ia nia ke du'a noima ka mae ka 'asia 'i ano.

KONA, ki saea logo 'ania GONA, 'ai ne'e ke doe liu mala, rauna raurau'a, takana ka kwao.
- ○ Nia ke bulao saena tolo.
- • Ti'iti'ilana ki saunga'i luma 'ania.
- • Ki kwa'ia logo fuana so'i.
- • Na 'ai doe ka bolo logo fuana 'olelana 'ania reba 'ai kī.

MALAKONA nia karangi ka di'ia logo kona bore ma noa'a la'u kona 'inoto'a. 'Ai ne'e ke doe liu mala, nonina gwagwā'a, rauna raurau'a, takana ka mela.
- ○ Nia ke bulao ana tolo.
- • Ti'iti'ilana ki saunga'i luma 'ania.
- • Ki kwa'ia fuana so'i.
- • Na 'ai doe ka bolo logo fuana 'olelana 'ania reba 'ai kī.

MALAIOLO, 'ai ne'e ke doe liu mala, nonina ka borabora'a, rauna te'e molimoli'a ka te'e raurau'a go'o.
- ○ Nia ke bulao ana ta kula go'o 'ana.
- • Ti'iti'ilana ki saunga'i luma 'ania .
- • Ki kwa'ia fuana so'i.
- • Na 'ai doe ka bolo logo fuana 'olelana 'ania reba 'ai kī.

RIRU, 'ai ne'e ke doe liu mala, nonina kwaokwao'a, rauna ka sisilia ka ketaketa'a, nia ka fungu 'ania fa'irū kī, fuana molimoli'a.
- ○ Nia ke bulao saena to'ona'oa ka tasa ana gwa'i kwaru ma nia ke bulao logo saena tolo goro ma kula kunukunu'a kī.

BRUGUEIRA, this tree doesn't get very big, its body is scaly, its leaf is longish and green, like a scraping (mangrove) leaf but a bit slender.
- ○ It grows along inlets and in swamps, especially in places where scraping grows.
- • When small we build houses with it.
- • We fell it for fuel if it is dried or dies and falls to the ground.

MABURA = BRUGUEIRA / *Bruguiera parviflora* (Roxb.) W. & A. ex Griff. (*Rhizophoraceae*)

BURCKELLA, this tree gets very big indeed, its leaf is slender, its flower is white.
- ○ It grows in the inland.
- • When small we build houses with it.
- • We also fell it for fuel.
- • The big tree is also suitable for cutting into wooden planks.

KONA / GONA = BURCKELLA / *Burckella obovata* (Forst.) Pierre (*Sapotaceae*)

FALSE-BURCKELLA is almost like burckella (*kona*) but it is not the most important burckella. This tree gets very big indeed, its body is blackish, its leaf is slender, its flower is brown.
- ○ It grows in the inland.
- • When small we build houses with it.
- • We fell it for fuel.
- • The big tree is also suitable for cutting into wooden planks.

MALAKONA = FALSE BURKELLA / *Burckella sorei* Royen / *B.* aff. *obovata* (Forst.) Pierre (*Sapotaceae*)

MALAIOLO, this tree gets very big indeed, its body is purplish, its leaf is quite rounded and quite slender.
- ○ It grows in any place at all.
- • When small we build houses with it.
- • We fell it for fuel.
- • The big tree is suitable for cutting into wooden planks.

MALAIOLO = *MALAIOLO* / *Mimusops elengi* L. / *Palaquium ambionense* Burck. / *P. galctoxylum* (Muell.) Lamk. / *P. morobense* Royen. / *P. Salomonense* C. T. White / *P. stehlinii* C. Chr. / *P. masuui* Roy.en. / *Planchonella torricellensis* (Schum.) Lamk. / *P. erythrospermum* Lamk. / *P. firma* (Miq.) Dub. / *P. macropoda* Lamk. (*Sapotaceae*)

PLANCHONELLA, this tree gets very big, its body is whiteish, its leaf is narrow and longish, it bears fruit and the fruit is rounded.
- ○ It grows in the lowland especially among rocks and it also grows in the misty inland and swampy places.

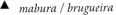

▲ *mabura / brugueira*

- 'Ai ne'e ngasi liu ma ka onaona liu, nia ne'e ki saunga'i 'ania rū di'ia ka'ika'ina kwa'ikwa'i ma fa'i kuba ma kafa saunga'ini'i ana ta'i reba 'ai.

- Ki saunga'i luma logo 'ania.

MALAGISO, 'ai ne'e ke doe liu mala, nonina te'e gwagwā'a, saena kasirū marako, buira ka'irū kwaokwao'anga. Rauna karangi ke di'ia logo gwarogwaro. Nia ke bulao ana takana.

- Nia ke bulao saena to'ona'oa ma saena logo tolo, saena dukwasi logo, bore ma fafona asi ma saena kunukunu ne'e noa'a.
- Ti'iti'ilana ki saunga'i luma 'ania.
- Ki kwa'ia fuana so'i.

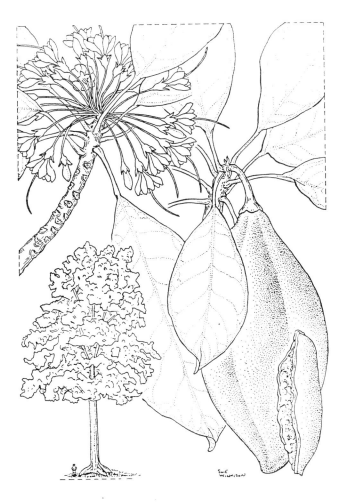

▲ *kona / burckella*

- This tree is very strong and tough, that's why we make things with it like axe handles and walking sticks and the combs made from one flat of wood.
- We also build houses with it.

RIRU = PLANCHONELLA / *Planchonella costata* (Endl.) Pierre ex. Lamk. / *P. chartacea* (Muell.) Lamk. / *P. linggensis* (Burck.) Pierre (*Sapotaceae*)

MALAGISO, this tree gets very big indeed, its body is quite blackish, the inside of the poles is green and behind the stems is whiteish. Its leaf is almost like calophyllum (*gwarogwaro*), it grows from its flower.

- It grows in the lowland and also in the inland, in wilderness, but not on the sea or in swamps.

- When small we build houses with it.
- We fell it for fuel.

MALAGISO = *MALAGISO*

MALANUNU, 'ai ne'e ke doe liu mala, nia to'o ana rō malita'irū kī.

MALANUNU saga, nonina te'e borabora'a bore ma kaida'i nia ū saena dukwasi ni'i kwaokwao'anga. Ta'eta'ena baba'ula, saena sakosako'a. Gwangona nia maramarako'a.
○ Nia ke bulao go'o 'i fafona kafo kī ma daudaurafia kī, ma saena logo tolo.
• 'Ai ne'e noa'a nia kesi ngasi go'o, no'a nia kesi bolo fa'inia saunga'inga.
• Ki tufua ke kwa'i, ka leleka nia ke fura, fuana gero ke ala ana 'i ki 'īnia fuana 'anilana.
• Ki kwa'ia fuana so'i.

MALANUNU FAU, ki saea logo 'ania BULUA, rauna bulubulu'anga ka reba liu mala, gwangona ka meomeo'a.
○ Nia ke bulao saena to'ona'oa ma saena tolo ka tasa ana ninimana kafo kī.
• 'Ai ne'e nia ngasi, ta ne'e ki saea 'ania malanunu fau. Ki tufua fuana diro ma fa'i gwaofa fuana luma kī sulia ni'i ke teo fa'asia ta talata'ingwae 'uana ta talata'ingwae.
• Ki saunga'i kafa 'ania, kafa nai'ari ki alasia go'o 'ania ta'i ma'erū.
• Nia le'a logo fuana so'i.
• Na 'ai doe ka bolo logo fuana 'olelana 'ania reba 'ai kī.

MAMALADE, 'ai te'e doe ne'e, nonina mamarako'anga, fa'i 'ai kī sasabe'a liu, ta'eta'ena ka nemanema go'o, fuana ketaketa'a ka marako. Rauna ti'iti'i go'o, fa'ina ka rebareba ka keta.
○ Nia ke bulao go'o 'ana ana kula kī sui.
• Nia le'a ka tasa fuana saunga'i luma'a sulia nia sagasaga'a ka ngasi logo.
• Ki tadilia logo fuana suba'e kī.
• Ki sabangi logo 'ania.
• Talina ngela kī ke danga 'ania saena mafu 'i ke busu di'ia fa'i kareke kī.

MUDU, 'ai ne'e ke doe liu mala, nonina gwagwā'a, rarana ka 'oro liu, rauna ka molimloli'a ka marako.

○ Nia ke bulao saena dukwasi saena to'ona'oa, nia 'oro logo saena tolo.

NEONAUCLEA, this tree gets very big indeed, and it has two kinds.

NEONAUCLEA proper, its body is quite purplish but when it stands in wilderness it is whiteish. Its skin is thick and yellow inside. Its leaf-shoot is greenish.
○ It grows on waters and steep slopes, and also in the inland.
• This tree is not strong and not suitable for building.
• We chop and fell it and eventually it rots for fungi to sprout on it and we pick them to eat.
• We fell it for fuel.

SOLID NEONAUCLEA, also called DARK, its leaf is darkish and very wide indeed and its leaf-shoot is reddish.
○ It grows in the lowland and in the inland, especially beside waters.
• This tree is strong, that's why we call it solid neonauclea. We chop it for posts and ridge-beams for houses because it remains from generation to generation.
• We make combs from it, the combs we shave from a single piece.
• It is also good for fuel.
• The big tree is suitable for cutting into wooden planks.

MALANUNU = NEONAUCLEA / *Neonauclea* sp. (3888 / 4100 / 19144 / DCRS 441) (*Naucleaceae*)
MALANUNU FAU / BULUA = SOLID NEONAUCLEA / DARK

ALANGIUM, this is a quite big tree, its body is greenish, the tree is very straight, its skin is thin, its poles are longish and green. Its leaf is small, its fruit is wideish and long.
○ It just grows in all places.
• It is especially good for house-building because it is straight and strong.
• We also trim it for dibbles.
• We also conduct (yam-vines) with it.
• Its pits children drop into the fire to burst like cartridges.

MAMALADE =ALANGUIM / *Alangium javanicum* (Bl.) Wang (*Alangiaceae*)

MUDU, this tree gets very big indeed, its body is blackish, it has very many branches, its leaf is rounded and green.
○ It grows in wilderness in the lowland and it is also plentiful in the inland.

- Ki 'oia uila fuana laungilana 'ania ngwa'i kī ka tasa fuana ngwae 'alako kī, sulia di'ia rauna ngwati'ula nia ke moko le'a ma ka lia le'a.
- Ki saunga'i luma 'ania.
- Ki du'a logo 'ania sulia nia le'a fuana so'i.
- 'Ai ne'e nia ngasi liu, na 'ai doe ka bolo fuana 'olelana 'ania reba 'ai kī.

RĀ 'ai ne'e ke doe mala, rauna ta'i reba. Nia ke fungu 'ania fa'irū doe ka molimoli'a, talirū ngasi nia 'i saena. Nia ke bulao ana fa'irū.
○ Nia ke bulao nama saena dukwasi.
- Talina fa'irū, ki saunga'i 'ania rā kī fuana ngwa'enga'a, ki itoa ana 'aeka. Kaida'i ki ngwa'engwa'e, rongolana ketekete ka rā, ta ne'e ki fa'asata 'uri ana.
- Nia le'a liu fuana saunga'i luma'a.
- Noa'a kisi du'a 'ania sulia ta'eta'ena nia momote.
- Rauna ki rarangia ki afua 'ania gwau 'i ngwae 'ūla kī 'i ke saungia 'ū.

MALASATA, 'ai ne'e ke doe mala, nonina te'e kwaokwao'anga, rauna ka te'e ketaketa'a ka te'e sisimi'a go'o.
○ Nia ke bulao go'o ana kula kī sui.
- Ki tufua ki tadilia fuana suba'e fuana kilu'a.

- Ki saunga'i luma 'ania.
- Ki kwa'ia fuana so'i.
- Ki gura logo 'ania ti mata'inga.

SALU ne'e 'ai doe keta mala, nonina te'e gwagwā'anga, rauna marako ka ti'iti'i go'o.
○ Nia ke bulao 'i fafona asi.
- Nia ngasi le'a fuana saunga'ilana rū kī di'ia kakina akisi ma alafolo, bore ma kaida'i afu 'ai nia faolu ki sofonga'inia fa'asia sina, nia kata foga.
- Nia ngasi le'a logo fuana saunga'ilana luma.
- Lalina ki saunga'inia 'ania atola fuana dēa saena kafo.

- We break off fronds to decorate bags with, especially for young men, because when the leaves dry out they smell good and look good.
- We build houses with it.
- We also burn with it because it is good for fuel.
- This tree is very strong and the big tree is suitable for cutting into wooden planks.

MUDU = MUDU / *Dillenia ingens* Burtt (*Dilleniaceae*)

CRASH, this tree gets really big, its leaf is quite wide. It bears big rounded fruit with hard pits inside. It grows from its fruit.
○ It must grow in wilderness.
- The pit of the fruit we make into crashers for dancing, we tie them to our legs. When we dance its sound rattles and crashes, that's why we name it thus.
- It is very good for house-building.
- We don't burn with it because its skin is scratchy.
- The leaf we warm and wrap the head of a lousy person with it to kill the lice.

RĀ = CRASH / football tree / *Pangium edule* Reinw. (*Flacourtiaceae*)

MALASATA, this tree gets really big, its body is a bit whiteish, its leaf is quite longish and quite narrow.
○ It grows in all places.
- We chop and trim it for dibbles for burying (planting tubers).
- We build houses with it.
- We fell it for fuel.
- We also cure some illnesses with it.

MALASATA = MALASATA / *Casearia grewiaefolia* Vent. / *Erythrospermum candidum* (Becc.) Becc. / *Homalium tatambense* Sleum. (*Flacourtiaceae*) / *Drypetes lasiogynoides* Pax & Hoffm. (*Euphorbiaceae*)

CASUARINA is a big tall tree, its body is a bit blackish, its leaf is green and small.
○ It grows on the sea.
- It is good and strong for making things like axe handles and deflector-clubs, but while the wood is new we hide it from the sun lest it splits.
- It is also good and strong for building houses.
- Its root we make traps from for fishing in the waters.

SALU = CASUARINA / south sea ironwood / she oak / beefwood / *Casuarina equisetifolia* J.R. & G. Forst. (*Casuarinaceae*)

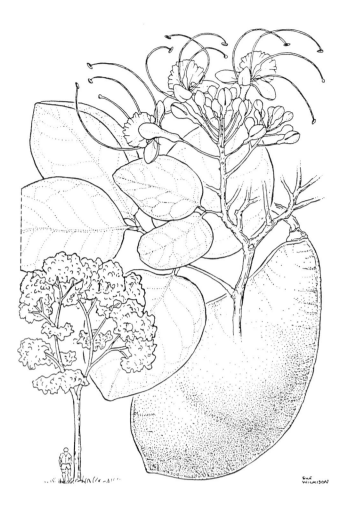

◀ *u'ula / ipil*

U'ULA,'ai ne'e ke doe mala, ta'eta'ena kwao rafurafu'a, saena ta'eta'ena ka meomeo'anga. Rauna ka molimoli'a, nia ke taka ka fungu logo, nia ngasi liu.
- ◦ Nia ke bulao ana kula kī ta'ifau, ka tasa go'o 'i fafo 'i asi.
- • Fa'i 'ai ti'iti'i kī ka le'a fuana saunga'i luma'anga ma ki saunga'i funu logo 'ani fuana luma sulia 'ai ne'e ona mala. Nia le'a ka tasa logo fuana diro kī.
- • Ki labu sakali logo 'ania.
- • Fa'i 'ai doe kī ka le'a logo fuana reba 'ai kī.
- • Ki gurā 'ania ti mata'inga.

'AIMARAKO, 'ai ne'e doe mala, nonina maramarako'a, rauna ka ketaketa'a ka te'e reba, takana kwao ka ti'iti'i.
- ◦ Nia ke bulao saena fafona asi
- • Ki saunga'i luma 'ania.
- • Ki kwa'ia fuana so'i.

IPIL, this tree gets really big, its skin has a white bloom, the inside of the skin is reddish. The leaf is rounded, it flowers and bears too, and it is very strong.
- ◦ It grows in all places, especially on the sea.

- • The small trees are good for house-building and we also make posts from it for houses because the tree is really tough. It is especially good for posts.
- • We also stake fences with it.
- • The big tree is also good for wooden planks.
- • We also cure some sicknesses with it.

U'ULA = IPIL / *Intsia bijuga* (Colebr.) Kuntze (*Fabaceae*)

GREEN-TREE, this tree gets really big, its body is greenish, its leaf is longish and quite wide, its flower is white and small.
- ◦ It grows on the sea.
- • We build houses with it.
- • We fell it for fuel.

'AIMARAKO = GREEN-TREE / *Mastixia kaniensis* Melch. / *Pongamia pinnata* (L.) Pierre (*Mastixiaceae*) / *Papil*(?)

AKWA, 'ai ne'e ke doe mala, nonina meomeo-'anga ma rauna ka te'e keta ma ka te'e reba ka marako, takana te'e kwao ma fa'irū kī ka te'e rebareba'a.
- ○ Nia ke bulao go'o ana kula kī sui saena to'onaoa ma ka tasa logo saena tolo. Nia ke bulao ke 'oro liu, ka tasa ana ti kula.
- • Nia le'a ka tasa fuana saunga'ilana luma.
- • Ki kwa'ia logo fuana so'i, nia ke du'a kwasukwasu, noa'a nia kesi du'a dangi go'o.
- • Ki 'olea logo rebana fuana saunga'inga.
- • Ki gura logo 'ania ti mata'inga kī.

SIMALAU, 'ai ne'e ka keta ka gwalogwalo'a. Nia matanga'a 'ania ka'ika'irū kī 'i gwauna, rauna keta ka sisilia go'o, fulina ka'ika'irū kī ki lisia 'i nonina 'ingata'i 'ai.
- ○ Nia ke bulao ana to'ona'oa ma saena logo tolo.
- • Ki kwa'ia fuana so'i.
- • Ki gura logo 'ania ti mata'inga.

AKWA, this tree gets really big, its body is brownish and its leaf is quite long and quite wide and green its flower is quite white and its fruit is quite wideish.
- ○ It grows in all places in the lowland and especially in the inland. It grows very plentifully, especially in some places.
- • It is especially good for building houses.
- • We also fell it for fuel, it burns flaming, it won't burn till day.
- • We also cut it into planks for building.
- • We also cure some sicknesses with it.

AKWA = *AKWA*

SIMALAU, this tree is tall and straight. It divides into stems at the head, its leaf is long and narrow and the sites (scars) of the stems can be seen on the body of the trunk.
- ○ It grows in the lowland and also in the inland.
- • We fell it for fuel.
- • We also cure some sicknesses with it.

SIMALAU = *SIMALAU* / *Gastonia spectabilis (Harms.) Philipson* / *Peekeliipanax spectabilis Harms* / *Polyscias neo-ebudanum (Guill.) B.C. Stone* (*Araliaxceae*)

'Ai ne'e kesi doe liu go'o kī

Trees which don't get very big

NGARA, 'ai ne'e kesi doe liu go'o, nonina ka te'e maramarako'a, rauna reba mala ma ka molimoli'a, takana kwao, fuana molimoli'a ka te'e doe. Nonina, di'ia nia du'a na'a nia momote liu, ta ne'e ki saea 'ania nia ne'e ngara, bore ma di'ia nia mauri 'ua nia kesi momote.

○ Nia ke bulao ana kula kī ta'ifau, saena fuli fanoa kī, te'e saena kunu ne'e noa'a. Nia bulao to'oto'o, nia kesi 'oro liu go'o.
• Ki saunga'i diro 'ania fuana luma kī, bore ma nia kesi le'a fuana saunga'i luma'a.
• Ki labu 'ania bā gwata logo sulia nia ke birabira, ki tufua itangana ma rarana ma fa'i 'ai ti'iti'i kī.

• Noa'a kisi kwa'ia fuana so'i sulia nia momote liu.
• Nia le'a fuana guragura'a fuana kini kesi ina.

'AIKAREFO, ta sata KAREFO, 'ai ne'e doe logo bore ma nia kesi doe liu go'o, nonina gwāgwā'a, ta'eta'ena ka ifiifi'a, rauna sisimi'a ka miga liu, takana ka kwao. Fuana ka bababa'a ka te'e ketaketa'a, ka di'ia fuana keresmasa bore ma nia ti'iti'i lala, di'ia nia make nia gwā ma di'ia ki salongā ma ki kwaila'inia ma magana ne'e kwatea ke ketekete. Kaida'i nia mae ka du'a ma rarana ka 'asia 'i ano, di'ia ki uria noima ki 'oia rarana nia ke mangingeda ka di'ia logo rongolana mafula ba ke du'a ke sikisiki, ta nini'a ki fa'asata 'uri ana sulia.

○ Nia ke bulao ka 'oro ana kula ki sui, ka tasa ana fuli raku faolu kī.
• Ki saunga'i luma 'ania, bore ma luma sasufi'i go'o ne'e bolo fa'inia sulia nia ngwara'u go'o ma suma ke 'ania.
• Nia le'a ka tasa fuana so'i sulia nia du'a kwasukwasu 'ali'ali ka liufia 'ai kī, ta ne'e ki saea 'ania aikarefo. Bore ma nia kesi du'adangi nia du'a maemaela.
• Ki guragura logo 'ania.

TANGAFENO, ti sata FINOFINO, FENOFENO, 'ai ne'e kesi doe liu go'o, nonina maramarako'a, rauna reba ka matanga'a, takana marako, fa'irū kī ka molimoli'a.

PRICKLY, this tree doesn't get very big, its body is a bit greenish, its leaf is really wide and rounded, its flower is white, its fruit is rounded and quite big. Its body, if it has dried out, is very scratchy, that's why we say it is prickly, but if it is alive it doesn't scratch.

○ It grows in all places, on home sites, only not in swamp. It grows individually and is not very plentiful.
• We make posts from it for houses but it is not very good for house-building.
• We also stake it for pig barriers because it sprouts, we chop its trunk, branches and small trees.
• We don't fell it for fuel because it is very scratchy.
• It is good for curing women not to be pregnant.
NGARA = PRICKLY / pua / *Fagraea racemosa* Jack. ex Wall. (*Potaliaceae*)

FLARE-TREE, also named FLARE, this tree gets big but not very big, its body is blackish, its skin is pithy, its leaf is narrow and very tiny, its flower is white. Its fruit is flat and quite wideish, like the fruit of Christmas tree (flame-tree / *Delonix*) but smaller, if it is ripe it is black and if we shake it and beat it, its seeds make it rattle. When it is dead and dried and its branches fall to the ground, if we tread on or break the branch it crackles like the sound of a fire sparking, that's what we name it after.

○ It grows plentifully in all places, especially in new shoots sites.
• We build houses with it, but it is only suitable for smoky houses because it is just soft and worms eat it.
• It is especially good for fuel because it burns flaming and fast, more than other trees, that's why we call it flare-tree. But it doesn't burn till day, it burns dying.
• We also cure with it.
'AIKAREFO / KAREFO = FLARE-TREE / FLARE / *Shleinitzia novo-guineensis* (Warb.) Verdc. (*Mimosaceae*)

MACARANGA, this tree doesn't get very big, its body is greenish, its leaf is wide and divided, its flower is green and its fruits are rounded.

▲ *ngara / prickly*

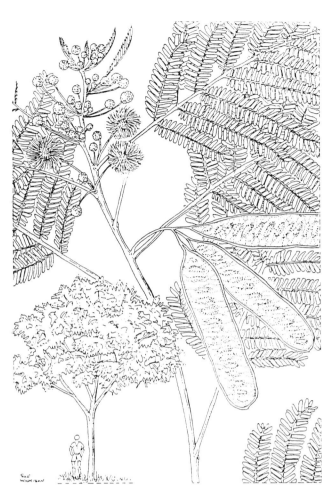

▲ *'aikarefo / flare-tree*

○   Nia ke bulao ana kula kī ta'ifau, te'e saena kunu ne'e noa'a, ka 'oro ana to'ona'oa. 'Ai ana raku faolu go'o, ke bulao ana fuila kula tabu'i ka buru kī, ka tasa 'i fuila o'olā kī, ma di'ia 'ai ana dukwasi nunufia ma nia ke mae logo.

• Rauna le'a ka tasa fuana gwa'abi'anga 'ania.
• Rauna ki solea logo 'ania onina ngela kī.
• Rauna ki 'afua logo 'ania subi 'i ne'e rū kī kesi karasia, nia bolo fa'inia sulia lisilana rauna nia bolo fa'inia subi.
• Ki saunga'i luma 'ania, noa'a suma kesi 'ania bore ma ka bolo go'o fa'inia luma sasufi'i ma gwaurau kī go'o sulia nia kesi ngasi liu go'o.
• Ki kwa'ia logo fuana so'i, nia le'a ka tasa sulia nia du'a kwasukwasu bore ma nia du'a maemaela go'o, noa'a kesi du'a dangi di'ia ti 'ai.
• Ki gura logo 'ania mata'inga kī.

○   It grows in all places, except not in swamp, it is plentiful in the lowland. It is just a tree of the new shoots and grows on cleared, dense (overgrown) sites, especially garden sites, and if the trees of the wilderness shades it, it dies.

• Its leaf is good for oven-cooking with.
• Its leaf we also wipe up children's shit with.
• Its leaf we also wrap an angle-club in so things won't scratch it, it is suitable because the leaf looks the same as an angle-club (a lozenge).
• We build houses with it, worms don't eat it but it is only suitable for smoky homes and leaf-shelters because it is not very strong.
• We fell it for fuel, it is especially good because it burns flaming but it just burns dying and doesn't burn till day like some trees.
• We also cure sicknesses with it.

TANGAFINO / FINOFINO / FENOFENO = MACARANGA / *Macaranga aleuritoides* Muell.   (*Euphorbiaceae*)

'AIDORI, 'ai ne'e kesi doe liu go'o, nonina te'e kwaokwao'a, rauna ka keta ka reba, takana kwao-kwao'anga, fa'irū kī te'e ketaketa'a ka ti'iti'i go'o.
- ○ Nia ke bulao fa'asia fafona asi 'uana 'i tolo, bore ma noa'a nia kesi bulao saena kunu-kunu'a. Nia bulao to'oto'o, ka tasa ana ti kula, ana ano bulu, noa'a nia kesi 'oro liu go'o.
- Siko ne'e satana fa'i dori kī ogā liua tua'a ana rauna, sulia lisilana di'ia fa'i dori kī. Ki lia 'uana fa'i dori ana rauna 'aidori nai'ari kī fuana 'anilani.
- Nia te'e le'a fuana saunga'inga sulia nia te'e ngasi bore ma nia ke suma'ala'a logo, nia bolo go'o fa'inia saunga'ilana luma sasufi'i kī.
- Ki kwa'ia logo fuana so'i bore ma noa'a kesi du'a dangi.
- Ki gurā 'ania ti mata'inga.

'ALABUSI nia 'ai ne'e kesi doe liu go'o, rauna marako ka molimoli'a.
- ○ Nia ke bulao saena to'ona'oa.
- Nia ngasi fuana saunga'i luma'a, bore ma nia bolo go'o fa'inia luma ti'iti'i di'ia luma ni du'urū'a ma babala gwata, si ne'e fa'irū kī dokodoko go'o.
- Ki tufua fuana sabangilana falisi, ki labua logo 'ania bā gwata, nia le'a sulia 'ai ne'e ke bulao ana 'itangana.
- 'Ali'alirū saga kī, ki tufu'i fuana raforafo fuana usa sao'anga ani'i.

KETO, 'ai ne'e noa'a kesi doe liu go'o, nonina gwagwa'a. Di'ia ki tufua nia ke birabira ana gwarirū. Nia bulao ana magana. Nia to'o ana rō malita'irū kī. KETO saga, rauna marako. KETO NGWANE, ngwasana meo, rauna meomeo'a logo.
- ○ Nia ke bulao ka 'oro liu ana ano kaolea kī saena to'ona'oa.
- Ki saunga'i luma 'ania, bore ma luma sasufi'i go'o ne'e bolo fa'inia si ne'e nia ke suma'ala'a.
- Ki kwa'ia logo fuana so'i.

REBAREBA, ta sata TAKASUI, 'ai ne'e rauna molimoli'a ka reba ma ka marako logo, nia to'o ana kakirū ne'e ra'irū fi'i sau ana. Ki saea 'ania rebareba sulia rauna reba. Takana sakosako'a ka nenere'a go'o.

DORI-TREE, this tree doesn't get very big, its body is quite whiteish, its leaf is long and wide, its flower is whiteish, its fruit is longish and just small.
- ○ It grows from on the sea to the inland, but it doesn't grow in swamp. It grows individually, especially in some places, on dark ground, it is not very plentiful
- The hoppers called *dori* like very much to live on the leaves, because they look like *dori*s. We look for *dori*s on the *dori*-tree leaves for eating.
- It is quite good for building because it is quite strong but it also becomes worm-eaten and is only suitable for building smoky houses.
- We fell it for fuel but it doesn't burn till day.
- We cure some sicknesses with it.

'AIDORI = *DORI*-TREE / *Bridelia minutiflora* Hook. f. / *B. penangiana* Hook. f. / *Antidesma olivaceum* Schum. / *A. rostrata* Muell. Arg. (*Euphorbiaceae*)

ACALYPHA is a tree which is not very big, its leaf is green and rounded.
- ○ It grows in the lowland.
- It is strong for house-building but it is only suitable for small houses like cooking houses and pig shelters, as the poles are just short.
- We chop it for conducting yam-vines and also stake pig barriers with it, it is good because the tree will grow from its (planted) trunk.
- The straight quick-growth we chop for battens for sewing sago (leaf) on (for roofing).

'ALABUSI =ACALYPHA / *Acalypha grandis* Benth. / *Mallotus tiliifolius* (Bl.) Muell. Arg. (*Euphorbiaceae*)

KETO, this tree doesn't get very big, its body is blackish. If we chop it down it sprouts from the stump. It grows from its seed. It has two kinds. *KETO* proper, its leaf is green. MALE *KETO*, its leaf shoot is red and its leaf is reddish too.
- ○ It grows very plentifully on clay ground in the lowland.
- We build houses with it, but it is only suitable for smoky houses as it becomes worm-eaten.
- We also fell it for fuel.

KETO = *KETO* / *Macaranga faiketo* Whitmore / *M. fimbriata* S. Moore / *M. inermis* Pax & Hoffm. / *M. lanceolata* Pax & Hoffm / *M. polyadenia* Pax & Hoffm. (*Euphorbiaceae*)
KETO NGWANE = MALE *KETO* / *Mallotus leucodermis* Hook.f. (*Euphorbiaceae*)

WIDEISH, also named FLOWER- FINISH, the leaf of this tree is rounded, wide and green and it has a stalk which the leaves develop from. We call it wideish because its leaf is wide. Its flower is yellow, tiny and multiple.

Nia ka taka ka sui, takana ni'i 'asi ta'ifau, noa'a nia kesi alua ti takarū la'u burina, nia ma'asia nama fuana kaida'i ana taka'a. Ta ne'e ki saea logo 'ania takasui. Fa'irū kī magarū'a ka ti'iti' go'o.

○ Nia ke bulao ana raku faolu ana kula kī ta'ifau go'o, ke 'oro saena to'ona'oa, te'e saena kunu ma gwa'i kwaru kī nia kesi bulao kesi 'oro liu go'o ani.

• Na rauna ki gwa'abi 'ania.
• Nia te'e le'a fuana saunga'i luma'a, bore ma luma sasufi'i go'o ne'e bolo fa'inia sulia suma ke 'ania ma gwagwao ke sotea.
• Ki kwa'ia logo fuana so'i, nia du'a kwasukwasu bore ma nia maemaela.

SU'AMANGO, 'ai ne'e kesi doe liu go'o, nonina kwaokwao'a, rauna ka reba ka konakona'a, takana ka kwao ka magamaga'a, fuana ka molimoli'a ka maramarako'a.

○ Nia ke bulao ana kula kī ta'ifau ka tasa saena raku faolu kī, ke 'oro liu di'ia logo ti 'ai, ka tasa saena to'ona'oa.

• Ki ngalia rauna fuana 'aralana 'ania nonika 'i ke faolu, ki 'inia logo rauna fuana 'asaboro'a, ma ki su'afia 'onina ngela kī 'ania rauna.
• Ki saunga'i luma 'ania, bore ma nia ngwarau go'o, na suma ke 'ania ma nia ke fura 'ali'ali, nia bolo go'o fa'inia luma sasufi'i.
• Nia le'a fuana so'i bore ma nia ke du'a maemaela.
• Ki gura 'ania mangotorotoro.
• Ki saea 'ania su'amango sulia ki su'afia 'ania ma ki guragura logo ngwae ne'e mata'i 'ania mango.

MADAKWARE'A, 'ai ne'e noa'a kesi doe liu go'o, nonina ka kwao, rauna kesi doe liu go'o.

○ Nia ke bulao saena dukwasi ma saena masu'u, ana ua 'i rū kī ma fafona asi, nia ka 'oro saena tolo.

• Di'ia 'ai ngasi kī di'ia mamalade ni'i 'ato, ki saunga'i bara 'ania madakware'a fuana ki alua so'i 'i saena fafona fu'a.
• Nia le'a logo fuana saunga'i luma'a.
• Nia le'a ka tasa fuana so'i sulia nia du'a kwasukwasua.

When it finishes flowering the flowers all fall and it doesn't produce more flowers afterwards, it waits for flowering time That's why we also call it flower-finish. The fruits are full of seeds and small.

○ It grows in the new shoots in all places, and is plentiful in the lowland, only in swamp and rocks will it not grow plentifully.

• Its leaf we oven-cook with.
• It is quite good for house-building but only suitable for smoky houses because worms eat it and wasps bore it.
• We also fell it for fuel, it burns flaming but dying.

REBAREBA / TAKASUI = Wideish / FLOWER-FINISH / *Macaranga clavata* Warb / *M. tanarius* (L.) Muell.Arg. (*Euphorbiaceae*)

BREATH-WIPE, this tree doesn't get very big, its body is whiteish, its leaf is wide and sharp-pointed, its flower is white and has seeds, its fruit is rounded greenish.

○ It grows in all places, especially in new shoots, and is as plentiful as other trees, especially in the lowland.

• We take the leaf for scrubbing our bodies clean, we also pick the leaf for bottom-wiping and we wipe up children's shit with the leaf.
• We build houses with it but it is just soft, worms eat it and it rots quickly, it is only suitable for smoky houses.
• It is good for fuel but it burns dying.

• We cure breathlessness with it.
• We call it breath-wipe because we wipe with it and we also cure a person who is sick with breath problems with it.

SU'AMANGO = BREATH-WIPE / *Macaranga densiflora* Warb. / *M. dioica* (Forst.) Muell.Arg. / *M. aff. involucrata* (Roxb.) Baill. / *M. similis* Pax & Hoffm. / *M. urophylla* Pax & Hoffm. (*Euphorbiaceae*)

CROTON, this tree doesn't get very big, its body is white, its leaf is not very big.

○ It grows in wilderness in forest, on hills and on the sea, it is plentiful in the inland.

• If strong trees like alangium (*mamalade*) are hard to get we make a rack from croton for putting fuel on above the hearth.
• It is also good for house-building.
• It is especially good for fuel because it burns flaming.

MADAKWARE'A = CROTON / *Croton aff. choristadenia* A. Shaw / *C. pusilliflorus* Croisat (*Euphorbiaceae*)

'AIKWADU, 'ai ne'e kesi doe liu go'o, nonina te'e kwaokwao'a, rauna te'e reba ka ketaketa'a ka nunura, nia ke fungu 'ania fa'irū te'e doe ma ka molimoli'a. Ki fa'asata 'uri ana sulia no'o kwadu ke saunga'inia nu'i 'i gwauna 'ai.
○ Nia ke bulao ana ano bulu ana to'ona'oa.
• Ki saunga'i luma 'ania.
• Nia le'a logo fuana so'i.

'AI'AFAE, 'ai ne'e noa'a kesi doe liu go'o, nonina melamela'a, nia ketaketa'a go'o, rauna sisilia ka marako ma kesi doe liu go'o. Di'ia ki tufua suluna ka sikilia nonika, ki meato'ona nia 'afae liu, ta ne'e ki fa'asata 'uri ana.
○ Nia ke bulao ana kula ta'ifau fa'asia fafona asi 'uana 'i tolo.
• Ki saunga'i luma 'ania, nia le'a logo.
• Ki kwa'ia logo fuana so'i.
• Ki gura 'ania ngwa'ala.

'AINGWANE nia 'ai ne'e kesi doe liu, ki fa'asata 'uri ana sulia nia ke bulao ka ū ti'ana. Nonina kwaokwao'a, rauna ka keta ka reba.
○ Nia ke bulao go'o 'ana ana kula kī ta'ifau ana tolo ma fafo'i asi kī, bore ma kaole na'a ne'e nia bulao ka 'oro liu ana.
• Ki kwa'ia fuana so'i ki du'a 'ania.
• Ki guragura 'ania.

DILO, 'ai ne'e noa'a kesi doe liu go'o, nonina te'e kwao, rauna ka reba ka nunura, nia ke fungu 'ania fa'irū molimoli'a, kaida'i nia ke make ke kwao. Nia ke bulao ana fuana.
○ Nia ke bulao go'o 'i fafona asi ma saena fuli raku kī.
• Lalina ma ta'eta'ena ki atongirū 'ania, 'i ne'e ni'i ke meo. Ki atongia 'ania rū kī di'ia taketake niu ma 'aba obi fuana saunga'ilana rū fuana laungi kī. Ki dodoa memena fa'inia 'abarū kī, ki do'ofia 'i ne'e 'abarū kī ke meo.
• Ki gurā 'ania ngwae ne'e 'abura'e saungida.

KIKIRI, 'ai ne'e noa'a kesi doe liu go'o, lisilana karangi ka di'ia logo dilo, rauna reba ka ketaketa'a. Nia ke fungu 'ania fa'irū ka kwao, nia ke bulao ana magana. Fa'irū ne'e mamata lala fa'asia dilo.
○ Nia ke bulao ana kula kī ta'ifau saena to'ona'oa ma saena raku faolo.

KWADU-**TREE**, this tree doesn't get very big, its body is a bit whiteish, its leaf is quite wide and longish and shiny, it bears quite big rounded fruit. We name it thus because the *kwadu* bird builds its nest at the head of the tree.
○ It grows on dark ground in the lowland.
• We build houses with it.
• It is also good for fuel.
'AIKWADU = KWADU-TREE / *Cryptocarya aureo-sericea* Kost. / *C. medicinalis* C.T. White / *C. weinlandii* Schum. (*Lauraceae*) / *Polyalthia rumphii* (Bl.) Merr. (*Annonaceae*)

BITTER-TREE, this tree is not very big, its body is brownish, it is tallish, its leaf is narrow and green and not very big. If we chop it and the sap splatters our body, if we taste it it is very bitter, that's why we name it thus.
○ It grows in all places from on the sea to the inland.
• We build houses with it, it is quite good.
• We fell it for fuel.
• We cure poisonous bites with it.
'AI'AFAE = BITTER-TREE

MALE-TREE is a tree which is not very big, we name it thus because it stands by itself. Its body is whiteish, its leaf is long and wide.
○ It just grows in all places in the inland and on the sea, but it is on clay that it grows plentifully.

• We fell it for fuel and burn with it.
• We cure with it.
'AINGWANE = MALE-TREE / *Tarenna buruensis* (Miq.) Merr. / *T. sambiciana* (Forst.) Durand. (*Rubiaceae*)

DYE, this tree doesn't get very big, its body is quite white, its leaf is wide and shiny, it bears rounded fruit and when ripe it is white. It grows from its fruit.
○ It just grows on the sea and in shoots sites.

• Its root and skin we stain things with to become red. We stain things like coconut cuticle and band (*Calamus*) strip for making things for decoration. We flask a paste with the strips and burn them so the strips become red.
• We cure with it a person who is struck down by blood-pressure.
DILO = DYE / indian mulberry / beach mulberry / *Morinda salomonensis* Engl. / *M. citrifolia* L. (*Rubiaceae*)

KIKIRI, this tree doesn't get very big, it looks almost like dye (*dilo / Morinda*), its leaf is wide and longish. It bears white fruits and grows from its seed. The fruit is different from dye.
○ It grows in all places in the lowland and in new shoots.

kikiri / morinda ▶

- Ti ngwae ke 'ania fa'irū, 'anilana asila liu. Ki do'ofi'i mala ki fi'i 'ania, bore ma ngwae kī ta'ifau kesi 'ania. (Fuana dilo noa'a kisi 'ania).
- Na fa'i 'ai saga kī ki saunga'i luma 'ania.
- Ki kwa'ia logo fuana so'i.

SAKOSIA, 'ai ne'e kesi doe liu go'o bore ma ti ai ke doe liu mala. Nonina melamela'anga, rauna keta ka sisili'a go'o.
○ Nia ke bulao saena to'ona'oa, ka 'oro liu saena tolo, ana fuli raku kī ma kula kaole'a noima ana gwa'i kwaru kī bore 'ani.
- Na numa kī ke 'ania rauna ma ki 'oia fuana 'anilana.
- Kaida'i nia ke kwa'i 'i ano, ka leleka nia ke fura, gero kī di'ia gero'ulau ni'i ke ala ana fuana 'anilana.
- Ki saunga'i luma 'ania.
- Ki kwa'ia fuana so'i, nia le'a sulia nia du'a dangi liu.
- Ki kwaigurai 'ania gwangona, ki damia fuana siri ke langalanga.

- Some people eat the fruit, it is very sweet to eat. We burn it then eat it, but not everyone eats it. (Dye fruit we don't eat.)
- The straight trees we build houses with.
- We also fell it for fuel.

KIKIRI = *KIKIRI* / indian mulberry / *Morinda citrifolia* L. / *M. umbellata* L. (*Rubiaceae*)

TIMONIUS, this tree doesn't get very big but some of them do get very big. Its body is brownish and its leaf is long and narrow.
○ It grows in the lowland and is plentiful in the inland, in shoots sites and clay places or even among rocks.
- Caterpillars eat the leaf and we pick them to eat.
- When it falls to the ground and eventually rots, fungi like *'ulau* fungus sprout on it for eating.

- We build houses with it.
- We fell it for fuel, it is good because it burns till day well.
- We cure with the leaf-shoot, we chew it for diarrhoea to dry up.

SAKOSIA = TIMONIUS / *Timonius timon* (Spreng.) Merr. (*Rubiaceae*)

'AITAFISI'ORO, 'ai ne'e noa'a nia kesi doe liu go'o, rauna ta'i rebareba'a, nia ke fungu 'ania fa'irū kī, fa'ina ta'i ti'iti'i go'o, nia ke bulao ana fa'ina.
○ Nia ke bulao saena to'ona'oa.
• Noa'a nia 'isi bolo fa'inia saunga'i'anga 'ani sulia nia 'isi ngasi go'o.
• Rauna, ki alu uta 'ania, nia ne'e fuana fa'alilana fanga'a ta ngwae, ta ne'e ki fa'asata 'uri ana.
• Ki gura logo 'ania.

'AITEA, 'ai ne'e noa'a kesi doe liu go'o, nonina gwagwā'a, rauna kesi doe liu go'o ma fa'irū kī ka ti'iti'i go'o.
○ Nia ke bulao go'o 'ana ana kula kī sui, nia 'oro saena to'ona'oa.
• Nia le'a ka tasa fuana fa'i sau'a fuana saungilana ka'aka'a sulia nia 'eke'eke ma ka ngasi ma ka maomao'a, noa'a kesi fa'alia ka'aka'a 'ania sūla, noa'a kesi fa'alia limaka kaida'i ki saungia ka'aka'a.
• Ki kwa'ia logo fuana so'i, nia le'a sulia nia ngasi ka onaonala'a fuana ne'e ke du'adangi logo, nini'a ki saea 'ania na 'aitea.
• Ana asoa sui kī, ki lalia ma ki bulia fuana fa'amāliulana fanoa noima luma 'i ki ke saungida.

ALANGIA, 'ai ne'e noa'a kesi doe liu, nia dokodoko go'o, nia ke fi'irū'a ke birabira 'ania 'ai 'oro kī ana te'e 'itanga'i'ai. Nonina ka kwaokwao'a, rauna ka molimoli'a. Nia ke fungu 'ania fa'irū kī, fuana molimoli'a. Na sakwalo ke 'ania fa'irū kī.
○ Nia ke bulao go'o 'i fafona kafo kī, nia 'oro saena to'ona'oa.
• Ki kwa'ia fuana so'i.

MANGOMANGO, 'ai ne'e kesi doe liu go'o, nonina melamela'a, rauna ka te'e ketaketa'a ma ke fungu 'ania fa'irū kī.
○ Nia ke bulao ana kula kī sui saena raku faolu kī.
• Di'ia nia ke teo 'i nonina fanoa, karai kī ke ra'e ke māliu 'i gwauna.
• Ki kwa'ia fuana so'i.
• Ki guragura logo 'ania mangomango, ta ne'e ki fa'asata 'uri ana.

RAINBOW-TREE, this tree doesn't get very big, its leaf is quite wideish, it bears fruit, and the fruit is quite small and it grows from its fruit.
○ It grows in the lowland.
• It is not suitable for building with because it is not strong.
• Its leaf we cause rain with, it's for spoiling a person's feast, that's why we name it thus.
• We also cure with it.
'AITAFISIORO = RAINBOW-TREE / *Ficus immanis* Corner (*Moraceae*)

CONTINUOUS-TREE, this tree doesn't get very big, its body is blackish, its leaf is not very big and its fruits are only small.
○ It just grows in all places, it is plentiful in the lowland.
• It is especially good for pounders for making mash because it is dry and strong and smooth, it won't spoil the mash with sap and it won't damage our hands while we pound the mash.
• We also fell it for fuel, it is good because it is hard with embers which will burn till day, that's why we call it the continuous-tree.
• In bygone days we invoked and dedicated it to send a home or house to sleep so we could kill them.
'AITEA = CONTINUOUS-TREE / *Ficus austrina* Corner / *F. erythrosperma* Miq. / *F. indigofera* Rech. / *F. verticillaris* Corner (*Moraceae*)

ALANGIA, this tree doesn't get very big, it is only short, it forms a clump and sprouts many trees from one trunk. Its body is whiteish, its leaf is rounded. It bears fruit, the fruit is rounded. Bats eat the fruit.
○ It just grows on waters, it is plentiful in the lowland.
• We fell it for fuel.
ALANGIA = ALANGIA / *Ficus adenosperma* Miq. / *F. mollior* Benth. (*Moraceae*)

BREATHING, this tree doesn't get very big, its body is brownish, its leaf is quite longish, and it bears fruit.
○ It grows in all places, in the new shoots.
• If it is in the area of a home, chickens go up to sleep at its head.
• We fell it for fuel.
• We also cure beathing (problems) with it, that's why we name it thus.
MANGOMANGO = BREATHING / *Ficus arfakensis* King / *F. baccaureoides* Corner / *F. macrothyrsa* Corner. ssp. *lancifolia* / *F.* aff. *pachyrrhachis* Ltb. & Schum / *F. profusa* Corner / *F. scaposa* Corner / *F. tanypoda* Corner / *F. virens* Ait. (*Moraceae*)

DEDELA, 'ai ne'e kesi doe liu go'o, nonina gwagwā'a, rauna ka reba ka te'e molimoli'a ma ka mole'a.

○ Nia ke bulao ana kula kī sui.
• Rauna ki gwa'abi 'ania, ki buta logo rū kī 'ania.
• Ki kwa'ia logo fuana so'i.

FA'ADI'ILA, 'ai ne'e kesi doe liu, nonina gwagwā'a ma rauna ka fisifisila ka dokodoko ka molimoli'a. Sūla ka kwao ka tongatonga'a.

○ Nia ke bulao go'o saena to'ona'oa, to'o ti'i kaida'i go'o ne'e ki lisia saena tolo.
• Ki tufua fuana fa'i sau'a, ka di'ia logo 'aitea.
• Ki saunga'i luma 'ania.
• Ki kwa'ia logo fuana so'i.

SALA, 'ai ne'e kesi doe liu go'o, nonina mela ma ka reforefo'a. Kaida'i ana sato ra'efilana 'afita'i sulia ne'e nonina maomao'a, ta ne'e ki fa'asata 'uri ana. Rauna ka reba ma sūlana ka tongatonga'a ka kwao. Nia ka fungu sulia rarana ma nonina, sakwalo ke tete ana fa'irū kī.

○ Nia ke bulao ka 'oro saena to'ona'oa, nia saena logo tolo.
• 'Uli'ulina fa'i 'ai fi'i doe kī ki diua fuana saunga'ilana la'ua.
• Noa'a kisi saunga'i 'ania si ne'e nia ngwara'u liu.
• Ki kwa'ia fuana so'i.
• Sūlana ki kwaigurai logo 'ania.

SAMOTA, 'ai ne'e noa'a kesi doe liu go'o, rauna ka reba ka keta ka marako, ilina ra'irū kī momote. Nia ka fungu 'ania fa'irū kī ka marako ma kaida'i ni'i make ni'i ke sakosako'a. Noa'a kisi 'ania fa'irū kī.

○ Nia ke bulao ana kula kī ta'ifau, fa'asia fafona asi ka dao 'i tolo.
• Rauna ki 'inia ki alua ka bala fuana samotālana rū kī di'ia dako ma ka'ika'ina akisi. Ta ne'e ki fa'asata 'uri ana.
• Kaida'i nini'ari mike 'ara sosobini logo 'ania.
• Nia ti'iti'i noa'a kesi totolia saunga'ilana luma.
• Ki du'a logo 'ania.

DEDELA, this tree doesn't get very big, its body is blackish, its leaf is wide and quite rounded and shiny-white.

○ It grows in all places.
• Its leaf we oven-cook with and wrap things in.
• We also fell it for fuel.

DEDELA = *DEDELA* / *Ficus cynaroides* Corner / *F. lancibracteata* Corner / *F. longibracteata* Corner (*Moraceae*)

FA'ADI'ILA, this tree doesn't get very big, its body is blackish and its leaf is thin and short and rounded. Its sap is white and gummy.

○ It just grows in the lowland, only sometimes do we see it in the inland.
• We chop it for pounders, like continuous-tree (*'aitea* / *Ficus*).
• We build houses with it.
• We also fell it for fuel.

FA'ADI'ILA = *FA'ADI'ILA* / *Ficus verticillaris* Corner (*Moraceae*)

SMOOTH, this tree doesn't get very big, its body is brown and scaly. When it is sunny it is difficult to climb because its body is smooth, that's why we name it thus. Its leaf is wide and its sap is sticky and white. It bears along its branches and body and bats eat the fruit.

○ It grows plentifully in the lowland and is also in the inland.
• The bark of the young tree we hammer to make cloth.
• We don't build with it as it is very soft.

• We fell it for fuel.
• Its sap we also cure with.

SALA = SMOOTH / *Ficus nodosa* T.et B. / *F. variegata* Bl. (*Moraceae*)

ABRASIVE, this tree doesn't get very big, its leaf is wide and long and green and the back of the leaf is scratchy. It bears green fruit and when ripe they are yellow. We don't eat the fruit.

○ It grows in all places, from on the sea to the inland.
• Its leaf we pick and leave to go pale for abrading things like bowls and axe handles. That's why we name it thus.
• At present we also scrub saucepans with it.
• It is small and not fit for building houses.
• We also burn with it (as fuel).

SAMOTA = ABRASIVE / *Ficus chrysochaete* Corner / *F. imbricata* Corner / *F. oleracea* ssp. *pugans* Corner / *F. oleracea* ssp. *villosa* Corner / *F. storckii* Seem. / *F. trachypison* ssp. *pallida* Ltb. & Schum. (*Moraceae*)

RARANGA, 'ai ne'e kesi doe liu go'o, nonina ka gwagwā'a ma rauna ka te'e reba ma ka molimoli'a, ka ta'i ketaketa'a go'o, saena ra'irū ngarangara'a ka di'ia logo samota.

- ○ Nia ke bulao go'o ana kula kī sui.
- • Rauna ki samota 'ania ka di'ia logo samota, ki fa'asinafia 'i ke bala mala , ki fi'i samotā 'ania rū di'ia ka'ika'i akisi ma ra'unga kī ma dako kī.
- • Noa'a kisi saunga'i 'ania sulia nia ke suma'ala.
- • Ki kwa'ia fuana so'i.
- • Ki guragura logo 'ania dulina ngwae 'i ke doe ma ka keta, ki rarangia rauna ki lalafia 'ania dulina. Ta ne'e ki fa'asata 'uri ana.

NGO'ONGO'O, 'ai ne'e noa'a kesi doe liu go'o, nonina maramarako'a, rauna te'e sisilia ka keta-keta'a. Nia ke fungu 'ania fa'irū kī ka molimoli'a ka sakosako'a, na fa'irū kī ka to'o ana ka'ika'irū ne'e sau ana itangana ma sulia logo rarana. Sakwalo kī kira ke 'ania fuana.

- ○ Nia ke bulao ana kula kī ta'ifau, fa'asia fafona asi ka dao 'i tolo, te'e saena kunu ne'e nia kesi bulao ana. Nia kesi 'oro liu go'o, ke bulao to'oto'o ma ka tasa ana ti kula.
- • Ki 'ania ngwasana sulia tatabu kwasi nini'a.
- • 'Ingatana ki saunga'inia logo 'ania luma ni du'urū.
- • Ki kwa'ia logo fuana so'i.

'AIUKA, 'ai ne'e kesi doe liu go'o, nonina kwao-kwao'anga, rauna ta'i sisilia go'o di'ia rauna ka'o. Lisilana nia di'ia logo kwalo uka, ta ne'e ki fa'asatā 'uri ana. Nia ke fungu 'ania fa'i rū ti'iti'i kī.

- ○ Nia ke bulao ana kula kī ta'ifau, fa'asia fafona asi ka dao 'i tolo, te'e saena kunukunua ne'e noa'a.
- • Ti'iti'ilana ki saunga'i luma 'ania.

BOLANGUNGU, ta sata 'ARASIBOLA, 'ai ne'e kesi doe liu go'o, nonina gwagwā'a, rauna ka reba ka keta mala, burina ra'irū ka kwao ma saena ka marako. Nia ke taka ka sui ka fi'i fungu 'ania fa'irū te'e keta ma kesi doe liu go'o. Bola kī ke 'ania fa'irū kī ma ki ke ngu, ta ne'e ki fa'asata 'uri ana.

- ○ Nia ke bulao saena to'ona'oa.
- • Ti'iti'ilana ki saunga'i luma 'ania.
- • Ki kwa'ia logo fuana so'i.
- • Ki guragura logo 'ania

WARMED, this tree is not very big, its body is blackish and its leaf is quite wide and rounded and a bit longish, the back of the leaf is prickly like abrasive (*samota* / *Ficus*).

- ○ It just grows in all places.
- • Its leaf we abrade with, as with abrasive, we sun it to go pale, we then abrade things such as axe handles and weapons and bowls with it.
- • We don't build with it as it gets worm-eaten.
- • We fell it for fuel.
- • We cure a man's penis with it so it will be big and long, we warm the leaf and tug it around his penis. That's why we name it thus.

RARANGA = WARMED / *Ficus pseudowassa* Corner *(Moraceae)*

NGO'O NGO'O, this tree doesn't get very big, its body is greenish, its leaf is quite narrow and longish. It bears rounded yellow fruit, the fruits have a stem which emerges from the trunk and also along the branches. Bats eat its fruit.

- ○ It grows in all places, from on the sea to the inland, only in swamp it won't grow. It is not very plentiful, it grows individually but especially in some places.
- • We eat its shoot, as it is a wild vegetable.
- • Its trunk we build cooking houses with.
- • We also fell it for fuel.

NGO'ONGO'O = *NGO'ONGO'O* / sandpaper cabbage / *Ficus wassa* Roxb. *(Moraceae)*

DERRIS-TREE, this tree doesn't get very big, its body is whiteish, its leaf is quite narrow like a bamboo leaf. It looks like derris vine (*'uka*) and that's why we name it thus. It bears small fruit.

- ○ It grows in all places, from on the sea to the inland, only not in swamp.
- • When small we build houses with it.

'AIUKA = DERRIS-TREE / *Archidendron lucyi* Mell. / *A. solomonense* Hemsl. *(Fabaceae)* / *Harpullia solomonensis* Vente. / *H. vaga* Merr.& Perry *(Sapindaceae)*

PIGEONS-SING, also named PIGEONS'-HAUL, this tree doesn't get very big, its body is blackish, its leaf is long and really wide, behind the leaf is white and in front it is green. It flowers and then it bears fruit, quite long and not very big. Pigeons eat the fruit and sing, that's why we name it thus.

- ○ It grows in the lowland.
- • When small we build houses with it.
- • We also fell it for fuel.
- • We also cure with it.

BOLANGUNGU / ARASIBOLA / PIGEONS-SING / PIGEONS'-HAUL / *Litsea flavinervis* Kost. / *L. collina* Moore *(Lauraceae)*

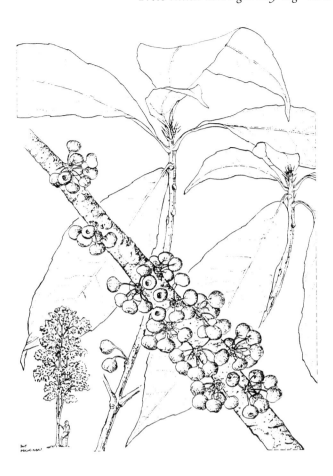

ngo'ongo'o / ngo'ongo'o ▶

'AITOTŌ, 'ai ne'e kesi doe liu go'o, nonina kwaokwao'anga, rauna ketaketa'a, nia ke fungu 'ania fa'īrū kī.
○ Nia ke bulao saena to'ona'oa.
• Ki salinga'inia fuana fa'ata'ilana ma'e biru ma tōtō kī ma fuli tua'a kī, ta ne'e ki fa'asata 'uri ana.
• Ki tufua diro ana fuana saunga'i luma'a.
• Na 'ai fi'i doe sasabe'a kī ki saunga'i luma logo 'ani'i.
• Ki kwa'ia logo fuana so'i.
• Na 'ai doe ka bolo logo fuana 'olelana 'ania reba 'ai kī.

'AI'U'UNIMANU, 'ai ne'e noa'a kesi doe liu go'o, nonina kwaokwao'a, rauna ka marako ka ketaketa'a ka 'iri reba liu go'o, nia ka fungu 'ania fa'īrū ma nia ka bulao ana fa'i rū kī.
○ Nia ke bulao fa'asia fafona asi 'uana 'i tolo.
• Ki kwa'ia fuana so'i.
• 'Ai ne'e, ki fa'asata sulia manu tolo, no'o ne'e inamaemū mala rongoa ma lisia, kwatea nia ke ngwangwane'a. Ki gura 'ania 'inamaemū ma ki agia logo 'ania ngwae 'i ne'e nia ke 'inamaemū logo.

MARKER-TREE, this tree doesn't get very big, its body is whiteish, its leaf is longish and it bears fruit.
○ It grows in the lowland.
• We transplant it to show boundaries and (land) marks and rest-sites, that's why we name it thus.
• We chop posts of it for house-building.
• The young straight trees we also build houses with.
• We also fell it for fuel.
• The big tree is also suitable for cutting into wooden planks.
'AITOTŌ = MARKER-TREE / *Weinmannia blumei* Planch. / *W. ysabelensis* Perry (*Cunoniaceae*) / *Tristiropsis acutangula* Radlk. (*Sapindaceae*)

***MANU*-COMPLAINT-TREE**, this tree doesn't get very big, its body is whiteish, its leaf is green and longish and not very wide, it bears fruit and it grows from its fruit.
○ It grows from on the sea to the inland.
• We fell it for fuel.
• We name this tree after the inland *manu*, the bird which a kinless person (orphan or widow) hears and sees, making him blessed. We cure kinlessness with it and we also afflict a person with it so he'll be kinless.
'AI'U'UNIMANU = *MANU*-COMPLAINT-TREE

'AIDA'AFI, ta sata 'AISATO, 'ai ne'e noa'a kesi doe liu go'o, nonina melamela'a, rauna te'e reba ma ka ketaketa'a, ti ai rauna sakosako'a, ti ai ka marako. Ki saea 'ania rō sata kī si ne'e kaida'i ana sina nia lia kwanga. Nia ke fungu 'ania màgana fingifingia ka marako, di'ia ni'i make magana balabala'a.
- ° Nia ke bulao saena fafona asi
- • Ki fasia fuana tua nunufi'anga, sulia nia satola ma ka lia le'a.
- • Ki kwa'ia fuana so'i.
- • Rauna, ki rao 'ania fuana musilana uta, nini'a logo ne'e ki saea 'ania rō sata nai'ari kī.
- • Ki guragura logo 'ania.

'AKO'AKO nia ne'e to'o ana ti malita'irū, ki fa'asata'i si ne'e di'ia ra'irū ni'i to'oto'oka nia ke 'akofia nonika.

'AKO'AKO saga, 'ai ne'e noa'a nia kesi doe liu go'o, nonina gwagwā'anga ma rauna ka reba. Nia ke bulao ana takana.
- ° Nia ke bulao ka 'oro saena to'ona'oa ma fafona kafo kī, ana ano kaole'a fa'inia ano gwagwā'a kī logo.
- • Di'ia ra'irū ni'i 'akofikia, nia ke 'ako ti'iti'i go'o.
- • 'Ai ne'e le'a liu fuana saunga'ilana bā gwata ma fasilana 'i nonina sakali kī, si ne'e nia ke bulao.
- • Ki gwa'abi logo 'ania rauna, kaida'i ki rarangia rauna, noa'a kesi 'akofikia na'a.
- • Noa'a kisi du'a 'ania si ne'e nia kesi langalanga, saena ifirū kī islia liu.
- • Ni'i 'iri bolo fuana saunga'i luma'a si ne'e nia 'isi ngasi.
- • Ki gurā 'ania ti mata'inga.

'AKO'AKO DINGA, 'ai ne'e ti'iti'i go'o, lisilana ka di'ia 'ofenga bore ma ruana te'e matanga'a, nonina gwagwā'a. Nia ke bulao ana takana.

- ° Nia ke bulao saena to'ona'oa.
- • Nia matamata fa'asia 'ako'ako saga sulia nia ka 'ako fifī ka fa'alia 'uli'uli ngwae, ta ne'e ki fa'asata 'uri ana.
- • Ki gurā 'ania ti mata'inga.
- • Ki gurā 'ania gwata mangomango'a, ka tasa ana fa'i uruuru rangerange'a kī.

CLEAR-SKY-TREE, also named SUNNY-TREE, this tree doesn't get very big, its body is brownish, its leaf is quite wide and longish, some have yellow leaves, some green. We call it by the two names as during sunshine it looks pretty. It bears bunches of green seeds, if they are ripe they are paleish.

- ° It grows on the sea.
- • We plant it for sitting in the shade, because it is pretty and looks nice.
- • We fell it for fuel.
- • Its leaf we use to stop rain, that's also why we call it by those two names.
- • We also cure with it.

'AIDA'AFI / 'AISATO = CLEAR-SKY-TREE / SUNNY-TREE / *Desmodium umbelatum* L. DC. (Papil??)

STINGER has several kinds and we name them because it the leaf touches us it stings (heats) our body.

STINGER proper, this tree doesn't get very big, its body is blackish and its leaf is wide. It grows from its flower.

- ° It grows plentifully in the lowland and on waters, on clay ground and on blackish ground too.
- • If its leaves sting us they only sting a little.
- • This tree is very good for building pig barriers and planting alongside fences, as it grows.
- • We also oven-cook with the leaf, when we warm the leaf it will not sting us.
- • We don't burn with it as it doesn't dry out, the inside of the logs are very wet.
- • It is not suitable for house-building as it is not strong.
- • We cure some sicknesses with it.

'AKO'AKO = STINGER / nettle / *Dendrocnide mirabilis* (Rech.) Chew / *D. nervosa* (Winkl.) Chew / *D. rechingeri* (Winkl.) Chew / *D. schlechter* Winkl. (*Urticaceae*)

EXTRA STINGER, this tree is just small, it looks like pseuderanthemum (*ofenga*) but its leaf is rather divided, and its body is blackish. It grows from its flower.

- ° It grows in the lowland.
- • It is different from stinger proper because it stings acutely and damages a person's skin, that's why we name it thus.
- • We cure some sicknesses with it.
- • We cure pigs with breathing (problems) with it, especially unhealthy-looking runts.

'AKO'AKO DINGA = EXTRA STINGER / *Dendrocnide kajewskii* Chew / *D. latifolia* (Gaud.) Chew (*Urticaceae*)

'AKO'AKO FULUMA ne'e laua, 'ai ti'iti'i go'o.
Nia ta'i raurau'a go'o saena ano, rauna sisili'a ka
keta, takana kwao, nia ke fungu 'ania fua'irū ti'iti'i
kī. Nia ke bulao ana takana.
o   Nia ke bulao saena raku faolu kī ka di'ia fuli
    fanoa kī, ana to'ona'oa ma ana kula kī ta'ifau.
    Ki saea 'ania fuluma sulia nia ke bulao ka tasa 'i
    fuli luma kī.
•   Di'ia ra'irū ke 'akofikia, nia 'ako ka liufia rū kī
    ma ka kwakwa'ini'ini.
•   Ki gurā 'ania ti mata'inga.

SUNGASUNGA, 'ai ne'e kesi doe liu go'o di'ia
akwa ma ba'ula, nonina bulu. Nia ke fungu 'ania
fa'irū ti'iti'i ma ka molimoli'a ka to'o ana magarū
kī, na no'o lofolofo kī ke 'ani'i.
o   Nia ke bulao saena to'ona'oa bore ma noa'a
    kesi 'oro liu. Nia ke bulao go'o saena o'olā di'ia
    laua kī ma saena raku ma fulina kula tufu'i kī
    ma kula 'ofo kī.
•   Ngwanga laulau gwau kī ka 'ania rauna, ki ke
    'ania ngwangarū nai'ari kī di'ia numa.
•   Ki saunga'i 'ania ana babala ma gwaurau bore
    ma noa'a nia kesi bolo fa'inia saunga'i luma'a.
•   Noa'a kesi le'a fuana so'i sulia nia du'a
    maemaela.
•   Ki gurā logo 'ania mata'inga 'oro kī.

ILOI, 'ai ne'e kesi doe liu go'o, 'itangana kwaokwao'anga go'o, rauna te'e molimoli'a go'o ma ka
marako, takana kwao ma nia ke alua fa'irū ti'iti'i kī.
o   Nia ke bulao ke 'oro liu ana busubusurū'a. Nia
    ke bulao go'o saena raku faolu kī, ana kula kī sui.
•   Noa'a nia 'iri bolo fa'inia saunga'inga sulia nia
    'iri ona, nia ngwara'u go'o, bore ma nia le'a ka tasa
    fuana labulana 'ania ma'e bā gwata sulia nia ke
    birabira.
•   Di'ia nia du'a ma kula so'i 'ato ana ma ki du'a
    logo 'ania.

LA'ELA'E,'ai ne'e to'o ana ro malita'i rū kī.

LA'ELA'E 'inoto'a, ki saea logo'ania LA'ELA'E
NGWANE, 'ai ne'e kesi doe liu go'o, nonina
gwagwā'a, rauna ka reba ma burina ra'irū ka kwao
ka momote.
o   Nia ke bulao go'o ana dukwasi ma raku buru,
    ana kula kī ta'ifau, fa'asia fafona asi ka dao 'i
    tolo, te'e saena kula kunu'a nia noa'a.
•   Ki sole oni ngela 'ania rauna.

HOUSITE STINGER is a weed, just a small tree.
It is only slight and near the ground, its leaf is
narrow and long, its flower is white and it bears
small fruit. It grows from its flower.
o   It grows in new shoots, like home sites, in the
    lowland and all places. We call it housite
    because it grows especially on house sites.

•   If its leaf stings us, it stings more than anything
    and causes a rash.
•   We cure some sicknesses with it.
'AKO'AKO FULUMA = HOUSITE STINGER / Laportea
interrupta (L.) Chew / L. ruderalis (Forst.f.) Chew (Urticaceae)

PIPTURUS, this tree doesn't get very big like
akwa or ba'ula (Callophylum), its body is dark. It
bears small rounded fruit with seeds and the birds
eat them.
o   It grows in the lowland but it is not very
    plentiful. It just grows in gardens as a weed and
    in shoots and on sites which are chopped down
    and light places.
•   Head-shaker grubs eat its leaf and we eat these
    grubs as caterpillars.
•   We build shelters and leaf-shelters with it but it
    is not suitable for house-building.
•   It is not good for fuel because it burns dying.

•   We also cure many sicknesses with it.
SUNGASUNGA = PIPTURUS / Pipturus argentus (Forst.f.)
Wedd. (Urticaceae)

ILOI, this tree doesn't get very big, its trunk is
whiteish, its leaf is quite rounded and green, its
flower is white and it bears small fruits.
o   It grows very plentifully as thickets. It just
    grows in the new shoots, in all places.
•   It is not suitable for building because it is not
    tough, it is just soft, but it is good for staking pig
    barriers with because it sprouts.

•   If it is dried and in a place where fuel is hard to
    get, we also burn with it.
ILOI = ILOI / Boehmeria platyphylla G.Don var. mollucana
Wedd / Cyphylophus trapula Winkl. (Urticaceae)

CELTIS, this tree has two kinds.

The important CELTIS, also called MALE
CELTIS, this tree doesn't get very big, its body is
darkish, its leaf is wide and the back of the leaf is
white and scratchy.
o   It grows in wilderness and in new shoots, in all
    places, from on the sea to the inland, only not
    in swampy places.
•   We wipe up children's shit with its leaf.

- Ki saunga'i luma 'ania sulia nia ngasi.
- Ki kwa'ia logo fuana so'i.
- Ki gura logo 'ania ti mata'inga.

MAMALALA'ELA'E, ki saea logo 'ania LA'ELA'E KINI, 'ai ne'e ke doe mala, nonina ka kwao ka doe, ta'eta'ena ka baba'ula, rauna ka keta ka sisili'a.

- Kula ne'e nia ke bulao ana nia bolo logo fa'inia la'ela'e saga.
- Ti'iti'ilana ki saunga'i luma 'ania .
- Ki kwa'ia logo fuana so'i.
- Kaida'i fa'i 'ai ke mae, safao ke fanga ana, ki tufu 'uani fuana 'anilani.
- Na 'ai doe ka bolo logo fuana 'olelana 'ania reba 'ai kī.

BALA, 'ai ne'e to'o ana ūlu malita'irū kī.
BALA saga, 'ai ne'e kesi doe liu go'o, rauna sako-sako'a ka fisifisila, fuana sakosako'a, kaida'i nia ke make ke gwā. Nia ke bulao ana fuana. Mokolana moko le'a liu mala, ka di'ia logo na mokofana ri'i.

- 'Ai fasia nini'a, ki fasia saena o'olā kī fuana ulikwa'ima kī 'i ne'e ke fa'amauria o'olā ka bulao le'a.
- Ki fasia logo saena fanoa ma māna kafo kī fuana lisilana kula kī ke kwanga ma ke moko le'a.
- Ūluna ki laungia 'ania ngwa'i kī 'i ke moko le'a.
BALA NI KWARU nia ke te'e doe, nonina itanga 'i rū nia melamela'a, rauna ka marako.
- Rū kwasi nini'a, nia ke bulao saena kula kwaru'a kī ma raku faolo kī ma fa'i ua kī, fa'asia fafona asi 'uana 'i tolo, nia 'oro saena to'ona'oa.
BALA KWAO, ki saea logo 'ania BALA FUFURI, 'ai ne'e ke doe liu ka liufia bala kī ta'ifau. Ki fa'asata 'uri ana sulia ne'e ta'eta'ena kwaokwao'a go'o ka fufuria. Rauna reba kesi keta liu go'o ka mamata fa'asia rauna ro bala lokiri.
- Nia ke bulao fa'asia fafona asi 'uana 'i tolo.
- Bala ne'e kī ta'ifau ki gura 'ani'i 'usia kelema ma mata'inga kī ta'ifau.

- We build houses with it because it is strong.
- We also fell it for fuel.
- We also cure some sicknesses with it.
LA'ELA'E NGWANE = CELTIS / MALE CELTIS / *Celtis kajewskii* Merr.& Perry / *Celtis philippensis* Bl. (*Ulmaceae*) [?]

PSEUDO-CELTIS, also called FEMALE CELTIS, this tree is really big, its body is white and big, its skin is thick and its leaf is long and narrow.

- The places where it grows are the same as for celtis proper.
- When small we build houses with it.
- We also fell it for fuel.
- When the tree dies *safao* grubs eat it and we chop them out to eat.
- The big tree is also suitable for cutting into wooden planks.
MAMALA LA'ELA'E / LA'ELA'E KINI = PSEUDO-CELTIS / FEMALE CELTIS / *Leucosyke australis* Unruh. var. *salomonensis* / *L. capitellata* (Poir.) Wedd. / *L. salomonenesis* Unruh. (*Urticaceae*)

EUODIA, this tree has three kinds.
EUODIA proper, this tree doesn't get very big, its leaf is yellow and narrow, its fruit is yellow, when ripe it is black. It grows from its fruit. Its smell smells very good indeed, like the smell of *ri'i* (*Euodia*).

- This one is a planted tree, we plant it in gardens as a protector so it will make the garden live and grow well.
- We also plant it in homes and water spouts for places to look pretty and smell good.

- Its fronds we decorate bags with to smell good.
EUODIA-OF-THE-ROCKS gets quite big, the body of its trunk is browish, its leaf is green.
- This one is wild, it grows in rocky places and new shoots and on hills, from on the sea to the inland, it is plentiful in the lowland.
WHITE EUODIA, also called PATCHY *EUODIA*, this tree gets much the biggest of all the euodia. We name it thus because its skin is whiteish and patchy. Its leaf is big and not very long and different from the leaves of the other two *bala*.
- It grows from on the sea to the inland.
- All the *euodia* we cure with against sorcery and all sicknesses.
BALA = EUODIA
BALA NI KWARU = EUODIA-OF-THE-ROCKS / *Euodia elleryana* Muell. (*Rutaceae*)
BALA KWAO / BALA FUFURI = WHITE EUODIA / PATCHY EUODIA

MAMU, 'ai ne'e kesi doe liu go'o, lisilana ka di'ia logo bala.
- Nia bulao ka 'oro saena to'ona'oa.
- Na numa kī ke 'ania rauna ma ki 'oia fuana 'anilana.
- Ki saunga'inia 'ania luma sasufi'i.
- Ki kwa'ia logo fuana so'i.

BA'ABA'A, 'ai ne'e kesi doe liu go'o, rauna marako ka matanga'a ana ulu ra'irū kī, takana marako, nia ke bulao ana takana. Nia ke fungu 'ania fuana, kaida'i nia ke make ke gwā.
- Nia ke bulao fa'asia fafona asi 'uana 'i tolo, nia 'oro saena to'ona'oa.
- Ki saunga'i 'ania bore ma ana luma sasufi'i go'o ka di'ia luma ni du'uru'a.
- Ki kwa'ia logo fuana so'i.
- Ki gurā logo 'ania ti mata'inga.

BALIU ne'e 'ai bore ma lisilana mamata dangalu, nia fi'irū'a sulia di'ia nia doe na birabirana ke ta'e ka bungubungu'a ana te'e kula. Nia kesi doe liu go'o, nonina ta'i kwaokwao'anga, rauna molimoli'a ka marako.
- 'Ai ne'e bulaolana nama saena tofongana tolo kī, nia 'oro 'i nai'ari, nia kesi bulao ata go'o 'ana.
- Na uila nia bolo fuana laungilana ngwa'i kī, 'i ke lia 'olo'olo ma ka mokomoko.
- Nia le'a fuana diro'anga sulia nia ngasi ma nia ka taliore'a.
- Ki saunga'i luma 'ania ma bā gwata logo.
- Nia le'a liu logo fuana so'i sulia nia ke du'a dangi.
- Na 'ai doe ka bolo logo fuana 'olelana 'ania rebarū.

GWA'UGWA'U, 'ai ne'e sasabe'a liu, nonina ka kwaokwao'a, rauna reba ma kesi keta liu go'o, takana kwao ma fa'irū kī ka rebareba'a.
- Nia ke bulao go'o ana kula ki sui ma nia kesi bulao kesi 'oro liu go'o.
- Ki tufua fuana ūlungalana sulia fa'i sao ma ngali 'i ki ra'efia, nia le'a ka tasa sulia nia keta ka sasabe'a ma ta'elana ka sasala.
- Ki du'a logo 'ania bore ma du'alana maemaela, noa'a kesi du'a dangi.

ODOUR, this tree doesn't get very big, it looks like euodia (*bala*).
- It grows plentifully in the lowland.
- Caterpillars eat the leaves and we pick them to eat.
- We build smoky houses with it.
- We also fell it for fuel.

MAMU = ODOUR / *Euodia bonwickii* Meull. / *E. elleryana* Muell. (*Rutaceae*)

BA'ABA'A, this tree doesn't get very big, its leaf is green and divided into three leaves, its flower is green and it grows from its flower. It bears fruit and when ripe it is black.
- It grows from on the sea to the inland and is plentiful in the lowland.
- We build with it, but only for smoky houses like cooking houses.
- We also fell it for fuel.
- We also cure some sickness with it.

BA'ABA'A = BA'ABA'A / *Euodia viridiflora* C.T.White / *E. elleryana* Muell. / *E. radlkoferiana* Ltb. / *E. silvatica* Merr.& Perry / *E. solomonensis* Merr.& Perry (*Rutaceae*)

ASCARINA is a tree but it looks completely different, it is a clump because when it is big its sprouts come up as a thicket over an area. It doesn't get very big, its body is quite whiteish, its leaf is rounded and green.
- This tree has to grow in the central inland, it is plentiful there and it won't grow elsewhere.

- Its frond is suitable for decorating bags as it looks right and smells.
- It is good for posts because it is strong and has heartwood.
- We build houses with it and also pig barriers.
- It is good for fuel because it burns till day.

- The big tree is also suitable for cutting into planks.

BALIU = ASCARINA / *Ascarina diffusa* A.C.Sm. / *A. maheshwarii* Swamy. (*Chloranthaceae*) [?]

STERCULIA, this tree is very straight, its body is whiteish, its leaf is wide and not very long, its flower is white and its fruit is wideish.
- It just grows in all places but it is not very plentiful.
- We chop it to stand against sago trees and nuts to climb them, it is especially good because it is long and straight and light to raise up.
- We also burn with it but it burns dying, it won't burn till day.

GWA'UGWA'U = STERCULIA / *Sterculia parkinsonii* Muell. (*Sterculiaceae*)

DADAME, ki saea logo 'ania DAMEDAME,'ai ne'e noa'a nia kesi doe liu go'o, nonina kwao-kwao'a, rauna keta ka reba. Nia ke bulao ana fa'irū kī.
- Nia ke bulao fa'asia fafona asi 'uana 'i tolo, nia 'oro saena to'ona'oa, bore ma nia 'i saena raku buru kī go'o, burina o'olā kī.
- Ki saunga'i luma 'ania, noa'a nia kesi le'a liu sulia noa'a kesi ngasi, nia totolia saunga'ilana 'ania luma ni du'urū'a.
- Ki kwa'ia logo fuana so'i.
- Ki guragura logo 'ania.

KWASIKWASI, 'ai ne'e kesi doe liu go'o ma kesi keta liu go'o, rauna ketaketa'a ka te'e doe ka marako.
- Nia ke bulao go'o ana raku kī, ana kula kī ta'ifau, fa'asia fafona asi ka dao 'i tolo.
- Ta'eta'ena ki aea fuana saunga'ilana ngwa'i fa'a, lisilana le'a si ne'e nia ka kwao le'a.
- Noa'a kisi saunga'i luma 'ania, noa'a kisi kwa'ia fuana so'i sulia nia ti'iti'i go'o.

LOFA, 'ai ne'e noa'a nia kesi doe liu go'o, nia kwaokwao'anga, rauna ka keta ka te'e reba. Nia ka fungu 'ania fa'irū kī sakosako'a. Nia ka bulao ana fa'ina ma rarana ma di'ia ki tufua nia ke birabira.
- Nia ke bulao saena dukwasi, bore ma ki fasia logo ana kula kī ta'ifau.
- Ki fasia sulia ngali kī ma fa'i sao kī fuana ra'enga'a sulia 'i ne'e ki ke loia fa'i ngali kī ma ki tufua rara sao kī.
- Ki saunga'i 'ania babala kī bore ma noa'a kesi bolo fa'inia saunga'i luma'a.
- Ki gura 'ania noni ngwae kaida'i ka mabe liu, nia ke gaga'ai.

DAE, 'ai ne'e noa'a kesi doe liu go'o, nonina gwagwā'anga, rauna keta ma kesi reba liu go'o. Nia ke fungu 'ania fa'irū kī sulia nonina, fuana ka te'ete'e ma ka ketaketa'a, ka talirū'a. Nia ke bulao ana fa'irū kī. Ti ai ki fasia, ti ai ka kwasi. Dae fasia nia doe ana dae kwasi ma fuana ka doe ka liufia fuana dae kwasi.
- Nia ke bulao fa'asia fafona asi 'uana 'i tolo.
- Ki 'ania fa'irū, 'anilana le'a ka asila ma ka 'ero'ero. Ki dodoa saena fa'i ka'o, ki du'atelea logo, 'i ne'e nia ke ngwara'u.
- Ki 'ania logo gwangona, ki dodoa ki du'afia fuana ādamilana fa'inia alo ma kumara.

COMMERSONIA, this tree is not very big, its body is whiteish, its leaf is long and wide. It grows from fruit.
- It grows from on the sea to the inland, it is plentiful in the lowland, but it is just in the thick shoots, after gardens.
- We build houses with it, it is not very good because it is not strong, it is fit for building cooking houses.
- We also fell it for fuel.
- We also cure with it.

DADAME / DAMEDAME = COMMERSONIA / *Commersonia bartramia* (L.) Merr. (*Sterculiaceae*)

ABROMA, this tree doesn't get very big and doesn't get very tall, its leaf is longish and quite big and green.
- It just grows in the shoots, in all places from on the sea to the inland.
- Its skin we peel for making hanging bags, it looks good because it is nice and white.
- We don't build houses with it and we don't fell it for fuel because it is only small.

KWASIKWASI = ABROMA / *Abroma augusta* (L.) Willd. / *A. mollis* DC. (*Sterculiaceae*)

LOFA, this tree doesn't get very big, it is whiteish, its leaf is long and quite wide. It bears yellow fruit. It grows from its fruit and branches and if we chop it down it sprouts.
- It grows in the wilderness but we also plant it in all places.
- We plant it alongside nuts and sagos for climbing by so we can pick the nuts and chop sago branches.
- We build shelters with it but it is not suitable for house-building.
- We cure a person's body with it when it is very limp so he will stiffen up.

LOFA = *LOFA* / *Sterculia conwentzii* Schum. / *S. fanaiho* Setch. / *S. schumanniana* Ltb. / *S. shillinglawii* Muell. (*Sterculiaceae*)

GNETUM, this tree doesn't get very big, its body is blackish, its leaf is long and not very wide. It bears fruit along its body, the fruit is small and long, with a pit. It grows from its fruit. Some are planted, some are wild. Planted gnetum is bigger than wild gnetum and its fruit is bigger than wild gnetum fruit.
- It grows from on the sea to the inland.
- We eat the fruit, it is good to eat and sweet and oily. We flask-cook it in a bamboo and also roast it, so it will be soft.
- We also eat its leaf-shoot, we flask it and burn it to eat with taro and potato.

▲ *dadame / commersonia*

- Ta'eta'ena ki aea fuana dadalo, dadalona nia ngasi liu, ka totolia fuana saunga'ilana 'ania rū di'ia 'abagwaro ma gwa'isusuru.

DANGISATO, 'ai ne'e kesi doe liu go'o, nonina kwaokwao'anga. Rauna ka sakosako'a liu, ka molimoli'a bore ma nia noa'a 'iri reba liu go'o, lisilani satola liu ana kaida'i ana da'afi kī, ta ne'e ki fa'a-sata 'uri ana. Nia ka fungu 'ania fa'i rū ne'e molimoli'a ma magarū 'oro kī ka ni'i 'i saena. Nia ke bulao ana fa'irū.
○ Nia ke bulao ana kula kī ta'ifau te'e kunkunua kī ne'e noa'a ana.
- Na 'ai efoa ne'e ki fasia kalikalia luma ma fanoa sulia nia lia kwanga. Ti kaida'i ki fasia logo saena o'olā fuana tua nunufi'anga.
- Ti kaida'i ki ngalia ūlirū kī fuana laungilana ngwa'i ngwangwane kī.
- Kaida'i ana mamalo'anga ana Keresmasi kī, ki laungia 'ania fera ni fo'o kī fa'inia luma kia kī.
- Ki kwa'ia logo fuana so'i.

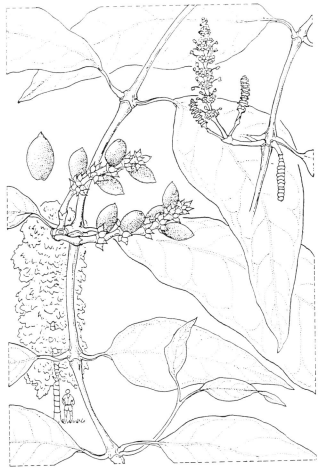

▲ *dae / gnetum*

- Its skin we peel for twine, the twine is very strong and ideal for making things like(bead-) patterned bands and *susuru* (women's) belts.
DAE = GNETUM / jointfir / *Gnetum gnemon* L. / *G. costatum* Schum. (*Gnetaceae*)

SUNNY-DAY, this tree doesn't get very big, its body is whiteish. Its leaf is very yellow, it is rounded but not very wide, it looks sunny during fine weather, that's why we name it thus. It bears fruit which is rounded and there are many seeds inside it. It grows from the fruit.

○ It grows in all places, only not in swamp.

- This tree is chosen to plant around the house and home since it looks pretty. Sometimes we also plant it in gardens for sitting in the shade.
- Sometimes we take fronds to decorate men's bags.
- During the Christmas holidays we decorate our prayer sanctums (churches) and houses with it.
- We also chop it for fuel.
DANGISATO = SUNNY-DAY

DAUKWAILIMA, 'ai ne'e kesi doe liu go'o, nonina marako, rauna ka rada ka tongatonga'a. Nia ke fungu 'ania fa'irū kī ne'e meo ka 'ere'a ka daukwailima.

- ○ Nia ke bulao saena to'ona'oa.
- • Ki fasia ana fuli tua'a ma māna kafo kī fuana go'o tua nunufi'anga ma fa'asaele'alana kaela ngela, kira ke masa 'ania fa'irū kī.

TOTONGWALA, 'ai ne'e noa'a nia kesi doe liu go'o, ta'eta'ena di'ia ki tufua nia ke tongatonga'a. Nia ke fungu, fa'irū kī ka ti'iti'i ka molimoli'a. Nia ke bulao ana fuana.

- ○ Nia ke bulao ana kula kaole'a, fa'asia fafona asi 'uana 'i tolo, saena logo kunu ko'a.
- • Na 'ai doe kī ki tufua fuana saunga'ilana 'ania sakali kī fuana sare gwata 'anga saena, nia le'a fuana saunga'i bā 'anga sulia nia ke birabira.

DILOMATE, 'ai ne'e noa'a kesi doe liu go'o, nonina te'e meomeo'anga, rauna reba di'ia fa'i mudu kī.

- ○ Na 'ai ana dukwasi nini'a, nia ke bulao go'o saena to'ona'oa ma fafona asi, saena tolo nia noa'a ana.
- • Ki saunga'i logo 'ania diro fuana luma kī, dirona ona di'ia fa'i mamufua.
- • Ki sakali 'ania fuana foka gwata, sulia kaida'i ki labunga'inia nia ke fi'i birabira ma ke bulao la'u.

DUDURU'USU, 'ai ne'e nia bulao kasi doe liu la'u di'ia ta 'ai doe, rarana 'oro ni'i kesi keta go'o ma rauni ka tolobabala go'o 'i ano. Rauna ka keta ka nunura, takana ka kwao ka di'ia ku'iku'ina kui kī, fa'irū kī kesi dau ngasi go'o, ka 'asi 'ali'ali go'o. Fa'irū ka le'a liu ka te'e meo ka te'e doe ana 'afi'o.

- ○ Nia ke bulao saena to'ona'oa ma saena logo tolo.
- • Rauna babala'a, kala siko ne'e satana 'usu, ta sata sikitau, nia duru 'i olofana rauna fuana 'anilana, nia ne'e ki fa'asata 'uri ana. Ti kaida'i ki la'ūmia rauna fuana 'usu nia durufia 'i olofana.
- • Noa'a kisi rao go'o 'ania bore ma fa'irū ne'e lia le'a liu, noa'a kisi 'ania go'o, rū go'o fuana ngela ti'iti'i kī fuana masa'a. Na ngela kī ke to'ia di'ia ngela kī sulia lisilana le'a, kira ke gelosia kwailiu bore ma kira kesi gelosia 'ania 'aeda sulia nia ngwara'u liu fuana foga'a.

HOLD-HANDS, this tree doesn't get very big, its body is green, its leaf is elongated and gummy. It bears fruits which are red and curved and (hook together as if to) hold hands.

- ○ It grows in the lowland.
- • We plant it at rest-sites and water spouts just for resting in the shade and making little children happy, they play with the fruit.

DAUKWAILIMA = HOLD-HANDS / *Lepinia solomonensis* Hemsl. (*Apocynaceae*)

STICKY-SAP, this tree doesn't get very big, its skin, if we chop it, is gummy. It bears and the fruits are little and rounded. It grows from its fruit.

- ○ It grows in clay places, from on the sea to the inland, and also in scraping swamp.
- • The big tree we chop for making fences for feeding (keeping) pigs inside, it is good for making barriers because it sprouts.

TOTONGWALA = *Cerbera manghas* L. (*Apocynaceae*)

DILOMATE, this tree doesn't get very big, its body is quite reddish and its leaf is wide like dillenia tree (*mudu*).

- ○ This one is a tree of the wilderness, it only grows in lowland and on the sea, not in the inland.
- • We make posts for houses with it, its posts are tough like securinega (*mamufua*) tree.
- • We fence with it for pig pens because when we stake it, it sprouts and grows again.

DILOMATE = *DILOMATE* / *Eugenia cincta* (Merr.& Perry) Whitmore / *Syzygium cinctum* Merr.& Perry (*Myrtaceae*)

'USU-CONGREGATES, this tree doesn't grow as big as a big tree, its branches are many and not long and its leaves shelter the ground. Its leaf is long and shiny, its flower is white and like a dog's tail, its fruit doesn't hold on strongly and quickly falls. The fruit is very nice and quite red, a bit bigger than an apple (*'afi'o / Eugenia*).

- ○ It grows in the lowland and also in the inland.
- • Its leaf is sheltering and the little hopper named *'usu*, also named leaps-far, congregates beneath the leaf for eating, that's why we name it thus. Sometimes we fold the leaf for the *'usu* to congregate beneath.

- • We don't work with it but the fruit looks very good, we don't eat it, it is something for small children to play with. Children cradle it like a child because it looks nice and roll it around with their feet because it is very easy to crack.

DUDURU'USU= 'USU-CONGREGATES / *Eugenia aff. nutans* Schum. / *Syzygium aff. aquem* (Burm.f.) Alston (*Myrtaceae*)

fo'oka / worship ▶

FO'OKA, ki saea logo 'ania FO'AKA, 'ai ne'e noa'a kesi doe liu go'o, rauna marako, nia ke taka ke sui ka fungu 'ania fa'irū kī molimoli'a. Nia mokole'a.

○ 'Ai fasia nini'a, nia kesi bulao ata go'o 'ana ana kula kī ta'ifau.

• Ki fasia 'i ke mokole'a ma ka lia le'a ana kula kī di'ia nonina fanoa ma fulitua'a 'inoto'a kī ma 'i māna kafo kī logo. Ki fasia logo kalikalia sulufaua ana fuliferaābu kī fuana fo'osi'anga, 'ai ne'e akalo ogā mokofana. Nia ke bulao logo saena dukwasi ana kula di'ia fuli fera kī. Ki fasia nama ana uta, kwate nia ka mauri le'a saena ano gwarigwari'a.

• Na ulina ki laungia 'ania ngwa'i kī sulia nia ke moko le'a.

• Ki 'oto 'ania fuana fonelana akalo kwasi kata dau ngwae.

• Rauna fuana logo gura'a.

WORSHIP, this tree doesn't get very big, its leaf is green, it flowers and then it bears rounded fruit. It smells good.

○ This is a planted tree, it won't grow at random in all places.

• We plant it to smell good and look good in places like home areas and important rest-sites and water spouts. We also plant it around the stone walling of tabu-sanctums for praying, it is a tree the ghosts like to smell. It also grows in the wilderness in places like sanctum sites. We have to plant it in the rain, so that it will live well in the damp ground.

• The fronds we decorate bags with because it smells good.

• We charm with it to block wild ghosts from grabbing people.

• Its leaf is also for curing.

FO'OKA / FO'AKA = WORSHIP / island musk / *Euodia hortensis* Forst. (*Rutaceae*)

FUFUDI, 'ai ne'e noa'a kesi doe liu go'o ma kesi keta liu go'o, rauna reba, nia ke fungu go'o 'i fūna ma ra'irū kī logo.
- Nia ke bulao go'o saena to'ona'oa fa'inia saena tolo.
- 'Ai ne'e ngasi, ki saunga'i luma 'ania.
- Ki kwa'ia logo fuana so'i.

GWALIFUNU, 'ai ne'e kesi doe liu go'o, rauna keta ka marako. Nia kesi ngasi bore ma nia kulu liu. 'Ai ne'e gwali'unu ke tua ana saena likolikorū kī 'i fuila rararū kī. Fa'irū kī kulu logo fuana ngalilani.

- Nia ke bulao ka 'oro go'o saena to'ona'oa.
- Ki saunga'i luma 'ania.
- Ki kwa'ia logo fuana so'i.
- Ki guragura logo 'ania.

ISU, 'ai ne'e noa'a kesi doe liu go'o, nonina kwaokwao'a, rauna reba, takana kwaokwao'a, fa'irū kī te'e ti'iti'i go'o ka bababa'a.
- Nia bulao ana masu'u sasala ma raku buru kī, fafona asi ma saena to'ona'oa ma saena logo tolo.
- Ki ba'o ana fuana mafula.
- Ki kwa'ia logo fuana so'i.

KWA'U, 'ai ne'e ka fi'irū'a, nonina balabala'a, rauna marako ka molimoli'a, ka moko kwa'ula'a. Takana kwao, nia fungu 'ania fingirū marako ti'iti'i kī, magarū kī kaida'i nia make ni'i ke gwā. Nia bulao ana fa'īrū kī.
- Nia bulao ana kula kī ta'ifau, saena raku ma dukwasi bore, saena fafona asi ma tofungana tolo bore, nia kesi 'oro go'o ana kula kī.
- Ki tufua diro kī ana fuana saunga'i luma'a.
- Ki saunga'i luma logo 'ania.
- Ki labua logo 'ania ma'e sakali.
- Ki kwa'ia fuana so'i, nia le'a ka tasa fuana du'anga'a.
- Ki ba'o logo ana fa'irū du'a kī.
- Rauna ma ta'eta'ena ki lalia 'ania ma'e fata'a fuana ki fa'agwaria ki fonea 'ania akalo ma kelema, rauna ki saita'inia ana gwa'i obi ana limaka.
- Ki guragura 'ania ana mata'inga 'oro, di'ia na gwau fī kī ma na sira fī kī fa'inia na gwari kī. Guralana 'ania kwa'u, ki kwa'ufia nama suluna, ta ne'e ki fa'asata 'uri ana.

ERYTHROXYLUM, this tree doesn't get very big or very tall, its leaf is wide, it bears at its base and its leaves too.
- It just grows in the lowland and in the inland.

- This tree is strong, we build houses with it.
- We also fell it for fuel.

FUFUDI = ERYTHROXYLUM / *Erythroxylum ecarinatum* Burk. (*Erythroxlaceae*)

BOERLAGIODENDRON, this tree doesn't get very big, its leaf is long and wide. It is not strong but it is very heavy. This tree *gwali*(lizards) live in, in holes on the sites of (fallen) branches. The fruit is also heavy to pick up.
- It grows plentifully in the lowland.
- We build houses with it.
- We also fell it for fuel.
- We also cure with it.

GWALIFUNU = BOERLAGIODENDRON / *Boerlagiodendron pachycephalum* Harms / *B. tetrandrum* C.T.White / *B. novo-guineensis* (Scheff.) Harms (*Araliaceae*)

CALLICARPA, this tree doesn't get very big, its body is whiteish, its leaf is wide, its flower is whiteish, its fruits are quite small and flat.
- It grows in light forest and dense shoots, on the sea and in the lowland and also in the inland.

- We rub with it for fire (making).
- We also fell it for fuel.

ISU = CALLICARPA / *Callicarpa pentandra* Roxb. (*Verbenaceae*)

DRINK, this tree forms a clump, its body is paleish, its leaf is green and rounded and it smells of drink (sharp smell). Its flower is white and it bears small green bunches with seeds which are black when ripe. It grows from its seeds.
- It grows in all places, whether in shoots or wilderness, whether on the sea or in the central inland, and is not plentiful in these places.
- We chop posts from it for building houses.
- We also build houses with it.
- We also stake it for fenceposts.
- We fell it for fuel, it is especially good for burning (food).
- We also rub (for fire) with the dry sticks.
- The leaf and skin we invoke with words to cool and block ghosts and sorcery, we insert the leaf in bands on our arms.

- We also cure many sicknesses with it, such as headaches and stomach aches and colds. To cure with drink we have to drink its sap, that's why name it thus.

KWA'U = DRINK / *Premna corymbosa* (Burm.f.) R.& W. / *P. nitida* Schum. / *P. obtusifolia* R.Br. (*Verbenaceae*)

SAIA, 'ai ne'e noa'a kesi doe liu go'o, nonina melamela'a, rauna keta ka sisilia go'o ma fuana ka doe ka molimoli'a ka melamela'a.

- Nia ke bulao fafona asi ma saena to'ona'oa ma ana ti kula logo saena tolo. Nia ke bulao ka 'oro liu ana ua 'i rū ki mala sulia nia ke bulao ana fa'ina.
- Fuana ki koria ki saungia saena titiu ke meme fuana ki mokea 'ania kula foga ana rū kī di'ia dako foga ma iolo ne'e te'e foga, fuana fonelana kafo kesi afe noima ke loto 'i saena.

- Kaida'i 'i na'o ki mokea logo 'ania kula foga safitana reba 'ai ana iolo kī.
- Ki atongia logo dako 'ania, ki dola fa'inia nanao 'i ke gwā, ki saia 'ania nonina dako 'i ne'e ke gwā.
- Ki saunga'i luma 'ania.
- Ki kwa'ia logo fuana so'i.

PUTTY, this tree doesn't get very big, its body is brownish, its leaf is long and narrow and its fruit is big and rounded and brownish.

- It grows on the sea and in the lowland and in some places in the inland. It grows very plentifully in hill-groves because it grows from its fruit.
- Its fruit we scrape and pound in a (coconut) cup into a paste for caulking cracks in things like cracked bowls and canoes which are a bit cracked, to stop water from flowing out or seeping in.
- In former times, we also caulked the cracks between the wooden planks of canoes with it.
- We also stain bowls with it, we mix it with charcoal to be black and putty the body of the bowl with it to become black.
- We also build houses with it.
- We also fell it for fuel.

SAIA = PUTTY / puttynut / *Parinari glaberrima* (Hassk.) Hassk. (*Chrysobalanaceae*)

▲ *kwa'u / drink*

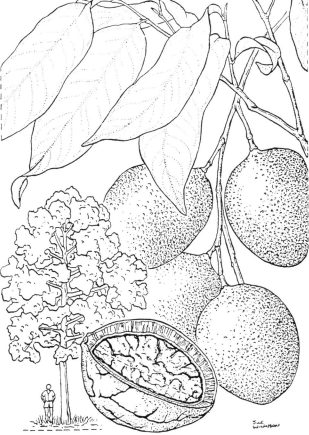

▲ *saia / putty*

SUSURA ne'e 'ai mala, nia kesi doe liu go'o, nonina kwaokwao'anga, rauna ka keta ka te'e reba, nia ke fungu 'ania fa'irū kī. Kaida'i nia mae ka du'a nia fura 'ali'ali liu.
○   Nia ke bulao ana kula kī sui.
•   Ki saunga'i luma 'ania.
•   Ki kwa'ia fuana so'i.

RIRIKO, 'ai ne'e kesi doe liu go'o, nonina furufuru'a, rauna ka marako ka te'e molimoli'a. Nia ke bulao ana lalina.
○   Nia ke bulao nama saena kunukunua ma fafona su'u kī, saena go'o dukwasi.
•   Ki saunga'i 'ania bā gwata, nia ke mauri ke bulao ke daua sakali ma ka fi'i ngasi le'a.

SAEBALA, 'ai ne'e noa'a kesi doe liu go'o, nonina melamela'a, rauna ka ketaketa'a ka sisili'a. Burina ra'irū kī ni'i kwao, ta ne'e ki fa'asata 'uri ana.

○   Nia ke bulao saena to'ona'oa fa'inia logo tolo.
•   Ki laungi ngwa'i 'ania ūlirū sulia mokolana le'a.

SASATO'O, 'ai ne'e noa'a kesi doe liu go'o, nonina di'ia fa'i lofa ma nia reforefo'a lala, rauna reba karangi ka di'ia rauna rā, kakina rauna dada go'o kesi ba'u la'u di'ia fa'i lofa.
○   Nia ke bulao nama ana dukwasi ma kaole, saena to'ona'oa ma tolo.
•   Ki fasia nonina fa'i labu ana fera, nia ke teo fuana fafato'o'anga ana malimae kī, ta ne'e ki saea 'ania sasato'o. Di'ia ki lisia ne'e rauna ni'i kuku, ta ne'e karangia ta mae ke fuli na'a.
•   Noa'a kisi du'urū 'ania, sulia 'ai fuana kū nini'a, ki gura 'ania kū.

TO'OMA, 'ai ne'e kesi doe liu go'o bore ma nia keta liu, nonina kwao, rauna ka marako ka ta'i ketaketa'a.
○   Nia ke bulao fa'asia fafona asi 'uana 'i tolo, saena raku faolu ma dukwasi logo. Ki fasia logo 'i nonina fanoa ma saena logo o'olā.
•   'Anilana fa'irū nia asila liu, fa'irū ngasi ki do'ofia, fa'irū make ki 'ania go'o.
•   Ki saunga'i luma 'ania.
•   Ki kwa'ia logo fuana so'i.

SUSURA is a tree, it is not very big, its body is whiteish, its leaf is long and quite wide, it bears fruit. When it is dead and dried it rots very quickly.
○   It grows in all places
•   We build houses with it.
•   We fell it for fuel.
SUSURA = *SUSURA* / *Crossostylis cominsii* Hemsl. / *Gynotroches axillaris* Bl. (*Rhizophoraceae*)

DOLICHANDRONE, this tree doesn't get very big, its body is gritty, its leaf is green and quite rounded. It grows from its root.
○   It must grow in swamp and on inlets, just in wilderness.
•   We make pig barriers from it, it lives and grows and will hold the fence good and strong.
RIRIKO = DOLICHANDRONE / mangrove trumpet tree / *Dolichandrone spathacea* (L.f.) Schum. (*Bignoniaceae*)

PALE-WITHIN, this tree doesn't get very big, its body is brownish, its leaf is longish and narrow. Behind the leaf is white, that's why we name it thus.
○   It grows in the lowland and also in the inland.
•   We decorate bags with its fronds because it smells good.
SAEBALA = PALE-WITHIN / *Aglaia argentea* Bl. (*Meliaceae*)

DEFENDER, this tree doesn't get very big, its body is like a *lofa* tree (*Sterculia*) but scaly, its leaf is wide and almost like a crash leaf (*rā* / *Pangium*), the stem of the leaf is flat and not thick like *lofa*.
○   It must grow in wilderness and on clay, in the lowland and the inland.
•   We plant it in the yard area of the sanctum, it is there for the prediction of enemies, that's why we call it defender. If we see its leaves wilt, then a feud is close to happening.
•   We don't burn with it because this is a tree for leprosy, we cure leprosy with it.
SASATO'O = DEFENDER / *Trichadenia philippinensis* Merr. (*Flacourtiaceae*)

TO'OMA, this tree doesn't get very big but it is very tall, its body is white, its leaf is green and quite longish.
○   It grows from on the sea to the inland, in new shoots and also in wilderness. We also plant it in the home area and also in gardens.
•   The fruit is very sweet to eat, the hard fruit we burn and the ripe fruit we just eat.
•   We build houses with it.
•   We also fell it for fuel.
TO'OMA = *TO'OMA* / *Terminalia megalocarpa* Exell / *T. solomonensis* Exell. (*Combretaceae*)

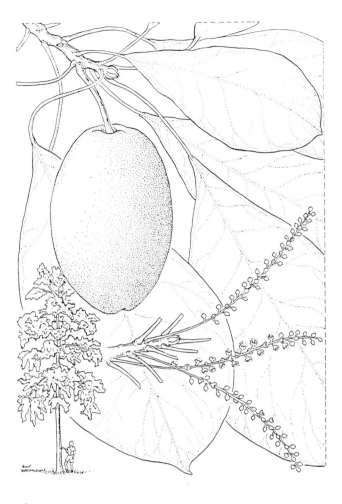

▲ to'oma / to'oma

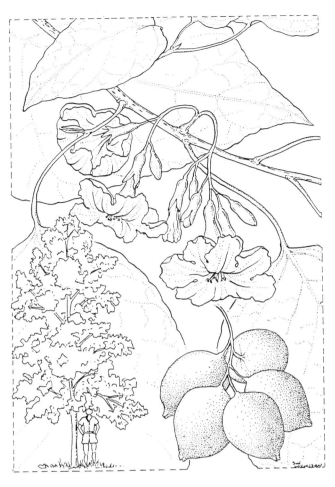

▲ uaua / lightweight

UAUA, ki saea logo 'ania MAUAUA, na 'ai ne'e noa'a kesi doe liu go'o, nonina ka ngwara'u ka te'e kwaokwao'a, rauna ka rebareba'a ma ka dokodoko go'o. 'Ai ne'e sasala liu, nia fa'ofa'o go'o, ta ne'e ki saea 'ania uaua.
- Nia ke bulao fafona asi, saena raku faolo kī.
- Kini kī kira ke raorū saena raku kī ma kira ke ū nunufi 'i 'aena.
- Fa'i 'ai du'a ki kwa'ia fuana so'i, nia ke du'a kwasukwasu ka di'ia logo 'aikarefo.

'AIKUKU, 'ai ne'e kesi doe liu go'o, nonina gwa-gwā'a, rauna rebareba'a. Nia ke fungu 'ania fa'irū ti'iti'i meo kī, kaida'i nia ke fungu bina ke 'ania, ta ne'e ki fa'asatā logo 'ania KOKOTA NA BINA.
- Nia ke bulao saena tolo.
- Ki saunga'i luma 'ania.
- Ki kwa'ia logo fuana so'i.

LIGHT-WEIGHT, this tree doesn't get very big, its body is soft and quite whiteish, its leaf is wideish and shortish. This tree is very light, it just floats, that's why we call it light-weight.
- It grows on the sea, in the new shoots.
- Women working in the shoots stand in the shade at its foot.
- The dried tree we fell for fuel, it burns flaming like flare-tree ('aikarefo / Schlienitzia).
UAUA / MAUAUA = LIGHTWEIGHT / kerosine wood / *Cordia aspera* Forst.f. / *C. subcordata* Lamk. (*Ehretiaceae*)

KUKU-TREE, this tree doesn't get very big, its body is blackish, its leaf is wideish. It bears small red fruits and when it bears hornbills eat them, so we also call it HORNBILL'S PRESENT.
- It grows in the inland.
- We build houses with it.
- We also fell it for fuel.
'AIKUKU / KOKOTA NA BINA = KUKU-TREE / HORNBILL'S PRESENT / *Myristica insularis* Kaneh. / *M. kajewskii* A.C. Sm. / *M. papinculata* (D.C.) Warb. / *M. petiolata* A.C. Sm. (*Myristicaceae*)

'AIALO, 'ai ne'e kesi doe liu go'o, nonina maramarako'a, rauna ka keta ka sisili'a go'o ka marako, takana kwao, ka bulao ana takana. Nia ke fungu 'ania fa'irū marako ka ketaketa'a kī ma kesi doe liu go'o, ni'i ngwara'u liu.

○   Nia ke bulao fafona asi, ka tasa ana kunu-kunu'a, nia logo saena to'ona'oa ma saena logo tolo. Noa'a nia kesi 'oro liu go'o, noa'a nia kesi bulao bubunga'irū'anga, nia ke bulao to'oto'o lala, ka tasa ana ti kula.

•   'Aialo nia le'a ka tasa fuana so'i. Nia sao ma nia ke du'a kwasukwasu, nia ke du'a sofonga'i ka du'a dangi, noa'a nia kesi du'a maemaela. Ka 'unari nia le'a ka tasa fuana ngalilana mafula 'uana o'olā ma kula kī sui. Ki saea 'ania satana SOFONGA'I MAFULA, nia di'ia masisi kia.

•   Nia ngwara'u bore 'ana ma nia le'a fuana saunga'ilana luma ni du'urūa sulia noa'a suma kesi 'ania.

'EBO, 'ai ne'e kesi doe liu go'o, lisilana 'itangana gwagwā'anga, rauna marako ka rebareba'a, ka ta'i ketaketa'a, takana kwao. Nia ke fungu logo 'ania fa'irū molimoli'a kī, kaida'i nia 'iri make 'ua nia marako, di'ia nia make ta ma ke meo.

Nia to'o ana rō malita'irū kī, ta ai ki fasia saena fanoa, ta ai ka kwasi go'o 'ana. Ai fasia, fuana doe mala, ai kwasi fuana rauraua go'o.

○   Nia ke bulao saena to'ona'oa, noa'a nia kesi bulao saena tolo. Ano kaole'anga ne'e nia bulao ka le'a ana. Nia kesi 'oro go'o, nia kesi bulao fiku ana te'e kula.

•   Rō 'ebo kī ta'ifau, ki 'ania fuani, 'anilana asila liu, kera'a asila ka bolo go'o. Ki 'ania fa'irū ma'a, ki dodoa logo saena fa'i ka'o ma ki do'ofia fuana 'anilana. Ki 'ania kaida'i ana fiolo'a kī, nia ke di'ia logo ne'e ki 'ania alo.

•   Noa'a kisi saunga'i luma 'ania sulia nia 'iri ona ma suma ke 'ania.

•   Ki kwa'ia logo fuana so'i, nia du'a kwasukwasu ma noa'a nia kesi du'a dangi, noa'a nia kesi du'a maemaela.

'IBO, 'ai ne'e kesi doe liu go'o. Fuana molimoli'a ka te'e doe, ka di'ia fa'i 'afi'o, nia ka bulao ana gwagina.

Nia to'o ana rō 'ibo kī. 'IBO KWAO, rauna marako balabala'a, fuana kwao. 'IBO MEO, rauna marako gwagwa'anga, fuana ka meo kwalakwala.

○   Nia ke bulao fa'asia fafona asi ka dao 'i tolo.

GOMPHANDRA-TREE, this tree doesn't get very big, its body is greenish, its leaf is long and narrow and green, its flower is white and it grows from its flower. It bears fruit which are green and longish and not very big, which are very soft.

○   It grows on the sea, especially in swamps, and also in the lowland and the inland. It is not very plentiful and does not grow in a thicket but grows individually, especially in some places.

•   Gomphandra-tree is especially good for fuel. It is soft and burns flaming, it burns hidden and burns till day, it doesn't burn dying. Hence it is especially good for taking fire to the garden and all other places. We give it the name FIRE-HIDER, it is like our matches.

•   Although it is soft it is good for building cooking houses because worms will not eat it.

'AIALO / SOFONGA'I MAFULA = GOMPHANDRA-TREE / FIRE-HIDER / *Gomphandra montana* (Schell.) Sleum. (*Icacinaceae*)

'EBO, this tree doesn't get very big, its trunk looks blackish, its leaf is green and wideish and quite longish, its flower is white. It bears rounded fruit, when not yet ripe it is green and when it is ripe it is red.

It has two kinds, one we plant in the home, one is just wild. The planted one has big fuit, the wild one the fruit is just slight.

○   It grows in the lowland, it will not grow in the inland. Clay ground is what it grows well on. It is not very plentiful and does not grow in groups in one place.

•   With both *'ebo* we eat the fruit, is is very sweet to eat and both are equally sweet. We eat the fruit raw and also flask it in bamboo and burn it to eat. If we eat it in times of hunger, it is as if we were eating taro.

•   We don't build houses with it because it is not tough and worms eat it.

•   We also fell it for fuel, it burns flaming but won't burn till day and won't burn dying.

'EBO = *'EBO*

CORYNOCARPUS, this tree doesn't get very big. Its fruit is rounded and quite big, like apple fruit (*'afio / Eugenia*), it grows from its core.

There are two kinds of corynocarpus. WHITE CORYNOCARPUS, its leaf is green and paleish, its fruit is white. RED CORYNOCARPUS, its leaf is green and blackish, its fruit is light red.

○   It grows from on the sea to the inland.

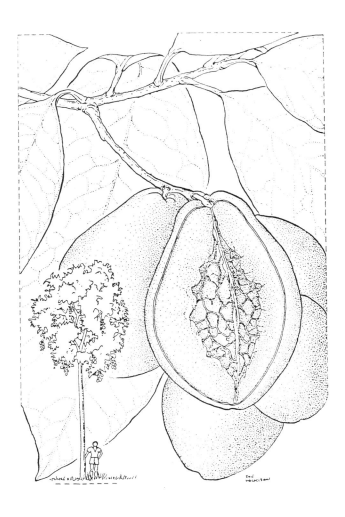

ibo / corynocarpus ▶

- Ki 'ania fa'irū kī.
- Noa'a kisi saunga'i go'o 'ania sulia nia kesi doe go'o ma ka ngwara'u.
- Ki du'a 'ania di'ia so'i ato.
- Ki gurā 'ania ti mata'inga.

'IBO'IBO, 'ai ne'e kesi doe liu go'o, nonina mela, rauna ka keta, takana ka lia le'a mala sulia nia meomeo'anga. Nia ke fungu 'ania fa'irū te'e doe kī.
- Nia ka bulao go'o saena to'ona'oa ma saena logo tolo, noa'a nia kesi 'oro liu go'o. Nia ke bulao to'oto'o, nia ka bulao ka le'a ana ti kula di'ia ano bū.
- Noa'a nia 'iri le'a fuana saunga'inga, nia kesi ona go'o sulia nia ke suma'ala.
- Du'alana, nia kesi du'a dangi, nia du'a maemaela.

- We eat the fruit.
- We don't build with it because it is not very big and is soft.
- We burn with it if fuel is hard to get.
- We cure some sicknesses with it.

'IBO = CORYNOCARPUS / *Corynocarpus cribbeanus* (F.M.Bail.) L.S.Sm. (*Corynocarpaceae*)

MERRILLIODENDRON, this tree doesn't get very big, its body is brown, its leaf is long, its flower looks good because is is reddish. It bears quite big fruit.
- It grows in the lowland and also in the inland, it is not very plentiful. It grows individually and grows well in places like on clotted ground.
- It is not good for building, it is not tough because it gets worm-eaten.
- To burn, it won't burn till day, it burns dying.

'IBO'IBO =MERRILLIODENDRON *Merrilliodendron megacarpum* (Hemsl.) Sleum (*Icacinaceae*)

'AI'ASAKA, 'ai ne'e kesi doe liu go'o, nonina melamela'anga. Rauna reba ka molimoli'a ka sakosako'a, lisilana karangia ka di'ia ra'ina asaka, ta ne'e ki fa'asata 'uri ana. Takana te'e meomeo'anga, fa'irū kī ka te'e molimoli'a.

○ Nia ke bulao fa'asia fafona asi 'uana 'i tolo, te'e saena kunukunua noa'a nia kesi bulao. Nia bulao to'oto'o, noa'a nia kesi 'oro liu, nia baru'a go'o bore ma ti kula ne'e nia ke bulao ka 'oro liu ani.

• Nia kesi le'a tasa go'o fuana saunga'inga sulia nia kesi ona liu go'o ma suma ke 'ania. Bore ma kaida'i nia mae nia ngasi liu mala, ki saunga'i diro 'ania fuana luma ma fuana logo sakali.

• Di'ia nia du'a ki kwa'ia logo fuana so'i, nia ke du'a kwasukwasu, noa'a kesi du'a dangi.

'AIBEBE, 'ai ne'e kesi doe liu go'o, nonina kwaokwao'a, rauna ka te'e ketaketa'a ma kesi reba liu go'o, lisilana di'ia logo 'ofenga. Takarū kī kwao ma di'ia nia taka bebe kī ke lofo ma'i kike to'o ana takana. Kaida'i nia fungu fa'irū kī lia kwanga ka le'a di'ia fatafata.

○ Nia ke bulao fafona asi ma noa'a nia kesi bulao saena kula kunukunu'a, noa'a nia kesi bulao saena tolo kī. Nia ke bulao to'oto'o, noa'a nia kesi 'oro liu go'o bore ma nia ke bulao ka tasa ana ti kula.

• 'Ai ne'e lisilana le'a liu, nia'a go'o fuana tua gwagwari'anga 'i olofana 'i fafona asi.

• Noa'a kisi saunga'i go'o 'ania sulia noa'a kesi doe liu go'o ma noa'a nia 'iri ona go'o.

• Noa'a kisi kwa'ia go'o fuana so'i, kisi oga go'o tufulana si ne'e 'ai ne'e noa'a kesi 'oro liu go'o.

'AIOFA, 'ai ne'e kesi doe liu go'o, nia fi'irū'a lala, nonina melamela'a, rauna ka di'ia logo rauna ofa. Di'ia ki tufua, mokofana karangia ka di'ia logo mokofani ofa.

○ Nia ke bulao ana kula kī ta'ifau, fa'asia fafona asi ka dao 'i tolo.

• Ki labunga'inia sulia sakali gwata kī, ni le'a sulia nia ke bulao ma ke daua sakali 'i ne'e kesi ofota'i.

• Ki saunga'i luma 'ania, nia le'a logo.

• Ki kwa'ia logo fuana so'i.

• Ki gura logo 'ania ti mata'inga.

COLEUS-TREE, this tree doesn't get very big, its body is brownish. Its leaf is wide and rounded and yellow, it looks almost like the leaf of coleus (*asaka*), that's why we name it thus. Its flower is quite reddish, its fruits are small and rounded.

○ It grows from on the sea to the inland, only in swamps it won't grow. It grows individually, it is not very plentiful, it is scarce, but in some places where it grows it is very plentiful.

• It is not especially good for building because it isn't very tough and worms eat it. But when it is dead it is very strong indeed and we make posts from it for houses and also for fences.

• If it is dried we also fell it for fuel, it burns flaming, it won't burn till day.

'AI'ASAKA = COLEUS-TREE / *Astronidium alatum* Veldk. / *A. aneityense* (1649) / *A. Bracteatum* Maxw. / *A. mammiformum* Maxw. / *A. miraculum-dei* Veldk. / *A. montanum* Merr.& Perry / *muscosum* Merr.& Perry / *A. palauense* (Kan.) Mgf. / *A. pallidum* Maxw. / *A. uncato-tessellatum* Maxw. (*Melastomataceae*)

BUTTERFLY-TREE, this tree doesn't get very big, its body is whiteish, its leaf is quite longish and not very wide, it looks like pseuderanthemum (*ofenga*). Its flower is white and when it flowers butterflies come flying to get to the flowers. When it bears the fruits look pretty and nice like speak (*fatafata*).

○ It grows on the sea but it won't grow in swampy places and it won't grow in the inland. It grows individually, it is not very plentiful but it grows especially in some places.

• This tree looks very good, it is just for sitting cool underneath on the sea.

• We don't build with it because it is not very big and not very tough.

• We don't fell it for fuel, we don't want to chop it down as the tree is not very plentiful.

'AIBEBE = BUTTERFLY-TREE / scaevola / saltbush / half-flower / *Messerschmidia argentea* (L.f.) Johnst. (*Boraginaceae*) / *Scaevola taccada* (Gaertn.) Roxb. (*Goodeniaceae*)

PEPPER-TREE, this tree doesn't get very big, it forms a clump, its body is brownish, its leaf is like a (betel) pepper leaf (*ofa / Piper*). If we chop it, its smell is also almost like the smell of pepper.

○ It grows in all places, from on the sea to the inland.

• We stake it for pig fences, it is good because it grows and holds the fence so that it won't tumble down.

• We build houses with it, it is quite good.

• We also fell it for fuel.

• We also cure some diseases with it.

'AIOFA = PEPPER-TREE / *Pittosporum ferrugineum* Ait / *P. sinuatum* Bl. (*Pittosporaceae*)

'AITAKALO, 'ai ne'e noa'a nia kesi doe liu, nonina kwaokwao'anga ma rauna ka molimoli'a ka rau-rau'a go'o. Ta'i kaida'i saena fa'i ngali na ra'irū kī ke 'asia ta'ifau ke takalo, nia ne'e ki fa'asatā 'uri ana
o Nia ke bulao saena to'ona'ona ma fafo'i asi.
• Ki tufua ki tadilia fuana suba'e fuana kilu'a.

• Ki saunga'i luma 'ania.
• Ki kwa'ia logo fuana so'i.

'AIBULU, 'ai ne'e kesi doe liu go'o, nonina bulu, rauna reba ka ketaketa'a, takana kwao ma nia ke fungu 'ania fa'irū molimoli'a kī.
o Nia ke bulao fa'asia fafona asi 'uana 'i tolo.
• Ki saunga'i luma 'ania.
• Ki kwa'ia fuana so'i.
• Ki guragura logo 'ania.

SIGORIA, 'ai ne'e noa'a kesi doe liu go'o, nonina kwaokwao'anga, rauna matanga'a ka reba ka ketaketa'a, ma ka sau ana ka'ika'irū. Fa'irū kī no'o lofolofo ke 'ania.
o Nia ke bulao saena to'ona'oa, ka 'oro saena tolo, noa'a kesi 'oro saena fafona asi.
• Noa'a kisi saunga'i 'ania sulia nia ngwara'u liu.
• Ki kwa'ia fuana so'i.
• Ki gura logo 'ania.

BORABORA, 'ai ne'e kesi doe liu go'o, nonina borabora'a, rauna reba ka dokodoko go'o, takana kwao ma nia ke fungu 'ania fa'irū molimoli'a kī.
o Nia ke bulao ana fa'asia fafona asi 'uana 'i tolo, ka 'oro saena to'ona'oa .
• Ki kwa'ia fuana so'i.
• Ki gura logo 'ania.

'AISISIU, 'ai ne'e kesi doe liu go'o, nonina gwagwā'a, rauna ka te'e ketaketa'a maramarako'a, takana ka kwao, fa'irū kī ka te'e ketaketa'a.
o Nia ke bulao saena raku faolu kī, ana ta kula bore 'ana.
• Ki sabangi 'ania.
• Ki saunga'i luma 'ania, nia le'a logo.
• Ki kwa'ia logo fuana so'i.
• Ki gura logo 'ania ti mata'inga.

SCATTER-TREE, this tree doesn't get very big, its body is whiteish and its leaf is rounded and slight. At one time in the year the leaves all fall and scatter, that's why we name it thus.
o It grows in the lowland and on the sea.
• We chop it and trim it for dibbles for burying (planting tubers).
• We build houses with it.
• We also fell it for fuel.
'AITAKALO = SCATTER-TREE

DARK-TREE, this tree doesn't get very big, its body is dark, its leaf is wide and longish, its flower is white and it bears rounded fruit.
o It grows from on the sea to the inland.
• We build houses with it.
• We fell it for fuel.
• We also cure with it.
'AIBULU = DARK-TREE / *Diospyros aibulu* Kost. / *D. ellipticifolia* (Stokes) Bakh. / *D. ferrea* (Willd.) Bakh. / *D. hebecarpa* A.Cunn. / *D. insularis* Bakh. / *D. maritima* Bl. / *D. Peeklii* Ltb. / *D. Pulchra* Bakh. / *Salomonensis* Bakh. Kost. (*Ebenaceae*)

PLERANDRA, this tree doesn't get very big, its body is whiteish, its leaf is divided and wide and longish and emerge from stems. Its fruit the birds eat.
o It grows in the lowland, it is plentiful in the inland, it is not plentiful on the sea.
• We don't build with it because it is very soft.
• We fell it for fuel.
• We also cure with it.
SIGORIA = PLERANDRA / *Plerandra solomonensis* / *P. stahliana* Warb. / *Schefflera stahliana* (Harms) Frodin (*Araliaxceae*)

PURPLE, this tree doesn't get very big, its body is purple, its leaf is wide and shortish, its flower is white and it bears rounded fruits.
o It grows from on the sea to the inland, it is plentiful in the lowland.
• We fell it for fuel.
• We also cure with it.
BORABORA = PURPLE / *Leea suaveolens* Burtt / *L. indica* (Burm.f.) Merr. / *L. tetramera* Burtt (*Leeaceae*)

EXCOICARIA-TREE, this tree is not very big, its body is blackish, its leaf is quite wideish and green-ish, its flower is white and its fruits are longish.
o It grows in the new shoots, in any place at all.

• We conduct (yam-vines) with it.
• We build houses with it, it is quite good.
• We also fell it for fuel.
• We also cure some diseases with it.
'AISISIU = EXCOICARIA-TREE / *Excoecaria agallocha* L. (*Euphorbiaceae*)

KATAFO, rū ne'e 'ai girogiro, noa'a kesi doe liu go'o, nonina kwaokwaoa, rauna te'e reba ma ka tongatonga'a, fa'irū kī ka doe ma ka ketaketa'a. Nia to'o ana rō malita'i rū kī, ta'i fa'irū kwao, ta'i fa'irū ka marako. Di'ia fa'irū kī kwasa ni'i meo kwalakwala.
- Rū faka ne'e, kira salinga'inia fa'asia 'i 'a'e asi. Di'ia ki taka 'ania magana nia ke bulao talana.
- Ki 'ania fa'irū kwasa kī, anilana asila ka le'a liu.

- Ki kukia gwangorū fuana guralana malaria.

FA'OLA, ki saea logo 'ania FA'OLO, FAKUSU, 'ai ne'e kesi doe liu go'o, ti kaida'i nia ke doe ka alua fi'i fa'ola doe. Nonina kwaokwao'anga, rarana ka 'oro liu ka usu ka 'ere 'i ano, rauna ka te'e reba ka marako. Takana di'ia logo takana tatali bore ma ti ai takana meomeo'a go'o, ti ai takana sakosako'a. Nia to'o ana fa'irū kī ma nia ke bulao logo ana 'itangana ma rarana.
- Nia ke bulao ana kula kī sui, kula kunukunu'a bore, nia 'oro liu ana ti kula.
- Ki aea ta'eta'ena fuana saunga'irū'anga, raolana ka bolo logo raolana 'abana sula ma malao. Ki tufua fa'i 'ai fi'i doe noima 'a'erū, ki aea 'abarū kī, ni'i bolo fa'inia fi'irilana foforū kī.

- Di'ia saunga'ilana 'ania rū kī, ki aea ta'eta'erū ngasi ki to'osia, ki ngalia 'abakwalo ngwara'u, ti kaida'i ki du'afia mala, ki fi'i saunga'inia 'ania dadalo fuana kwa'ilana furai ma dadalona basi, ki foli ngwa'i logo 'ania.
- Ki saunga'i luma logo 'ania bore ma noa'a nia kesi ona liu go'o, nia bolo fa'inia luma ni du'urū kī go'o.
- Na 'ai bulao 'ua kī ne'e ona ka le'a fuana saunga'inga. Ki tufua diro ana fuana saunga'i luma'a.
- Ki saunga'i logo 'ania sakali gwata, nia le'a sulia nia ke bulao.
- Ki kwa'ia logo fuana so'i.
- Ki gurā 'ania ti mata'inga.
- Ki gura logo 'ania fuana fa'agwarilana manatana ngwae kaida'i ana saeta'a.

PAWPAW, this is a tender tree, it doesn't get very big, its body is whiteish, its leaf is quite wide and it is gummy, its fruits are large and longish. It has two kinds, one with white fruit, one with green fruit. When the fruits are ripe they are lightish red.
- This is foreign, they transferred it from overseas. If we scatter its seeds it grows by itself.
- We eat the ripe fruit, it is sweet and very good to eat.
- We boil the leaf-shoots to cure malaria.
KATAFO =PAWPAW / papaya / *Carica papaya*

MALLOW, this tree doesn't get very big, sometimes when big it forms a big mallow clump. Its body is whiteish, its branches are very plentiful and long and curl on the ground, its leaf is quite wide and green, its flower is like the flower of hibiscus (*tatali*) but some have a reddish flower and some have a yellow flower. It has fruit and it also grows from its trunk and branches.
- It grows in all places, even swampy places, and it is plentiful in some places.
- We peel its skin for making things, to work with it is equivalent to working with *sula* and *malao* (both *Trichospermum*). We chop a slender tree or stock and peel off strips, they are suitable for binding bundles.
- If making things with it, we peel off the hard skin and throw it away and take the soft vine-strip, sometimes we burn (cook) it, then we make it into twine for nets and bowstrings, and we also plait bags from it.
- We also build houses with it but it is not very tough, it is suitable just for cooking houses.

- The longer-growing trees are good and tough for building. We chop posts from them for house-building.
- We also make pig fences with it, it is good because it grows.
- We also fell it for fuel.
- We cure some sicknesses with it.
- We also cure with it for cooling down a man's thoughts in time of anger.
FA'OLA / FA'OLO / FAKUSU = MALLOW / beach mallow / beach hibiscus / sea hibiscus / *Hibiscus tiliaceus* L. (*Malvaceae*)

fa'ola / mallow ▶

FA'OLA ASI, 'ai ne'e kesi doe liu go'o, rauna ka molimoli'a ka matanga'a, takana ka sakosako'a ka di'ia logo ba'era, takana ke afufu 'ali'ali go'o, fa'irū kī ka sau 'i fuila. Aelana ta'eta'ena ka talangwara'u liu.

○ Nia ke bulao go'o 'i fafona asi, ta ne'e ki fa'asata 'uri ana.
• Ta'eta'ena, ki aea ki fi'i du'afia 'i ke ngwara'u ma ke mabe fuana saunga'i 'ania dadalo ma gwa'i nili, ki faosia ngwa'i logo 'ania.
• Ti'iti'ilana ki saunga'i luma 'ania, bore ma luma sasufi'i go'o ne'e nia bolo fa'inia, sulia nia ke suma'ala.
• Ki labua 'ania ma'e bā, nia le'a sulia nia ke bulao ke birabira logo.
• Nia le'a logo fuana so'i.
• Ki gura 'ania 'afe 'i ke kale noa'a nia kesi nonifī.

SEA MALLOW, this tree doesn't get very big, its leaf is rounded and divided, its flower is yellow like cabbage (ba'era / Hibiscus), the flowers quickly drop and fruit emerge in their place. The skin is very easy to peel.

○ It just grows on the sea, that's why we name it thus.
• The skin we peel and then burn to become soft and flexible for making twine and braided cord, and we also plait bags from it.
• When small we build houses with it, but it is only suitable for smoky houses because it becomes worm-eaten.
• We stake barriers with it, it is good because it grows and sprouts.
• It is also good for fuel.
• We cure a woman with it so she'll give birth without pain.

FA'OLA ASI = SEA MALLOW / *Thespesia populnea* (L.) Sol. ex Correa (*Malvaceae*)

TATALI, 'ai ne'e ti'iti'i go'o, nonina kwaokwao-'anga, rauna te'e ketaketa'a ma ka te'e reba, ka girigiri'a raku kalikalia, takana doe ka kwanga liu. Nia to'o ana bara malita'irū kī, rauda karangia bobolo bore ma takana takarū kī lala ne'e mamata, ti ai takana meo, ti ai taka ka kwao, ti ai ka sako-sakoa. Ka 'unari bore ana satana ne'e tatali go'o.

- ○ Rū fasia ne'e, ki salinga'inia fuana laungilana nonina fanoa, si ne'e nia ke taka ka kwanga liu.
- • Ki sakali gwata 'ania, nia ke mauri ke bulao ka doe fuana fonea logo bā.
- • Ki aea ta'eta'ena fuana itolana 'ania babala ma gwaurau bore ma fuana luma 'inoto'a noa'a kesi bolo fa'inia sulia noa'a nia kesi ngasi le'a.
- • 'Abarū fuana logo saunga'ilana kalibeta fuana ra'e niu'a.
- • Takana ki silifa'inia saena gwauka ma ki sa'ingia ana angilaka fuana laungi'anga 'ania.

HIBISCUS, this tree is small, its body is whiteish, its leaf is quite longish and quite wide, it has pointed serrations around it, its flower is big and very pretty. It has several kinds, their leaves are almost the same but their flowers are different, some have red flowers, some the flower is white, some are yellow. Even so its name is just hibiscus.

- ○ This is planted, we transfer it to decorate the home area, as it flowers and is very pretty.
- • We fence pigs with it, it lives and grows big to block off a barrier.
- • We peel its skin to tie shelters and leaf-shelters with, but for important houses it is not suitable because it is not good and strong.
- • Its strips (of bark) are also for making foot-straps for climbing coconut (palms).
- • Its flower we stick in our heads (hair) and insert behind our ears for decoration.

TATALI = HIBISCUS / red hibiscus / chinese hibiscus / *Hibiscus rosa-sinensis* L. (*Malvaceae*)

KAKAFAE, 'ai ne'e ti'iti'i go'o, nia di'ia tatali. Fuana te'e molimoli'a ka marako, nia ke bulao ana fa'irū. Nia to'o ana rō malita'irū kī.
KAKAFAE KWAO, nonina kwaokwao'a, rauna ka reba liu ka marako.
KAKAFAE MEO, ki saea logo 'ania KINIOLO, nia di'ia logo ai kwao te'e rauna ne'e mela-mela'a, takana ka meo.

- ○ Nia ke bulao saena raku faolu ana kula kī ta'ifau, ka tasa ana fuli fanoa kī.
- • Ti kaida'i ki fasia saena fanoa sulia takana ka lia le'a liu ma 'i nia ke teo karangi fuana guragura'anga.
- • Ki gurā 'ania folofolo'aigwari ma du'afu'ufu'u.

CLERODENDRUM, this tree is just small, it is like hibiscus (*tatali*). Its fruit is quite rounded and green and it grows from its fruit. It has two kinds.
WHITE CLERODENDRUM, its body is whiteish and its leaf is very wide and green.
RED CLERODENDRUM, also called *KINIOLO*, is like the white one only its leaf is brownish and its flower is red.

- ○ It grows in the new shoots in all places, especially at home sites.
- • Sometimes we plant it in the home because the flower looks very good and it will be nearby for curing.
- • We cure consumption or tuberculosis with it.

KAKAFAE KWAO / KINIOLO = WHITE CLERODENDRUM / *Clerodendrum inerme* (L.) Gaertn.
KAKAFAE MEO = RED CLERODENDRUM / *Clerodendrum buchanani* (Roxb.) Walp. (*Verbenaceae*)

FATAFATA, 'ai ne'e ti'iti'i go'o, nonina kwao-kwao'a, rauna ka marako ka ketaketa'a, kaida'i karangia ni'i ke mae, rauna ke meo na'a. Takana kwao ma fuana kesi doe liu go'o ka marako.

- ○ Rū salinga'inia mala, ki fasia nonina fanoa fuana lisilana rauna ne'e ke meo ma ka kwanga ma fuana ki rao 'ania.

SPEAK, this tree is just small, its body is whiteish, its leaf is green and longish and when it is almost dead the leaf goes red. Its flower is white and its fruit is not very big and is green.

- ○ This has to be transferred, we plant it about the home to see the leaves go red and pretty, and for us to work with.

- Ra'irū ne'e meo ma ka tala 'asia 'i ano, ne'e ki ngalia ma ki tirufia ana kwakwana ngela ma ki fa'atalama'inia saelana satana rū kī, fuana kwakwana ke sasala fuana fata'a noima ala'anga. Ta ne'e ki saea 'ania fatafata.

'ALA'ALA ne'e 'ai ti'iti'i go'o, nia to'o ana malita'irū to'oto'o kī.
'ALA'ALA MARAKO, rauna marako mala.
'ALA'ALA SAKO, rauna sakosako'a.
'ALA'ALA MEO, rauna meo.
'ALA'ALA FI'IRODO, rauna ka meo ka rorodo'a.

'ALA'ALA OGAMU, ta sata 'ALA'ALA FI'IMU, rauna rikirikimu'a.

- Rū fasia ne'e, ki fasia nonina fanoa ma fuli tua'a, sulia ta'i tala kī, māna sakasaka'a kī, māna logo kafo kī. Nia ke bulao kwasi logo saena to'ona'oa fa'inia fafona asi saena fuli fanoa kī ma fuli tua'a kī.
- Ki fasia fuana laungilana kula nai'ari kī, ma ki fasia logo fuana 'oto'a 'ania 'usia ma'e akalo ma gwa'i mae'a ne'e ke fa'alia fanoa. 'Ai ne'e, di'ia ki sasia 'ania ta rū, nia ramo'ala liu, ta ne'e ki saea 'ania 'ala'ala.
- Ki 'inia ūluna fuana laungilana nonika kaida'i ana ngwa'enga kī. Kaida'i 'i na'o ngwae kī ke fonea 'ania latoda kaida'i ana laungi noni'anga.

TATA'I ne'e kala 'ai, nia ke doe ka bolo fuana sabangi falisi'anga, nonina ta'i melamela'a, rauna ti'iti'i miga ka sisimia go'o. Fa'irū kī, kaida'i isi make 'ua ni'i ta'i marako, di'ia nia make ni'i gwā na'a, na no'o ki saea 'ania bibisu ne'e ke lofo ma'i fuana 'anilana fa'irū kī.
- Nia ke bulao saena raku faolo kī, saena to'ona'oa bore ma nia kesi 'oro liu go'o ana.
- Ki tufua fuana kilua noima afita'anga fuana kumara ma falisi bore.
- Ki labunga'inia fa'i 'ai kī sulia sakali 'au kī sulia nia ke bulao talangwara'u ma ke birabira.
- Ki kwa'ia fuana so'i kaidai nia ke du'a.

- The leaf which is red and falls to the ground by itself, this we take and fan it on a child's mouth and train him to know the names of things, so that his mouth will be light for speech or conversation. That's why we call it speak.
FATAFATA = SPEAK

INSTANT, this tree is just small, it has different kinds.
GREEN INSTANT, its leaf is really green.
YELLOW INSTANT, its leaf is yellow.
RED INSTANT, its leaf is red.
GETTING-DARK INSTANT, its leaf is red and darkish.
WANTS-TO-BREAK INSTANT, also named ABOUT-TO-BREAK INSTANT, its leaf has breaking-points.
- This is planted, we plant it about homes and rest-sites, along paths, at (home) entrances and water spouts. It also grows wild in the lowland and on the sea on village sites and rest-sites.

- We plant it for decorating these places and we also plant it to charm against magic and epidemics damaging the home. This tree, if we do something with it, it is very active, that's why we call it instant.
- We pick its fronds for decorating our bodies during dances. In former times men shut off their genitals with it when decorating the body.
'ALA'ALA = INSTANT / croton / *Codiaeum variegatum* ssp. *moluccanum* (L.) Bl. (*Euphorbiaceae*)

TATA'I is a little tree, it gets big enough to conduct yam (vines), its body is brownish, its leaf is minutely small and narrow. The fruits, when not yet ripe are quite green, if they are ripe they are black and the bird called *bibisu* comes flying to eat the fruits.
- It grows in the new shoots, in the lowland, but it is not very plentiful there.
- We chop it (as a dibble) for burying or mounding potato or yam.
- We stake the trees along bamboo fences because it grows easily and sprouts.
- We fell it for fuel when it is dried.
TATA'I = *TATA'I* / *Phyllanthus microcarpus* (Benth.) Muell. Arg. / *P. reticulatus* Poir. / *Breynia cernua* (Poir.) Muell.Arg. / *B. racemosa* Muell.Arg (*Euphorbiaceae*)

SIKIMĀ, ta sata NUNUBA, 'ai ne'e ti'iti'i go'o, nonina melamela'a, rauna molimoli'a ka ti'iti'i go'o nia ke sau ana ka'ika'irū, ma ra'irū kī īla nunura. Rauna marako, di'ia rauna ke mae nia ke meo na'a go'o ka 'asi na'a 'i ano. Takana maramarako'a, afuna ka magamaga'a go'o ka maramarako'a logo. Na 'ai ne'e ngasi, nia ke birabira ana nonina kaida'i ki tufua. Di'ia ki 'oia gwangona, suluna ke siki ana māka, nia ne'e ki fa'asata 'uri ana. Di'ia noa'a kisi ta'ufia 'ali'ali ma māka ke rodo.

Nia to'o ana rō malita'irū kī, SIKIMĀ MARAKO fa'inia SIKIMĀ MEO, lisilana raudaro'o lala ne'e mamata, tai rauna marako, tai rauna ka meomeo'a, ma kera'a bolo go'o.

○ Nia ke bulao nama ana raku faolo ma ana masu'u sasala logo, ana kula kī ta'ifau fa'asia fafona asi ka dao 'i tolo, nia kesi bulao kesi 'oro liu go'o bore ma nia te'e 'oro saena to'ona'oa. Di'ia nia bulao saena o'olā saena fa'i alo ne'e mau'a na'a kī, lisilana le'a mala.

• Ki saunga'i 'ania bore ma nia 'iri le'a liu go'o sulia 'ai ne'e kesi doe go'o ma nia kesi ngasi logo, nia ke suma'ala logo. Ki saunga'i 'ania luma sasufi'i ma babala bore ma nia kesi bolo fa'inia saunga'i luma'a.

• Di'ia kini kī ke fofori kira ke lafua alo kī kika fikua alo kī 'i 'aena nunuba fuiri 'i ne'e ke fofori olofana noima kika ūnunufi 'i nunuba, nia ne'e ki saea 'ania nunuba.

• Ki kwa'ia fuana so'i, nia du'a kwasukwasu bore ma nia maemaela go'o.

KASIBULU ne'e 'ai ti'iti'i go'o, nonina gwā, ta ne'e ki fa'asata 'uri ana. Rauna ka marako ka te'e doe-doe'anga, noa'a kesi reba liu go'o.

○ Nia ke bulao saena raku faolu, fa'asia fafona asi 'uana 'i tolo, bore ma noa'a kesi 'oro go'o. Di'ia raku faolu ke dukwasi'a na'a, ma kasibulu kī ke mae logo.

• Ta'eta'ena ki aea fuana ito lakeno'anga, ma ito tatafe'anga ma ito babala'anga, bore ma fuana itolana luma 'inoto'a ne'e noa'a kesi bolo fa'inia.

• Ki saunga'i luma 'ania bore ma nia ngwara'u go'o, di'ia nia isila nia ke fura 'ali'ali.

• Ki kwa'ia fuana so'i, nia du'a ka kwasukwasu.

SQUIRT-EYE, also named SHADY, this tree is just small, its body is brownish, its leaf is rounded and small and emerges from a stem, and the leaf has a shiny back. Its leaf is green, if the leaf dies it goes red and then falls to the ground. Its flower is greenish and its fruit is full of seeds and greenish too. This tree is strong and sprouts from its body when we chop it down. If we snap the leaf-shoot, its sap squirts in our eyes, that's why we name it thus. If we don't wash it quickly our eyes go blind.

It has two kinds, GREEN SQUIRT-EYE and RED SQUIRT-EYE, the leaves of the two look different, one has green leaves, one has reddish leaves, but they are both the same.

○ It must grow in new shoots and light forest, in all places from on the sea to the inland, it doesn't grow very plentifully but it is quite plentiful in the lowland. If it grows in a garden in a plot of taros which are mature it looks really nice.

• We build with it but it is not very good because the tree doesn't get very big and is not very strong either, and it becomes worm-eaten too. We build smoky houses with it and shelters but it is not suitable for (dwelling) house-building.

• If women are harvesting they lift the taros and gather them at the foot of the shady to harvest under it or they stand in the shade of the shady, that's why we call it shady.

• We fell it for fuel, it burns flaming but also dying.

SIKIMĀ / NUNUBA = SQUIRT-EYE / SHADY / *Homalanthus novo-guineensis* (Warb.) Ltb. & Schum. / *H. papuanus* Pax. & Hoffm. / *H. populifolius* Grah. / *H. populneus* (Griset.) Pax / *H. trivalvis* A.Shaw (*Euphorbiaceae*)

DARK-SECTION is just a small tree, its body is black, that's why we name it thus. Its leaf is green, quite big and not very wide.

○ It grows in the new shoots, from on the sea to the inland, but it is not very plentiful. If the new shoots become wilderness, dark-sections will die.

• Its skin we peel for tying up pudding, tying platforming and tying shelters, but for tying important houses it is not suitable.

• We build houses with it but it is only soft and if it is wet it rots quickly.

• We fell it for fuel, it burns flaming.

KASIBULU = DARK-SECTION / *Melochia umbellata* (Houtt.) Stapf. (*Sterculiaceae*)

BEROBERO nia 'ai ti'iti'i, noa'a kesi doe liu go'o ma kesi keta liu go'o. Nia to'o ana rō malita'irū kī, na ai fasia fa'inia na ai kwasi. Berobero fasia rauna molimoli'a ka keta ka sakosako'a, ta'i ai fasia ne'e rauna fisifisi'a ka keta. Berobero kwasi rauna molimoli'a ka marako.

○ Berobero fasia ki fasia saena fanoa 'i māna fera kī ma ti kula bore 'ani, sulia nia lia le'a liu ma ka kwanga ma si ne'e ki laungi logo 'ania ngwa'i kia kī. Ki fasia go'o 'itanga 'i rū noima 'a'erū di'ia kaibia. Berobero kwasi nia ke bulao saena fuli fanoa kī.

• Gwangona ai sakosako'a ki kōngia 'ania gwata ma ki 'ania.

• Ki gura logo 'ania mata'inga kī.

BEROBERO is a small tree, it doesn't get very big and doesn't get very tall. It has two kinds, the planted one and the wild one. Planted *berobero*, its leaf is rounded and long and yellow, and one planted one has a thin long leaf. Wild *berobero*, the leaf is rounded and green.

○ Planted *berobero* we plant in homes in front of sanctums and anywhere else, because it looks very nice and pretty so we can also decorate our bags with it. We just plant its trunk or stock, like *bia*-yam (cassava). Wild *berobero* grows on home sites.

• The leaf-shoot of the yellow one we bake with pig and eat it.

• We also cure sicknesses with it.

BEROBERO = *BEROBERO* / *Mackinlaya celebica* (Harms) Philipson / *Delarbrea collina* Vieill. / *Polyscias filicifolia* (L.Moore) Bail. / *P. fructicosa* (L.) Harms / *P. guilfoylei* L.H.Bailey / *P. rumphiana* Harms / *P. scutellaria* (Burm.f.) Fosb. / *P. verticillata* B.C.Stone (*Araliaceae*)

▲ *berobero* / berobero

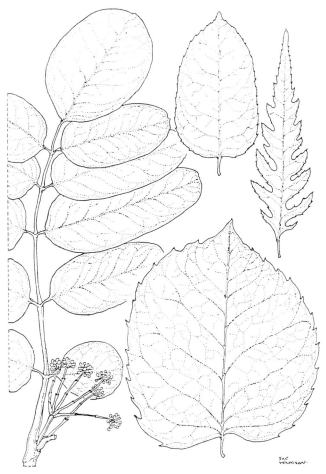

▲ *ti malita'i rauna berobero kī* / *some kinds of berobero leaf*

'AMAU, ki saea logo 'ania SAKWARI, nia 'ai ti'i bore 'ana, nonina gwagwā'a ka mamarako'a, rauna te'e ketaketa'a ma ka lia mole'a. Nia ke fungu 'ania fa'irū molimoli'a, magana ka 'oro. Nia ke ala ana kaida'i fa'i ngalia ke make, kike saea 'ania rongorongo 'i kata. Nia to'o ana malita'irū to'oto'o, ta ai rauna molilmoli'a, ta ai rauna ketaketa'a.
- o   Nia ke bulao ka 'oro saena to'ona'oa, nia logo saena tolo. Nia bulao kwasi go'o, bore ma saena o'olā kī noa'a kisi sungia, ki ogani ani fuana tatabu, di'ia ni'i 'oro liu ki sungi'a go'o ti ai.

- •   Kaida'i nia ka fi'i ala, kike 'inia ngwasana fuana 'anilana sulia tatabu kwasi nini'a.
- •   Safao kī ke fanga 'i saena nonina ni'i ke tete kaida'i nia mauri bore 'ana, go'o ki tufu 'uani fuana 'anilana.

BUNABUNA ne'e 'ai ti'iti'i go'o, ka'ika'ina dokodoko liu go'o, rauna molimoli'a ka reba ka rodo'a, ka to'o ana kakirū.
- o   Nia ke bulao saena dukwasi ana kula kī sui.
- •   Rauna ki atongia 'ania rū kī di'ia ta'eta'e 'ai ma kwalo 'abe fuana saunga'i dadalo'anga, ka di'ia logo dilo.
- •   Itangana ka'ika'ina ki dalofia 'ania dadalo ne'e ti'iti'i liu ka ngasi liu.
- •   Ki aea 'abarū fuana faosilana 'ania sangesange ne'e ki gwaro 'ania 'adi ma taketake niu, ki faosia logo 'ania fo'osae, ki obia logo 'ania usuusu.

'OFENGA ne'e 'ai ti'iti'i, nia to'o ana ti malita'irū.

'OFENGA to'o, nonina te'e sakosako'a ma rauna ka sakosako'a mala.
- o   Ki fasia saena o'olā kī ma nonina fanoa kia kī, nia ke bulao ana kaki'i rū kī ne'e ke teoteo ka buru fāfia ma nia ke kwasi logo.
- •   Rauna ne'e tatabu, 'anilana le'a liu.

'OFENGA 'AI, nonina ka maramarako'a, rauna ka keta. Ketalana ka tasa ana ofenga to'o, nia mauri ka tau liu.
- o   Nia ke bulao kwasila'a ana ano to'o ma ki fasia logo di'ia 'ofenga to'o.
- •   Rauna ne'e tatabu logo bore ma 'anilana ka 'afae liu.

'OFENGA KŌNGWAE, nonina te'e meomeo'anga ma rauna ka kerekere'a.
- o   Nia ke bulao nama ana kula ne'e bolo fa'inia saena nama kula te'e tolo'a kī, saena to'ona'oa kī ma karangia kafo kī. Ki fasia logo saena o'olā.

'AMAU, also called *SAKWARI*, is a tree but small, its body is darkish and greenish, its leaf is quite longish and looks round. It bears rounded fruit with many seeds. It sprouts when the nuts are ripe, we call it the sound of nut-pudding (being pounded). It has different kinds, one has rounded leaves, one has longish leaves.
- o   It grows plentifully in the lowland and it is also in the inland. It just grows wild, but in gardens we don't scorch it, we conserve it for vegetables and if it is very plentiful we just scorch some of them.
- •   When it is just sprouting we pick its leaf-shoot to eat because it is a wild vegetable.
- •   *Safao* (grubs) eat the inside of the body, they knaw it even while it's alive and we chop them out to eat.

'AMAU / SAKWARI = 'AMAU / sandpaper cabbage / *Ficus copiosa* Steud. (*Moraceae*)

BUNABUNA is a small tree, its stem is very short, its leaf is rounded and wide and dark and has a stem.
- o   It grows in wilderness in all places.
- •   The leaf we stain things with, like tree skin and anodendron-vine ('*abe*) for making twine, it is like dye (*dilo* / *Morinda*).
- •   Its main stem we twine into twine which is very small and very strong.
- •   We peel strips for plaiting into (arm) rings which we pattern with '*adi*-orchid and coconut cuticle, we also plait girdles with it and band nose-pins with it.

BUNABUNA = *BUNABUNA* / *Cyclosorus inivisus* (Forst.) Copel (*Thelypteridaceae*)

PSEUDERANTHEMUM is a small tree, it has several kinds.

PSEUDERANTHEMUM proper, its body is a bit yellow and its leaf is really yellow.
- o   We plant it in gardens and home areas, it grows from stalks which make a thicket, and it is also wild.
- •   Its leaf is a vegetable, it is very good to eat.

TREE PSEUDERANTHEMUM, its body is greenish, its leaf is long. It is taller than pseuderanthemum proper and it is very long lived.
- o   It grows wild on proper ground and we also plant it like pseuderanthemum proper.
- •   Its leaf is also a vegetable but it is very bitter to eat.

MAN-BAKING PSEUDERANTHEMUM, its body is a bit reddish and its leaf has markings.
- o   It must grow in places which suit it, in places a bit inland in the lowland and close to waters. We also plant it in gardens.

- Rauna ne'e tatabu, 'i na'o ma'i ki kōngia fa'inia ngwae fuana 'anilana.
- Rauna 'ofenga kī ta'ifau, ki dodoa ma ki kukia, ki lulungā logo fa'inia gwata ma karai ma sibolo kī ta'ifau.

RONGORONGOLUA ne'e 'ai ti'iti'i go'o, ka di'ia logo ofenga, nonina te'e maramarako'a, rauna keta ka sisili'a, rauna marako fifī logo.

- Nia ke bulao sulia kafo kī ma kula kunukunu'a kī, ta ne'e ki saea 'ania nia rongo lua.
- Gwa'irū kī ne'e tatabu kwasi, ki gwa'abia fa'inia kōnge gwata ma karai kī, nia 'iri 'afae liu logo.

- Its leaf is a vegetable, formerly we baked it with man to eat.
- The leaves of all pseuderanthemum we flask-cook and we boil them, we also parcel-cook them with pig and chicken and all proteins.

'OFENGA 'AI = TREE PSEUDERANTHEMUM / *Pseuderanthemum whartonianum* Hemsl. / *P.* ssp. (2 ssp.) (*Acanthaceae*)

HEARS-THE-TIDE is just a small tree, it is like pseuderanthemum (*'ofenga*), its body is a bit greenish, its leaf is long and narrow, its leaf is also intense green.

- It grows along waters and in swampy places, that's why we say it hears the (high) tide.
- The crown is a wild vegetable, we oven-cook it with baked pig and chicken, it is not very bitter.

RONGORONGOLUA = HEARS-THE-TIDE / *Graptophyllum pictum* (L.) Griff. / *Pseuderanthemum bicolor* Radlk. / *P.* aff. *whartonianum* Hemsl. (*Acanthaceae*)

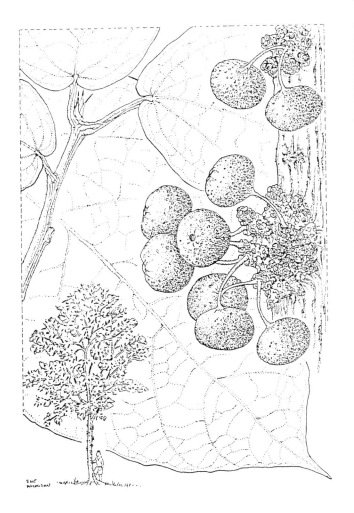

▲　*'amau / 'amau*

▲　*'ofenga 'ai / tree pseuderanthemum*

DADA ne'e 'ai ti'iti'i go'o, rauna ketaketa'a, takana ka meo.
- ○ Nia ke bulao saena to'ona'oa ma saena tolo, saena dukwasi kī go'o.
- • Ki saunga'i 'ania rū di'ia ka'ika'ina akisi ma fa'i kuba kī.
- • Ki saunga'i luma 'ania.
- • Ki kwa'ia logo fuana so'i.
- • Ki guragura logo 'ania.

DILI, 'ai ne'e ti'itit'i go'o, rauna keta ka te'e reba. Ti ai takarū kwao liu, ti ai meo, ti ai ka sakosako'a. Nia ke bulao ana 'a'erū ma ana takana logo.

Nia to'o ana rō malita'irū kī. DILI MEO, ki saea logo 'ania SANGO, nia rū fasia, ki fasia saena fanoa kī, nia ke bulao logo saena fuli fanoa kī. DILI MARAKO ne'e ai kwasi, nia ke bulao logo saena fuli raku ma saena masu'u, ti ai ki fasi'i logo.
- ○ Rō dili ta'ifau ni'i bulao ka 'oro saena tolo.
- • Ki fasia si nia lia le'a ma ka kwanga fuana laungilana fanoa, fuana logo oto'a 'usia ma'e akalo.
- • Dili marako fa'inia dili meo, ki laungi logo 'ania nonika ma ngwa'i kia kī.
- • Kaida'i 'i na'o, fataābu ke ilala 'ania ra'i dili, ki saea 'ania sango ni ilala'a.
- • Rauna ki dodoa 'ania ngongora kī 'i 'anilana ke moko le'a liu.
- • Ki gura 'ania du'afu'ufu'u.

DILI LALABE, nia mamata fa'asia dili saga sulia rauna tatala'asi'a ka kwanga.
- ○ Rū fasia logo, ki fasia ana kula kī ta'ifau.
- • Ki fasia kalikalia fanoa sulia bā. Ki barua fa'i ka'o sulia dili lalabe kī, go'o ki labunga'inia ti 'ifi 'ai ana ta bali mala ki fi'i fi'iria 'ania fa'i kwalo di'ia kwalo rara, sata, kalitau.

DADA is a small tree, its leaf is longish and its flower is red.
- ○ It grows in the lowland and in the inland, only in wilderness.
- • We make things from it like axe handles and walking sticks.
- • We build houses with it.
- • We also fell it for fuel.
- • We also cure with it.

DADA = *DADA* / *Crudia papuana Kost.* / *Cynometra ramiflora* L. / *Kingiodendron alternifolium* (Elmer) Merr. & Rolfe / *K. micranthum* Burtt / *K. platycarpum* Burtt / *Maniltoa grandiflora* (A.Gray) Scheff. (*Ceasalpiniaceae*)

CORDYLINE, this tree is just small, its leaf is long and quite wide. Some have very white flowers, some red, some are yellow. It grows from its base and also from its flower.

It has two kinds. RED CORDYLINE, also called *SANGO*, is planted, we plant it in homes and it also grows on home sites. GREEN CORDYLINE is a wild one, it grows in shoots sites and in the forest, and some we also plant.
- ○ Both cordylines grow plentifully in the inland.
- • We plant it to look good and pretty to decorate the home, and also for a charm against magic.

- • Green and red cordyline we also decorate our bodies and bags with.
- • In former times a tabu-speaker (priest) would divine with a cordyline leaf, we call it divination by *sango*.
- • The leaf we flask-cook *ngongora*(lizards) with so they'll smell very nice to eat.
- • We cure tuberculosis with it.

DILI = CORDYLINE / ti-plant / *Cordyline fruticosa* (L.) A. Chev. (*Lilliacae*)

***LALABE*-CORDYLINE** is different from cordyline proper because its leaf is striped and pretty.
- ○ It is also planted, we plant it in all places.
- • We plant it around the home as a barrier. We stack bamboos along the *lalabe* cordylines and we stake some tree logs on one side, and we then bind them with vines like *rara* vine (*Stenochlaena*), lygodium (*sata*) and winds-far.

DILI LALABE = *LALABE* CORDYLINE / *Cordyline terminalis* L. (*Liliaceae*)

MALADILI, ki saea logo 'ania MAMALADILI, 'ai ne'e ti'iti'i go'o, ka di'ia logo dili saga bore ma nonina ta'i maramarako'a. Nia to'o ana rō malita'i rū kī. Ai fasia, rauna keta ka marako, tatala'asia kwao kī ana rauna. Ai kwasi, rauna noa'a kasi tatala'asia go'o nia marako fīfī ka nunura logo.

o Ai kwasi nia ke bulao saena dukwasi ma saena logo raku, saena to'ona'oa ma tolo.

• Ki tufua fuana saunga'i sakali'anga. Nia le'a fuana bā gwata si ne'e nia ke birabira 'ali'ali.

• Noa'a kisi saunga'i 'ania ma kisi du'urū go'o 'ania.

MAOA ne'e 'ai ti'iti'i go'o, nia lia kwaokwao'a, nonina mela, saena mela, rauna marako fīfī. Di'i kī ragia ma ki daua 'ani fanga, ki 'ania ki moa, sulia nia moko fīfī.

o Nia ke bulao saena dukwasi.

• Ki saunga'i luma 'ania.

• Ki saunga'irū 'ania di'ia kafa ma sua.

• Ki kwaigurai 'ania ta'eta'ena.

SIMIDI, kala 'ai ne'e, nonina te'e borabora'a, rauna ka marako ka sisilia go'o ka te'e ketaketa'a.

o Nia ke bulao go'o saena tolo ma ana ti kula go'o 'i fafona asi, noa'a nia kesi bulao saena kunu. 'Ai go'o ana masu'u nini'a, nia kesi 'oro liu go'o ana kula kī.

• Nia le'a ka tasa fuana saunga'i'anga fuana bā gwata.

• Ki saunga'i 'ania luma.

• Ki kwa'ia logo fuana so'i.

BIALA, ki saea logo 'ania FIRI, nia 'ai ti'iti'i, rauna ti ai keta ka sisilia, rauna ti ai dokodoko ka reba. Nia ke bulao ana fuana.

o Rū fasia ne'e, kira salinga'inia ma'i 'i 'a'e asi. Ki takaloa taka rū dele kī, ka bulao ki fi'i fasia to'oto'o ani.

• Ki biala 'ania. Ki 'inia rauna, ki eta tafia ra'i 'ai etaeta kī ka tali ana ra'i 'ai 'i sae, ki ogani ana nia ke lango ki fi'i sikilia ki tafia ra'ina ki silia sisilina. Ka sui ki daura'inia ana 'aba kwalo ke du'a mala ki fi'i bulasia 'ania afu 'ai, ki saea 'ania ra'i firi. Ki fi'i biala 'ania.

FALSE-CORDYLINE, also called PSEUDO-CORDYLINE, this tree is just small, it is like cordyline proper but its body is a bit greenish. It has two kinds. The planted one has white stripes on its leaf. The wild one doesn't have stripes, it is intense green and shiny too.

o The wild one grows in wilderness and also in new shoots, in the lowland and the inland.

• We chop it for making fences with. It is good for pig barriers as it sprouts quickly.

• We don't build with it and we don't burn with it.

MALADILI / MAMALADILI = FALSE-CORDYLINE / PSEUDO-CORDYLINE / *Dracaena angustifolia* (Roxb.) (*Agavaceae*) *Pleomele angustifolia* (Roxb.) N. E. Brown (*Liliaceae*)

MAOA is a just small tree, it looks whiteish, its body is brown and brown inside, its leaf is intense green. If we strip the bark and hold food, when we eat we vomit because it has an intense smell.

o It grows in wilderness.

• We build houses with it.

• We make things with it like combs and spears.

• We cure with its skin.

MAOA = AMOORA / *Amoora cucullata* Roxb. / *Dysoxylum kaniense* Hemsl. (*Melastomataceae*)

SIMIDI is a little tree, its body is a bit purplish, its leaf is green and narrow and quite longish.

o It just grows in the inland and some places on the sea, it won't grow in swamp. This is a tree of the forest, it is not very plentiful in most places.

• It is especially good for building for pig barriers.

• We build houses with it.

• We also fell it for fuel.

SIMIDI = *SIMIDI*

TOBACCO, also called TIED, is a small tree, the leaves of some are narrow, the leaves of others are shortish and wide. It grows from its fruit.

o This is planted, they transferred it here from overseas. We scatter the parched flowers, they grow and we then plant them out separately.

• We (smoke) tobacco with it. We pick its leaf, we first strip off the first tree leaves and remove the leaves inside, we store them to dry out and then cut off and strip the leaf and split off the spine. Then we hang it on a vine-strip to dry out well and then roll it on a piece of stick and call it tied leaf. We then (smoke) tobacco with it.

BIALA / FIRI = TOBACCO / TIED / *Nicotiana tabacum* L. (*Solanaceae*)

'ASAKA nia ta laua go'o, noa'a kesi keta liu go'o, rauna ti ai molimoli'a, rauna ti ai ka ketaketa'a, takana kwao. Na 'asaka kī to'oto'o, ti ai rauna ka kwao, ti ai rauna ka meo kwalakwala'a, ti ai ki saea 'ania 'ASAKA BULU, ti ai rauna sakosako'a, ki saea 'ania 'ASAKA SAKOSAKO'A, ti ai rauna ka marako.

o   Na 'asaka kī ta'ifau ki fasi'i, te'e ai marako ne'e kisi fasia, nia kwasi. Ki fasia go'o 'a'erū kī.
•   Ki fasia tatala'a ana kalikalia luma kī 'i ke lia kwanga saena fanoa.
•   Ki fasia logo saena o'olā kī 'i ke lia kwanga ma fuana logo ulikwa'imā fuana tagi'a sulia alo ma falisi kī.
•   Ulirū ma takarū, ki laungia 'ania saena siosi.

•   Ki siu ki ongoa nonika 'ania ra'irū kī 'i ke faolo.

KWAKWALU BEBE ne'e laua go'o, nia kesi keta liu go'o, rauna marako ke te'e reba. Takana ka rata'i ka kwakwalubebe'a ana nonika di'ia ki liua ana.

o   Nia ke bulao ke 'oro liu ana ti kula fa'asia fafona asi ka dao saena tolo, ana ta kula bore 'ana ne'e fuli raku'a.
•   Nia le'a ka tasa fuana guragura'a.

BA'ERA, ki saea logo 'ania DE'E, ne'e laua go'o, nonina kwaokwao'a, takana sakosako'a. Nia ka to'o ana malita'irū 'oro kī, ti ai rauni dokodoko ka matanga'a, ti 'ai rauni keta ka sisili'a ti ai ke doe liu, ti ai kesi doe go'o di'ia BA'ERA OGA GWATA.

o   Rū fasia ne'e, kira salinga'inia ma'i 'i 'a'e asi. Nia ke bulao ana 'itangana noima rarana ma 'a'erū kī. Ki fasia saena fanoa ma o'olā ma ta kula bore 'ana.
•   Tatabu 'inoto'a nini'a, ki 'inia rauna fuana 'anilana, ki kukia, ki dodongia logo ma ki lulungā logo.

COLEUS is just a weed, it is not very tall, the leaf of some is rounded, the leaf of others is longish, the flower is white. Of the different coleus, some have white leaves, some have light red leaves, some we call DARK COLEUS, some with yellow leaves we call YELLOW COLEUS, some have green leaves.

o   All the coleus we plant, only the green one we don't plant, it is wild. We plant the stocks.
•   We plant it in a line around houses to look pretty in the home.
•   We also plant it in gardens to look pretty and also for a protector to look after taros and yams.
•   The fronds and flowers we decorate inside the church with.
•   When we bathe we rub our bodies with the leaf to get clean.

'ASAKA = COLEUS / *Blumea sylvatica* (Bl.) DC. (*Asteraceae*) / *Coleus scutellarioides* (L.) Benth. (*Lamiaceae*)

CLINGERS is just a weed, it is not very tall, its leaf is green and quite wide. Its flower sticks and clings to our bodies if we pass it by.

o   It grows plentifully in some places from on the sea to in the inland, but in places which are shoots sites.
•   It is especially good for curing.

KWAKWALU BEBE = CLINGERS / *Adenostema lavenia* (L.) Kuntze. / *Wedelia* aff. *rechingeriana* Muschler (*Asteraceae*)

CABBAGE, also called *DE'E*, is just a weed, its body is whiteish, its flower is yellow. It has many kinds, some the leaves are short and divided, some the leaves are long and narrow and some very big, some are not very big, like WANTS-PIG CABBAGE

o   This is planted, we transferred it here from overseas. It grows from its trunk or its branch and stock. We plant it in the home and garden and any other places.
•   This is an important vegetable, we pick the leaf to eat, we boil it and flask-cook it and also parcel-cook it.

BA'ERA / DE'E = CABBAGE / hibiscus cabbage / hibiscus spinach / slippery cabbage / *Hibiscus manihot* L. (*Malvaceae*)

GISOBALA ne'e laua go'o, nia ka kwaokwao'a, rauna ti'iti'i go'o, takana ketaketa'a ka moko le'a, nia ke bulao ana takana.

○ Rū fasia ne'e, nia kesi bulao ata.
• Ki fasia nonina fanoa kī sulia nia ke moko le'a.

• Ki laungia 'ania ngwa'i kī 'i ke moko le'a.
• Ki gurā 'ania ti mata'inga.

MAMALA'ALAKO ne'e laua, nonina kwaokwao'a, rauna molimoli'a ka ti'iti'i go'o, rauna īla kwao, saena ka marako.

○ Nia ke bulao go'o 'ana ana kula kī ta'ifau. Ti kaida'i go'o ne'e ki salinga'inia ki fasia ana kula ne'e ni'i noa'a ani kī, sulia 'ai mokomoko nini'a ma kami ke gurā 'ania ti mata'inga.
• Di'ia na gwaufī saungi 'oe ki 'oia ūlirū kī noima gwa'irū kī fuana itolani 'i māna dara ka 'iri gwauka ke aroaro ma kasi fī.

OCIMUM is just a weed, it is whiteish, its leaf is small, its flower is longish and smells good, it grows from its flower.

○ This is planted, it won't grow at random.
• We plant it round homes because it smells good.
• We decorate bags with it to smell good.
• We cure some sickness with it.

GISOBALA = OCIMUM / *Ocimum sanctum* L. (*Lamiaceae*)

MAMALA'ALAKO is a weed, its body is whiteish, its leaf is rounded and small, the back of its leaf is white and the front is green.

○ It just grows in all places. Sometimes we transfer it and plant it in a place where it is not, because this is a tree which smells and we cure some sickness with it.
• If a headache strikes us we pick fronds or crowns to tie at the brow so our head will be soothed and not ache.

MAMALA'ALAKO = *MAMALA'ALAKO*/ *Vitex negundo* L. (*Verbenaceae*)

▲ *ba'era / cabbage*

▲ *kwalu malita'i rauna ba'era / eight kinds of cabbage leaf*

UFUUFU ne'e laua, nia ke bulao go'o 'i ano, rauna ka marako ka reba, takana kwaokwao'a, nia to'o go'o ana magarū nenere'a kī. Nia to'o ana rō malita'irū kī. UFUUFU saga nia marako, UFUUFU BULU nia gwagwā'a lala.
- ○ Nia ke bulao ke 'oro liu ana kula kī ta'ifau, ka tasa saena tolo.
- • Nia kesi le'a go'o fuana ta rū sulia na laua go'o nini'a.

UFUUFU is a weed, it just grows on the ground, its leaf is green and wide, its flower is whiteish and it has a batch of small seeds. It has two kinds. *UFUUFU* proper is green but DARK *UFUUFU* is blackish.
- ○ It grows very plentifully in all places, especially in the inland.
- • It is no good for anything because it is just a weed.

UFUUFU = *UFUUFU* / *Cyrtandra heintzelmaniana (3017)* *(Gesneriaceae)* / *Elatostema feddeanum* H.Schroter / *Procris penduculata* (Forst.) Wedd. (*Urticaceae*)
UFUUFU BULU = DARK *UFUUFU* / *Elatostema aff. novae-britanniae* Ltb. (*Urticaceae*)

KU'IKU'ITA ne'e laua, nia'a te'e di'ia na 'ai ti'iti'i kī, rauna marako ka reba ma ka ketaketa'a. Kaida'i ki liu ana, fa'irū kī ke rata'i ana ifuka ma nonika, ki saea 'ania nia di'ia logo lango ke ku'ia ta rū mae.
- ○ Nia ke bulao ana kula kī sui 'i fuila raku kī, sulia ta'itala kī ma ana kula tabu'i kī bore.
- • Nia'a 'iri le'a go'o fuana ta rū.

SWARM is a weed, it is a bit like a small tree, its leaf is green and wide and longish. When we pass by, its fruits stick to our hair and bodies, we say it is like flies swarming on something dead.
- ○ It grows in all places in shoots sites, along pathways and cleared places.
- • It is no good for anything.

KU'IKU'ITA = SWARM

MARABURABU ne'e laua go'o, rauna marako ka molimoli'a ka ti'iti'i go'o, takana kwao.

- ○ Nia ke bulao saena fuli raku kī ma sulia ta'itala kī ana kula kī ta'ifau, ke 'oro ana kula ki tabu'i fuana o'olā kī.
- • Nia le'a go'o fuana guralana mata'inga kī.

CRASSOCEPHALUM is just a weed, its leaf is green and rounded and small and its flower is white.
- ○ It grows in shoots sites and along pathways in all places, it is plentiful in places we clear for gardens.
- • It is just good for curing sicknesses.

MARABURABU = CRASSOCEPHALUM / *Crassocephalum creidoedes* (Benth.) S. Moore (*Asteraceae*)

MAMANI ne'e laua, nia fi'irū'a, rauna ka te'e ketaketa'a ka marako, takana molimoli'a ka marako logo, nia ke alua magarū marako kī, bore ma nia sau go'o 'i 'aena ra'irū kī.
- ○ Nia ke bulao 'i fafona asi, saena to'ona'oa ma ka 'oro saena tolo, te'e kunu go'o ne'e noa'a.
- • Nia kesi le'a go'o fuana ta rū sulia laua go'o nini'a.

MAMANI is a weed, it is a clump, its leaf is quite longish and green, its flower is rounded and green too, it produces green seeds, but they just emerge from the foot of the leaves.
- ○ It grows on the sea, in the lowland and plentifully in the inland, only not in swamp.
- • It isn't good for anything because it's just a weed.

MAMANI = *MAMANI* / *Elatostema neticulatum* Wedd. / *E. sesquifolium (Reinw.)* Hassk. / *Procris frutescens* Bl. / *P. obovata* Beck. (*Urticaceae*)

BULAO RAUNA ne'e laua, nonina marako, rauna te'e keta ka te'e reba ma ka nunura. Nia ke bulao ke 'oro liu sulia nia ke bulao ana rauna.
- ○ Ki fasia fuana 'i ke lia le'a saena fanoa.
- • Ki guragura 'ania ra'irū.

LEAF GROWER is a weed, its body is green, its leaf is quite long and quite wide and shiny. It grows plentifully because it grows from its leaf.
- ○ We plant it to look good in the home.
- • We cure with the leaf.

BULAO RAUNA = LEAF GROWER

LAI ne'e ta karasi bore ma nia bulao ka te'e ra'e ana karasi kī, rauna keta mala ka ti'iti'i. Nia ke lalisusu saena ano ma lalirū bulao kī raku liu.

○ Nia ke bulao ana kula kī ta'ifau, fa'asia fafona asi ka dao 'i tolo.
● Noa'a kesi bolo fa'inia ta rū.

NGWANO ne'e fi'irū, nia di'ia karasi bore ma nia kesi momote, rauna keta liu ma ka sislia, nia ka marako ta'ifau.
○ Nia ke bulao saena kunukunua kī.
● Ki saunga'i 'ania mata kī

MAMAFU'AI, laua go'o ne'e, nia kwaokwao'a. Nia ke susu fafia kula, lafulana nia ngasi liu.
○ Rū ne'e kira salinga'inia ma'i fa'asia 'i 'a'e asi, nia ke bulao go'o 'i fafona asi.
● Ki fo'ota ai 'oro kī fuana saloa na sasalo.

● Ki guragura logo 'ania.

'AMA'AMA ne'e laua ti'iti'i go'o, 'aena noa'a kesi doe liu go'o, rauna marako ka matanga'a ka nenere'a go'o ka ta'i fisifisi'a ka di'ia logo takuma, bore ma nia ta'i ngasi. Kaida'i nia fi'i doe nonina marako bore ma kaida'i nia ngwaro nonina sakosako'anga na'a. Nia ke leforū'a ka susu fafia ano. Rō 'ama'ama kī, 'AMA'AMA AFA nia doe mala ana 'AMA'AMA saga.
○ Nia ke bulao go'o 'i fafona asi ma saena to'ona'oa, saena lalano ma sulia ta'itala kī, nia 'oro saena to'ona'oa. Nia ke bulao ka buru ka leforū'a fafia afu masu'u ti'iti'i kī, masu'u ne'e bulao ka nenere'a saena o'olā ki fa'asata 'ania 'ama'ama ta'a.
● Kula nia bulao susuto'o nia le'a fuana kilulana alo, si ne'e nia fa'ata'inia kula gwari ne'e.

● Ki 'oia ūlina fuana laungi'anga 'i ke lia le'a, ki daura'ini'i sulia ngwa'i.
● Ki alua logo saena gwauna ngwae, fada 'ania ngwae nai'ari nia saungia ngwae. Ta ne'e ki saea ngwae ta'a 'ania "ae loi 'ama'ama,' satana ne'e fa'i loi ne'e saungia ngwae, ma'e fata'a nai'ari ke kwatea ngwae ke saeta'a liu.
● Ki sasi logo 'ania rū 'oro kī ana bali akalo.

IMPERATA is a grass (Pijin *karasi*) but it grows a bit higher than other grasses, its leaf is really long and small. It roots firmly in the ground and the growing roots put out shoots.
○ It grows in all places, from on the sea to the inland.
● It is not suitable for anything.
LAI = IMPERATA / *Imperata conferta (Presl) Ohwi. / I. cylindrica (L.) Rauesch. / I. exaltata (Roxb.) Brongn.* (Poaceae)

ELEOCHARIS is a clump, it is like grass but it is not scratchy, its leaf is very long and narrow and it is all green.
○ It grows in swamps.
● We make matting from it.
NGWANO = ELEOCHARIS / *Eleocharis dulcis* (Burm.f.) Henschel / *E. geniculata* (L.) Roem. & Schult. / *E. variegata var. latiflora* (Thur.) C.B.C.I. (*Cyperaceae*)

MAMAFU'AI, this is just a weed, it is whiteish. It covers over a place, it is very hard to pull up.
○ This is something they transferred from overseas, it just grows on the sea.
● We lash many of them together for sweeping, as a broom.
● We also cure with it.
MAMAFU'AI = *MAMAFU'AI / Sida rhombofolia* L. (*Malvaceae*) / *Ludwigia octovalis* (Jacq.) Raven (*Onagraceae*)

SELAGINELLA is a small weed, its foot is not very big and its leaf is green, divided, multiple and quite thin, like fern (*takuma / Diplazium*) but quite strong. When part grown its body is green but when old its body is yellow. It forms a thicket and covers the ground. Of the two selaginellas, EAGLE SELAGINELLA is bigger than SELAGINELLA proper.
○ It just grows on the sea and in the lowland, in forest and along pathways, it is plentiful in the lowland. It grows densely and thickets over a small piece of forest, and the forest which grows and multiplies over a garden we call bad selaginella.
● The places it grows and covers are good for burying (planting) taro, since it shows the place is damp.
● We snap off its fronds for decoration to look good and hang them from bags.
● We also put them in a man's head (hair), meaning that the man has killed someone. That's why we call a bad man 'you selaginella viper', the name of a snake which kills people, and these words will make a man very angry.
● We also do many things with it to do with ghosts.
'AMA'AMA = SELAGINELLA / *Selaginella rechingeri* Hieron (*Selaginellaceae*)

NINIU, saena 'abafola ne'e nia ke ū fuana ti malita'i 'ai ne'e kira bolo logo. Niniu nia ke keta gwalogwalo'a ma i'ikorū ke aboe 'afia, go'o rarana ka 'asia na'a. Ra'irū sau ana 'ai'ai'irū.

- Nia ke bulao logo saena kunukunua kī ma kula 'eke'eke kī, ka 'oro liu saena to'ona'oa ma tolo, nia saena tolo goro logo.
- Noa'a kisi 'ania, ka noa'a kisi du'a logo 'ania di'ia so'i, bore ma nia 'inoto'a fuana saunga'irū-'anga.
- 'Itangana ki kwa'igasia 'ania rebarū kī, nia le'a liu fuana tatafe'anga ma 'odo'anga, fuana logo raforafo fuana 'oilana ra'i sao fafia fuana to'osilana luma ma logo fuana bakasilana 'odo'a.
- Fifikona, 'i na'o ma'i ki tufua fuana gwaru'a fafona saena luma ma 'i'iko fuana alua fanga'a.

- Na ūlina le'a logo fuana sasalo.
- Nia le'a logo fuana guralana ti mata'inga.

'A'ATARE ne'e malita'irū logo ana niniu, lisilana di'ia logo niniu, doelana ma ketalana bolo logo fa'inia. Rauna go'o te'e mamata ka doe ka doko-doko go'o ana niniu, lisilana di'ia rauna sao bore ma ka ti'iti'i ana.

- Nia ke bulao sulia kunukunu'a kī.
- Rauna ki usa fuana to'osilana luma, ka di'ia logo ra'i sao.
- 'Itanga'irū, raolana di'ia logo niniu.

KIKIRU, ki saea logo 'ania 'OTA, nia malita'irū logo ana niniu, nia ke keta gwalogwalo'a, nonina gwagawā'a, rauna doe liu mala ma ka keta. Nia fungu 'ania fingirū kī.

Kikiru ka to'o ana rō malita'irū kī.
KIKIRU 'inoto'a, ki saea logo 'ania MĀLUA.

- Ai fasia nini'a, ki fasia 'i nonina fanoa ma ana ta kula bore 'ana, fa'asia fafona asi ka dao 'i tolo.

'A'AFAE, ki saea logo 'ania KIKIRU KWASI, nia di'ia logo kikiru bore ma lisilana raurau'a go'o fa'asia mā lua, rauna bore ki lia sai ana ni'i ti'iti'i lala ana malua, fuana ni'i ti'iti'i logo ana fa'i malua.

- Ai kwasi nini'a, noa'a kisi fasia. Nia ke bulao ana kula kī ta'ifau.

PALM in this book stands for some kinds of trees which are similar. Palm is tall and erect and its frond-sheaths drop off around it, then the branch falls. The leaves emerge from a stave (mid-rib).

- It grows both in swamps and in dry places, it is plentiful in the lowland and inland and it is also in the misty inland.
- We don't eat it, nor do we burn with it as fuel, but it is important for making things.

- Its trunk we tear into flats, it is very good for platforming and walling, and also for battens for thatching sago leaf for roofing houses and also for clamping walling.

- Its frond-base, formerly we chopped it off for sitting on in the house, and the frond-sheaths for putting food on.
- The frond is also good for brooms.
- It is also good for curing some sicknesses.

NINIU = PALM / *Gulubia macrospadix* (Burret) H. E. Moore / *G. niniu* H.E. Moore (*Arecaceae*)

ACTINORHYTIS is a kind of palm, it looks like palm, its size and length are similar. Just its leaf is a bit different, it is bigger and shorter than palm, it looks like sago leaf but smaller.

- It grows along by swamps.
- Its leaf we stitch for roofing houses, like sago leaf.
- The trunk, its uses are like palm.

'A'ATARE = ACTINORHYTIS / *Actinorhytis callapparia* (Bl.) Wendl.& Drude (*Arecaceae*)

BETEL, also called 'OTA, is a kind of palm, it is tall and erect, its body is blackish, its leaf is very big and long. It bears bunches (of fruit).

Betel has two kinds.
Important BETEL we also call EYE-BULGER.

- This is the planted one, we plant it in the home area and anywhere else, from on the sea to the inland.

BITTER, also called WILD BETEL, is like betel but it looks slighter than betel, and we can see that even its leaf is smaller than betel and its fruit is also smaller than eye-bulger.

- This is the wild one, we don't plant it. It grows in all places.

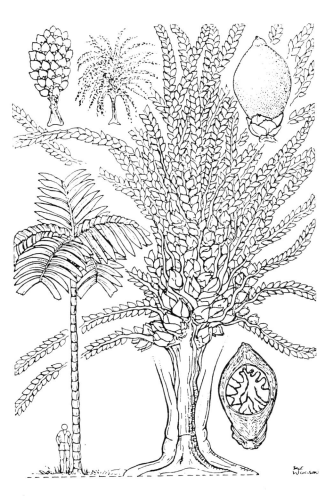

▲ *kikiru / betel*

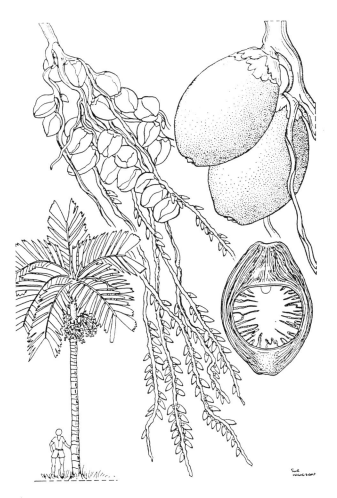

▲ *'a'afae / bitter*

- Ki damia fa'i kikiru. Ki 'alea ta'eta'ena fuana 'anilana sa'erū, ki damia fa'inia fena ma 'ofa, go'o ki fa'asata 'ania dami'a. Di'ia ngwae ngado, nia ke saungia sa'e kikiru saena kakata fa'inia 'ofa ma fena. Di'ia fa'i 'agiru, fada 'ania ne'e ki ke 'ala giroa go'o māna fa'irū; di'ia mālua, fada 'ania ne'e ta'eta'ena ngasi, di'ia ki 'alea māka fasi ke lua mala. Ki damia logo fa'i ukulu ma di'ia 'agiru nia 'ato ki damia logo fa'i 'agiru lufi'a. Ki damia logo fa'i 'a'afae, bore ma 'anilana nia 'afae liu ana kikiru 'inoto'a.

- 'Itangana kikiru ki kwa'igasia 'ania rebarū kī, ka tasa 'ana kikiru kwasi. Rebarū nai'ari kī fuana tatafe'anga, ki 'oia logo ra'i sao fafia fuana to'osi-lana logo luma. Ki gasia logo 'itangana 'ania rebarū ti'iti'i kī fuana usalana sao, ka di'ia logo 'aba kalitau noima ma'e midi.

- Ūlina ki to'osia 'ania gwaurau saena o'olā kī ma ta kula bore 'ana fuana tua nunufi'anga.

- We chew betel fruit. We bite off the skin to eat the inner part and chew it with lime and pepper (*òfa / Piper betel*) and we call it (betel) chewing. If a person is toothless he pounds the inside of the betel in a mortar with pepper and lime. If it's tenderbite it means we can easily bite into the fruit; if it's eye-bulger it means the skin is hard and if we bite it our eyes seem to bulge. We also chew soft ones and if tenderbites are difficult to get we also chew immature tenderbites. We also chew bitter but it is much more bitter to eat than important betel.

- The betel trunk we tear into flats, especially wild betel. These flats are for platforming, and we also fold sago leaf over it for roofing houses. We also tear the trunk into small flats for stitching sago (leaf), as with winds-far strip or (sago) leaf-spines.

- Its fronds we roof leaf-shelters with in gardens and anywhere else, for sitting in the shade.

KIKIRU / 'OTA / MĀLUA = BETEL / EYE-BULGER / betelnut / areca palm / *Areca catechu* L

'A'AFAE / KIKIRU KWASI = BITTER / WILD BETEL / *Areca macrocalyx* Zipp. ex Bl. (Arecaceae)

DI'A, ki saea logo 'ania FUFURI, FUNGUTOLI, ne'e malita'irū logo ana niniu, lisilana ka di'ia logo fa'i kikiru bore ma nia keta ka doe liu mala. Nonina kwaokwao'anga, rauna sisili'a ka ta'i ketaketa'a. Nia ke fungu ana 'itangana, fuana talirū'a, fingirū ke dau tatara 'i sulia, nia ne'e ki saea 'ania fungu toli.

○   Nia ke bulao go'o ana to'ona'oa.
•   Ki botakolekolea mafora'irū fuana tatafe.
•   Rebana ki tadilia fuana bakasilana 'odoa.
•   Kaida'i nia ke 'asia, ganafu kī ke fanga 'i saena ka di'ia logo sao, ki tufu 'uani fuana 'anilani.
•   Ki guragura logo 'ania.

BASIBASI ne'e malita'irū logo ana niniu, nia keta liu mala ka te'e doedoe'anga, 'itangana gwagwā'a.

○   Nia bulao saena to'ona'oa ma saena kunu-kunu'a ma saena mutana ua kī logo. Noa'a nia kesi 'oro, noa'a kisi takiloa tufulana go'o, ki ognani ana fuana saunga'irū 'ania sulia ki raorū 'ania.
•   Rū 'inoto'a ne'e fuana saunga'inia 'ania rū di'ia 'ai'ai 'i basi fa'inia logo sua kī ma ma'e sima kī.
•   Nia bolo logo fa'inia saunga'ilana rebarū di'ia raforafo.
•   Ki tolea logo gwaurau kī 'ania uila.

BŌFAU nia bolo logo fa'inia basibasi, ka keta ma kesi doe liu go'o, rauna ketaketa'a ka marako. Nia ke fungu 'ania fa'irū molimoli'a kī ni'i talirū'a, fa'irū nia marako, kaida'i nia ke make ke meo. Nia ke bulao ana fa'irū.

○   Nia ke bulao fafona kunukunua kī ma ano 'eke-'eke kī logo, saena to'ona'oa ma saena logo tolo.
•   Saunga'inga 'ania bōfau nia di'ia logo saunga'inga 'ania basibasi, bore ma kaida'i fa'i 'ai ke doe ka 'ua na'a ma tufulana ka ona liu, lisilana saena fa'i rū ka gwā ka ailoko'a mala. Fa'i 'ai nai'ari ne'e ngasi ka bolo fa'inia saunga'ilana rū di'ia sua kī ma basi ma ma'e sima kī ma ma'erū fuana ma'e 'aranga kī. Ki saunga'inia logo 'ania ma'ena kafa gwaroa kī.
•   'Itangana ki kwaigasia 'ania rebarū ne'e le'a ka tasa fuana tatafe'anga.
•   Ki saunga'i sakai logo 'ania fuana gwa'abi'anga, ka tasa fuana du'urū'a ana kaida'i ana maoma, sulia nia le'a ka liufia sakai ana ka'o.

CARYOTA, also called *FUFURI* and BEARS-DOWNWARD, is a kind of palm, it looks like betel (*kikiru* / *Areca*) but it is tall and very big indeed. Its trunk is blackish. It bears on its trunk, its fruits have pits and the bunches hang along it, that's why we call it bears downward.

○   It just grows in the lowland.
•   We smash lengths of it flat for platforming.
•   Its flats we trim for clamping walling.
•   When it falls down *ganafu* (grubs) eat inside it, as with sago, and we chop them out to eat.
•   We also cure with it.

DI'A / FUFURI / FUNGU TOLI = CARYOTA / BEARS DOWNWARDS / fishtail palm / *Caryota rumphiana* Bl. ex Mart. (*Arecaceae*)

BOW is a kind of palm, it is very tall indeed and quite big, its trunk is blackish.

○   It grows in the lowland and in swamp and also on the ridges of hills. It is not very plentiful and we don't chop it down wastefully, we save it for making things because we work with it.

•   It is important for making things like bow staves and also spears and arrows.
•   It is also suitable for making flats, like battens.

•   We also thatch leaf-shelters with the fronds.

BASIBASI = BOW / *Clinostigma haerestigma* H.E.Moore / *Drymophloeus pachycladus* (Burret) H.E.Moore / *D. rehderopheonix* Sub. / *D. subdistichus* H.E.Moore / *Rehderopheonix subdisticha* H.E.Moore (*Arecaceae*)

SET-SOLID is similar to bow (*Arecaceae*), it is tall and not very big, its leaves are longish and green. It bears rounded fruit with pits, the fruit is green and when ripe it is red. It grows from its fruit.

○   It grows on swamp and dry ground also, in the lowland and also in the inland.
•   Working with set-solid is like working with bow, but when the tree is big and old it is very tough to chop, and the inside of it looks black and deep red. This tree is strong and suitable for making things like spears, bows, arrow foreshafts and prongs for liester-spears. We also make the sticks of patterned combs from it.

•   Its trunk we tear into flats which are especially good for platforming.
•   We also make tongs of it for oven-cooking, especially for burning (food) during festivals, because it is better than tongs of bamboo.

BŌFAU = SET-SOLID / *Ptychosperma salomonense* Burret / *Strongylocaryum latius* Burret (*Arecaceae*)

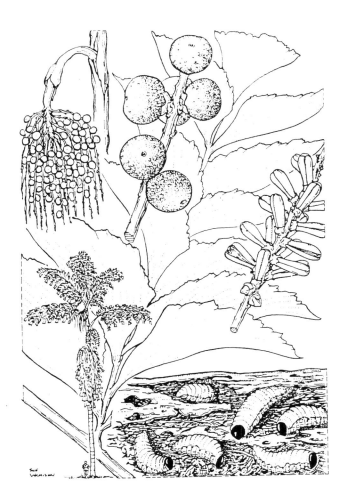

▲ *di'a / caryota*

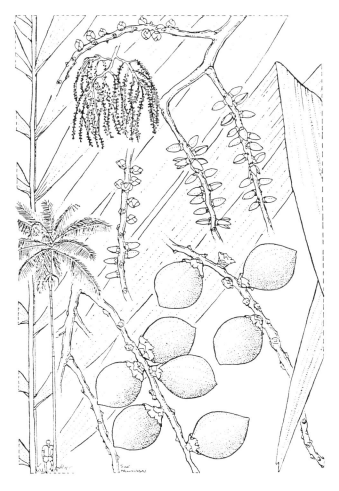

▲ *dai'i / rhopaloblast*

DAI'I, ta sata 'AGARIRU, ne'e bolo logo fa'inia basibasi ma niniu, 'itangana borabora'a, nia to'o ana 'aba'abarū kī, go'o rauna ka marako ka keta liu ka sisili'a, burina ra'irū kī kwaokwao'anga. Nia to'o ana gwa'i bula'irū kī di'a niniu ma ka fi'i takara'a ka alua fa'irū molimoli'a kī ma kesi doe liu go'o, na taila to'o go'o 'ana te'e sa'erū. Nia ke bulao ana fuana.

○ Nia ke bulao ana kula kī ta'ifau, fa'asia fafona asi ka dao 'i tolo, nia 'oro liu mala saena dukwasi.

• 'Itangana ki kwa'igasia 'ania rebarū fuana saunga'i luma'a, na rebana ngasi ka agariru'a ka liufia fa'i niniu, ta ne'e ki fa'asata 'uri ana. Rebarū ki 'oia ra'i sao fafia fuana to'osilana luma, ki bakasia 'ania 'odoa, ki tatafe logo 'ania. Nia bolo logo fa'inia rebarū rokoa fuana māna fera gwaroa.

• Na ūlirū kī ki tolea logo gwaurau kī 'ania 'i māna o'olā kī.

RHOPALOBLAST, another name HARDWOOD, is equivalent to bow (*Arecaceae*) and palm, its trunk is purplish, it has fronds and the leaf is green, very long and narrow, and the back of the leaf is whiteish. It has frond-shoots like palm and it then flowers and sets fruit which are rounded and not very big, and the pits have a bit inside (kernel). It grows from its fruit.

○ It grows in all places, from on the sea to the inland, and it is plentiful in wilderness.

• Its trunk we tear into flats for building houses, the flats are strong and a hardwood, more than palm. The flats we fold sago leaf over for roofing houses, we clamp walls with them and we also platform with them. It is also suitable for incised flats for the front of a patterned sanctum.

• The fronds we also thatch leaf-shelters with beside gardens.

DAI'I / 'AGARIRU = RHOPALBLASTE / HARDWOOD / *Rhopaloblaste elegens* H.E.Moore (*Arecaceae*)

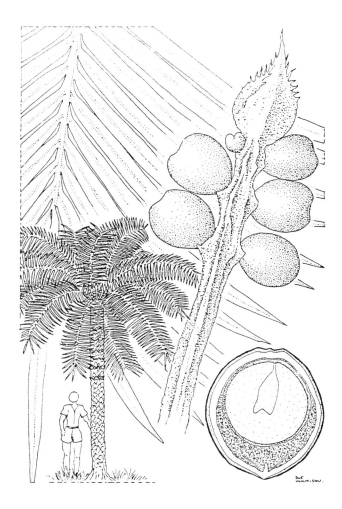

◀ *baibai / cycad*

BAIBAI ne'e malita'irū logo ana niniu, noa'a kesi doe liu go'o, nonina gwagwā'anga ka furufuru'a, rauna ka karangi ka di'i na fa'i basibasi kī. Nia ke fungu 'ania fa'irū kī, fuana rebareba'a ka ninini'a, ka to'o ana ta'i talirū, nia ke bulao ana talirū.
○   Nia ke bulao 'i fafona asi.
•   Ūlirū kī ki laungi 'ania luma kī kaida'i ana fafanga'a, ki silifa'inia ana 'odoa 'i māna sinama kī.
•   Fuana, kaida'i nia ke make, ngela kī ke sotea fuana lalafilana. Ki tafangia fa'irū, ki to'osia sa'erū, ki fi'i itoa gwa'i dadalo ana rō bali kī, ki lalafia 'i ne'e ke abula, go'o nia ke angi ka kodi ma ka koko na'a, ki saea 'ania nia ke baibai.

FILU ne'e malita'irū logo ana niniu, noa'a nia kesi doe liu bore ma nia keta liu. Bore ma ra'irū nia mamata fa'asia niniu kī, ta'i ra'irū sau ana ka'ika'irū. Nia to'o ana rō malita'i filu kī. Ai ne'e rauna reba, ki saea 'ania FILU saga, ai ne'e rauna sisilia, na satana ne'e FILU TALI.
○   Nia ke bulao go'o saena to'ona'oa.

 CYCAD is a kind of palm, it is not very big, its body is blackish and gritty and its leaf is almost like bow (*Arecaceae*). It bears fruit, the fruit is flattish and thin and has one pit, it grows from its pit.
○   It grows on the sea.
•   Its fronds we decorate houses with during feasts, we insert them in the walling in front of doorways.
•   The fruit, when it is ripe, children bore it for pulling. We open up the fruit and throw away the inner part, we then tie a twined cord to the two ends, we pull on it so it turns, then it cries and whistles and shouts, we say it cycads.
BAIBAI = CYCAD / palm fern / *Cycas rumphii* Miq. (*Cycadaceae*)

BRIGHT is a kind of palm, it is not very big but it is very tall. But its leaf is different from the palms, a single leaf emerges from the stem. There are two kinds of bright. The one with a wide leaf we call BRIGHT proper, the one with a narrow leaf we call SPLIT BRIGHT.
○   It just grows in the lowland.

- Ki rao 'ania rauna. Di'ia ki 'olea 'abana ki fa'asinafia nia ke kwao ka utifilu'a, ta ne'e ke saea 'ania filu.
- Ai rauna reba, ki 'afu 'ania rauna fuana butalana mani kī ma lifa ī'a kī. Nia le'a si ne'e rauna ngasi kesi ta'a 'ali'ali kaida'i nia ke sasufia saena bara, ka teo bore sulia ta bara fa'i ngali mani kī kesi bulibuli ma kesi mū.

- Rauna filu saga ki sū logo 'ania fa'asia uta.

- Filu tali, ki talia rauna ki fa'asinafia ke kwao 'i ki laungia 'ania ngwa'ī kī.
- 'Itangana nia ona liu, ki saunga'i 'ania basi ma ma'e sima kī.
- Ki saunga'i luma logo 'ania, ki kwaigasia logo 'ania rebarū ki fuana bakasilana odo'a.

- We work with the leaf. If we cut up the frond and sun it, it goes bright white, that's why we call it bright.
- The wide leaf one, we wrap with the leaf to parcel shell-money and fish (porpoise) teeth. It is good as the leaf is strong and will not go bad quickly when we smoke it on the rack, and even if it lies there for several years the money won't go dirty and (the string) won't break.
- The leaf of bright proper we also cover up with from the rain.
- Split bright, we split the leaf and sun it white to decorate bags with.
- Its trunk is very tough, we make bows and arrow foreshafts from it.
- We also build houses with it, we tear it into flats for clamping walling.

FILU = BRIGHT / fan-palm / *Livistona woodfordi* Ridl. / *Pritchardia pacifica* Seem. & Wendl. (*Arecaceae*)
FILU TALI = SPLIT BRIGHT / *Licuala lauterbachii* Damm. & Schum. (*Arecaceae*)

SAO nia mamata fa'asia niniu kī, nia ke doe, nonina ka ngarangara'a, rauna keta ka reba, rarana ke aboe 'afia, nia ke keta ngwaololo, na katakatarū ka fungu 'ania fa'irū molimoli'a kī.
○ Nia ke bulao ana kula fungufungu'a ma kula langalanga kī. Ki fasia logo saena tolo ma ti kula bore 'ana.
- Sao nia rū 'inoto'a, ki saunga'i 'ania fuana rū 'oro kī.
- Ki usa rauna fuana to'osi luma'anga ma odo'a logo, ki efoa ma'e midina fuana logo usalana 'ania.
- Sisilikwa ana fuana saunga'i sasalo'anga.
- Sisilina ki saunga'inia logo 'ania ma'e tari kī fuana fana no'onga.
- 'Itangana ki kwa'igasia 'ania rebarū kī fuana tatafe'anga.
- 'I na'o ki tufua ofiofina fuana gwaru'a 'i fafona saena ano, ka di'ia logo bae.
- Na sa'esa'e sao fuana sare gwata'anga, kaida'i ana fiolo'a ki kōngia logo fuana 'anilana.
- Kaida'i fa'i sao ka 'asia noima ki tufua, ki folofolo ana nonina fuana sīsī ke alua fakelana, ka teo ana leleka nia ka ganafu'a logo, ki tufu 'uana ganafu kī fuana 'anilani.
- Kaida'i fa'i sao nia fura, na gero sao nia ke 'ala logo ana fuana 'anilana.
- Na sa'esa'ena rarana ngela kī ke saunga'i masamasa ana 'ani faka, subi, alafolo ma ta rū bore 'ana.
- Na gwangona ki atongia fuana fa'i sangesange kī ana obi kī.

SAGO is different from the palms, it gets big, its body is prickly, its leaf is long and wide, its branches drop around it, it is tall and bendy, and its spike bears rounded fruits.
○ It grows in swampy places and dry places. We also plant it in the inland and anywhere else.

- Sago is important, we make many things with it.
- We stitch its leaf for roofing houses and walling and extract its leaf-spine for stitching (the leaf) with.
- Leaf-spines from it are for broom-making.
- The leaf-spines we also make into darts for shooting birds.
- Its trunk we split into flats for platforming.

- Formerly we chopped its sheath (frond-base) for sitting on on the ground, like bark-board.
- The inner part of the sago (trunk) is for feeding pigs, in times of hunger we also bake it to eat.
- When the sago tree falls or we chop it down, we score across the body for beetles to lay eggs and eventually it becomes full of *ganafu* (grubs), and we chop out the *ganafu* for eating.
- When the sago tree rots, sago fungus also sprouts on it for eating.
- The inner part of the branch children play at making into ships, angle-clubs, deflector-clubs, and anything else.
- Its leaf-shoot we stain for (arm)ring bands.

SAO = SAGO / ivory nut palm / *Metroxylon bougainvillense* Becc. / *M. salomonense* (Warb.) Becc. (*Arecaceae*)

NIU ne'e rū 'inoto'a ana falafala kia 'i Kwara'ae.

○   Rū fasia ne'e, nia ke bulao 'i fafona asi fa'inia saena to'onaoa, ki fasia logo saena tofungana tolo bore ma bulaolana 'i nai'ari kesi le'a liu.

•   Fasilana, ki ngali fa'i rū dele ki alua ka bulao, ki fi'i fasia saena ano, ki tabu 'afia 'i ke doe. Nia ke doe sulia lima fa'i ngali'anga, ka fi'i fungu.

•   Fuana, kaida'i nia kwa'ukwa'unga ki loia fuana kwa'ufilana suluna ma 'anilana, nia asila liu ma ka 'ero'ero.

•   Kaida'i fa'irū nia dele na'a, ki koria, ki losia logo fuana lofa, fuana saugwasu'a ma saulakeno'anga fa'inia saunga'ilana sufusufu kī.

•   Lasina, ki saunga'i titiu 'ania fuana fanga ma kwa'unga 'i saena.

•   'Itangana ki gasia ki tufua 'ania rebarū fuana tatafe'anga, nia ngasi liu bore ma tadililana te'e ato.

•   Ki saunga'i logo'ania rū kala'i di'ia ra'unga kī.

•   Ūlirū kī, ki tolobabala 'ani'i fuana gwarū nunufi'a.

•   Rauna ki faosia 'ania rū fuana gonilana fanga ma ta rū bore 'ana, di'ia kukudu, 'ita, lafa, bebete, fa'i sakusaku.

•   Ki 'afu ī'a 'ania rauna fuana gwa'abilani.

•   Ma'e midi, ki saunga'i sasalo 'ania fuana salo'a.

•   Gwangorū kī, ki aea taketakena fuana folilana rū di'ia gwarosangesange kī.

•   Taketakena niu fuana kwa'ilana rū fuana laungi'a kī, ki atongia 'ania dilo fuana gwarolana 'ania rū di'ia kafa gwaroa ma fa'i rade kī. Ana to'a buri kī, ki saunga'inia logo 'ania 'aba obi fuana kini sari'i kī kira ke abisi'i 'i gwauna alada.

•   Lalirū girogiro kī, ki atongia 'ania gwaro sangesange kī.

•   Ta'eta'ena ki gura logo 'ania ti mata'inga, ki tufua ki kukia di'ia lif ti.

COCONUT is important in our tradition in Kwara'ae.

○   It is planted, it grows on the sea and in the lowland and we also plant it in the central inland but its growth there is not very good.

•   To plant it we take a parched fruit and put it to grow and then plant it in the ground and clear around it for it to become big. It gets bigger for five years and then bears.

•   The fruit, when it is drinkable, we pick it to drink the juice and to eat, it is very sweet and oily.

•   When the fruit is parched we scrape it and wring it out for cream, for pounding coconut-pudding and cream-pudding and also for making stews.

•   Its shell we make cups with for eating and drinking from.

•   Its trunk we tear and chop into flats for platforms, it is very strong but quite difficult to trim.

•   We also make carved things with it, like weapons.

•   The fronds we shelter under for sitting in the shade.

•   Its leaves we plait into things for storing food and other things, like baskets, pouches, trays, flaps and balls (for play).

•   We wrap fish in its leaf to oven-cook them.

•   The leaf-spines we make brooms with for sweeping.

•   Its leaf-shoot we peel the cuticle off for weaving things like ring-patterns (armbands).

•   Coconut cuticle is for making things for (personal) decoration, we stain it with dye (*dilo / Morinda*) for patterning things like patterned combs and (ear)reeds. Old-fashioned people also make it into bands for maidens to wear on the hips.

•   The soft roots we stain ring-patterns (armbands) with.

•   Its skin we also cure some sicknesses with, we chop it and boil it like tea.

NIU = COCONUT / *Cocos nucifera* L. (*Arecaceae*)

6
Fi'irū ne'e boeboena ka ofi fafia fa'ina kī

6
Clumps with leaf-tubes sheathing the stem

'AGE, saena 'abafola ne'e nia ke ū fuana ti malita'irū kī ne'e kira bolo logo. 'Age ne'e fi'irū, fa'ina ka keta, boeboena ka ofi fafia fa'ina, rauna ka keta logo ke te'e reba ka nunura. Takana ke fingifingi'a ka kwao, ti ai ka meo, ka alua fa'irū molimoli'a kī.

- Nia ke bulao go'o 'ana ana kula kī sui. Rū kwasi ne'e bore ma ta 'age ne'e rauna kwanga ka kwao ma ka marako, ki salinga'inia 'i 'a'e asi fuana kwanga'a saena fanoa.
- Rauna ki sigora 'ania ka'o fuana kwa'ufilani kī.

- Ki buta 'ania ti fanga di'ia sa'e ngali kī, ki kutua logo 'ania rū di'ia bibi gwata fuana ngalilana. To'a asi go'o ne'e ke buta ī'a ti'iti'i kī 'ania fuana usi'a 'ani'i.
- Gwa'abi'a, ki rao go'o 'ania ūlina ta'ifau ma ki safa'a talana 'ania fanga kī, sulia ra'irū ni'i ti'iti'i go'o, bore ma noa'a 'iri le'a kesi bolo fa'inia ti ra'irū doe kī.
- Ūlirū kī ki to'osia 'ania gwaurau saena o'olā kī ma ta kula bore 'ana fuana tua nunufi'anga.

'IU ne'e fi'irū, nia di'ia logo 'age, nonina meo kwalakwala'a, rauna keta ka sisilia, takana kwao, fingina tatara, fuana ka meo kwalakwala'a. Nia bulao ana afuna saena ano fa'inia fuana.

- Nia ke bulao 'i fafo 'i asi ma saena to'ona'oa.
- Ki gurā 'ania ti mata'inga.

FIU ne'e fi'irū, nia ta malita'irū logo ana 'age bore ma ka dokodoko go'o 'i ano, go'o ka alua afurū saena ano. Nia to'o ana rō malita'irū kī.
FIU saga nia marako, rauna ka ti'iti'i go'o ka sisilia ka ta'i ketaketa'a go'o. Nia ke bulao ana 'itanagana ma afurū.
FIU RAKO, ki saea logo 'ania FIU RĀRĀ, ni'i di'ia logo ai saga bore ma nia keta ana ma rauna ka doe ka ketaketa'a ka di'ia rauna rako, ta ne'e ki fa'asata 'uri ana. 'Afurū sakosako'a.

- Rō rū ne'e kī ki fasi'i 'i nonina fanoa kī ma ana kula kī ta'ifau, nia ke lalisusu saena ano ma ka 'oro liu mala.

ALPINIA, in this book it stands for some things which are similar. Alpinia is a clump, its stem is long, its leaf-tube sheaths the stem, its leaf is also long and quite wide and shiny. Its flowers are bunched and white, some are red, and produce rounded fruit.

- It just grows in all places. It is wild, but an alpinia which has pretty leaves, white and green, we transferred from overseas to be pretty in the home.
- Its leaf we roll (into spouts) for bamboos for drinking.
- We parcel food with it, like inner nuts (kernels) and also wrap things in it like baby pigs for carrying. The sea people parcel small fish in it for marketing.
- For oven-cooking, we just work with the whole frond and we spread a place for food with it, because the leaf is just small, but it is not good compared to some big leaves.
- The fronds we roof leaf-shelters with in gardens and anywhere else for sitting in the shade.

'AGE = ALPINIA / red ginger / *Alpinia oceanica* Burk. / *A. purpurata* (Vieill.) Schum. (*Zingiberaceae*)

'IU is a clump, it is like alpinia (*'age*), its body is light red, its leaf is long and narrow, its flower is white, its bunches hang down and its fruit is light red. It grows from its tuber in the ground and its fruit.

- It grows on the sea and in the inland.
- We cure some sickness with it.

'IU = 'IU / *Alpinia aff. nutans* Rosc. (*Zingiberaceae*)

GINGER is a clump, it is a kind of alpinia (*'age*) but it is low on the ground and it produces tubers in the ground. It has two kinds.
GINGER proper is green, its leaf is small, narrow and quite longish. It grows from its trunk and the tuber.
HELICONIA GINGER , also called RĀRĀ GINGER, is like the proper one but it is taller and its leaf is big and wideish like heliconia (*rako*) leaf, that's why we name it thus. The tuber is yellow.

- Both of them we plant in home areas and in all places, it spreads its roots in the ground and becomes plentiful.

- Ki dami 'ania ma ki 'ania, 'anilana 'ako'ako ka le'a liu. Ki 'ilia ki tabu le'a ana ma ki damia kaida'i afurū kī ke 'eke'eke.
- Nini'ari ki saungia afurū kī ma ki alua saena sufusufu, ka di'ia kari.
- Rauna ki to'osia fāfona barabara 'ai ana babala saena o'olā.
- Rū fuana fonelana akalo nini, na ngwae tua fuana akalo kī ke lalia afurū kī 'ania ma'e fata'a ka damia ka busura'inia 'usia akalo kwasi ma rū ke takisi kia kī.
- Nia le'a ka tasa fuana guralana 'ania mata'inga kī.

GWANGO'ASI, ki saea logo 'ania GWAGWANGO, nia ke fi'irū'a 'i ano, ka di'ia logo fiu bore ma rauna reba ana ka te'e ketaketa'a. Fingina sau go'o ana ka'ika'irū kī 'i ano ka ra'e, takana ka sakosako'a ka sau ana fingina. Takana sulu'a ka giragira'a di'ia gwangona ngwae, ta ne'e ki saea 'ania gwango'asi.
○ Nia ke bulao ana kula kī ta'ifau, ana ano kaole'a.
- Ki gurā 'ania ti mata'inga.

FOLOTA ne'e fi'irū, nia ta malita'irū logo ana 'age, rauna keta mala ka marako. Nia ke taka, na fingina 'afu'afua takarū ka sau ana. Fuana molimoli'a, nia ke bulao ana fuana.
○ Rū ana raku faolu nini'a, nia ke bulao 'i fafona asi, nia 'oro saena to'ona'oa ma saena logo tolo.

- Ki 'inia rauna fuana 'afulana fanga di'ia kata ma ta rū bore 'ana, ki gwa'abi logo 'ania, nia moko le'a. Ki safa logo 'ania rauna talana fanga kī, rauna fuana logo gu'utalana bi'i fanga.

- Ki ninia logo ke ti'iti'i 'i ke bolo fa'inia sigora'anga ka'o fuana kwa'unga'a.
- Rauna ki to'osia 'ania babala fuana tua nunufi'a 'i saena o'olā.
- Ki guragura logo 'ania 'a'erū girogiro kī fuana māla kī.

- We chew it (with betel) and eat it, it is hot to eat and very good. We dig it up and clean it up well and chew it when the tubers are dry.
- At present we pound the tubers and put them in stew, it is like curry.
- The leaf we roof over the frames of shelters in the garden.
- This is something for blocking ghosts and men who live for the ghosts invoke the tubers with words and chew it and spray it out against wild ghosts and things which attack us.
- It is especially good for curing sickness with.
FIU = GINGER / *Zingiber*
FIU RAKO / FIU RĀRĀ = HELICONIA GINGER / RĀRĀ GINGER / turmeric / *Curcuma longa* L. (Syn. *C. domestica* Val.) (*Zingiberaceae*)

SNOT-FALL, also called SNOTTY, forms clumps at the ground, it is like ginger (*fiu* / *Zingiber*) but its leaf is wide and quite long. Bunches emerge from stems at the ground and come up, its flower is yellow and emerges from the bunch. Its flower has a slimy juice like human snot, that's why we call it snot-fall.
○ It grows in all places, on clay ground.

- We cure some sickness with it.
GWANGO'ASI / GWAGWANGO = SNOT-FALL / SNOTTY / *Costus* sp. (*Zingiberaceae*)

GUILLANIA is a clump, it is also a kind of alpinia (*àge*), its leaf is really long and green. It flowers, its bunch has a wrapping and the flower emerges from it. Its fruit is rounded and it grows from its fruit.
○ This is a thing of the new shoots, it grows on the sea, it is plentiful in the lowland and also in the inland.
- We pick its leaf for wrapping food like nut-pudding and anything else, and we also oven-cook with it, it smells good. We also spread the leaf as a place for food, and the leaf is also for plugging tubes of food.
- We also slice it small to be suitable for rolling (spouts) for bamboos for drinking.
- Its leaf we roof shelters with for sitting in the shade in the garden.
- We also cure with the tender base for wounds.
FOLOTA = GUILLANIA / *Guillainia purpurata* Vieill. (*Zingiberaceae*)

KAKALI ne'e fi'irū , rauna ka keta, takarū ka meo, ka sau ana fingirū ne'e meomeo'a kī. Nia bolo fa'inia folota bore ma nia mamata fa'asia sulia nia ke fungu 'i ano 'ania fingirū ne'e ofiofina fafia magarū gwā kī ni'i 'oro liu. Lisilana magarū ka di'ia logo maga kwalo kakali.

○ Nia ke bulao saena raku faolu kī ma sulia kafo kī, fa'asia fafona asi ka dao 'i tolo.
• Di'ia fingirū nia make ma ka bisibisila na'a, ta ma ki suia fuana 'anilana. Ki efoa ofiofirū, ki to'osia ta'eta'ena ki fi'i 'ania magarū, 'anilana mamasia liu ka asila, noa'a kisi do'ofia.
• Di'ia ki lafua takana ki loto fi'i ma nia asila liu logo.

HORNSTEDTIA is a clump, its leaf is long, the flower is red and emerges from bunches which are reddish. It is similar to guillainia (*folota*) but different from it because it bears bunches at the ground which enclose black seeds which are very plentiful. The seeds look like hornstedtia vine (*kwalo kakali / Passiflora*) seeds.

○ It grows in the new shoots and along waters, from on the sea to the inland.
• If the bunches are ripe and shiny, then we gather them to eat. We remove the sheath and throw away the skin and then eat the seed, it is very tasty and sweet, we don't burn it.
• If we pull up the the flower and suck it, it is also very sweet.

KAKALI = HORNSTEDTIA / *Hornstedtia lycostoma* (Ltb. & Schum.) Schum. (*Zingiberaceae*)

kakali / hornstedtia ▶

KAKARA, ki saea logo 'ania MAFUSU noima MAFUSI, ne'e fi'irū nia di'ia logo folota, rauna reba ka keta di'ia kakali. Nia to'o ana rō malita'irū kī. KAKARA saga, ta sata KAKARA MEO, nonina meomeo'anga ma rauna bore sisilina ra'irū ka meomeo'a logo. KAKARA KWAO nonina kwaokwao'a ma sisilina bore kwaokwao'a logo, fingirū kī bore kwaokwao'a logo.

o   Nia ke bulao saena to'ona'oa ma tolo, ka 'oro saena tolo.

•   Ki silia gwangona fuana laungi'anga 'i ne'e ke moko le'a.

•   Rauna ki saunga'inia 'ania babala 'i māna o'olā ma saena masu'u kī.

KAKARA, also called *MAFUSU* or *MAFUSI*, is a clump like guillainia (*folota*), its leaf is wide and long like hornstedtia (*kakali*). It has two kinds. *KAKARA* proper, another name RED *KAKARA*, its body is reddish and even the spine of its leaf is reddish too. WHITE *KAKARA*, is body is whiteish and even the spine of its leaf is whiteish and its bunches are whiteish too.

o   It grows in the lowland and inland, it is plentiful in the inland.

•   We shred the leaf-shoot for decoration as it smells good.

•   The leaf we make into shelters facing gardens and in the forest.

KAKARA / MAFUSU/ MAFUSI = *KAKARA* / *Alpinia pulchra* (DCRS 235)
KAKARA MEO = RED *KAKARA* / *Alpinia stapfiana* Schum.
KAKARA KWAO = WHITE *KAKARA* / *Catimbium novae-pommeraniae* Schum. (*Zingiberaceae*)

RAKO, ta sata RĀRĀ, ne'e fi'irū, itanga'irū ofiofina keta liu ka fi'ifi'i'nga ka fi'i alua ra'irū doe ma ka keta. Nia to'o ana bara malita'irū kī. RAKO TO'ONA'OA, rako ne'e ki saea 'ania rako saga, rauna marako, ilina ra'irū kī marako logo, sui ka mamarigawaila'a mala.

o   Nia ke bulao saena raku faolu, saena to'ona'oa ka tasa sulia dodo kī, ma nia saena logo tolo.

RAKO TOLO, rauna marako ka ta'i ti'iti'i ana rauna ai saga, ilina ra'irū kī rafurafu'a ka kwao.

o   Nia ke bulao go'o 'i tolo.

KURAKO, fi'irū ne'e nia'a ta rako logo, nonina meomeo'a, rauna te'e reba ka marako ka rafurafu'a.

o   Nia ke bulao go'o saena tolo.

RAKO FASIA, fi'irū noa'a kesi doe liu go'o bore ma 'aba'abarū kī doe go'o 'i ano. Rū salingani lala, di'ia ta kula ne'e rako kī kasi teo bore 'ana ki ngalia ma'i fuana fasilana. Di'ia ki fasia bore 'i fanoa nia kasi doe liu kasi ogamusia la'u ta kula, nia ne'e nia le'a fuana fasilana.

•   Rako kī ta'ifau, rauni ki safa talana 'ania fanga kī, ki gwa'abi logo 'ania, nia totolia sulia nia moko le'a. Ki rao 'ania ka tasa ana tolo gwari, kula ne'e rau kesi 'oro liu ana.

•   Siko kī ke tua ana tegotego rau kī fuana 'anilana.

HELICONIA, another name *RĀRĀ*, is a clump, the sheath of its trunk is very long and its clump produces big long leaves. It has several kinds. LOWLAND HELICONIA, this heliconia we call heliconia proper, its leaf is green, the backs of the leaves are also green, and all really shiny-smooth.

o   It grows in the new shoots, in the lowland and especially along gullies, and it is also in the inland.

INLAND HELICONIA, its leaf is green and the backs of the leaves are powdery white.

o   It just grows in the inland.

KU-HELICONIA, this clump is also a heliconia, its body is reddish, its leaf is quite wide and green with a bloom.

o   It just grows in the inland.

PLANTED HELICONIA, this clump doesn't get very big but the leaves are big at the ground. This is transferred, if there is a place with no heliconia we bring it for planting. Even if we plant it in a home it is not very big and doesn't spread all over the place, that's why it's good for planting.

•   All the heliconias, we spread their leaves to make way for food and also oven-cook with it, it is fit because it smells good. We use it especially in the cool inland, the place where leaf is not very plentiful.

•   Hoppers live in the shrivelled leaf for eating.

RAKO / RĀRĀ = HELICONIA / *Heliconia indica* ssp. *indica* Lamk. / *H. lanata* (P.S. Green) Kress. / *H. solomonensis* Kress.(*Heliconiaceae*)

LĀ nia fi'irū ka leforū'a, nia to'o ana rō malita'irū.

LĀ saga, ki saea logo 'ania LĀ MARAKO, rauna doe ka reba liu mala ka marako, takana fa'inia fingina ni'i kwao, fingina keta 'oro.

○ Nia ke bulao fa'asia fanona asi ka dao 'i tolo, sulia edeedea kī ma gwa'i kafo ti'iti'i kī. Ki salinga'inia logo fuana fasilana saena kula kunukunua kī ma kula gwarigwari kī.

• Rauna ki 'afua 'ania sau'a kī ma ta fanga bore 'ana. Rauna keta ka bolo fa'inia sulia nia lia le'a la'u ma kaida'i fanga du'a 'anilana ka moko le'a.

• Ki gwa'abi logo 'ania rauna bore ma nia kesi le'a liu go'o sulia ti ra'irū ti'iti'i go'o, ki rao 'ania saena tolo gwari, kula nai'ari rauna le'a kesi 'oro liu go'o.

COMINSIA is a clump forming a thicket, it has two kinds.

COMINSIA proper, also called GREEN COMINSIA, its leaf is big and very wide and green, its flower and bunches are white and the bunches are many and long.

○ It grows from on the sea to the inland, along wastelands and small waters. We also transplant it to plant in swampy places and damp places.

• Its leaf we wrap puddings and any other food with. The long leaf is suitable because it looks best and when the food is burned it smells good to eat.

• We also oven-cook with the leaf but it is not very good because some leaves are just small, we use it in the damp inland, the place where good leaf is not very plentiful.

LĀ = COMINSIA / *Cominsia gigantea* (Schellenb.) Schum. (Marantaceae)

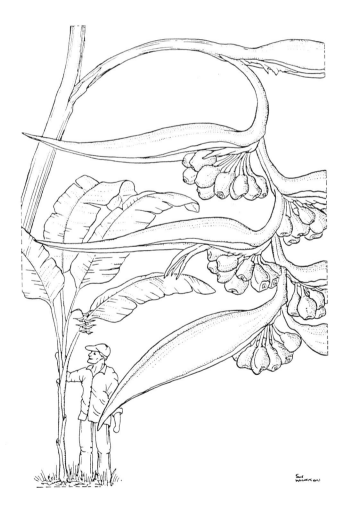

rako / heliconia ▶

LĀ 'IKI'IKI, nia bolo logo lā saga bore ma nia dokodoko go'o 'i ano, rauna ka ti'iti'i logo, ilina rauna meo.
- Nia ke bulao ana kula ne'e 'iki'iki kī ke tua ana, ta ne'e ki fa'asata 'uri ana. Noa'a kisi fasia go'o.

- Lā 'iki'iki ne'e 'aurafu 'i lā go'o, noa'a la'u lā 'inoto'a. Ki butā 'ania fanga kī bore ma lā saga nia le'a ka tasa sulia ra'irū la 'iki'iki marako fīfī.

- Lā kī ta'ifau, siko kī ke tua ana tegotego rau kī fuana 'anilana.
- Rauna ki tolea 'ania babala kī.

BA'U ne'e fanga 'inoto'a kia, boeboena ka ofi fafia itangana, rauna doe ka keta ka reba, nia ke fungu 'ania fingirū. Nia bulao go'o ana galana.
- Rū fasia ne'e, ki fasia 'i nonina fanoa kia ma saena o'olā kia kī.
- Ki 'ania fuana, 'anilana le'a sulia ti ai asila liu mala.
- Ra'i rau kī, ki buta fanga 'ania, ki gwa'abi 'ania, ki safa talana logo fanga kī 'ania, ka tasa logo fuana sau'a kī di'ia lakeno. Nia le'a logo bore ma mokolana ka te'e 'afa'afa'anga. Kaida'i ki buta 'ania ki sisia sisilirū 'i ke mabe ki fi'i la'umia fuana ke kwalakoni fuana ngalilani.

Ki to'o ana ti ba'u 'oro, satani to'oto'o, ti ai rū nama ana fanoa, ti ai kira salaiga'ini'i ma'i 'i 'a'e asi. 'I na'o ki to'o go'o ana ba'u ne'e kī:
BA'U 'U'UNIMANU, fuana 'ere di'ia u'una no'o lofolofo, nia le'a fuana 'anilana.
BA'U MEO, fuana molimoli'a.
BA'U NGWADALA, fa'irū kī keta.
BA'U NGWAFILA, fa'irū kī 'oro liu ka di'ia 'aena ngwafila.
BA'U FOKALINGWANE, fa'irū kī te'e keta ma ka doe.
BA'U LOBO, fa'irū kī doe ka keta.
BA'U LOBOMU'U nia ke doe liu mala, nonina ka gwagwā'a, fa'irū kī ka doe mala bore ma nia to'o ana rō i'irū kī go'o ka sui.
BA'U BABA, fuana ka keta ka 'ere ka marako, 'anilana ka ngwara'u, ki du'atelea ki saungia fuana gwasu ba'u.
BA'U ANOASA, fa'irū kī anoasa'anga.
BA'U 'ASOFE MAE, fa'irū kī ke dokodoko ma kesi doe liu go'o. Di'ia fingirū nia mau'a na'a, ābarū kī mae ta'ifau na'a 'afia fuana, lisilana di'ia na'a ta bara 'asofe ba teo tatala'a ma ka mae ka gwā na'a.
BA'U KWALU NGWENGWELA, fa'irū kī te'e 'ere ka doe. Fadalana satana ki kina.

'IKI'IKI COMINSIA is similar to cominsia proper but it is low on the ground, its leaf is small too and the back of the leaf is red.
- It grows in the places that 'iki'iki (marsh frogs) live, that's why we name it thus. We don't plant it.
- *'Iki'iki* cominsia is a useless cominsia, not an important cominsia. We parcel food in it but cominsia proper is the best because the leaf of *'iki'iki* cominsia is intense green.
- Both cominsias, hoppers live in the shrivelled leaves for eating.
- The leaf we thatch shelters with.

LĀ 'IKI'IKI = *'IKI'IKI* COMINSIA / *Cominsia guppyi* Hemsl. (*Marantaceae*)

BANANA is an important food, its leaf-tube sheaths its trunk, its leaf is big and long and wide, and it bears bunches. It just grows from its suckers.
- This is planted, we plant it in our home areas and in our gardens.
- We eat the fruit, it is good to eat because some are very sweet.
- The leaf we parcel food with, we oven-cook with and spread the way for food with, especially for puddings like cream-pudding. It is quite good but smells a bit bitter. When we parcel with it we split out the leaf-spine to be flexible, and then fold it ready for carrying.

We have many bananas with separate names, some must be from home, some they transferred from overseas. Formerly we only had these bananas:
EAGLE-CLAW BANANA, its fruit is curved like the claw of a bird, it is good to eat.
RED BANANA, its fruit is rounded.
SNAKE BANANA, the fruit is long.
CENTIPEDE BANANA, the fruit are very plentiful like centipede legs.
FOKALINGWANE BANANA, the fruit is quite long and big.
LOBO BANANA, the fruit is big and long.
CUT-OFF-*LOBO* BANANA is very big indeed, its body is blackish and the fruits are really big, but it has only two rows (of fruit), then ends.
BABA BANANA, its fruit is long and curved and green, it is soft to eat, we roast and pound it for banana pudding.
FILTHY BANANA, the fruit is filthy.
DEAD RAT BANANA, the fruit is short and not very big. If the bunch is ripe and the leaves are all dead around the fruit, it looks like several rats lying in rows, dead and black.
EIGHT-IRIS BANANA, its fruit is quite curved and big. We don't know the meaning of its name.

Ti ba'u ne'e kira salinga'inia ma'i 'i 'a'e asi satani 'uri:
BA'U ASILA, nonina gwagwā'a ma kesi keta liu go'o, fa'irū kī ketaketa'a ka kesi doe liu go'o.
BA'U RERESIA, fuana doe ka molimolia ka keta. Ti kaida'i ki du'atelea ki resia.
BA'U TANGA'AI, fa'īrū kī doe ka keta.
BA'U ROBIANA, kira salinga'inia ma'i 'i Roviana. Fa'irū kī kubu ka doe.

BA'U SIKAIANA, kira salinga'inia ma'i ana bubunga 'i Sikaiana, fuana bobea ka ta'i doe.
BA'U LA'ULIMA, fa'irū kī te'e la'umi di'ia la'umi limana ngwae.
BA'U SUSUTATARA, fingirū nia doe, lisilana ka tatara mala.
BA'U LIFAĪ'A, fi'irū kī nonina ka balabala'a, sisilina rauna balabala'a logo, fingirū bore balabala'a logo, ka doe liu mala, fuana di'ia lifa kirio.
BA'U SASAO, fi'irū ka doe liu ka tasa ana ba'u kī ta'ifau, fingirū nia ū 'ala'a, fuana doe ka tasa mala ana fuana ba'u kī.
BA'U FAKA, fuana dokodoko ka asila liu.

SASAO, lisilana nia di'ia logo fi'i ba'u, rauna ka nunura ma ka marako, bore ma fingirū ka ti'iti'i go'o ana fingi ba'u, suluna gwāborabora'a.
○ Rū kwasi ne'e, nia ke bulao saena raku faolo kī ma saena dododoa kī fa'inia logo na gwauna 'ua kī, ne'e ano to'onga'a.
• Fuana sasao nia mamata fa'asia ba'u to'o kī, noa'a kisi 'ania.
• Rauna ka di'ia logo rauna ba'u, ki safa talana fanga kī 'ania, ki gwa'abi logo 'ania ma ki 'afua rū logo 'ania, nia le'a logo fuana 'afu lakeno 'anga, fuana lakeno ka moko le'a ma ka moko rakufa.
• Rauna ki saunga'i babala logo 'ani'i.
• Na boeboena ki sabangia logo 'ania kafo fuana siu'a ma kwa'unga, bore ma sulia go'o kaida'i dokodoko.
• Sūla fuana atongi rū 'anga di'ia dako kī ma la'ua fuana sofonga'ilana na'ofana kini kaida'i 'i na'o ma fa'i singisingi kī, rū fuana laungi'anga ana maoma kī. Ti ngwae bili ke atongia māna, kwatea ngwae kī noa'a kesi lia sai ada.

Some bananas which we transferred here from overseas are named:
SWEET BANANA, its body is blackish and not very tall, its fruit is longish and not very big.
SCRAPING BANANA, its fruit is big and rounded and long. Sometimes we roast it and scrape it.
FORKED BANANA, the fruit is big and long.
ROVIANA BANANA, we transferred it here from Roviana (Western Solomons). The fruit is stout and big.
SIKAIANA BANANA, we transferred it from the island of Sikaiana, its fruit is swollen and quite big.
BENT-ARM BANANA, the fruit is a bit bent like the bend of a man's arm.
HANGING-BREAST BANANA, the bunch is big with a hanging look.
FISH-TOOTH BANANA, the body of the clump is paleish, the spine of the leaf is also paleish and even the bunch is paleish, it is very big and the fruit is like a porpoise tooth.
SASAO BANANA, the clump is very much bigger than all bananas, the bunch stands up, its fruit is much bigger than all banana fruits.
FOREIGN BANANA, its fruit is short and very sweet.
BA'U = BANANA / *Musa* sp. (*Musaceae*)

SASAO looks like banana (*ba'u*), its leaf is shiny and green, but its bunches are smaller than banana bunches, its sap is purple-black.
○ This is wild, it grows in the new shoots and in gullies and also at the tops of hills, on proper ground.
• *Sasao* fruit is different from banana proper, we don't eat it.
• Its leaf is like banana leaf, we spread the way for food with it, we oven-cook with it and we wrap things in it, it is quite good for wrapping cream-pudding for the pudding to smell good and appetising.
• Its leaf we also make shelters with.
• Its leaf-tube we also duct water with for bathing and drinking, but only for short periods.
• Its sap is for staining things like bowls and (bark)cloth for concealing women's fronts in former times and (arm) rings, things for decoration at festivals. Some thieves stain their faces so that people won't recognise them.
SASAO = *SASAO* / wild banana / *Musa* sp. (*Musaceae*)

Fi'irū ne'e kasirū'a kī

KA'O nia'a 'au 'inoto'a, ki saea 'ania ka'o saga. Saena 'abafola ne'e nia ke ū fuana ti malita'i ka'o ne'e kira bolo logo. Ka'o ne'e fi'irū'a ka kasirū'a, lalana ke keta liu, kasina keta logo, ti kasirū doe mala, ti kasirū ti'iti'i go'o, nonina ka marako, rauna keta ka sisilia, nia ke leforū'a.

○ Nia ke bulao ka 'oro saena to'ona'oa ma saena logo tolo. Di'ia nia noa'a ana ta kula, ti kaida'i ki salinga'inia 'i nia ke bulao karangia fanoa kia, ki fasia go'o gwagirū noima fū'irū.
• Ka'o nia 'inoto'a fuana tualaka, ki saunga'i 'ania rū 'oro kī.
• Lalarū doe kī fuana saunga'i luma'a. Ki 'odo luma 'ania, ki 'ato logo 'ania.
• Lalarū doe kī ki sakalia logo 'ania o'olā ma fanoa kia kī.
• Ki botakwalekwalea logo lalarū fuana saunga'i-lana 'au kara, rū ne'e fuana 'odo'a ma tatafe-'anga, nia totolia sulia fa'i 'au ke doe, kasina keta, gwagina noa'a kesi doe liu go'o, rebana noa'a kesi baba'ula go'o.
• Lalarū ki gasia logo 'ania 'aba 'au, di'ia raforafo fuana usa sao'anga ma 'au kara fuana bakasilana 'odoa.
• 'Aba 'au fuana logo saunga'i lana sakai 'au kaurefe fuana du'urū'anga.
• Kasirū ki saunga'i logo 'ania ka'o ma ladelade ma 'aurua fuana kwa'unga ma ta'ufilana rū kī.

• Na lalarū ki saunga'inia logo 'ania 'abasasaba kī.
• Lala 'au du'a ki unu logo 'ani'i ana rodo.
• Ki sisia nini 'au ana fa'i ka'o fuana tarilana 'uligwata.
• Kasirū doe, ki dodongia fanga kī 'i saena fuana du'afilana, ki gu'utā 'ania ra'i rau, ki fi'i du'afia bi'irū saena mafula. Ki dodoa logo sa'e ngali ma manumanu'a kī 'i saena fuana fa'asasufilana saena bara.
• Kasirū kī logo fuana gonilana rū 'oro kī di'ia rū fuana noni laungi'a kī ma fena ma rū ābu kī, ki fonotā logo 'ania ana ma'e ka'o. Di'ia fa'i fena, ti kaida'i ki rokoa logo fuana laungilana 'i ke lia kwanga.

• Kasirū kī ki saunga'inia 'ania tala'au fuana ūfilana fuana ngwa'enga. Ki saunga'inia logo 'ania fa'i kudi fuana kini sari'i ke kwa'i kudi 'ania 'i ke inua 'alako kī.

Clumps which are sectioned

BAMBOO is the important bamboo, we call it bamboo proper. In this book it stands for other kinds of bamboos which are similar. Bamboo is a clump, it has sections (internodes), its poles are very long and its sections are also long, some sections are big (in diameter), some sections are small, its body is green, its leaf is long and narrow, and it forms thickets.

○ It grows plentifully in the lowland and also in the inland. If there is none in a place, sometimes we transfer it to grow near to our homes, we just plant the node or the base.
• Bamboo is important for our living, we make many things with it.
• The big poles are for house-building. We wall houses with it and we also rafter with it.
• The big poles we also fence our gardens and homes with.
• We also smash the poles flat to make scored bamboo (board), something for walling and platforming, it is fitted because the bamboos are big, its sections are long, its nodes are not very big and its flats are not thick.
• The poles we also tear into bamboo strips, like battens for stitching sago (leaf) on and scored bamboo for clamping walling.
• Bamboo strip is also for making bamboo tongs for burning (cooking) things.
• The sections we also make into (water) bamboos and knocked-through-lengths and double-bamboos for drinking and washing.
• The poles we also make into (water) ducts.
• The dry poles we also use for flares at night.
• We split bamboo knives from bamboo for slicing pig-flesh.
• The big sections we flask food in for burning, we plug it with leaf and then burn the tube-full on the fire. We also flask inner nuts (kernels) and blanched-nuts in it for smoking on the rack.
• The sections are also for storing many things, like things for body decoration and lime (for betel) and tabu things, and we also stop it up with a piece of bamboo. If a lime-flask, sometimes we also engrave it for decoration to look pretty.
• The sections we also make bamboo-rows (panpipes) from for blowing for dances. We also make whistles for maidens to whistle with to attract youths.

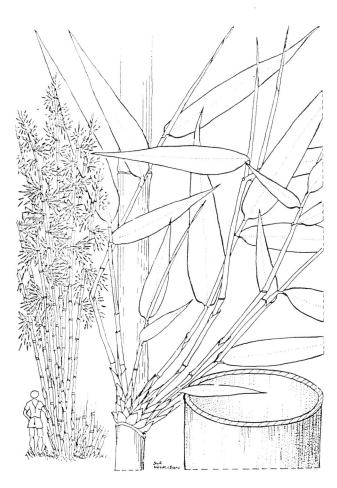

ka'o / bamboo ▶

- Lalarū keta kī, ki saunga'i logo 'ania rū di'ia 'au ni dē'a ma kauala fuana loilana fa'irū kī di'ia fa'i ngali ana 'ai keta kī.
- Lalarū ti'iti'i kī ki saunga'inia 'ania rū di'ia fa'i 'au gwaroa fuana laungilana alingana ngwae.

KA'O ASI nia to'o ana rō malita'irū kī. Ai saga ne'e fi'irū, nia di'ia logo ka'o saga te'e nonina kasirū ne'e sakosako'a ma ka ti'iti'i ana ka'o saga. Ruana ka'o asi nia ti'iti'i ana ai saga, doelalana ka fi'ifi'i'inga.
- Rū fasia ne'e, noa'a nia kesi 'oro di'ia ka'o saga. Ruana ka'o asi nia ke bulao 'i fafona asi.
- Ki fasia fuana laungilana fanoa kī.
- Ki saunga'i luma 'ania bore ma noa'a kesi bolo fa'inia 'au kara sulia nia ti'iti'i go'o ma nia ke fenala'a.

- The long poles we also make into things like fishing bamboos (rods) and hooks for picking fruit like nuts from tall trees.
- The small poles we make into things like patterned bamboos for decorating a person's ears.

KA'O = BAMBOO / *Nastus obtusus* Holtt. (*Poaceae*)

SEA BAMBOO has two kinds. The proper one is a clump, it is like bamboo proper only the body of the section is yellow and smaller than bamboo proper. The second sea bamboo is smaller than the proper one and it forms a big clump.
- This is planted, it is not plentiful like bamboo proper. The second sea bamboo grows on the sea.
- We plant it for decorating homes.
- We build houses with it but it is not suitable for scored bamboo (board) because it is only small and it gets mouldy.

KA'O ASI = SEA BAMBOO

KEKETO, ka'o ne'e ke fi'iru'a, lalana ti'iti'i ana ka'o saga, na ofeoferū nia ana kasirū kī, nonina momote, takana kwao ma ka alua fa'irū kī. Nia ke leforū'a ka susu mala, ka nu'inu'irū'a ana lalana ma ūluna. Nia ke bulao ana fa'irū ma 'itanga'irū kī logo.

○ Nia ke bulao ana kula kī ta'ifau, ana kula dukwasia ma raku kī, nia 'oro saena to'ona'oa.
• Na lalana ki sakalia 'ania gwata kī ma karai kī.
• Ki sabangi logo 'ania falisi fuana kai ma fana ke ango sulia.

• Lalarū saga kī ki usa sao logo ani, ki alua logo fuana tatafe'anga.
• Ti kaida'i ki tufua logo fuana raforafo fuana bakasilana 'odoa 'i sao ma itolana kokoba. Lalana nia ngasi ana 'aba ka'o ma noa'a kesi gasia si ne'e fa'i keketo nia ti'iti'i go'o, noa'a nia kesi bolo fa'inia 'abarū fuana saunga'inga.
• Ki gasia fa'irū kī 'ania rebarū kī, ki saunga'i 'ania korefe fuana du'urū'anga.
• Ki saunga'inia logo sauka'e ana rebarū kī.
• Lalarū nia le'a logo fuana ki bilinga ma'e oea kī ana fuana aranga fuana fana ī'anga. Ki tadilia logo lalana fuana labulabu'a, rū fuana masa'anga go'o.
• Ngela ti'iti'i kī ke furia fa'i keketo fuana fa'abusula'inia di'ia fa'i kwanga kī. Ki 'inia ra'irū kī, ki bulasi'i ka ngiringiri, ki ru'unga'inia saena ta bali ana fa'i keketo, ka sui ki ru'unga'inia ta ma'e keto ti'iti'i saena fā'i keketo doe fuiri, mala ki fi'i ladea 'i ne'e ke busula'inia. Ti kaida'i ki ngalia logo fingi dili kī ma fingi kwalekwale kī, fuana fa'abusula'inia.
• Ki saunga'i 'ania fa'i rade fuana laungilana alinga. Ki ko'ā ka sui, ki gwaroa kasirū 'ania na adi fa'inia na takataka niu ma na luluka.

'AU FĪRŪ, ka'o ne'e fi'irū, nonina marako, doelana nia di'ia logo fi'i ka'o bore ma kasirū kī dokodoko liu, rauna ti'iti'i liu ka sisimia ana rauna ka'o. Di'ia nia ke bulao ana ta kula, nia ke susu fāfia kula fuiri ke susuto'o go'o fāfia, ka kwate ru'unga'a saena ka 'afita'i liu. Di'ia ki ke leka ru'u gwata kwasi 'ania kui kī na gwata ke tafi ka ago na'a saena 'au fīrū, 'unari ki fata na'a 'uri, na gwata kwasi ne'e kī kira ato liu na'a saena fi'i 'au fīrū ne'e kī.
○ Nia ke bulao fafona kunukunua kī ma ta kula bore 'ana, saena to'ona'oa ma saena tolo.
• Noa'a kisi sasia go'o ta rū 'ania, te'e ti kaida'i ki sakali 'ania fuana rokisilana go'o na ka'o saga.

SCHIZOSTACHYUM, this bamboo becomes a clump, its pole is smaller than bamboo proper, there is a sheath on the section, its body is scratchy, its flower is white and it produces fruit. It becomes a covering thicket, a tangle of poles and fronds. It grows from the fruit and the trunk too.
○ It grows in all places, in wilderness places and shoots, it is plentiful in the lowland.
• The poles we fence pigs and chickens with.
• We also conduct yam-gardens with it for yam and pana-yam (*kai, fana / Dioscorea*) to creep along.
• The straight poles we also stitch sago (leaf) on (for thatch) and also lay it for platforming.
• Sometimes we chop it for battens for clamping sago walling and tying the ridge-crest. Its poles are stronger than bamboo strip but we don't tear it (into strips) as schizostachyum is just small and not suitable for strips for building.
• We tear lengths into flats and make tongs from it for burning.
• We also make (coconut) scrapers from the flats.
• The poles are also good to tip with wire for leister-spears for shooting at fish. We also trim the poles for spears, just for playthings.

• Small children saw off schizostachyum to make it explode like guns. We pick leaves, roll them tight and insert them in one end of the schizostachyum, then we insert a small piece of schizostachyum into the big schizostachyum, and then we stab it so it explodes. Sometimes we also take cordyline (*dili*) or *kwalekwale* (*Flagellara*) fruits to make it explode.
• We make reeds from it for decorating the ears. We scrape it then pattern a section with orchid (*adi*), coconut cuticle and gleichenia (*luluka*).

KEKETO = SCHIZOSTACHYUM / native bamboo / aboriginal bamboo / *Schizostachyum stenocladum* A. Camus / *S. tessellatum* A. Camus (*Poaceae*)

TANGLE BAMBOO, this bamboo is a clump, its body is green, its size is like a bamboo clump but the sections are very short, its leaf is very small and narrower than bamboo leaf. If it grows in a place it completely covers it over, it makes entering it very difficult. If we go after wild pigs with dogs the pig will flee and hide in tangle bamboo so, we say, wild pigs are very hard to get in these clumps of tangle bamboo.
○ It grows on swamps and anywhere else, in the lowland and in the inland.
• We don't do anything with it, only sometimes we fence with it instead of bamboo proper.

'AU FĪRŪ = TANGLE BAMBOO / *Nastus* aff. *productus* / *Racembambos holttumii* Dransf. (*Poaceae*)

DODOLA ne'e fi'irū, nia ta ka'o logo, ka mamata fa'asia ka'o saga sulia kasina dokodoko go'o, gwagina ka doe. Nia to'o ana rō malita'irū kī. DODOLA saga, lalana ke doe ka keta, rauna bolo go'o ana di'ia ka'o saga. Nonina ka talasia ka marako ma ka sakosako'a, ta ne'e ki saea 'ania dodola. KAKO, ki saea logo 'ania DODOLA MARAKO, kasina dokodoko go'o ka marako.

- ○ Ro dodola kī ta'ifau ke bulao go'o 'ada ana kula kī sui fa'asia fafona asi ka dao 'i tolo.
- Rō dodola kī, ki fasia logo gwagirū noema fū'irū 'i ne'e nia ke bulao karangia fanoa kia kī fuana saunga'ilana 'ania rū kī, di'ia logo ka'o.
- Kasina dodola nia ngasi mala. Ki saunga'i luma 'ania, ki botakwalekwalea fuana tatafe'anga, ki gasia logo 'ania reba 'au fuana raforafo ma bakasilana 'odoa, ki sabangia logo 'ania kafo. Saunga'irū'anga 'ania nia bolo logo fa'inia ka'o saga bore ma ka'o nia le'a liu ka liufia dodola, si ne'e dodola, kasina dokodoko, gwagina ka doe, na rebana ka baba'ula, ma suma ke 'ania.
- Ki ulungā ki fo'otā logo 'ania fa'i ngali kī ma fa'i sao kī fuana ra'efilani, nia le'a sulia nia sasala ka ngasi.
- Ki furia fa'irū fuana fa'i fena roko'i kī.
- Dodola noa'a kesi bolo fa'inia ufi ka'onga sulia saena kasirū ni'i furafura.

MIXTURE is a clump, it is also a bamboo and different from bamboo proper because its sections are short and its nodes are big. It has two kinds. MIXTURE proper, its poles are big and long, its leaf is the same as bamboo proper. Its body is striped green and yellow, that's why we call it mixture. *KAKO*, also called GREEN MIXTURE, its section is short and green.

- ○ Both mixtures just grow in all places from on the sea to the inland.
- Both mixtures we plant the node or the base to grow near our homes for making things, like bamboo.
- Mixture section is really strong. We build houses with it, we smash it flat for platforming, we also tear it into bamboo flats for battens and clamping walling, and also duct water with it. Working with it is equivalent to bamboo proper but bamboo is much better than mixture as with mixture the section is short, the node is big, the flats are thick, and worms eat it.
- We stand it up and lash it to nut trees and sago trees for climbing, it is good because it is light and strong.
- We saw pieces for engraved lime-bottles.
- Mixture is not suitable for bamboo containers because inside the sections are rotten.

DODOLA = MIXTURE / *Bambusa* aff. *blumeana* Schultes. KAKO / DODOLA MARAKO = *KAKO* / GREEN MIXTURE / common bamboo /feathery bamboo / *Bambusa vulgaris* Schrad. ex Wendl. (*Poaceae*)

ONGI, ta ka'o ti'iti'i ne'e fi'irū 'ania fi'ifi'inga 'i ano. Nia ke bulao ana fa'ina ma 'itangana.

- ○ Nia ke bulao go'o 'ana saena masu'u, fa'asia fafona asi ka dao 'i tolo.
- Lalana ki efoa fuana saunga'ilana sisimā, ki diua nia ke mangisi ka reba fuana ki kwa'ia 'ania sisimā fa'inia 'aba kwasakwasa kī.

ONGI is a small bamboo which clumps in clusters on the ground. It grows from its fruit and its trunk.

- ○ It just grows in wilderness, from on the sea to the inland.
- Its poles we select for making narrow-eye (walling), we hammer it to break it flat for making narrow-eye with *kwasakawasa* (*Flagellaria*) strips.

ONGI = *ONGI*

RADE ne'e fi'irū ka kasirū'a, nonina fa'irū kī kwao-kwao'a ma rauna ka sisili'a ka keta ka momote, takana kwao. Nia ke bulao ana 'a'erū, ke leforū'a.

- ○ Nia bulao saena raku faolu kī ana kula ki sui, ka 'oro saena to'onaoa, te'e saena kunu ne'e noa'a. Ki fasia logo fuana saunga'irū'anga.
- Fa'irū kī ki usa sao ani, nini'ari go'o na'iri'a.
- Ti kaida'i ki alua fuana tatafe'anga.
- Fa'irū ki saunga'i logo 'ania 'ingatana ma'e sima kī ma ma'e 'aranga kī fuana fana ī'anga ma no'onga, bore ma ki bilinga ma'e bōfau 'i māna.

REED is a clump with sections, its stem body is whiteish and its leaf is narrow, long and scratchy, its flower is white. It grows from the base as a thicket.

- ○ It grows in the new shoots in all places, it is plentiful in the lowland, only not in swamp. We also plant it for making things.
- The stems we stitch sago (leaf) on, at present.
- Sometimes we lay it for platforming.
- The stems we also make into shafts of arrows and leister-spears for shooting fish and birds, but we tip it with set-solid(palm)(*bōfau* / *Arecaceae*) at the end.

RADE = REED / *Miscanthus floribulus* Warb. / *Phragmites karka* (Retz.) Trin. ex Steud. (*Poaceae*)

SILA, fi'irū ne'e lisilana karangia ka di'ia logo fi'i rade bore ma nia ti'iti'i go'o ana, rauna ka keta-keta'a ka di'ia logo rauna rade, nia ke fungu 'ania magarū kī.
- ○ Nia ke bulao fulina fuli raku kī ma sulia kafo kī, ana kula oneone'a kī, fa'asia fafona asi ka dao 'i tolo.
- • Ki ngalia magana ki usafia 'ania kwala kekefa fuana laungi'anga kī.

UFU nia fi'irū'a ka kasirū'a, ka 'oro liu mala, kasirū kī ke doe mala, rauna ka sisilia ka keta. Nia to'o ana malita'irū 'oro kī.
UFU BULU, nonina 'a'erū kī bulubulu'anga.
UFU TABA'A, nonina kwao ma rauna ka sisili'a go'o ma ka marako.
UFU 'AI, nonina melamela'a, rauna ka te'e reba. 'Alilana nia ngasi liu ka di'ia 'ifi 'ai.
UFU MALASISI, nonina ta'i melamela'a maramarako'a, rauna ka sisili'a ka marako.
UFU SURAO, nonina tatalaasi'a 'ania noni'irū to'oto'o 'uri kī, marako, meomeo'a, boraboara'a ma ka sakosako'a.
Ki to'o la'u ana malita'i ufu 'oro ne'e noa'a kisi fa'asata'i ta'ifau.
- ○ Ufu 'oro nini ki fasi'i kī, rū faka kī ta'ifau go'o, ki salinga'ini'i ma'i 'i 'a'e asi. Ki fasia sulia na biru kī saena o'olā ma 'i nonina fanoa ma gwa'i alialia kī.
- • Ki 'oia ma ki totofia kasirū kī, totofilana asila liu ka gwarigwaria liu ma ka mamasia la'u go'o.

LOSI ne'e fi'irū, nia di'ia logo ufu bore ma 'a'erū kī ti'iti'i go'o ka keta ka ona, rauna di'ia logo ufu bore ma nia raurau'a lala ka keta. Nia ka taka 'ania gwa'irū kī.
- ○ Ki fasia saena o'olā kī.
- • Tatabu nini'a, ki 'ania gwa'irū kī kaida'i nia kasi takara'a 'ua, ki 'oia ki du'afia noema ki efoa ofiofina ki fi'i dodoa, ki sasi logo 'ania lulunga kī ma sufusufu kī. 'Anilana ta'i ngwatakataka ka le'a ka tasa.
- • 'A'erū noa'a kisi totofia di'ia ufu sulia nia ngasi go'o.

COIX, this clump looks almost like reed clump (*rade* / *Poaceae*) but it is smaller, its leaf is longish like reed leaf and it bears seeds.
- ○ It grows in the sites of shoots and along waters, in sandy places, from on the sea to the inland.
- • We take the seeds and thread them on strings of beads for decoration.
SILA = COIX / job's tears / *Coix lachryma-jobi* L. (*Poaceae*)

SUGAR is a clump with sections which are very plentiful, its sections are really big, its leaf is narrow and long. It has many kinds.
DARK SUGAR, the body of the stock is dark.
GIGANTIC SUGAR, its body is white and its leaf is long and narrow.
TREE SUGAR, its body is brownish and its leaf is quite wide. It is very hard to bite, like a tree-stick.
STRIPY-SUGAR, its body is a bit brownish and greenish, its leaf is narrow and green.
SURAO SUGAR, its body is of many separate colours; green, reddish, purplish and yellow.

We also have many kinds of sugar which we don't all name.
- ○ We plant all these sugars, they are all foreign, we transferred them from overseas. We plant them along the borders in gardens and in home areas and boundaries.
- • We snap and suck the sections, it is very sweet to suck and very cooling and tasty too.
UFU = SUGAR / sugarcane / *Saccharum*

PITPIT is a clump, it is like sugar (*ufu*) but its stock is small and tall and tough, its leaf is like sugar but it is slender and long. It flowers at the crowns.
- ○ We plant it in gardens.
- • This is a vegetable, we eat the crowns when not yet flowering, we snap them off and burn them or we remove the sheath and flask it, and we also make it into parcels and stews. To eat, it is a bit granular and especially good.
- • The stock we don't suck it like sugar because it is hard.
LOSI = PITPIT / fiji asparagus / *Saccharum edule* Hassk. (*Poaceae*)

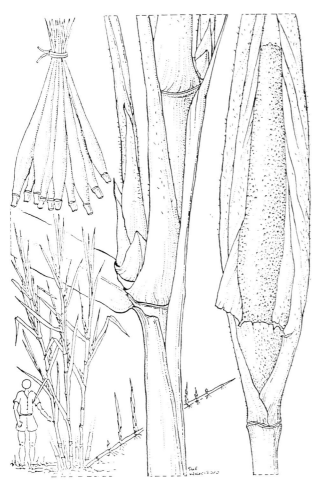

▲ *losi / pitpit*

▲ *kalitau / winds-far*

KALITAU ne'e kasirū'a, fa'ina doe ka keta liu mala. Kaida'i nia fi'i doe lisilana di'ia fi'irū kī, satana ki saea 'ania FELOFELO, bore ma nia ke teo ke doe ka alua na'a fa'i kalitau, go'o nia ka ra'e kalia na'a 'ai kī.

- ○ Nia ke bulao 'i fafona asi ma nia 'oro saena to'ona'oa ma saena logo tolo.
- • Kalitau ne'e rū 'inoto'a fuana ito'a 'ania ana luma. Ki sikilia mala 'ania bara afurū'a ki fi'i sisia 'ania 'abarū ne'e ngasi le'a ma ka mabe le'a fuana ito'a, fuana logo usalana sao. Te'e felofelo ne'e noa'a kesi bolo fa'inia itolana luma si ne'e noa'a 'iri ngasi ma nia ka mafusifusi.
- • 'Aba kalitau ki saunga'inia logo 'ania rū di'ia fo'osae ma obi kī.
- • Kalitau ki saunga'i logo 'ania fuana atola fuana dēlana saena kafo kī.
- • Rauna felofelo ki buta ī'a 'ania ka di'ia logo ra'irū kī. Ti kaida'i ki to'osia 'ania babala.
- • Ki kwa'i onga 'ania ma'erū kī, ki fo'ota fikua ulu ma'erū'anga, go'o ki tonga'inia saena onga, go'o ki labua ana nonika.

WINDS-FAR is sectioned, its stem is big and very long. When it is part-grown it looks like a clump and the name we call it by is *FELOFELO*, but if it gets big it produces winds-far, then it climbs winding round trees.

- ○ It grows on the sea and it is plentiful in the lowland and also in the inland.
- • Winds-far is an important thing for tying houses with. We cut it into several pieces and then split it into strips which are good, strong and flexible for tying, and also for stitching sago (leaf). Only *felofelo* is not suitable for tying houses because it is not strong and it snaps.
- • Winds-far strip we also make into things like (men's) girdles and (plaited) rings.
- • Winds-far we also make into traps for fishing in the waters.
- • *Felofelo* leaf we wrap with, like other leaf. Sometimes we roof shelters with it.
- • We do tatooing with the thorns, we lash together three thorns, then we smear it with ink and stab it on our bodies.

KALITAU = WINDS-FAR/ rattan / lawyer-cane / *Calamus* aff. hollrungii Becc. (*Arecaceae*)

OBI ne'e ta kalitau logo bore ma fa'ina doe liu ana kalitau saga.

o Nia ke bulao go'o saena tofungana tolo saena go'o dukwasi, nia kesi 'oro liu go'o.

• Ta'eta'ena ki aea fuana saunga'ilana 'ania obi ma fo'osae fuana laungilana nonina ngwae.

• Ti kaida'i ki ito 'ania ana luma bore ma noa'a kesi tatakola'a.

KALITAU ALO, lisilana di'ia logo kalitau saga bore ma nia marako fifī ma nia ka dada mala.

o Nia ke bulao saena dukwasi ma saena kula kunukunua kī ka tasa 'i gwauna gwa'i kafo kī kula dukwasi'anga kī.

• Noa'a kisi ito 'ania ana luma si ne'e noa'a nia 'iri ngasi, di'ia ki sisia 'abarū kī ke mafusifusi, ki saea 'ania nia di'ia logo afuna alo.

ASIASI, rū ne'e karangi ka di'ia logo kalitau bore ma nonina dada mala ma ka ti'iti'i go'o bore ma boeboena ngarangara'a liu, nia ka leforū'a ka 'ato fuana ngwae ke ru'u 'i saena.

o Nia ke bulao 'i fafona asi ma saena logo to'ona'oa.

• Ka matamata fa'asia kalitau, noa'a kisi usa sao go'o 'ani sulia sisilana ta'a, nia ke lae tabasi.

• Ki gurā 'ania ti mata'inga.

KWAKWAKO nia fi'iru'a, nonina marako ka kasirū'a, nia ke atobirabira 'ania rararū 'oro kī. Rauna te'e reba ka molimolia go'o ka marako, di'ia rauna du'a na'a ta ma nia meo kwala-kwala'a.

o Nia ke bulao saena raku faolu, 'i fafona kafo kī ma fafona dodo kī ma saena tolo ma to'ona'oa logo. Nia ke bulao kesi 'oro liu go'o.

• Noa'a kisi saunga'i 'ania, noa'a kisi du'a 'ania, sulia saena kwakwa go'o, ka 'iri ona noima ka ngasi.

• Sali ki gurā 'ania ti mata'inga.

BAND is also a winds-far but its stem is much bigger than winds-far proper.

o It just grows in the central inland, just in wilderness, and it is not very plentiful.

• We peel its skin for making (plaited) bands and girdles for decorating a person's body.

• Sometimes we tie houses with it but it is not abundant.

OBI = BAND / rattan / *Calamus stipitatus* Burret (*Areceae*)

TARO WINDS-FAR looks like winds-far proper but it is intense green and really smooth.

o It grows in wilderness and in swampy places, especially at the heads of waters in wilderness places.

• We don't tie houses with it as it is not strong, if we split it the strips snap, we say that it's like a taro tuber.

KALITAU ALO = TARO WINDS-FAR

ASIASI is a thing almost like winds-far but its body is smooth and small, but its leaf-tube is very prickly and its thickets are difficult for a person to enter inside.

o It grows on the sea and also in the lowland.

• It is different from winds-far, we don't stitch sago (leaf) with it because it splits badly and off-course.

• We cure some sickness with it.

ASIASI = *ASIASI*

KAVA is a clump, its body is green and has sections, it sprouts with many branches. Its leaf is quite wide and rounded and green, and if the leaf is dry then it is light red

o It grows in the new shoots, on the sea and in gullies and in the inland and lowland too. It doesn't grow very plentifully.

• We don't build with it, we don't burn with it, because its inside is hollow, it is not tough or strong.

• Maybe we cure some sickness with it.

KWAKWAKO = KAVA / *Piper wichmannii C.DC.* (*Piperaceae*)

8
Fi'irū ne'e di'ia takuma kī

8
Clumps like fern

TAKUMA, ki saea logo 'ania SAKUMA, saena 'abafola ne'e nia ke ū fuana ti malita'irū ne'e kira bolo logo. Takuma ne'e fi'irū'a, 'ifitana ka doko-doko ka gwā, rauna ka keta ka kwa'i, ma gwa'irū ka 'ere'ererū'a. Nia ke bulao ke leforū'a ka susu fāfia kula. Rū di'ia fi'i takuma kī, noa'a ni'i kesi taka, noa'a ni'i kesi fungu go'o ani ti fa'irū, ni'i ke bulao ana rararū kī.

o   Nia ke bulao 'i ninimana kafo kī, ka tasa logo saena kunukunu'a kī, saena to'ona'oa ma saena logo tolo ana kula gwari kī ma kula kī ta'ifau go'o. Noa'a nia kesi 'oro liu go'o.

•   Tatabu kwasi nini'a, ki 'ania gwa'irū.

FERN, in this book it stands for some kinds of things which are similar. Fern is a clump, its bole is short and black, its leaf is long and bends over and its crown is a coil. It grows in a thicket and covers a place. Things like fern do not flower, they do not bear fruit, they grow from the branches.

o   It grows beside waters, especially in swamps, in the lowland and also in the inland in damp places and all places. It is not very plentiful.

•   This is a wild vegetable, we eat the crown.
TAKUMA / SAKUMA = FERN / *Diplazium proliferum* (Lamk.) Kaulf. (*Athyriaceae*)

takuma / fern ▶

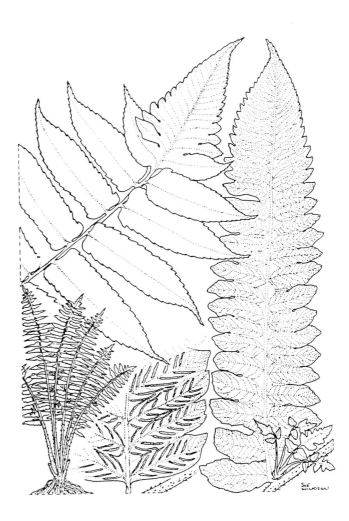

'UNU'UNU nia ta takuma logo, nia doe ana takuma saga, nia fi'irū'a, 'ifita'irū doe ka gwā, rauna fisifisi'a, gwa'ina marako ka 'ere'ere'a ka doe. Nia to'o ana rō malita'irū kī.
'UNU'UNU TO'OFU ne'e 'unu'unu 'inoto'a.

'UNU'UNU TABA'A nia doe ana 'un'unu saga, nonina ka te'e bala ki saea 'ania ne'e nia kwao.

○ Nia ke bulao 'i ninimana kafo kī ma sulia dodo kī ma kula gwari kī go'o ma saena to'ona'oa ma saena tolo. Nia ke bulao to'oto'o, ka le'a liu ana ti kula, noa'a nia kesi 'oro liu di'ia takuma.
• Tatabu kwasi logo nini'a, gwa'ina 'ere'ere'a nia le'a ka tasa fuana 'anilana, bore ma 'unu'unu taba'a 'anilana ka te'e 'afae.
• Ngela ti'ti'i kī ke masa logo 'ania gwa'irū kī fuana fa'ama'ulada ma fuana logo fa'aga'anga.

TATARAKWASI nia di'ia logo 'unu'unu bore ma rauna marako, nia fi'irū'a, ka'ika'ina ka keta mala ma ra'irū marako ka sisimia ma ka matanga'a.
○ Nia ke bulao go'o saena tolo, noa'a nia kesi 'oro liu go'o.
• Gwangona nia le'a ka tasa fuana laungilana ngwa'i kī. Ki sikilia ra'irū kī, ki fa'asinafi'i, ki sili'i mala, ki fi'i laungia 'ania ngwa'i kī.
• Ki labunga'inia logo fuana saunga'ilana 'ania bā gwata.

MĀBILI, ki saea logo 'ania MĀMĀBILI, takuma nini'a, bore ma rū ne'e kwate ka mamata ne'e nonina kwaokwao'a nia ka doe mala, rauna reba lala ma gwa'irū kī ka doe mala ma ka ifuifu'a ma ka bili'a.
○ Nia ke bulao saena dodo kī
• Ki 'ania gwa'irū kī, bore ma di'ia ne'e rauna beta na'a ma noa'a kisi 'ania na'a. 'Anilana nia 'iri 'afae bore ma 'anilana gwari lala.

'ORO KWADI, ta sata DIDILAKOME, ne'e ta takuma, nia fi'irū'a, nonina marako, nia 'aba'aba'a di'ia gwa'u. 'Ere'ererū ana gwa'irū nia didila ka molimoli'a di'ia fa'i kome, ta ne'e ki fa'asata 'uri ana.
○ Nia ke bulao saena tolo kī ma dodo kī.
• Tatabu kwasi nini'a, ki 'ania gwa'irū kī.

DENNSTAEDTIA is also a fern, it is bigger than fern proper, it is a clump and its bole is big and black, its leaf is thin, its crown is green, coiled and big. It has two kinds.
TO'OFU DENNSTAEDTIA is the important dennstaedtia.
GIGANTIC DENNSTAEDTIA is bigger than dennstaedtia proper, its body is quite pale, we call it white.

○ It grows besides waters and along gullies and damp places in the lowland and in the inland. It grows individually, it is good in some places and not very plentiful, like fern.
• This is also a wild vegetable, its coiled crowns are especially good to eat, but gigantic dennstaedtia is rather bitter to eat.
• Small children play with the crowns to frighten others and also to make them laugh.
'UNU'UNU = DENNSTAEDTIA / *Dennstaedtia samoensis* (Brack.) Moore (*Dennstaedtiaceae*)

PLEOCNEMIA is like dennstaedtia (*'unu'unu*) but its leaf is green, it is a clump, its stalk is long and its green leaf is tiny and divided.
○ It just grows in the inland, it is not very plentiful.
• Its leaf-shoot is especially good for decorating bags. We cut off the leaves, we sun them and shred them and then decorate bags with them.
• We also stake it for making pig barriers.
TATARAKWASI = PLEOCNEMIA / *Pleocnemia aff. tripinnata* Holtt. (*Aspidiaceae*)

DIRTY-EYE, this is a fern but what makes it different is that its body is whiteish and really big, its leaf is wide and its crown is really big and hairy and dirty.

○ It grows in gullies.
• We eat the crowns, but if its leaf is withered we don't eat it. To eat, it is not bitter but is cold to eat.
MĀBILI = DIRTY-EYE / *Diplazium stipitipinnula* Holtt. (*Athyriaceae*)

'ORO KWADI, also named SLIPPERY-RING, is a fern, it is a clump, its body is green and it has a stem like head (*Cyclosorus / gwau*). The coil at its crown is slippery and rounded like a (shell) ring, that's why we name it thus.
○ It grows in the inland and in gullies.
• This is a wild vegetable, we eat the crowns.
'ORO KWADI / DIDILAKOME = SLIPPERY-RING / *Cyclosorus sp.* (*Thelypteridaceae*)

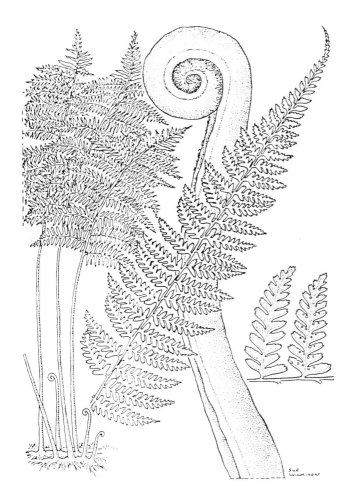

▲ *'unu'unu / dennstaedtia*

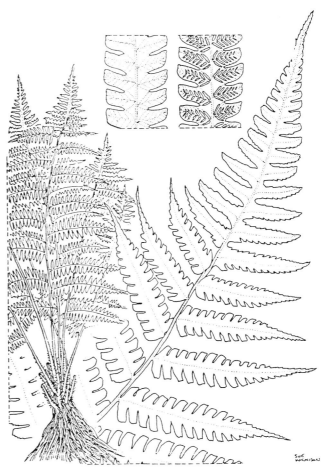

▲ *mā bili / dirty-eye*

SISIRABA'U ne'e ta takuma logo, nia fi'irū'a, nia ke ra'e logo di'ia fi'i goea kī, bore ma kesi doe liu go'o. Rauna sisili'a go'o ka sau ana gwa'irū kī. Na bibirū kī ke bulao logo sulia ulirū kī kaida'i ni'i ke ngwaro ka 'asia 'i ano.

○   Nia ke bulao sulia kafo kī.
•   Tatabu kwasi nini'a, ki 'ania gwa'irū fi'i ra'e kī.

SITOI ne'e ta takuma logo, nia fi'irū'a, 'ifitana ka dokodoko go'o 'i ano, rauna keta ka fisifisi'a ka kwa'i, gwa'irū 'ere'ere'a kī di'ia logo gwa'i takuma kī bore ma ni'i meomeo'a lala.

○   Nia ke bulao ana kaole saena kula tolo'a kī.
•   Tatabu kwasi nini'a, ki 'ania gwa'irū kī.

SISIRABA'U is also a fern, it is a clump, it comes up like *gwaea* (treefern) clumps, but it is not very big. Its leaf is narrow and emerges from the crowns. Baby ones grow along the fronds and when they are old they fall to the ground.

○   It grows along waters.
•   This is a wild vegetable, we eat the crowns coming up.
SISIRABA'U = *SISIRABA'U*

SITOI is also a fern, it is a clump, its bole is low on the ground, its leaf is long and narrow and droops, its coiled crowns are like fern crowns but they are reddish.

○   It grows on clay in inland places.
•   This is a wild vegetable, we eat the crowns.
SITOI = *Blechnum* sp. (4 sp.) (*Blechnaceae*)

GWAU nia di'ia logo takuma, nia fi'irū'a. Rauna nia di'ia logo takuma kī, bore ma kaida'i ni'i ti'iti'i gwa'irū kī ereere'a, ki saea 'ani'i gwau kī. Nia ke bulao ana ūlirū kī, ke 'oro liu mala ana ti kula ana lefo gwau kī. Gwau nia to'o ana ti malita'irū.
Fi'i GWAU saga.
- ○ Nia ke bulao ana ododo'a ma babara'oa kī, saena tolo noa'a kesi 'oro liu ana.
- • Ki 'ania logo di'ia na tatabu kwasi, 'anilana le'a ka tasa ka te'e matamata fa'asia takuma. Ki 'ania gwa'irū fi'i ra'e kī.
Fi'i GWAU BALA, ta sata GWAU MĀRODO, 'ifitana ka dokodoko, rauna keta ka kwa'i, nonina maramarako'a ka bala.
- ○ Nia ke bulao go'o sulia kafo kī ma kula ano to'onga kī.
- • Tatabu kwasi logo nini'a, ki 'ania gwa'ina ma ki tafangia māna gwa'irū kī mala kī fi'i dodoa saena fa'i ka'o fuana do'ofilana, sasi 'ubani ki 'ania ma māka ke rodo.
Fi'i GWAU BULU, fi'irū kī gwā, rauna ka marako ka keta logo. Nia ke bulao ana matangana ra'irū kī.
- ○ Nia ke bulao ke 'oro liu, nia ke leforū'anga, nia 'oro saena tolo.
- • Noa'a kisi 'ania, nia 'iri le'a go'o fuana ta rū, nia'a di'ia go'o laua.

FITAFITA nia di'ia logo gwau, nia fi'irū'a go'o saena ano, nia rararū'anga di'ia logo gwau, rauna marako ka keta logo ma ka nura. Nia ke bulao logo ana matangana rauna.
- ○ Nia ke bulao ka 'oro saena tolo ma saena logo to'ona'oa.
- • Ki 'ania gwa'irū kī di'ia ta tatabu, ki dodoa noima ki lofa fuana, 'anilana le'a ka tasa.

- • Kaida'i uta ke to'o ki 'inia ulirū kī ki sū logo 'ania.

GARAGARA ne'e ta gwau, nia gwā, rauna sisilia go'o ka te'e keta. Nia ke bulao ana 'aena, ka lalisusu mala ma lafulana ka ta'a liu.
- ○ Nia ke bulao di'ia laua saena buru faolu saena fuli o'olā kī ma sulia ta'itala kī, nia ka fafi kula ana leforū kī. Ti kaida'i nia ke bulao logo 'i gwauna 'ai kī. Nia ke bulao 'i fafona asi ma saena logo to'ona'oa ma ana logo ti kula saena tolo.
- • Laua go'o nini'a, nia 'iri le'a go'o fuana ta rū.
- • Sali ti ngwae ke rao 'ania fuana guralana ti mata'inga, noima ka noa'a go'o.

HEAD is also like fern, it is a clump. Its leaf is like the ferns but when they are small the crowns are curved and we call them heads. It grows from its fronds and is very plentiful indeed in some places in head thickets. Head has several kinds.
HEAD clump proper.
- ○ It grows on lowlands and hillsides, in the inland, it is not very plentiful.
- • We also eat it as a wild vegetable, it is especially good to eat but a bit different from fern. We eat the crowns coming up.
PALE HEAD, another name BLIND-EYE HEAD, its bole is short, its leaf is long and droops and its body is greenish and pale.
- ○ It just grows along waters and in places with proper soil.
- • This is a also wild vegetable, we eat the crown but we extract the eye (coil) of the crown and only then flask it in bamboo for burning, in case we eat it and our eyes go blind.
DARK HEAD, the clump is black, its leaf is green and long. It grows from forks in the leaves.
- ○ It grows very plentifully and becomes thickets, it is plentiful in the inland.
- • We don't eat it, it is no good for anything, it is just like a weed.
GWAU = HEAD / *Cyclosorus magnificus* (Copel.) Ching
GWAU BULU = DARK HEAD / *Cyclosorus truncatus* (Poir.) Farwell. (*Thelypteridaceae*)

BLENCHNUM is also like head (*gwau / Cyclosorus*), it is a clump at the ground and it is branching like head, its leaf is green and long and shiny. It also grows from the forks in its leaves.
- ○ It grows plentifully in the inland and also in the lowland.
- • We eat the crowns as a vegetable, we flask-cook it or make cream for it, it is especially good to eat.
- • When rain falls we pick fronds to cover with.
FITAFITA = BLENCHNUM / *Blechnum procerum* (Forst.) Sw. (*Blechnaceae*)

NEPHROLEPIS is a head (*gwau / Cyclosorus*), it is black, its leaf is narrow and quite long. It grows from its foot, is firmly rooted and hard to pull up.
- ○ It grows like a weed in new dense growth on garden sites and along pathways, it covers a place with thickets. Sometimes it also grows at the heads of trees. It grows on the sea and also in the lowland and some places in the inland.

- • This is just a weed, it is no good for anything.
- • Maybe some people may use it for curing sicknesses, or maybe not.
GARAGARA = NEPHROLEPIS / *Nephrolepis salinga* Carruth. (*Oleandraceae*)

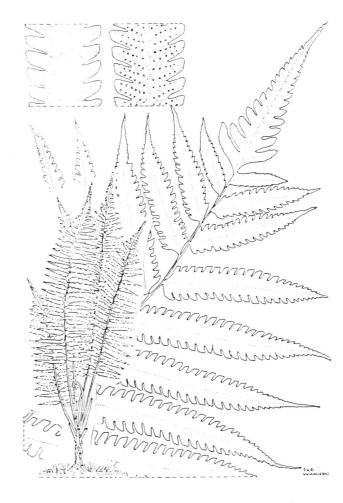

head / gwau ▶

GWA'IGWA'I nia di'ia logo gwau bore ma nia doe ana, nia fi'ifi'ila ma ka 'aba'abarū'a, rauna ka sisilia ka keta. Di'ia ki sikili dangulua rarana nia ke giragira ma ke orea nama 'i māna rararū sikili'i kī.
○ Nia ke bulao 'i fafona kafo doe kī ma babara'oa kī, n ia 'oro saena tolo.
• Di'ia nia teo ana kula ni o'o, kī tufua rarana ki alua sulia fa'i biru kī 'i ne'e nia ke kwatea kula fuiri ke ngwangwakwa'a ma alo kī ka bulao le'a ma ka 'inoi.

MUMUDALA ne'e fi'irū, nia ke fi'ifi'ila ka moli-moli'a, nia di'ia logo gwa'igwa'i bore ma nonina dada lala. Rauna keta ka kakirū'anga ka marako.
○ Nia ke bulao go'o ana kula kī ta'ifau, nia 'oro saena tolo.
• Nia le'a fuana guragura'a ma fuana logo guralana fanga, ki koria buta memerū, ki 'ui 'ania saena o'olā 'i ke su'usia mata'inga di'ia 'eo kesi takisia o'olā.

GWA'IGWA'I is also like head (*Cyclosorus*) but bigger, it is clumpy and leafy, its leaf is narrow and long. If we cut off its branches completely a slime remains on the end of the cut branches.
○ It grows on big waters and hillsides, it is plentiful in the inland.
• If we are in a gardening area we chop the branches and lay them along the boundaries so they will make the place soft and moist and taro will grow well and plump.
GWA'IGWA'I = *GWA'IGWA'I* / *Angiopteris erecta* (Forst.) *Hoffm.* (Angiopteridaceae)

MUMUDALA is a clump, it is clumpy and rounded, it is like *gwa'igwa'i* (*Angiopteris*) but its body is smooth. Its leaf has a stalk and is green.
○ It just grows in all places, it is plentiful in the inland.
• It is good for curing and also for curing food (crops), we scrape a parcel of paste and throw it on the garden to protect against sickness like poison damaging the garden.
MUMUDALA = *MUMUDALA*

KATAKATA ne'e laua, nia di'ia logo takuma kī bore ma nia ti'iti'i go'o, 'ingatana gwā. Nia ke bulao go'o 'i ano ka susu fafia kula.
○ Nia ke bulao ana kula kī sui.
• Ki guragura 'ania.

LULUKA ne'e fi'irū, nonina gwagwā'a, rauna di'ia takuma ma gwau bore ma nia mamata lala fa'asia sulia rarana ka ladolado lala.

○ Nia ke bulao saena to'ona'oa, bore ma noa'a kesi 'oro liu.
• Ki gwaroa 'ania fa'inia na 'adi ma na takataka niu.
• Ki gaua 'ania ma'e kafa, ki saunga'i logo 'ania kafa kī di'ia gau adi'o.

KWA'E ne'e sata 'afu'afu bore ma ni'i to'o ana kwa'e to'oto'o kī ne'e satani mamata lala. Rauni ka di'ia rauna takuma ma gwau bore ma 'itangani ka ra'e lala di'ia 'ai kī.
○ Na kwa'e kī ni'i ke bulao ana kula kī sui, fa'asia fafona asi ka dao 'i tolo.
KWA'E saga ne'e ai 'inoto'a, 'itangana ka gwā, rarana ka keta, rauna ka sisilia.
KWA'E BULU nia di'ia logo kwa'e 'inoto'a te'e nia'a ne'e ti'iti'i go'o ma nonina ka gwagwā'a.
○ Nia ke bulao ka 'oro liu saena tolo.
KWA'E KURAKO nia di'ia logo kwa'e 'inoto'a te'e nia ne'e doe mala ka liufia kwa'i kī ta'ifau, nonina ka melamela'a.
DINGODINGO, nia ne'e ta kwa'e logo, doelana noa'a kesi doe liu la'u di'ia kwa'e kī, nia raurau'a go'o, 'ingatana ka ta'i gwāgwā'a, rauna ka di'ia logo kwa'e.
○ Nia ke bulao saena dukwasi ana ano kaole ma ano bulu logo, nia kesi 'oro liu go'o.
GWAEA, ki saea logo 'ania **GOEA**, ta kwa'e logo nini'a bore ma ka fi'irū'a lala, 'itangana ke atoabirabira 'ania fi'irū 'oro kī, ni'i bulao ana ta'i ifita'irū ka susu ka doe liufia mala kwa'e saga kī. Nonina melamela'a, rauna ka di'ia rauna kwa'e.
○ Nia ke bulao ana ano to'o ana kula kī ta'ifau, ka 'oro liu saena tolo, te'e fafona asi ne'e nia kesi bulao ana.
• Rao'a 'ania kwa'e kī ta'ifau ni'i bolo go'o.

KATAKATA is a weed, it is like the ferns but it is just small, its trunk is black. It just grows on the ground and covers a place.
○ It grows in all places.
• We cure with it.
KATAKATA = *KATAKATA* / *Nephrolepis biserrata* (Sw.) Schott. / *N. hirsutula* (Forst.) Presl. (*Oleandraceae*)

GLEICHENIA is a clump, its body is blackish, its leaf is like fern and head (*gwau* / *Cyclosorus*) but it is different from them because its branches are joined.
○ It grows in the lowland but it is not very plentiful.
• We pattern with it, with orchid (*'adi*) and coconut cuticle.
• We bind comb-sticks with it, and also make combs like *adi 'o* (*Vitaceae*)-bound (combs) with it.
LULUKA = GLEICHENIA / *Gleichenia kajewskii* Copel. / *G. milneri* Baker (*Gleicheniaceae*) / *Histiopteris herbacea* Copel. (*Dennstaedtiaceae*)

TREEFERN is a general name but there are individual treeferns with separate names. Their leaves are like fern and head (*gwau* / *Cyclosorus*) but their trunks go up like trees.
○ Treeferns grow in all places, from on the sea to the inland.
TREEFERN proper is the important one, its trunk is black, its branches are long and its leaf is narrow.
DARK TREEFERN is like the important treefern only it is small and its body is blackish.
○ It grows plentifully in the inland.
KURAKO TREEFERN is like the important treefern only it is very big, more than all the treeferns, its body is brownish.
DINGODINGO is also a treefern, its size is not very big like the treeferns, it is only slender, its trunk is a bit blackish and its leaf is also like treefern.
○ It grows in wilderness on clay ground and dark ground, it is not very plentiful.
GWAEA, also called *GOEA*, this one is also a treefern but it is a clump, its trunk sprouts into many clumps, they grow from one bole and cover much more than proper treeferns. Its body is brownish, its leaf is like treefern leaf.
○ It grows on proper ground in all places, it is very plentiful in the inland, only on the sea it won't grow.
• Working with all the treeferns is the same.

- 'Itangana ki saunga'i 'ania fuana rū 'oro kī. Ki saunga'i luma 'ania di'ia 'ai kī. Nia totolia logo diro'anga, ka tasa saena tolo, kula ne'e 'ai fuana diro'a noa'a kasi 'oro ana. Ki bōngia 'ania talana 'odoa 'i 'au kī, ki bō 'ania fuana fa'i alo kī, ki sakali logo 'ania 'usia gwata kī, ki bōngia logo 'ania kabara kī. Nia le'a fuana rū kī sui sulia nia ke teo ta'u ka teo bore 'ana sulia ta fita fa'i ngali nia kesi fura.
- Na kula taliore'a gwā ki saunga'i 'ania rū kī di'ia ma'e kafa, ka tasa fuana kafa gwaroa kī.
- Gwangorū fi'i ra'u bako ki 'inia fuana 'anilana di'ia ta tatabu kwasi, ka di'ia gwa'i takuma kī.
- Kwa'e 'inoto'a, ki 'ania logo sa'esa'erū. Kaida'i ki saungia ma nia ka lango ki ke tadilia 'itangana ma ki fi'i kōngia sa'esa'erū fuana 'anilana. 'Anilana kwa'e inoto'a ka le'a ka di'ia kai kī, bore ma kwa'e mamata kī noa'a kisi 'ani'i.
- Kwa'e kī ta'ifau, kaida'i nia du'a ki kedea logo 'ania mafula, nia ke du'a dangi sulia nia ka onaonala'a.

- Its trunk we make into many things. We build houses with it like trees. It is also fit for posts, especially in the inland, the place where trees for posts are not very plentiful. We fix bamboo walls in position with it, we border taro plots with it, we also fence with it against pigs and set latrines with it. It is good for everything because it is long lasting and however many years it lies it won't rot.
- The black heartwood we make into things like comb sticks, especially for patterned combs.
- The tender leaf-shoots we pick for eating as a wild vegetable, like fern crowns.
- With the important treefern we also eat the inside. When we pound it and it is dry we trim the trunk and bake the inside to eat. To eat, important treefern is like yam, but the other treeferns we don't eat.

- All the treeferns, when burned, we also kindle fire with, it burns till day because it makes embers.

KWA'E = TREEFERN / *Cyathea lunulata* (Forst.) Copel. / *C. vittata* Copel.
KWA'E BULU = DARK TREEFERN / *Cyathea brackenridgei* Mett.
KWA'E KURAKO = *KURAKO* TREEFERN / *Cyathea whitmorei* Baker
DINGODINGO = *DINGODINGO* / *Cyathea hornei* (Baker) Copel. GWAEA / GOEA = *GWAEA* / *Cyathea alta* Copel. (*Cytheaceae*)

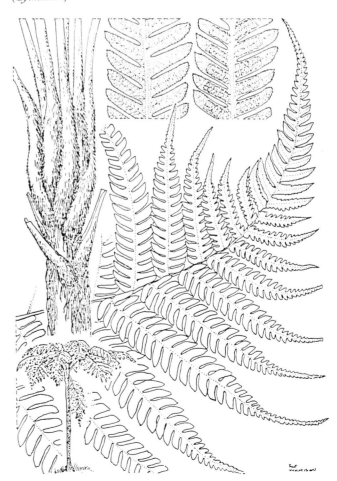

kwa'e / treefern ▶

FA'U, saena 'abafola ne'e nia ke ū fuana ti malita'irū ne'e kira bolo logo.

FA'U saga ne'e fi'irū'a, nonina ngarangara'a, lalina keta liu, rauna keta liu ka te'e reba. Nia ke fungu, ke bulao ana fuana. Nia to'o ana ti malita'irū kī.
FA'U TAFAI, ta sata FA'U FAFADA, rauna kesi keta liu go'o ka marako fīfī, ma nonina ra'irū kī ka te'e maramarako'a go'o, ma rauna ka mabe.
○ Rū fasia nini'a, ki fasia saena fanoa kī.
FA'U TOLO, rauna keta liu mala ma rauna ka marako fifi mala ma ka gaga'ai.
○ Rū kwasi nini'a, kisi fasia. Nia ke bulao ana kula kī ta'ifau, fa'asia fafona asi ka dao 'i tolo, saena go'o 'ana masu'u ma saena kunukunua kī bore.
FA'U DA'I nia di'ia logo fa'u tolo bore ma nonina kwaokwao'a lala.
○ Nia ke bulao 'i fafona asi.
• Fa'u nai'ari kī, aba'abana ki saunga'i 'ania fa'u fuana dukurū'anga 'ania ma fua'a 'ania, fuana logo sū fa'asia uta ma fonelana sina, ma ki teo logo 'i saena.
• Ki 'olea 'aba'abana fa'u fuana 'afulana rū kī di'ia buta ko'a ma karusulana gwa'i fara kī fa'inia imola kī.
• 'Aba'abarū, ki saunga'inia logo 'ania rū kī di'ia 'abakwalo ni fua ma kabileta fuana ra'efilana 'ai kī.
• Ki karia logo fuana 'afulana ngwae mae fuana kwaiatolana.

MOMOLE ne'e ta malita'i fa'u, nia fi'irū'a ke doe ka keta mala, bore ma rauna ka sisilia ka keta ka di'ia logo tara kī.
○ Rū fasia ne'e, ki fasia nonina fanoa. Ki salinga'inia nini'a 'i 'a'e asi.
• Ti to'a mamata kira rao 'ania, bore ma kia'a Kwara'ae noa'a kisi sasi go'o 'ania ta rū. Noa'a kisi taia fuana fa'u sulia rauna kesi reba ma kesi ngasi le'a.
• Nini'ari ne'e ki faosia 'ania mata ma ngwa'i kī.

MAT, in this book it stands for some kinds of things which are similar.

MAT proper is a clump, its body is prickly, its root is very long, its leaf is long and quite wide. It bears and grows from its fruit. It has several kinds.
TAFAI MAT, another name *FAFADA* MAT, its leaf is not very long and is intense green, the body of the leaf is greenish and the leaf is flexible.
○ This one is planted, we plant it in homes.
LOCAL (inland) MAT, its leaf is very long indeed and the leaf is intense green and stiff.
○ This one is wild, we don't plant it. It grows in all places, from on the sea to the inland, only in the forest and even in swamps.

DA'I MAT is like local mat (*fa'u tolo / Sararanga*) but its body is whiteish.
○ It grows on the sea.
• These mats, their strips (leaves) we make into mats for bundling and carrying burdens, and also for covering up from the rain and shutting off the sun, and we also lie on them.
• We cut up mat strips for wrapping things like parcels of scraping (mangrove pudding) and packaging *fara*(fish) and *imola*(fish).
• The strips we also make into things like burden vine-strips and foot-straps for climbing trees.

• We also split it (the sewn mat) open to wrap a dead person for disposal.
FA'U = MAT/ pandanus / screw pine / *Pandanaceae*
FA'U TOLO = LOCAL MAT / *Sararanga sinuosa* Hemsl.
FA'U DA'I = *DA'I* MAT / pandanus / screw pine / *Pandanus aff. compressus* Martelli
(*Pandanaceae*)

PANDANUS is a kind of mat (*fa'u / Pandanus*), it is a clump and gets big and really tall, but its leaf is narrow and long like *tara* (*Pandanus*).
○ This is planted, we plant it round the home. We transferred it from overseas.
• Some other people work with it, but we Kwara'ae don't do anything with it. We don't sew it for mats because the leaf is not wide and not very strong.
• At present we plait it into matting and bags.
MOMOLE = PANDANUS / *Pandanus rubellus* B.C. Stone / *P. sp.* (*Pandanaceae*)

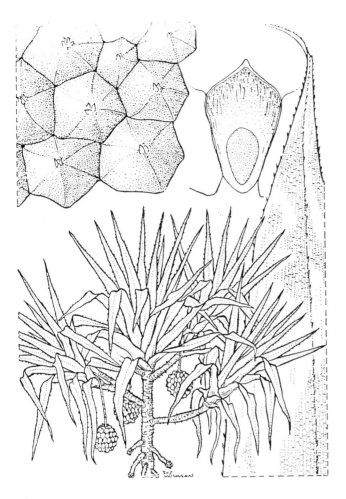

▲ *fa'u da'i / da'i* mat

TARA, nia di'ia logo fa'u kī, fi'irū kī marako fīfī ma 'abana ka sisilia ka keta liu mala.

○ Nia ke bulao ke susu go'o ana te'e kula 'i fafona asi.
• Noa'a kisi sasia go'o 'ania ta rū.

AFOLE, ta sata A'AFOLE, ne'e fi'irū, lisilana di'ia fa'u bore ma nia mamata logo ana, rauna nia afole, ka kwanga ma ke sau kalikalia 'itangana. Takana kwao, nia ke fungu ka bulao ana fuana.
○ Nia ke bulao 'i fafona asi.
• Ki 'olea boeboena ke di'ia ī'a kī fuana alulana ana ma'e fina'u fuana dē'a saena asi.

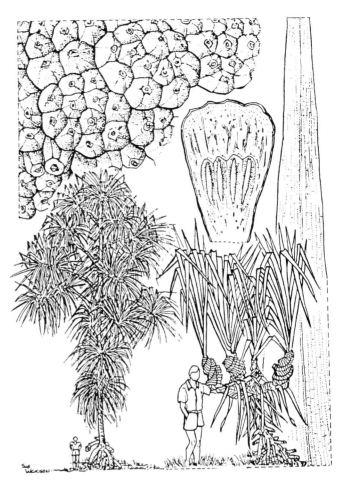

▲ *momole / pandanus*

TARA is like the mats (*fa'u / Pandanus*), the clumps are intense green and the leaf is narrow and very long indeed.
○ It grows and covers at a few places on the sea.

• We don't do anything with it.
TARA = *TARA / Pandanus croceus* St.John / *P. echinatus* St.John / *P. erinaceus* B.C.Stone / *P. polycephalus* Lamk. / *P. rechingeri* (Martelli) St.John / *P. upoluensis* Martelli (*Pandanaceae*)

CURVED is a clump, it looks like mat (*fa'u / Pandanus*) but is different, its leaf curves over, it is pretty and emerges around the trunk. Its flower is white, it bears fruit and grows from its fruit.
○ It grows on the sea.
• We cut its leaf-tube to be like fishes for putting on hooks for fishing in the sea.
AFOLE = CURVED / *Pandanus decus-montium* B.C.Stone / *P. paludosus* Merr & Perry (*Pandanaceae*)

TASISI ne'e fi'irū, nonina keta liu, rauna keta, lisilana ka di'ia fi'i fa'u kī. Nia fungu ana magarū ti'iti'i ka bulu ma ka ngasi.
○ Nia ke bulao saena maguru.
• Magana ki loia ki sote'e fuana saunga'inia 'ania na maga mani bulu ki saea 'ania fulu.
• Rauna ki to'osia gwaurau 'ania saena o'olā.

FULU ne'e fi'irū, nia di'ia logo fi'i tasisi kī, rauna marako ka keta di'ia rauna tasisi. Nia ke fungu 'ania fingirū kī, kaida'i nia 'iri make 'ua ni'i marako, di'ia nia make na'a ta ma nia gwā.
○ Nia ke bulao go'o 'i tolo ana kula gwari.
• Magana ki saunga'inia 'ania na maga mani bulu logo, ni'i doe ana maga tasisi kī. Ki usu'ia dola 'ania maga mani kwao kī fuana laungilana 'ania na rō bali kī ana tafuli'ae.

AFAAFAMANU, ki saea logo 'ania ARAKAO, nia fi'irū'a ka kwaokwao'anga, 'itanga'irū ka doe, rauna ka marako ka keta liu, takana kwao ka meomeo-'anga ma ka lia di'ia lili. Nia ke fungu, fa'irū kī marako ka molimoli'a, nia ke bulao ana faruna. Nia to'o ana rō malita'irū kī, ta ai sakosako'a, ta ai ka marako nia ke doe liufia mala ai sakosako'a.
○ Ai marako ne'e rū kwasi. Nia ke bulao ana kula kī ta'ifau, fa'asia fafona asi ka dao 'i tolo, ka tasa ana ti kula. Nia ke bulao to'oto'o, ka tasa ana ano gwagwā'a kī.
• Afaafamanu sakosako'a, rū ne'e ki fasia fuana laungilana fanoa, nia le'a liu go'o fuana lisilana.
• Ki 'olea boeboena fuana alulana ana ma'e fina'u fuana dē'a saena asi, sulia lisilana ka di'ia logo ī'a, ki saea 'ania arakao.
• Siko kī ke tua ana ra'irū kī fuana 'anilana.

GWAGWASU, ki saea logo 'ania 'ABURA, BULU, ne'e fi'irū nia doe fi'ifi'ila go'o 'i ano, nia ke doe ke keta ke dao bolo go'o fa'inia gwauna alaka ka sui. Nia ke taka ka alua magarū ti'iti'i kī, ka make ni'i ka 'asi mala 'i ano ka fi'i bulao 'ania bibirū kī. Na gwagwasu to'o ana rō malita'irū kī, GWAGWASU BULU fa'inia GWAGWASU BALA.
○ Rū fasia ne'e, ki fasia saena o'olā kī ma fanoa kī 'i ne'e nia ke moko le'a ma ka lia kwanga.

TASISI is a clump, its body is very long, its leaf is long and it looks like the mats (*fa'u / Pandanus*). It bears small seeds which are dark and hard.
○ It grows in the mangroves.
• Its seeds we pluck and bore for making into the dark money beads called *fulu* (Gesneriaceae).
• Its leaf we roof shelters with in the garden.
TASISI = *TASISI / Hypolytrum nemorum* (Vahl.) Spreng / *Mapania cuspidata* (Miq.) Vitt. / *Paramapania parribractea* (Clarke) Vitt. (*Cyperaceae*)

FULU is a clump, it is like *tasisi* clump (Cyperaceae) its leaf is green and long like *tasisi* leaf. It bears bunches and when they are not yet ripe they are green, when they are ripe they are black.
○ It just grows in the inland in damp places.
• Its seeds we make into money beads also, they are bigger than *tasisi* seeds. We thread them among white shell-money beads to decorate the two ends of a ten-string (shell-money).
FULU = *FULU / Boea hemsleyana* (Bl.) Burtt / *B. magellanica* Lamk. / *Mapania palustris* (Hassk. ex Streud.) Vitt. (*Gesneriaceae*)

AFAAFAMANU, also called LURE, is a clump and is whiteish, the trunk is big, its leaf is green and very long, its flower is white and reddish and looks like a waterlily. It bears and the fruits are green and rounded, and it grows from its pips. It has two kinds, one is yellow and one is green and bigger than the yellow one.
○ The green one is wild. It grows in all places, from on the sea to the inland, especially in some places. It grows individually, especially on blackish ground.
• Yellow *afaafamanu* is something we plant to decorate the home, it is just very nice looking.
• We cut off the leaf-tube for putting on fish-hooks for fishing in the sea, because it looks like a fish, we call it a lure.
• Hoppers live in the leaves for eating.
AFAMANU / 'ARAKA'O = *AFAMANU / LURE / Crinum asiaticum* L. (*Amaranthaceae*) / *Hanguana malayana* (Jack) Merr. (*Flagellariaceae*)

HEDYOTIS, also called *'ABURA* or DARK, is a clump which is big and clumpy on the ground, it gets big and tall and reaches to our chins. It flowers and produces small seeds, when ripe they fall to the ground and then grow into seedlings. Hedyotis has two kinds, DARK HEDYOTIS and PALE HEDYOTIS.
○ This is planted, we plant it in gardens and homes so it will smell good and look pretty.

- Sulia alo ne'e marako fifī, gwagwasu ne'e ke gwagwā'a 'i safitana ka fi'i lia kwanga fa'inia. Ma fa'inia logo saena fa'i alo kī, mokofana gwagwasu ke fonea mata'inga ne'e satana 'eo noima alo mae kesi fa'alia alo kī, 'i ne'e alo kesi simora'a.
- Ki laungia logo 'ania nonika ma ngwa'i fa'ani kī fuana ke moko le'a, fuana logo bulasilana manatana ngela kini 'i nia ke manata fifī to'ona ngwae.
- Rauna gwagwasu bulu, 'i na'o ma'i ki du'afia kwate sasuna ke fa'amāliua malimae kia kī, fuana saungilada. Ngwae sai ani ke lalia 'ania ma'efata'a ne'e ki saea 'ania fa'abulu.
- Ki gurā logo 'ania ti mata'inga.
- Rū nai'ari kī, gwagwasu bulu nia ngasi ana gwagwasu bala.

DIUDIUDARA ne'e fi'irū, nia to'o ana rō malita'irū kī. Ta'i rauna reba ka te'e molimoli'a, fa'irū ka molimoli'a ka te'e doe, di'ia nia kwasa ke meo. Ta'i rauna ti'iti'i ka keta ka matanga'a.
- Rō ai ta'ifau ni'i ke bulao saena raku faolu ma sulia ta'i tala kī ma ana agi kafo gwa'u kī.
- Ai rauna reba, kaida'i fa'irū kī ni'i afuafu'a 'ua ngela kī ke fisu'ī ma kira ke diu 'i māna darada 'i ke busu, nia nini'a ki fa'asata sulia.
- Ai rauna ti'iti'i ne'e tatabu, ki 'ania gwa'irū kī, ki dodoa, kukia, gwa'abia, 'anilana nia di'ia logo ba'era.

KOKO'OE ne'e fi'iru, rauna te'e reba ka ketaketa'a ka marako, takana sakosako'a, nia ke bulao ana fa'irū kī.
- Nia bulao saena raku buru ma logo 'i ninimana kafo kī, ana to'ona'oa ma saena tofongana tolo.
- Gwa'irū ne'e tatabu fuana 'anilana.

FARAFARA ne'e fi'irū, nia di'ia logo koli bore ma nia kesi alua fingirū, nia taka go'o. Nonina mamarako'a ka momote, rauna ketaketa'a ka sisili'a, nia ke bulao ana takana.
- Nia ke bulao 'i fafona asi ma 'i ninimana kafo kī, bore ma agi kafo kesi dukwasi'a kī.
- Nia ta'a liu si ne'e nia ngarangara'a ma ke momotea nonina ngwae. Noa'a kisi sasia go'o 'ania ta rū.

- Because taro is an intense green, the dark hedyotis among it looks pretty with it. And besides, in taro gardens the smell of hedyotis blocks the sickness named poison or taro-death from damaging the taro, so the taro won't be stunted.
- We also decorate our bodies and shoulder bags with it to smell good and also to turn the minds of the girls so they will think intensely of a man.
- The leaf of dark hedyotis, formerly we burned it so that its smoke would make our enemies sleep, to kill them. A man who knew would invoke with words which we call making-dark.
- We also cure some sickness with it.
- For these things, dark hedyotis is stronger than pale hedyotis.
GWAGWASU = HEDYOTIS / *Hedyotis lapeyrousii DC.* (*Rubiaceae*)

SMASH-BROW is a clump, it has two kinds. One, its leaf is wide and quite rounded, its fruit is rounded and quite big and if it is ripe it becomes red. One, the leaf is long and divided.
- Both of them grow in the new shoots and along pathways and on stretches of empty (dry) waters.
- The wide leafed one, while the fruit are still whole, children pluck and smash them against the brow to burst them, which is what we name it after.
- The small leafed one is a vegetable, we eat the crowns, we flask-cook it, boil it and oven-cook it, it is like cabbage (*ba'era / Hibiscus*) to eat.
DIUDIUDARA = SMASH-BROW

WEDELIA is a clump, its leaf is quite wide and longish and green, its flower is yellow and it grows from its fruit.
- It grows in the new shoots and beside waters, in the lowland and in the central inland.
- The crown is a vegetable for eating.
KOKO'E / TOTOI = WEDELIA /*Wedelia biflora* (L.) DC. (*Asteraceae*)

FARAFARA is a clump, it is like maize but it doesn't produce a bunch, it just flowers. Its body is greenish and scratchy, its leaf is longish and narrow, it grows from its flower.
- It grows on the sea and beside waters, but on stretches of water which are not in wilderness.
- It is very bad because is it is prickly and scratches a person's body. We don't do anything with it.
FARAFARA = *FARAFARA*

RI'I ne'e fi'irū ti'iti'i go'o, rauna marako ka sisilia ka keta, nia moko fīfīī ma ka le'a, mokofana di'ia logo fo'oka. Nia to'o ana rō malita'irū kī. RI'I NGWANE, rauna doe ka keta, RI'I KINI, rauna ka sisili'a ka ti'iti'i ana ai ngwane.

- ○ Rū fasia ne'e, ki fasia fuana laungilana fanoa ma nonina logo feraābu kī ma fulitua'a kī. Nia ke bulao kwasila'a logo ka tasa saena tolo.
- • Ri'i kini na'a ne'e 'inoto'a fuana rū ana akalo kī. Ki 'oto 'ania 'usia akalo.
- • Nia moko le'a, ki laungia 'ania ngwa'i fa'ani kī, ti kaida'i ki 'oia ulirū, 'i ki fa'abala'i fuana laungi'anga.
- • Ti kaida'i ngwae ke 'ilua 'ania manatana ngela kini kī 'ania 'i ne'e kira ke ogā ngwae.

BEBE, fi'irū ne'e nia nenere'a go'o 'i ano, nonina bulu, rauna ka di'ia 'aba'abana bebe, nia ma'e toto'anga.

- ○ Nia ke bulao saena to'ona'oa fafona kafo kī ma saena logo tolo, bore ma 'i fafona asi ka noa'a go'o.
- • Noa'a kisi sasia go'o 'ania ta rū.

'ADI ne'e fi'irū, nonina sakosako'a ta'ifau, rauna sisilia, takana kwao ka te'e sakosako'a, nia ke bulao ana takana. Nia to'o ana rō malita'irū kī, ta'i kasina doe ka keta, ta'i kwalona ka ti'iti'i go'o.

- ○ Nia ke bulao lala 'i gwauna 'ai kī, ana ta 'ai go'o 'ana ana ta kula bore 'ana. Noa'a kesi 'oro liu go'o ma ke bulao to'oto'o, ka tasa saena tolo fa'inia logo gwauna totoloa kī.
- • Rō malita'i 'adi ne'e kī, kwaloni ngasi liu, ki efoa fuana gwarolana 'ania rū kī 'i ke kwanga, rū di'ia kafa gwaroa ma fa'i rade ma fo'osae, fuana laungi'anga. Ki faosia fa'inia taketake niu ne'e ki atongia ke meomeo'anga, 'i ne'e lisilani rō rū ne'e kī ke kwanga liu.

FARI ne'e fi'irū, 'aba'abana sakosako'a, rauna marako, takana sakosako'a logo, nia ke fungu 'ania magarū sakosako'a kī. Nia ke bulao 'i matangana rara 'ai kī ma gwauna gwari 'ai kī.

- ○ Nia ke bulao ana kula kī ta'ifau sulia no'o ke ngalia magana ka alua ana 'ai kī, ka 'oro saena tolo.
- • Nia le'a ka tasa fuana no'o akaka'u ke tua ni fuli saena fi'irū, na luma no'o akaka'u mala nini'a. Ti kaida'i rō rū'anga ma ulu rū ke teo 'i saena te'e fi'i fari.

RI'I is a small clump, its leaf is green and narrow and long, it smells intensely and good, its smell is like worship (*fo'oka* / *Euodia*). It has two kinds. MALE *RI'I*, its leaf is big and long, FEMALE *RI'I*, its leaf is narrow and smaller than the male one.

- ○ This is planted, we plant it to decorate the home and also round tabu-houses and rest-sites. It also grows wild, especially in the inland.
- • Female *ri'i* is important for things to do with ghosts. We charm with it against ghosts.
- • It smells good and we decorate hanging bags with it, sometimes we snap a frond to bleach it for decoration.
- • Sometimes a man attracts girls' minds with it so they'll want the man.

RI'I =*RI'I* / *Eodia aff. anisodora* (*Rutaceae*)

BUTTERFLY, this clump just clusters at the ground, its body is dark, its leaf is like a butterfly wing, it is spotted.

- ○ It grows in the lowland on waters and also in the inland, but not on the sea.

- • We don't do anything with it.

BEBE = BUTTERFLY

ORCHID is a clump, its body is all yellow, its leaf is narrow, its flower is white and a bit yellow and it grows from its flower. It has two kinds, one the sections are big and long, one its vine is just small.

- ○ It grows at the heads of trees, on any tree in any place. It is not very plentiful and it grows individually, especially in the inland and also on hill-tops.
- • Both these kinds of orchids, the vine is very strong and we choose it for patterning things with so they'll be pretty, things like patterned combs and ear-reeds and (men's) girdles, for decoration. We plait it with coconut cuticle which we dye reddish, so the two things look very pretty.

'ADI = ORCHID / *Cadetia hispida* (A.Rich.) Schltr. / *Diplocaulobium meckynosepalum* (Schltr.) Kraenzl. / *D. solomonense* Carruth. (*Orchidaceae*)

LIPARIS is a clump, its strip (stem) is yellow, its leaf is green, its flower is also yellow and it bears yellow fruit. It grows in the forks of tree branches and at the head of tree stumps.

- ○ It grows in all places because birds take its seeds and leave them on trees, it is plentiful in the inland.
- • It is especially good for cuscus to settle in the clump, this is indeed the cuscus' house. Sometimes two or three will live in one liparis clump.

FARI = LIPARIS / *Liparis condylobulbon* Rchb.f. (*Orchidaceae*)

DIONGA nia di'ia logo 'adi, fi'irū kī rarara'a, rauna molimoli'a ka marako, takana ka sakosako'a, fa'irū kī ka sakosako'a logo.

○ Nia ke bulao ana 'ai kī, ke 'oro ana 'ado'a ka liufia ti 'ai bore 'ani, ka 'oro saena tolo.

• Nia lia kwanga liu ka di'ia logo ti rū sulia nia sakosako'a, bore ma noa'a kisi sasia go'o 'ania ta rū.

DIONGA is like orchid (*'adi*), the clumps are branching, its leaf is rounded and green, its flower is yellow and its fruits are also yellow.

○ It grows on trees, it is plentiful on joined (nut)(*'ado'a* / *Canarium*), more than on any other tree, it is plentiful in the inland.

• It looks as pretty as anything, but we don't do anything with it.

DIONGA = *DIONGA* / *Amyema artensis* (Montre.) Danser / *A. rigidiflora* (Krause.) Danser / *Amylotheca angustifolia* Teigh. / *A. insularum* (A.Gray.) *Danser* / *A. triflora* Danser / *Dactyliophora angustifolia* (Teigh.) *Barlow* / *D. salomonia* Danser / *D. verticillata* Teigh. / *Decaisnina holrungii* (Schum.) Barlow / *Notothixos leiophyllus* Schum. / *Sogerianthe sessiliflora* Danser / *S. versicolor* Danser / *Dendrophthoe falaca* Danser (*Loranthaceae*) / *Dendromyza salomonia* Danser (*Santalaceae*)

ARAKOI nia fi'irū'a, rauna ka sisilia ka marako, takana kwao ka lagolago'a. Nia ke bulao ana ifuifuna takana

○ Nia ke bulao saena tolo goro.

• Ki gura 'ania ti mata'inga.

ARAKOI is a clump, its leaf is narrow and green, its flower is a white plume. It grows from the hairs of its flower.

○ It grows in the misty inland.

• We cure some sicknesses with it.

ARAKOI = *ARAKOI*

TATALE'OLE'O ne'e fi'irū'a, rauna ka reba ma ka keta mala.

○ Nia ke bulao tofungana 'ai kī di'ia logo fi'i fari, ana ta kula bore 'ana.

• Na no'o akaaka'u kī ke tua ana fa'inia logo 'unu kī.

• Ki tufua ki alua logo ana saena fanoa 'i ke lia le'a.

• Ki guragura 'ania.

TATALE'OLE'O is a clump, its leaf is wide and really long.

○ It also grows on the middle of trees, like liparis (*fari*), in any place at all.

• Cuscus also live in it as well as lizards.

• We chop it down and put it in the home to look good.

• We cure with it.

TATALE'OLE'O = *TATALE'OLE'O* / birdsnest fern / *Asplenium Nidus* L. (*Aspleniaceae*) / *Merinthosorus drynaroides* (Hook.) Copel (*Polypodiaceae*)

RĪDO ne'e fi'irū, nia molimoli'a mala di'ia fa'i babakini doe molimoli'a kī. 'Aba'abana kī ke sau ana fi'i rīdo ka fi'i alua ra'irū kī, rauna marako, takana meomeo. Nia to'o ana rō malita'irū kī, RĪDO saga fa'inia logo RĪDO FAU.

○ Nia ke bulao 'i gwauna 'ai kī, ana ta kula bore 'ana.

• Nia le'a ka tasa go'o fuana lolo ke buri ma ka tua 'i saena.

HYDNOPHYTUM is a clump, it is really rounded like a big round pumpkin. Stalks emerge from the hydonphytum clump and produce leaves, the leaf is green, its flower is red. It has two kinds, HYDNO-PHYTUM proper and SOLID HYDNOPHYTUM.

○ It grows at the heads of trees, in any place at all.

• It is especially good for ants to inhabit and live inside.

RĪDO = HYDNOPHYTUM / antplant / *Hydnophytum* sp. RĪDO FAU = THICK HYDNOPHYTUM / *Hydnophytum formicarum* Jack. / *H. guppianum* Becc. / *H. hahlii* Rech. / *H. hellwigii* Warb. / *H. kajewsky* Merr.& Perry / *H. longipes* Merr.& Perry / *H. longistylum* Becc. / *H. Stewartii* Fosb. / *H. tortuosum* Becc. (*Rubiaceae*)

SALU, kwalo ne'e nonina marako, lalina ke alua logo fa'i ngwako fuana ra'efilana 'ai kī. Rauna marako, takana kwao ma nia ke fungu 'ania fingirū kī, fa'ina ka keta. Nia to'o ana rō malita'irū kī, ta'i rauna reba liu mala, ta'i rauna keta ka noa'a 'iri reba liu go'o.

- ○ Nia ke bulao go'o ana kula kī ta'ifau, nia kesi 'oro liu bore ma ti kula nia ke bulao ke tasa ani.
- • Ngwakona nia le'a ka tasa fuana firi'a 'ania sulia 'aba ngwako ngasi liu. Ki aea fuana fi'iri 'ania ana luma fuana susu'ilana 'odoa, ki usu'ia 'ania sao kī fuana to'osi luma'a, ka di'ia logo 'aba kalitau.
- • Kaida'i ki ogā ki lalafia ngwako ki agofia, ki dau ana, go'o ki lalafia 'ali'ali fuana nia ke mū ma'i, ka 'asia ta'ifau.
- • Ka'ika'ina kaida'i nia ngwaka ki aea logo 'abarū fuana gwa'i nili ma dadalo sulia nia ngasi liu.
- • Rauna ki gwa'abi 'ania ma ki 'afua logo 'ania buta ko'a kī.
- • 'Unu ma no'o akaaka'u ni'i ke 'ania rauna.

SALU, this vine's body is green, its root also produces tendrils for climbing trees. Its leaf is green, its flower is white and it bears bunches of long fruit. It has two kinds, one the leaf is really very wide, the other the leaf is long and not very wide.

- ○ It grows in all places, it is not very plentiful but it grows especially in some places.
- • Its tendril is especially good for tying because the tendril strip is very strong. We peel it for tying houses with to secure walling and stitch sago (leaf) with it for house roofing, like winds-far strip.
- • When we want to tug the tendril we sneak up on it, we hold it, then we tug it quickly for it to break off and all fall down at once.
- • Its stalk, when it is soft we also peel strips for braided cord and twine since it is very strong.
- • Its leaf we oven-cook with and wrap scraping (mangrove pudding) parcels with.
- • Lizards and cuscus eat its leaf.

SALU = *SALU* / *Epipremnum amplissimum* Schott Engl. / *Rhaphidophora australasica* F.M.Bail. / *R. novo-guineense* Engl. / *R. aff. stolleana* Schott / *Spathiphyllum solomonense* Nicholson, *Scindapsus altissimus* V. Au.R. / *S. cuscuara* (Aubl.) Presl. / *Pothos Albertisii* Engl. / *P. rumphii* Engl. / *P. helwigii* Engl. (*Araceaea*)

SATA, fa'i kwalo ne'e nia kalia 'ai kī, nia di'ia logo kalitau bore ma kwalona dokodoko go'o, noa'a kesi bolo fa'inia ta'i tafanga'anga. Rauna matanga'a ka marako fīfī. Nia to'o ana malita'irū to'oto'o kī. Ta'i ai ki saea 'ania SATA 'U'I AFA sulia lalina ka di'ia 'u'una afa kī.

- ○ Nia ke bulao ana kula kī sui, saena raku faolu ma saena logo dukwasi, fa'asia fafona asi ka dao 'i tolo.
- • Ki toea kwalona fuana faosilana 'ania rū kī di'ia kukudu ngasi ma kokofi. Ki kalia fa'i kwalo kī, ki firi 'adoa kalikalia rō kwakwa 'i rū kī.
- • Ki itoa luma 'ania, ngasilana ka bolo fa'inia kalitau bore ma nia dokodoko go'o ana. Ki ito 'ania fa'i kwalo la'ula'u si ne'e nia ti'iti'i go'o ma di'ia ki sisia nia ke fura. Nia totolia susu'ilana ra'itai ma kokoba si ne'e uta ke to'ea bore 'ana, noa'a nia kesi fura 'ali'ali. Te'e sata 'ae 'afa ne'e noa'a kasi bolo fa'inia ito'a sulia fa'i kwalo la'ula'u nia mafusifusi.
- • Nia bolo logo fuana itolana 'ania sakali sulia noa'a nia kesi fura 'ali'ali ana kula isila.

LYGODIUM is a vine which winds round trees, it is like winds-far but its vine is short, not as much as a fathom. Its leaf is divided and intense green. It has separate kinds. One we call EAGLE'S CLAW LYGODIUM because its root is like an eagle's claws.

- ○ It grows in all places, in new shoots and also in wilderness, from on the sea to the inland.

- • We pare its vine for plaiting into things like strong baskets and trays. We wind the vines round and bind two together around the edges.
- • We also tie houses with it, its strength is equivalent to winds-far but it is shorter. We tie with the whole vine since it is only small and if we split it, it rots. It is fit for securing the ridge and crest (of a roof) since even when rain soaks it, it won't rot quickly. Only eagle's claw lygodium is not suitable for tying because the entire vine snaps.
- • It is also suitable for tying fences because it won't rot quickly in a wet place.

SATA = LYGODIUM / *Lygodium dimorphum* / *L. microphyllum* (Cav.) R.Br. / *L. palmatum* / *L. trifurcatum* Baker (*Schizaeaceae*)
SATA 'U'I AFA = EAGLE'S CLAW LYGODIUM / *lygodium circinnatum* (Burm.f.) Sw. / *L. versteeghii* C. Chr. (*Schizaeaceae*)

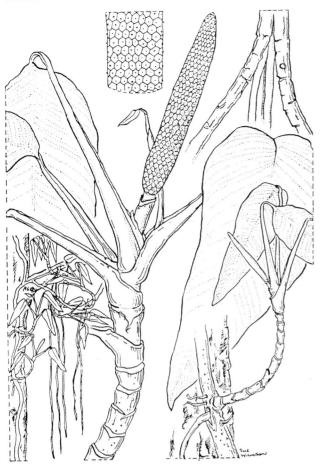

▲ *salu* / salu

▲ *kwalekwale* / kwalekwale

KWALEKWALE, fa'i kwalo ne'e fi'irū, nia ūsulia na'a kwasakwasa bore ma kwasakwasa ne'e doe ana. Lalana ka ti'iti'i ka ngwaladada'a ka keta liu logo di'ia fa'i kalitau, rauna keta ka sau laelae sulia fa'ina. Nia ke ra'e sulia 'ai kī.

○ Nia ke bulao ana kula kī ta'ifau, nia 'oro saena to'ona'oa.

• Lalana ki aea 'ania 'abarū fuana itolana luma di'ia logo kalitau, fuana logo usalana sao.

• Ki itoa logo 'ania sakali kī.

• Ki gura 'ania du'a fu'ufu'u.

KWASAKWASA nia di'ia logo kwalekwale bore ma nia doe ana. Nonina mela ka gwā, rauna keta ka sau laelae sulia lalarū.

○ Nia ke bulao ana kula kī ta'ifau, nia 'oro saena tolo.

• Lalana ki aea 'ania 'abarū fuana itolana luma, fuana logo usalana sao di'ia logo 'aba kwalekwale ma 'aba kalitau.

• Ki sisia 'ania 'abarū kī fuana kwa'ilana 'ania sisimā fuana 'odo'a, ki faosia 'aba kwasakwasa kī gwagwā'a fa'inia 'aba ka'o kwaokwao'anga.

KWALEKWALE is a vine which is a clump, it resembles *kwasakwasa* but *kwasakwasa* is bigger. Its canes are small and and snaky and very long like winds-far, its leaf is long and emerges all along its stem. It climbs along trees.

○ It grows in all places, it is plentiful in the lowland.

• Its canes we peel into strips for tying houses like winds-far, and also for stitching sago (leaf).

• We also tie fences with it.

• We cure tuberculosis with it.

KWALEKWALE = *KWALEKWALE* / *Flagellara indica* L. (*Flagellariaceae*)

KWASAKWASA is like *kwalekwale* but it is bigger. Its body is brown and black, its leaf is long and emerges all along its canes.

○ It grows in all places, it is plentiful in the inland.

• Its cane we peel into strips for tying houses and also for stitching sago (leaf) like *kwalekwale* strip and winds-far strip.

• We split it into strips for doing narrow-eye for walling, we plait the blackish *kwasakwasa* strip with whiteish bamboo strip.

KWASAKWASA = *KWASAKWASA* / *Flagellaria gigantea* Hook.f. (*Flagellariaceae*)

'ABU, kwalo ne'e, nonina kwaokwao'a, rauna marako ka reba ka molimoli'a go'o, takana kwao ma ka te'e ti'iti'i, nia ke bulao ana takana. Suluna meo ka di'ia 'abu, ta ne'e ki fa'asata 'uri ana. Nia ke kalia 'ai kī ma fafona logo ano.
○ Nia ke bulao fa'asia fafona asi 'uana 'i tolo.
• Kaida'i nia ma'ā nia le'a ka tasa fuana fo'ota-lana 'ania rū di'ia fofo sao kī ma ta rū bore 'ana.

'ABUI, kwalo ne'e nonina langa ka kwaokwao'a ma fa'i ai gerogero ka marako, rauna reba liu ka moli-moli'a ka marako, takana ka di'ia takana tatali, ka fungu go'o ka afumae, nia ke bulao ana fa'irū ti'iti'i kī. Nia ke bulao ke susu fāfia kula kī 'ania leforū, nia ke kalia logo 'ai kī ma ka ango logo saena ano.
○ Nia ke bulao ana kula kī sui, fa'asia fafona asi ka dao 'i tolo, ana ano 'eke'eke, saena kunu-kunu'a, saena ano to'o. Bore ma noa'a kesi 'oro liu go'o.
• Ki fi'iri 'ania kwalona.
• Ki gura 'ania ma'e māla kī.

'ABE, kwalo ne'e nonina ka kasirū'anga ka borabora'a, rauna te'e reba ka ketaketa'a, fa'irū ti'iti'i go'o. Nia kalia 'ai kī.
○ Nia ke bulao go'o saena to'ona'oa, nia kesi 'oro liu go'o bore ma to'o ta'i kula nia ke bulao ke 'oro liu.
• Nonina kwalo ne'e ngasi liu, ta ne'e ki efoa fuana saunga'ilana dadalo. Ki sikilia kasirū kī, ki aea ta'eta'ena fuana rebarū sisili'a kī, ki do'ofia, ki fi'i koria, ki fa'alangā, ka sui ki dalofia. Dadalona nia ti'iti'i ma ka ngasi liu, lisilana ka kwaokwao'a, nia ka bolo fa'inia usufilana maga mani kī ma kwa'ilana furai kī. Ki dalofia logo fuana dadalona basi ma saunga'ilana rū di'ia fo'osae.
• Ki saunga'inia logo 'ania gwarosangisangi, ki karasia kwalona, ki ngalia 'abana fuiri, ki fa'alanga ka sui, ki fi'i atongia 'ania bunabuna noima dilo, ki alua ke langalanga la'u, ki fi'i faosia 'ania gwarosangisangi kī.

MAEMAE, kwalo ne'e nonina ti'iti'i go'o ka bala-bala'a, rauna ti'iti'i go'o ka di'ia kwalo oli. Di'ia nia ango kwau nia ke 'akofolo tofungana, gwangorū ke mauri la'u ana ta bali, ta ne'e ki fa'asta 'uri ana.
○ Nia ke bulao saena masu'u ana kula kī ta'ifau, fa'asia fafona asi ka dao 'i tolo.
• Noa'a kisi sasia go'o 'ania ta rū.

BLOOD, this vine's body is whiteish, its leaf is green and wide and rounded, its flower is white and quite small and it grows from its flower. Its sap is red like blood, that's why we name it thus. It winds round trees and also on the ground.
○ It grows from on the sea to the inland.
• When fresh it is especially good for lashing things, like sago (leaf) bundles and anything else.
'ABU = BLOOD

CONVOLVULUS, this vine's dry body is whiteish but the tender one is green, its leaf is very wide, rounded and green, its flower is like hibiscus (*talali*) flower, it bears and then dies off and grows from small fruits. It grows to cover places with a thicket, it also winds round trees and creeps on the ground.
○ It grows in all places, from on the sea to the inland, on dry ground, on swamp and on proper ground. But it is not very plentiful.

• We bind with its vine.
• We cure wounds with it.
'ABUI = CONVOLVULUS / morning glory / *Ipomoea illustris* (Clarke) Prain / *Merremia bracteata* P. Bacon / *Merremia peltata* (L.) Merr. (*Convolvulaceae*)

ANODENDRON, this vine's body is in sections and is purplish, its leaf is quite wide and longish and its fruit is just small. It winds round trees.
○ It just grows in the lowland, it is not very plentiful but has places where it grows very plentifully.
• The body of the vine is very strong, so we select it for making twine. We cut off sections and peel the skin for narrow strips, we burn it and then scrape it and sun it, then we twine it. Its twine is small and very strong, it looks whiteish and it is suitable for threading shell-money beads and making nets. We also twine it for bow string and making things like (men's) girdles.
• We also make it into ring-patterns (armbands), we scrape the vine, take the strip and sun it then we stain it with *bunabuna* (*Cyclosorus*) or dye (*dilo* / *Morinda*), we lay it to dry again and then plait it into ring-patterns.
'ABE = ANONDENDRON / *Anodendron paniculatum* (Roxb.) DC. (*Apocynaceae*)

DIE, this vine's body is small and paleish, its leaf is small like return vine (*oli* / *Ipomoea*). As it creeps it withers in the middle and the leaf-shoot is alive again at the side, that's why we name it thus.
○ It grows in the forest in all places, from on the sea to the inland.
• We don't do anything with it.
MAEMAE = DIE

'AFAAFAFOLA, ta sata A'AFOLA, kwalo ne'e nonina meomeo'anga, rauna nunura ka baba'ula ka marako, takana kwao, nia ke bulao go'o ana takana. Nia ke kalia 'ai kī. Nia to'o ana rō malita'irū kī. AFAAFOLA NGWANE rauna moli-molia ka doe. AFAAFOLA KINI rauna ketaketa'a.

○ Nia ke bulao go'o sulia one ma 'i fafona asi, nia kesi 'oro liu go'o.
● Ki laungi 'ania takana, nia le'a fuana laungilana 'ania ngwa'i, nini'ari ki laungia logo 'ania luma.

OLI, kwalo ne'e nia ke kali 'i ano ma kula kī sui, rauna kesi reba liu go'o ka te'e molimoli'a go'o, takana ti'iti'i go'o ma nia to'o go'o ana fa'irū ti'iti'i kī, nia ke bulao ana fa'irū kī.

○ Nia ke bulao ke 'oro liu mala ana kula kī sui, ka tasa ana fuli fanoa kī ma raku faolu kī.
● 'I na'o ma'i, di'ia ki saeta'a ma ki saungia ta ma'e fanoa, ta ngwae kasi mauri na'a, ta'ifili ana go'o gwa'i fau kī ke teo ma kwalo oli ka la'u na'a fafia fuila fanoa fuiri. Nia funi'a ka tasa liu mika fa'asatā kwalo oli 'unari.
● Ki gurā 'ania kui rakana bonobono.

INA, kwalo ne'e ango go'o 'i ano, kwalana marako, rauna ka reba ka ketaketa'a.

○ Nia ke bulao ana kula kī ta'ifau fa'asia fafona asi ka dao 'i tolo, saena raku faolu go'o, saena dukwasi ma kunukunu'a ne'e noa'a.
● Gwangona ne'e tatabu kwasi, ki dodoa ma lulunga ma kukia fuana 'anilana.

SUSURU, kwalo ne'e ke kalia 'ai kī, kwalona gwā, rauna matanga'a, karangia ka di'ia rauna sata bore ma nia marako.

○ Nia ke bulao ana ta kula bore 'ana, fuila 'ai fura kī.
● Ki to'ea fa'i kwalo 'ania 'abarū kī fuana saunga'irū'anga, noa'a kesi dafofia go'o. Ki saunga'inia 'ania obi ma 'abagwaro ne'e gwā, ki to'o tala'irū'anga 'ania maga mani kwao ma maga mani gwā kī. Na gwa'isusuru, 'abarū ne'e fuana laungilana 'afe kaida'i 'i na'o, ki faosia 'abakwalo ma ki usu'ia maga mani kwao kī 'i safitana.

IPOMOEA, this vine's body is reddish, its leaf is shiny and thick and green, its flower is white and it grows from its flower. It winds round trees. It has two kinds. MALE IPOMOEA, its leaf is rounded and big. FEMALE IPOMOEA, its leaf is longish.

○ It just grows along the sand and on the sea, it is not very plentiful.
● We decorate with its flower, it is good for decorating bags with, and at present we also decorate the house with it.
AFAAFAFOLA = IPOMOEA / *Ipomoea pes-caprae* ssp. *brasiliensis* (L.) R.Br. (*Convolvulaceae*)

RETURN, this vine winds on the ground and all places, its leaf is not very wide and quite rounded, its flower is small and it has small fruits, it grows from its fruits.

○ It grows very plentifully indeed in all places, especially on village sites and new shoots.
● Formerly, if we were angry and killed a home, no-one was left alive, stones alone remained and vine (not people) returned again to cover the site of the home. It was especially because of this that we name return vine thus.
● We cure a dog with a blocked nose with it.
OLI = RETURN / *Ipomoea accuminater* (Vahl) R.&J. / *I. congester* R.Br. / *I. learii* Stevens (*Convolvulaceae*)

OPERCULINA, this vine just creeps on the ground, its vine is green, its leaf is wide and longish.

○ It grows in all places from on the sea to the inland, just in new shoots, not in wilderness or swamp.
● Its leaf-shoot is a wild vegetable, we flask-cook it and parcel-cook it to eat.
INA = OPERCULINA / *Operculina turpethum* (L.) S.Manso (*Convolvulaceae*)

SUSURU, this vine winds round trees, its vine is black, its leaf is divided and almost like lygodium leaf (*sata*) but it is green.

○ It grows in any place at all, on the sites of rotten trees.
● We pare the vine into strips for making things, we don't twine it. We make (arm) bands and pattern-rings (armbands) which are black and have rows of white and black shell-money beads. A *susuru*-belt is a strip for decorating a married woman in former times, we plait (twine) the vine-strip and thread white money beads among it.
SUSURU = *SUSURU* / *Ficus tinctoria* Forst.f. (*Moraceae*)

ADI'O, kwalo ne'e nonina gwagwā'anga ma nonina fa'irū funia sau ana fa'i kwalo doe kī nonini melamela'a, rauna ti'iti'i go'o ma ni'i ka sau ana te'e kakirū. Takana kwao ka ti'iti'i go'o, fa'irū kī ti'iti'i go'o. Nia ke kali sulia 'ai ki.
- Nia ke bulao ana to'ona'oa ana kula kī ta'ifau, nia kesi 'oro liu go'o.
- Ki firi 'ania kwalona, nia le'a ka tasa fuana fo'otalana fofo 'i rū, sulia nia 'alata'a noa'a kesi didilia, nia kesi langalanga bore ki fi'iri go'o 'aka 'ania.
- Di'ia ki ogā itolana rū le'a kī, ki aea ta'eta'ena, ki saunga'i rū 'ania sa'esa'erū, ki susu'ia 'ania tala'au fuana ūfilani, ki susu'ia 'ania kafa, ki bulasia 'ania fo'osae kī, kī obia logo 'ania kauala fuana loi ngali'a.

- Ki rara'o logo 'ania.

GWARI, kwalo ne'e kali sulia 'ai kī, nonina mela, rauna ka molimoli'a, takana ka kwao, fuana ka marako, nia bulao ana fuana.
- Nia ke bulao ana raku buru.
- Ki fi'iri 'ania ta rū bore 'ana di'ia foforū kī, bore ma noa'a nia kisi itoa 'ania luma sulia nia ke fura 'ali'ali.

ONGAONGA, kwalo ne'e nia gwā ma sūla bore ka gwā logo.
- Nia ke bulao fa'asia fafona asi 'uana 'i tolo.
- Ki faosia 'ania sangesange ne'e ki gwaro 'ania 'adi ma taketake niu, ki faosia logo 'ania 'aba obi fuana saunga'ilana fo'osae.

GOGOLOME, ta sata KOKOLOME, kwalo ne'e ka ango go'o saena ano, nia kesi kali sulia 'ai kī. Rauna keta ka marako, nia ke fungu 'ania fa'irū ti'iti'i meo kī, nia ke bulao ana fuana.
- Nia ke bulao saena to'ona'oa ma saena logo tolo.
- Ki afua 'ania ī'a ma denge saena kafo. Ki 'inia rauna ki diua ki fi'i danga 'ania saena kafo fuana afulana ī'a.

'ADI'O, this vine's body is blackish and the body of those which emerge from the big vine, the body is brownish, its leaf is small and they emerge from a little stalk. Its flower is white and small and its fruit is small. It winds along trees.
- It grows in the lowland in all places, it is not very plentiful.
- We bind with the vine, it is especially good for lashing bundles, because it grips and won't slip and even if it is not dry we bind with it.

- If we want to tie good things with it, we peel the skin and make things with the inner part, we secure bamboo-rows (panpipes) for blowing, we secure combs with it, we wind it round (men's) girdles and ring pole-hooks with it for picking nuts.
- We also make string-figures with it.

'ADI'O = 'ADI'O / *Cayratia japonica* (Thunb.) Gagnep. / *C. trifolia* (L.) Domin. / *Tetrastigma gilgianum* Ltb. (*Vitaceae*)

TETRASTIGMA, this vine winds round trees, its body is brown, its leaf is rounded, its flower is white, its fruit is green and it grows from its fruit.
- It grows in the new shoots.
- We bind anything with it as bundles, but we don't tie houses with it because it rots quickly.

GWARI = TETRASTIGMA / *Tetrastigma* sp. (*Vitaceae*)

ONGAONGA, this vine is black and even its sap is black.
- It grows from on the sea to the inland.
- We plait armbands from it which we pattern (embroider) with orchid ('adi) and coconut cuticle, and we also plait strips of band (obi / *Calamus*) with it for making (men's) girdles.

ONGAONGA = ONGAONGA

GEOPHILA, this vine just creeps on the ground, it doesn't wind round trees. Its leaf is long and green, it bears small round fruits and it grows from its fruit.
- It grows in the lowland and also in the inland.

- We dope fish and eels with it in the waters. We pick its leaf and hammer it and then drop it into the water to dope the fish.

GOGOLOME / *KOKOLOME* = GEOPHILA / *Geophila repens* (L.) Johnst. / *Geophila* sp. (*Rubiaceae*)

BABĀ, kwalo ne'e ke ango sulia ano, ti kaida'i nia ke ra'efia 'ai ki, nonina maramarako'a, rauna ka keta ka matanga'a.
- Nia ke bulao ana kula kī ta'ifau.
- Kula ne'e rau le'a ni'i ato ana, ki gwa'abi 'ania rauna babā.
- Ki gurā 'ania ba'eko tolo ne'e ke ale kia.

KWALO 'AFI'O, nonina kwaokwao'a, ka kalia 'ai kī, rauna ka reba ka ketaketa'a. Nia ka fungu 'ania fa'irū molimoli'a kī, ni'i di'ia logo 'afi'o bore ma fuana kwalo 'afi'o nia ti'iti'i go'o ma nia te'e 'afae.
- Nia ka bulao ana kula kī ta'ifau.
- Ki 'ania fa'irū kī.

KWALO ROTO, nonina gwagwā'a ka doe, rauna marako ka te'e molimoli'a, takana kwao, fa'irū kī bābābā'a go'o ka molimoli'a ka gwagwā ka nunura liu.
- Nia ke bulao saena to'ona'oa ma tolo logo, nia ke kalia 'ai kī.
- Na ngwangwa ngwarimadeko nia ke fanga saena kwalona, ka bubuta, ki tufua fuana 'anilana.
- Fa'irū kī, ngela kī ke masa 'ania, kira ke gelosia.

KAULATA, kwalo ne'e ka doe dangalu ana kwalo kī ta'ifau, nonina kwaokwao'a, ka ketaketa ka te'e reba, nia kali sulia 'ai kī.
- Nia ke bulao saena dukwasi, saena to'ona'oa, ka 'oro saena tolo.
- Saena fa'i kwalo nia kafo'a fuana kwa'ufilana, ki tufu 'uana di'ia ki leka ana kula noa'a ta kafo ana.
- Na fa'irū du'a kī ni'i le'a liu fuana so'i sulia nia du'a dangi.
- Ki 'ui 'o'a logo 'ania abala 'i rū ki sulia nia ngwafeafea.

BABĀ, this vine creeps on the ground, sometimes it climbs trees, its body is greenish, its leaf is long and divided.
- It grows in all places.
- In places where good leaf is hard to get, we oven-cook with *babā* leaf.
- We cure with it when an inland menace (poisonous snake) bites us.

BABĀ = *BABĀ*

APPLE VINE, its body is whiteish, it winds round trees, its leaf is wide and longish. It bears rounded fruits, they are like apple (*'afi'o* / *Eugenia*) but apple vine fruit is just small and rather bitter.
- It grows in all places.
- We eat the fruit.

KWALO 'AFI'O = APPLE VINE / *Medinilla anisophylla* Merr.& Perry / *M. halogeton* S. Moore / *M. mortonii* Hemsl./ *M. quadrilfolia* Bl./ *M. rubescens* Merr.& Perry / *M. vagans* Merr.& Perry (*Melastomataceae*)

ENTADA VINE, this vine's body is blackish and big, its leaf is green and quite rounded, its flower is white, its fruits are flat, rounded, blackish and very shiny.
- It grows in the lowlands and also in the inland, it winds round trees.
- The *ngwarimadeko* grub eats inside the stem, it swells up and we chop them out for eating.
- The fruit, children play with them, they roll them.

KWALO ROTO = ENTADA VINE / *Entada phaseoloides* (L.) Merr / *Entada scandens* Benth. (*Mimosaceae*)

UNCARIA, this vine is absolutely the biggest of all vines, its body is whiteish, longish and quite wide and it winds round trees.
- It grows in wilderness, in the lowland and is plentiful in the inland.
- Inside the vine is water for drinking, we chop to get it if we go to a place where there is no water.
- The dry lengths are very good for fuel because they burn till day.
- We beat gongs with a length of it because it is flexible.

KAULATA = UNCARIA / *Uncaria appendiculata* Benth. ssp. *glabrescens* / *U. longiflora* (Poir.) Merr. ssp. *longiflora* / *U. nervosa* Elmer ssp. *valetoniana* / *U. orientalis* Guill. (*Rubiaceae*)

UKA, kwalo ne'e nonina kwaokwao'a, rauna ka ti'iti'i ka keta, ilina ra'irū kī ka kwao, saena ka marako.

○   Nia ke bulao saena tolo ma saena gwa'i kwaru ki. Ki fasia logo.

•   Ki uka 'ania kafo fuana ī'a ma dolo ke mae, kī losia 'i gwauna kafo, go'o sūla ka saungia ī'a kī ma dolo kī ma ti rū la'u.

A'ATA, kwalo ne'e nonina ka te'e kwao-kwao'anga, rauna ka molimoli'a ka te'e dokodoko ma ka marako. Takana kwao ka magamaga'a, na takana go'o ne'e ke alua bibirū kī.

○   Nia ke bulao go'o 'i fafona asi ma saena kabara, saena to'ona'oa nia ke bulao go'o ana kula kunukunu'a, nia kesi bulao saena tolo. Nia ke bulao ka 'oro liu ma ka tasa ana ti kula.

•   Kwalana le'a ka tasa fuana firi'a noima ito'a sulia nia ngasi liu. Ki ito rū 'ania ma ki fo'ota rū 'ania, di'ia kaida'i ana kwa'isao'anga ki fo'ota 'ania fofo sao kī. Ki saunga'inia logo 'ania kabileta kī fuana ra'e'ai'anga. Ki rao 'ania ana 'afutana fa'i kwalo ne'e bore ma di'ia fa'i ai doe sali ki sisia fuana ito'a.

•   Suluna 'afae, ki diua kwalona ki afua logo 'ania 'ego'egora kī 'uana ī'a, ka di'ia logo uka.

•   Ki gurā logo 'ania ti mata'inga.

'OFA, ki saea logo 'ania ANGOANGO, fa'i kwalo ne'e ke ango sulia 'ai kī, nonina maramarako'a, rauna ka reba ka molimoli'a, nia ke fungu logo 'ania fa'irū kī.

○   Nia ke bulao ana kula kī ta'ifau, fa'asia fāfona asi ka dao'i tolo, te'e saena kunu ne'e noa'a. 'Ofa to'o ana malita'i rū to'oto'o kī:

OFA to'o, ki fasia logo 'i 'aena fa'i 'ai du'a ne'e ū saena o'olā faolu ma nonina logo fanoa kī, go'o nia ke bulao rū fuana tae raku faolu ka buru ka doe fafia, nia ke bulao olisirū'a. Nia bulao kwasila'a logo saena dukwasi, ana ano to'o noima ana kula ano to'onga kī saena to'ona'oa.

•   Ki damia fa'inia 'agiru, ki 'ania rauna ma fa'ina ma ta'eta'ena bore na suli karikari kī. Damilana to'o ka meo liu.

•   Nia le'a logo fuana guralana ti mata'inga.

•   Rauna fuana logo 'ilulana 'ania kini. Ngwae ke lalia 'aba 'ofa ke fi'i kwatea fuana ngela kini 'i ne'e nia ke damia mala ka burasia manatana kini 'i ke ogā.

DERRIS, this vine's body is whiteish, its leaf is small and long, the back of the leaves are white and the fronts are green.

○   It grows in the inland and on rocks. We also plant it.

•   We derris the water with it for fish and eels to die, we squeeze it out at the head of the water and then the juice kills the fish and eels and other things.

UKA = DERRIS / *Derris* sp. (*Fabaceae*)

A'ATA, this vine's body is quite whiteish, its leaf is rounded and quite short and green. Its flower is white and has seeds and the flower produces baby ones.

○   It just grows on the sea and in the stilt-roots, in the lowland it just grows in swampy places, it doesn't grow in the inland. It grows especially plentifully in some places.

•   Its vine is especially good for binding and tying because it is very strong. We tie things with it and lash things with it, as when cutting sago (leaf) we lash bundles of sago (leaf) with it. We also make footstraps with it for tree climbing. We work with the whole vine but if it is a big one we may split it for tying.

•   Its sap is bitter, we hammer its vine and dope tidal pools with it for fish, like derris (*uka*).

•   We also cure sicknesses with it.

A'ATA = A'ATA / three-leaved sea derris / *Derris heterophylla* (Willd.) Bakh. / *D. elegens* Benth (*Fabaceae*)

PEPPER, also called CREEPER, this vine creeps along trees, its body is greenish, its leaf is wide and roundish, and it also bears fruits.

○   It grows in all places, from on the sea to the inland, only not in swamp.
Pepper has separate kinds:

PEPPER proper, we plant it at the foot of burned trees which stand in new gardens and also round homes, then it grows and however big and thick the new shoots, it will revert (to the wild). It also grows wild in the wilderness, on proper ground or areas of proper ground in the lowland.

•   We chew it with betel (*'agiru / Areca*), we eat its leaf and fruit and skin and even the stem. In chewing it gets very red.

•   It is also good for curing sicknesses.

•   Its leaf is also for attracting women. A man will invoke a pepper leaf and then give it to a girl so when she chews it, it afflicts the girl's mind to want him.

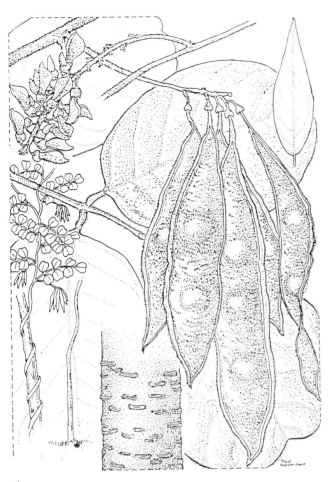

▲ *uka / derris*

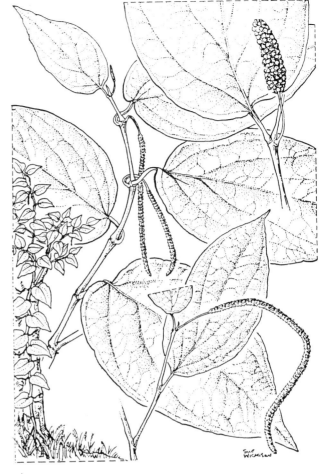

▲ *ofa / pepper*

'OFA LALAMUA, malinga'ilana nia di'ia 'ofa to'o bore ma nia kwanga lala sulia nonina ma rauna nia meo kwalakwala'a ma nia kesi fungu.

• Ki damia fa'inia 'agiru, nia le'a liu sulia damilana te'e gwari. Nia ka bulao kwasila'a ma ki fasia logo, 'anilana ma mokofana bolo go'o 'ana. Damilana 'ofa lalamua noa'a kesi to'o liu noima kesi meo liu go'o. Di'ia ngwae damia ma ka meo liu na'a ta ma ki saea lalamua ke ba'a saungia na'a, nia'a fu ki fa'asata sulia.

'OFA 'ABU, malinga'ilana nia di'ia ofa to'o bore ma īla ra'irū kī lia 'abu'abura'a noima nia meo kwalakwala. Bulaolana nia di'ia logo 'ofa to'o bore ma rū kwasi lala. Noa'a kisi damia fa'inia 'agiru, sulia di'ia ngwae ke 'ania suli doe sa ilina ke fī liu mala. Noa'a kisi sasia go'o 'ania ta rū.

ENEMY PEPPER, this kind is like pepper proper but it is pretty because its body and leaf is light red and it doesn't bear fruit.

• We chew it with betel, it is very good because it is quite cool to eat. It grows wild and we also plant it, but to eat and smell it is the same. To chew, enemy pepper is not very normal or very red. If a person chews and it becomes very red, then we say an enemy will later kill him, which is what we name it after.

BLOOD PEPPER, this kind is like pepper proper but the back of the leaf looks bloody or light red. It grows like pepper proper but is wild. We don't chew it with betel because if a person eats it the big bone in his back will become very sore. We don't do anything with it.

'OFA KWASI, malinga'ilana di'ia 'ofa to'o, bulaolana nia di'ia logo 'ofa to'o, bore ma nia kwasila'a. Noa'a kisi sasia go'o 'ania ta rū.

'OFA DIO, ti sata 'OFA 'ODOFEO TUKU, malinga'ilana ne'e nia mamata logo fa'asia 'ofa 'inoto'a kī, rauna doe ka reba ana 'ofa kī.

○ Rū kwasi lala, bulaolana nia mamata logo fa'asia 'ofa to'o, nia ke angoango go'o 'i ano.
• 'Anilana fa'inia 'agiru ta'a liu ma ki moata'inia sulia nia moko ta'a, ma 'anilana ka gwari liu na'a.
• Ki sae 'inoto'a ana si ne'e ki gura 'ania mata'inga ne'e ki saea 'ania lagasia noima tuku, nia ne'e ki fa'asatā 'uri ana.

FAUDUMU, kwalo ne'e nonina meomeo'a, rauna ka rebareba'a.
○ Nia ke bulao ana kula kī ta'ifau.
• Ki fi'iri rū 'ania, di'ia fofo sao kī, fofo 'ai kī, ma ta rū go'o 'ana ne'e fuana fi'irilana. Fa'i kwalo doe ki gasia 'ania ro 'abarū kī fuana fi'iri'anga.
• Ki gurā 'ania ti mata'inga.

'ARI'ARI, kwalo ne'e kalia 'ai kī, nonina marako, rauna ka sisili'a ka keta.
○ Nia ke bulao ana kula ki sui.
• Ki firi 'ania fa'irū kī. Ki sisia 'ari'ari di'ia kalitau bore ma na rō afurū'anga go'o ne'e bolo fa'inia ki firi 'ania. Bore ma kisi aea saena 'aba rū ma kisi firi 'ania ta'eta'e rū. Ki rao 'ania fuana fo'otalana fofo sao kī ma fofo 'ai kī ma fofo ka'o kī ma ti rū la'u.

BULA, kwalo ne'e fa'irū kesi doe liu go'o, nonina kwaokwao'anga, takana sakosako'a ka moko le'a.

○ Nia ke bulao go'o 'ana ana 'ai doe kī ana ta kula bore 'ana.
• Ki lulua fuana laungi'anga 'ania. Kaida'i takana ke 'asi ki usu'ia sulia 'aba kwalo ka sui ki fa'ā 'i luaka 'i ke lia kwanga ma ke moko le'a. Ngwae kī ke saunga'inia fuana kini, kwate nia ke manata ma ka angi ke leka ma'i fuana.

WILD PEPPER, this kind is like pepper proper, it grows like pepper proper, but it is wild. We don't do anything with it.
'OFA = PEPPER / betel pepper / *Piper betel* L.

DIO PEPPER, also named *'ODOFEO* RHEUMATISM PEPPER, is a different kind from the important peppers, its leaf is bigger and wider than other peppers.
○ It is wild and it grows differently from pepper proper, it just creeps on the ground.
• To eat with betel it is very bad and we vomit it up because it smells bad, and it is very cool to eat.
• We call it important since we cure the sickness called arthritis or rheumatism with it, that is why we name it thus.
'OFA DIO / 'OFA 'ODOFEO / TUKU = DIO PEPPER / *'ODOFEO* / RHEUMATISM PEPPER / *Piper bosnicanum* C.DC / *P. sclerophloeum* C.DC. var. scandens (*Piperaceae*)

CLEMATIS, this vine's body is reddish, its leaf is wideish.
○ It grows in all places.
• We bind things with it, like bundles of sago (leaf) and anything that we want to tie. The big vines we tear into two strips for binding.
• We also cure sicknesses with it.
FAUDUMU = CLEMATIS / *Clematis smilacifolia* Wall. (*Ranunculaceae*)

FREYCINETIA, this vine winds round trees, its body is green, its leaf is narrow and long.
○ It grows in all places.
• We bind with lengths of it. We split freycinetia like winds-far but only into two pieces suitable for binding with. But we peel off the inside of the strips and don't bind with the skin. We use it for lashing bundles of sago (leaf) and wood and bamboo and other things.
'ARI'ARI = FREYCINETIA / *Freycinetia* sp. (more than 20 ssp.) (*Pandanaceae*)

FAGRAEA, this vine's lengths are very big, its body is whiteish, its flower is yellow and smells good.
○ It just grows on big trees in any place at all.

• We seek it out for decorating with. When the flowers fall we thread them on a vine-strip and then we hang them on the neck to look pretty and smell good. Men make it for a woman, to make her think and cry and come for him.
BULA = FAGRAEA / *Fagraea berteriana* Benth. / *F. ceilanica* Thunb. / *F. salomonensis* Gilg. & Benth. (*Potaliaceae*)

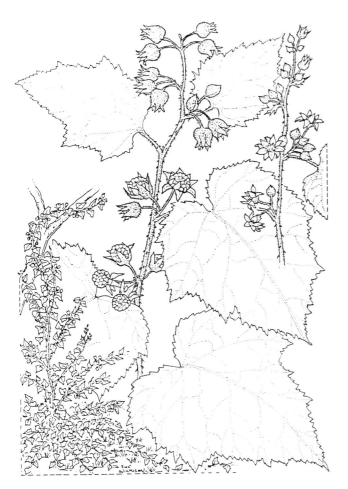

▲ *farakau / raspberry*

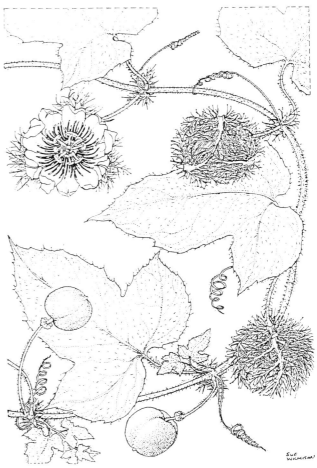

▲ *kwalo kakali / hornstedtia vine*

FARAKAU, kwalo ne'e ke kalia 'ai kī, nonina ngarangara'a ka melamela'anga, rauna marako, nia ke fungu 'ania fa'irū meo kī, lisilana ka di'ia fa'i 'afi'o kī. Nia ke bulao ana fa'irū kī.
○   Nia ke bulao ana raku faolu, nia 'oro saena tolo.
●   Ki fisua go'o fa'irū kī fuana 'anilani, 'anilani asila liu.

KWALO KAKALI, kwalo ne'e ke kali ana 'ai kī. Fa'i kwalo fi'i doe kī ifuifu'a, ilina ra'irū kī bore te'e ifuifu'a logo. Na fa'i kwalo langa kī kwaokwao-'anga. Nia ke fungu, di'ia fa'irū kwasa ni'i saksako'a, ofiofirū ifula nia buta fafia, saena ka to'o ana magarū ti'iti'i 'oro kī, lisilani di'ia magarū saena fingi kakali saga kī.
○   Nia ka bulao saena raku buru kī.
●   Ki 'ania fa'irū kī, 'anilani asila liu ma ki 'ania go'o no kisi do'ofia.
●   Ki fi'iri logo 'ania fa'i kwalo langa kī.

RASPBERRY, this vine winds round trees, its body is prickly and brownish, its leaf is green, it bears red fruit looking like apples (*'afi'o / Eugenia*). It grows from its fruit.
○   It grows in the new shoots, it is plentiful in the inland.
●   We pluck the fruits to eat, they are very sweet to eat.
FARAKAU = RASPBERRY / *Rubus moluccanus* L. (*Rosaceae*)

HORNSTEDTIA VINE, this vine winds round trees. The part-grown vine is hairy and even the backs of the leaves are a bit hairy too. The dried-out vine is whiteish. It bears and when the fruit is ripe it is yellow, a hairy casing wraps it and inside it has many small seeds, they look like the seeds in a bunch of hornstedtia proper (*kakali*).
○   It grows in the dense shoots.
●   We eat the fruits, they are very sweet to eat and we just eat them, we don't burn them.
●   We also bind with the dried out vines.
KWALO KAKALI = HORNSTEDTIA VINE / wild passion fruit / stinking passionflower / *Passiflora foetida* L. (*Passifloraceae*)

RĀRĀ TOLO, kwalo ne'e ke kalikalia 'ai kī, nonina marako, rauna ka keta ka sisili'a.
- Nia ke bulao ka tasa 'i fafona asi, saena to'ona'oa ma saena logo tolo, saena dukwasi go'o, ne'e noa'a saena raku faolu.
- Kwalona ki itoa 'ania luma, ki rao 'ania di'ia logo kalitau, ki rokisia 'ania kalitau di'ia nia 'oro ka liufia kalitau nonina fanoa.
- Ki 'ania gwa'irū kī, ki sufusufu'i ma ki lulunga'i logo, ki lofa fuani.

KWALO UFUUFU, kwalo ne'e nonina kwao-kwao'a ka ti'iti'i go'o, rauna sisilia ka marako.
- Nia ke ango go'o 'i ano, saena to'ona'oa ma tolo logo.
- Ngela ki ke totofia kwalona ka di'ia ufu, ta ne'e ki fa'asata 'uri ana.

KWALO'AI, kwalo ne'e doe liu, nonina kwaokwao'a ka doe karangia ka di'i fa'i 'ai, tufulana ka ngasi liu, ta ne'e ki fa'asata 'uri ana.
- Nia ke ra'e sulia 'ai doe liu kī, ka liufia kwalo kī ta'ifau.
- Noa'a kisi sasia 'ania ta rū.

LOCAL RĀRĀ, this vine winds round trees, its body is green, its leaf is long and narrow.
- It grows especially on the sea, in the lowland and also in the inland, just in wilderness, not in new shoots.
- Its vine we tie houses with, we use it like winds-far and exchange it for winds-far if it is more plentiful than winds-far in the home area.
- We eat the crowns, we stew them and parcel-cook them and make cream for them.
RĀRĀ TOLO = LOCAL RĀRĀ / *Stenochlaena laurifolia* Presl (*Blechnaceae*)

SUGAR VINE, this vine's body is whiteish and small, its leaf is narrow and green.
- It just creeps on the ground, in the lowland and also in the inland.
- Children suck the vine like sugar(cane), that's why we name it thus.
KWALO UFUUFU = SUGAR VINE

TREE-VINE, this vine is very big, its body is whiteish and almost as big as a tree, it is very hard to cut, that's why we name it thus.
- It climbs up very big trees, more than all other vines.
- We don't do anything with it.
KWALO'AI = TREE-VINE / *Connarus pickeringii* A. Gray / *C. salomonensis* Schellenb. / *C. semidecandrus* Jack (*Connaraceae*) / *Erycibe aff. floribunda* Pilger (*Convolvulaceae*) / *Loesneriella macrantha* (Korth.) A.C.Smith / *Salacia chinensis* L. / *S. erythroparca* Schum. / *S. forsteniana* Miq. / *S. Parkinsonii* Schum. / *S. sororia* Miq. (*Celastraceae*) / *Lophopyxis maingayi* Hook. f. / *Polyporandra scadens* Becc.(*Icacinaceae*) / *Smythea lanceata* (Tul.) Summerh. (*Rhamnaceae*) / *Strychnos colubrina* L. / *S. aff ledermannii* Gilg.&Benn. / *S. minor* dennst. (*Loganiaceae*)

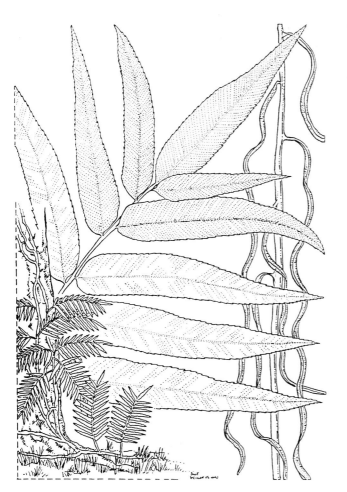

◀ *rārā tolo / local* rārā

LOLOSI ne'e ta kwalo,, rauna te'e keta ka 'iri reba liu go'o, takana kwao ka ti'iti'i go'o, nia to'o logo ana fa'irū ti'iti'i kī. Ki fa'asatā logo ania KALIALO sulia fa'i kwalo ne'e ke kalia alo kī. Nia ke bulao ana fa'irū kī.
○ Rū ne'e fi'i dao go'o ma'i 'i Malaita fa'asia bubunga mamata kī. Nia ke bulao go'o saena raku faolu, ana kula kī sui, ke 'oro liu ana busubusurū kī.
• Nia le'a ka tasa fuana guralana mata'inga kī, di'ia ki tufukia ki 'inia rauna, ki ranangia, ki 'asa'asangā ki losia saena ma'e māla 'i ke mafo.

RA'UKWALO, nonina kwaokwao'a, rauna ka ketaketa'a.
○ Nia ke bulao saena to'ona'oa ma fafo'i asi kī.
• Noa'a nia kesi ngasi ka bolo fuana firilana rū kī, ta ne'e ki saea 'ania ra'u kwalo du'ungana nia mūmūla go'o di'ia ra'i rau go'o kī
• Ki kwaigurai 'ania sulia nia bolo ma ka le'a liu fuana gura'a.

DOLO, kwalo ne'e nonina kwaokwa'a ka ngangara'a, rauna ka reba.
○ Nia ke nuku fafia 'ai kī ana kula kī ta'ifau, nia 'ato fuana ki ru'u 'i saena nukunukurū.
• Ki guragura 'ania.

DILADILA, kwalo ne'e noa'a nia kesi doe liu bore ma nia kali ka ra'e liu. Nonina melamela'a, rauna ka keta ka reba mala.
○ Nia ke bulao ana kula kī sui.
• Noa'a kisi sasia go'o 'ania ta rao'a.

SA'A, kwalo ne'e nonina kwaokwao'a, rauna ka te'e reba.
○ Nia ke kalia 'ai kī ana kula kī sui.
• Kwalona nia le'a ka ngasi fuana fi'iri'anga 'ania rū kī di'ia fofo 'i sao kī, fa'inia logo to'osi'anga ngali kī fuana ra'efilana.

DAUDAU, kwalo ne'e nonina melamela'a, rauna ka ta'i molimoli'a ka sisimia, nia to'o ana ngonga-ngongarū kī ne'e nia dau 'ania rarana 'ai kī, ta ne'e ki fa'asata 'uri ana.
○ Nia ke ke kalia 'ai kī 'i fafona asi.
• Ki guragura 'ania.

MIKANIA is a vine, its leaf is quite long and not very wide, its flower is white and small and it also has small fruits. We also name it WINDS-TARO because the vine winds round taros. It grows from its fruits.
○ This has just come to Malaita from other islands. It just grows in new shoots, in all places, it is very plentiful in thickets.

• It is especially good for curing sicknesses, if we cut ourselves we pick a leaf, we warm it, rub and squeeze it into the wound to soothe it.
LOLOSI / KALI ALO = MIKANIA / *Mikania micrantha* H.B.K (*Asteraceae*)

VINE-LEAF, its body is whiteish and its leaf is longish.
○ It grows in the lowlands and on the sea.
• It's not strong enough for tying things, that's why we call it vine-leaf, on account of it breaking like leaves.
• We cure with it because it is suitable and very good for curing.
RA'UKWALO = VINE-LEAF

CAESALPINIA, this vine's body is whiteish and prickly, its leaf is wide.
○ It canopies over trees in all places, it is difficult to enter the canopy.
• We cure with it.
DOLO = CAESALPINIA / *Caesalipina bonduc* L. Roxb. / *C. major* (Medik.) Dandy & Exell. (*Caesalpiniaceae*)

DILADILA, this vine is not very big but it winds and climbs a lot. Its body is brownish and its leaf is long and really wide.
○ It grows in all places.
• We don't have any use for it.
DILADILA = *DILADILA*

SA'A, this vine's body is whiteish, its leaf is quite wide.
○ It winds round trees in all places.
• Its vine is good and strong for binding things like sago (leaf) bundles and also for throwing onto nut trees for climbing.
SA'A = *SA'A* / *Canavalia microcarpa* (DC.) Mree. / *Oxyrhynchus papuanus* (Pulle.) Verdc. / *Pueraria phaseoloies* (Roxb.) Benth. / *Pueraria pulcherrima* (Koord.) Koord. & Schum. / *Rynchosia accuminatissima.* Miq.

HOLD-ON, this vine's body is brownish, its leaf is quite rounded, tiny and narrow, and it has tendrils which hold on to the branches of tree, that's why we name it thus.
○ It winds round trees on the sea.
• We cure with it.
DAUDAU = HOLD-ON

ALO nia fanga inoto'a ko'o kia kī 'i na'o, ka tasa ana fanga kī. Ki to'o ana alo 'oro kī, satani to'oto'o, ti ai ki saea 'ania alo ngwane kī, ti alo kini kī. Alo ngwane nia doe ka ra'e ka ūlua ka liufia mala alo kini kī. 'Anilana alo ngwane nia le'a ma ka moko le'a liu ka tasa ana alo kini kī, ti alo ngwane ni'i alo sata mala. Ta rū bore, eo kata fa'alia alo ngwane, nia ke dula. Alo kini, noa'a ni'i kasi alo sata'anga bore 'ana maurilana nia ngasingasi'a, noa'a 'iri talangwara'u fuana 'eo ke saungia ana kaida'i gwa'i mata'inga ne'e 'eo ka liu.

ALO NGWANE kī, ti malita'irū satani 'uri:
'ANIGAO, nia fi'irū'a, a'una 'oro, 'anilana le'a liu ka tasa. Alo ne'e, kaida'i ana ngwae etaeta kī ne'e kira saea 'ania Gao kī, kira salinga'ia ma'i. 'Anigao ne'e alo lalifū, ka alo 'inoto'a ma ka alo aofia. 'I na'o ma'i nia ābu fuana ki kī kesi 'ania.

LO'OSILA, nia fi'irū'a, a'una ka te'e meo kwalakwala'a, 'anilana le'a logo. Ki fa'asata 'uri ana sulia 'i na'o ta ngwae nia folia ngwa'i alo ana ta ngwae 'ania kwala sila, nia saea 'ania la'usu'u lala.

KŌNARE, nia fi'irū'a, a'una 'oro, 'anilana le'a, mokofana le'a liu. Ki salinga'inia ma'i fa'asia kula kira saea 'ania 'i Fulikōngare, saena tolo ana bali 'i sulana sina 'i Kwara'ae.

KETEKETE, nia fi'irū'a, a'una noa'a kesi 'oro,'anilana ngwara'u ma ka moko le'a.

TAKASINA, nia fi'irū'a, nonina a'u nia takasina'a, 'oni'onina ka doe ka tasa ana fi'i ketekete.

KWAKWA, nia to'o go'o ana ta'i a'u, 'oni'onina nia molimoli'a ka doe liu. Ki fa'asata 'uri ana sulia kaida'i ki kilua saena afu ano, ka teoteo ke doe safitana alo kī, noa'a ta afu ano kasi teo 'i safitana.

KWAOBULU, nia to'o go'o ana ta'i a'u, 'oni'onina nia molimoli'a ka doe liu. 'A'erū nia bulu kaida'i nia ma'a bore ma kaida'i ki du'atelea ma ki resia, nonina ke kwao.

MADAMOTA'E, nia fi'irū'a, nonina a'u nia kwaokwao'a. Kaida'i ki lafua fuana 'anilana, lisilana 'oni'onirū kī doe ka molimoli'a ka di'ia madamo fu ke ra'e ma'i.

KWAUFA, nia fi'irū'a, nonina a'u nia gwāborabora'a, 'oni'onina molimoli'a ka doe logo.

OSIMAKU, nia fi'irū'a, kaida'i ki garasia 'oni'onina, sa'erū nia marako ka kwaokwao'a. Kaida'i ki resia fuana 'anilana, mokofana ufiufima'e, 'anilana ngwagafu ka rakufa liu.

TARO was the important food of our ancestors formerly, more than other foods. We have many taros with separate names, some we call male taros and some female taros. Male taro is big and rises to stand up more than female taro. To eat, male taro is good and smells much better than female taro, and some male taros are really prime taro. However poison may damage male taro and it may rot. Female taro is not prime taro but its life is stronger, it is not easy for poison to kill it when an epidemic of poison comes along.

MALE TAROS, some kinds are named:
EAT-GAO is a clump with many stocks, it is especially good to eat. This taro, in the time of the first people who they called the Gaos, they transferred it here. Eat-Gao is a major taro, an important taro and a paramount taro. Formerly it was tabu for women to eat it.

ELBOW-OF-COIX is a clump, its stock is quite light red and it is also good to eat. We name it thus because formerly a man bought a bag of taro from a man for a vine of coix-seeds (*sila* / job's tears) and called it an elbow-length (shell-money).

KŌNARE is a clump, it has many stocks, it is good to eat and smells very good. We transferred it here from a place called Fulikōngare, in the inland to the sunset-side of Kwara'ae.

KETEKETE is a clump, it does not have many stocks, it is soft to eat and smells good.

STRIPED, the body of the stock is striped and its bottom is bigger than *ketekete*.

HOLE has just one stock, its bottom is rounded and very big. We name it thus because when we bury it in the ground and it lies and gets big among the taros, there is no ground (space) between them.

DARK-AND-WHITE has just one stock, its bottom is rounded and very big. The base is dark when it is raw, but when we roast and scrape it, its body is white.

RISING-MOON is a clump, the body of the stock is whiteish. When we lift it for eating, the bottoms look big and rounded, like the full moon coming up.

KWAUFA is a clump, the body of its stock is black-purple, its bottom is rounded and big.

OSIMAKU is a clump and when we scrape its bottom the inner part is green and whiteish. When we scrape it for eating, its smell is delicious and it is tasty and very appetising to eat.

UNU'UANA, nia to'o go'o ana ta'i a'u, 'onionina molimoli'a ka kwaokwao'a, kaida'i ki karasia nia meomeo'a, kaida'i ki 'olea sa'erū nia go'o kwao. Ki fa'asata 'uri ana sulia kaida'i ki leka ana fofori'anga, ki unu 'uana o'olā saena rodo fuana saka asi'a ana usia.

NGOLININIU, a'una te'e gwagwā'a ma 'aena ka molimoli'a, 'oni'onina ka molimoli'a bore ma ka inoi ka liufia mala alo kī, lisilana ka di'ia fūna fa'i niniu kī.

BERONUNUFI, a'una marako ma 'oni'onirū ka te'e keta.

TOLI'ANI'AENA, nia to'o go'o ana ta'i a'u, a'una gwāgwā'a, 'oni'onirū ka molimoli'a. Satana, fada 'ania ne'e kaida'i ki daroia ana fafanga'a kī ngwae daro kī kira ke kiria kabu 'i rū 'ania 'aeda.

FAKALA'IDEODEO, nia to'o go'o ana ta'i a'u, a'una sisilirū'a, 'oni'onirū ka molimoli'a ka inoi mala, ka di'ia fakalana geogeo.

'UBUNI, 'oni'onina ka molimolia ka doe ka inoi liu, 'anilana nia ngwara'u, nia noa'a la'u alo sata. Ki fasia go'o fuana folilana fuana to'a ni asi.

ALO KINI kī ni'i to'o ana ta'i a'u'anga, a'uni kwaokwao'a ma 'oni'onirū ka molimoli'a ma kesi doe liu go'o. Ti malita'i alo kini, satani 'uri:

MOMOLESAKO, 'oni'onina ka molimoli'a, noa'a kesi doe liu, sa'erū nia sakosako'a, ne'e ki saea satana 'ania.

AKALOMAMALE, ta sata MAMALA 'INOTO'A, 'oni'onina te'e keta ma a'una ka meo sisili'a. Ki saea satana 'ania sulia kaida'i kini ke fofori, uta ka to'o, ka isila nonina ka mamalea, nia saeta'a fuana alo'funi'a nia ka 'uri 'E, akalo ne'e mamale!'

MAMALA SA'OGA, ta sata SAKOSAKO, lisilana rauna bolo logo fa'inia akalomamale, te'e saena afuna sakosako lala, karangia nia di'ia logo molemolesako.

MANGIO, nonina a'una ka maramarako'a, 'oni'onina di'ia ki karasia nia ke kwao.

DAOFA'ISIRANA, nonina a'una ka maramarako'a, 'oni'onina ka ketaketa ka noa'a kesi inoi liu go'o. Ki fa'asata sulia na ngwae fuiri liu ka fanga leleka ka abusu mala ka fi'i dao ma'i 'i luma.

NGE'E, nonina a'una ka marako, 'oni'onina ka keta. Kaida'i ana dodolana 'anilana ka te'e mamale, ma 'aba kwakena nia mamale liu, noa'a ki kesi 'ania.

'USI'USI, nonina a'una ka marako, 'aena a'u ka borabora'a, 'oni'onina ka ketaketa'a. 'Anilana ka te'e mamale ka di'ia nge'e, 'aba kwakena nia mamale liu, noa'a ki kesi 'ania.

MUDIMUDI, a'una gwagwā'a, 'oni'onina te'e ketaketa'a, saena afurū lisilana midimidi'a. Ki 'ania logo 'abana. Na alo ne'e kesi 'inoto'a liu go'o.

TORCH-TO-IT has just one stock, its bottom is rounded and whiteish and when we scrape it, it is reddish, when we cut up the inside part it is just white. We name it thus because when we go to harvest it we use a torch to get to the garden in the night to go to the sea for market (at dawn).

PALM-LIKE, its stock is quite blackish and its foot is rounded, its bottom is rounded but it is more plump than other taros and it looks like the base of a palm.

BERONUNUFI, its stock is green and its bottom is quite long.

DISTRIBUTE-BY-FOOT has only one stock, its stock is blackish and its bottom is rounded. Its name means that when we distribute it at feasts the men who distribute it push portions with their feet.

MEGAPODE'S-EGG has only one stock, its stock is narrow, its bottom is rounded and really plump, it is like a megapode's egg.

'UBUNI, its bottom is rounded and big and very plump, it is soft to eat and it is not a prime taro. We just plant it to sell to the sea people.

FEMALE TAROS have only one stock, their stocks are whiteish and the bottom is rounded and not very big. Some kinds of female taro are named:

YELLOW-ROUND, its bottom is rounded, it is not very big, the inner part is yellow, which is why we call it this name.

GHOST-ITCH, another name IMPORTANT ITCH, its bottom when we scrape it is purplish. We call it this name because when a woman harvested it, rain fell and wet her body, it itched, she was angry with the taro and said 'Eh, it's a ghost itching!'

YELLOW-ITCH, another name YELLOW, its leaf is equivalent to ghost-itch, only the inside of the tuber is yellow, it is almost like yellow-round.

MANGIO, the body of the stock is greenish, the bottom if we scrape it is white.

COMES-WITH-BELLYFUL, the body of its stock is greenish, its bottom is longish and not very plump. We name it after a man who goes off and eats his fill and then comes (home) to the house.

NGE'E, the body of its stock is green and its bottom is long. When flask-cooked it is quite itchy to eat and the leaf is very itchy, we don't eat it.

'USI USI, the body of its stock is green, the foot of the stock is purplish and the bottom is longish. It is quite itchy to eat, like *nge'e*, and its leaf is very itchy, we don't eat it.

MUDIMUDI, its stock is blackish, its bottom is quite longish, the inside of tuber is mixed colours. We also eat its leaf. This taro is not very important.

○ O'ofilana alo nama ana kula ne'e bolo fa'inia, kula gwarigwari'a kī go'o, ano te'e moge go'o, ano gwā bore 'ana, ano kaole'a, ano nakinaki'a, ano sango, ma kula ano to'onga. Saena kula 'eke'eke noa'a nia kesi ūlua le'a ana, noa'a kisi kilua la'u ana ano ne'e kwaru'a ma ka rerede'a ma ka gwara ofoofo. Alo ngwane, ki kilua nama saena gwa'italafa kī, alo kini ki kilua bore ma saena langa ani kula.

• Do'ofilana alo, ki kōngia noema ki dodongia, noema 'i ta'ena ki kukia. Ki saungia logo fuana lakeno ma gwasu, ki saunga'i logo 'ania kata ma tadili.

• 'Aba kwake ani kī ki 'ania logo, nia ke ta'i mamale. Fanga nai'ari le'a fuana kaida'i ana fiolo'a. Bara alo go'o ne'e kwakena mamale liu, noa'a kisi 'ani'i.

KAKAMA, ki saea logo 'ania ALO KUNU, nia ta malita 'i alo, na kakina ka keta, rauna ka reba ka doe liu, nia ka to'o ana 'oni'onirū saena ano.

○ Nia ke bulao saena kunukunu'a kī, ki fasia logo saena kula fungu. Rū faka nini'a, kira salinga'inia ma'i fa'asia 'i 'a'e asi.

• Ki 'ania 'oni'onirū, ki tadilia ki kwa'i ti'iti'i ana ka sui ki du'afia ki 'ania ka di'ia logo alo.

• Ki gwa'abi 'ania rauna, ki safa logo 'ania ma ki afua logo 'ania buta ko'a kī.

• Ki fua logo 'ania 'aba'abarū mae kī.

FILA, ki saea logo 'ania SANGAI, ta sata EDU, lisilana ka di'ia logo alo bore ma nia ka doe ka di'ia mala fi'i kakama kī, rauna reba liu ka baba'ula. Di'ia ki liu ana ma ki tufua, di'ia nia to'o ana nonika nia ke mamale liu mala. 'Oni'onina doe ka keta liu, takana magamaga'a ka meo, na fa'irū kī fingifingi'a, nia ke bulao ana fuana. Nia to'o ana rō malita'irū kī, kera'a bolo go'o bore ma mamata'anga ne'e nonidaro'o lia mamata.

FILA FASIA, ki saea logo 'ania FILA NGWA'E-NGWA'E, rauna abana birubiru.

○ Noa'a nia kesi bulao ata go'o 'ana, ki kilu'i nama saena o'olā 'i safitana rū di'ia alo kī, nia ke teo saena raku faolu 'i burina o'olā. Di'ia ki kilua fa'irū kī nia ke bulao ke 'oro liu.

• Ki 'ania 'oni'onina, 'anilana ka di'ia logo alo. Kaida'i ki susulia, ki lia 'uana ma'erū kī ni'i kwao, ki susulia nama fa'asia 'i kesi mamale. Ki gwa'abia ma ki dodoa ma ki kukia logo.

○ Taro gardening must be in a suitable place, a damp place, quite soggy ground, whether black ground, clay ground, flinty ground, normal ground or a place with proper ground. In a dry place it won't stand up well, nor do we bury it in rocky ground or gravel ground or landslides. Male taro we have to plant on the ash patches but female taro we plant in dry (unfertilized) areas.

• To burn taro we bake it or flask-cook it or at present we boil it. We also pound it for cream-pudding and coconut-pudding and also make it into nut-pudding and cured(nut)-pudding.

• The leaf we also eat, it is quite itchy. This food is good for times of hunger. A few taros have very itchy leaves and we don't eat them.

ALO = TARO / cocoyam / *Colocasia esculenta* (L.) Schott. (*Araceae*)

CYRTOSPERMA, also called SWAMP TARO, is a kind of taro, its stalk is long, its leaf is wide and very big and it has a bottom in the ground.

○ It grows in swamps and we also plant it in full (waterlogged) places. This one is foreign, they transferred it here from overseas.

• We eat the bottom, we trim and cut it small and then burn it and eat it like taro.

• We oven-cook with the leaf, we also make a spread with it (for food etc.) and wrap parcels of scraping (mangrove pudding) in it.

• We also wrap burdens in the dead leaf.

KAKAMA = CYRTOSPERMA / SWAMP TARO / *Cyrtosperma chamissonis* (Schott.) Merr. (*Araceae*)

ALOCASIA looks like taro (*alo / Colocasia*) but it is big and really like a cyrtosperma (*kakama*) clump, its leaf is very wide and thick. If we pass by and chop it, if it touches our bodies it is really very itchy. Its bottom is big and very long, its flower has seeds and is red, its fruit is in bunches and it grows from its fruit. It has two kinds, they are similar but the difference is that their bodies look different.

PLANTED ALOCASIA, also called THRIVING ALOCASIA, its leaf-stems are close together.

○ It doesn't grow just anywhere, we have to plant it in the garden among things like taro and it remains in the new shoots after the garden. If we plant its fruit it grows very plentifully.

• We eat its bottom, it is like taro to eat. When we pare it we look for the bits which are white and pare them away so it won't be itchy. We oven-cook it, flask-cook it and also boil it.

'Anilana, ti kaida'i ti ai ke mamale di'ia ne'e nia
teo gwari, di'ia nia ta'i du'a ma'a 'ana, 'anilana
ta'i mamale logo.
- Rauna ki gwa'abi logo 'ania.
FILA KWASI, rauna abana la'ala'a.
○ Nia ke bulao ana kula kī sui, saena raku faolu
ma saena masu'u logo, fa'asia fafona asi ka dao
'i tolo.
- Fila kwasi noa'a kisi 'ania sulia nia mamale liu.

- Fingina rō fila kī ta'ifau, na kila ke 'ania, bore
ma noa'a kisi 'ania sulia 'anilana mamale liu.

- Ki gura logo 'ania ti mata'inga.

TEKO ne'e ta alo kwasi, lisilana maramarako'a
ta'ifau. Nia teo ka liufia na'a kaida'i fuana
maua'anga, rauna ka teko ma ka tengela na'a, ta
ne'e ki fa'asata 'uri ana.
○ Nia ke bulao 'i ninimana kafo kī ma ana kula
kunukunu'a kī logo.
- Sali ti ngwae ke 'ania 'abarū di'ia tatabu, bore
ma sulana mamale liu mala. Di'ia ki ogā ki
'ania, ki alua 'abana saena kokofi niu ke teo
sulia rō asoa kī fuana sulana ke 'afe, sui mala ki
fi'i do'ofia saena fa'i ka'o noema ki kukia.
- Noa'a kisi 'ania onionina sulia nia mamale liu.

BONO nia ta alo kwasi bore ma lisilana ka
matamata ana alo saga ma nia alua logo 'oni'onirū.
Rō bono kī, ta ai ne'e marako, ta ai lisilana rauna
ka di'ia alo kī.
○ Rū kwasi ne'e, noa'a kisi fasia. Nia ke bulao
go'o ana dodo'a kī saena tolo.
- 'I na'o ma'i 'afe kī ke toro 'ania rauna fuana
fonelana na'ofada ana kaida'i dokodoko ana
tua bisi'a ma tua go'o 'i bisi kale, ta ne'e ki saea
'ania bono.
- Ruana bono nai'ari, ki 'ania rauna di'ia logo
'aba kwake kī, bore ma nia mamale liu. Ki 'ania
logo gwa'i fulana. Afuna, noa'a kisi 'ania.

To eat, sometimes some are itchy if they go
cold, and if it is a bit burned and raw it is also
a bit itchy to eat.
- Its leaf we also oven-cook with.
WILD ALOCASIA, its leaf-stems are wide-spaced.
○ It grows in all places, in new shoots and also in
forest, from on the sea to the inland.

- Wild alocasia we don't eat because it is
very itchy.
- The fruit-bunches of both alocasias, *kila*-parrots
eat, but we don't eat them because they are
very itchy.
- We also cure some sickness with it.
FILA / SANGAI / EDU = ALOCASIA / giant taro / *Alocasia sp.*
FILA FASIA / FILA NGWA'ENGWA'E = PLANTED
ALOCASIA / THRIVING ALOCASIA / *Alocasia macrorrhiza*
(L.) G.Don
FILA KWASI = WILD ALOCASIA
(*Araceae*)

SHRIVEL is a wild taro, it looks greenish all over.
If it stays past the time of ripening its leaf shrivels
and stiffens, that's why we name it thus.

○ It grows besides waters and also in swampy
places.
- Maybe some people eat the leaf as a vegetable
but the juice is really very itchy. If we want to
eat it we put the leaf in a coconut-leaf basket to
lie for two days for the juice to flow away, and
after that we burn it in a bamboo or boil it.
- We don't eat its bottom because it is
very itchy.
TEKO = SHRIVEL

SHUT is a wild taro but it looks different from
taro proper and it produces a bottom. There are
two shuts, one is green, the other the leaf looks
like a taro.
○ This is wild, we don't plant it. It just grows in
gullies in the inland.
- Formerly, women would dress in the leaf to
shut off their fronts for a short time while in
menstrual seclusion and birth seclusion, that's
why we call it shut.
- The second shut, we eat the leaf like taro leaf,
but it is very itchy. We also eat its flower-
spathe. Its bottom we don't eat.
BONO = SHUT / *Homalomena alba* Hassk. / *H. cordata* Schott. /
Schismatoglottis calyptrata (Roxb.) Zoll.& Mor. (*Araceae*)

KAI nia fanga 'inoto'a ko'o kia kī, ma alo go'o ne'e tasa ana. Saena 'abafola ne'e nia ke ū fuana ti malita'irū ne'e kira bolo logo. Kai ne'e kwalarū, nia kalia 'ai ma sabangi kī, kwalana nia maramarako'a, kwalana ti ai nia borabora'a ma ti ai ka melamela'a. Rauna ti ai ti'iti'i ka molimoli'a, kaida'i nia fi'i bulao ma'i, lisilana meo, bore ma kaida'i rauna beta na'a nia marako. Takana kwao ka ti'iti'i go'o, nia kesi fungu 'ania fa'irū kī bore ma 'oni'onirū kī ke sau 'i 'aena ra'irū kī ana kwalarū ke fungu saena ano fuana 'anilana. Nia ke bulao ana afuna ma 'oni'onirū saena ano ma ki fasia logo fa'irū ne'e ke sau ana kwalarū.

- O'ofilana kai, na o'olā faolu ana kai ma fana ma arakai go'o, ki saea 'ania fa'i falisi, ma di'ia ki fasi fuli ana ta ma ki saea 'ania fa'i kukuli. Ti kaida'i ki fasi'i logo safitana alo. Kula ne'e bolo fa'inia falisi, ano bū'a ne'e noa'a kasi moge, kula ngwangwakwa'a kī, ma ti kula 'i fafona asi ne'e ano oneone'e ma afu ano fulako'a kī. Noa'a kai kesi bulao saena kunukunu'a.
- Ki susulia 'oni'onirū fuana 'anilana, rū isila nia mamalea nonika. Ki du'atelea, ki dodoa, ki gwa'abia, ki kukia logo.

Kai to'o logo ana malita'irū 'oro kī, satani to'oto'o ni'i 'uri:

KWARU'ABU, 'oni'onina molimoli'a, kaida'i ki susulia saena ta'eta'ena meo kwalakwala'a. Kwalana ka marako, rauna bore marako logo ka te'e molimoli'a ma kesi reba liu go'o.

KWARUBALA, 'oni'onina nia keta ka doe, kaida'i ki susulia saena ka kwaokwao'anga. Kwalana ka maramarako'a, rauna reba ka ketaketa'a ka marako.

LUDABAOSI, 'oni'onina nia keta liu, ka gwā ma saena ka meomeo'a, rauna ketaketa'a ka sisili'a go'o. Ki saea 'ania ludubaosi si ne'e ngwae ne'e to'ongia ma'i nia ludangia saena baosi nia fuana agota'ilana.

LULUKA nia ka fi'irū'a, lisilana fi'irū nia di'ia logo fi'i luluka kī. 'Oni'onina rebareba'a ma ka 'inoi, ka kwaokwao'anga. Rauna reba ka te'e molimoli'a.

IDUBIRU, 'oni'onina doe liu ka rebareba'a ma ka gwagwā'a. Kwalana kwaokwao'a ma rauna ka keta, ka marako. Kaida'i nia ke doe saena ano, afuna ke iku olofana biru ana falisi, ta ne'e ki fa'asata 'uri ana.

BOROSURA, 'oni'onina doe ka ta'i 'ere, ka kwaokwao'anga. Kwalana kwaokwao'a, rauna te'e molimoli'a ka marako. Kaida'i nia teo saena ano ma ka doe, afuna ka sikira'inia ma'i na afita 'i ano.

YAM is an important food of our ancestors and only taro surpasses it. In this book it stands for some kinds of things which are similar. Yam is a vine, it winds round trees and conductors (props), its vine is greenish, the vines of some are purplish and of others are brownish. The leaves of some are small and rounded and when about to grow they look red, but when the leaf is mature it is green. Its flower is white and small, it doesn't bear fruit but a bottom emerges at the foot of the leaves on the vine and bears in the ground for eating. It grows from its tuber or bottom part in the ground and we also plant fruit that emerge from the vine.

- In gardening yam, the new garden of yam and pana and *arakai* we call a yam-plot (*falisi*), and if we replant the site then we call it *kukuli*. Sometimes we plant them among taro. A place that is suitable for yams is clotting ground which is not soggy, soft and moist places and some places on the sea where the ground is sandy with silty parts. Yam won't grow in swamp.
- We pare the tuber to eat, the wet parts itch our skin. We roast it, flask-cook it and oven-cook it, and also boil it.

Yam has many kinds and their individual names are:

SCRAPE-BLOOD, its tuber is rounded and when we pare it, inside the skin is light red. Its vine is green and even its leaf is green and quite rounded and not very wide.

SCRAPE-PALE, its tuber is long and big and when we pare it, inside it is whiteish. Its vine is greenish, its leaf is wide and longish and green.

POUCH-LOAD, its tuber is very long, black and reddish inside, its leaf is longish and just narrow. We call it pouch-load as the man who got it here loaded it in his pouch to hide it.

GLEICHENIA is a clump, it looks like clumps of gleichenia (*luluka*). Its tuber is wideish and plump and whiteish. Its leaf is wide and quite rounded.

BOUNDARY-MOVER, its tuber is very big and wideish and blackish. Its vine is whiteish and its leaf is long and green. When it gets big in the ground, its tuber shifts the boundary of the yam garden from underneath, that's why we name it thus.

BOROSURA, its tuber is big and a bit curved and whiteish. Its vine is whiteish and its leaf is quite rounded and green. When it lies in the ground and is big, its tuber pushes up a mound of ground.

KAI = YAM / greater yam / *Dioscorea alata* L. (*Dioscoreaceae*)

FANA, nia di'ia logo kai bore ma nia ta'i mamata lala. Nia ka fi'irū'a, 'oni'onirū nia ketaketa'a, fi'irū ke alua mala 'oni'onirū 'oro kī. Kwalana marako ka ngarangara'a ma ka ta'i 'oro mala ana kwalana kai, rauna molimoli'a ka marako. Nia to'oa ana kwana-kwanarū kī ni'i bulao ana ifita'irū funia 'oni'onirū sau logo ana, nia to'o ana ma'e ona kī, di'ia nia ru'u saena 'aeka nia ke ubu. Fana, ngwae ne'e salinga'i ma'i, nia ngalia fa'asia 'i Gela, ma ka mero fafia bonga ana fana ne'e nia ka fasia 'i Malaita.

Fana nia to'o ana rō malita'irū kī, ta'i ne'e ki saea 'ania FANA LUSU, afuna ka doe nia kasi keta liu go'o, FANA KWALO, afuna doe ka keta ka liufia mala fana lusu.

○ Ki fasia 'ania fa'irū kī ne'e ki saea 'ania falisi.
• Ki 'ania 'oni'onirū ka di'ia logo kai.

SAULU nia ta kai ne'e kwasi, nia matamata fa'asia kai fasia sulia kwalona ka doe malama 'oni'onirū doe liu ka ketaketa'a ma ka ifuifu'a, nonina kwao-kwao'anga, saena ka kwao. 'Oni-'onirū kī sau ana kwalarū kī. Rauna keta ka sisili'a ma ka marako.

○ Nia ke bulao saena to'ona'oa ka tasa ana fafona kafo kī ma saena fuli raku kī. Nia ke bulao ata go'o 'ana ana kula gwara ofoofo kī bore 'ana. Ki salinga'inia fuana fasilana saena falisi, leleka nia ke bulao la'u saena fuli falisi. Kwalana ke ra'e ka tasa sulia 'ai keta liu kī , ta ne'e ki fa'asata 'uri ana.
• 'Oni'onirū ki do'ofia fuana 'anilana di'i logo kai fasia.

GWA'UFI, ki saea logo 'ania GU'UFI, nia di'ia logo kai. Kaida'i ki fasia na afita'irū nia fafabusu ka silolo liu mala. Afuna gwagwā'a bore ma di'ia ki olea saena afurū kwao lala di'ia saena afuna fana. Nia to'o ana malata'irū to'oto'o kī.
GWA'UFI 'inoto'a, kwalana marako ka doe mala ka ngarangara'a, rauna marako ka reba ka te'e keta, afuna goligoli'a. Nia ke bulao to'oto'o ma nia ke bulao ka fi'irū'a ka tasa ana ti kula.
GWA'UFI SUSUA, ta sata GWA'UFI FISUFISU-GWAU, afuna ka molimoli'a di'ia logo ti kai, kwalana gwagwā'anga, rauna molimoli'a. Kaida'i ki 'ilia fuana 'anilana ki fisua afuna māna 'ifita'irū, ka sui ki fi'i susua logo 'ifita'irū fuiri ki ke ukua anoana fuila afurū fuana la'u ta kaida'i ne'e ki 'ilia la'u. Noima ki 'ilia ki lafua go'o ti afurū ma ti afurū ka teo logo, di'ia go'o ne'e ki fisua afuna. Nia ne'e ki fa'asatā 'uri ana.
GWA'UFI LAELAE, ta sata GWA'UFI KU'IKU'I-NGWARI, afuna kwaokwao'anga ka doe ma ka keta ka di'ia fana kwalo, gwauna ka keta.

PANA is like yam but it is a bit different. It is a clump, its tuber is longish, the clump produces many tubers. Its vine is green and prickly and a bit more plentiful than yam vines and its leaf is rounded and green. It has thorns growing from the bole which the bottom also emerges from, it has spikes and if they go into our legs they swell up. Pana, the man who brought it here took it from Gela (islands) and pulled his foreskin over a pana seed (to conceal it) which he planted in Malaita.

Pana has two kinds, one called *LUSU* PANA, its tuber is big and not very long, and VINE FANA, its tuber is big and long, much more than *lusu* pana.

○ We plant it in areas called yam-plots.
• We also eat the bottom as with yam.
FANA = PANA / lesser yam / chinese yam / *Dioscorea esculenta* (Lour.) Burk. (*Dioscoreaceae*)

HIGH is a wild yam, it is different from planted yam because the vine is really big and the tuber is very big and longish and hairy, its body is whiteish and inside it is white. The bottom emerges from the vines. Its leaf is long and narrow and green.

○ It grows in the lowland especially on waters and in new shoots and landslide areas. It grows just anywhere, even on landslide areas. We transfer it to plant in yam-plots and eventually it grows again on (abandoned) yam-plot sites. Its vine grows beyond the tall trees, that's why we name it thus.
• The tuber we burn to eat as with planted yam.
SAULU = HIGH

GWA'UFI, also called *GU'UFI*, is like yam. Its tuber is blackish but if we cut it up its inside is white like the inside of pana-yam. When we plant it the mound erupts and gets massive. It has separate kinds.
Important *GWA'UFI*, its vine is green, really big and scratchy, its leaf is green and wide and quite long and its tuber is wrinkled. It grows individually and grows in a clump, especially in some places.
MOUNDED *GWA'UFI*, another name PLUCK-HEAD *GWA'UFI*, its tuber is rounded like some yams, its vine is blackish and its leaf is rounded. When we dig it up to eat we pluck off the tuber at the base, then we mound over the base and heap ground on the site of the tuber for the time when we will dig it up again. Or we dig and lift some tubers and some tubers remain if we pluck off the tuber. That's why we name it thus.
RUNNING *GWA'UFI*, another name RAT-TAIL *GWA'UFI*, its tuber is whiteish and big and long and like vine pana (*fana kwalo*) and its head is long.

Kwalana ne'e lae saena ano ka tau mala fa'asia ifita'irū, ka fi'i alua afurū, ta ne'e ki saea 'ania gwa'ufi laelae. Kaida'i ki 'ilia, afuna sau ana lalirū keta liu, ki saea 'ania nia di'ia ku'iku'ina ngwari. MALAFAU, karangia ka di'ia logo gwa'ufi laelae, te'e afuna ta'i molimoli'a go'o, noa'a kesi doe liu go'o ma kesi 'oro. Kwalarū ke lae saena ano ka tau mala ka fi'i alua afurū kī, afuna lisilana ka di'ia gwa'i fau molimoli'a kī, ta ne'e ki fa'asata 'uri ana. FAFALIFAU ne'e fi'irū'a, kwalana ke te'e doe ka dada ka marako, rauna reba ma ka ketaketa'a, afuna ketaketa'a ma ka te'e ififula. Nia ke bulao ka tasa ana ano kaole'a, kwala ke kalikalia gwa'ifau rara kī

- Di'ia gwa'ufi nia teo ma'i saena masu'u ki saea 'ania kai kwasi, ma ki fasia logo saena o'olā, kwatea nia ke bulao ke 'oro. Nia ke bulao kwasila'a saena to'ona'oa ma saena logo tolo, di'ia ki salinga'inia ki fasia, nia ke bulao logo 'i fafona asi. Fi'i gwa'ufi ke bulao le'a ana ano nakinaki, ano bubū, ano dafudafu fa'inia ano kaole'anga.
- Ki fasia sulia ngali kī ma ta fa'i 'ai ngasi kī, sulia nia kesi lango 'ali'ali. Nia ke teo sulia rō fa'i ngali'anga noema ulu fa'i ngali'anga, leleka ana kaida'i nia lango ana July, ki lisia kwalana ke balabala'a ma ke lango mū ma ano nia fafabusu ka gwaubusu 'i ne'e 'oni'onina nia to'osi ka doe mala, ka fi'i bolo fa'inia 'ililana.
- Afuna gwa'ufi, 'anilana le'a ka tasa. Ki du'atelea ki kukia bore ma di'ia ki dodoa afuna ma ki fasia ifitana ma nia kesi bulao.

'AFĀ, ki saea logo 'ania 'AFAE, ta sata la'u MOTE, kai kwasi nini'a ne'e di'ia logo gwa'ufi kwasi. Nia ke fi'irū'a, kwalarū kī ka te'e ngarangara'a, ta ne'e ki saea 'ania mote. Rauna ka reba liu mala ma ka te'e molimoli'a ka marako. Nia ke alua 'oni'onirū sulia kwalana ne'e teo saena ano. 'Oni'onina ka ngatangata'a ka bababa'a, nonina ka ngarangara'a ka sakosako'a, saena ka kwao. Nia ke bulao ana gwa'irū.

- Nia ke bulao saena to'ona'oa ma saena tolo, ti kaida'i nia ke bulao 'i fafona asi ana ti kula, nia 'oro liu ana ti kula ma ti kula nia ke barū'a go'o. Malita'i ano kaolea ne'e nia ke bulao ka tasa ana.
- Ki 'ania afuna ana ta kaida'i go'o 'ana, 'anilana le'a ka tasa bore ma ti afu ai te'e 'afa'afae'anga, ta ne'e ki saea 'ania 'afā. Ki dodoa noima ki kukia logo saena sosobini, ke du'a ki fi'i songea fuana 'anilana.

Its vine runs in the ground far from the bole and then produces the tuber, that's why we call it running *gwa'ufi*. When we dig it, its tuber emerges from a very long root, we say it is like a rat's tail. FALSE-STONE is almost like running *gwa'ufi* only its tuber is quite rounded, it is not very big and not very plentiful. The vine runs really far in the ground and then produces tubers, the tubers look like rounded stones, that's why we name it thus. OVER-STONES is a clump, its vine is quite big and smooth and green, its leaf is wide and longish, its tuber is longish and a bit hairy. It grows especially on clay ground, its vine winds round bare stones.

- If *gwa'ufi* is in the forest we call it a wild yam but we plant it in gardens to make it grow plentifully. It grows wild in the lowland and also in the inland and if we transfer and plant it, it also grows on the sea. *Gwa'ufi* clump grows well on flinty ground, clotted ground, dusty ground and also clay ground.

- We plant it alongside nut trees and strong trees because it doesn't wilt (ripen) quickly. It will lie for two or three years until the time when it dies back in July and we see its vine go pale and die back and the ground swells and erupts as it puts down a really big tuber, and it is then suitable to dig up.
- *Gwa'ufi* tuber is especially good to eat. We roast it and boil it but if we flask-cook the tuber and plant the bole it will not grow.

GWA'UFI / GU'UFI = *GWA'UFI* / *Dioscorea aff. alata* L. (*Dioscoreaceae*)

BITTER another name SCRATCHY, this is a wild yam which is like wild *gwa'ufi*. It is a clump, the vines are a bit prickly, that's why we call it scratchy. Its leaf is very wide and quite rounded and green. It produces bottoms along its vine which lies in the ground. The bottom is knobbly and flat, its body is scratchy and yellow, the inside is white. It grows from its crown.

- It grows in the lowland and in the inland, sometimes it grows on the sea in some places, it is very plentiful in some places and in others it is scarce. Clay is the kind of ground it grows on especially.
- We eat the tuber at any time, it is especially good to eat but some tubers are quite bitter, that's why we call it bitter. We flask-cook it or boil it in a saucepan and when it is burned we peel it to eat.

'AFĀ / ĀFAE / MOTE = BITTER / SCRATCH / *Dioscorea aff. esculenta* (Lour.) Burk. (*Dioscoreaceae*)

LEO ne'e ta gwa'ufi bore ma nia ai ngwane lala, noa'a nia kesi fungu ma noa'a kesi alua go'o ti afu-rū, ta ne'e ki fa'asata 'uri ana. Nia fi'irū'a, kwalana doe ka di'ia logo kwalana gwa'ufi bore ma nia ngarangara'a liu lala, rauna marako ka reba ka keta.

○   Nia ke bulao go'o 'ana ana kula kī sui, te'e kula one'a ne'e nia kesi bulao ani.

•   Ti kaida'i ki itoa sakali 'ania kwalana.

•   Gwata kī ke 'ania lalina.

ARAKAI nia di'ia logo kai, nia ka fi'iru'a, 'oni'onina 'inoi ka molimolia ka sakosako'a ma saena ka kwao. Kwalana te'e doe ka kwaokwao'anga, rauna matanga'a 'ania ūlu ra'irū kī.

○   Ki fasia saena falisi, nia ke bulao kwasi'a logo. Nia ke bulao ata go'o 'ana ana kula gwara ofoofo kī bore 'ana.

•   Ki 'ania logo 'oni'onirū di'ia kai.

KAMO nia ta kai kwasi, nia di'ia logo kai fasia te'e kwalana go'o ne'e doe ma rauna ka te'e doe mala. Afuna keta liu mala saena ano ma ka doe mala, kaida'i ki 'ilia kiluna 'ato liu, karangia ke bolo fa'inia ketelana ngwae.

○   Nia ke bulao saena fuli raku kī saena to'ona'oa ma fafona kafo kī.

•   Ki du'afia fuana 'anilana di'ia logo kai fasia.

DA'U, ta sata EME, nia ta'i di'ia logo kai bore ma nia mamata lala fa'asia. Kwalana nia ke ra'e sulia sabangi ma ka nukunukua na'a gwari 'ai doe fuiri, rauna molimoli'a, gwauna ra'irū kī ka raku. Nia ke fungu sulia fa'i kwalona 'i gwauna sabangi kī. Nia ke alua 'oni'onirū bore ma nia kesi doe la'u di'ia kai. Nia to'o ana rō malita'i da'u kī. DA'U FASIA ki fasia saena o'olā. Ki sabangi sulia gwari 'ai 'iri nia ke fungu ma ki loia fuana, ki dodoa fuana 'anilana. DA'U KWASI nia ke bulao ata go'o 'ana ana kula ki sui.

•   Fuana 'afae liu, ki emea mala fuana 'anilana, ta ne'e ki saea logo 'ania eme. Ki emea, ki alua saena ngwa'i, ki alua māna sasaba ana kafo ke to'ea sulia ulu asoa kī, ka sui ki fi'i ngalia 'i luma ki losia sūla ka afe fa'asia, ki fi'i dodoa fuana 'anilana. Rū fuiri fuana kaida'i ana fiolo'a go'o.

•   'Oni'onina da'u ki 'ania logo, bore ma noa'a nia kesi le'a di'ia kai sulia nia ti'iti'i go'o.

•   Gwata kī ke 'ania fuana ma lalina.

•   Ki gura logo 'ania ti mata'inga.

BARREN is a *gwa'ufi* but it is a male one, it doesn't bear and it doesn't produce tubers, that's why we name it thus. It is a clump, its vine is big and like *gwa'ufi* vine but is is very scratchy, its leaf is green and wide and long.

○   It just grows in all places, only in sandy places it won't grow.

•   Sometimes we tie fencing with its vine.

•   Pigs eat its roots.

LEO = BARREN / *Dioscorea nummularia* Lamk. (*Dioscoreaceae*)

ARAKAI is like yam, it is a clump, its tuber is plump, rounded and yellow, and the inside it is white. Its vine is quite big and whiteish and its leaf is divided into three leaves.

○   We plant it in yam-plots and it also grows wild. It grows just anywhere, even on landslide areas.

•   We also eat the bottom like yam.

ARAKAI = *Dioscorea pentaphylla* L. (*Dioscoreaceae*)

KAMO is a wild yam, it is like planted yam only its vine is big and its leaf is really quite big. Its tuber is very long in the ground and big and when we dig it up the hole is very deep, almost equivalent to the height of a man.

○   It grows in shoots sites in the lowland and on waters.

•   We burn it to eat like planted yam.

KAMO = *KAMO* / *Dioscorea alata* L.

DA'U, also named GRATE, is quite like yam but it is different from it. Its vine climbs along conductors (props) and overgrows big tree stumps, its leaf is rounded and the tip of the leaf is pointed. It bears (fruit) along its vine at the head of the conductors. It produces a tuber but it is not as big as yam. There are two kinds of *da'u*. PLANTED *DA'U* we plant in the garden. We conduct it along tree stumps so it bears and we can pick the fruit and flask-cook them to eat. WILD *DA'U* just grows anywhere in all places.

•   Its fruit is very bitter, we have to grate it to eat, that's why we also call it grate. We grate it, put it in a bag and leave it under a water spout to soak for three days, then we take it to the house and squeeze the bitter juice from it, then flask-cook it to eat. This is just something for times of hunger.

•   *Da'u* bottom we also eat, but it is not as good as yam because it is just small.

•   Pigs eat the fruit and the root.

•   We also cure some illnesses with it.

DA'U / EME = *DA'U* / GRATE /aerial yam /*Dioscorea bulbifera* L.

UFI 'ABE, ki saea logo 'ania KWALA'ASI, nia ta kai kwasi, kwalana ke kalia 'ai kī, nonina marako, rauna ka te'e reba ka marako logo ma kaida'i nia raku na ngwasana meo. Kaida'i nia maua, kwalana ke mae ka 'asi kwailiu go'o 'ana saena ano, ta ne'e ki saea 'ania kwala'asi. Karangi ka di'i logo gwa'ufi bore ma rauna ka ta'i fisifisi'a lala go'o, afuna ka gwā ma ka keta lala. Nia ke bulao ana gwa'irū.
  ○ Nia ke bulao saena to'ona'oa ma saena tofonga'i tolo, ka tasa saena tolo gwarigwari'a, ma fafona asi ne'e noa'a. Ti kula nia ke 'oro liu mala, ti kula noa'a go'o, nia kesi bulao saena kunukunua.
  • Afuna 'inoto'a liu fuana 'anilana, 'anilana le'a liu, to'o ti'i kaida'i suma ma 'oro'oro ke 'ania logo. Ki du'atelea noema ki dodoa, bore ma di'ia ngwae fiolo ka noa'a ta mafula fuana du'uru'a nia ke 'ani ma'ā go'o ana, ka tasa na'a ana ngwae tolo kī.
  • Nia le'a logo fuana guragura'a.

GWAUGWAUMELA, ki saea logo 'ania 'OBA'OBA, ne'e ta kai, kwalana doe, rauna ka marako ka reba ma ka ketaketa'a. Afuna doe ka keta saena ano bore ma gwauna mela lala.
  ○ Rū kwasi ne'e, nia ke bulao ka tasa ana kula ano to'o kī saena kwaru.
  • Ki 'ania go'o 'oni'onirū, 'anilana le'a liu mala, bore ma gwauna afurū kasi bolo fa'inia 'anilana sulia nia ngasi ma ka melamela'a ma ka iliilia.

KUMARA, ki saea logo'ania BUTETE, ne'e kwalarū'a, nia ango go'o saena ano, ka alua 'oni'onirū kī. Kumara to'o ana bara malita'i rū, ti ai rauni molimoli'a ka reba, ti ai rauni matanga'a. Ki to'o ana malita'i kumara 'oro kī, ti satani to'oto'o ni'i 'uri: SITANAI, BANIKEFO, MOLEMOLE, BIRABIRA, WESITENE, FORISI, TIRIMANISI.
  ○ Rū fasia nini'a ne'e ko'o kia kī ne'e leka 'i Fiti ma 'i Kwinslan kira ka salinga'inia ma'i fa'asia 'a'e asi. Ki fasia kwalana fa'inia logo 'oni'onirū kī. Nia bolo fa'inia kula kī ta'ifau, kula nakinaki'a bore, kula ano bū bore, kula kwaru'a bore, te'e saena ano rerede'anga noema ka one'a noema ka moge ne'e noa'a kesi bolo ana.
  • Fanga 'inoto'a na'a 'i nini'ari nini'a. Ki kōngia, ki dodoa, ki du'atelea, ki kukia logo.

  • Ki sare gwata logo 'ania.

UFI 'ABE, also called FALLING-VINE, is a wild yam, its vine winds round trees, its body is green, its leaf is quite wide and green too and when it shoots its leaf-shoots are red. When it is ripe its vine dies and falls about on the ground, that's why we call it falling-vine. It is almost like *gwa'ufi* but its leaf is quite thin. It grows from its crown.
  ○ It grows in the lowland and in the central inland, especially in the cool inland, but not on the sea. In some places it is very plentiful, in others it is not, and it won't grow in swamp.
  • Its tuber is very important for eating, it is very good to eat, but occasionally worms and so-manys (*'oro'oro* / taro-beetle) also eat it. We roast it or flask-cook it, but if a person is hungry and has no fire for burning he can just eat it raw, especially among the inland people.
  • It is also good for curing.
UFI 'ABE / KWALA'ASI = *UFI'ABE* / FALLING-VINE

BROWN-HEAD, also called 'OBA'OBA, is a yam, its vine is big, its leaf is green and wide and longish. Its tuber is big and long in the ground but its head is brown.
  ○ This one is wild, it grows especially in places with normal soil in rocky areas.
  • We just eat the bottom, it is very good indeed to eat, but the head of the tuber is not suitable to eat because it is hard and brown and full of roots.
GWAUGWAUMELA / 'OBA'OBA = BROWN HEAD

(SWEET) POTATO, also called KUMARA, is a vine, it just creeps on the ground and produces tubers. Kumara has several kinds, some the leaves are rounded and long, some the leaves are divided. We have many kinds of potato and some individual names are: *SITANAI, BANIKEFO*, ROUNDED, SPROUTING, WESTERN, *FORISI*, THREE-MONTHS.
  ○ This is a planted thing which our ancestors who went to Fiji and Queensland transferred here from overseas. We plant its vine and also its tuber. It is suitable for all places, whether flinty places, clotting ground, rocky places, only gravel or sand or soggy ground are not suitable for it.
  • This is an important food of the present. We bake it, we flask-cook it, we roast it and also boil it.
  • We also feed pigs with it.
KUMARA / BUTETE = POTATO / sweet potato

KAIBIA ne'e fi'irū, kakina gwaligwali'a, rauna matanga'a ka keta, afuna keta. Kaibia to'o ana ti malita'irū di'ia KAIBIA MEO, KAIBIA NGWANE, kasina doe ka keta, KAIBIA KWAO.

○   Rū fasia nini'a, kira salinga'inia ma'i fa'asia 'i Fiti. Nia ke bulao ana kakina, ki afita talana saena ano fuana fasilana kakirū kī saena.

•   Ki 'ania afuna, ki du'atelea, ki dodoa, ki kōngia, ki kukia, ki 'ara logo fuana lakeno 'i rū ki saea 'ania 'ara, ki saungia logo fuana gwasu 'i rū.

•   Ki sare gwata logo 'ania.

BIA-YAM is a clump, its stalk is ringed, its leaf is divided and long and its tuber is long. Tapioca has kinds like RED *BIA*-YAM, MALE *BIA*-YAM, its stalk is big and long, and WHITE *BIA*-YAM.

○   This is planted, they transferred it from Fiji. It grows from its stalk, we dig a mound for it in the ground for planting the stalk in.

•   We eat its tuber, we roast it, we flask-cook it, we bake it, we boil it, and we grate it for a cream-pudding called grating and also pound it for coconut-pudding.

•   We also feed pigs with it.

KAIBIA = *BIA*-YAM / cassava / tapioca / *Manihot esculenta* (*Euphorbiaceae*)

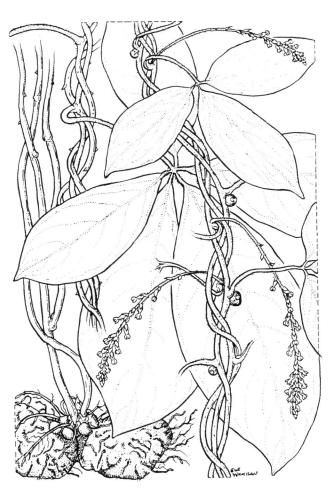

▲ *arakai* / arakai

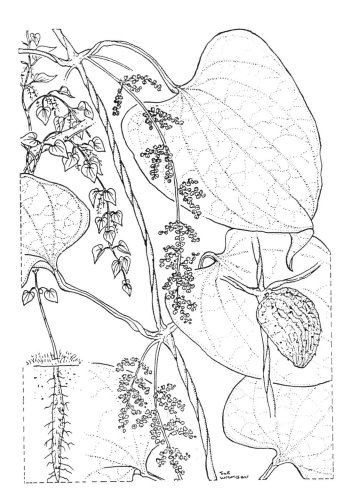

▲ *kamo* / kamo

Leaves of forest trees, drawn by Michael Kwa'ioloa,
as explained by advisor Frank Ete Tuaisalo.

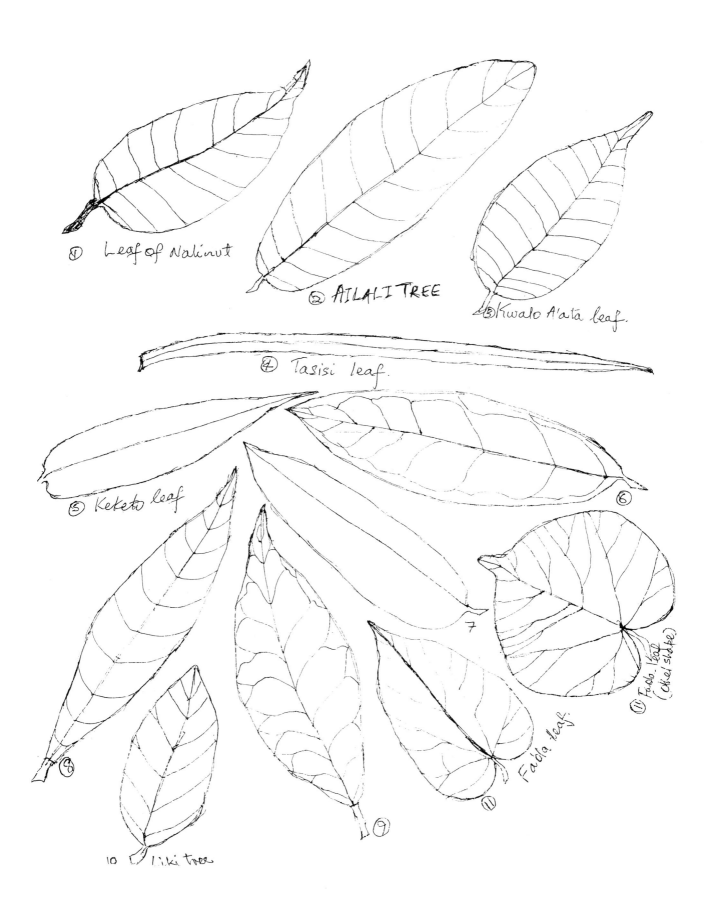

① Leaf of Nalinut

② AILALI TREE

③ Kwalo A'ata leaf.

④ Tasisi leaf.

⑤ Keketo leaf

⑥

7

⑧

⑨

⑩ Iliki tree

⑪ Faola leaf.

⑪ Faola leaf (Okel shape)

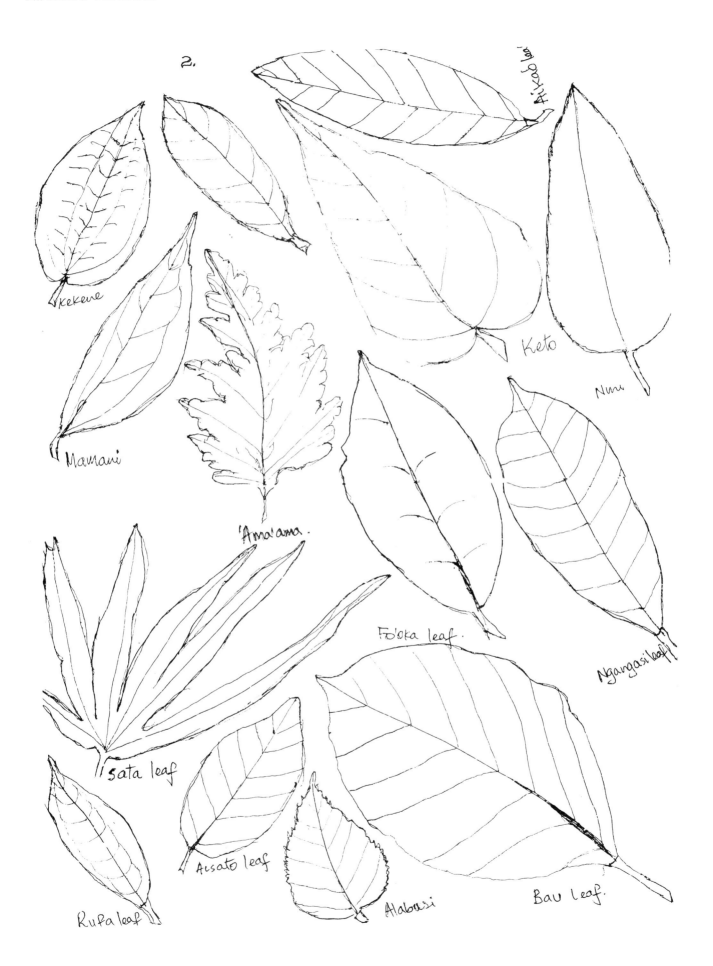

2.

Kekeve

Mamani

'Ama'ama.

A'ikabu'ae'

Keto

Nunu

Ngangasi leaf

Fo'oka leaf.

I sata leaf

A'sato leaf

Alabusi

Bau leaf.

Rufa leaf

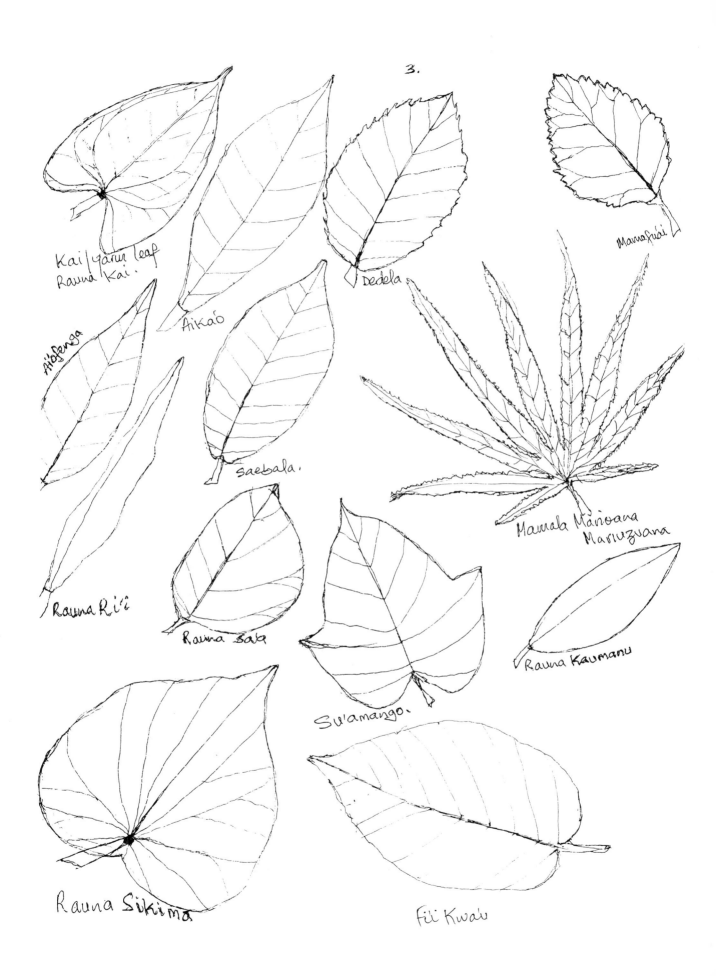

3.

Kai/yarui leaf
Rauna Kai.

Dedela

Mamafuai

Alofenga

Aikaó

Mamala Manoana
Mariuzuana

saebala.

Rauna Ri'i

Rauna Sala

Rauna Kaumanu

Su'amango.

Rauna Sikima

Fii Kwao

Index to Part 2

This index lists growing things by their principal Kwara'ae names, as used in the text, with page references to their descriptions in Part 2 of the book. It repeats the alternative Kwara'ae names, the translations used in the English text, other English names and botanical names, as given in Part 2.

The rationale for the use of the English text names is explained in the Introduction (page 19). The botanical names are taken from Henderson and Hancock's *A Guide to the Useful Plants of Solomon Islands* (1988), where fuller indexes may be found, by species and family as well as by Kwara'ae names.

There are some Kwara'ae names in our list which do not appear in Henderson and Hancock's book and some where the spelling differs or the identification is uncertain. Bearing this in mind, and the years which have passed since the book was published, the botanical information given here should not be taken as definitive or up to date. It is provided primarily as an aid to understanding Kwara'ae culture.

Names in the index are arranged as follows:

KWARA'AE NAME
    ENGLISH TEXT NAME
      other English name
      botanical species (botanical family)   page no.

'AMA / 'AMA KAREFO
  'AMA / SOFTWOOD *'AMA*
  swamp oak
  Terminalia microcarpa Decne. / *T. aff. rubiginosa*
  Schum. / *T. complanta.* K Schum.   107
'AMA FAU / 'AMA RODO
  SOLID *'AMA* / NIGHT *'AMA*
  Terminalia Diels. / *T. rerei* Coode / *T. whitmorei* Coode
  (*Combretaceae*)   108
'AMA'AMA
  SELAGINELLA
  Selaginella rechingeri Hieron (*Selaginellaceae*)   185
'AMAU / SAKWARI
  'AMAU
  sandpaper cabbage
  Ficus copiosa Steud. (*Moraceae*)   178
ARAKAI
  ARAKAI
  Dioscorea pentaphylla L. (*Dioscoreaceae*)   239
ARAKAO see AFAAFAMANU
ARAKOI
  ARAKOI   219
ARAKOKO
  GMELINA
  white beech
  Gmelina moluccana (Bl.) Baker (*Verbenaceae*)   114
'ARASIBOLA see BOLANGUNGU
'ARI'ARI
  FREYCINETIA
  Freycinetia (more than 20 sp.) (*Pandanaceae*)   228
'ASAI
  MANGO
  Mangifera indica L. / *M. minor* Bl. (*Anacardiaceae*) 120
'ASAKA
  COLEUS
  Blumea sylvatica (Bl.) DC. (*Asteraceae*) /
  Coleus scutellarioides (L.) Benth. (*Lamiaceae*)   182
ASIASI
  ASIASI   206
'ASIRUFARUFA
  SALTMARSH
  Eugenia effusum A. Gray / *Syzygium decipiens* (Koord.
  & Val.) Amsh. (*Myrtaceaea*)   110
'AU FĪRŪ
  TANGLE BAMBOO
  Nastus aff. productus / *Racembambos holttumii* Dransf.
  (*Poaceae*)   202
'AURIDI
  'AURIDI / *Decaspermum fruticosum* J.R. & G. Forst. /
  D. salomonense Scott / *Metrosideros eugenioides* (Schltr.)
  Steere / *Metrosideros salomonense* C.T. White
  (*Myrtaceae*)   130
BA'ABA'A
  BA'ABA'A
  Euodia viridiflora C.T.White / *E. elleryana* Muell. /
  E. radlkoferiana Ltb. / *E. silvatica* Merr.& Perry /
  E. solomonensis Merr.& Perry (*Rutaceae*)   159
BABĀ
  BABĀ   225

BA'ERA / DE'E
  CABBAGE
  hibiscus cabbage/ hibiscus spinach / slippery
  cabbage
  Hibiscus manihot L. (*Malvaceae*)   182
BAIBAI
  CYCAD
  palm fern
  Cycas rumphii Miq. (*Cycadaceae*)   190
BALA
  EUODIA   158
BALA NI KWARU
  EUODIA OF THE ROCKS
  Euodia elleryana Muell. (*Rutaceae*)   158
BALA KWAO / BALA FUFURI
  WHITE EUODIA / PATCHY EUODIA   158
BALE'O
  BREADFRUIT
  Artocarpus communis Forst. / *A. altilis* (Park.) Fosb.
  (*Moraceae*)   126
BALIU
  ASCARINA
  Ascarina diffusa A.C.Sm. / *A. maheshwarii* Swamy.
  (*Chloranthaceae*)   159
BAOLA
  BANYAN
  strangler fig
  Ficus microcarpa L.f ssp. *naumannii* Engl. /
  F. prasinicarpa Elmer. / *F. glandulifera* Summerh.
  (*Moraceae*)   126
BAOLA FAU
  SOLID BANYAN
  Ficus drupacea Thunb. ssp. *glabrata* Corner /
  F. obliqua Forst. f./ *F. xylosycia* spp. *cylindricarpa* Diels /
  F. crassiramea Miq. ssp. *patellifera* Warb.
  (*Moraceae*)   127
BAOLA GARAGARA / BAOLA LĀLĀ
  SPREAD BANYAN / TUG BANYAN
  Ficus benjamina L. var *nuda* (Miq.) Braith. /
  F. subcordata Bl. (*Moraceae*)   127
BAOLA SUSUSU / SIRIFENA
  SUSUSU BANYAN
  Ficus tinctoria Forst. f. (*Moraceae*)   127
BASIBASI
  BOW
  Clinostigma haerestigma H.E.Moore / *Drymophloeus*
  pachycladus (Burret) H.E.Moore / *D. rehderopheonix*
  Sub. / *D. subdistichus* H.E.Moore / *Rehderopheonix*
  subdisticha H.E.Moore (*Arecaceae*)   188
BA'U
  BANANA
  Musa sp. (*Musaceae*)   198
BA'ULA
  BA'ULA
  Calophyllum kajewskii A.C.Sm. (*Clusiaceae*)   130
BEBE
  BUTTERFLY   218

Sources for the illustrations

Drawings, Part 1
The drawings in Part 1 are by Ben Burt, and their sources are noted here as a record of Kwara'ae material culture. Unless otherwise stated, the photographs and artefacts they are based on are from East Kwara'ae. In the list below, names and dates indicate when objects were documented, but for most we cannot say when, where and by whom they were made. Artefacts which the Kwara'ae remember but no longer possess, especially decorative objects which they associate with the traditional religion, are illustrated mostly by examples from Kwaio to the south, where they continue to be made.

page
65 *A home of the old fashioned people*: based on the home of Timi Ko'oliu in 'Ere'ere, 1984
71 *Walling section of stripy*: from the sanctum of Aisah Osifera of 'Aimomoko, at Fi'ika'o, 1979
Walling section of narrow-eye: from the Anglican church at Fa'iketo 1984
73 *Fronts of patterned churches*: both from photographs in the archives of the South Sea Evangelical Mission, undated and unattributed, but probably taken in Kwara'ae in the 1920s or 30's
75 *Platformed house with cooking house*: from the home of Stephen Binalu at Dingodingo, 1993 *Inside a cooking house*: composed from several photos, 1980s
77 *adze*: heirloom belonging to Timi Ko'oliu of 'Ere'ere, 1979
walking stick: heirloom belonging to Andrew Gwa'itafa of Ubasi 1983
angle club: heirloom belonging to Andrew Gwa'itafafa of Ubasi, 1983
deflector-club: made by Arumae Bakete of 'Ere'ere, perhaps in 1890s -1900s
bowls: large; made by Adriel Rofate'e; small, made by Ben Temakao, 1960s-1970s
78 *canoe*: from photograph in South Sea Evangelical Mission archive, probably 1900s-1910s, of canoes made in Santa Ana, Makira Province. Other photos from the coasts of Kwara'ae show exactly the same style of construction and decoration.
bamboo section: from East Kwaio, 1980s
lime container: East Kwaio 1979 belonging to Ben Burt
79 *pudding slicer*: belonging to Aisa Osifera of 'Aimomoko, 1983
dance baton: belonging to Riomea of Fakula'e,1979
comb: 1979
betel mortar: from Diosi, 1979, belonging to Ben Burt
81 *arm bands*: 1987
(man's) girdle: made by William Kware, 1979, belonging to the British Museum
83 *panpipes*, from Takangwane of Latea, 1984, belonging to Ben Burt
comb: 1979, belonging to Ben Burt
susuru belt: 'Ere'ere, 1979 (of glass beads)

85 *(waist) band strip for a maiden*: made by Gala'a of Uogwari, West Kwaio, 1983 belonging to David Akin
87 *pouch*: East Kwaio, 1976, belonging to the British Museum
coconut baskets: 1979, 1984, belonging to Ben Burt
strong basket: made by Jemiel Misialo of Sulaifau 1984, belonging to Ben Burt
89 *satchel*: 1979 belonging to Ben Burt
sack: made by Adriel Rofate'e of Gwauna'ongi, 1979 belonging to Ben Burt
90 *ring-patterns*: East Kwaio, 1979, belonging to Ben Burt
91 *ear reeds*: East Kwaio, 1979, belonging to Ben Burt
patterned combs: small, East Kwaio, 1979; large, origin unknown, both belonging to Ben Burt

Drawings, Part 2
The botanical drawings in Part 2 are by Susan Wickison, as published in Henderson and Hancock's *Guide to the Useful Plants of Solomon Islands* (1988). We have reproduced the drawings to scale so that the details of the plants appear at approximately 50% of natural size.

Most of the drawings were made from living examples at various sites on Guadalcanal, including the Honiara Botanic Gardens, as documented in Henderson and Hancock's book. As they explain, 'The general principles of botanical line drawings have been adhered to, that is, to show as much information as possible whilst keeping the actual drawings simple and accurate in scale. Features regarded as important are, leaf size, shape, venation, arrangement, and also inflorescence / fruit structure and habit.' (1988:16)

We are particularly grateful to the artist, the authors and the Solomon Islands Ministry of Agriculture for enabling us to illustrate the book with such excellent drawings.

The drawings of leaves on pages 242 to 244, from Michael Kwa'ioloa's research notes, are also reproduced at approximately 50% of natural size.

Photographs
All the photographs were taken in East Kwara'ae and all are by Ben Burt, except nos. 4, 13 and 17, which are by Pauline Khng, and no. 23, by an unidentified friend.

The stamps in no. 10 are reproduced courtesy of the Solomon Islands Philatelic Bureau.

Glossary of Kwara'ae botanical terms

Parts of growing things

In this list, translations used as standard in the book are in italics, followed by alternative translations or meanings. When referring to parts of growing or living things, the Kwara'ae words as given below usually have the inalienable possessive suffix -*na* (its / his / hers) meaning that it is part of a particular object or person. Many are also used as classifiers, particularly with the suffix -*rū* (thing), implying that the object is being referred to in the abstract.

fa'i = *tree, stem, stick*, etc., item
fi'i = *clump*, cluster of items
lali = *root*
afu = *tuber*, piece, part
'oni'oni = *bottom*, tuber, arse, shit
'a'e = *stock*, base
a'u = *stock* of taro
'ae = *foot*, base of tree
'ifita = *bole*, base of clump or tree
kobakoba = *buttress*-root
noni = *body*, trunk or stem and limbs
'itanga = main *trunk*, main stem, principal
gwa'i = *crown*, rounded top
gwau = *head*, top
lala = *pole*, full length of bamboo etc.
kasi = *section*, internode of bamboo etc.
gwagi = *node* of bamboo etc., *core* of fruit, knot
kwalo = *vine*, rope
kwala = *vine* of edible tuber
ta'eta'e = *skin*, bark, husk
'uli'uli = *bark*, skin with flesh (thicker than ta'eta'ena)
'aba = *strip*, strip-like leaf, strip of bark, wing etc
taketake = *cuticle*, thin outer skin of coconut frond
rara = *branch*
boeboe = *leaf-tube*, base of leaf sheathing parent stem
ofiofi = *sheath* covering stem or fruit, palm frond-base
fifiko = *frond-base*, boeboe of palm
i'iko = *frond-sheath*, ofiofi of palm frond
'ai'ai = *stave*, mid-rib of palm-frond
ūli /uila = *frond*, leafy branch or twig
ngwili = *sprig*, shoot with leaves
ka'ika'i = *stem* supporting leaf or fruit, handle
ngongangonga / ngwako = *tendril*
ngwasa = *shoot*, young root
gala = *sucker* of banana
raku = *shoot*, point
gwango = *leaf-shoot*

birabira = *sprout*
rau = *leaf*
ra'i = *leaf*
taka = *flower*
fua = *fruit*
fa'i = *fruit*, item
fingi = *bunch* of flowers, fruit etc.
tali / taila = *pit*, fruit-stone, hard *heartwood*
faru = *pip*
maga = *seed*, bead
lasi = *shell* of coconut etc., skull
sa'e = *inside* of nut etc., kernel
sula = *sap*, juice

Descriptions of growing things

Descriptive words are often reduplicated to make them less forceful than the simple form given here (in which case we have usually translated them with the suffix -ish), and they may also take suffixes distinguishing them as qualifiers.

marako = *green*
meo = *red*
sakosako = *yellow*
kwao = *white*
gwā = *black*
mela = *brown*
bulu = *dark*
bora = *purple*, dark blue-black
bala = *pale*
kwalakwala = *light* coloured

doe = *big*
ti'iti'i = *small*
reba = *wide*
keta = *long, tall*
dokodoko = *short*
sisili = *narrow*
molimoli = *rounded*
gwalogwalo = *erect*, tall and unbranching
ra'ura'u = *slight*, slender
'ere'ere = *coiled*
raku = *pointed*, sharp
ngara = *prickly*
momote = *itchy*
maomaoa = *smooth*
nunura = *shiny*